WINDOWS
NT

Professional
Library

WINDOWS NT

Windows NT 4
Advanced Programming

About the Authors...

Raj Rajagopal has more than 17 years of professional experience covering all phases of software development, including requirements, architecture, high-level design, coding, testing, maintenance, and project and line management. He is Senior Computer Scientist at Illinois Institute of Technology-Research Institute involved with Technology Assessments. He is the author of *Windows NT, UNIX, NetWare: Migration and Coexistence* and is the principal or co-author of more than a dozen technical reports on topics such as Unix vs. Windows NT, modeling/simulation, standards, and other topics. He has written articles for *Computer Technology Review* and *Application Development Trends*. He is also the co-author of many patents in computer software. Mr. Rajagopal previously worked at IBM for nearly 10 years and has taught computer science and management courses at the University of Maryland, Johns Hopkins University, and University of D.C. He can be reached by e-mail at **rrajagop@capaccess.org**.

Subodh P. Monica is an Advisory Programmer at IBM Corporation with more than 14 years of experience in the areas of software product development, programming, and design. He has extensive experience with graphical user interfaces and developing products for Windows, Unix, and OS/2 environments. Mr. Monica has also done extensive work in the area of icon-based authoring tools, editors, and document imaging systems.

WINDOWS NT

Windows NT 4
Advanced Programming

RAJ RAJAGOPAL
AND
SUBODH P. MONICA

Osborne **McGraw-Hill**

Berkeley New York St. Louis San Francisco
Auckland Bogotá Hamburg London Madrid
Mexico City Milan Montreal New Delhi Panama City
Paris São Paulo Singapore Sydney
Tokyo Toronto

Osborne/**McGraw-Hill**
2600 Tenth Street
Berkeley, California 94710
U.S.A.

For information on translations or book distributors outside the U.S.A., or to arrange bulk purchase discounts for sales promotions, premiums, or fund-raisers, please contact Osborne/**McGraw-Hill** at the above address.

Windows NT 4 Advanced Programming

1234567890 DOC DOC 901987654321098

ISBN 0-07-882357-9

Publisher	**Proofreader**
Brandon A. Nordin	Stefany Otis
Editor-in-Chief	**Indexer**
Scott Rogers	David Heiret
Acquisitions Editor	**Computer Designer**
Wendy Rinaldi	Michelle Galicia
Project Editor	**Illustrator**
Cynthia Douglas	Leslee Bassin
Editorial Assistant	**Series Design**
Ann Sellers	Peter Hancik
Technical Editor	**Cover Design**
Herbert Schildt	Adrian Morgan
Copy Editor	
Jan Jue	

To my daughter Sheila,
who is eager to see her name in print,
to my son Venkat
who I hope one day will be equally eager
to see his name, to my wife Chitra, and to my parents.

—Raj

To Indu and Kapish for their understanding and
putting up with all the long hours.

—Subodh

WINDOWS
NT
Professional
Library

AT A GLANCE

WINDOWS
NT
Professional
Library

CONTENTS

PART II

NT Advanced GUI and OS Services Programming

PART III

NT Communications Programming

PART IV

NT Multimedia and Database Programming

PART V

Appendixes

ACKNOWLEDGMENTS

We would like to thank Arthur 'Choon' Choi for his help in the area of database programming, Keng T. Loh in the area of ActiveX programming and Donald Asonye in the area of sockets programming; Herb Schildt for his technical reviews and useful tips; the staff at Osborne including Scott Rogers, Wendy Rinaldi, Ann Sellers, Cynthia Douglas, and Jan Jue—without whose support and hard work, this book would not have been possible.

Introduction

In our experience of developing applications, we have found that, in a given project, selected parts of the operating system are used more heavily than others. For example, in a communications-oriented Windows NT project, one may use sockets a lot, while in an Internet-oriented application, one may use WinInet and ISAPI a lot. We have always felt the need for a book that provides a quick introduction to a topic concerning the operating system and that includes some examples that we could use to become productive quickly. This book is aimed at fulfilling these needs for the advanced programmers who have used Windows NT for a while, but who still are looking for something to jumpstart their learning a new Windows NT topic. With this in mind, this book addresses a number of programming topics in Windows NT including OLE 2, ActiveX, WinSock2, ODBC, DAO, WinInet, ISAPI, TAPI, OpenGL, Advanced Controls, Audio, Video, 3D, Animation, GDI, and more. Each topic is introduced at such a level that experienced programmers can easily pick up the concepts of the topic and immediately follow with the examples, allowing them to be productive in a very short time.

As programmers, we also spend a bit of time looking for and using utilities that help in our everyday program development. We have included many such utilities in the CD accompanying this book. We encourage you to take a look at Appendix B, which provides a brief description of the utilities we've provided. You may find a utility or two that you may not have come across and that will help you in your work.

Happy Programming!!

WINDOWS NT
Professional
Library

PART I

Windows NT Programming
Foundations

WINDOWS
NT
Professional
Library

CHAPTER 1

Windows
NT Overview

W indows NT is the place to be for programmers. Windows NT is outselling competing operating systems (OSs) and network operating systems (NOSs) such as UNIX and NetWare. Microsoft has done a good job of fixing the problems of prior versions of Windows NT. While Windows 95 still enjoys a huge install base, the distinction between it and Windows NT is narrowing. Starting with version 4.0, Windows NT has the same end-user interface as Windows 95. The Win32 API (Application Programming Interface) is becoming a common development mechanism for both Windows 95 and Windows NT. With "Cairo," Microsoft's code name for the next version, Windows NT will start getting all the benefits of being an object-oriented system. With the prices of memory, processors, and other hardware continuing their downward spiral, the minimum system requirements to run Windows NT are getting more and more affordable. Windows NT does not have any 16-bit code and is more stable than Windows 95. Windows NT is the base for Microsoft's BackOffice set of products. Although UNIX still has a sizable mission-critical application base, many UNIX application vendors have ported or developed equivalent applications to run on Windows NT. There are third-party products that let customers port their UNIX applications to Windows NT. Windows NT, with the Internet Information Server (IIS) and the ability to access data from corporate databases, can be a strong player in the fast-growing corporate intranets. Are you sold on Windows NT yet? This book is for and by Windows NT programmers. The focus is to give you the Windows NT programming concepts you need along with sample code you can cut and paste into programs you will be writing. The CD is packed with tools programmers use every day to be more productive.

Part 1 presents a quick overview of Windows NT from a programmer's perspective. Windows NT comes in two flavors—Windows NT Workstation and Windows NT Server. For the most part, programming for Windows NT Workstation is the same as programming for Windows NT Server. As such, all programming topics presented apply to both Windows NT Workstation and Windows NT Server unless specifically noted. A summary of the similarities and differences between Windows NT Workstation and Windows NT Server is included later in this chapter.

The purpose of this chapter and other chapters in Part 1 is to provide you with a list of Windows NT topics that you should be familiar with before getting into advanced NT programming. If you have been working with NT for a while, then you may be familiar with some of the topics presented. Since the rest of the book presumes that you are familiar with these topics, you may want to peruse the list in this chapter and ensure that you are comfortable with the list of topics. If you need a more detailed coverage of any individual topic, refer to an introductory book such as *Windows NT Programming from the Ground Up*, by Herbert Schildt, published by Osborne/McGraw-Hill, 1997.

Microsoft provides programming languages, APIs, SDKs (software development kits), class libraries, a development environment , and so on, to facilitate programming for Windows NT. The topics that a Windows NT programmer should be familiar with or aware of include

▼ Windows NT architecture overview

■ Programming languages and development environment

- Application Programming Interfaces
- Software development kits (SDKs)
- Microsoft Foundation Class (MFC) library
- Graphical device interface (GDI)
- Internet and network programming
- Component Object Model (COM) and Distributed COM
- Object linking and embedding (OLE)
- Multimedia
- Data access
- ▲ Registry

Let us now look at each of the topics in greater detail.

WINDOWS NT ARCHITECTURE OVERVIEW

Windows NT architecture is best explained using Figure 1-1. This shows the different components that make up the Windows NT architecture, the modes in which they operate, the interaction between the components, and so on.

Kernel and Microkernel

The operating system (OS) is the one program that is always running when the computer is on. It uses real memory, disk space, and other resources. It is the necessary "overhead" to keep the computer up. The aim of operating system designers is to keep this overhead as low as possible while still delivering all the services an OS should deliver. The way NT keeps the overhead low is by keeping the base operating system as small and as tight as possible. Only those functions that could not reasonably be performed elsewhere remain in the base operating system or *kernel*. This microkernel-based approach of NT is similar to Mach, a microkernel-based operating system developed at Carnegie-Mellon University.

The kernel is the nucleus of the operating system. (See Figure 1-1 for the relationship of the kernel to the other parts of the operating system. The kernel is just above the layer of code that shields the hardware, the *Hardware Abstraction Layer (HAL)*, which will be discussed later in this chapter.)

The kernel is resident in memory and cannot be preempted (except by some interrupts). Some of the functions the kernel performs are

- ▼ Handles hardware exceptions and interrupts
- Schedules, prioritizes, and dispatches *threads,* the basic unit of execution
- ▲ Synchronizes execution across processors in a multiprocessor environment

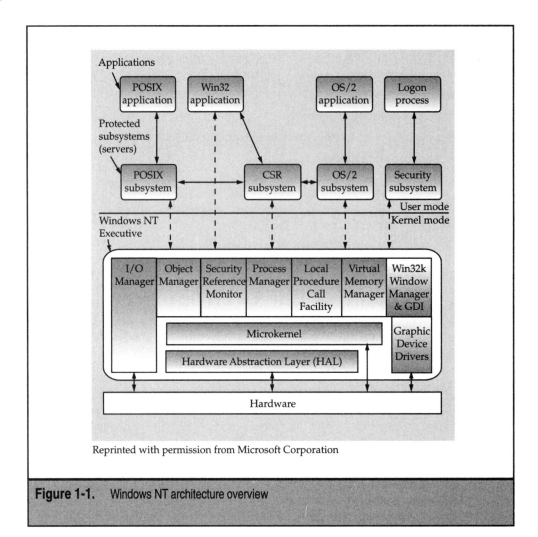

Reprinted with permission from Microsoft Corporation

Figure 1-1. Windows NT architecture overview

Operating Modes

A simple programming principle to keep in mind as a programmer is that your program takes turns with other programs and the NT operating system during the execution of your program. If your program runs in a multiprocessor system, then more than one program (or even threads of the same program) can be simultaneously executing in multiple processors. But the concept of programs taking turns still applies. Memory, disk space, and other resources are shared by all the executing programs. Mechanisms are necessary to keep applications separate from the operating system and other applications.

> ## Note for UNIX Programmers
> Though UNIX and Windows NT are similar in many ways, one of the differences is the kernel. Windows NT uses a *microkernel*-based approach, where the core kernel functions are kept as small as possible and the other functions of the operating system are performed in nonprivileged portions of the operating system called *protected subsystems*. This approach is in contrast to UNIX, where it is not uncommon for the kernel to be a lot bigger and encompass many more operating system functions. One consequence of a bigger kernel is that it needs to be changed more often compared with the Windows NT kernel.

Windows 95 application separation was not very good, and it caused application memory to be corrupted, resulting in the infamous General Protection Faults (GPFs).

The way NT solves this problem is to run the operating system code in a privileged processor mode known as *kernel mode.* Operating system code running in the kernel mode has access to system data and hardware. Applications run in a nonprivileged processor mode known as *user mode* and have limited access to system data and hardware. Thus, if an errant program misbehaves, the operating system gets control and can terminate the errant program without other programs being affected. Windows NT uses the protection mechanisms (also called *rings*) provided by the processor (also known as the central processing unit or CPU) to implement mode separation. When an application program is executing, the operating system is not using the CPU and really does not know what the application is trying to do. However, the operating system gets the CPU to check if the application attempts to execute at a ring level not appropriate for the application. If the application misbehaves, the CPU raises an exception and invokes the operating system, which is now in control, to deal with the application.

When an application needs to have access to the hardware—for example, when an application wants to print or read data from a disk—it invokes the operating system services, usually through a set of well-defined interfaces, called *Application Programming Interfaces (APIs).*

Hardware Abstraction Layer (HAL)

Operating systems, including Windows NT, are designed to run on more than one hardware platform, and platform-specific details are masked to the rest of the operating system by the Hardware Abstraction Layer (HAL). Windows NT is designed to run Intel, Alpha, and PowerPC, although IBM and others have recently announced that they are dropping support for Windows NT on the PowerPC. Hardware could be different in instruction sets (reduced instruction set computing, or RISC, versus non-RISC), word sizes (64-bit versus 32-bit, and so on), and even the number of processors. Most parts of the operating system are not concerned about these hardware differences, thanks to the Hardware Abstraction Layer.

Processor Support

Up until recently, most computing at the desktop and server level used machines that had only one CPU. *Multiprocessing*, where multiple processors exist on the same physical machine, have been used in mainframes for some time. With the advent of cheaper processors and operating systems that support multiple processors, multiprocessing is becoming more commonplace in desktops and servers.

Asymmetric multiprocessing (*ASMP*) is where the operating system uses one or more processors for itself, and schedules and runs the application programs in the remaining processors. Operating systems that support *symmetric multiprocessing* (*SMP*) do not impose such restrictions on processors. The ability to run any program on any processor provides better load balancing (in ASMP, the processor that runs the operating system may be idle while applications are waiting to use the other processor(s)). Fault tolerance is also improved in SMP because the failure of a processor dedicated for the operating system in ASMP means the machine is not operational, even though other processor(s) may be operational. The price to pay for improved load balancing and fault tolerance is complexity. SMP operating systems are more complex to build and maintain. Windows NT and many UNIX operating systems support SMP. SMP support is usually transparent to applications.

Executive

In Windows NT, the *Executive*, refers to the operating system code that runs in kernel mode. Besides the kernel and the Hardware Abstraction Layer, the Executive includes modules that provide services for applications such as memory management, I/O handling, object handling, process management, security monitoring, and a local procedure call facility. These modules are not implemented as a layered hierarchy, one on top of the other. Rather, they are implemented as peer managers which interact with each other.

Note for UNIX Programmers

Unlike UNIX, this portion of the operating system in Windows NT is not changed locally by a system administrator and is updated only by upgrades issued by Microsoft.

Process Manager

A *process* is the execution instance of a program. Each process has its own memory address space (4 gigabytes (Gb) in Windows NT and many UNIX systems) where the code that makes up the process resides. Each process also owns resources required for the process, such as files, threads, and so on. The Process Manager portion of the Executive manages the creation, management (including suspending and resuming processes), and deletion of processes (and threads). The Process Manager, like other key operating systems

Note for UNIX Programmers

Unlike UNIX, processes in Windows NT are not executable by themselves. Also unlike UNIX, Windows NT does not automatically establish a parent/child relationship when one process creates another.

services such as the Security Reference Monitor, gathers valuable performance data that helps system administrators monitor the system performance.

Even though a process is an execution instance, the process itself does not execute. A process is made up of one or more threads. Threads are the basic units of execution. A process has at least one thread. Multiple threads can be created. Each thread has its own memory. Threads are a convenient and efficient way to split functions that can be done in the background, while the main thread continues with other processing. In multiprocessor systems, two or more threads of the same process can be executing in parallel, thereby having portions of the same program executing in parallel. However, the price to pay for the convenience and efficiency is the need to *synchronize* threads. If you use a thread to perform a big sort in the background, your main thread has to ensure that the sort input data has not changed, and the main thread must be notified when the sort is done. As you will see in Chapter 10, using threads is one way to take advantage of the programming facilities in Windows NT, and you can synchronize threads using communication techniques such as semaphores.

Memory Manager

As mentioned earlier, each process gets its own address space of 4Gb. Most desktops and servers do not have that amount of real memory. Considering that there will be multiple processes at the same time, it is obvious that there must be a mechanism that maps the process address space to real memory. This mapping is done by the Virtual Memory Manager. The "virtual" in "virtual memory" indicates that most (or all) of a process memory is not real memory. Contents of the address space that are not held in real memory are held on the disk (see Figure 1-2).

During the course of execution, programs may need additional memory. A program requests additional memory either because program control gets transferred to part of the code that is not resident in memory, or because the program needs more memory for application data storage. In either case, since real memory is limited, some contents of real memory have to be swapped out. The process of swapping memory contents is called *demand paging.* A *page* is the minimum amount of memory that will be swapped in or out. The typical page size is 4 kilobytes (K). Both the process address space and the real memory are divided into pages. Each process thus has (4Gb/4K) a million pages. If you have 32 megabytes (MB) of real memory, then you have (32MB/4K) 8,000 real memory pages. The technique of selecting which pages will be moved out is called *first in, first out* (*FIFO*). The operating system keeps track of which pages came in first and selects those for swapping out. The idea behind this technique is that the more recent a page, the greater the chances that it will be used and needs to be kept in real memory. The Virtual

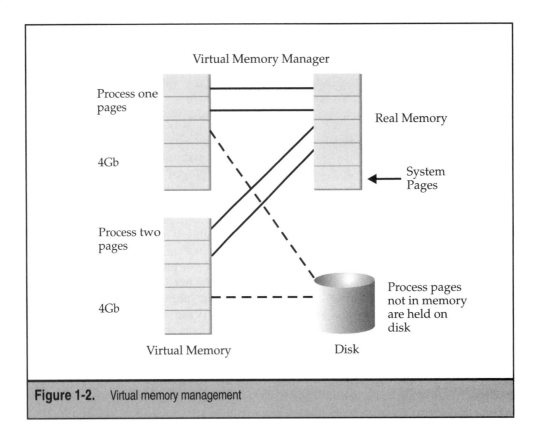

Figure 1-2.   Virtual memory management

Memory Manager uses a *page table* (actually the page table is a multilevel table), which holds status information about all memory pages. A business application programmer normally does not have to worry about how the operating system internally manages memory using memory management routines.

Virtual memory management attempts to strike the proper balance. If too much memory is allocated to processes, fewer processes will run and real memory occupied by some processes will not be accessed fast enough and will be wasted. Allocating too little memory to processes may cause frequent swapping of pages, resulting in a situation where the operating system is taking up a lot of CPU time that could have otherwise been used by application processes (the system is said to be *thrashing* when this occurs). To compound the situation, the memory access patterns will vary between processes, and what is optimal for one will not be for another. The operating system monitors the number of pages allocated and used by each process (also called the *working set*) and automatically fine-tunes memory allocation.

Windows NT uses 32-bit linear memory addressing. *Linear memory* means that the whole memory is considered one big layout, and each memory address is one value in the 32-bit address space. Contrast the linear memory model with the segmented memory

Note for UNIX Programmers

UNIX uses linear memory addressing, too. In addition, Windows NT and UNIX also use demand paging. Both systems also support *memory-mapped files,* which is a technique of speeding up file access by keeping files in memory rather than on disk. In addition, both systems also use *heaps,* which are unstructured memory. However, there are differences. Windows NT has a richer API set for virtual memory management and for managing heaps.

model of Windows 3.1, where memory is considered to be composed of 64K segments. If you are familiar with programming using segmented memory, then consider the 4Gb memory as one *huge* segment where you don't have to worry about far and near pointers. The 4Gb limit comes from the 32-bit address (2^{32}). Half of the process address space (2Gb) is used for the application process, and the other half, for system functions (related to the application process).

Input/Output Manager

This part of the NT Executive deals with all input and output, including input from and output to displays, disks, CD-ROM drives, and so on. The I/O Manager uses what is called a *uniform driver model.* In this model every I/O request to a device is through an *I/O request packet* (IRP), regardless of the specific type of I/O device. The device specifics are handled at a level below the I/O Manager. The I/O Manager performs the I/O task asynchronously. The process that issued the I/O request is preempted by the operating system, and it waits until it gets a signal that the I/O has been completed.

The I/O Manager of Windows NT uses a number of subcomponents such as the network redirector/server (Remote Access Server or RAS), the cache manager, file systems, network drivers, and device drivers:

▼ *Network redirector/server (RAS)*   This is covered in Chapter 3.

■ *Cache Manager*   In both Windows NT and UNIX, the *cache* is used to store frequently accessed data from disk (such as file data) to speed up future requests for data. Unlike some other fixed cache-size systems, the cache size in Windows NT varies depending on the amount of available memory.

▲ *Device drivers*   The need for device drivers is very simple. Windows NT can have hundreds of printers, disk drives, CD-ROM drives, and other peripherals attached to it. The low-level code to drive each of these devices is unique to the

Note for UNIX Programmers

Both Windows NT and UNIX consider all forms of I/O data as a string of bytes or a file. Both systems also implement task preempting for I/O requests.

device. For example, the line-feed command for an HP printer would be different from the command from an Epson printer. It could even be different for different printer models from the same manufacturer. If a word processing application wants to print, it wouldn't make sense for the Windows NT base operating system to format the output including the device-unique codes. The job of formatting output for the specific device is taken care of by device drivers (see Figure 1-3).

The Windows NT base operating system interacts with all device drivers in a standard way. By contrast, Windows 95 supports two ways—a device driver could be a protected-mode device driver, or it could be a real-mode device driver. As discussed earlier, Windows NT restricts low-level hardware access, and not supporting real-mode drivers is another example of the same design principle. Windows NT includes *device driver kits* (*DDKs*), which are equivalent to SDKs, for writing device drivers. Device drivers are normally written only by peripheral manufacturers or software companies that specialize in writing device drivers. Device drivers are low-level programs that business application programmers do not normally worry about.

The *file system* subcomponent deals with accessing, reading, and updating files. File systems are covered in Chapter 4.

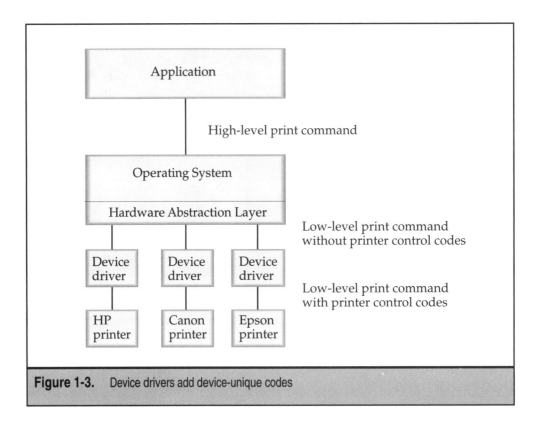

Figure 1-3.   Device drivers add device-unique codes

Object Manager

This part of the Executive creates, manages, and deletes objects. Almost everything in the Windows NT operating system is an object. For example, memory, processes, devices, and so on, are all objects. Objects have properties associated with them, and the functions of the object are invoked by *methods*. From the time an object is created to the time it is deleted, it has an associated *handle* that uniquely identifies the object.

Security Reference Monitor

Security in computer systems is getting a lot more attention thanks to hacking and viruses. With the increasing popularity of the Internet, the scope of hacking and of viruses has increased dramatically. Virtually any computer with external connections and/or floppy disk drives is susceptible to hacking and viruses. To combat this, operating systems have been increasing their security functions. Many agencies of the federal government have been working on the security problem along with interested groups in the computer industry for a long time. One result of these efforts is a scale indicating the level of security functions provided by an operating system. The scale ranges from D (least secure level) to A (most secure level), with intermediate classifications. The level most operating system vendors aim for and that is required in many federal computer procurements is C2. Windows NT meets the requirements for the C2 security level.

Windows NT implements a security system wherein all resources such as files have an associated security level. All users of the operating system, including system administrators, other users, and applications, have an associated security level. The security information is specified in an *access control list.* When a user wants to access a resource, the security levels are compared to determine if the user will be allowed to access the resource. Of course, security is a lot more complicated than that. Security is pervasive throughout Windows NT and is a part of many APIs and MFC classes. APIs and MFC classes will be covered throughout this book. Most of the setup and maintenance of security functions are handled by the system administrator.

Local Procedure Call Facility

Applications (*clients*) request services from the protected subsystems (*servers*). For example, a Win32 application requests services from the Win32 subsystem. Although the phrase "client/server" may conjure up the vision of a small Windows desktop accessing a big server across a network, there is no restriction that clients and servers cannot coexist on the same physical machine. For clients and servers distributed across a network, the most common communication mechanism is the industry standard *remote procedure call* (*RPC*). When the client and the server are on the same physical machine with common resources like shared memory, there is scope for optimizing the communication mechanism. Such an optimization is called the *local procedure call.*

Protected Subsystems

The operating system functions not performed by the kernel are performed by a set of nonprivileged servers known as protected subsystems (see Figure 1-1). When your application makes an NT API call, these calls are handled by the protected subsystems. One of the advantages of the protected subsystems approach is that it permits modular development of new protected subsystems without affecting either the base operating system or the other existing protected subsystems. The same is true for enhancements to protected subsystems. For example, if Microsoft wants to drop support for OS/2 or POSIX applications, then essentially all that needs to be done is to drop the code contained in those protected subsystems. Although Windows NT is designed to run POSIX and OS/2 applications, do not expect to be able to pass data or files between a Windows and a POSIX (or OS/2) application. Nor can you expect to see the graphical user interface Windows is famous for—both POSIX and OS/2 support only character mode applications. This is because the Win32 subsystem is the primary subsystem and supports the programming of text, graphics, networking, and all other functions available in Windows NT. The OS/2 and POSIX subsystems, on the other hand, are "compatibility mode" subsystems with just text support, and without graphics or network support. The lines between the OS/2 or POSIX subsystems and the Win32 subsystem in Figure 1-1 indicate that for many application calls, the OS/2 and POSIX subsystems actually call the Win32 subsystem. Microsoft documentation is specific on the differences in how Windows NT handles Win32 and POSIX (or OS/2) applications.

Quoting from "Microsoft Windows NT from a UNIX Point of View," a white paper from Microsoft:

"The POSIX and OS/2 subsystems provide 'compatibility-mode' environments for their respective applications and, by definition, are not as feature-rich as the Win32 subsystem."

A more technical quote from the Windows NT resource kit:

"With this release of Windows NT, POSIX applications have no direct access to any of the facilities and features of the Win32 subsystem, such as memory mapped files, networking, graphics, or dynamic data exchange."

Translated, no access to graphics means that the popular Windows graphical user interface is not natively available for a POSIX application, and you are restricted to console text applications. No networking means no WinSock, Point-to-Point Protocol (PPP) support, and the like. You get the picture. In providing POSIX support the way it did, Microsoft ensured that Windows NT can be used in federal and state acquisitions bids that mandate POSIX compliance, while ensuring that there is enough incentive for users to switch and take advantage of the other Win32 features.

Besides the protected subsystems, Windows NT also supports *virtual machines*. All the DOS programs, for example, run in a virtual DOS machine (VDM). The same mechanism is also used to run 16-bit Windows applications (also called *WOW* for Windows on Win32 applications). The same 16-bit Windows application that may run and cause a GPF and shut down Windows 3.1 will not be able to do that here, since the application only affects the virtual machine, not the whole operating system. The price for this protection is that some 16-bit applications (games and other applications that access the hardware or attempt to enhance performance through nonstandard means), will not run in Windows NT. There can be more than one virtual machine active at the same time.

PROGRAMMING LANGUAGES AND DEVELOPMENT ENVIRONMENT

Microsoft supports program development by providing a number of language compilers and an integrated development environment. Languages supported include general-purpose programming languages such as Visual C++, Visual Basic, Fortran, and special-purpose languages such as HTML, Visual J++, and PERL (Practical Extraction and Report Language).

Hypertext Markup Language (HTML) is the language used for developing World Wide Web pages and supports embedding multimedia content such as graphics into web pages. HTML also supports *hyperlinks,* which viewers use by clicking on the link (typically displayed in a different color than the rest of the text) and go to the address (*URL*, or Universal Resource Locator) pointed to by the hyperlink.

PERL had its origins in UNIX. PERL is a free-form interpreted language. PERL is used to scan and extract information from text files and to print reports using the extracted information. Windows NT supports PERL 5.

Fortran is used primarily for many scientific and some engineering applications. Microsoft's Fortran PowerStation supports the latest Fortran standard—Fortran 90.

Java is the programming language developed by Sun Microsystems and differs from traditional programming languages in one important way. Java compilers do not produce run-time executables for a specific environment, unlike traditional programming languages. The Java compiler outputs *Java byte codes.* These byte codes are interpreted by a Java Byte Code Interpreter, which can be embedded into many applications. The most common example of applications that embed Java interpreters are the World Wide Web browsers. Visual J++ is Microsoft's implementation of Java. Visual J++ allows you to create, edit, compile, run, and debug Java programs within an integrated development environment.

Visual Basic provides the ability to build applications without a lot of programming by use of prebuilt programming components or objects. It has many features of other programming languages such as branching, condition evaluations, assignments, and so on. Visual Basic, however, uses English-like constructs rather than terse programming constructs.

Keep in mind that you are not tied to any programming language. For the most part, you can invoke programs written in one language from another language. All major development efforts typically use more than one language. Learning programming languages is like learning to drive cars. Once you get a basic feel for the road, you can drive most cars relatively easily. Once you have learned to program in one language and understand logic, algorithms, and the like, you can program in any other language after a short learning curve.

Microsoft provides an integrated program development environment called the *Developer Studio*. The Developer Studio supports development of Visual C++ and other languages. The functions provided by the Developer Studio include

▼ Source code management

■ Editing and compiling program source

■ Link editing and makefiles

■ Project management

▲ Debugging

Microsoft integrates new functions related to program development into the Microsoft Developer Studio. Most of the programming examples in this book will be written in C++ and developed and tested by use of the Developer Studio.

Other software vendors also provide development environments. Borland International, for example, produces language compilers, environments, and tools such as C++ compiler, Object Window Library (OWL), and so on.

APPLICATION PROGRAMMING INTERFACES

Windows Application Programming Interfaces started with Win16, the 16-bit API, used by Windows 3.1 applications. Win32 is the 32-bit version used by Windows NT. Win32s was a subset of the Win32 API set that could be called by 16-bit applications. Wing is an API set for graphics. Although there is a huge install base of 16-bit applications, advances in hardware and software make it likely that most future programming will use the Win32 API. This book will focus on the Win32 API. You can tell whether system files and DLLs are 16-bit or 32-bit versions by looking for "32" in the filename. For example, *Kernel32.dll*, *Gdi32.dll*, *User32.dll*, and *Regedt32.exe* are all 32-bit functions.

The Win32 APIs are categorized as shown in Table 1-1.

Win32 Extensions

Microsoft has extended the Win32 APIs and included support to

▼ Develop desktop applications that integrate telephone functions by use of the Telephony Application Programming Interface (TAPI)

■ Develop asynchronous communications applications by use of the Remote Access Server (RAS)

■ Provide applications with database access by use of Data Access Objects (DAO)

▲ Develop electronic commerce applications by use of Exchange SDK

Category	Functions
Controls	Combo box, dialog box, edit, header, hot-key, image lists, list box, list view, progress bar, property sheet, rich edit, scroll bar, status, tab, toolbar, toolkit, track bar, tree view, and up-down controls Example: CreateUpDownControl
Graphics (GDI)	Advanced graphics functions including animation Example: CAnimateCtrl
Windows management	Windows, window class, window properties, and window procedures; cursors; menus; hooks; icons; Multiple Document Interfaces (MDIs); keyboard accelerators; keyboard inputs; mouse input messages; message queues; timers; and clipboards Example: InsertMenuItem
Console	Shell-related functions Example: TextOut
System services	Access files and databases, exception handling, network transports, performance monitoring, processes, threads, and security Example: GetOpenFileName
Network	Handle network connections, manage network configuration, domain administration, network management, remote access service, and Windows Socket interface Example: GetExtensionVersion
Multimedia	Audio, media control, video, joystick, and other special inputs/outputs Example: mciSendString

Table 1-1.   Win32 API Categories and Functions

SOFTWARE DEVELOPMENT KITS

Microsoft provides a number of *software development kits* (*SDKs*). SDKs are self-contained kits including specifications, programmer reference documentation, example source code, and so on. Each SDK focuses on one topic. Windows NT provides a number of SDKs. These include

▼ *Win32 SDK*   The Win32 SDK enables you to develop code using the Win32 API (refer to the "Application Programming Interfaces" section earlier in this chapter).

■ *MAPI SDK*   The MAPI SDK enables you to develop MAPI-compliant applications. The MAPI SDK is available in 16- and 32-bit versions. The 32-bit version is part of the Win32 SDK. C, C++, and Visual Basic examples are included in the MAPI SDK.

■ *OLE SDK*   The OLE SDK contains the COM specification. The OLE SDK enables you to develop code using the Microsoft object linking and embedding (OLE) interface.

■ *ODBC SDK 2.1*   This enables you to develop Open Database Connectivity (ODBC) drivers and ODBC-compliant applications.

■ *DAO SDK*   The DAO SDK enables you to develop DAO applications.

■ *RAS SDK*   The RAS SDK enables you to develop applications by use of the RAS API. You can use the RAS API to write applications to establish, communicate, and terminate connections with remote machines.

■ *Exchange SDK*   The Exchange SDK enables you to develop client and server programs based on the Microsoft Exchange Server.

■ *SMS SDK*   This SDK is used for developing applications for the Systems Management Server. The SMS Server and the SNA Server are add-on server products that run on top of Windows NT. These are covered later in this chapter.

■ *Systems Network Architecture (SNA) SDK*   This SDK is used for developing applications for the SNA Server.

▲ *Active Directory Service Interfaces (ADSI) SDK*   This SDK enables users, such as administrators, or applications to access and manipulate LDAP, NetWare, and NT directories. ADSI also includes Active Data Object (ADO) and OLE DB interfaces. ADSI itself is not language specific and will work with Visual Basic, Visual J++, and Visual C/C++.

MICROSOFT FOUNDATION CLASSES (MFC)

The Microsoft Foundation Class library (MFC) is an application framework for developing applications by use of the Win32 API. The framework is a collection of C++ classes. Classes simplify programming and promote code reuse. Using MFC classes will save you a lot of time. MFC is integrated within the Visual C++ development environment. For example, if you develop an application using AppWizard, you have the MFC classes available for your use. MFC is built on top of the Win32 API and attempts to shield the programmer from some of the details of API programming. Programs developed using MFC port well across the different Windows platforms, unless there are platform-specific constraints. If you have some old 16-bit code, Microsoft has an MFC migration kit that assists you in migrating the old 16-bit code. MFC has been keeping pace with the development technologies Microsoft has been coming up with. The latest version of MFC includes full OLE support, Data Access Objects (DAO) support, common controls support, thread synchronization support, and so on.

This book will include a lot of programming samples and exercises using the MFC.

GRAPHICAL DEVICE INTERFACE (GDI)

Graphical device interface deals with the subject of graphical end-user interface (as opposed to character-based interfaces) that Windows and Microsoft have become famous for. Windows includes a lot of support for you to develop GDI applications including Win32 APIs, MFC classes, prebuilt controls, and so on. Some of the common GDI objects you will use include

- ▼ Pens
- ◼ Brushes
- ◼ Fonts
- ◼ Bitmaps
- ▲ Metafiles

User interface programming is covered in more detail in Chapter 2.

While Windows is famous for its graphical interface, Windows NT does support character-based applications. Character-based applications run in a Windows NT *shell*. The Windows NT shell is an enhancement for the command prompt. The shell supports running character-based applications and is a good alternative to regular graphical windows programming for quick-and-dirty applications.

INTERNET AND NETWORK PROGRAMMING

Microsoft provides a number of ways to help you develop programs involving the Internet. Some of the ways include

- ▼ Internet server classes
- ◼ AppWizard for creating Internet applications
- ▲ World Wide Web access from the Developer Studio

The latest release of MFC has added five new Internet server classes. These classes implement the Internet Server API (ISAPI). These classes and their functions are

- ▼ **CHttpServer** Creates an Internet server extension.
- ◼ **CHttpServerContext** **CHttpServer** uses this to handle multiple concurrent requests.

■ **CHttpFilter**   Creates an Internet server filter to screen messages to and from an Internet server.

■ **CHttpFilterContext**   **CHttpFilter** uses this to handle multiple concurrent requests.

▲ **CHtmlStream**   **CHttpServer** uses this to send an HTML stream back to the client.

You can create Internet server extensions and filters using these classes and the ISAPI extension wizard. Visual C++ includes the example MFCUCASE, which illustrates creating Internet filter DLLs using MFC classes. Visual C++ also includes the example HTTPSVR, which illustrates using MFC and WinSock classes to implement a simple World Wide Web HTTP server. The HTTP server supports form creation and execution of Common Gateway Interface (CGI) server applications by use of the standard HTML constructs.

Network Programming

Besides the Internet, Windows NT also includes functions to support network programming. These functions include

▼ Windows Sockets (WinSock) support

■ Remote Access Server (RAS) support

■ Messaging Application Programming Interface (MAPI) support

▲ Telephony Application Programming Interface (TAPI) support

TAPI includes the APIs to integrate telephone functions with your applications. For example, using TAPI you can programatically place or receive a telephone call, hang up, place a call on hold, transfer calls, enable conference calls, and monitor calls. Of course, you need a line device such as a phone, fax card, modem, or an Integrated Services Digital Network (ISDN) card and a connection to the public phone network.

MAPI is more than an API. MAPI is a messaging architecture that is designed to bridge multiple applications on one side to multiple messaging systems on the other across heterogeneous hardware platforms and networks. MAPI shields users from the differences of various messaging systems—in particular, mail systems.

For example, you can use MAPI to develop applications that communicate with different messaging systems for fax, voice, and so on.

You can use MAPI in different ways:

▼ You can use Simple MAPI by using the Visual C++ (or Visual Basic) API interface.

■ You can use Common Messaging Calls (CMC), which is another form of API that supports the XAPIA standard.

▲ You can use OLE messaging.

COMPONENT OBJECT MODEL (COM) AND DISTRIBUTED COM

COM specifies how objects interact. It does not matter whether the objects are within a single application or spread across different applications. COM specifies basic interfaces that are used by all COM-based technologies such as OLE and ActiveX. One of the important elements of COM is its specification for component interoperability at the binary level. Binary components imply that the source language used to generate the binary or even the platform/vendor used to generate the binary is not relevant. All that is necessary is that the binary follows COM interoperability rules for it to use and be used by other COM-based binaries. Besides the binary nature of components, COM also specifies the communication rules between COM components. There is no restriction that the components be restricted to a machine or process. Thus, you have the communications between objects across networks, the basis for networked OLE functions. COM also specifies the rules for sharing memory between components, handling exceptions in the case of errors, and dynamic loading of components as required.

Distributed COM (DCOM) extends the COM model and constructs to let objects interact seamlessly across a network. DCOM is the new name for what used to be called networked OLE. Each DCOM object provides useful functions, and a set of functions is called an *interface* (which, in reality, is a table of pointers to the functions). Each DCOM object can have multiple interfaces. When an application that you are developing wants to use functions available in a DCOM object, you can invoke the DCOM object. The exact invoking mechanism is handled transparently by the operating system. Your application does not know where the object resides, which could be across a network or in the same process. In addition, the interfaces to the objects your application invokes can be changed and your application will remain unaffected (unless you want to take advantage of the interface changes). DCOM objects functions are implemented as dynamic link libraries (DLLs). This means that your application need not be recompiled if the DCOM object functions are changed. DCOM builds on remote procedure calls (RPCs).

OLE

The following describes a user's view of OLE. Your job is to provide the programming to make this happen. Let's start with a very brief recap of OLE basics and OLE 1.0. OLE provides the ability of an application like Word to include a spreadsheet object and to permit editing of the spreadsheet using Excel, but without quitting Word.

The object—the spreadsheet in this case—can be *linked* from or *embedded* into the Word document. If the object is linked, it remains as an independent spreadsheet and can be independently edited by use of Excel. But if you open the Word document that has the spreadsheet linked to it, the Word document will reflect the updates made to the spreadsheet. This behavior is an advantage if this is what you wanted, and a problem if you opened the Word document and were surprised to find the updated spreadsheet.

When the Word document embeds the spreadsheet, it completely contains the spreadsheet. The size of the Word document increases (approximately) by the size of the embedded spreadsheet. You can send the Word document to another Windows machine (across the world), and you can still see the document including the spreadsheet (assuming that machine has the right versions of Word and Excel). The Word document is also called a *compound document.*

OLE is based on the Component Object Model (COM). OLE lets you write platform- and language-independent objects. It specifies the interaction rules between objects. OLE lets you programatically implement the preceding scenario in your own application.

OLE has since expanded beyond compound documents. It is used for a variety of component software-based programming functions such as reusable custom controls, data transfer, drag-and-drop embedding, OLE automation, and in-place activation. As mentioned before, OLE is based on COM; an OLE-compatible application should follow the COM rules for functions and interfaces. There are many interfaces that are available for OLE applications, and many OLE applications use only a small subset of the interfaces. The one interface all OLE applications should implement is the **IUnknown** interface, which is like an entry point for all other interfaces. In fact, it includes the **QueryInterface** function that provides the list of the other interfaces available. Another important programming concept associated with OLE that you should be familiar with is called *OLE automation.* OLE automation is the mechanism by which one application can access, control, and manipulate another application's objects. OLE is covered in more detail in Chapter 13.

MULTIMEDIA

Windows NT includes support for you to develop multimedia applications. Multimedia applications are those that incorporate video, sound, and complex graphics. You can program at a high level using the MCIWnd window class or can have more control and program using the Media Control Interface (MCI) API, or even use multimedia structures such as **AVIFilePrevKeyFrame**. Other services provided by Windows NT for multimedia programming include a multimedia timer and I/O support such as joystick services. You can write sophisticated graphics programs in Windows NT using OpenGL.

OpenGL

OpenGL was originally developed by Silicon Graphics Incorporated (SGI) for its graphics workstations. Using OpenGL you can create applications with high-quality color images and animated 3-D graphics. OpenGL is independent of the windowing systems, operating system, and hardware.

Windows NT OpenGL components include

▼ OpenGL commands

■ OpenGL utility library (GLU)

▲ OpenGL programming guide auxiliary library

The Windows Graphic Library APIs and the new Win32 APIs for pixel formats and double-buffering also help in OpenGL programming. Microsoft Visual C++ has some OpenGL examples.

DATA ACCESS

Windows NT provides a number of ways for applications to store and retrieve data. Applications could use files. Windows NT supports multiple file systems such as New Technology File System (NTFS), File Allocation Table (FAT), and so on, and these are covered in Chapter 4.

Windows NT applications can also store and retrieve data from many databases, including smaller ones such as Access or enterprise databases such as SQL Server or Oracle. One popular way to access databases is the *Open Database Connectivity* (*ODBC*) using the standard language for database retrieval, the *Structured Query Language* (*SQL*). Microsoft has recently introduced *Data Access Objects* (*DAO*), which improves upon the functionality of ODBC. ODBC is covered in Chapter 20. DAO is covered in Chapter 21.

REGISTRY

The *Registry* is the configuration information database in Windows 95 and Windows NT (although at this point they are not compatible). The Registry is an alternate and better method of dealing with configuration information about hardware, applications, users, and so on, and is a replacement for the INI files used in prior versions of Windows. Note that for compatibility reasons, the old INI files are still supported. Registry can be updated by use of a built-in Registry Editor. The Registry can also be programatically accessed by use of APIs.

NT SERVER AND NT WORKSTATION

As mentioned earlier, Microsoft Windows NT actually comes in two flavors: Windows NT Workstation and Windows NT Server. The NT Workstation is designed to be the client machine, with fewer resource (memory and disk space) requirements compared with the NT Server. There is more commonality between the two NT products than there are differences. You can think of the NT Server functions as a superset of the NT Workstation functions. Both NT products provide rich networking capabilities including Transmission Control Protocol/Internet Protocol (TCP/IP) support and remote access services. Both products also have the same file systems support, basic NetWare integration functions, and provide basic security functions. Probably the most important from a programming perspective, both products support the Win32 API, including GDI support for end-user interfaces. This means that the same Win32 program that you write will work on both products.

Note for UNIX Programmers

There are third-party tools that let you run an application written using the Win32 API on many UNIX systems. Microsoft has a licensing program called *Windows Interface Source Environment* (*WISE*). The goal of WISE is to enable programs written to the Win32 API to run on different platforms such as UNIX and Macintosh. WISE SDKs provides source code compatibility, and the application source code must be recompiled for the different systems the application needs to run on. Examples of WISE SDKs include MainWin from Mainsoft and Wind/U from Bristol Technologies.

There are differences between the two Windows NT products, however, and the important ones from a programming perspective are summarized here:

▼ If you develop server applications—for example, using the BackOffice products or the Internet Information Server—then those may not work on the NT Workstation.

■ Windows NT Server includes a special disk device driver called *Ftdisk.sys*, which takes advantage of the fault-tolerant capabilities such as disk mirroring, duplexing, and parity striping of Redundant Array of Inexpensive Disks (RAID).

■ Windows NT Server includes TCP/IP-related networking enhancements such as Dynamic Host Configuration Protocol (DHCP) support (which permits dynamic IP addresses assignment), Windows Internet Naming Service (WINS) support (which provides dynamic NetBIOS name registration and resolution), and a Dynamic Domain Naming Service, which adds on the benefits of dynamic support to regular Domain Naming Service functions.

■ Another networking difference concerns RAS. The RAS service in Windows NT Server supports up to 256 simultaneous RAS connections, while the RAS service in NT Workstation allows only a single connection.

■ Windows NT Server provides Internet support using the Internet Information Server (IIS). IIS is a full-fledged Internet server that supports HyperText Transfer Protocol (HTTP), file transfer protocol (FTP), Gopher, and other Internet services. The Windows NT Workstation, on the other hand, uses Peer Web Services, which is functionally equivalent to the IIS, with one important difference being that it limits the number of incoming connections to ten. This limitation restricts the number of users and Internet functions that can be supported by use of a Windows NT Workstation.

▲ Windows NT Server can integrate Macintosh clients, has extensible security functions, supports integration with and migrating from NetWare, supports "roving" users by storing user-profile information and letting the user have the same environment wherever he or she logs on, can provide a single logon for multiple domains, and so on.

There are more differences between the two NT products. To summarize: the Windows NT Workstation is not designed to run such server applications, and the two products are designed for different requirements. If an NT Server is used where an NT Workstation would suffice, it would amount to cracking a nut with a sledgehammer. On the other hand, if you attempt to save money and try to run server applications on the Workstation, chances are that there will not be enough horsepower for the NT Workstation to run the application (if it were possible to run at all).

ADD-ON SERVER FUNCTIONS FOR THE WINDOWS NT SERVER

Besides the Windows NT Server product itself, there are a number of add-on server products that Microsoft produces which add unique functions to the Windows NT Server. These unique functions include database access, systems management functions, functions for the Internet, and so on. Your programming tasks are likely to include one or more of these add-on products. The following presents a brief summary of these add-on products. Figure 1-4 shows an overview of the add-on products and the common programming tools for the add-on products.

SQL Server

The Structured Query Language (SQL) Server is a relational database management system. It is comparable to and is a competitor of database systems from Oracle, Sybase, and Informix. Some of the functions provided by the SQL Server are

▼ Storing and retrieving data

■ Ability to run application logic common to many applications in one place, instead of each application duplicating the logic

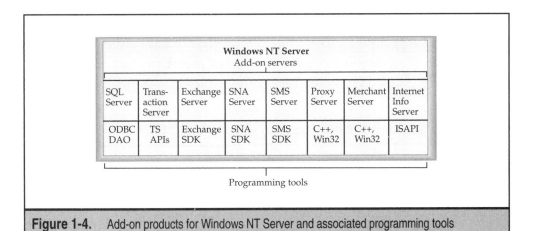

Figure 1-4.   Add-on products for Windows NT Server and associated programming tools

■ Database administration functions such as backup and recovery

■ Communication between databases when data required for an application is in another database

▲ Interface support to permit applications to access data (such as ODBC, DAO, and so on)

Common programming tools for the SQL Server include SQL, ODBC, and DAO.

Systems Management Server

The Systems Management Server (SMS) is a tool for administrators to manage servers and client workstations from a central location. Some of the functions provided by the SMS are

▼ SMS stores and updates configurations of hardware and software for servers and clients on a network.

■ Remote software distribution permits clients' software to be automatically updated from the SMS. Besides the actual program files, configuration information for the client could be provided as well.

■ SMS provides an end-user interface as well as the ability to access its functions programatically.

▲ SMS helps desk support functions, including the ability to monitor client workstations remotely.

The SMS SDK, which includes System Management APIs, is used to program the SMS.

Proxy Server

The Microsoft Proxy Server acts as a gateway on top of the Windows NT Server and the Internet Information Server to provide a secure access to the Internet. All Internet users' requests are routed through the Proxy Server. The Proxy Server includes caching functions and will attempt to satisfy a user's request with a cached copy. The Proxy Server eliminates having a dedicated Internet gateway, since it (and IIS) can run on any Windows NT Server. The Proxy Server supports TCP/IP and Novell's Internetwork Packet Exchange/Sequenced Packet Exchange (IPX/SPX) protocols, the Secure Sockets Layer (SSL) interface, and the European Laboratory for Particle Physics (CERN) Proxy standard.

Merchant Server

This is a new add-on server function from Microsoft designed to facilitate transaction processing and exchanges between merchants online. Both the Proxy Server and the Merchant Server can be programmed by use of the C++ and Win32 APIs.

Microsoft Transaction Server

The Microsoft Transaction Server is a recent addition to the Microsoft BackOffice family. Microsoft Transaction Server is a transaction processing system. It includes different components such as a Transaction Server run-time environment, a graphical user interface, and so on. Of interest to the programmer is an Application Programming Interface specifically meant for developing applications for the Transaction Server. Some of the important features of the Transaction Server of interest to the programmer include

▼ Developers can build Transaction Server applications as software components using tools that support ActiveX, including Microsoft Visual Basic, Visual C++, and Visual J++.

■ Transaction Server includes a component packaging service to facilitate integration, installation, and deployment of many components as a single application.

■ Transaction Server manages a pool of ODBC connections to a database.

■ Transaction Server automatically provides transparent transaction support to applications running on the server. The application does not need to use low-level transaction control primitives (or fundamental elements) to accomplish this.

■ Transaction Server uses DCOM for component-to-component communications across a network. Microsoft is trying to license DCOM as an open-industry standard through the Open Group.

■ Transaction Server works with many resource managers, including relational databases, file systems, and image stores, that support a transactional two-phase commit protocol. This enables businesses to leverage existing investments in UNIX and mainframe data stores.

■ Win32 "fat" clients and HTML "thin" clients can access Transaction Server applications concurrently.

▲ Administrators can easily partition an application across multiple servers by deploying an application's components into several packages, with each package running on its own server.

IIS Server

The Internet Information Server (IIS) provides Internet-related functions for its Internet clients including

▼ File transfer using the file transfer protocol (FTP)

■ Searching the Internet through a Gopher

▲ Domain Naming Service (DNS) to translate lookup Universal Resource Locators (URLs)

The ISAPI is used to program Internet-related functions. MFC also includes new Internet-related classes.

SNA Server

The SNA Server is used to interface with IBM's networks that use the Systems Network Architecture. The SNA Server enables applications to interface with legacy applications and to retrieve legacy data.

The SNA SDK is used to program the SNA server functions.

CONCLUSION

We have looked at a range of Windows NT topics that provide an overview of the different functions in Windows NT. These topics lay the groundwork for future chapters, and you should be familiar with the programming topics mentioned. The remainder of the book builds on these topics. For example, ODBC is covered in Chapter 20; DAO, in Chapter 21; ISAPI, in Chapter 16; OLE, in Chapters 12 and 13; and TAPI is covered in Chapter 18.

WINDOWS
NT
Professional
Library

CHAPTER 2

User Interface Programming

Programming the user interface is one of the most challenging and rewarding areas of Windows NT programming. You already know that people can understand a lot better what they can *see*. Coming up with a well-designed user interface and demo helps to show the application you are developing much better than reports, charts, and other documentation about the application. The good news for you is that Microsoft is standardizing the user interfaces of its primary products. First, Windows NT got the same interface as Windows 95. Second, Microsoft is trying to further standardize the desktop to an Explorer-based desktop where it doesn't matter whether the items on the desktop are from the local machine or from the network. This interface is already becoming available in the Visual Developer Studio, the Microsoft Developers Network, and so on. Why is this standardization important to you? One obvious reason is that if you have used one Microsoft product, you can be comfortable with others. More importantly, Microsoft includes a lot of prebuilt code to support user interface programming, and use of the prebuilt code will lead to the same standardized interface. This means that even without seeing a single dialog box in your application, your end users are already trained in many end-user aspects of your application.

THE WINDOWS USER INTERFACE

User interface programming involving Windows NT differs from other programming environments, such as mainframes and even many UNIX environments, in Windows NT's ability to customize and in its built-in support for the customization. Most mainframe and some UNIX environments show the application screens to the user, but the user can do little to customize them. Many of the functions that are taken for granted in Windows NT user interfaces, such as adjusting the size of the window, changing background and foreground colors, changing fonts, scrolling, moving the position of a window on the desktop, reducing a window to an icon, and so on, are either not available or restricted in the other environments. The good news on customization for you as a programmer is that you get all of this functionality for very little effort. Windows NT has a lot of built-in code that provides much of the functionality for supporting the Windows NT user interface.

Besides the window management and customization support, Windows NT includes a number of built-in standard user-interface elements to ease the task of user interface programming. These include standard functions to ask the user to choose from a list of alternatives, to provide the user with a list of available choices for a field, and so on. These built-in elements are the bread and butter of Windows NT user interface programming.

In this chapter we will review the basics of user interface programming for Windows NT, including a few of the built-in controls. Windows NT had always included a number of built-in APIs and controls to support user interface programming. Windows NT 4 expands on the built-in APIs and controls. Windows NT includes support for advanced user interface features, such as common controls and world transforms. These advanced features add pizzazz to your user interface. A more detailed discussion of some of the built-in elements, together with programming examples, appears in Chapter 7.

As a programmer, you are not constrained to use any of these built-in elements. However, unless you want to try things on your own, use these built-in elements as much as possible. If you use them, you have already in effect trained your end user in some aspects of using your application. For example, if you open a Windows application that you may not know how to use, you still may have some idea where to find the application functions if you see File, Edit, Window, and Help on the menu bar. Since your application end user has most likely used other Windows applications at home or work, you make his or her life a lot easier by being consistent with other Windows applications.

WINDOWS NT USER INTERFACE PROGRAMMING

Windows NT provides different ways that you can program to support user interfaces:

▼ Windows basic and common controls

■ Programming interfaces to support graphics (GDI support)

■ ActiveX controls

■ OpenGL support

■ Control classes supplied by the MFC

▲ Windows NT shell and shell extensions

This chapter covers the basic controls, and using the MFC to program controls. Chapter 5 will address GDI programming. Chapter 7 will address advanced controls and the shell and its extensions. Chapter 12 will address ActiveX controls, and Chapter19 will address OpenGL programming. Before we start looking at programming simple controls, let's look at two ways that you can program these controls.

APIS VERSUS THE MFC PROGRAMMING

You can program user interfaces (and most other functions) in Windows NT either directly using the Win32 API or by using the MFC. Win32 APIs were summarized in Chapter 1.

Programming using the MFC is the same as C++ programming using classes. In fact, the MFC is a class library. The MFC encapsulates or wraps Windows NT programming elements such as dialog boxes in the MFC classes. You program using the MFC by using an existing class (or deriving from an existing class) and creating an object of the existing or derived class. Once an object has been created, you call member functions of the class to manipulate the object. It is important to note that use of the MFC is not a completely different way of programming. The MFC calls the same Win32 APIs that you can write to directly. The MFC shields some of the details associated with APIs and in some cases performs some small housekeeping functions that tend to save you time and effort compared with programming directly to the Win32 APIs. Also note that the MFC encapsulates most of the Win32 API. Note that there are some APIs that the MFC doesn't encapsulate. This is because the MFC provides classes for the anticipated needs of most programmers, but it is not meant to be a C++ run-time library. In cases where the MFC does not have the classes for some function that you want to program, you can use the MFC for the other functions and call the Win32 API directly from within the MFC.

While many programmers use the MFC for the added convenience, as an advanced Windows NT programmer, you should be familiar with both Win32 API and MFC programming. Let's review some basic controls, their characteristics, and programming aspects.

BASIC CONTROLS

It is impossible to use Windows NT for a while and not come across the word "control." *Controls* are the building blocks of user interface programming. The interaction between a user and your program takes place in the form of passing messages back and forth between your program and controls. Controls are child windows to let the user make selections, input or edit data, and so on. Controls are typically used in dialog boxes, although they are used in other windows as well. Some common examples of controls include check boxes, combo boxes, edit boxes, list boxes, scroll bars, and so on. The Windows NT operating system has always provided a number of predefined controls, and more controls were added for Windows NT 4.0. The advanced controls are called *common* controls; let us call the older, simpler ones *basic* controls.

Windows NT provides the programming tools for you to include controls in your program. You can add controls to your dialog box using the Visual C++ dialog editor. The MFC includes a class for each of the controls. **CWnd** is the base class for all control classes (and all other window classes as well).

Next, let's look at how to program controls—predefined and custom controls, disabling controls, and stand-alone controls.

PROGRAMMING CONTROLS

You can create a control in two ways. You can specify a control's associated windows class to the **CreateWindowEx** function. Alternately, you can specify the controls to be included in the dialog box template. Typically, you would include more than one control in your dialog box or window. To distinguish one control from another, each control has a unique identifier called a *control identifier*. If you use **CreateWindowEx**, the control identifier is specified using the *hMenu* parameter. If you use a dialog box template, the control identifier is specified in the ID member of the **DLGITEMTEMPLATE** structure.

Once created, a control sends messages when it is accessed by the user (these are **WM_COMMAND** messages). These messages, called *notification messages,* are sent to the parent window. The notification messages include the control identifier and information about the event that caused the notification message. The control includes the control identifier in the notification message by using either the **GetDlgCtrlID** function or by retrieving the identifier from the *hMenu* member in the **CREATESTRUCT** structure while processing the **WM_CREATE** message. The application receives these messages and takes appropriate action. The application can manipulate the control using functions such as **ShowWindow** or **EnableWindow**, or can send control messages (if the control's window class supports control messages). Control messages could be predefined, such as **WM_SETFONT**, or application defined. Application-defined messages are sent using a function such as **SendDlgItemMessage** to send messages. All messages from the application to the control go through to the window procedure.

Predefined Versus Custom Controls

Controls can either be predefined by Windows NT, or you can create your own custom controls. There are a lot of programming advantages in using predefined controls. *Predefined* controls have a set of built-in *styles* that you can choose from. Styles specify the appearance and behavior variations for the control. Windows NT also provides a lot of code to support the built-in controls, which translates into less work for you. To get a custom look, you can use your own custom controls.

The most elaborate and time-consuming way to do this is to define your own window class. You then register your window class the same way you would register any other window class. (Remember, each window class must have a unique name.) You then specify the name of your window class in the **CreateWindowEx** function or in the dialog box template. You must also write the window procedure to draw the control, process any input messages from the keyboard and mouse, and send notification messages to the parent window. In addition, your window procedure may need to process control messages sent by the parent window or other windows.

There are a couple of easier ways to get custom controls. First, you can create a subclass of a predefined control class. In this case, instead of writing a window procedure to handle all the messages, you can write a subclass procedure to handle selected messages and pass all other messages to the original window procedure for the control. Finally, for some predefined controls such as list boxes and combo boxes, you can designate them as owner-drawn controls by specifying the appropriate style. Windows NT still does most of the work associated with the control, such as detecting and notifying if the user interacts with the control. The drawing of the control, however, is left to the parent window of the control. Thus, you can choose to vary the appearance of your control.

USING PREDEFINED CONTROLS

Having looked at different controls and some programming aspects in general, let's look at some common predefined controls and user interface programming functions provided by Windows NT.

TIP: There are excellent examples of different user interface elements and how to navigate. You already have the example—just refer to your Windows NT and your Visual C++ program interfaces.

Menu

You probably will never develop a Windows NT user interface application without a menu. Your menu, which typically is the first one your user sees, provides a snapshot of all functions provided by your application. Windows NT provides a lot of support to help you in creating your menu.

The menu (or more accurately the *menu bar*) is the bar displayed just below the *caption bar* displaying the choices your program provides to the user. For example, the Microsoft Word menu is shown in Figure 2-1.

Menu Characteristics

The menu shows a list of items that the user can select by clicking on them (or selecting them by means of the keyboard). When selected, each item typically brings up a *pull-down menu* (also called a *submenu*) indicating more choices. Menu bars have consistency

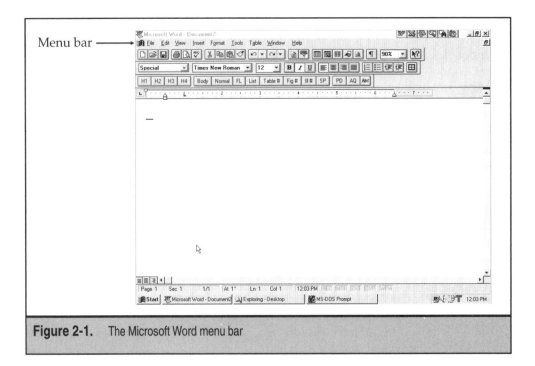

Figure 2-1. The Microsoft Word menu bar

guidelines that are a good idea for you to follow in your application. For example, File is typically the first item and Help, the last. Within each pull-down menu, horizontal bars group similar items together. Items that have additional levels of choices are indicated by an ellipsis (...). Typically, a description for each item in the menu bar shows up either as a tooltip or as text in the status bar. It is also common for a menu item to be selected by typing a letter when the menu or submenu is active (usually the first letter, unless the letter is already being used). Each window (except for some very simple ones) typically has a menu, but having a window is not a prerequisite for a menu. You can program *floating menus* to appear anywhere on the desktop. The pop-up menu that appears when you click the right mouse button on an empty area of the desktop is an example of a *floating pop-up menu*. You can dynamically add or change menu items based on the context in your application.

Programming Menus

From a programming perspective, you can consider each menu item as a command that you have to process. Windows NT passes the command menu item, and your program processes the command and responds to the message. The steps involved in adding and processing a menu in your program are as follows:

1. Create the menu.
2. Display the menu at program startup.
3. Handle messages from the menu.
4. Destroy the menu (if necessary).

You can create a menu by defining it in a resource file. You can edit a resource file using resource editors built into Microsoft Visual C++, or you can edit them by hand. You can also create menus dynamically and by using the Visual C++ AppWizard. You can edit the menu resource AppWizard generates to add or delete menu items. When creating a menu, you should ensure that the ID for each menu item is unique. The ID of each item tells your application which item you are working with. Submenus do not have IDs. When you create a menu, you also create the items that belong to the menu. Some items may have other items nested below them, and these are called *submenus* or *pop-ups*. You create pop-ups when you create the menu as well. You also specify options associated with menu items, such as if the item is to be inactive or grayed (you can programmatically turn these on later—for example, in Word some of the edit options are grayed out until you open a file).

In step 2, you cause a menu to be displayed at your program startup by specifying the name of the menu in the *lpszMenuName* parameter of the window class.

In step 3, you start using the menu. The user makes a selection by clicking on a menu item (or using the keyboard). This causes a **WM_COMMAND** message to be sent to the window that owns the menu. One of the parameters passed in the message is the ID of the menu item selected by the user. This lets you take appropriate action in your program and respond. Your response depends on your application. If you are using the MFC, the

MFC framework converts the **WM_COMMAND** message into a function call that can be used in your program's other classes, such as document or view classes.

Lastly, if your menu is associated with a window, then the menu is destroyed and its memory released when the window is closed. If your menu is not associated with a window, then you should explicitly destroy your menu using **DestroyMenu**.

You can change a menu by adding or deleting menu items. If you add a menu item, you modify the menu resource to add the item and add message-handling functions to process the new menu item. Message-handling functions can be developed by use of the ClassWizard.

Dialog Box

A dialog box permits more complex interaction, including the ability for the user to input text using the keyboard.

A dialog box (or dialog, for short) is actually a placeholder wherein other controls such as list boxes, edit boxes, and so on, can reside. As such the dialog box is the parent for the other controls that reside in the dialog box.

Dialog Box Characteristics

There are two types of dialog boxes: *modal* and *modeless*. The user must respond to a modal dialog box before he or she can switch focus to another window in the application (and this includes the parent window of the modal dialog box). Figure 2-2 shows the Save As dialog box in Word, which is a modal dialog box. You can move a modal dialog box around on the desktop.

A modeless dialog box permits the user to switch focus to another window in the application. Figure 2-3 shows the Find dialog box in Word, which is a modeless dialog box.

Modeless dialog boxes provide more options to the user, and they are also more difficult to program, since you have to cater to more possibilities of user actions compared with the modal dialog box.

Programming Dialog Boxes

Before you can use a dialog box in your program, you must define it. The common method to define a dialog box is by use of the dialog editor. Some of the parameters you specify for defining a dialog box are the dialog name, a caption for the dialog, and the style of the dialog. The style specifies such things as whether support for Maximize and Minimize should be included, whether the dialog box should include a system menu when created, and so on. By default, a modal dialog box is visible when created, whereas a modeless dialog box is not. If you are creating a modeless dialog box and want it automatically visible, ensure that you have made it visible.

A dialog box is created (displayed) by your program by calling either the **DialogBox** API (for modal dialog boxes) or **CreateDialog** (for modeless dialog boxes). You pass the name of the dialog box as a parameter, and Windows NT looks for a dialog box with the name you specify in your program's resource file. **DialogBox** returns control to your

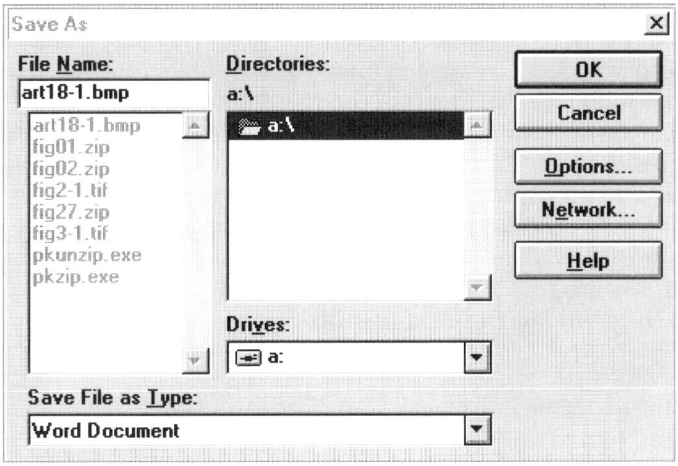

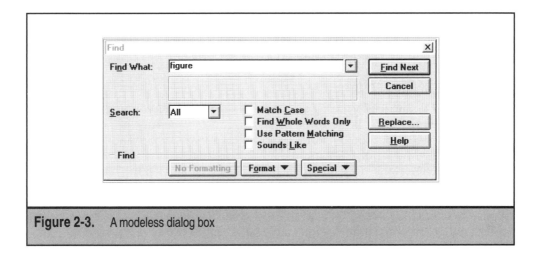

Figure 2-2. A modal dialog box

program with an exit status. **CreateDialog** returns a handle that your program should use for future requests associated with the dialog box.

A dialog box has its own message queue, and the messages from the dialog box are not sent to your program's main window function. Dialog box messages are handled by

Figure 2-3. A modeless dialog box

dialog functions (also called *dialog procedures*). Although we refer to the messages the dialog box function receives as dialog box *messages,* keep in mind that the messages are actually triggered by the user accessing one of the controls within the dialog box. Each dialog box has its own dialog function. The dialog function is a *callback* function. The message sent to the dialog function includes the ID of the control that caused the message to be sent. The main difference in programming between modal and modeless dialog boxes comes in message processing. For a modeless dialog, your main window function may receive messages while the modeless dialog is active. So you need to check if the messages are actually meant for the modeless dialog box and not process them in your main window function. You use the **IsDialogMessage** function to check and route dialog box messages.

When you no longer need the dialog box, destroy it using **EndDialog** (for modal dialogs) or **DestroyWindow** (for modeless dialogs).

TIP: You may be creating dialog boxes outside WinMain (for example, in the window procedure). Since the dialog box needs access to the current instance handle, you have to ensure that a copy of the current instance handle is available to the dialog box. You could use a global variable for this purpose.

DIALOG BOXES USING THE MFC   If you use the MFC, you can create a dialog box either by hand or by using the dialog editor. When you create the dialog box, you also include the controls that are part of the dialog. Then you use the ClassWizard to derive a class from **CDialog**. You code your message-handling functions as required. Depending on where the dialog box is invoked, you may need to modify your existing resources and message-handling functions to include the new dialog.

Message Box

Another common control you will use in your program is the *message box,* which is actually a special and simple form of a dialog box. You are likely to use this often.

A message box is a simple window used to show a message to a user. The message box is removed after the user has acknowledged the message. Figure 2-4 shows a message box.

Message Box Characteristics

The severity of the message varies. It can convey information or a warning, or even notify the user of a serious error. Besides one or more buttons, a message box can include an icon, and you can color code the icon to indicate its severity. For example, you can use red to indicate serious errors. When you display a message to a user, you want to ensure that the user has read the message. The way to ensure that the user has read the message is to get the user to acknowledge the message (using a mouse click, for example). You should include at least one button (usually this is the OK button). You can also provide more button choices for user acknowledgment, where appropriate. For example, if the user's request cannot be fulfilled due to a resource not being available (printing when the printer is out of paper, or reading a floppy disk drive which has no floppy disk), then

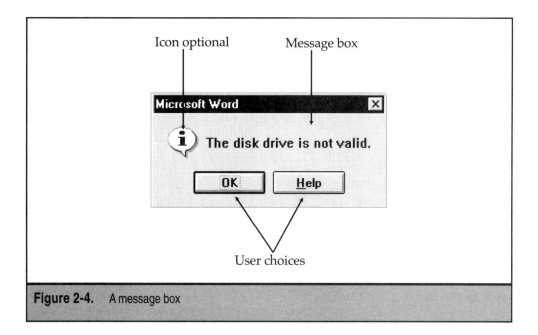

Figure 2-4.   A message box

you can ask the user if the operation is to be retried. A message box commonly provides the user with Abort, Retry, and Ignore options. (Ignore skips that particular request, but proceeds with other requests.)

While it is a good programming practice to get the user to acknowledge messages you display, there are some exceptions. An acknowledgment from the user may be optional, for example, in a status message that indicates progress of the user's request (such as a print request). If you don't want your program to wait for an acknowledgment, you can program to display the message for a certain amount of time or for an event (such as successful completion of printing) and programmatically remove the message. Keep in mind, though, that you cannot use a modal dialog (including a message box) if you plan to do this, since by definition the modal dialog will wait for the user's response.

Programming Message Boxes

You can program a message box using the **MessageBox** API. You can pass the title of the message box window as a parameter. You can also use styles to ask Windows NT to include some buttons automatically. The most common button is the OK button, which is specified by including the MB_OK style. Including the OK button lets the user click on the OK button to acknowledge the message. Other buttons you can include are Abort, Retry, Cancel, and so on. The message box returns the user's choice of acknowledgment.

MESSAGE BOXES USING THE MFC   Using the MFC, you invoke a message box using one of the MFC classes like **AfxMessageBox**. You can pass as parameters the text that is to be displayed in the message box and the styles you want. There are two forms of **AfxMessageBox**. The one whose prototype is shown next lets you provide a string pointed to by a pointer to display in the message box.

```
int AfxMessageBox( LPCTSTR lpszText,

                   UINT nType = MB_OK,

                   UINT nIDHelp = 0 );
```

where *lpszText* points to a **CString** object or null-terminated string containing the message to be displayed in the message box, *nType* is the style of the message box, and *nIDHelp* is the Help-context ID for the message (0 indicates the application's default Help context will be used).

The other form of **AfxMessageBox** uses an *nIDPrompt* parameter of type UINT, which is a unique ID used instead of the *lpszText* parameter to reference a string in the string table.

Scroll Bar Controls

A scroll bar is a very important control and one that you are most likely to use in programming user interfaces. This is the bar to the right and at the bottom of many windows, with arrows at the ends and a small box in the middle that can slide along the scroll bar.

Scroll Bar Characteristics

Scroll bars are used to scroll the contents of the window they border on. The vertical scroll bar moves the window contents up or down. The horizontal scroll bar moves the contents right and left. The scroll bar can be used to move the contents in one of two ways—either by clicking on the arrows or by clicking, holding, and dragging the sliding small box. The latter method tends to be faster than the former. The scroll bars that are present in almost all windows are called the *standard scroll bars.* Scroll bars can also be used as stand-alone controls, providing the same functionality as standard scroll bars. When used in this manner, the controls are referred to as *scroll bar controls.* Standard scroll bars have a default range of 100, while scroll bar controls do not have a default range and have to be set programmatically.

Programming Scroll Bars

To include a standard vertical scroll bar, you can specify the WS_VSCROLL style in **CreateWindow**. Use WS_HSCROLL to include a horizontal scroll bar. When the user uses the scroll bar in one of the two ways mentioned earlier, your program gets a **WM_VSCROLL** message for a vertical scroll bar or a **WM_HSCROLL** message for a horizontal scroll bar. The parameters passed with **WM_VSCROLL** or **WM_HSCROLL** indicate whether the scrolling was for a line or a page, and the direction of the scroll (Up, Down, Right, Left). Unlike some other controls, Windows NT does not automatically update the scroll bar's position. You have to do that in your program. Windows NT provides you the **SetScrollInfo** and **GetScrollInfo** APIs to help you update the scroll bar position. **SetScrollInfo** and **GetScrollInfo** work for both standard scroll bars and scroll bar controls.

Static Control

The use of the word "control" in "static control" is actually inaccurate, because a static control doesn't do anything. That is, it doesn't generate or receive any messages. Once you define a static control and it shows up on the display, that's it. Sometimes you need to put up some text on dialogs, or group a bunch of controls to indicate to the user that the controls belong to a group. You would use a static control for these purposes. Static controls are summarized in Table 2-1.

As their names suggest, CTEXT, RTEXT, and LTEXT are used to display static text in a centered, right-aligned, or left-aligned manner. GROUPBOX can be used judiciously to make your dialogs more intuitive and are another way to spruce up your user interface.

Figure 2-5 shows the Page Setup dialog in Word. Besides the text, it shows that the header and footer margins are a group, since both share a common property that they are measured from the edge of the page. When you change one margin, the grouping makes you think about the other margin as well.

OTHER BASIC CONTROLS

Windows NT provides many more basic controls. Some of these controls are listed in Table 2-2. If you are not familiar with programming any of these, refer to *Windows NT 4 Programming from the Ground Up*, by Herbert Schildt, Osborne/McGraw-Hill, 1997.

Note for UNIX Programmers

If you have programmed user interfaces using X Window/Motif in the UNIX environment, then programming for the Windows environment is similar. Window sizing and navigation functions are very similar between Windows NT and UNIX.

ADDING CONTROLS BY HAND

As stated earlier, you can either add controls to a dialog box with the dialog editor, or add them yourself with code. You can create your own control object by embedding the C++ control object in a C++ dialog or frame-window object. Like many other objects in the MFC framework, controls require two-stage construction. You should call the control's Create member function as part of creating the parent dialog box or frame window. For dialog boxes, this is usually done in **OnInitDialog**, and for frame windows, in **OnCreate**.

Static Control	Function of the Control	Parameters
CTEXT	Display text centered in a predefined area	Text to be displayed, area where the text is to be displayed
RTEXT	Display text left-justified in a predefined area	Text to be displayed, area where the text is to be displayed
LTEXT	Display text right-justified in a predefined area	Text to be displayed, area where the text is to be displayed
GROUPBOX	Draw a box to group other controls	Title of box, area where the box is to be displayed

Table 2-1. Static Controls

DISABLING CONTROLS

One of the ways you can make your program really user friendly is by making it impossible for users to select options that don't apply to their situation. From your program's context, you know what valid input your user can provide at a given time. It would be too expensive to create a separate dialog for the controls a user needs at each

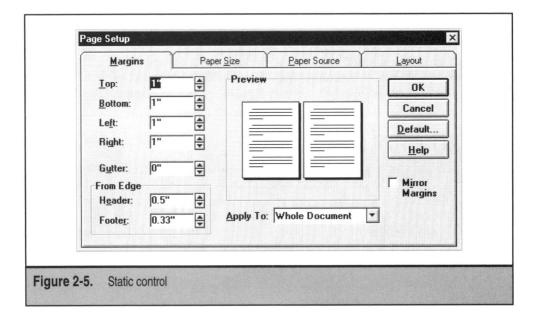

Figure 2-5. Static control

Control	Function of the Control
List Box	Provides a list of alternatives for the user to choose from
Edit Box	Lets user input data
Check Box	Provides the ability to turn an option on or off
Radio Button	Provides a list of mutually exclusive options
Combo Box	Combines the functionality of a list box and an edit box

Table 2-2.   Other Basic Controls

point. A more effective solution is to use an existing dialog and to disable the controls that are not applicable. Disabling a control causes that control to be displayed in gray. The user cannot select a grayed control. Figure 2-6 and Figure 2-7 are two output screens from Windows NT diagnostics that illustrate disabling controls. The buttons for Properties and Refresh are grayed out in Figure 2-6, as they are not applicable. The same buttons are enabled in Figure 2-7.

STAND-ALONE CONTROLS

Although controls are normally used within a dialog box, you can program controls to be stand-alone. Of course, stand-alone controls must still be within the client area of the main window. The control could be a basic control such as Button, ComboBox, ListBox, and so on. You can also customize the control by using the styles associated with the controls, just as you would if the control were within a dialog. You create a stand-alone control using **CreateWindow**. You pass the name of the control and the associated style you want as parameters. Messages from a stand-alone control are handled by the control's parent window procedure.

USER INTERFACE: BEYOND CONTROLS

We have seen some basic controls, and we have also seen how to derive custom controls. Besides basic and custom controls, there are other ways you can spruce up your user interface.

Windows NT also lets you include your own icons, bitmaps, and other graphics in the user interface you program. You can significantly enhance the usability of your program by suitably using these graphical elements in your program. You can use icons for programs, resources such as printers, operations, and so on. Some programs include a small icon and a slightly larger icon to represent the same object in different situations.

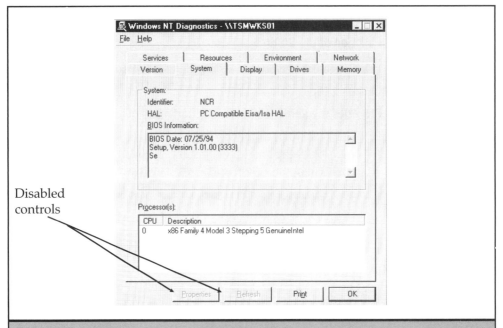

Disabled controls

Figure 2-6. Disabled controls

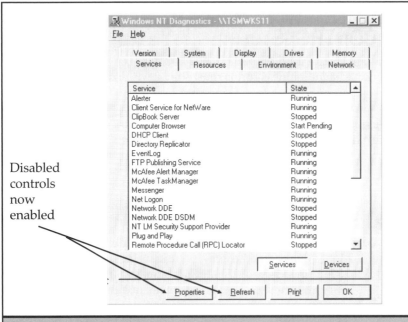

Disabled controls now enabled

Figure 2-7. Enabling disabled controls

For example, the small icon is typically used when the window of a program (that the icon represents) is minimized. You can also use bitmaps. A *bitmap* is a pixel-level representation of a graphic image. Bitmap sizes vary. Small bitmaps (about the size of thumbnails) are used for menu choices. You can use the built-in graphics functions to draw lines, rectangles, circles, and so on. Windows NT provides support for GDI, and this is addressed in Chapter 5.

THE MFC CONTROL CLASSES

As is the case with programming in other areas, the MFC includes a lot of support for developing user interface programs. The MFC provides control classes that you can use when you want to implement the controls. The MFC also provides classes that provide variations that add pizzazz to your controls, such as the ability to include bitmaps instead of text for buttons, and support for dragging list items. Table 2-3 lists three such classes.

These classes let you spruce up your user interface using bitmaps, draggable lists, and so on.

ACCELERATOR KEYS

Another way to spruce up your user interface in Windows NT is to use *accelerator keys*.

When you program user interfaces, you invariably come across a dilemma—how to structure your user interface so that a first-time user can use it easily *and* so that it supports power users. You can optimize for one user set, but that invariably means affecting the other user set. For example, if you make your interface flow easily through a bunch of

Control Class	Function
CBitmapButton	Permits you to use bitmaps instead of text for button labels. You can use up to four bitmaps for each button to show the different states of the button (normal, selected, focused, disabled).
CCheckListBox	Provides the functionality of a list box with added check boxes that the user can check. Used only for owner-drawn controls.
CDragListBox	Improves on the functionality of a regular list box by including the ability for the user to drag items in the list. By default, the dragged items are moved, but you can customize the drag to perform a copy instead of a move.

Table 2-3.   Additional MFC Control Classes

windows, the power users may have to navigate more windows than necessary. Of course, the choices are application dependent, and you may have a simple way out. For example, if your application is designed primarily for decision-support purposes and is used occasionally by managers and executives, you want a very simple user interface, one that is very tolerant of user errors. But more often than not, your user base is likely to be a combination of users with varying degrees of familiarity with computers.

This dilemma is not unique to business application programming. Programmers who write software for games face a similar problem: how to make the game interesting for the first-time player, while still keeping it challenging for the power user. Their solution is to alter the program behavior using play skill levels. For business programming, you normally do not want to ask (or otherwise figure out) if the user is a beginner or an advanced user. But you can develop the user interface more toward the beginner and program some functions that will help the power user. One such function is accelerator keys.

You can let a user branch to another window in your application, bypassing the menu system by using accelerator keys. Often an experienced user knows where to branch to within the menu system, but he or she has to make a bunch of tedious menu selections to get there. For the users who are paid by the number of transactions they process, going through the menu system is more than an annoyance, it is loss of productivity and money. Pressing the accelerator keys jumps the user directly to the window and brings the window to the top of the Z order. (The Z order of a window indicates the window's position in a stack of overlapping windows along an imaginary z-axis.) Besides the alphabet and number keys, accelerator keys can also include *virtual keys*—keys that do not have an ASCII equivalent, such as the SHIFT key, CTRL key, and so on.

Programming Accelerator Keys

Programming for accelerator keys involves two steps:

1. Define the accelerator keys.

2. Include the accelerator keys in your program.

You can define accelerator keys using an accelerator key table in your resource file.

You can include the accelerator keys in your program by using two APIs—**LoadAccelerators** and **TranslateAccelerator**. You call **LoadAccelerators** right after creating a window, and it loads the accelerator table and returns a handle. **TranslateAccelerator** sends a **WM_COMMAND** message including the ID associated with the translated accelerator key. This is transparent to your program and will appear to your program that the **WM_COMMAND** was generated by the user making a menu selection. However, there is a difference. You should ensure that when you get a message as a result of **TranslateAccelerator**, you don't call **TranslateMessage** and **DispatchMessage** as you normally would in processing messages. For the most part, it should not make any difference to your program whether the user pressed an accelerator key or used the menu. But you can figure it out if you need to by looking at **WM_COMMAND** parameters.

Note that while the primary use for accelerator keys is with menus, the accelerator-key mechanism is general enough for you to perform any function you want that is triggered by the accelerator key. The accelerator key concept is very similar to hot keys. Both accelerator keys and hot keys enable some keyboard combination to be used as kind of a shortcut to perform a function. The HotKey control lets you define a keyboard combination that can be pressed by the user to perform some immediate function in your application. The HotKey control is covered in Chapter 7.

Besides standard and common controls, Windows NT provides other controls, the most notable of which is ActiveX controls. ActiveX controls, formerly known as OLE controls, can be used in dialog boxes in your applications for Windows NT or in HTML pages on the World Wide Web. ActiveX controls are covered in Chapter 12.

TEXT SUPPORT IN USER INTERFACES

Although the graphical interfaces with windows, icons, bitmaps, and so on, are the ones most programmed for and used, Windows NT has special support for text. There are two ways that text can be displayed under Windows NT. Older character-based programs can be run in the Windows NT shell. This is more of a compatibility mode solution for the older programs, which are usually DOS-based and assume that the whole screen is available to them. If you want to develop programs that have just a text interface under Windows NT, there is a better method—one that lets you display text in a window. You can use the APIs Windows NT provides for text support.

APIs for Text

The most common API for text is **TextOut**. You can pass the character string you want displayed and the (x,y) coordinate locations to **TextOut** (coordinates are relative to the window and not absolute coordinates). The coordinates are logical coordinates, and Windows NT maps these logical coordinates to physical coordinates, based on the mapping mode. In the default mapping mode of MM_TEXT, logical coordinates and physical coordinates are the same—pixels—and thus you specify the coordinates in pixels. For example, if your coordinates are (x,y), Windows NT locates the starting point for the text display by moving x pixels horizontally and y pixels vertically (going downward, since the coordinate origin is the upper-left corner).

When you display text, Windows NT uses the default colors for the text and the background, but you can change them using **SetTextColor** and **SetBkColor**, respectively. In cases where the physical display is not capable of displaying the color selected, Windows NT chooses the closest color that the device is capable of. In Windows NT, as with many other systems, different colors are specified as different combinations of the three fundamental colors—red, green, and blue (RGB). Windows NT provides a macro, the RGB macro, that helps you specify the color of your choice. The macro accepts three parameters, one for each of the three colors. Each parameter is a value between 0 and

255, with 0 being the lowest intensity and 255 being the highest intensity. Thus, RGB(0,0,0) is the absence of red, green, and blue-black color, and RGB(255,255,255) is a combination color that has the maximum of red, green, and blue-white. The RGB macro returns a 32-bit value, which has a special type called COLORREF. You use this type in your program to specify your color choice. You can also set the background mode (which is either Opaque or Transparent) using **SetBkMode**.

Text Metrics

One of the differences between Windows NT and other operating systems is the evolution in support for text and graphics. Many other operating systems supported text and were subsequently enhanced to display graphics and color. Windows NT, on the other hand, always had graphics support as a primary objective, and text support is also present. One consequence of this difference in evolution is that in other systems you will not find functions that you would normally take for granted, such as a text cursor. If you display text in a window, you (not Windows NT) have to worry about whether there is enough space to display additional text. There is no concept of a cursor that automatically advances based on the number of characters. In addition, knowing the number of characters you displayed is not enough, since most text you display will be proportional. The actual space occupied on the display will be different for two strings with the same number of characters (as long as the characters themselves are different). What you need to do is calculate the actual space occupied by what you displayed and adjust the starting coordinates of your next display request accordingly. You need to know the font characteristics (height, distance between lines in pixels). The API that you use to get font characteristics is **GetTextMetrics**. Windows NT also provides another API called **GetTextPoint32**, which computes the length of a character string.

NOTE: Windows NT provides a set of features (through the Win32 API) that you can use to program special user-interface functions that make it easier for persons with disabilities to use your program. These features are beyond the scope of this book.

CONCLUSION

Designing and writing good user-interface programs is more an art than a science. As a user interface programmer, your job is similar to that of an artist. You have the tools (basic controls, custom controls, icons, bitmaps, graphics, and so on), and you have a set of blank screens. Using the tools, you paint a set of screens that constitutes your program user interface. You can make a big difference in your users' perception of your application by what you do with your user interface. As mentioned before, you can also make a difference in user productivity.

In Chapters 1 and 2, we have looked at an overview of Windows NT and user interface programming aspects. Continuing to lay the groundwork for NT programming foundations, we will look at the communication mechanisms that Windows NT provides in Chapter 3.

WINDOWS
NT
Professional
Library

CHAPTER 3

NT Communications and Networking

Although PCs started out as personal, self-contained computers, it soon became apparent that communicating with other computers is highly desirable, since that is how many tasks related to the PC get accomplished—by communication and collaboration. Thus, while DOS had limited communications features and you typically bought communication software packages, Windows NT has integrated networking with built-in functions to communicate in a variety of ways. For example, Windows NT not only supports dial-up networking, but it also includes support for a number of clients (including Apple Macintosh) and protocols. The ever increasing use of e-mail and the Internet have given communications programming an important role, one that you should be familiar with as an advanced Windows NT programmer.

In terms of computers, the word "communications" has different meanings. There are communications between different programs (processes) *within* a computer—*interprocess* communications. There can also be functions requiring communications (such as file transfers) between two programs each running in a different computer. The link between the two computers could be a cable or telephone lines. There are software packages that provide such links, and you normally do not program for such applications (unless you are a developer of one of the communication packages).

Then there are communications where the computer is attached to a network with a *network adapter card,* and you write business applications that communicate using the adapter card and communication facilities provided by the operating system. This is the type of communications discussed in this chapter. Using this, you can have both peer-to-peer and other forms of communication for distributed computing, including client/server communications.

Even if you have programmed with Windows NT, there are many business applications where communication functions are limited and there is little chance to program communication-related functions. If such has been your experience, then this chapter will help you understand the communication mechanisms available in Windows NT and set the stage for an in-depth study in Part 3.

We will start with the International Standards Organization (ISO) model for communications between two applications. This is also called the *seven-layer model* or the *Open System Interconnection (OSI) model.* We will briefly review the communication mechanisms that Windows NT provides. We will then look at *distributed computing,* a programming paradigm in which communications plays a key role. Then we will look at some Windows NT communication functions associated with the Internet.

Note for UNIX Programmers

If you have programmed using UNIX communication mechanisms, then it will be easy for you to write communications programs using Windows NT. Windows NT provides TCP/IP support and includes the Windows version of Sockets, called *WinSock.* WinSock (short for "Windows Sockets") is compatible with Berkeley Software Distribution (BSD) sockets. WinSock includes BSD-style sockets as well as Windows-unique extensions.

THE ISO COMMUNICATIONS MODEL

Figure 3-1 shows the ISO seven-layer communications model. Although strictly speaking there are eight layers (0–7), from a programming perspective you don't have to worry about the bottom layer—the *media layer*. This model has been used for quite a while. Note that this is a reference model, not a commercial product or design. The beauty of this model is that you can fit the role of any communications-related program into one or more of the seven layers.

Before we look at the other layers, let's review some characteristics that are true for all the layers above the media layer. The purpose of each of the other layers is to provide services to the next higher layer. The aim is to provide services that are transparent. If you call a Win32 API, you know you pass control and get control back. Your program doesn't know exactly what happens in between. The same concept applies here. Lower layers shield the higher layers from the actual implementation details. There is also division of labor between the layers. When an application in one computer communicates with another application in another computer, there are several functions to be taken care of. These functions include breaking down the data into manageable *packets*, ensuring that data has been properly transmitted (including retransmission, if necessary), translating between *communication protocols* if required, and so on. The different layers are meant to take on different functions. In practice, a product that primarily addresses

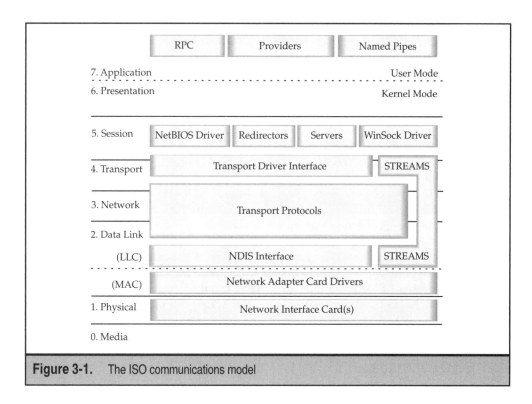

Figure 3-1.   The ISO communications model

the functions of one layer may include some functions in other layers. Transport protocols span the functions of multiple layers. Let's look briefly at the services of each layer.

The Media Layer

The bottom layer is the *media layer,* which is all the media used to connect computers and networks—whether these are copper or fiber-optic cable or even wireless. From a programming perspective, there is no software in this layer.

The Physical Layer

The *physical layer* is where the *network interface card* (*NIC*) (also called *network adapter card*) fits in. The NIC has the physical hardware connectors to connect to a network external to the computer. It shields device drivers from the propreties of the media.

The Data Link Layer

The *data link layer* is divided into two sublayers—the *media access control (MAC) layer* and the *logical link control (LLC) layer*. The MAC sublayer hosts the device drivers that control the NIC as mentioned in the physical layer section. The MAC sublayer sends and receives data in *frames* (which is just a way of grouping bits). One of the added functions of the MAC sublayer is to ensure that the communications are error free. For example, it retransmits frames if it does not receive positive acknowledgment that the frames it sent were received. The LLC hosts the Network Device Interface Specification (NDIS), a specification jointly developed by Microsoft and 3Com. As with other layers, NDIS shields the details of the NIC from the transport protocols.

The Network and Transport Layers

The *network* and *transport layer* functions are provided by transport protocols. The transport protocols fit in both the network layer and the transport layer. Windows NT supports many transport protocols—TCP/IP, NetBEUI Frame (NBF), NWLink, Microsoft Data Link Control (DLC), and AppleTalk.

The TCP/IP protocol is the de facto protocol standard that is common in the Internet. TCP/IP includes an addressing mechanism and routing based on the addresses. The ability to route avoids the need to broadcast messages. Avoiding broadcasting and sending messages to portions of the network helps reduce network traffic. The NBF protocol is derived from *NetBEUI* (NetBIOS Extended User Interface). NetBEUI is the protocol used in older Microsoft networks, such as those for Windows for Workgroups, and is an extension of NetBIOS (Network Basic Input Output System). The NWLink protocol is an NDIS-compliant version of the transport protocol used in Novell networks—IPX/SPX (Internetwork Packet Exchange/Sequenced Packet Exchange). AppleTalk is the protocol used by Apple Macintosh networks. The unit of data that is moved in the network and transport layers is a *packet*, which is not related to or dependent upon frames. The functions provided by the network and transport layers include adjusting packet-routing based on network traffic, checking for errors in packets, and retransmitting them, if necessary.

Windows NT also supports STREAMS, developed by AT&T for UNIX System V, Release 3.2. Windows NT includes STREAMS support for the same reason it supports the POSIX subsystem—compatibility. Inclusion of STREAMS support enables existing STREAMS-based transport protocol drivers to work with Windows NT.

The Transport and Session Layers

The Transport Driver Interface (TDI) enables software at the *session layer,* such as a network director, to choose from different lower-level transport mechanisms, such as TCP/IP or IPX/SPX. This illustrates the power of the ISO model. Lower-level mechanisms are shielded from the upper layers, and software at one level is not tied to the details of the software at another level. TDI lies between the *transport layer* and the session layer. Transport protocol device drivers are written to the TDI interface.

At the session layer level are the drivers such as WinSock (short for "Windows Sockets") and NetBIOS drivers.

WinSock

A *socket* is a connection's endpoint. Two sockets, one at each end, form a complete communication path. A communication path formed by sockets provides a bidirectional communication mechanism. WinSock 1.1 supports two types of sockets—*stream sockets* and *datagram sockets.* Stream sockets are used for the bidirectional transmission of a large stream of data. Streams are normally used for transmitting and receiving unduplicated data (packets are sent and received only once) and sequenced data (the order in which the data packets are sent is preserved). Stream sockets guarantee data delivery. As mentioned before, grouping the data into packets is handled by the lower-level transport layer. Datagram sockets are connectionless, unreliable communication mechanisms suitable for data communications where you don't care about guaranteed data delivery. The message buffers allocated for datagram-type sockets are small. Datagram sockets use the User Datagram Protocol.

WinSock has had two releases. The first release aimed at providing independence from TCP/IP stacks. That was a stepping stone for the next release, which not only supports TCP/IP, but also supports other protocols including DECnet.

WinSock 2 not only expands on the socket types, but also provides a dynamic way for applications to query the available transport protocols and their properties using the **WSAEnumProtocols** function. Socket type definitions appear in *Winsock2.h.*

PROGRAMMING WINDOWS SOCKETS   Windows Sockets is implemented as a DLL—*Winsock.dll.* You can use the MFC for Windows Sockets programming. The MFC includes socket objects, with encapsulated handles of the type SOCKET. Socket handles are similar to window handles. You use the handle to get to an instance of the socket or window. You then use socket classes to perform the actual messaging functions. The MFC includes two classes for sockets programming—**CAsyncSocket** and **CSocket**. **CAsyncSocket** is more advanced and includes all the functionality of sockets APIs. **CSocket** is a simplified version for serialized data communications such as packing and unpacking data for stream sockets. You can derive your own classes from these two classes and override the member functions they contain such as **OnConnect**, **OnSend**, **OnAccept**, and so on.

NetBIOS

NetBIOS stands for Network Basic Input Output System. As with WinSock, NetBIOS fits in the session layer. The functions that NetBIOS provides include establishing logical network names and establishing connections between the logical names. The Win32 NetBIOS function is primarily for compatibility. You would use this function for porting current NetBIOS applications that are not being rewritten. If you have programmed using IBM's NetBIOS specifications, note that there some minor differences in the way Microsoft implemented the specification.

Redirector

When you communicate, you access resources on another computer and vice versa. *Redirector* and server are a pair that provide complementary communication functions. The redirector handles accessing the remote computer, and the server responds to remote requests. The redirector provides transparency. It redirects an I/O request to the right device across the network when the file or device to be accessed is not on the local machine. It interfaces with the server on the remote machine. The redirector is a file system driver. The application's file I/O request does not change whether the file is local or remote. The redirector also redirects print requests in the same manner. The redirector interfaces with the I/O Manager Executive component. The Windows Executive and its components were covered in Chapter 1. Redirectors also perform some network housekeeping functions.

Note for UNIX Programmers

The ability of the redirector to provide transparent file access is similar to the functionality in UNIX file systems such as the Network File System (NFS) and the Andrew File System (AFS). File systems are covered in Chapter 4.

Server

The term "server" is used to denote different things. In Windows NT Server, the term refers to the whole operating system (and sometimes includes the machine the operating system is running on). In SQL Server, the server refers to the software that is on top of the Windows NT Server that provides database services. In the context of this paragraph, the server is the component that talks to redirectors. When a server receives a request from a redirector, it accesses the local resources and returns the result to the requesting redirector. The server is also a file system driver and handles print requests as well as file I/O requests.

Both the redirector and server execute in the kernel mode for a reason. Both could be handling large amounts of data, and it is easier to handle large amounts of data with other kernel-mode components like I/O Manager and Cache Manager executing in the kernel mode than in the user mode (such as a protected subsystem). At any given time, many redirectors and servers can be active.

Redirector/server pairs are a modular way to expand the network connectivity of Windows NT. Windows already includes such software to let Windows NT coexist in NetWare networks. Third-party redirector/server pairs are also available.

The Presentation Layer

The *presentation layer* handles formatting and translating data including such functions as code and character set conversion. For example, this layer handles ASCII to EBCDIC (which stands for Extended Binary Coded Decimal Interchange Code and is commonly used in IBM mainframes) translation, compression/decompression, and encryption/decryption of data. This layer also establishes and terminates sessions. This layer allows the layer above, the application layer, to interpret the meaning of the data.

The Application Layer

The top layer, the *application layer*, is where the business application you write fits in. All your program knows (and cares about) is the interface to the layer just below—the presentation layer. All the other layers are concerned only about the successful transmission of data. The actual content of the data and its meaning are relevant only at this level.

We looked at the different layers of the ISO's OSI model. Now let's take a step-by-step look at how the different layers of the model are used when two applications communicate.

THE OSI MODEL AND A WINDOWS NT APPLICATION

Having looked at the ISO's OSI model, let's look at what happens when a Windows NT application issues a request for a remote file I/O access. The sequence of events that happen when your program requests an I/O operation is as follows:

1. Your program (at the application layer level) makes an I/O request, using a Win32 API for file I/O, and the I/O Manager gets the request.

2. The I/O Manager formats your request into an I/O request packet (IRP). The IRP is sent to the redirector (at the session level) through a *provider* (for each redirector there is a provider at the application level). The right provider is selected by a multiple provider router.

3. The redirector determines if the request can be satisfied locally or whether the request needs to be sent to a remote computer (let's go with the remote version).

4. The redirector sends the request to a network transport driver (at the transport level).

5. The network transport driver adds header information for the network and transport and invokes the NDIS driver (at the data-link layer level).

6. The NDIS driver adds data-link headers and invokes the lower level.

7. The physical layer and the media layer carry the IRP plus all the other headers to the server (on the remote machine).

8. The NDIS driver on the server removes the data-link headers and passes the rest of the data to the server network transport driver.

9. The server network transport driver removes the headers its counterpart on the requesting machine added and passes the rest of the data up the chain.

10. The server completes the I/O and sends the data back. Now it follows the same path described in the previous steps, except that the data flow is from the remote machine's server to the requesting machine's redirector. For brevity, let's skip the lower layer steps and assume that the data has come back to the redirector of the requesting machine.

11. The redirector gets the results (including the requested data, hopefully) and passes the results to the I/O Manager.

12. The I/O Manager returns the data to your program.

While the number of steps and the whole operation may seem time-consuming and complex just for a file I/O, in practice it is very fast and not that complex. The added headers and checks at different levels ensure not only an error-free transmission, but also retransmissions that are transparent to the application. Your application will never know that it got its data on the second attempt, because the first attempt had a recoverable error.

COMMUNICATIONS MECHANISMS IN WINDOWS NT

Having looked at a generic reference model and an application scenario of how that model is used with Windows NT components, let's look at all communication mechanisms in Windows NT. Windows NT supports a number of communications mechanisms to facilitate you writing programs that require communication services. The mechanisms include

▼ *Win32 API*—such as the one we looked at for file I/O.

■ *WinSock APIs*—covered in Chapter 15.

■ *WNet*—provides a network-independent interface for managing network connections.

■ *Remote procedure calls (RPCs)*—the ability to invoke procedures that are physically resident on another machine as though they were present in the local machine.

■ *Remote Access Server (RAS) services—lets remote users have the same functionality as if they were connected directly to a computer network, by the use of one or more RAS servers.*

■ *Named pipes*—to connect two Windows applications and to facilitate communication between the applications.

■ *Mailslots—are* similar to named pipes. You can use mailslots to let your process communicate with other processes.

■ *Support for protocols*—including TCP/IP, NBF, NWLink, Microsoft Data Link Control (DLC), and AppleTalk.

■ *Internet-related communication mechanisms*—such as:

   ■ *Telnet*, which lets your computer become a terminal to a remote server.

   ■ *FTP*, which allows for file transfers between remote computers.

   ■ *Ping*, which checks if a remote server is responding.

■ *Microsoft SNA Server*—provides communication with legacy systems that support IBM's Systems Network Architecture. SNA Server supports programming using the Common Programming Interface for Communications (CPI-C) and Advanced Program-to-Program Communications (APPC) interfaces. The SNA Server was briefly covered in Chapter 1.

■ *Open Database Connectivity (ODBC)*—enables applications to communicate with databases to retrieve, store, and update data. ODBC is covered in Chapter 20.

▲ *Object linking and embedding (OLE)*—allows applications to communicate with each other and to make functions of one program available to another. OLE can also be used to provide complex communication functions between applications across networks. OLE is covered in Chapter 13.

Let's briefly look at some of the communication mechanisms.

WNet

WNet functions let you connect and disconnect network resources and the associated end-user interfaces. For example, the **WNetAddConnection2** function makes a persistent connection or redirects a local device to a network resource. The local device could be any local resource such as a disk or printer. WNet also includes functions to enumerate resources (**WNetEnumResource**) or even the current network user name (**WNet-GetUser**). The WNet end-user interface includes **WNetConnectionDialog**, which displays a network-connection dialog box. **WNet** enumeration functions use the NETRESOURCE structure shown next:

```
typedef struct _NETRESOURCE {  /* network resource structure */
    DWORD   dwScope;
    DWORD   dwType;
    DWORD   dwDisplayType;
    DWORD   dwUsage;
    LPTSTR  lpLocalName;
    LPTSTR  lpRemoteName;
    LPTSTR  lpComment;
    LPTSTR  lpProvider;
} NETRESOURCE;
```

dwScope defines the enumeration scope. It could be RESOURCE_CONNECTED to get currently connected resources, RESOURCE_GLOBALNET for all network resources, or RESOURCE_REMEMBERED for remembered (persistent) connections.

dwType indicates whether the resource is disk, printer, or any. Type is specified as a bitmask.

dwDisplayType specifies how the network object is displayed in the user interface. It could be RESOURCEDISPLAYTYPE_DOMAIN to display the object as a domain, RESOURCEDISPLAYTYPE_GENERIC to indicate that the display type does not matter, RESOURCEDISPLAYTYPE_SERVER to display the object as a server, or RESOURCEDISPLAYTYPE_SHARE to display the object as a share.

dwUsage is only applicable when *Scope* is RESOURCE_GLOBALNET. It could be RESOURCEUSAGE_CONNECTABLE to indicate a connectable resource whose name is pointed to by *RemoteName* or RESOURCEUSAGE_CONTAINER to indicate a container resource.

lpLocalName is the name of a local device if *Scope* is RESOURCE_CONNECTED or RESOURCE_REMEMBERED. It is NULL if the connection does not use a device. Otherwise, it is undefined.

lpRemoteName is the remote network name if the resource is a network resource or the network name associated with the name pointed to by *LocalName*, if the resource is a current or persistent connection.

lpComment is a provider-supplied comment, and *lpProvider* is the name of the provider owning this resource. *Provider* can be NULL.

Remote Access Server (RAS) Services

RAS allows two-way communications between the Windows NT Server and clients supported by the Windows NT Server. RAS lets a remote computer provide all the functions as if it were directly connected to the network. Functions provided by RAS at the client include an end-user interface, starting and ending RAS connections between the remote computer and the Windows NT Server, and providing RAS status and configuration information. At the server, RAS provides administration, security, and connection-management functions.

Named Pipes

A *named pipe* is a high-level communication mechanism you can use in your process to communicate to another process. The process you are communicating to can be anywhere on the network (unlike an anonymous pipe) and need not be related to your process. Windows NT implements a named pipe as a file object. If you are familiar with accessing files using file system drivers, then you know how to use named pipes. In fact, you use read and write operations on named pipes as you would for files.

TIP: The file-system object and driver analogy is applicable in many other areas of Windows NT programming such as mailslots.

Usually a server opens a named pipe with a name clients already know, or passes the handle or the name of the pipe to clients through an InterProcess Communication (IPC) mechanism. Once a client knows the name, it opens the named pipe (provided it has the authorization to do it), and the server and the client communicate using read and write on the pipe. Named pipes can support both one-way and two-way communications. When clients open a named pipe by using its name, separate instances of the named pipe are created, even though the pipes may have the same name. These separate instances have unique handles and memory buffers (you can also have unbuffered pipes if you want to). The use of separate instances permits more multiple clients to simultaneously communicate using the same pipe name. Pipe access can be overlapped or synchronous. Named pipes can use any underlying transport protocols that are available for communication between a client and a server. One of the nice features of named pipes is *impersonation*, which lets a server impersonate a client. This has security implications. When a server impersonates a client, it is the client's access privileges that determine whether an access can be performed.

Programming Named Pipes

Some of the functions you may use for communicating using named pipes are **CreateNamedPipe**, **TransactNamedPipe**, and **CallNamedPipe**. The typical programming sequence would be to call the functions **CreateFile**, **TransactNamedPipe**, and **CloseHandle**. You can use **WaitNamedPipe** if **CreateFile** cannot open the pipe immediately. Alternatively, you can call one function—**CallNamedPipe**. The **CallNamedPipe** function connects to a message-type pipe, writes to and reads from the pipe, and then closes the pipe. **CallNamedPipe** waits for an instance of the pipe, if one is not available. The prototype for **CallNamedPipe** is shown next:

```
BOOL CallNamedPipe( /* Connect , Write, Read, and Close a named pipe */
                LPCTSTR  lpNamedPN,
                LPVOID   lpInBuf,
                DWORD    nInBufSize,
                LPVOID   lpOutBuf,
                DWORD    nOutBufSize,
                LPDWORD  lpBytesRead,
                DWORD    nTimeOut

);
```

lpNamedPN is the named pipe name, *lpInBuf* is a pointer to the input buffer that contains the data written to the pipe, *nInBufSize* is the input buffer size in bytes, *lpOutBuf* is the pointer to the output buffer that holds the data read from the pipe, *nOutBufSize* is the output buffer size in bytes, *lpBytesRead* is a pointer to a variable that stores the actual number of bytes read from the pipe, and *nTimeOut* is the time to wait for the named pipe to be available. You can specify the time-out duration in milliseconds, or specify to wait indefinitely (NMPWAIT_WAIT_FOREVER), to not wait if the pipe is not available (NMPWAIT_NOWAIT), or to wait for the default specified when the pipe was created using the **CreateNamedPipe** function (NMPWAIT_USE_DEFAULT_WAIT). The return value is nonzero if the function succeeds and zero otherwise.

Note for UNIX Programmers

If you have programmed using named pipes in UNIX, then Windows NT named pipes are very similar. Note, however, that named pipes in Windows NT and UNIX are not compatible.

Mailslots

Mailslots are similar to named pipes in that by using mailslots your process can communicate with other processes. The file system analogy of named pipes applies to mailslots as well. But there are differences between the two (otherwise you wouldn't need two different communication mechanisms). The similarities and differences between named pipes and mailslots are summarized in Table 3-1.

When you create a mailslot, you are a mailslot server. Other programs (mailslot clients) can store messages in the mailslot, and the messages are appended to the end and remain in the mailslot until you retrieve them. You can be a mailslot server and a client at the same time. There are basically two classes of mailslots—first class and second class. Windows NT implements only second-class mailslots. Second-class mailslots are a connectionless messaging mechanism. When you use second-class mailslots, keep in mind that the message delivery is not guaranteed. This absence of a guarantee makes

Feature	Named Pipes	Mailslots
Communication type	Two way	One way
Message delivery	Processes know if messages sent	Processes don't know for sure if messages sent
Programming	Using file system APIs	Using file system APIs
Scope	Between any two processes	Local to the creating process and to processes that inherit from the creating process
Typical use	Between two processes	Broadcast

Table 3-1. Differences Between Named Pipes and Mailslots

mailslots suitable for broadcast messaging and for identifying computers and services available on a network. You can broadcast to one computer or all computers in a domain. (A *domain* is a group of workstations and servers that have a common group name.)

TIP: If you are familiar with programming using Microsoft OS/2 LAN Manager, then using mailslots should be easy, since mailslot APIs in Windows NT are a subset of those in Microsoft OS/2 LAN Manager.

Programming Mailslots

You can use mailslots in your program by using the mailslot APIs. The mailslot APIs are **CreateMailslot** to create a mailslot, **GetMailslotInfo** to read a message from a mailslot, and **SetMailslotInfo** to set the mailslot's time-out value for a read. You create a mailslot and set a time-out, if applicable. Other programs write messages to the mailslot using **CreateFile** and **WriteFile** functions, and you read them using **GetMailslotInfo**. The prototype for **CreateMailslot** is shown next:

```
HANDLE CreateMailslot(LPCTSTR lpszName, DWORD cbMaxMsgSz,

                      DWORD dwRdTimeout,

                      LPSECURITY_ATTRIBUTES lpSecAttr);
```

lpszName is the mailslot's name. *lpszName* can include multiple directory levels and must be unique.

cbMaxMsgSz is the maximum message size allowed for a message (in bytes). Set *cbMaxMsgSz* to zero if you do not want a limit.

dwRdTimeout specifies the time to wait for a mailslot message (if the mailslot is empty) in milliseconds. If *dwRdTimeout* is zero, the function returns immediately if there is no message. You can also wait until a message arrives in the mailslot (use MAILSLOT_WAIT_FOREVER).

lpSecAttr is the pointer to a SECURITY_ATTRIBUTES structure (shown next) that determines whether the returned handle can be inherited by child processes.

```
typedef struct _SECURITY_ATTRIBUTES { /* Security Attribute Structure */
            DWORD   nLength,

            LPVOID lpSecurityDescriptor,

            BOOL bInheritHandle
} SECURITY_ATTRIBUTES;
```

PROTOCOLS

Protocols are an important part of communications. Let's review some common protocols supported by Windows NT, such as TCP/IP, NetBEUI, and IPX/SPX.

TCP/IP

TCP/IP actually comprises two major functions. *TCP*, which stands for Transmission Control Protocol, covers messaging details, while *IP*, which stands for Internet Protocol, covers addressing and routing messages. TCP/IP is probably the most commonly used protocol today due to two related developments: the adoption of TCP/IP as the protocol when Berkeley UNIX started including network functions, and the growing popularity of the Internet, which was already using TCP/IP.

TCP/IP Features

TCP/IP is a robust protocol that has proven itself. Some of its robustness comes from its support for transmission reliability features. Compared with competing protocols such as NetBEUI, TCP/IP has proven itself in demanding applications. It includes support for applications to interface with sockets. The socket support enables higher-level functions such as FTP, Ping, and firewalls to be built on top of TCP/IP. Consistent with the OSI model, it shields the functions built on top of it from the details of the lower-level layers. It is a general-purpose protocol and is used for a wide range of applications—unlike, for example, IPX/SPX, which is used heavily for network file and print services in Novell

NetWare networks. TCP/IP supports message routing by including a routing *gateway address* for all messages not meant for a specific TCP/IP network segment.

TCP/IP Addressing

Each computer running TCP/IP must have three addresses—a unique address that lets other computers locate it, another address to indicate the network that it is a member of (called the *subnet mask*), and the gateway address to route messages, as mentioned before. Each of these addresses is a 32-bit number expressed in dotted decimal format (such as 112.233.34.115). This addressing scheme provides for scalability. The explosive growth of the Internet has caused the number of IP addresses to run out, and efforts are under way to increase the address size. A TCP/IP network can be segmented so that each segment carries the traffic only for addresses within the segment.

TCP/IP, while popular, does have some drawbacks. TCP/IP requires a good deal of configuration work. If you have tried to get connected to an Internet service provider (ISP) and played around with WinSock to get connected, then you have a good idea of the configuration work involved in setting up TCP/IP.

NetBEUI

NetBEUI stands for NetBIOS Extended User Interface. IBM introduced NetBEUI in 1985 to support communications across PC networks. The protocol is old (at least in terms of computer years) and has some problems associated with an old design. For example, NetBEUI allows only 254 simultaneous sessions, which was probably a large number when NetBEUI was designed. In addition, NetBEUI was not designed to provide reliable connectionless communications.

NetBEUI Features

NetBEUI is not as robust as TCP/IP. Unlike TCP/IP, which is a general-purpose protocol, NetBEUI is optimized for print and file sharing within the local network. Also, NetBEUI is not as standardized as TCP/IP. Windows NT uses the NetBEUI Frame (NBF) protocol, which is an extension of the NetBEUI. One of the extensions supported by NBF is the removal of the 254-session limit. NetBEUI doesn't support routing, so if you segment your network, you lose communications functions across segments. This also means that NetBEUI is not very scalable. But NetBEUI is easy to configure.

IPX/SPX

IPX stands for Internetwork Packet Exchange, and *SPX* stands for Sequenced Packet Exchange. IPX/SPX is the protocol suite widely used in Novell networks. Novell recently provided TCP/IP support for NetWare (which is a testimony to the popularity of the TCP/IP protocol). IPX/SPX is similar to NetBEUI in that both are primarily used in small networks, and file and print sharing are the major applications. IPX/SPX is a connection-oriented, routable protocol. It is easy to configure.

The features of TCP/IP, NetBEUI, and IPX/SPX are compared in Table 3-2.

As mentioned before, TCP/IP has complex configuration and setup procedures. Let's now look at some functions provided by Windows NT to mitigate this problem.

TCP/IP CONFIGURATION AND SETUP SOLUTIONS

As noted earlier, configuration and setup is a major issue with TCP/IP. One of the solutions to the system administrator having to set up TCP/IP configuration in each client machine is to set up the configurations in a server and download the configurations to clients. This is the idea behind Dynamic Host Configuration Protocol (DHCP). The system administrator sets up one (or more) DHCP server that stores the configuration information for the entire network, including client configurations. This works fine for client workstations that are in-house. For dial-up remote clients, a RAS server can be set up to act on behalf of a remote computer as a DHCP client. The RAS server requests and gets a pool of IP addresses and configuration information from a DHCP server. RAS manages this pool by allocating and deallocating addresses when remote computers log on and log off.

Programming Using DHCP

A DHCP client broadcasts a Discover request on startup. Any DHCP server that receives the Discover can respond with an Offer, which among other things contains configuration information, including a proposed IP address. The Offer is not broadcast, but is sent directly to the client issuing the Discover. If the DHCP client and DHCP server are not on the same subnet, the Offer is sent through a router back to the DHCP client. The client receives the Offer and accepts with a Request. The Request is broadcast and includes the accepted IP address. If more than one DHCP server responded to the Discover, the server

Features	TCP/IP	NetBEUI	IPX/SPX
Initial design purpose	General communications	File and print sharing	File and print sharing
Setup and configuration	Complex	Simple	Simple
Robustness in handling demanding applications	Robust	Not so robust	Robust
Routing support	Routable	Not routable	Routable

Table 3-2. TCP/IP, NetBEUI, and IPX/SPX Features Compared

which issued the accepted IP address is the one that will carry on future communications with the client.

The DHCP server completes the setup with an ACK. ACK includes complete configuration information. When the client receives the ACK, it completes setting up the TCP/IP stack and is now a *bound* DHCP client that can start using the IP address. The client is said to have *leased* the configuration from the server, since there is a time limit specified for the usage of the IP address given to the client. The client can renew the lease or get a new lease from another server (if the server that issued the first lease is unavailable, for example). DHCP protocol caters to network interruptions. The client and server periodically exchange information to keep configuration updated. For example, if a client with an active lease moves from one subnet to another (for example, when a portable or even a desktop machine is moved around), the ongoing lease is terminated and a new lease is set up. The ongoing lease cannot be used because the subnet address is part of the IP address, and moving to another subnet causes the IP address to change.

Note for UNIX Programmers

If you have programmed using NFS or Domain Naming Service (DNS), then the concepts of centralizing configuration information are the same. However, in NFS the configuration information is locally held and is periodically downloaded. In DNS, a server stores the configuration information, but the address-name mapping is static. Also, unlike DNS, WINS doesn't support a network hierarchy or *zones.*

WINDOWS INTERNET NAMING SERVICE (WINS)

WINS provides dynamic name registration and resolution on TCP/IP. WINS complements DHCP, but DHCP is not a prerequisite for WINS. WINS provides a dynamic name resolution method along with DHCP. The functions of WINS are similar to that of DNS, with one major difference. DNS resolves TCP/IP host names to static IP addresses. WINS is specifically designed to resolve NetBIOS names on TCP/IP to dynamic addresses assigned by DHCP. WINS is fully interoperable with other NetBIOS Name Servers (NBNS).

When a WINS client is started, it contacts a WINS server directly (unlike a broadcast used by a DHCP client). WINS primary and secondary server names are specified in the client's TCP/IP properties sheet. The information sent by the WINS client includes the computer name, an IP address, and so on. If the WINS client is also DHCP enabled, then the IP address would have been obtained dynamically from a DHCP server. If the WINS client is not DHCP enabled, the IP address is a static number obtained from a network administrator and manually entered as part of the TCP/IP configuration information. IP addresses must be unique. If DHCP assigns the addresses, then it ensures the addresses are unique. If DHCP is not used, then they are manually assigned and the person assigning the addresses (usually the network administrator) has to ensure that they are unique.

WINDOWS NT MACINTOSH SUPPORT

Windows NT Server includes functions to be an AppleShare file server for Macintosh clients. File server functions are provided by the Macintosh Services component. Macintosh Services also includes the AppleTalk print server and fully functional, native AppleTalk router functions. Macintosh Services supports the AppleTalk Filing Protocol (AFP). Using Windows NT as an AppleShare file server enables some of the other functions built into Windows NT such as RAID support, multiprocessor support, security functions, and so on. Using Windows NT as an AppleTalk print server lets Mac clients print to any printer that can be attached to Windows NT, including network printers and non-PostScript printers. Windows NT includes a PostScript interpreter to convert the data stream into a (bitmap) format that can be handled by a non-PostScript printer. Since the number of printers supported is large, this provides a significant advantage for Windows NT compared with many other print servers. As an AppleTalk router, you can use a variety of network cards including Ethernet, FDDI, and so on.

DISTRIBUTED COMPUTING

Distributed computing is the next logical step in the evolution of communications. First you have peer-to-peer, where the communication is between two peers, such as applications. Then you have client/server communications, the next step, where a client application talks to different server applications for application, print, and file services. Distributed applications are applications where portions of the applications can reside on heterogeneous systems at different nodes in a network, but work together to fulfill the functions of the applications. To accomplish this, the applications need an environment that will provide distributed services, a mechanism to pass messages between applications, mechanisms to accomplish distributed transaction processing, the ability to access data from different databases, and so on. Such an environment has been specified by the Open Software Foundation (OSF), a nonprofit industry consortium formed to further the use of open distributed computing, and is called the Distributed Computing Environment (DCE). While distributed computing systems are a better match to the real world and have some advantages, keep in mind that they also tend to be more complex. The DCE specifies six core services:

▼ *Remote procedure call* (*RPC*) services to let an application access services provided by another computer on the network

■ *Distributed directory* services to locate any named object on the network by use of a single naming model

■ *Threads* service to be able to execute multiple threads

■ *Distributed time* services to maintain one time across all computers on the network by synchronizing the system clocks of different computers

■ *Security* services to authenticate users, authorize access to resources, and provide user and server account management on a distributed network

▲ *Distributed file* services to access files anywhere on a network

Windows NT natively includes only full RPC support. Microsoft is working on providing directory services. At this time, you need third-party software to provide the other services. For example, Digital Equipment Corporation (DEC, also referred to as Digital) has a product known as Digital DCE Services for Windows NT that provides RPC services, cell directory services, DCE threads services, distributed time services, and DCE security services. Gradient Technologies has DCE products that provide the core DCE services as well as distributed file services.

Remote Procedure Call (RPC)

RPC was invented by Sun Microsystems. Based on this initial work, the Open Software Foundation issued DCE RPC. DCE is the heterogeneous distributed computing environment envisioned by OSF, and RPC is the mechanism in DCE for interprocess communications.

RPC gives you the ability to invoke procedures that are resident on another machine as if they were present in the local machine. The details of the network are transparent to your application. Your application also does not have to worry about data translation that may need to occur in heterogeneous environments—for example, between Windows' *little-endian* convention and UNIX's *big-endian* convention. RPC fits in the application layer of the ISO model. As with other layers, RPC is dependent on other lower-level mechanisms. In Windows NT, RPC can use named pipes, NetBIOS, or Windows Sockets to communicate with remote systems. RPC interfaces are specified by use of the Interface Description Language (IDL) and compiled by use of Microsoft's IDL language compiler (MIDL). MIDL converts IDL into C syntax. When you compile your interfaces using the IDL compiler, *stub functions* (which are dummy functions that call the actual functions on the remote machine at run time) are generated on the local machine. Your program calls only these stub functions. The stubs convert the passed procedure parameters into the network data representation (NDR) format. At run time, RPC run-time libraries and the underlying network code call the real remote procedures with the NDR-formatted parameters. A *binding* is established between the RPC client and the RPC server at run time. A variation of the RPC called LPC (local procedure call) is used for communication across local systems within a computer.

> ## Note for UNIX Programmers
> If you have programmed using ONC RPC or DCE RPC, then you can easily program using Windows NT RPC. Windows NT RPC is interoperable with DCE RPC, and there are porting tools that let you port ONC RPC to DCE RPC.

DIAL-UP NETWORKING AND RAS

Dial-up networking, as the name suggests, offers networking capabilities normally available to LAN-attached desktops to remote dial-in computers. For example, your laptop could function as your desktop and perform the same functions—access mail, file, and printers. You can also access the Internet by dialing in and using the RAS server as an Internet gateway. Some limitations do apply to RAS-based network connections. Dial-up networking is the client portion of RAS. The server portion of RAS is remote access administration. RAS connections can be made using regular phone lines and a modem. RAS also supports X.25 and ISDN connections. RAS supports up to 256 concurrent sessions (in the Windows NT Server). These sessions can be incoming or outgoing. RAS supports IPX, TCP/IP, and NetBEUI at the network layer and Point-to-Point Protocol (PPP) and Serial-Line Internet Protocol (SLIP) at the transport layer. While RAS connections can use any combination of the network layer protocols, the transport layer protocol has to be either PPP or SLIP.

Some common RAS functions are in Table 3-3 .

CONCLUSION

In this chapter we looked at the OSI reference model, which is the "granddaddy" of computer communications. We looked at the communication mechanisms provided by Windows NT and how these mechanisms relate to the OSI model. We took a step-by-step look at how communications work. We then looked at some of the Windows NT communication mechanisms in more detail. This chapter lays the groundwork for Part III, where we will look at sockets, Internet-related programming, MAPI, and RAS in greater detail.

RAS Function	Action Performed
RASADFunc	Application-defined callback function
RasConnectionNotification	Specifies an event object that the system sets to signaled state when creating/terminating a RAS connection
RasDial	Establishes a RAS connection between a RAS client and a RAS server
RasDialFunc2	Application-defined callback function invoked by RasDial on state changes
RasDialDlg	Establishes a RAS connection using a specified phone-book entry
RasEntryDlg	Property sheets to manipulate phone-book entries
RasEnumConnections	Lists active RAS connections including handle and phone book
RasGetConnectStatus	Status of a current RAS connection
RasGetEntryDialParams	Retrieves connection information from last successful call for a phone-book entry
RasGetErrorString	Converts RAS error code to an error string
RasMonitorDlg	Property sheet that describes the status of RAS connections
RasHangUp	Terminates a RAS connection

Table 3-3. Summary of RAS

CHAPTER 4

Windows NT
File Systems

Continuing with Windows NT programming foundations, let's take a look in this chapter at the support in Windows NT for accessing data such as file systems and databases. Windows NT supports multiple file systems. Besides the file systems themselves, Windows NT also includes features such as *memory-mapped files* and *asynchronous input/output* that you can take advantage of in your programs to speed up file processing. We will also briefly look at Windows NT support for Redundant Array of Inexpensive Disks (RAID), which provides better fault tolerance and performance compared to regular disks

FILE SYSTEMS

Separating data from executable code so that the same executable can run using different sets of data probably began when programmers first started to program. The early data storage was through files of different types. Now it is more common to use databases, particularly for business mission-critical data (although many databases internally use files to store the data). This trend has become even more popular with the advent of desktop databases. Database programming using ODBC is covered in Chapter 20. MFC support for databases and the DAO SDK is covered in Chapter 21. As a business programmer, you may still use files occasionally when the effort and cost of setting up and using a database system outweighs the benefits of using a database.

Windows NT support for file systems lets your applications create, read, write, update, and delete files and directories. Windows NT supports multiple file systems. The file systems supported by Windows NT include the *New Technology File System (NTFS)*, the *File Allocation Table (FAT) file system* (and some variations of FAT such as *protected-mode FAT* and *FAT32*), the *Compact Disc File System (CDFS)*, and, up to Windows NT 3.51, the *High Performance File System (HPFS)*. Keep in mind that file systems are not mutually exclusive. You can have one partition in your hard drive formatted for FAT and the other formatted for NTFS, and Windows NT can access and write to both.

FILE ALLOCATION TABLE (FAT)

The FAT file system had its origins in the DOS operating system and suffers from the problems of an old design not keeping pace with advances. One of the problems is the FAT file-naming system. All files handled by FAT should follow what is called the *8-dot-3 system*, where the filename can be up to 12 characters—with the first part up to 8 characters followed by an optional dot (mandatory, if there is an extension) followed by an extension up to 3 characters. Actually, the full name of a FAT file is *drive:\ directory\filename.ext* (*directory* could include subdirectories). All other fields except *filename* are optional. This design may suffice when disk capacities are very small and there are only a few files. It becomes a major problem with many software development efforts where there typically are hundreds of files. In addition, FAT is not case sensitive. One solution to this problem was a variation of FAT called *VFAT* or *protected-mode FAT.* VFAT supports long filenames up to 255 characters and other file data, such as date last accessed, in extended FAT structures. VFAT is compatible with FAT.

Another problem with FAT is clustering. Available disk space is usually broken down into *clusters,* which are further broken down into *sectors.* A sector typically is a half kilobyte (512 bytes). The number of sectors per cluster varies (for example, the sectors per cluster is 4 for a 1.2MB floppy disk and 32 for a 512MB hard drive). Allocations are usually in cluster multiples. So a 1K data file that occupies 4 sectors in a 1.2MB floppy will take up 32 sectors or 16K in the 512MB hard drive. The rest of the space is usually wasted. Thus, if you have a lot of small files on a big hard drive, there will be a lot of wasted space using FAT. Microsoft introduced FAT32, a variation of FAT that addresses this clustering problem. FAT32 uses only 4K clusters (for disks up to 8Gb) to avoid wasting disk space. FAT32 also supports disks with capacity up to 2 terabytes. Unfortunately, FAT32 is supported only by Windows 95. FAT32 is compatible with FAT.

FAT's big advantage is its low overhead, and for this reason it is the only file system available to support floppies and very small hard drives. In fact, on small drives, FAT access will even be faster than NTFS or HPFS. Since FAT has been around a while, there are many volumes and floppy disks with the FAT file system. To maintain compatibility, all operating systems since DOS, including Windows 3.x, Windows 95, Windows NT, and OS/2, support FAT.

NEW TECHNOLOGY FILE SYSTEM (NTFS)

NTFS is the file system designed to address many of the limitations of FAT. Probably the most significant is the removal of the FAT requirement that filenames use the 8-dot-3 format. But that is just the beginning. NTFS also includes much better recovery (without having to use stand-alone file recovery utilities), security features (consistent with NT's C2 security classification), support for Unicode filenames, and so on. NTFS not only supports multiple extended attributes, but it also allows applications to define their own extended attributes.

While Windows NT (using NTFS) supports long filenames, it also supports the 8-dot-3 filenames. In fact, whenever a file is created with a long filename, it internally generates a short name in the 8-dot-3 format. Table 4-1 compares the features of FAT and NTFS.

NOTE: UNIX systems have their own file systems, such as the Network File System (NFS) and the Andrew File System (AFS). There are third-party tools that let Windows NT applications access these file systems and vice versa.

HIGH PERFORMANCE FILE SYSTEM (HPFS)

Microsoft dropped support for HPFS in Windows NT 4.0. HPFS is similar to NTFS in that it allows long filenames, extended attributes, and so on. Windows NT supported HPFS

File System Feature	FAT	NTFS
File naming	8-dot-3	255-character maximum, no extension required
Security	Not secure	Enhanced security
Multiple data stream	No	Yes
File recovery	Poor—need stand-alone recovery tools	Good—don't need stand-alone utilities in most cases
Unicode support	No	Yes
Special functions for POSIX	No	Yes
MS-DOS aliases	NA	Automatic
Floppy disk support	Yes	No
Extended attributes	No	Yes
Overhead	Low	High

Table 4-1.   Comparison of FAT and NTFS Features

(up to version 3.51) primarily for backwards compatibility (for systems that dual-boot OS/2 and Windows NT).

COMPACT DISC FILE SYSTEM (CDFS)

With increasing program sizes and large multimedia content, CD-ROMs have become the most common distribution mechanism for software. CDFS is the file system used to store files on a CD-ROM. Windows NT supports the ISO 9660 standard (level 2).

Note for UNIX Programmers

Thanks to an international standard (ISO 9660), CDFS is supported by many UNIX operating systems and Windows NT. You should be able to exchange CDs between two operating systems supporting CDFS.

We've looked at different file systems. Now let's take a look at programming aspects of file systems.

FILE SYSTEM PROGRAMMING

File system programming falls into three categories:

▼ Volume- and drive-related programming

■ Directory-related programming

▲ File-related programming

Let's review each of these categories.

Volume and Drive Functions

The functions available for your applications related to volumes and drives are summarized in Table 4-2.

Let's look at the prototype of one of the volume and drive functions—**GetDiskFreeSpace**—which you would use anytime you want to ensure that there is enough space on the disk for what you want to store.

```
BOOL GetDiskFreeSpace( LPCTSTR  lpRootPathName,
                       LPDWORD  lpSectorsPerCluster,
                       LPDWORD  lpBytesPerSector,
                       LPDWORD  lpNumOfFreeClusters,
                       LPDWORD  lpTotalNumOfClusters
                     );
```

The parameters for **GetDiskFreeSpace** are as follows:

▼ *lpRootPathName* points to a string that specifies the root directory of the disk to return information about. Use NULL for the root of the current directory.

■ *lpSectorsPerCluster* points to a variable that has the number of sectors per cluster.

■ *lpBytesPerSector* points to a variable that has the number of bytes per sector.

■ *lpNumOfFreeClusters* points to a variable that has the total number of free clusters on the disk.

▲ *lpTotalNumOfClusters* points to a variable that has the total number of clusters on the disk.

GetDiskFreeSpace returns nonzero if it succeeds and returns zero otherwise.

If you want to show a list of available drives and let the user pick a drive, you can call **GetLogicalDriveStrings**, which shows the user the available root directories (such as C:\, D:\,...). Once the user picks a drive, you can ensure that the drive is a valid drive for the application's purpose (you may not want to let the user pick a CD-ROM drive to write to) by calling **GetDriveType**. Once a valid drive has been picked, you can ensure that there is enough space on the drive by calling **GetDiskFreeSpace**.

Function	Information Returned or Action Performed
GetVolumeInformation	Retrieves volume name, volume serial number, file system name (FAT, NTFS), file system flags (whether the file system is case sensitive, supports Unicode, and so on), maximum filename length, and so on
SetVolumeLabel	Sets or deletes the label of a file system volume
GetDiskFreeSpace, GetDiskFreeSpaceEx	Retrieves volume organizational data such as bytes/sector, sectors/cluster, number of free clusters, and total number of clusters
GetDriveType	Indicates whether the drive (specified drive letter) is a removable, fixed, CD-ROM, RAM, or network drive
GetLogicalDrives	Identifies the volumes present
GetLogicalDriveStrings	Retrieves a null-terminated string for each volume present

Table 4-2. Volume and Drive Functions

TIP: Do not assume or hard code filename lengths in your program. Use the *lpMaximumComponent-Length* parameter of **GetVolumeInformation**, which tells you the maximum filename length.

Directory Functions

The functions available for your applications related to directories are summarized in Table 4-3.

Let's look at the prototype of one of the directory functions—**GetCurrentDirectory**.

```
DWORD GetCurrentDirectory( DWORD nBufLen,
                           LPTSTR lpBuf
                         );
```

The parameters for **GetCurrentDirectory** are as follows:

▼ *nBufLen* specifies the length of the buffer current directory string (in characters and including space for a terminating null character).

▲ *lpBuf* is a pointer to the buffer that holds the fully qualified path of the current directory string.

Function	Information Returned or Action Performed
CreateDirectory, CreateDirectoryEx	Creates new directories. You can specify a security descriptor. Directory names can use Unicode or Uniform Naming Convention (UNC) format. CreateDirectoryEx can use a directory template.
RemoveDirectory	Deletes existing directories. Directories should be empty and the calling process must have delete access.
GetCurrentDirectory	Retrieves the current directory (directory at the end of the active path) for the calling process as a fully qualified path.
SetCurrentDirectory	Changes the current directory for the current process. You can supply a relative path or a fully qualified path.
ReadDirectoryChangesW	Retrieves information about changes occurring within a directory you specify synchronously or asynchronously. Refer to "File System Notifications" later in this chapter.
GetSystemDirectory	Retrieves path to the Windows system directory.
GetWindowsDirectory	Retrieves path to the Windows directory.

Table 4-3. Directory Functions

GetCurrentDirectory returns the number of characters written to the buffer if successful, and zero if it fails. If the failure is caused by insufficient buffer size to hold the results of the call, the return value specifies the required size of the buffer.

TIP: In instances where you do not know the buffer size (as in the case of *lpBuf* earlier) you can code zero for the buffer length parameter (*nBufLen* earlier). The function call will fail, but the return value will indicate the length of buffer required. You can then repeat your call using the correct buffer size.

File Functions

The common functions available for your application related to files are summarized in Table 4-4.

Function	Information Returned or Action Performed
AreFileApisANSI	Determines whether a set of Win32 file functions uses the American National Standards Institute (ANSI) or Original Equipment Manufacturer (OEM) character set *code page*. The function returns nonzero for the ANSI code page and zero for the OEM code page. You can set the code page using SetFileApisToANSI and SetFileApisToOEM.
CancelIO	Cancels all pending and in-progress overlapped I/O operations issued by the calling thread for a specified file handle.
CopyFile, CopyFileEx	Copies an existing file to a new file. You can choose to overwrite an existing file. File attributes are copied to the new file, but security attributes are not copied to the new file. CopyFileEx also preserves extended attributes, OLE structured storage, and NTFS alternate data streams.
CopyProgressRoutine	Application-defined callback routine that is called when a portion of a copy operation started by CopyFileEx is completed. You can use the callback routine to display a progress bar indicating copy progress.
CreateFile	Creates or opens a file and returns a handle. Filenames can use Unicode or Uniform Naming Convention (UNC) format. You can use the attributes of an existing template file. CreateFile is also used to create pipes, mailslots, consoles, and so on.
CreateIoCompletionPort	Associates an instance of an opened file with an I/O completion port to let applications receive notification of asynchronous I/O completion.
DeleteFile	Deletes a file (that is not open or is not a memory-mapped file).
FileIOCompletionRoutine	Routine that is called when an asynchronous I/O function (such as ReadFileEx) is completed and the calling thread is waiting for an alert.

Table 4-4.   File Functions

Function	Information Returned or Action Performed
FindClose	Closes the search handle used by the FindFirstFile and FindNextFile functions.
FindFirstFile, FindFirstFileEx	Searches a directory for a file. Filenames can use Unicode or UNC format. The function returns a handle that can be used to find the next file that matches the same name criteria using FindNextFile. FindFirstFile uses filenames only. FindFirstFileEx uses filenames as well as attributes.
FindNextFile	Locates the next file that matches a given search criteria using the handle returned by FindFirstFile or FindFirstFileEx.
FlushFileBuffers	Writes all buffered data to the file and clears the buffers.
GetBinaryType	Determines if a file is executable and the appropriate subsystem (32-bit Windows, 16-bit Windows, OS/2, POSIX, and so on).
GetFileAttributes, GetFileAttributesEx	Retrieves attributes (such as hidden, system, archive, compressed, and so on) for a specified file or directory. GetFileAttributesEx retrieves attribute information that is more than the FAT-style attribute information retrieved by GetFileAttributes.
GetFileInformationBy Handle	Retrieves information about a specified file.
GetFileSize	Retrieves the uncompressed file size in bytes. (To get the compressed file size, use GetCompressedFileSize.)
GetFileType	Retrieves the file type, which could be FILE_TYPE_UNKNOWN (for an unknown file type), FILE_TYPE_DISK (for a disk file), FILE_TYPE_CHAR (for a character file such as an LPT device or a console), or FILE_TYPE_PIPE (for a named or anonymous pipe).
GetFullPathName	Retrieves the full path and filename by merging the name of the current drive and directory with the specified filename (but doesn't verify to see if the path is valid or if the file is actually present).

Table 4-4. File Functions (*continued*)

Function	Information Returned or Action Performed
GetShortPathName	Obtains the short path form of a specified input path. You can obtain a file's long name from the short name by calling FindFirstFile.
LockFile, LockFileEx	Locks and prevents other processes from accessing a region or byte range in an open file.
MoveFile, MoveFileEx	Moves (renames) a file or directory. Renaming a directory renames all children. MoveFileEx adds other options such as moving a file across volumes, delaying the move until reboot, and so on.
ReadFile, ReadFileEx	Reads data from a file synchronously or asynchronously. ReadFileEx performs only asynchronous reads and calls an application completion routine upon read completion.
SearchPath	Searches for the specified file.
SetEndOfFile	Truncates or extends a file by moving the end-of-file.
SetFileAttributes	Sets a file's attributes (such as Hidden, Normal, System, Read-only, and so on).
SetFilePointer	Sets the file pointer forward or backward. Exercise caution if you use this function in a multithreaded application.
UnlockFile, UnlockFileEx	Unlocks a region or byte range of a file previously locked by LockFile or LockFileEx.
WriteFile, WriteFileEx	Writes data to a file synchronously or asynchronously. WriteFileEx performs only asynchronous writes and calls an application completion routine upon write completion.

Table 4-4.   File Functions (*continued*)

Let's look at the prototype of one of the file functions—**WriteFileEx**.

```
BOOL WriteFileEx( HANDLE hFile,
                  LPCVOID lpBuf,
                  DWORD nNumOfBytesToWrite,
                  LPOVERLAPPED lpOvrlap,
```

```
    LPOVERLAPPED_COMPLETION_ROUTINE lpCompletionRoutine
);
```

The parameters for **WriteFileEx** are as follows:

▼ *hFile* is the file handle for a file opened with the FILE_FLAG_OVERLAPPED and with GENERIC_WRITE access by the **CreateFile** function.

■ *lpBuf* points to the buffer containing the data to be written to the file.

■ *nNumOfBytesToWrite* specifies the number of bytes to write to the file.

■ *lpOvrlap* points to an OVERLAPPED (shown later in the chapter) data structure that supplies data to be used during the asynchronous write operation.

▲ *lpCompletionRoutine* points to your application completion routine that is called when the write operation is complete and the calling thread is in an alertable wait state (fAlertable flag set to TRUE for **SleepEx**, **WaitForSingleObjectEx**, or **WaitForMultipleObjectsEx** function).

WriteFileEx returns nonzero if successful, and zero if it fails.

Programming Notes

Let's take the example of reading data from disk, let the user make updates, and write the data back to the file. You call **CreateFile** to open the file. If it is a shared file and you want to prevent other accesses, you use **LockFile** to lock the file. You then call **ReadFile** as many times as you need to get the data from the file that you want to display to the user. When the user has completed the updates, you call **WriteFile** and **UnlockFile**. You can call the "Ex" version in the preceding calls where appropriate.

In the previous scenario, if you are unable to **CreateFile** because it doesn't exist, then the file could have been moved. You can give the user the option to search for the file using **SearchPath** and **FindNextFile**. If there are multiple files that match the search criteria provided by the user, you can get more details about the files using **GetFileSize**, **GetFileType**, and **GetFileInformationByHandle** to help the user pick the specific file.

Windows NT stores the long filenames on disk in Unicode. This means that the original long filename is always preserved, even if it contains extended characters, and regardless of the code page that is active during a disk read or write operation. The case of the filename is preserved, although the file system itself is not case sensitive.

MEMORY-MAPPED FILES

The use of memory-mapped files is a way of associating the contents of a file with a process' virtual memory through a file-mapping object. Although a memory-mapped file appears to be resident in virtual memory to the process using it, a memory-mapped file's contents are actually held in real memory associated with a file-mapping object. Thus, memory mapping is a much faster way to access the file's contents compared with disk I/O. Since a file-mapping object can be shared between processes, memory-mapped files can also be used as shared memory between processes in Windows NT (remember that in Windows NT, each process has its own address space, unlike the shared memory that is available in other Windows operating systems). The portion of a process' virtual address space that is mapped to the file's contents is called *file view*. Since a file view is part of the virtual memory, you can use read and write using pointers.

You can memory map any file, including the system pagefile. The file-mapping object can be for all or any part of a file, and similarly the file view can be for all or any part of a file-mapping object. The ability to map only a portion of a file makes it easy to process very big files by mapping portions of the file at a time. Different processes can have different views, and a process can have multiple views. Windows NT ensures *coherence* between the different views (all the views display the same data even if a process updates the data in one view), except when the file is a remote file, or if you simultaneously update the file using views and APIs. For example, if you map a complete file and the size of the physical file grows after the mapping object has been created, the mapping object will no longer reflect the complete file. A process can access a file randomly or sequentially using a file mapping (by setting the pointer where you want).

Windows NT internally uses memory-mapped files to speed up the loading of EXE and DLL files. Just as you can use locking functions such as **LockFile** when you access files on disk, you can use the **VirtualProtect** function to control access to file view. Having looked at the characteristics of memory-mapped files, let's look at the programming aspects of memory-mapped files.

Programming Memory-Mapped Files

You can use the functions shown in Table 4-5 to program memory-mapped files.

Let's look at the prototype of one of the memory-mapped file functions—**CreateFileMapping**.

```
HANDLE CreateFileMapping( HANDLE hFile,
                          LPSECURITY_ATTRIBUTES lpFileMappingAttributes,
                          DWORD flProtect,
                          DWORD dwMaxSizeHigh,
                          DWORD dwMaxSizeLow,
                          LPCTSTR lpName
);
```

The parameters of **CreateFileMapping** are as follows:

▼   *hFile* identifies the file for which a mapping object is to be created. *lpFileMapping Attributes* is a pointer to a **SECURITY_ATTRIBUTES** structure. If this parameter is NULL, the default security descriptor is used.

Function	Information Returned or Action Performed
CreateFileMapping	Creates a file-mapping object for a file and optionally lets you name the file-mapping object.
FlushViewOfFile	Flushes the cached writes to the file.
MapViewOfFile, MapViewOfFileEx	Maps a view of a file into calling a process' address space. MapViewOfFileEx lets you pass a starting address for the map.
OpenFileMapping	Opens a named file-mapping object. Used by other processes to access a file-mapping object once it has been created.
UnmapViewOfFile	Unmaps a view created by MapViewOfFile or MapViewOfFileEx.

Table 4-5. Memory-Mapped Files Programming Functions

■ *flProtect* specifies the desired protection for the file view. The valid values for this parameter are PAGE_READONLY (for read-only access), PAGE_READWRITE (for read-write access), and PAGE_WRITECOPY (for copy-on-write access where a new copy of the page is created for a write).

■ *dwMaxSizeHigh* is the maximum size of the file-mapping object (the High-Order 32 bits).

■ *dwMaxSizeLow* is the maximum size of the file-mapping object (the Low-Order 32 bits). Specify *dwMaxSizeLow* and *dwMaxSizeHigh* as zero to make the maximum size of the file-mapping object the same size as the file you are creating a mapping for.

▲ *lpName* is the name for the file-mapping object. Specifying NULL creates the file-mapping object without a name. Using a name of a file-mapping that already exists causes the function to access the existing object.

CreateFileMapping returns a handle to the file-mapping object if it succeeds, and NULL upon failure.

To use a memory-mapped file, you perform the following steps:

1. Create (or open) a file by use of **CreateFile**. If you want exclusive access to prevent others from using the file (for example, to preserve coherence), set the *dwShareMode* parameter of **CreateFile** to zero.

2. Create a file-mapping object using **CreateFileMapping**. **CreateFileMapping** will use the handle returned by **CreateFile** in step 1. You can name the file-mapping object using the *lpName* parameter of **CreateFileMapping** if the file-mapping object will be shared by use of its name.

3. Create a file view using **MapViewOfFile** or **MapViewOfFileEx** using the handle of the file-mapping object returned by **CreateFileMapping** in step 2. Keep track of the base address.

4. If the file-mapping object is to be shared by processes, the other processes can use the **OpenFileMapping** function using the name of the file-mapping object from step 2. Using a name is one of three ways to share a file-mapping object. The other ways you can share a file-mapping object are by duplicating a handle or by getting a handle at process creation time.

5. You read and write by dereferencing the pointer to the view(s). The data from the writes is normally cached to improve efficiency and save time, but you can cause the *dirty pages* (pages that have been modified since the file view was mapped) to be flushed using **FlushViewOfFile**.

6. Once you have finished using a view, you unmap it using **UnmapViewOfFile**. You pass the base address of the mapped view of a file that is to be unmapped. This base address value is returned by a previous call to the **MapViewOfFile** in step 3.

7. You close the file-mapping object using its handle (from step 2) in a call to **CloseHandle**.

Note for UNIX Programmers

Most UNIX systems support memory-mapped files. If you have programmed using *mmap* in UNIX, then you can program memory-mapped file functions in Windows NT using **CreateFileMapping**, **MapViewOfFile**, and other functions as mentioned earlier.

FILE SYSTEM NOTIFICATIONS

We talked about showing the user a list of files to choose from (under "File Functions"). If you have displayed a list of files, the user can switch to another window and actually create a file or directory that invalidates the file list being displayed by your application. It would be nice for you to be able to detect file system changes and update your list. You can do this using file system notification functions. Windows NT provides the file system notification functions listed in Table 4-6.

You can use file system notifications in the following manner:

First, you use **FindFirstChangeNotification** to set up the triggers you want to watch for. The prototype for **FindFirstChangeNotification** is shown next:

Function	Information Returned or Action Performed
FindFirstChangeNotification	Creates a change notification handle and sets up initial change notification filter conditions. Filters can be changing of a filename, directory name, and so on.
FindNextChangeNotification	Signals a change notification handle the next time an appropriate change is detected.
FindCloseChangeNotification	Stops change notification handle monitoring.
ReadDirectoryChangesW	Retrieves information about changes occurring in a directory.
SignalObjectAndWait	Allows the caller to signal one object and wait for another object.
WaitForSingleObject, WaitForSingleObjectEx	Waits for an object to be signaled (or for a time-out). WaitForSingleObjectEx also waits for an I/O completion routine or *asynchronous procedure call (APC)* to be queued.
WaitForMultipleObjects, WaitForMultipleObjectsEx	Same as preceding, except that the wait is for multiple objects instead of one object.
MsgWaitForMultipleObjects, MsgWaitForMultipleObjectsEx	Waits for the specified objects to be in the signaled state. The objects can include different types of input event objects such as mouse event, hot key event, and so on.

Table 4-6. File System Notification Functions

```
HANDLE FindFirstChangeNotification( LPCTSTR lpPathName,
                                    BOOL bWatchSubtree,
                                    DWORD dwNotifyFilter
);
```

▼ *lpPathName* specifies the path of the directory to watch. Here the directory could be at any level (that is, it could be a subdirectory).

■ *bWatchSubtree* specifies whether the scope of the watch is limited to the directory (or subdirectory) specified, or whether the watch should include all levels starting with the directory (or subdirectory) specified and further down the tree hierarchy.

▲ *dwNotifyFilter* specifies the trigger conditions to watch out for. The values for this parameter are listed in Table 4-7.

NOTE: The trigger occurs when the operating system detects the changes in the file system, which will be slightly delayed compared with when an application changes it (due to caching). Normally this delay is insignificantly small.

FindFirstChangeNotification returns a handle if successful, and INVALID_HANDLE_VALUE if it fails.

Now that you have set up the triggers, you can detect if a file system change has happened by using one of the wait functions, such as **WaitForSingleObject**, whose prototype is shown next:

```
DWORD WaitForSingleObject( HANDLE hHandle,
                           DWORD dwMillisecs

);
```

Parameter Value	Triggered By
FILE_NOTIFY_CHANGE_FILE_NAME	A filename change within the watch scope—for example, when a file is created, moved (renamed), or deleted
FILE_NOTIFY_CHANGE_DIR_NAME	A directory name change within the watch scope—for example, when a directory is created, moved (renamed), or deleted
FILE_NOTIFY_CHANGE_ATTRIBUTES	A file attribute change within the watch scope—for example, from hidden to normal
FILE_NOTIFY_CHANGE_SIZE	A file-size change for files within the watch scope
FILE_NOTIFY_CHANGE_LAST_WRITE	A change to the last write-time of files within the watch scope
FILE_NOTIFY_CHANGE_SECURITY	A security-descriptor change for files or directories within the watch scope

Table 4-7.   File or Directory Change Triggers

hHandle identifies the file system change notification object.

dwMillisecs is the time-out interval, in milliseconds. Code zero to return immediately without waiting and INFINITE to wait until the object is signaled.

Once **WaitForSingleObject** returns, you can scan the directory for changes or call **ReadDirectoryChangesW** to get a list of the changes. You can use the changes to update your user interface, if appropriate. If you think there could have been further changes to the directory while you were performing the user interface update, then you can call **FindNextChangeNotification**, which will indicate if there have been changes to your triggers since the time of **FindFirstChangeNotification**. When you have finished processing, you call **FindCloseChangeNotification**. **WaitForSingleObject** returns a value that indicates the event that caused the function to return (for example, the state of the waited upon object or time-out is signaled if it succeeds and WAIT_FAILED if it fails).

ASYNCHRONOUS I/O

It is well known that of all the subsystems in a computer system, the I/O subsystem is the slowest. Reading and writing to disks, tapes, and CDs take a lot of time. (We are talking relative computer time here. A disk I/O may only take a few milliseconds, which is a lot less than the time for you to blink an eye, but milliseconds are a lot longer compared with the microseconds or nanoseconds it takes for executing instructions or accessing real memory. If you have a 120MHz Pentium, then its clock speed is 120×10^6 cycles/sec. In other words, the time for one cycle is 1/120 microsecond. Since each instruction takes only a few cycles, you can see that executing instructions is a lot faster than I/O access.)

Solutions to ensure that the central processing unit (CPU) wasn't idle have included preemptive scheduling and multiprocessing. Windows NT preempts the thread requesting I/O and schedules another thread. Another solution to the slow I/O problem is the use of memory-mapped files, covered earlier, where you substitute fast memory access for slow disk access. Yet another solution is *asynchronous I/O*. What if, instead of automatically scheduling *another* thread to execute, Windows NT lets *your own* thread that requested the I/O continue to do other things (presuming you have other things to do) and notifies your thread when the I/O is complete? Windows NT lets you do precisely that with its support for asynchronous I/O. Asynchronous I/O is also called *overlapped I/O*.

Let's start with the data structure that plays a central part in overlapped I/O—the **OVERLAPPED** structure shown next:

```
typedef struct _OVERLAPPED { // Overlapped Data Structure
                    DWORD   Internal;
                    DWORD   InternalHigh;
                    DWORD   Offset;
                    DWORD   OffsetHigh;
                    HANDLE  hEvent;
} OVERLAPPED;
```

Internal, reserved for Windows NT, specifies a system-dependent status when the **GetOverlappedResult** function returns without setting the extended error information to ERROR_IO_PENDING.

InternalHigh, reserved for Windows NT, specifies the length of the data transferred when the **GetOverlappedResult** function returns TRUE.

Offset specifies the file position to start the transfer, which is a byte offset from the start of the file. You set this member before calling **ReadFile** or **WriteFile**.

OffsetHigh specifies the high word of the byte offset at which to start the transfer.

hEvent is the event that is set to the signaled state when the transfer has been completed. You set this member before calling **ReadFile** or **WriteFile**.

To use overlapped I/O in your program, start with **CreateFile** and specify the FILE_FLAG_OVERLAPPED parameter as shown in the prototype that follows:

```
HANDLE CreateFile(LPCTSTR lpFileName,
                  DWORD dwDesiredAccess,
                  DWORD dwShareMode,
                  LPSECURITY_ATTRIBUTES lpSecurityAttributes,
                  DWORD dwCreationDistribution,
                  DWORD dwFlagsAndAttributes,
                  HANDLE hTemplateFile
);
```

Let's look at the only parameter of interest for asynchronous I/O—the *dwFlags AndAttributes* parameter—and the values you can specify that affect asynchronous I/O.

▼ FILE_FLAG_OVERLAPPED—I/O operations that take a significant amount of time return ERROR_IO_PENDING. When the operation is finished, the specified event is set to the signaled state. With this flag, the system does not maintain the file pointer. The file position must be passed as part of the *lpOverlapped* parameter to the **ReadFile** and **WriteFile** functions. This flag also enables more than one operation, such as simultaneous read and write, to be performed with the handle.

▲ FILE_FLAG_NO_BUFFERING—Opens the file with no intermediate buffering or caching. If you also specify FILE_FLAG_OVERLAPPED, then I/O operations do not use the synchronous operations of the memory manager, and thus some overhead is reduced. On the other hand, benefits of caching, such as delayed writes, are not available.

Once you have created or opened the file, you initialize the overlapped structure and specify the portion of the file you want to read using the *Offset* and *OffsetHigh* parameters described earlier. You then call **ReadFile** with the *lpOverlapped* parameter. Control will be immediately returned, and you can perform other functions. Once you are ready to check if the asynchronous I/O is complete, you can use the **WaitForSingleObject** function covered earlier in the chapter. When the I/O is complete, **WaitForSingleObject** returns.

You can check the results of your read using the **GetOverlappedResult** function. You can use the **CancelIO** function to cancel an asynchronous I/O operation.

The console program that follows demonstrates asynchronous I/O. It creates a large stream of data, encrypts it, and saves it to a file. But instead of encrypting all the data and then writing to the file, it tries to encrypt blocks of data while the program is writing another encrypted block. Every time it takes a long time to finish I/O, the program proceeds to encrypt the next block of data. It displays a message on the console to indicate this. Since only a small amount of data is written by this program, it is difficult to simulate a long I/O operation that will take considerable time. For you to experiment, some of the data in the program is defined using #define, and you can vary these data parameters and try them out. In my local test, I was able to overlap I/O and encryption 10 to 15 times out of 200 I/O attempts. Of course, your results will vary depending on your computer configuration, other programs you are running, and so on.

```
#include <windows.h>
#include <iostream.h>


#define TOTAL_BUFFER_SIZE          200000
#define BYTES_PER_WRITE            100
#define SAMPLE_STRING_LENGTH       100
```

Instead of hard coding the buffer size and number of bytes that are written to the disk in each block, these values are #defined.

```
void EncryptNextSegment();
char *pOutBuf;
```

For simplicity, the pointer to the buffer that is written out is defined to be global.

```
int main ()
{
    char *szString = "This is a long string. It will be encrypted and stored in\
the file. This string is 100 bytes long...";
    char *pStrTemp;
    char *pOutBufTemp;

    pOutBuf = new char[TOTAL_BUFFER_SIZE];
    pOutBufTemp = pOutBuf;
    // make repetitive copy of szString into pOutBuf
    for(int i = 0; i < TOTAL_BUFFER_SIZE/SAMPLE_STRING_LENGTH; i++)
    {
      pStrTemp = szString;
      for (int j = 0; j < SAMPLE_STRING_LENGTH; j++)
      {
```

```
        *pOutBufTemp++ = *pStrTemp++;
        }
    }
    HANDLE hFile = CreateFile ("a:Out.enc", GENERIC_WRITE, 0, NULL,
CREATE_ALWAYS, FILE_FLAG_OVERLAPPED, NULL);
    // Return code should be checked here.  But assume it is OK for this
    // sample.
    // Prepare to write data to the file.
```

A buffer is allocated from the heap and the data is initialized. The file *a:Out.enc* is created. Drive A is used to attempt to slow down the I/O. Note that the FILE_FLAG_OVERLAPPED parameter is used while creating the file (by use of **CreateFile**).

```
    DWORD dwWrite;
    OVERLAPPED      ov;
    ov.Offset = 0;
    ov.OffsetHigh = 0;
    ov.hEvent = NULL;

    const int iTotalEncryptSegment = TOTAL_BUFFER_SIZE/BYTES_PER_WRITE;
    pOutBufTemp = pOutBuf;
    EncryptNextSegment();      // Encrypt first segment
```

The total number of blocks to be encrypted and written to the file is calculated and the first block is encrypted.

```
for (int k = 0; k < iTotalEncryptSegment; k++)
    {
      BOOL      fWriteResult;

      fWriteResult = WriteFile(hFile, pOutBufTemp, BYTES_PER_WRITE, NULL, &ov);
      for(;;)
      {
          DWORD dwResult = WaitForSingleObject(hFile, 20);
          if(dwResult == WAIT_TIMEOUT)
          {
          // The I/O is still going on - Proceed to encrypt the next block
              cout << "Proceed to encrypt while waiting for the IO to\
complete." << endl;
              EncryptNextSegment();
          }
          else if(dwResult == WAIT_OBJECT_0)
          {
```

```
            // Write is completed. Do at least one more encryption if we did
            // not time out the first time
            cout << "IO completed." << endl;
            EncryptNextSegment();
            break;
        }
        else if(dwResult == WAIT_FAILED)
        {
            cout << "WAIT_FAILED" << endl;
            break; //Check error by calling GetLastError() and process.
        }

    }
```

The encrypted block is written to the file asynchronously. The program then goes in a loop, periodically checking to see if the I/O has been completed. If the I/O is still pending, it proceeds to encrypt the next block of data. If the I/O is completed, it still tries to encrypt one more block just in case the first try to check the I/O completion was successful without a wait. It breaks out of the *for* loop, proceeds to get the overlap I/O result, and writes the next block of data. When all the data is written, it closes the file.

```
    pOutBufTemp += BYTES_PER_WRITE;
    GetOverlappedResult(hFile, &ov, &dwWrite, TRUE);
    ov.Offset += dwWrite;


    }
    CloseHandle(hFile);
    return(1);
}
```

The function **EncryptNextSegment** does a trivial encryption, where it increments the character by one. So "A" is rotated to "B," "B" to "C," and so on. This is a simplified version of more complex rotation encryption algorithms. **EncryptNextSegment** remembers which block is to be encrypted, and if all the blocks are encrypted, it just returns without doing anything.

```
void EncryptNextSegment()
{
    static int iCurrentEncSegment = 0; // Remember which segment is to be encrypted
    char *pBuf;
    if (iCurrentEncSegment < TOTAL_BUFFER_SIZE/BYTES_PER_WRITE)
    {
      // We still have more data to encrypt
```

```
        pBuf = pOutBuf + iCurrentEncSegment*BYTES_PER_WRITE;
        for (int i = 0; i < BYTES_PER_WRITE; i++)
        {
                *pBuf = *pBuf+1;      //Rot 1 encryption. Just increase the value
                                      //by 1. So 'A' will be 'B'

                pBuf++;
        }
        iCurrentEncSegment++;
    }
}
```

RAID SUPPORT

You've probably noticed two things about disk drives. First, the prices keep falling, as with many other computer components. Second, occasionally you have problems. I don't necessarily mean a crash, but you have files that have to be recovered, bad disk sectors, and on occasion your computer won't boot up because the boot sector is damaged. The problems of getting a magnetic head so close to a disk while ensuring that the two don't actually touch each other (with at least one of them moving at a high speed) has been likened to flying a Boeing 747 just a few feet off the ground. I started my floppy disk backup seriously since I read that.

The first solution to the disk problems is backups and an uninterruptible power supply (UPS). A UPS is good, but it only takes care of disk problems attributable to power failures. Backups are good and if you have mission-critical data, you want to ensure that at least one copy of the backup is physically stored away from the building where the original is (in the event of a fire in the building). But backups are a separate step, and it typically takes time to locate and get at the backup data. There is another solution. If disk prices are cheap and one disk may have problems, why not write the same data to more than one disk at the same time? The data in one disk is like a backup to the data in another disk, and vice versa. Since the data is written to all the disks at the same time, there is no extra step involved. That is the idea behind using a Redundant Array of Inexpensive Disks (RAID) instead of just one disk. Windows NT supports the RAID technology. The device driver *Ftdisk.sys* supports RAID.

There are six levels of RAID that are possible, and these are summarized in Table 4-8. Windows NT supports RAID in two ways—hardware and software:

▼ Hardware support for RAID disks

▲ *Ftdisk.sys* support for RAID levels 0, 1, and 5

Using RAID is primarily the job of a system administrator. When the system administrator mirrors a partition, another partition with the same drive letter as the one being partitioned is created. All data written to one partition is also written to the other. As an advanced programmer, you ought to be familiar with RAID and its benefits.

RAID Level	Function
0	Striping. Data that is written to the disk is split and written (striped across) to multiple disks.
1	Mirroring and duplexing. All data written to one disk is duplicated (mirrored) in another disk.
2	Bit-level striping with error-correction code (ECC). This technique is proprietary, using multiple parity drives.
3	Byte-level striping, also with ECC for parity. This is similar to RAID 2, except that only one parity drive is used.
4	Block-level striping, with single-drive parity. Drives are not synchronized.
5	Block-level striping with parity information distributed across multiple drives.

Table 4-8.   RAID Levels and Functions

CONCLUSION

We looked at the characteristics of the different file systems supported by Windows NT including FAT and its variations, NTFS, HPFS, and CDFS. We looked at the programming functions provided by Windows NT for volumes, drives, directories, and files. We looked at some advanced file system features, such as asynchronous input/output and memory-mapped files. We also looked at how your program can be notified of changes in the file system. Finally, we briefly looked at the characteristics of RAID.

The first four chapters surveyed the major features of Windows NT from a programming perspective. We looked at NT's architecture and related topics in Chapter 1. We looked at user interface-related topics in Chapter 2. We looked at communications-related topics in Chapter 3 and file-related topics in this chapter.

This concludes Part 1. In Part 2, we look at advanced GUI and OS services programming

WINDOWS NT
Professional Library

PART II

NT Advanced GUI and OS Services Programming

CHAPTER 5

GDI Programming

Part 1 of this book laid the programming foundations. The remainder, Parts 2 through 4, will build on those foundations. Here in Part 2 we will look at one of the most important programming areas in Windows NT—the user interface. Part 3 deals with communications programming, and Part 4 covers multimedia and database programming.

In this chapter, we will look at graphics programming using the graphical device interface (GDI). Chapter 6 will focus on advanced user interface programming. Chapter 7 will look at an animation programming method that uses controls, as well as other advanced controls availabale in Windows NT 4.0; and Chapter 8 will look at animation using bitmaps. Chapters 9 and 10 will cover advanced OS services such as dynamic link libraries (DLLs) and threads.

GDI BASICS

Windows NT includes a number of tools to facilitate graphics programming. We will review the basics briefly. By using the programming tools, you can draw regularly shaped objects, such as lines and circles, as well as irregularly shaped objects, such as irregular polygons. The programming tools include *pens* to draw lines, arcs, circles, ellipses, and so on. You can use *brushes* to fill in enclosed spaces. If you want to see a sample graphics program in action, check the paint accessory included with Windows.

The Graphics Coordinate System

Windows NT uses a graphics coordinate system to draw graphics. For example, if you draw a line, it is from the current coordinate of the cursor (the cursor is not visible, unlike it is with text) to the coordinate where the line terminates. When your program begins, the current cursor coordinate is set to (0,0). By default, (0,0) is the coordinate of the upper-left corner of the screen. You specify the drawing units (for example, the length of the line you want to draw) in *logical units*. By default, logical units are pixels. Remember, you can change the defaults for both the coordinate system and the logical units by using mapping modes (see the "Mapping Modes" section later in this chapter).

Device Context

A *device context* (*DC*) is a structure that Windows maintains when it outputs information to a device or collects information about a device. The device could be a display, printer, or a memory area. The DCs that access memory area are also called *compatible DCs,* and the DCs used to collect information are also called *informational DCs.* The MFC library provides classes that support DCs. The MFC DC classes and their descriptions are summarized in Table 5-1.

Output Mode

Windows copies the graphics output of your program as is and overwrites current window contents by default. However, you can AND, OR, or XOR your output with the

MFC DC Class	Description
CDC	This is the base class for all DC classes such as CPaintDC, CMetafileDC, and so on.
CPaintDC	This class is derived from CDC. It performs a CWnd::BeginPaint and constructs a CPaintDC object at construction time. It performs CWnd::EndPaint at destruction time. CPaintDC is typically used when you respond to the WM_PAINT message.
CMetaFileDC	This is used to create a CMetaFileDC object. A Windows metafile consists of GDI commands such as MoveTo and LineTo, and is an alternate way to reproduce images (compared with storing the whole image in a bitmap and reproducing the image).
CWindowsDC	This is used to access the entire screen area (both client and nonclient areas) of a window. CWindowsDC calls GetWindowDC at construction time and ReleaseDC at destruction time.
CClientDC	This is used to access the client area of a window. CClientDC calls GetDC at construction time and ReleaseDC at destruction time.

Table 5-1.   MFC Library DC Classes

current window contents by setting the appropriate mode. You can set the output mode using the **SetROP2( )** function. You can also choose the mode parameter values of **SetROP2( )**. The resulting colors when you subsequently use a pen or brush are shown in Table 5-2.

Mapping Modes

As mentioned earlier, the windows default is to map one logical unit to one pixel. You can change this mapping using the **SetMapMode** function. GDI uses the mapping mode to convert logical coordinates into the appropriate device coordinates. The mapping mode defines the unit of measure used to convert logical units to device units. It also defines the orientation of the device's X and Y axes. The **SetMapMode** function prototype is shown next:

```
virtual int SetMapMode( int nMapMode );
```

Mode Parameter Value	Drawing Mode
R2_BLACK	Black
R2_COPYPEN	Output copied to the window, overwrites the current contents
R2_MASKNOTPEN	AND of the inverse of the pen color and the current screen color
R2_MASKPEN	AND of the pen color and the current screen color
R2_MASKPENNOT	AND of the pen color and the inverse of the current screen color
R2_MERGENOTPEN	OR of the inverse of the pen color and the current screen color
R2_MERGEPEN	OR of the pen color and the current screen color
R2_MERGEPENNOT	OR of the pen color and the inverse of the current screen color
R2_NOP	No effect
R2_NOT	Inverse of the current screen color
R2_NOTCOPYPEN	Inverse of the current pen color
R2_NOTMASKPEN	Inverse of R2_MASKPEN
R2_NOTMERGEPEN	Inverse of R2_MERGEPEN
R2_NOTXORPEN	Inverse of R2_XORPEN
R2_WHITE	White
R2_XORPEN	Exclusive-OR of pen color with the current screen color

Table 5-2. Parameter Values to Choose Output Modes

The valid values of *nMapMode* and the resulting mode are summarized in Table 5-3. Having covered some graphics programming basics, let's look at some of the graphics programming topics in depth. As an advanced Windows programmer, you probably are already familiar with regular graphics programming using pens to draw lines, arcs, ellipses, and so on, and the use of brushes to fill in enclosed areas. We will not go into the programming details here. However, the sample program in this chapter draws an

nMapMode Value	Mode
MM_ANISOTROPIC	Maps logical units to programmer-defined units with arbitrarily scaled axes. You can use SetWindowExtEx or SetViewportExtEx to specify the units, scaling, and so on.
MM_HIENGLISH	Maps each logical unit to 0.001 inch.
MM_HIMETRIC	Maps each logical unit to 0.01 millimeter.
MM_ISOTROPIC	Maps logical units to programmer-defined units with equally scaled axes resulting in a 1:1 aspect ratio.
MM_LOMETRIC	Maps each logical unit to 0.1 millimeter.
MM_LOENGLISH	Maps each logical unit to 0.01 inch.
MM_TEXT	Maps each logical unit to one device pixel.
MM_TWIPS	Maps each logical unit to 1/20 of a printer's point, or approximately 1/1440 inch.

Table 5-3.   nMapMode Values and Resulting Mode

irregular polygon, an ellipse, and a rectangle. You can follow the code to see how this is done. If you want to read more about these topics, please refer to *Windows NT Programming from the Ground Up,* by Herbert Schildt, published by Osborne/ McGraw-Hill.

FONTS

Our discussion of graphics would be incomplete without covering the topic of text. You invariably need text in most graphics for titles, descriptions, notes, and so on. As an advanced programmer, you may already be familiar with different programming aspects of displaying text, such as specifying the color of the text you display as well as setting the background color, specifying the exact portion of the screen where your text will be displayed using Window coordinates and text metrics, setting the display mode, and so on. These topics will not be covered in this book. We will cover one key text aspect that can turn a simple-looking program into a professional-looking one—using font features. Windows NT provides multiple types of fonts and several built-in fonts within each type for your use. You can also create custom fonts. We will cover the different font types, how to choose a specific font, and creating custom fonts in the following sections. There are a number of attributes associated with fonts. Since many of the attributes are used in the rest of the chapter and examples, let us quickly review these terms in Table 5-4.

Raster, Vector, and TrueType Fonts

While the attributes listed in Table 5-4 deal with a font's appearance, it is left to the operating system to decide *how* to create and display or print a font. There are three types

Attribute	Description
Character set	This identifies which of the different character sets (ANSI, UNICODE, OEM, Symbol, and so on) is used by the font. The examples in this chapter will use the standard Windows character set, which is based on the ANSI character set.
Typeface	This defines the shaping features, such as the line slopes, curves, and so on, that visually set one font apart from other fonts.
Style	This is the style of the font, such as bold, italics, normal, and so on.
Weight	This is the thickness of the lines that make up the font. Windows NT supports several thickness levels.
Size	This is the size of a font measured in *points* (approximately 1/72 inch).
Font family	This is the family that a font belongs to. Windows NT supports the following font families: Decorative, Modern, Roman, Script, and Swiss.
Pitch	This is the width of each font character.
Proportional	The pitch of characters in the same font may vary, thus proportional fonts are also called *variable-pitch fonts*. For example, a "W" will not occupy the same width as an "I."
Nonproportional	This is the opposite of proportional. The pitch of all font characters is the same (also called *fixed-pitch* or *monospace*).
Serif	Serifs are the short lines found at the character endpoints (*sans serif* characters do not have a serif).

Table 5-4.   Font Attributes

Font Type	Creation Method	Advantages/ Disadvantages	Typical Use
Raster font	This font type stores bitmaps for each font character, and displays or prints bitmaps.	No additional work is needed in displaying or printing. Scaling is a problem, since scaling bitmaps leads to loss of resolution.	This is used in displays and in printers supporting bitmaps.
Vector font	This font type stores the endpoints to the line segments that make up each glyph and draws the segments to display each character.	This type takes less space than raster fonts.	This is well suited to plotters.
TrueType font	This font type stores information about the lines and arcs that make up each glyph and drawing instructions for them.	This type scales well.	This is used in applications that need WYSIWYG (what you see is what you get).

Table 5-5.   Font Types and Characteristics

of fonts corresponding to three ways of creating and displaying a font. These are summarized in Table 5-5. Windows NT supports all three font types.

USING BUILT-IN FONTS

Windows NT includes six built-in fonts as shown in Table 5-6.

As with all other Windows versions after 3.0, Windows NT uses a variable-pitch system font. System fonts are an example of a *stock object*, which is an existing object that is ready for use in your GDI application. Other stock objects included with Windows NT are brushes, pens, and palettes.

Font	Description
ANSI_FIXED_FONT	Monospace (fixed-pitch) font
ANSI_VAR_FONT	Proportional (variable-pitch) font
DEVICE_DEFAULT_FONT	Default device font, normally the system font
OEM_FIXED_FONT	OEM-defined font based on an OEM character set
SYSTEM_FONT	Proportional default font used by Windows NT for menus, dialog boxes, and so on
SYSTEM_FIXED_FONT	Font used by older versions of Windows (prior to Windows 3.0), included for compatibility purposes

Table 5-6.   Built-in Fonts in Windows NT

FONT PROGRAMMING EXAMPLE

Let's look at a sample program to illustrate the font-related concepts discussed so far. The program uses the **LOGFONT** structure. The **LOGFONT** structure defines the attributes of a font.

The **LOGFONT** structure has the following form:

```
typedef struct tagLOGFONT { /* lf */
    LONG Height;
    LONG Width;
    LONG Escapmnt;
    LONG Orient;
    LONG Weight;
    BYTE Italic;
    BYTE Underln;
    BYTE StrikeOut;
    BYTE CharSet;
    BYTE Outprecis;
    BYTE Clipprecis;
    BYTE Qual;
    BYTE PitchFam;
    CHAR TypeFaceName[LF_FACESIZE];
} LOGFONT;
```

Height is the height of the font in logical units. If *Height* is zero, a default size is used. If *Height* is nonzero, then Windows NT tries to locate a font that is as close in height as possible to the requested height without exceeding the requested height.

Width is the width of the font in logical units. If *Width* is zero, then Windows picks a font that is closest to the requested width by comparing the digitization aspect ratio of available fonts to the aspect ratio of the device where the font will be used.

You can output text at an any angle with reference to the X axis of the device where your text is displayed using the *Escapmnt* parameter. Imagine a line that goes through the base of all the text characters you want to display. The *Escapmnt* parameter specifies the angle between this line and the X axis of the device. The angle is specified in tenths of a degree ("10" for 1 degree, "20" for 2 degrees, and so on) in a counterclockwise direction. For regular text display (where the text is horizontal), there is no angle and the *Escapmnt* parameter is 0. Specify 900 (90 degrees) for text going up, 2700 (270 degrees) for text going down, and so on.

Unlike *Escapmnt,* which specifies the angle for all the characters of the text you are displaying, *Orient* specifies the angle of individual text characters. *Orient* is also specified in tenths of a degree in a counterclockwise direction.

Weight specifies the font weight. You can either specify a number in the range 0 to 1000 or you can use predefined macros. Typical values are 400 for normal and 700 for bold. If you specify zero, it means that you want Windows NT to pick a default weight. The predefined macros you can use and their weight values are as follows:

Predefined Macro	Weight Value
FW_DONTCARE	0
FW_THIN	100
FW_EXTRALIGHT or FW_ULTRALIGHT	200
FW_LIGHT	300
FW_NORMAL or FW_REGULAR	400
FW_MEDIUM	500
FW_SEMIBOLD or FW_DEMIBOLD	600
FW_BOLD	700
FW_EXTRABOLD or FW_ULTRABOLD	800
FW_HEAVY or FW_BLACK	900

A nonzero value for *Italic* specifies an italic style. If you do not want the italic style, specify this parameter as zero.

A nonzero value for *Underln* creates an underlined font. If you do not want underlines, specify this parameter as zero.

A nonzero value for *StrikeOut* creates a strike-through font. If you do not want strike-through, specify this parameter as zero.

CharSet indicates the character set you want to use. Some commonly used values are predefined. ANSI_CHARSET is a common value. Other values that can be specified include DEFAULT_CHARSET, SYMBOL_CHARSET, OEM_CHARSET, and so on. If you specify DEFAULT_CHARSET, Windows NT picks a font based on the font's name (see discussion of *TypeFaceName*, later in this section) and size. If a font with the specified *TypeFaceName* does not exist, Windows NT will pick a font from any character set. You should be consistent between this parameter and the *TypeFaceName* parameter.

Outprecis is the desired output precision. Precision reflects how closely the selected font's characteristics should match the requested font characteristics such as height, width, and so on. The valid values for this parameter and their descriptions of how Windows NT maps the fonts are as follows:

Precision Value	Description
OUT_CHARACTER_PRECIS	Not used
OUT_DEFAULT_PRECIS	Uses the default way of mapping the closest font
OUT_DEVICE_PRECIS	Chooses a device font when there are multiple fonts with the same font name
OUT_OUTLINE_PRECIS	Chooses from TrueType (and other outline-based) fonts when there are multiple fonts with the same font name
OUT_RASTER_PRECIS	Chooses a raster font when there are multiple fonts with the same font name
OUT_STRING_PRECIS	Value returned when raster fonts are enumerated
OUT_STROKE_PRECIS	Value returned when TrueType (and other outline-based) fonts or vector fonts are enumerated
OUT_TT_ONLY_PRECIS	Chooses a TrueType font (only) and uses the default mapping when no TrueType fonts are available
OUT_TT_PRECIS	Chooses a TrueType font when the system contains multiple fonts with the same name

Clipprecis specifies how each character that extends outside the clipping region is to be clipped (or truncated). The commonly used value for this parameter is CLIP_DEFAULT_PRECIS, which specifies the default clipping action. Other values for this parameter include CLIP_LH_ANGLES, which specifies whether the coordinate system orientation is left-handed or right-handed, and CLIP_EMBEDDED, which is specified when you're using embedded read-only fonts.

Qual determines how closely the logical font will match the actual physical fonts provided for the requested output device. The values you can specify and their descriptions are as follows:

Qual Value	Description
DEFAULT_QUALITY	This quality is a "don't care" (the font appearance is not significant).
DRAFT_QUALITY	This is draft quality level. Uses scaling for raster fonts where needed to match the required font characteristics. While this option permits more font choices, the quality of a scaled font may not be as good as a font that is not scaled, due to scaling distortions.
PROOF_QUALITY	This is the highest quality level. It does not use scaling and instead picks the font that matches the closest in size. This avoids scaling distortions.

PitchFam specifies the OR values of the pitch and family of the font. For pitch, you can specify DEFAULT_PITCH (which uses the default of the family such as fixed pitch for MODERN), FIXED_PITCH, or VARIABLE_PITCH. If you specify a typeface (see following paragraph on *TypeFaceName*), then Windows NT attempts to use it if available. If the specific typeface is not available, the font family value will be used. The font family value is one of five families and a "don't care" as follows:

Font Family/Value	Description
FF_DECORATIVE	Fonts used for decorative purposes and old manuscripts, such as Old English
FF_MODERN	Fixed-pitch fonts, such as Courier
FF_ROMAN	Proportional fonts with serifs (short lines at the character endpoints), such as MS Serif
FF_SCRIPT	Fonts that mimic handwriting, such as Cursive
FF_SWISS	Proportional fonts without serifs, such as MS Sans Serif
FF_DONTCARE	Lets the system pick any font family

TypeFaceName is a pointer to the name of the typeface. When you specify a *TypeFaceName*, Windows NT will try to locate a font with the specified typeface name in the system where your application executes. You should be consistent between this parameter and the character set you specify. This name is limited to 32 characters. If you specify NULL for this parameter, Windows NT automatically selects the first font that matches the other font characteristics you specify.

Figure 5-1 shows the output from the *Font* sample program and illustrates a small font height and the bold style. Figure 5-2 shows another output from the same program with a bigger font height and italic style.

The Font sample program shows how to enumerate all the fonts available in the system by use of **EnumFontFamilies** and **EnumFontProc**. It also shows how to set a font to a window by use of the **CFont** class and the **LOGFONT** structure. The sample when run displays a window with a menu. If Font is selected from the File menu, a dialog panel is displayed that lists all the font families available in the system. It also displays a sample text in the selected font in a multiline edit control. To display text in a font of your choice, select the font and then select the style. For example, Figure 5-3 shows the result of selecting Algerian font and normal style. It gives the option of changing the font height and applying basic styles like normal, bold, or italic to the sample text in the selected font. The multiline edit control also accepts entered text, which would help you try other text strings in the selected font, height, and style.

In most of the samples that will be discussed here and elsewhere, the AppWizard that comes with Visual C++ is used to generate some code. ClassWizard is a convenient and easy way to generate the code for the dialog boxes. One of the advantages of ClassWizard is that you do not have to remember the function signatures. However, this book does not expect the reader to have knowledge of generating code through this method. Furthermore, some of the samples are extended in other samples.

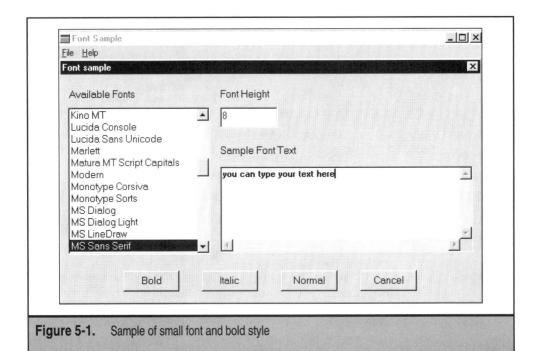

Figure 5-1.　Sample of small font and bold style

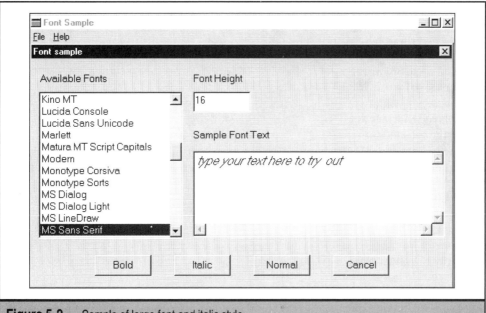

Figure 5-2.   Sample of large font and italic style

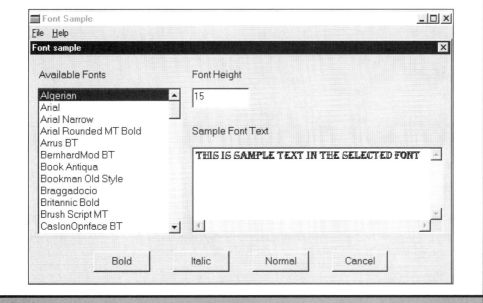

Figure 5-3.   Sample of Algerian font in normal style

The main application code is simple and functionally minimal. It has code to create the main application deriving from the **CWinApp** class and to run it. The code is shown and discussed next.

```
#include <afxwin.h>
#include <afxdlgs.h>
#include "FontDlg.h"
#include "Resource.h"
```

The header files *Afxwin.h* and *Afxdlgs.h* have definitions concerning window- and dialog-related information. The other two files are header files related to this application.

```
// Define the application object class
class CApp : public CWinApp
{
public:
        virtual BOOL InitInstance ();
};
```

The application object class is defined by deriving from the **CWinApp** class, and overriding the **InitInstance** method. During **InitInstance** the main window object is constructed, shown, and updated.

```
// Define the window class
class CWindow : public CFrameWnd
{
public:
    CWindow();
    afx_msg void OnAppAbout();
    afx_msg void OnFontDlg();
    afx_msg void OnExit();
    DECLARE_MESSAGE_MAP()
};
```

The main window is of class type **CWindow**, which is derived from **CFrameWnd**. All the menu-related functions are defined here. The **OnAppAbout** function processes the About menu item, the **OnFontDlg** function processes the Font menu item, and the **OnExit** function processes the Exit menu item. The message map next tells the system to call these functions when the respective menu items are selected.

```
/////////////////////////////////////////////////////////////////////////
// CWindow
BEGIN_MESSAGE_MAP(CWindow, CFrameWnd)
        ON_COMMAND(ID_APP_ABOUT, OnAppAbout)
```

```
                ON_COMMAND(ID_FONTDLG, OnFontDlg)
                ON_COMMAND(ID_APP_EXIT, OnExit)
END_MESSAGE_MAP()


//////////////////////////////////////////////////////////////////////
/////
//  CWindow  construction

CWindow::CWindow()
{
        Create( NULL, "Font Sample",
        WS_OVERLAPPEDWINDOW,
          rectDefault, NULL, MAKEINTRESOURCE(IDR_MAINFRAME) );
}
```

A new window is created with the title "Font Sample," taking the default initial size and associating the IDR_MAINFRAME resource to it. The main application object is defined next and is followed by the **InitInstance** function.

```
//////////////////////////////////////////////////////////////////////////
// The one and only CApp object
CApp theApp;

// CApp initialization

BOOL CApp::InitInstance()
{
        m_pMainWnd = new CWindow();
        m_pMainWnd -> ShowWindow( m_nCmdShow );
        m_pMainWnd -> UpdateWindow();
        return TRUE;
}
```

When the About menu item is selected, the **OnAppAbout** function is called, which creates a **CAboutDlg** object and displays the dialog box. This **CAboutDlg** class, which derives from the **CDialog** class, is defined next. It is followed by the **OnAppAbout** function, which displays the About dialog panel as a modal dialog box.

```
//////////////////////////////////////////////////////////////////////////
// CAboutDlg dialog used for App About
class CAboutDlg : public CDialog
{
public:
        CAboutDlg();
```

```
        enum { IDD = IDD_ABOUTBOX };
};

CAboutDlg::CAboutDlg() : CDialog(CAboutDlg::IDD)
{
}
// App command to run the dialog
void CWindow::OnAppAbout()
{
        CAboutDlg aboutDlg;
        aboutDlg.DoModal();
}


/////////////////////////////////////////////////////////////////////////////
// CWindow commands
// App command to run the dialog

void CWindow::OnFontDlg()
{
        CFontDlg fontDlg(this);
        fontDlg.DoModal();
}
// On Exit handles the void
void CWindow::OnExit()
{
        DestroyWindow();
}
```

When the Font menu item is selected, **OnFontDlg** is called, which creates a **CFontDlg** object and displays it modally. **OnFontDlg** is discussed in detail shortly. When the user selects Exit, the application destroys the window and closes the application.

The dialog resource file for the font dialog is shown next; note the style of the edit control, which is set to multiline edit.

```
IDD_FONTDLG DIALOG DISCARDABLE  0, 0, 292, 153
STYLE DS_MODALFRAME | WS_POPUP | WS_VISIBLE | WS_CAPTION | WS_SYSMENU
CAPTION "Font sample"
FONT 11, "MS Sans Serif"
BEGIN
    LISTBOX     IDC_FONTLIST,5,22,100,99,LBS_SORT | LBS_NOINTEGRALHEIGHT |
                WS_VSCROLL | WS_HSCROLL | WS_TABSTOP
    EDITTEXT    IDC_FONTHEIGHT,112,22,40,14,ES_AUTOHSCROLL
    EDITTEXT    IDC_MLE,112,62,175,58,ES_MULTILINE | ES_AUTOHSCROLL |
```

```
                        WS_VSCROLL | WS_HSCROLL
        PUSHBUTTON      "Bold",IDC_BOLD,44,132,39,14
        PUSHBUTTON      "Italic",IDC_ITALIC,99,132,39,14
        PUSHBUTTON      "Normal",IDC_NORMAL,154,132,39,14
        PUSHBUTTON      "Cancel",IDCANCEL,209,132,39,14
        LTEXT           "Available Fonts",IDC_STATIC,6,9,117,8
        LTEXT           "Font Height",IDC_STATIC,112,9,51,8
        LTEXT           "Sample Font Text",IDC_STATIC,112,47,69,8
END
```

The **CFontDlg** that displays a dialog box with all the font families in the system is defined next. It has members that correspond to the controls in the Font dialog box. These are the m_ListBox for the list control, m_MLE for the multiline edit control, and m_FontHeight for the edit control that lets the user enter the font height. It also has functions that are called when various push buttons in the panel are pressed. The constructor takes the pointer parent window and saves it for future use.

```
// FontDlg.h : header file
// CFontDlg dialog
#include "Resource.h"

class CFontDlg : public CDialog
{
private:
        int       iFontFeature;   // 0 = Normal, 1 = Bold, 2 = Italics
        CFont     *psaveFont;
        CWnd      *pParentWnd;

        CListBox  m_ListBox;
        CEdit     m_MLE;
        CEdit     m_FontHeight;

        void ChangeFont();
// Implementation
protected:

        // Generated message map functions
        virtual BOOL OnInitDialog();
        afx_msg void OnBold();
        afx_msg void OnItalic();
        afx_msg void OnNormal();
        virtual void DoDataExchange(CDataExchange* pDX);         // DDX/DDV
// Construction
public:
```

```
        CFontDlg(CWnd* pParent)
                : CDialog(IDD_FONTDLG, pParent)
                { pParentWnd = pParent;}
        ~CFontDlg();

DECLARE_MESSAGE_MAP()

};
```

The code that processes the font dialog panel is shown next. The message map section maps the button-click messages of Bold, Italic, and Normal push buttons to the respective functions.

```
#include <afxwin.h>
#include <afxdlgs.h>
#include "FontDlg.h"
#include "Resource.h"

// Function declaration for EnumFontFamilies callback
int  CALLBACK EnumFontsProc(LPLOGFONT, LPTEXTMETRIC, DWORD, LONG) ;

BEGIN_MESSAGE_MAP(CFontDlg, CDialog)
        //{{AFX_MSG_MAP(CFontDlg)
        ON_BN_CLICKED(IDC_BOLD, OnBold)
        ON_BN_CLICKED(IDC_ITALIC, OnItalic)
        ON_BN_CLICKED(IDC_NORMAL, OnNormal)
        //}}AFX_MSG_MAP
END_MESSAGE_MAP()


/////////////////////////////////////////////////////////////////////////////
// CFontDlg message handlers
```

Dialog data exchange (DDX) is an easy way to initialize the controls in the dialog panel and to gather data entered by the user. The initial values of the dialog object's member variables are typically set during **OnInitDialog** or the dialog constructor. Just before the dialog box is displayed, the framework's DDX mechanism transfers the values of the member variables to the controls in the dialog box. It also transfers values from the controls to the member variables when the user clicks on the OK button or when the **UpdateData** member function of the class **CWnd** is called.

```
void CFontDlg::DoDataExchange(CDataExchange* pDX)
{
        CDialog::DoDataExchange(pDX);
        DDX_Control(pDX, IDC_FONTLIST, m_ListBox );
```

```
        DDX_Control(pDX, IDC_FONTHEIGHT, m_FontHeight);
        DDX_Control(pDX, IDC_MLE, m_MLE);
}
/////////////////////////////////////////////////////////////////////////////
// CFontDlg message handlers
BOOL CFontDlg::OnInitDialog()
{
    CDC     *hdc;
    CFont      *defaultFont;
    LOGFONT    lf;

    CDialog::OnInitDialog();
    psaveFont = NULL;

    hdc = pParentWnd->GetDC();
    EnumFontFamilies(hdc->GetSafeHdc(), (LPSTR)NULL, (FONTENUMPROC)
    EnumFontsProc, (LONG)&m_ListBox);
    ReleaseDC(hdc);

    defaultFont = m_MLE.GetFont();    // Get the default font for the edit control
    defaultFont->GetLogFont(&lf);    // Get the pointer to the LOGFONT structure
    m_ListBox.SelectString(0, lf.lfFaceName); // Select the default font in the
    list box.
    SetDlgItemInt(IDC_FONTHEIGHT, -lf.lfHeight, FALSE);

    m_MLE.LimitText(256);
    m_MLE.SetWindowText((LPCTSTR)"This is sample text in the selected font and
    height.");
    return TRUE;   // return TRUE unless you set the focus to a control
}
```

During **OnInitDialog,** the **EnumFontFamilies** function is called to enumerate the fonts in a specified font family that are available for the display device. The handle to the device control is taken from the parent window. A specific font family could have been given here, but giving a value of NULL randomly selects and enumerates one font of each available type family. The next parameter is the procedure instance address of the application-defined callback function. For each font, this function retrieves information about that font and passes it to the **EnumFontFamProc** function. This continues until there are no more fonts or until the callback returns zero. Application-specified data can be passed to the procedure function as the last parameter. This feature is utilized and the list box class member data is passed. This is later used inside the procedure function to enter the font name in the list box. After displaying all the fonts inside the list box, the initialization procedure gets the current font of the multiline edit control and selects that font in the list box. It also displays a sample text in the multiline edit control.

When the style push buttons are pressed, the respective style is recorded in the private member variable **iFontFeature** and the text is updated by calling **ChangeFont( )**.

```
void CFontDlg::OnBold()
{
    iFontFeature = 1;
    ChangeFont ();
}


void CFontDlg::OnItalic()
{
    iFontFeature = 2;
    ChangeFont ();
}


void CFontDlg::OnNormal()
{
    iFontFeature = 3;
    ChangeFont ();
}
void CFontDlg::ChangeFont()
{
    char     newFace[LF_FACESIZE];
    int         index;
    int         iFontSize;
    CFont    *poldFont;
    CFont    *pnewFont;
    LOGFONT    lf;
```

The **CFont** class encapsulates a Windows GDI font and provides member functions for manipulating the font. The **LOGFONT** structure defines the attributes of a font. A new **CFont** object is created, and the existing font attributes are collected. The new font and the new font height are substituted in the font attribute structure. The font style is changed based on the user selection.

```
    pnewFont = new CFont ();
    memset (&lf, 0, sizeof(LOGFONT));
    poldFont = m_MLE.GetFont();
    poldFont->GetLogFont(&lf);

    index = m_ListBox.GetCurSel();
    m_ListBox.GetText(index, newFace);
```

```
    strcpy (lf.lfFaceName, newFace);
    if (iFontFeature == 1)
    {
    lf.lfWeight = FW_BOLD;
    lf.lfItalic = FALSE;
    }
    else if (iFontFeature == 2)
    {
    lf.lfWeight = FW_NORMAL;
    lf.lfItalic = TRUE;
    }
    else
    {
    lf.lfWeight = FW_NORMAL;
    lf.lfItalic = FALSE;
    }
    iFontSize = GetDlgItemInt(IDC_FONTHEIGHT, NULL, FALSE);
    if (iFontSize <= 0)
        iFontSize = 10;
    lf.lfHeight = -iFontSize;
    pnewFont->CreateFontIndirect(&lf);
```

The new font is set to the multiline edit control. The **LOGFONT** structure has many more attributes that can be modified. The results can be viewed by making additional changes to other attributes. Finally, the old font object is deleted, freeing up the resource. The destructor of the **CFontDlg** deletes the last font object.

```
    m_MLE.SetFont(pnewFont, TRUE);
    if (psaveFont)
        delete psaveFont;
    psaveFont = pnewFont;
}


CFontDlg::~CFontDlg()
{
    delete psaveFont;
}
```

For every font that the **EnumFontFamilies** function retrieves it calls **EnumFontsProc** to pass the information about the font. The member variable for the list box control is also passed in. The function adds the font name to the list box and asks for more fonts if available by returning 1. To terminate font enumeration, a zero can be returned.

```
////////////////////////////////////////////////////////////////////////////

// CFontDlg dialog

int CALLBACK EnumFontsProc (LPLOGFONT lplf, LPTEXTMETRIC lptm, DWORD
dwStyle, LONG lParam)
{
        CListBox        *pLBox;

        pLBox = (CListBox *)lParam;
        pLBox->AddString((LPCTSTR)lplf->lfFaceName);    // Add this font
        to the list box.
        return 1;

}
```

You can add *tooltips* to make the program easier to use and to make it look more professional. An enhanced version of the font enumeration program including the tooltips is shown on the next page. Figures 5-4 and 5-5 illustrate adding tooltips. You can

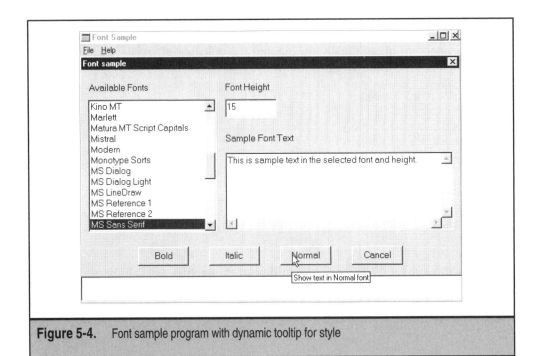

Figure 5-4.   Font sample program with dynamic tooltip for style

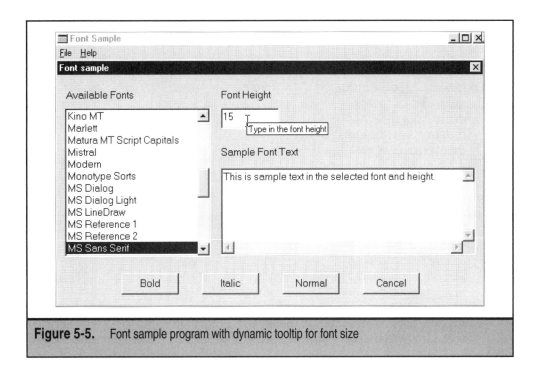

Figure 5-5.   Font sample program with dynamic tooltip for font size

add tooltips to many Windows user-interface components based on the technique illustrated in the example to come.

The functioning of the tooltip control is shown by modifying the Font sample program that was discussed earlier. The function of the Font sample program remains the same, except that it now shows tooltips for all the controls in the dialog box. When the cursor is moved over various controls, tooltip text appears. The tooltip text is static for all controls except the Font list box, where the tooltip changes every time a new font is selected from the list box. Only the changes made to the Font sample program are highlighted here. The **CToolTipCtrl** class, which encapsulates the functionality of a tooltip control, is used in the sample program.

Shown next is the header file for the **CFontDlg** class. *Afxcmn.h*, the header file that defines **CToolTipCtrl**, is included. **CToolTipCtrl** member data is added to correspond to the tooltip control, and two member functions to show the tooltip are also added.

```
// FontDlg.h : header file
//////////////////////////////////////////////////////////////////////////////
// CFontDlg dialog
#include <afxcmn.h>
#include "Resource.h"

class CFontDlg : public CDialog
```

```
{
private:
        int       iFontFeature;  // 0 = Normal, 1 = Bold, 2 = Italics
        CFont     *psaveFont;
        CWnd      *pParentWnd;
        CListBox  m_ListBox;
        CEdit     m_MLE;
        CEdit     m_FontHeight;
        CToolTipCtrl m_ToolTips;

         void ChangeFont();
// Implementation
protected:
        // Generated message map functions
        virtual BOOL OnInitDialog();
        afx_msg void OnBold();
        afx_msg void OnItalic();
        afx_msg void OnNormal();
        virtual void DoDataExchange(CDataExchange* pDX);        // DDX/DDV
        virtual BOOL PreTranslateMessage(MSG* pMsg);
        BOOL OnToolTipNotify ( UINT id, NMHDR * pTTTStruct, LRESULT * pResult );
// Construction
public:
        CFontDlg(CWnd* pParent)
                : CDialog(IDD_FONTDLG, pParent)
                { pParentWnd = pParent;}
        ~CFontDlg();
DECLARE_MESSAGE_MAP()
};
```

The code that handles the Font dialog box is shown next. This code is similar to the font sample that was discussed earlier, and the changes made to add a tooltip are highlighted. To show the tooltip, a **CToolTipCtrl** is created and various tools are added. The **PreTranslateMessage** method is handled, and information is relayed to the tooltip control to show the tooltip text. If the tooltip text is dynamic, then the **TTN_NEEDTEXT** notification message is handled.

```
//*************************************************************
// This sample demonstrates the class/functions related to
// Fonts.  This module implements the font dialog class.
// FontDlg.cpp : implementation file

#include <afxwin.h>
#include <afxdlgs.h>
```

```
#include <afxcmn.h>
#include "FontDlg.h"
#include "Resource.h"

// Function declaration for EnumFontFamilies callback
int  CALLBACK EnumFontsProc(LPLOGFONT, LPTEXTMETRIC, DWORD, LONG) ;

BEGIN_MESSAGE_MAP(CFontDlg, CDialog)
        //{{AFX_MSG_MAP(CFontDlg)
        ON_BN_CLICKED(IDC_BOLD, OnBold)
        ON_BN_CLICKED(IDC_ITALIC, OnItalic)
        ON_BN_CLICKED(IDC_NORMAL, OnNormal)
        ON_NOTIFY_EX(TTN_NEEDTEXT, 0, OnToolTipNotify)
        //}}AFX_MSG_MAP
END_MESSAGE_MAP()
```

As part of enabling the tooltips, the **TTN_NEEDTEXT** message is handled by adding an entry in the message map. The ID of the tooltip is always 0. You'll see later in the code that the tooltip text for the list box control is requested by the system from the application. The system requests the tooltip text by sending this notification message. The system would call **OnToolTipNotify** to get the text.

```
//////////////////////////////////////////////////////////////////////
// CFontDlg message handlers

void CFontDlg::DoDataExchange(CDataExchange* pDX)
{
        CDialog::DoDataExchange(pDX);
        DDX_Control(pDX, IDC_FONTLIST, m_ListBox );
        DDX_Control(pDX, IDC_FONTHEIGHT, m_FontHeight);
        DDX_Control(pDX, IDC_MLE, m_MLE);
}
//////////////////////////////////////////////////////////////////////
// CFontDlg dialog

int CALLBACK EnumFontsProc (LPLOGFONT lplf, LPTEXTMETRIC lptm, DWORD
dwStyle, LONG lParam)
{
        CListBox        *pLBox;
        pLBox = (CListBox *)lParam;
        pLBox->AddString((LPCTSTR)lplf->lfFaceName);
        return 1;
}
```

```
/////////////////////////////////////////////////////////////////////////
// CFontDlg message handlers
BOOL CFontDlg::OnInitDialog()
{
    CDC *hdc;
    CFont   *defaultFont;
    LOGFONT lf;

    CDialog::OnInitDialog();
    psaveFont = NULL;
```

In the next section **CToolTipCtrl** is created, and the tools are added to the tooltip control. For all controls except the list box, static text is used for the tooltip. For the list box tooltip, the goal is to show which font has been selected. Since this is dynamic text, the value LPSTR_TEXTCALLBACK is given. When the mouse pointer moves over the list box control, a **TTN_NEEDTEXT** notification message is sent to the parent of the list box control window. The handling of this message will be discussed later in this chapter. The delay between the time the mouse pointer moves over the control and the time the tooltip text appears can be set by calling the **SetDelayTime** member function. It is set to 50 milliseconds here. The default is 500 milliseconds. The length of time to display the tool text can be controlled by sending a **TTM_SETDELAYTIME** message to the tooltip control and specifying the delay time in milliseconds. Here it is set to SHRT_MAX milliseconds, which is approximately 33 seconds. Since **CToolTipCtrl** is derived from **CWnd** class, the member functions of **CWnd** can be used to change other attributes of the tooltip text and window like font, color, and so on.

```
m_ToolTips.Create(this);
        m_ToolTips.AddTool (&m_FontHeight, "Type in the font height");
        m_ToolTips.AddTool (&m_ListBox,   LPSTR_TEXTCALLBACK);
        m_ToolTips.AddTool (&m_MLE, "You may type your own text");
        m_ToolTips.AddTool (GetDlgItem(IDC_BOLD), "Show text in Bold font");
        m_ToolTips.AddTool (GetDlgItem(IDC_ITALIC), "Show text in Italic font");
        m_ToolTips.AddTool (GetDlgItem(IDC_NORMAL), "Show text in Normal font");
        m_ToolTips.AddTool (GetDlgItem(IDCANCEL), "Close the dialog box");
        m_ToolTips.SetDelayTime(50);
        m_ToolTips.SendMessage(TTM_SETDELAYTIME, TTDT_AUTOPOP, SHRT_MAX);

        hdc = pParentWnd->GetDC();
        EnumFontFamilies(hdc->GetSafeHdc(), (LPSTR)NULL,
                        (FONTENUMPROC) EnumFontsProc, (LONG)&m_ListBox);
        ReleaseDC(hdc);

        defaultFont = m_MLE.GetFont();  // Get the default font for the edit
```

```
                                      // control
    defaultFont->GetLogFont(&lf);   // Get the pointer to the logfont
    m_ListBox.SelectString(0, lf.lfFaceName); // Select the default font in
                                              // the list box.
    SetDlgItemInt(IDC_FONTHEIGHT, -lf.lfHeight, FALSE);
    m_MLE.LimitText(256);
    m_MLE.SetWindowText((LPCTSTR)"This is sample text in the selected font
                              and height.");
    return TRUE;  // return TRUE unless you set the focus to a control
}
```

When the tooltip for the list box is needed, a **TTN_NEEDTEXT** notification message is sent. It is handled by the **OnToolTipNotify** function shown next. The first parameter, *id*, is the control ID associated with the **WM_NOTIFY** message; since this ID is not unique, it is not used. The ID is taken from the NMHDR structure. If it is a handle to the window, the control is queried by calling the **GetDlgCtrlID** function and passing the handle to the window. Based on this control ID the tooltip text is decided. In this example we have only one control that would request the tooltip. So this text is created by finding out which font has been selected and appending a textual string. Either the pointer to the string can be sent in *lpsxText*, or the string can be copied in *szText*—provided it can fit in 80 bytes. Since in this example the text will be less than 80 bytes, it is copied in the *szText* buffer.

```
BOOL CFontDlg::OnToolTipNotify ( UINT id, NMHDR * pNMHDR, LRESULT *
pResult )
{
TOOLTIPTEXT *pTTT = (TOOLTIPTEXT *) pNMHDR;

    UINT nID =pNMHDR->idFrom;
    if ((pTTT->uFlags & TTF_IDISHWND))
      {
      nID = ::GetDlgCtrlID((HWND)nID);
      if(nID)
        {
        char     szFontFace[80];
        int index = m_ListBox.GetCurSel();
        m_ListBox.GetText(index, szFontFace);
        strcat (szFontFace, " font has been selected");
        pTTT->lpszText = szFontFace;
        return (TRUE);
        }
      }
return (FALSE);
}
```

Finally, the **PreTranslateMessage** method overrides the default handling. The **RelayEvent** method of the tooltip control is called to handle mouse button moves (up, down, dragging). This method triggers the display of the tooltips for the control. If the tooltip control already has the tooltip text, it will display; if not, it will send a notification message.

```
BOOL CFontDlg::PreTranslateMessage(MSG * pMsg)
{
   switch(pMsg->message)
   {
     case WM_LBUTTONDOWN:
     case WM_RBUTTONDOWN:
     case WM_MBUTTONDOWN:
     case WM_LBUTTONUP:
     case WM_MBUTTONUP:
     case WM_RBUTTONUP:
     case WM_MOUSEMOVE:
        m_ToolTips.RelayEvent(pMsg);
        break;
   }
   return CDialog::PreTranslateMessage(pMsg);
}

void CFontDlg::ChangeFont()
{
        char    newFace[LF_FACESIZE];
        int     index;
        int     iFontSize;
        CFont   *poldFont;
        CFont   *pnewFont;
        LOGFONT lf;

        pnewFont = new CFont ();
        memset (&lf, 0, sizeof(LOGFONT));
        poldFont = m_MLE.GetFont();
        poldFont->GetLogFont(&lf);

        index = m_ListBox.GetCurSel();
        m_ListBox.GetText(index, newFace);

        strcpy (lf.lfFaceName, newFace);
        if (iFontFeature == 1)
        {
```

```
        lf.lfWeight = FW_BOLD;
        lf.lfItalic = FALSE;
        }
        else if (iFontFeature == 2)
        {
        lf.lfWeight = FW_NORMAL;
        lf.lfItalic = TRUE;
        }
        else
        {
        lf.lfWeight = FW_NORMAL;
        lf.lfItalic = FALSE;
        }
        iFontSize = GetDlgItemInt(IDC_FONTHEIGHT, NULL, FALSE);
        if (iFontSize <= 0)
                iFontSize = 10;
        lf.lfHeight = -iFontSize;
        pnewFont->CreateFontIndirect(&lf);

        m_MLE.SetFont(pnewFont, TRUE);
        if (psaveFont)
                delete psaveFont;
        psaveFont = pnewFont;

}

void CFontDlg::OnBold()
{
        iFontFeature = 1;
        ChangeFont ();
}

void CFontDlg::OnItalic()
{
        iFontFeature = 2;
        ChangeFont ();
}

void CFontDlg::OnNormal()
{
        iFontFeature = 3;
        ChangeFont ();

}
```

```
CFontDlg::~CFontDlg()
{
        delete psaveFont;
}
```

Now let's take a look at some other functions introduced in Windows NT 4.0 that let you manipulate the graphics you display. With these functions you can rotate, translate, shear, reflect, and scale graphics. Windows calls these manipulations *world transforms*.

WORLD TRANSFORMS

To understand the programming of world transforms, we should start with understanding coordinate spaces.

Coordinate Spaces

Windows NT defines three *coordinate spaces*. They are as follows:

▼ *World space* is used to perform world transformations.

■ *Page space* is logical coordinate space used by your program.

▲ *Device space* is used to map to the physical device. This space uses physical coordinates.

The mapping of output (which is specified in logical units) to the physical units for the output device starts at page space unless you are using world transforms. If you are using world transforms, then the output mapping begins at world space. To use world transforms, you must do two things. First, you must enable Windows NT's advanced graphics mode using the **SetGraphicsMode( )** function whose prototype is shown here:

```
nt SetGraphicsMode(HDC hdc,
                   int GraphMode);
```

Here, *hdc* is the device context, and *GraphMode* specifies the graphics mode to be set. It must be either GM_COMPATIBLE or GM_ADVANCED. The function returns the previous mode or zero on failure. To use **SetWorldTransform( )**, you must set the mode to GM_ADVANCED. The default is GM_COMPATIBLE.

Second, you specify world transforms using **SetWorldTransform( )** as shown in the next section.

TIP: Once you have set the mode to GM_ADVANCED and specified transformations using **SetWorldTransform( )**, you can return to the GM_COMPATIBLE mode only if you reset your transformations using **SetWorldTransform( )** or **ModifyWorldTransform( )**.

SetWorldTransform( )

SetWorldTransform( ) sets a two-dimensional linear transformation (such as rotation) between world space and page space.

Its prototype is shown here:

```
BOOL SetWorldTransform(HDC hdc,
                       CONST XFORM *lpTrnsfrm);
```

Here, *hdc* is the handle to the device context, and *lpTrnsfrm* points to the **XFORM** structure (see next), which specifies the actual transformations. The function returns nonzero if successful and zero on failure.

Transformations are specified by use of an **XFORM** structure as follows:

```
typedef struct  tagXFORM
{
  FLOAT eM11;
  FLOAT eM12;
  FLOAT eM21;
  FLOAT eM22;
  FLOAT eDx;
  FLOAT eDy;
} XFORM;
```

The exact transformation that takes place is determined by the values you place in the matrix defined by **XFORM**. Let's see how each type of transformation can be achieved.

For any coordinate (x,y) in world space, the transformed coordinate in page space (x′,y′) is determined by the following algorithm:

```
x' = x * eM11 + y * eM21 + eDx,
y' = x * eM12 + y * eM22 + eDy,
```

where the transformation matrix is represented by the following:

```
| eM11 eM12 0 |
| eM21 eM22 0 |
| eDx  eDy  1 |
```

Transformations

Let's see how to perform each of the world transformations.

Translation To translate output, specify the following:

Field	Value
eDx	X offset
eDy	Y offset

Rotation To rotate output through an angle θ, specify the following:

Field	Value
eM11	Cosine of θ
eM12	Sine of θ
eM21	Negative sine of θ
eM22	Cosine of θ

Scaling To scale output, specify the following:

Field	Value
eM11	Horizontal scaling factor
eM12	Zero
eM21	Zero
eM22	Vertical scaling factor

Shearing To shear output, specify the following:

Field	Value
eM11	Zero
eM12	Horizontal shear factor
eM21	Vertical shear factor
eM22	Zero

Reflection To reflect output along the X axis, specify the following:

Field	Value
eM11	–1
eM12	Zero
eM21	Zero
eM22	1

To reflect output along the Y axis, specify the following:

Field	Value
eM11	1
eM12	Horizontal shear factor
eM21	Vertical shear factor
eM22	–1

To reflect output along both axes, specify the following:

Field	Value
eM11	–1
eM12	Horizontal shear factor
eM21	Vertical shear factor
eM22	–1

TIP: You can combine transformations. For example, you can combine rotation and translation. The following screen shots show the results of combinations. You can achieve the same effect programmatically.

World Transformation Example

Figure 5-6 shows the window with an overlapping polygon, an ellipse, and a rectangle when the sample program is executed. Figure 5-7 shows the effect of rotation, and Figure 5-8 shows the effect of translation. Figure 5-9 shows the effect of shearing, and Figure 5-10 shows the effect of combined shearing and rotation. Many more effects and combinations are possible. Try them on your own!

The *WrldXForm* sample program illustrates the world coordinate transformation. The sample displays an overlapping polygon (which appears like a five-pointed star), an ellipse, and a rectangle. Using menu selection and arrow keys, you can manipulate these

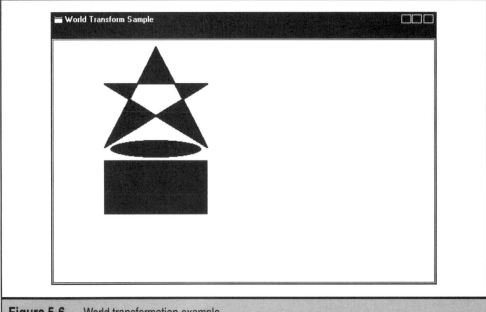

Figure 5-6.   World transformation example

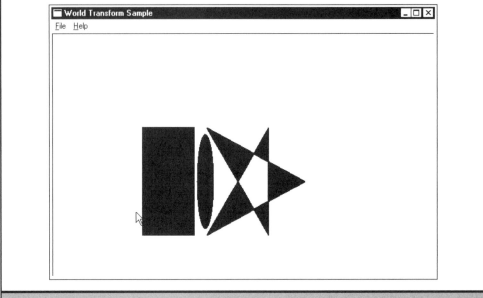

Figure 5-7.   World transformation example—rotation

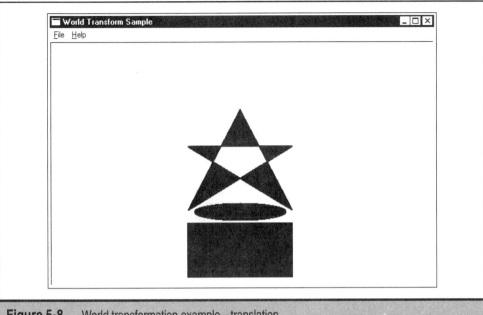

Figure 5-8. World transformation example—translation

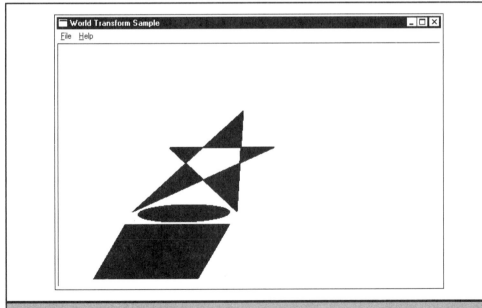

Figure 5-9. World transformation example—shearing

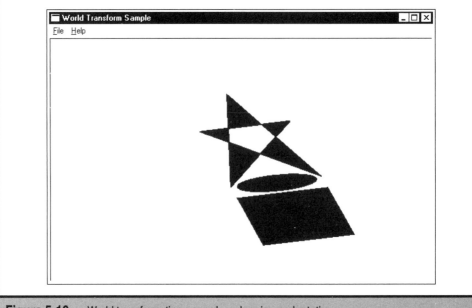

Figure 5-10. World transformation example—shearing and rotation

graphic objects. It shows the use of the **XFORM** structure and the **SetWorldTransform** API. The shell code for the *Font* sample is taken as the basis for this sample. When the program is executed, it displays a window with these three graphic objects. From the File menu you can select transformations like Rotate, Translate, Shear, Reflect, and Scale. After being selected, the graphic objects can be manipulated with the arrow keys. Selecting Original from the File menu would initialize the graphic objects to their initial state. Some of the transformations can be combined. The objects could be translated to a different location and then their reflection taken. The code for this sample is shown later in this chapter.

The *Math.h* header file is included for the trigonometric functions. A set of transformations is defined with values ranging from 1 to 6. This is followed by the global variable **xForm**, which specifies a world space to a page space transformation. Various functions in the program modify this structure, and the paint section of the code picks up the change and sets the world transform accordingly. There are two variables that keep the state information of the current and previous transforms the user selected, and another variable keeps track of the incremental angle by which the graphic objects are rotated.

```
//****************************************************************
// This sample demonstrates the class/functions related to
// World Transform
//****************************************************************
// WRLDXFORM.CPP
```

```
#include <afxwin.h>
#include <afxdlgs.h>
#include <math.h>
#include "Resource.h"

#define ORIGINAL    1
#define ROTATE      2
#define TRANSLATE   3
#define SHEAR       4
#define REFLECT     5
#define SCALE       6

XFORM    xForm;
int      iCurrentTransform;
int      iPreviousTransform;
short    sAngle;


// Define the application object class
class CApp : public CWinApp
{
public:
    virtual BOOL InitInstance ();
};
```

The **CWindow** class defines the application window and defines all the class member functions.

```
// Define the application's window class
class CWindow : public CFrameWnd
{
public:
    CWindow();
    afx_msg void OnPaint();
    afx_msg void OnKeyUp(UINT, UINT, UINT);
    afx_msg void OnAppAbout();
    afx_msg void OnOriginal();
    afx_msg void OnRotate();
    afx_msg void OnTranslate();
    afx_msg void OnShear();
    afx_msg void OnReflect();
    afx_msg void OnScale();
    afx_msg void OnExit();
```

```
    void UncheckMenu();
    void CheckMenu();
    DECLARE_MESSAGE_MAP()
};
```

The message map declares the action for various menu selections. It also declares a message map for the key-up message. Every time a key is pressed and released, this message is sent to the application. This message is used to manipulate the graphic objects.

```
//////////////////////////////////////////////////////////////////////////
// CWindow

BEGIN_MESSAGE_MAP(CWindow, CFrameWnd)
    ON_WM_PAINT()
    ON_WM_KEYUP()
    ON_COMMAND(ID_APP_ABOUT, OnAppAbout)
    ON_COMMAND(IDM_ORIGINAL, OnOriginal)
    ON_COMMAND(IDM_ROTATE, OnRotate)
    ON_COMMAND(IDM_TRANSLATE, OnTranslate)
    ON_COMMAND(IDM_SHEAR, OnShear)
    ON_COMMAND(IDM_REFLECT, OnReflect)
    ON_COMMAND(IDM_SCALE, OnScale)
    ON_COMMAND(ID_APP_EXIT, OnExit)
END_MESSAGE_MAP()
```

During the construction of the **CWindow** object, the global variables are initialized to represent no transformation.

```
//////////////////////////////////////////////////////////////////////////
// CWindow construction

CWindow::CWindow()
{
    LoadAccelTable(MAKEINTRESOURCE(IDR_MAINFRAME));
    Create( NULL, "World Transform Sample",
    WS_OVERLAPPEDWINDOW,
    rectDefault, NULL, MAKEINTRESOURCE(IDR_MAINFRAME) );
    xForm.eM11 = 1.0;
    xForm.eM12 = 0.0;
    xForm.eM21 = 0.0;
    xForm.eM22 = 1.0;
    xForm.eDx  = 0.0;
    xForm.eDy  = 0.0;
    iCurrentTransform = ORIGINAL;
```

```
                iPreviousTransform = ORIGINAL;
}


//////////////////////////////////////////////////////////////////////
// Create the application class object
CApp theApp;


//////////////////////////////////////////////////////////////////////
// Application initialization

BOOL CApp::InitInstance()
{

    m_pMainWnd = new CWindow();
    m_pMainWnd -> ShowWindow( m_nCmdShow );
    m_pMainWnd -> UpdateWindow();
    return TRUE;
}


//////////////////////////////////////////////////////////////////////
// CAboutDlg dialog triggered by About... menu item.

class CAboutDlg : public CDialog
{
public:
    CAboutDlg();

    enum { IDD = IDD_ABOUTBOX };
};

CAboutDlg::CAboutDlg() : CDialog(CAboutDlg::IDD)
{
}
// About... menu item command handler.
void CWindow::OnAppAbout()
{
    CAboutDlg aboutDlg;
    aboutDlg.DoModal();
}
```

OnPaint is called every time the window needs to be repainted. A **CPaintDC** object is created. This paint device context will perform the **BeginPaint( )** and **EndPaint( )** functions during construction and destruction, respectively. A red pen and a red brush are selected for drawing. The graphic mode is set to advanced graphics mode to allow world transformations. The mode must be GM_ADVANCED in order to perform world transformation. The **SetWorldTransform** function sets a two-dimensional linear transformation between world space and page space. We will be using this transformation for rotation, translation, shear, reflection, and scale by specifying appropriate values in the **XFORM** structure.

```
// Paint message handler
void CWindow::OnPaint()
{
    CPaintDC dc(this);
    // Change the pen and the brush
    CPen pen(PS_SOLID, 2, RGB(255,0,0));
    CBrush brush(RGB(255,0,0));
    dc.SelectObject(&pen);
    dc.SelectObject(&brush);

    SetGraphicsMode(dc.GetSafeHdc(), GM_ADVANCED);
    SetWorldTransform(dc.GetSafeHdc(), &xForm);
```

A *polygon* is a versatile function that can be used to construct various shapes such as a pentagon or star depending on how the points are connected. Here the polygon is used to construct a five-point star. The polygon fill mode is set to ALTERNATE, which, in fact, is the default mode. In the ALTERNATE mode the system fills the area between odd-numbered and even-numbered polygon sides on each scan line. The other option is to set the mode to WINDING, where the system uses the direction in which the graphic object is drawn to determine whether to fill an area. The **Polygon( )** function draws the polygon based on the array of points passed to the function. The polygon is drawn by connecting all the points given. Notice that the order of selection of the points creates a five-point star. By changing the selection order of the points, you can change the shape of the polygon.

Following the five-point star, a rectangle and an ellipse are drawn. Also note that the objects are drawn with the same values every time. When the program is run, though the specified coordinate is the same, the graphic objects appear different depending on the transformation used.

```
    CPoint a[5];
    a[0] = CPoint(80,160);
    a[1] = CPoint(160,10);
    a[2] = CPoint(240,160);
    a[3] = CPoint(80,40);
    a[4] = CPoint(240,40);
    dc.SetPolyFillMode(ALTERNATE);
    dc.Polygon(a, 5);
```

```
    dc.Rectangle(80,180,240,260);
    dc.Ellipse(90,150,230,175);
}
```

As you know, every time a key is pressed and released, a key-up message is sent by the system. The **OnKeyUp** function is called every time this message is sent. This function ignores all keys except the arrow keys. Depending on the currently selected transform, the transform structure is updated and the window is forced to repaint.

For *rotation*, the LEFT ARROW and the RIGHT ARROW keys are ignored. When the UP ARROW or DOWN ARROW key is pressed, the graphic objects are rotated counter clockwise or clockwise by 10 degrees. The check to see if the angle is between 0 and 360 degrees is just cosmetic and is not necessary trigonometrically. The eM11 and eM22 values in the transformation structure take the cosine of the angle of rotation. The eM12 value takes the sine of the angle, and eM21 takes the negative of the sine of the angle of rotation.

For *translation*, pressing the UP ARROW key decreases the y coordinate by 10, while pressing the DOWN ARROW key increases it by 10. The LEFT ARROW and RIGHT ARROW keys decrease and increase the x coordinate by 10.

For *shear*, pressing the UP ARROW or DOWN ARROW key decreases or increases the proportionality constant along the y coordinate, and the LEFT ARROW or RIGHT ARROW key does the same along the x coordinate.

For *reflection*, pressing the UP ARROW or DOWN ARROW key reflects vertically, while the LEFT ARROW or RIGHT ARROW key reflects horizontally.

For *scale*, pressing the UP ARROW or RIGHT ARROW keys increases the scale, while the DOWN ARROW or LEFT ARROW keys decreases the scale. Scaling both x and y coordinates is done for visual effect, and they can both be independently scaled. Scaling is done at an increment of 0.1; when the scaling factor reaches 0, it is reset to 1.0.

```
void CWindow::OnKeyUp(UINT c, UINT repCount, UINT Flags)

{
        switch (c)
        {
            case VK_UP:
            {
                switch(iCurrentTransform)
                {
                case ROTATE:
                    sAngle -= 10;
                    if (sAngle < 0)
                        sAngle += 360;
                    xForm.eM11 = (float) cos((sAngle*3.14159)/180.0);
                    xForm.eM12 = (float) sin((sAngle*3.14159)/180.0);
                    xForm.eM21 = (float) -sin((sAngle*3.14159)/180.0);
                    xForm.eM22 = (float) cos((sAngle*3.14159)/180.0);
```

```
                  break;
              case TRANSLATE:
                  xForm.eDy -= (float)10.0;
                  break;
              case SHEAR:
                  xForm.eM21 -= (float)0.1;
                  break;
              case REFLECT:
                  xForm.eM22 = (float)-1.0;
                  break;
              case SCALE:
                  xForm.eM11 += (float)0.1;  // Remove this line for
                                             //disproportionate scaling

                  xForm.eM22 += (float)0.1;
                  break;
          }
      Invalidate(TRUE);
      }

      break;
      case VK_DOWN:
      {
          switch(iCurrentTransform)
          {
          case ROTATE:
              sAngle += 10;
              if (sAngle > 360)
                  sAngle -= 360;
              xForm.eM11 = (float) cos((sAngle*3.14159)/180.0);
              xForm.eM12 = (float) sin((sAngle*3.14159)/180.0);
              xForm.eM21 = (float) -sin((sAngle*3.14159)/180.0);
              xForm.eM22 = (float) cos((sAngle*3.14159)/180.0);

              break;
          case TRANSLATE:
              xForm.eDy += (float)10.0;
              break;
          case SHEAR:
              xForm.eM21 += (float)0.1;
              break;
          case REFLECT:
              xForm.eM22 = (float)1.0;     // Reset to original
```

```
            break;
        case SCALE:
            xForm.eM11 -= (float)0.1; // Remove this line for
                                      // disproportionate scaling
            xForm.eM22 -= (float)0.1;
            if(xForm.eM11 < 0.0)    // If scaling becomes negative reset
                                    // to original size
                xForm.eM11 = 1.0;
            if(xForm.eM22 < 0.0)
                xForm.eM22 = 1.0;
            break;
        }
    Invalidate(TRUE);
    }

    break;
    case VK_LEFT:
    {
        switch(iCurrentTransform)
        {
        case ROTATE:
            break;
        case TRANSLATE:
            xForm.eDx -= (float)10.0;
            break;
        case SHEAR:
            xForm.eM12 += (float)0.1;
            break;
        case REFLECT:
            xForm.eM11 = (float)-1.0;
            break;
        case SCALE:
            xForm.eM22 -= (float)0.1; // Remove this line for
                                      // disproportionate scaling
            xForm.eM11 -= (float)0.1;
            if(xForm.eM22 < 0.0)    // If scaling becomes negative reset
                                    // to original size
                xForm.eM22 = 1.0;
            if(xForm.eM11 < 0.0)
                xForm.eM11 = 1.0;

            break;
        }
```

```
            Invalidate(TRUE);
        }
        break;
        case VK_RIGHT:
        {
            switch(iCurrentTransform)
            {
            case ROTATE:
                break;
            case TRANSLATE:
                xForm.eDx += (float)10.0;
                break;
            case SHEAR:
                xForm.eM12 -= (float)0.1;
                break;
            case REFLECT:
                xForm.eM11 = (float)1.0;      // Reset to original
                break;
            case SCALE:
                xForm.eM22 += (float)0.1; // Remove this line for
                                          //disproportionate
                                          //scaling

                xForm.eM11 += (float)0.1;
                break;
            }
        Invalidate(TRUE);
        }
        break;
    }

}
```

The following functions process the menu item commands. When the Original menu item is selected, the transform structure is reset and the global variables are set to their initial value. For all selections the current and previous selections are stored in the global variable and the menu selections are visually indicated by unchecking and checking the menu items. This is done by calling the **UnCheckMenu( )** and **CheckMenu( )** functions.

```
// Handle the menu commands.
void CWindow::OnOriginal()
{
    sAngle = 0;
    xForm.eM11 = 1.0;
    xForm.eM12 = 0.0;
```

```
        xForm.eM21 = 0.0;
        xForm.eM22 = 1.0;
        xForm.eDx  = 0.0;
        xForm.eDy  = 0.0;
        iPreviousTransform = iCurrentTransform;
        iCurrentTransform = ORIGINAL;
        UncheckMenu();
        CheckMenu();
        Invalidate(TRUE);
    }


void CWindow::OnRotate()
    {
        iPreviousTransform = iCurrentTransform;
        iCurrentTransform = ROTATE;
        UncheckMenu();
        CheckMenu();
        Invalidate(TRUE);
    }
void CWindow::OnTranslate()
    {
        iPreviousTransform = iCurrentTransform;
        iCurrentTransform = TRANSLATE;
        UncheckMenu();
        CheckMenu();
        Invalidate(TRUE);
    }
void CWindow::OnShear()
    {
        iPreviousTransform = iCurrentTransform;
        iCurrentTransform = SHEAR;
        UncheckMenu();
        CheckMenu();
        Invalidate(TRUE);
    }


void CWindow::OnReflect()
    {
        iPreviousTransform = iCurrentTransform;
        iCurrentTransform = REFLECT;
        UncheckMenu();
        CheckMenu();
        Invalidate(TRUE);
    }
```

```
void CWindow::OnScale()
{
    iPreviousTransform = iCurrentTransform;
    iCurrentTransform = SCALE;
    UncheckMenu();
    CheckMenu();
    Invalidate(TRUE);
}
```

UncheckMenu( ) removes the checkmark that appears against the menu item. It determines which menu item needs to be unchecked based on the previous transform state. It then calls **CheckMenuItem( )** to remove the check. **CheckMenuItem( )** determines the menu item based on the command. **CheckMenu( )** does the opposite—it checks the menu items.

```
void CWindow::UncheckMenu()
{
    CMenu    *Menu;

    Menu = GetMenu();
    switch(iPreviousTransform)
    {
        case ORIGINAL:
            Menu->CheckMenuItem(IDM_ORIGINAL, MF_BYCOMMAND | MF_UNCHECKED);
            break;
        case ROTATE:
            Menu->CheckMenuItem(IDM_ROTATE, MF_BYCOMMAND | MF_UNCHECKED);
            break;
        case TRANSLATE:
            Menu->CheckMenuItem(IDM_TRANSLATE, MF_BYCOMMAND | MF_UNCHECKED);
            break;
        case SHEAR:
            Menu->CheckMenuItem(IDM_SHEAR, MF_BYCOMMAND | MF_UNCHECKED);
            break;
        case REFLECT:
            Menu->CheckMenuItem(IDM_REFLECT, MF_BYCOMMAND | MF_UNCHECKED);
            break;
        case SCALE:
            Menu->CheckMenuItem(IDM_SCALE, MF_BYCOMMAND | MF_UNCHECKED);
            break;
    }
}
```

```
void CWindow::CheckMenu()
{
    CMenu    *Menu;

    Menu = GetMenu();
    switch(iCurrentTransform)
    {
        case ORIGINAL:
            Menu->CheckMenuItem(IDM_ORIGINAL, MF_BYCOMMAND | MF_CHECKED);
            break;
        case ROTATE:
            Menu->CheckMenuItem(IDM_ROTATE, MF_BYCOMMAND | MF_CHECKED);
            break;
        case TRANSLATE:
            Menu->CheckMenuItem(IDM_TRANSLATE, MF_BYCOMMAND | MF_CHECKED);
            break;
        case SHEAR:
            Menu->CheckMenuItem(IDM_SHEAR, MF_BYCOMMAND | MF_CHECKED);
            break;
        case REFLECT:
            Menu->CheckMenuItem(IDM_REFLECT, MF_BYCOMMAND | MF_CHECKED);
            break;
        case SCALE:
            Menu->CheckMenuItem(IDM_SCALE, MF_BYCOMMAND | MF_CHECKED);
            break;
    }

}

// On Exit handles the void
void CWindow::OnExit()
{
    DestroyWindow();
}
```

CONCLUSION

In this chapter you looked at graphics programming in Windows NT using the GDI. Besides creating simple graphical objects such as circles, rectangles, arcs, and so on, you can also use GDI for more complicated shapes such as irregular polygons as illustrated in the example. You also learned how to perform functions such as rotation on the graphical objects. You also looked at another area that you are likely to use—fonts. The programming sample uses one of the most important programming tools to add to your utility collection—a utility to figure out the available fonts in a computer. Tooltips will be covered in the advanced controls chapter, but you got a preview of how you can use tooltips to add pizzazz to your user interface. You can have tooltips with static text as well as dynamically changing text as illustrated in the example.

In the next chapter we will look at advanced user interface programming.

CHAPTER 6

Advanced User Interface Programming

ontinuing our discussion on advanced user interfaces, we will explore two important aspects of programming user interfaces—how to accelerate window repainting (which makes the difference between an ordinary program and a professional-grade program) and how to handle output to the screen that doesn't fit in the visible area of the screen.

As you know, each time a window receives a **WM_PAINT** message, it must restore its contents. The management and optimization of window repainting is fundamental to all Windows NT programs. At first glance, you might be wondering why a book on advanced Windows NT programming examines this seemingly rudimentary topic. The answer is straightforward: while nearly all programmers understand the need to handle **WM_PAINT** messages, few know the high-powered techniques required when professional, commercial-grade applications need to be produced. The proof of the foregoing statement is that it is easy to find examples of programs that respond poorly to **WM_PAINT** messages! When an application does not efficiently handle repaint requests, it appears both sluggish and unprofessional to the user. This makes the proper management of **WM_PAINT** one of the most important advanced techniques that a Windows NT programmer must put into his or her bag of tricks.

This chapter describes four important **WM_PAINT**-related techniques. First, it discusses a general-purpose method by which any program can quickly and efficiently repaint a window when a **WM_PAINT** message is received. This general method is based on the concept of a *virtual window*. Second, using the virtual window technology, you will see how to optimize your program's response to a repaint request. Third, you will learn how to use a virtual window to utilize a display workspace that is larger than the dimensions of the screen. Finally, you will see how to dynamically add scroll bars when contents of a window no longer fit within its current size.

THE REPAINT PROBLEM

As you know, Windows NT programs must repaint a window (that is, redisplay the information contained in the window) each time a **WM_PAINT** message is received. **WM_PAINT** messages are sent to your program whenever the contents of a window need to be restored. For example, when a window is overlaid by another and then uncovered, your program is sent a repaint request. To satisfy this request, your program must redisplay the contents of the window. Windows NT will not do this for you. It is your responsibility. Of course, this gives rise to the larger question: what mechanism should you use to restore the contents of a window when a **WM_PAINT** message is received? This question has haunted programmers since the early days of Windows. To some extent, its answer depends on the exact nature of your application. However, over time, three basic methods have emerged. Let's examine each now.

The first way that your program can repaint a window is by *regenerating* the output. This method will only work if that output is created by some computational means. For example, a program that displays the square roots of the integers between 1 and 100 could simply redisplay the values when a **WM_PAINT** message is received. Unfortunately, few programs fall into this category.

The second way your application can repaint its window is by storing a record of display events and then *replaying* those events when a repaint request is received. For example, such an approach may work for some types of games. For most programs, this approach is not feasible.

The third, and most versatile, method by which you can repaint a window is by keeping a *copy* of the window (that is, a virtual window) in memory. Each time a **WM_PAINT** message is received, the contents of the virtual window are copied to the screen. One important advantage of this method is that it will work for any and all programs. For this reason, it is the method that will be developed here. As you will see, Windows provides substantial support for this approach to repainting.

NOTE: If you are already familiar with the fundamentals of using a virtual window to accomplish fast and easy repaints, you may want to skip ahead to the section entitled "Optimizing Repaints."

VIRTUAL WINDOW THEORY

A virtual window is a bitmap that is compatible with the device context defined by your program. Thus, it will behave in the same way as the physical window that is displayed on the screen. The only difference is that the virtual window exists in memory. In general, a virtual window can be used to respond to a repaint request as follows. All output is written to the virtual window. Of course, you are free to simultaneously write output to the physical window, too. However, at all times, the virtual window must hold a complete copy of whatever is displayed on the screen. This ensures that there is always a record of the current contents of the window. Each time a **WM_PAINT** message is received, the contents of the virtual window are copied into the physical window, restoring the contents of the physical window. For example, if the physical window is overwritten and then uncovered by removing one or more windows that are on top of it, a **WM_PAINT** message will be received and the window's contents will be automatically restored.

The advantages to the virtual window approach are many. First, as mentioned earlier, it works for all programs. Second, it is easy to implement. Third, it can be efficiently implemented. Finally, once the virtual window mechanism is in place, it helps solve other output-related problems.

Creating the Virtual Window

To create a virtual window, use the following procedure. First, create a virtual *device context* (*DC*) that is compatible with your program's actual device context. This will be done only once, when the program begins execution—typically, when the **WM_CREATE** message is received. This compatible device context will exist the entire time the program is executing. Once you have created a compatible DC, you must create a compatible bitmap that will act as the virtual window. The dimensions of this bitmap must be large enough to handle a maximized window. Finally, this bitmap must be selected into the compatible DC and given the same brushes and pens used by the physical window that it is emulating.

Here is a sample of code that creates a virtual window:

```
case WM_CREATE:
  /* get screen coordinates */
  maxX = GetSystemMetrics(SM_CXSCREEN);
  maxY = GetSystemMetrics(SM_CYSCREEN);

  /* create the virtual window */
  hdc = GetDC(hwnd);
  memdc = CreateCompatibleDC(hdc);
  hbit = CreateCompatibleBitmap(hdc, maxX, maxY);
  SelectObject(memdc, hbit);
  hbrush = GetStockObject(WHITE_BRUSH);
  SelectObject(memdc, hbrush);
  PatBlt(memdc, 0, 0, maxX, maxY, PATCOPY);

  /* ... */

  ReleaseDC(hwnd, hdc);
  break;
```

Let's examine this code closely. First, the dimensions of the screen are obtained by use of **GetSystemMetrics( )**. They will be used to create a compatible bitmap. The prototype for **GetSystemMetrics( )** is shown here:

```
int GetSystemMetrics(int what);
```

Here, *what* will be a value that specifies the value that you want to obtain. (The function can obtain several different values.) Here is a sampling of macros for some common values:

Macro	Metric Obtained
SM_CXFULLSCREEN	Width of maximized client area
SM_CYFULLSCREEN	Height of maximized client area
SM_CXICON	Width of standard icon
SM_CYICON	Height of standard icon
SM_CXSMICON	Width of small icon
SM_CYSMICON	Height of small icon
SM_CXSCREEN	Width of entire screen
SM_CYSCREEN	Height of entire screen

In the preceding example, the values SM_CXSCREEN and SM_CYSCREEN are used to obtain the screen extents.

After the dimensions of the screen have been obtained, the current device context is acquired by use of the function **GetDC( )**. Next, a compatible device context is created in memory, by use of **CreateCompatibleDC( )**. The handle to this device context is stored in **memdc**, which is a global variable. The prototype for **CreateCompatibleDC( )** is shown here:

```
HDC CreateCompatibleDC(HDC hdc)
```

This function returns a handle to a memory device context that is compatible with the device context of the physical window specified by *hdc*. The function returns NULL if an error occurs.

Next, a compatible bitmap is created by use of **CreateCompatibleBitmap( )**. This establishes a one-to-one mapping between the virtual window and the physical window. The dimensions of the bitmap are those of the maximum screen size. This ensures that the bitmap will always be large enough to fully restore the window, no matter how large the window. (Actually, slightly smaller values could be used, since the borders aren't repainted, but this minor improvement is left to you as an exercise.) The handle to the bitmap is stored in the global variable **hbit**. The **CreateCompatibleBitmap( )** function creates a bitmap that is compatible with the specified device context. This bitmap can be used by any compatible device context. The prototype for **CreateCompatibleBitmap( )** is shown here:

```
HBITMAP CreateCompatibleBitmap(HDC hdc,
                               int width,
                               int height);
```

Here, *hdc* is the handle for the device context for which the bitmap will be compatible. The dimensions of the bitmap are specified in *width* and *height*. These values are in pixels. The function returns a handle to the compatible bitmap or NULL on failure.

After the bitmap has been created, it must be selected into the memory device context by use of **SelectObject( )**, which has this prototype:

```
HGDIOBJ SelectObject(HDC hdc,
                     HGDIOBJ hObject);
```

Here, *hdc* specifies the device context, and *hObject* is the handle of the object being selected into that context. The function returns the handle of the previously selected object (if there is one), allowing it to be reselected later if desired.

Next, a stock white brush is obtained, and its handle is stored in the global variable **hbrush**. This brush is selected into the memory device context, and then **PatBlt( )** paints the entire virtual window using the brush. Thus, the virtual window will have a white background. Since no pen is selected, the default pen will be used. These choices are arbitrary. In this case, the white background matches the background of the physical window in the example program that follows. (Remember, these colors are under your control. The colors used here are examples.) **PatBlt( )** function fills a rectangle with the color and pattern of the currently selected *brush*. The **PatBlt( )** has this prototype:

```
BOOL PatBlt(HDC hdc,
            int X,
            int Y,
            int width,
            int height,
            DWORD dwRaster);
```

Here, *hdc* is the handle of the device context. The coordinates *X* and *Y* specify the upper-left corner of the region to be filled. The width and height of the region are specified in *width* and *height*. The value passed in *dwRaster* determines how the brush will be applied. It must be one of these macros:

Macro	Meaning
BLACKNESS	Region is black (brush is ignored)
WHITENESS	Region is white (brush is ignored)
PATCOPY	Brush is copied to region
PATINVERT	Brush is ORed to region
DSTINVERT	Region is inverted (brush is ignored)

Therefore, if you wish to apply the current brush unaltered, you would select PATCOPY for the value for *dwRaster*. The function returns nonzero if successful, zero otherwise.

Finally, the physical device context is released. However, the memory device context stays in existence until the program ends.

Outputting to the Virtual Window

To output to the virtual window, do so just as you would to a normal window: just direct the output to the memory device context. For example, the following statement writes the sentence "This is a test" to the virtual window created by the code fragment in the preceding section.

```
strcpy(str, "This is a test");
TextOut(memdc, 0, 0, str, strlen(str)); /* output to virtual window */
```

Of course, this only outputs the sentence to the virtual window. A separate output statement must be used if you also want the output to appear in the physical window prior to a **WM_PAINT** message being received.

Responding to WM_PAINT

To use the virtual window to process a repaint request, your program must copy the contents of the virtual window to the physical window each time a **WM_PAINT** message is received. The best way to accomplish this is by using the **BitBlt( )** function. **BitBlt( )** copies a bitmap from one device context to another using a very fast bit-block transfer. It has this prototype:

```
BOOL BitBlt(HDC hDest,
            int X,
            int Y,
            int Width,
            int Height,
            HDC hSource,
            int SourceX,
            int SourceY,
            DWORD dwRaster);
```

Here, *hDest* is the handle of the target device context, and *X* and *Y* are the upper-left coordinates at which point the bitmap will be drawn. The width and height of the bitmap are specified in *Width* and *Height.* The *hSource* parameter contains the handle of the source device context, which in this case will be the memory context obtained by use of **GetCompatibleDC( )**. *SourceX* and *SourceY* specify the upper-left coordinates in the bitmap at which point the copy operation will begin. The value of *dwRaster* determines how the bit-by-bit contents of the bitmap will actually be copied. Some of its most common values are shown here:

dwRaster Macro	Effect
DSTINVERT	Inverts the bits in the destination bitmap
SRCAND	ANDs bitmap with current destination
SRCCOPY	Copies bitmap as is, overwriting previous contents
SRCERASE	ANDs bitmap with the inverted bits of destination bitmap
SRCINVERT	XORs bitmap with current destination
SRCPAINT	ORs bitmap with current destination

The function returns nonzero if successful and zero otherwise.

By use of **BitBlt( )**, here is one way to respond to a **WM_PAINT** message:

```
case WM_PAINT: /* process a repaint request */
  hdc = BeginPaint(hwnd, &ps); /* get DC */
```

```
/* copy virtual window to screen */
BitBlt(hdc, 0, 0, maxX, maxY, memdc, 0, 0, SRCCOPY);

EndPaint(hwnd, &ps); /* release DC */
break;
```

As you can see, the **BitBlt( )** function is used to copy the image from **memdc** into **hdc**. Remember, the parameter *SRCCOPY* simply means to copy the image as is, without alteration, directly from the source to the target. Because all output has been stored in **memdc**, this statement causes that output to actually be displayed. More importantly, if the window is covered and then uncovered, **WM_PAINT** will be received, and this code causes the contents of that window to be automatically restored.

In this example, the entire virtual window is copied to the physical window. However, later in this chapter you will see how to repaint only those parts of the physical window that actually need to be restored.

A Virtual Window Demonstration Program

Here is the complete program that demonstrates use of a virtual window. Sample output is shown in Figure 6-1.

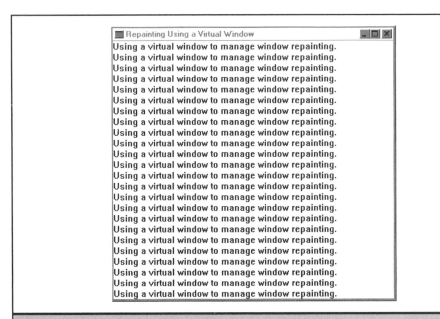

Figure 6-1.   Sample output from the virtual window program

```
/* Repainting using a virtual window. */
#include <windows.h>
#include <string.h>
#include <stdio.h>

LRESULT CALLBACK WindowFunc(HWND, UINT, WPARAM, LPARAM);

char szWinName[] = "MyWin"; /* name of window class */

int X=0, Y=0; /* current output location */
int maxX, maxY; /* screen dimensions */

HDC memdc; /* store the virtual device handle */
HBITMAP hbit; /* store the virtual bitmap */
HBRUSH hbrush; /* store the brush handle */

int WINAPI WinMain(HINSTANCE hThisInst, HINSTANCE hPrevInst,
                   LPSTR lpszArgs, int nWinMode)
{
  HWND hwnd;
  MSG msg;
  WNDCLASSEX wcl;

  /* Define a window class. */
  wcl.hInstance = hThisInst; /* handle to this instance */
  wcl.lpszClassName = szWinName; /* window class name */
  wcl.lpfnWndProc = WindowFunc; /* window function */
  wcl.style = 0; /* default style */

  wcl.cbSize = sizeof(WNDCLASSEX); /* set size of WNDCLASSEX */

  wcl.hIcon = LoadIcon(NULL, IDI_APPLICATION); /* standard icon */
  wcl.hIconSm = LoadIcon(NULL, IDI_APPLICATION); /* small icon */
  wcl.hCursor = LoadCursor(NULL, IDC_ARROW); /* cursor style */
  wcl.lpszMenuName = NULL; /* no main menu */
  wcl.cbClsExtra = 0;
  wcl.cbWndExtra = 0;

  /* Use white background. */
  wcl.hbrBackground = GetStockObject(WHITE_BRUSH);

  /* Register the window class. */
  if(!RegisterClassEx(&wcl)) return 0;
```

```
    /* Create the window. */
    hwnd = CreateWindow(
      szWinName, /* name of window class */
      "Repainting Using a Virtual Window", /* title */
      WS_OVERLAPPEDWINDOW, /* window style - normal */
      CW_USEDEFAULT, /* X coordinate - let Windows decide */
      CW_USEDEFAULT, /* Y coordinate - let Windows decide */
      CW_USEDEFAULT, /* width - let Windows decide */
      CW_USEDEFAULT, /* height - let Windows decide */
      HWND_DESKTOP, /* no parent window */
      NULL, /* no override of class menu */
      hThisInst, /* handle of this instance of the program */
      NULL /* no additional arguments */
    );

    /* Display the window. */

    ShowWindow(hwnd, nWinMode);
    UpdateWindow(hwnd);

    /* Create the message loop. */
    while(GetMessage(&msg, NULL, 0, 0))
    {
      TranslateMessage(&msg); /* translate keyboard messages */
      DispatchMessage(&msg);  /* return control to Windows */
    }
    return msg.wParam;
}

/* Window Procedure */
LRESULT CALLBACK WindowFunc(HWND hwnd, UINT message,
                            WPARAM wParam, LPARAM lParam)
{
  HDC hdc;
  PAINTSTRUCT ps;

  TEXTMETRIC tm;
  char str[255];
  int i;

  switch(message) {
    case WM_CREATE:
      /* get screen coordinates */
      maxX = GetSystemMetrics(SM_CXSCREEN);
```

```
    maxY = GetSystemMetrics(SM_CYSCREEN);

    /* create the virtual window */
    hdc = GetDC(hwnd);
    memdc = CreateCompatibleDC(hdc);
    hbit = CreateCompatibleBitmap(hdc, maxX, maxY);
    SelectObject(memdc, hbit);
    hbrush = GetStockObject(WHITE_BRUSH);
    SelectObject(memdc, hbrush);
    PatBlt(memdc, 0, 0, maxX, maxY, PATCOPY);

    /* get text metrics */
    GetTextMetrics(hdc, &tm);

    /* output to the virtual window */
    for(i=0; i<24; i++) {
      strcpy(str, "Using a virtual window to manage window repainting.");
      TextOut(memdc, X, Y, str, strlen(str)); /* output to memory */

      /* advance to next line */
      Y = Y + tm.tmHeight + tm.tmExternalLeading;
    }

    ReleaseDC(hwnd, hdc);
    InvalidateRect(hwnd, NULL, 0); /* force a repaint */
    break;
  case WM_PAINT: /* process a repaint request */
    hdc = BeginPaint(hwnd, &ps); /* get DC */

    /* copy virtual window to screen */
    BitBlt(hdc, 0, 0, maxX, maxY, memdc, 0, 0, SRCCOPY);

    EndPaint(hwnd, &ps); /* release DC */
     break;
  case WM_DESTROY: /* terminate the program */
    DeleteDC(memdc); /* delete the memory device context */
    PostQuitMessage(0);
    break;
  default:
   return DefWindowProc(hwnd, message, wParam, lParam);
  }
  return 0;
}
```

When you run this program, try covering and then uncovering the window. As you will see, the contents of the window are automatically restored.

Notice that inside **WM_CREATE**, output is only written to the virtual window. That is, the calls to **TextOut( )** only send output to the virtual window—not to the physical window. To cause that output to actually be displayed, **InvalidateRect( )** is called. As you probably know, **InvalidateRect( )** causes a **WM_PAINT** message to be sent to your application. Its prototype is shown here:

```
BOOL InvalidateRect(HWND hwnd,
                    CONST RECT *lpRect,
                    BOOL bErase);
```

Here, *hwnd* is the handle of the window that will receive the **WM_PAINT** message. The **RECT** structure pointed to by *lpRect* specifies the coordinates within the window that must be redrawn. If this value is NULL, the entire window will be specified. If *bErase* is TRUE, the background will be erased. If it is zero, the background is left unchanged. When you're using the virtual window technique, *bErase* will normally be zero. Specifying *bErase* as zero also helps eliminate "flicker" when repaints occur. The function returns nonzero if successful, zero otherwise. (In general, this function will always succeed.)

RECT is a structure that specifies the upper-left and lower-right coordinates of a rectangular region. This structure is shown here:

```
typedef tagRECT {
  LONG left, top; /* upper left */
  LONG right, bottom; /* lower right */
} RECT;
```

One unrelated, but interesting point about outputting text: Inside the **WM_CREATE** case, lines of text are output to the screen by use of **TextOut( )**. As you probably know, when outputting text, you must specify the starting point for each string. Therefore, to write several lines of text, you must manually advance the vertical coordinate to the starting point of each line. However, since Windows NT allows character fonts of differing sizes, you need to obtain the distance between lines dynamically, at run time. To accomplish this, the function **GetTextMetrics( )** is used. It obtains a copy of all the information related to text and puts it into a **TEXTMETRIC** structure. The two members of this structure that are needed to compute the starting point of the next line are **tmHeight** and **tmExternalLeading**. These members contain the height of the character set and the space between lines, respectively. Both values are in terms of pixels. If you are particularly interested in text output, you will want to learn more about text metrics. You can get more information about **GetTextMetrics( )** and other text related API from Microsoft documentation.

OPTIMIZING REPAINTS

In the preceding program, each time a **WM_PAINT** message is received, the entire contents of the window are restored—whether or not they need to be. This is the way most beginning Windows programmers handle a repaint request. It is, of course, not the best way. It is important to understand that restoring a window is expensive in terms of time. The larger the window, the longer it takes to restore it. Therefore, it is to your benefit to repaint only those parts of the window that actually need it. For example, it is quite common to cover only a corner of a window. When that corner is uncovered, it will be faster to restore only that portion than to repaint the entire window. Fortunately, Windows NT provides information that will allow us to do precisely that. By repainting only those portions of a window that actually require it, repaints take less time and your application has a much snappier feel. Optimizing window repainting is one of the most important performance improvements that you can make to your program.

All Windows NT programmers know that when a **WM_PAINT** message is processed, you must call **BeginPaint( )** to obtain a device context. However, what is sometimes overlooked is that in addition to acquiring a device context, **BeginPaint( )** also obtains information about the display state of the window. The prototype for **BeginPaint( )** is shown here:

```
HDC BeginPaint(HWND hwnd, PAINTSTRUCT *lpPS);
```

BeginPaint( ) returns a device context if successful or NULL on failure. Here, *hwnd* is the handle of the window for which the device context is being obtained. The second parameter is a pointer to a structure of type **PAINTSTRUCT**. The structure pointed to by *lpPS* will contain information that your program can use to repaint the window. **PAINTSTRUCT** is defined like this:

```
typedef struct tagPAINTSTRUCT {
  HDC hdc; /* handle to device context */
  BOOL fErase; /* true if background must be erased */
  RECT rcPaint; /* coordinates of region to redraw */
  BOOL fRestore;  /* reserved */
  BOOL fIncUpdate; /* reserved */
  BYTE rgbReserved[32]; /* reserved */
} PAINTSTRUCT;
```

Here, *hdc* will contain the device context of the window that needs to be repainted. This DC is also returned by the call to **BeginPaint( )**. *fErase* will be nonzero if the background of the window needs to be erased. However, as long as you specified a background brush when you created the window, you can ignore the *fErase* member. Windows NT will erase the window for you.

In **PAINTSTRUCT**, the *rcPaint* element contains the coordinates of the window region that needs to be repainted. We can take advantage of this information to reduce the time needed to restore a window.

The coordinates in *rcPaint* also define a *clipping region*. No output is allowed to be written outside the current clipping region. However, it is not an error to *attempt* to write output outside the clipping region. It simply will not be displayed. This is essentially a safety measure provided by Windows, but is of little value in optimizing repaint times. Our challenge is to utilize the coordinates provided by **BeginPaint( )** to restore the window by copying only as much information from the virtual window as is necessary. Put differently, the fact that the coordinates in *rcPaint* define a clipping region is essentially irrelevant to improving the performance of a repaint request.

Reducing Repaint Time

The key to decreasing the time it takes to restore a window when a **WM_PAINT** message is received is to restore only the portion of the window defined by *rcPaint*. This is easy to accomplish when you're using a virtual window. Simply copy the same region of the virtual window to the physical window. Don't copy the entire virtual window. Since the two device contexts are identical, so are their coordinate systems. The coordinates that are contained in *rcPaint* can be used for both the physical window and the virtual window. For example, here is one way to respond to **WM_PAINT**:

```
case WM_PAINT: /* an improved response to a repaint request */
  hdc = BeginPaint(hwnd, &ps); /* get DC */

  /* copy a portion of the virtual window */
  BitBlt(hdc, ps.rcPaint.left, ps.rcPaint.top,
          ps.rcPaint.right-ps.rcPaint.left, /* width */
          ps.rcPaint.bottom-ps.rcPaint.top, /* height */
          memdc,
          ps.rcPaint.left, ps.rcPaint.top,
          SRCCOPY);

  EndPaint(hwnd, &ps); /* release DC */
  break;
```

To see the effectiveness of this version, substitute it into the program from the preceding section. Because this version only copies the rectangle defined by *rcPaint*, no time is wasted copying information that has not been overwritten.

Notice how easy it is to optimize the repainting of a window when you're using the virtual window method. Almost no additional programming effort is required. As mentioned at the start of this chapter, the virtual window method of repainting is an elegant solution to many repaint-related operations.

ACCESSING AN OVERSIZED VIRTUAL WINDOW

In addition to achieving faster and more convenient repaints, a virtual window also helps you manage two other common programming situations. First, most windows may have their size changed by the user. For example, a user may resize a window by dragging its borders. The window may also be maximized, minimized, or restored to its original size. When a window is reduced in size, it is possible that all of its contents will not fit in the remaining client area. For some types of applications, it is acceptable to simply allow the information to be clipped. For others, scroll bars are added to the window to allow access to all of the information. In this case, there must be some mechanism to move the information through the remaining portion of the window. The second situation relates to the first. In some cases your application will require a very large workspace for its output. However, because of limits to the size of the screen, only a portion of this workspace can be displayed at a time. This type of situation is common in computer-aided design programs. The challenge is how best to manage this situation.

The common thread that links these two problems is the need to access a bitmap that is larger than the physical window. As you will see, by use of a virtual window, both of these situations can be dealt with easily.

Virtual Window Scrolling Basics

Before developing a complete example that scrolls the contents of the virtual window through the physical window, we will give an example of the basic mechanisms involved. Once these have been mastered, the details will be filled in.

In principle, accessing a larger virtual window through a smaller physical window is quite easy. The physical window simply displays a subregion of the larger space. That is, the physical window displays whatever portion of the virtual window that it is currently "over." When the physical window is scrolled, the physical window is moved to another location within the virtual window. This process is similar to using a microfilm reader. It is depicted in Figure 6-2.

The easiest way to scroll through a large virtual window is to use scroll bars. Each time a scroll bar is moved, the position of the physical window is changed relative to the virtual window. In this way, it is possible to scroll into view any part of a large virtual window.

Before you see how to implement such a procedure, a short digression is required which briefly reviews how scroll bars are managed under Windows NT.

Receiving Scroll Bar Messages

When a scroll bar is accessed by the user, it sends either a **WM_VSCROLL** or a **WM_HSCROLL** message, depending on whether it is the vertical or horizontal scroll bar, respectively. The value of the low-order word of *wParam* contains a code that describes the activity. For the standard window scroll bars, *lParam* is zero. However, if a

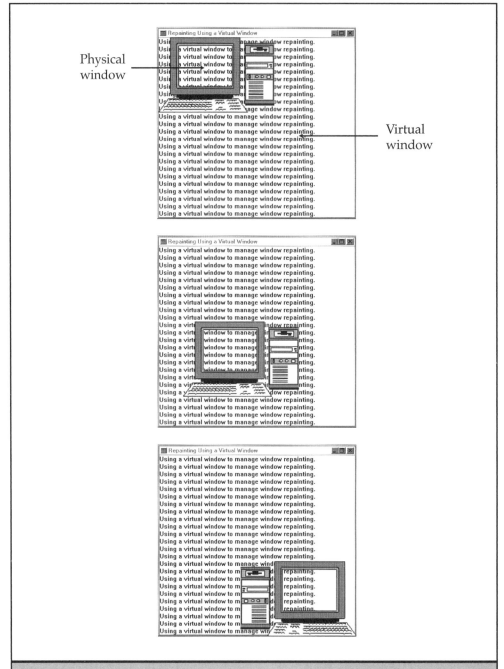

Figure 6-2. Accessing a large virtual window through a small physical window

scroll bar control generates the message, then *lParam* contains the handle of the scroll bar control.

As mentioned, the value in **LOWORD(***wParam***)** specifies what type of scroll bar action has taken place. Here are some common scroll bar values:

SB_LINEUP	SB_LINERIGHT
SB_LINEDOWN	SB_PAGELEFT
SB_PAGEUP	SB_PAGERIGHT
SB_PAGEDOWN	SB_THUMBPOSITION
SB_LINELEFT	SB_THUMBTRACK

For vertical scroll bars, each time the user moves the scroll bar up one position, SB_LINEUP is sent. Each time the scroll bar is moved down one position, SB_LINEDOWN is sent. SB_PAGEUP or SB_PAGEDOWN is sent when the scroll bar is moved up or down one page.

For horizontal scroll bars, each time the user moves the scroll bar left one position, SB_LINELEFT is sent. Each time the scroll bar is moved right one position, SB_LINERIGHT is sent. SB_PAGELEFT or SB_PAGERIGHT is sent when the scroll bar is moved left or right one page.

F or both types of scroll bars, the SB_THUMBPOSITION value is sent each time the slider box (*thumb*) of the scroll bar is dragged to a new position. The SB_THUMBTRACK message is also sent when the thumb is dragged to a new position. However, it is sent each time the thumb passes over a new position. This allows you to "track" the movement of the thumb before it is released. When SB_THUMBPOSITION or SB_THUMBTRACK is received, the high-order word of *wParam* contains the current slider box position.

Using the Scroll Bar API Functions

Scroll bars are, for the most part, manually managed controls. This means that in addition to responding to scroll bar messages, your program will also need to update various attributes associated with a scroll bar. For example, your program must update the position of the slider box manually using Windows NT's scroll bar API functions. Windows NT supports two sets of scroll bar functions: the Windows 3.1 style and the Win32 style. Because the Windows 3.1-style scroll bar functions are obsolete for use with Windows NT, we will be using the Win32 style functions. Since you may not be familiar with the new style functions, they are briefly described next.

SetScrollInfo( ) is used to set various attributes associated with a scroll bar. Its prototype is shown here:

```
int SetScrollInfo(HWND hwnd,
                  int Which,
                  LPSCROLLINFO lpSI,
                  BOOL repaint);
```

Here, *hwnd* is the handle that identifies the scroll bar. For window scroll bars, this is the handle of the window that owns the scroll bar. For scroll bar controls, this is the handle of the scroll bar itself. The value of *Which* determines which scroll bar is affected. If you are setting the attributes of the vertical window scroll bar, then this parameter must be SB_VERT. If you are setting the attributes of the horizontal window scroll bar, this value must be SB_HORZ. However, to set a scroll bar control, this value must be SB_CTL, and *hwnd* must be the handle of the control. The attributes are set according to the information pointed to by *lpSI* (discussed shortly). If *repaint* is TRUE, then the scroll bar is redrawn. If FALSE, the bar is not redisplayed. The function returns the position of the slider box.

To obtain the attributes associated with a scroll bar, use the second new scroll bar function, **GetScrollInfo( )**, which is shown here:

```
BOOL GetScrollInfo(HWND hwnd,
                   int Which,
                   LPSCROLLINFO lpSI);
```

The *hwnd* and *Which* parameters are the same as those just described for **SetScrollInfo( )**. The information obtained by **GetScrollInfo( )** is put into the structure pointed to by *lpSI*. The function returns nonzero if successful and zero on failure.

The *lpSI* parameter of both functions points to a structure of type **SCROLLINFO**, which is defined like this:

```
typedef struct tagSCROLLINFO
{
  UINT cbSize;    /* size of SCROLLINFO */
  UINT fMask;     /* operation performed */
  int nMin;       /* minimum range */
  int nMax;       /* maximum range */
  UINT nPage;     /* page value */
  int nPos;       /* slider box position */
  int nTrackPos;  /* current tracking position */
} SCROLLINFO;
```

Here, *cbSize* must contain the size of the **SCROLLINFO** structure. The value or values contained in *fMask* determine which of the remaining members contain valid information. *fMask* must be one or more of the following values. (To combine values, simply OR them together.)

fMask Value	Meaning
SIF_ALL	Same as SIF_PAGE I SIF_POS I SIF_RANGE I SIF_TRACKPOS.

fMask Value	Meaning
SIF_DISABLENOSCROLL	Scroll bar is disabled rather than removed if its range is set to zero.
SIF_PAGE	*nPage* contains valid information.
SIF_POS	*nPos* contains valid information.
SIF_RANGE	*nMin* and *nMax* contain valid information.
SIF_TRACKPOS	*nTrackPos* contains valid information.

nPage contains the current page setting for proportional scroll bars. *nPos* contains the position of the slider box. *nMin* and *nMax* contain the minimum and maximum range of the scroll bar. *nTrackPos* contains the current tracking position. The tracking position is the current position of the slider box while it is being dragged by the user. This value cannot be set.

As stated, scroll bars are manually managed controls. This means that your program will need to update the position of the slider box within the scroll bar each time it is moved. To do this, you will need to assign *nPos* the value of the new position, assign *fMask* the value SIF_POS, and then call **SetScrollInfo( )**.

The range of the scroll bar determines how many positions there are between one end and the other. By default, window scroll bars have a range of 0 to 100. However, you can set the range to meet the needs of your program. Control scroll bars have a default range of 0 to 0, which means that the range needs to be set before the scroll bar control can be used. A scroll bar that has a zero range is inactive.

Obtaining the Dimensions of the Client Area

To allow a smaller physical window to access all parts of a larger virtual window requires the use of both horizontal and vertical scroll bars. As you have probably noticed, in a professionally written program, the range of a scroll bar precisely matches the amount of information to be scrolled. That is, when the slider box has reached its full extent, the end of the information has also been reached. To achieve this, it is necessary to set the scroll bar's range appropriately. For our purposes, when the physical window is over the virtual window's upper-left corner, both scroll bars will be at their minimum position. When the physical window is over the virtual window's lower-right corner, the scroll bars will be at their maximum position. However, setting the ranges of the vertical and horizontal scroll bars appropriately requires the current dimensions of the physical window's client area.

To obtain the dimensions of the client area, call **GetClientRect( )**. It has this prototype:

```
BOOL GetClientRect(HWND hwnd,
                   LPRECT rect);
```

Here, *hwnd* is the handle of the window in question, and *rect* is a pointer to a **RECT** structure that will receive the current coordinates of the client area of the window. The function returns nonzero if successful and zero on failure. This function is useful whenever you need to know the current size of the client area of a window. In this case, it is used to determine how to set the range of the scroll bars when the physical window is first created.

Responding to WM_SIZE

Since a window can be resized, the dimensions of its client area may change during the execution of the program. Whenever this happens, the window will receive a **WM_SIZE** message. In this case, **LOWORD**(*lParam*) contains the new width and **HIWORD**(*lParam*) contains the new height of the client area. *wParam* contains a code describing the nature of the resize event. It will be one of the following:

SIZE_MAXHIDE	Another window has been maximized.
SIZE_MAXIMIZED	The window has been maximized.
SIZE_MAXSHOW	Another window has been returned to its previous size.
SIZE_MINIMIZED	The window has been minimized.
SIZE_RESTORED	The window has been resized (but not minimized or maximized).

For our purposes, the value of *wParam* can be ignored, but it might be of value to you in your own applications.

Each time a **WM_SIZE** message is received, the ranges of the scroll bars must be reset appropriately. If they are not, then the slider box position will not accurately reflect the physical window's location relative to the virtual window.

A Sample Program

Here is a program that scrolls a physical window through a larger virtual window. Sample output is shown in Figures 6-3 through 6-5.

```
/* Scrolling through the virtual window. */
#include <windows.h>
#include <string.h>
#include <stdio.h>

LRESULT CALLBACK WindowFunc(HWND, UINT, WPARAM, LPARAM);

char szWinName[] = "MyWin"; /* name of window class */
```

```
int X=0, Y=0; /* current output location */
int maxX, maxY; /* screen dimensions */
int orgX=0, orgY=0;

HDC memdc; /* store the virtual device handle */
HBITMAP hbit; /* store the virtual bitmap */
HBRUSH hbrush; /* store the brush handle */

int WINAPI WinMain(HINSTANCE hThisInst, HINSTANCE hPrevInst,
                   LPSTR lpszArgs, int nWinMode)
{
  HWND hwnd;
  MSG msg;
  WNDCLASSEX wcl;

  /* Define a window class. */
  wcl.hInstance = hThisInst; /* handle to this instance */
  wcl.lpszClassName = szWinName; /* window class name */
  wcl.lpfnWndProc = WindowFunc; /* window function */
  wcl.style = 0; /* default style */

  wcl.cbSize = sizeof(WNDCLASSEX); /* set size of WNDCLASSEX */
  wcl.hIcon = LoadIcon(NULL, IDI_APPLICATION); /* standard icon */
  wcl.hIconSm = LoadIcon(NULL, IDI_APPLICATION); /* small icon */
  wcl.hCursor = LoadCursor(NULL, IDC_ARROW); /* cursor style */
  wcl.lpszMenuName = NULL; /* no main menu */
  wcl.cbClsExtra = 0;
  wcl.cbWndExtra = 0;

  /* Use white background. */
  wcl.hbrBackground = GetStockObject(WHITE_BRUSH);

  /* Register the window class. */
  if(!RegisterClassEx(&wcl)) return 0;

  /* Now that a window class has been registered, a window
     can be created. */
  hwnd = CreateWindow(
    szWinName, /* name of window class */
    "Using a Large Virtual Window", /* title */
    WS_OVERLAPPEDWINDOW | WS_HSCROLL | WS_VSCROLL,
    CW_USEDEFAULT, /* X coordinate - let Windows decide */
    CW_USEDEFAULT, /* Y coordinate - let Windows decide */
```

```
      CW_USEDEFAULT, /* width - let Windows decide */
      CW_USEDEFAULT, /* height - let Windows decide */
      HWND_DESKTOP, /* no parent window */
      NULL, /* no override of class menu */
      hThisInst, /* handle of this instance of the program */
      NULL /* no additional arguments */
    );

    /* Display the window. */
    ShowWindow(hwnd, nWinMode);
    UpdateWindow(hwnd);

    /* Create the message loop. */
    while(GetMessage(&msg, NULL, 0, 0))
    {
      TranslateMessage(&msg); /* translate keyboard messages */
      DispatchMessage(&msg); /* return control to Windows */
    }
    return msg.wParam;
}

/* Window Procedure */
LRESULT CALLBACK WindowFunc(HWND hwnd, UINT message,
                            WPARAM wParam, LPARAM lParam)
{
  HDC hdc;
  PAINTSTRUCT ps;

  TEXTMETRIC tm;
  char str[255], str2[255];
  int i;
  static SCROLLINFO si; /* scroll bar info */

  static RECT curdim;

  switch(message) {
    case WM_CREATE:
      /* get screen coordinates */
      maxX = GetSystemMetrics(SM_CXSCREEN);
      maxY = GetSystemMetrics(SM_CYSCREEN);

      /* create virtual window that is twice as large */
      maxX += maxX;
      maxY += maxY;
```

```
   /* initialize scroll bar ranges */
   GetClientRect(hwnd, &curdim);

   si.cbSize = sizeof(SCROLLINFO);
   si.fMask = SIF_RANGE;
   si.nMin = 0; si.nMax = maxX-curdim.right;
   SetScrollInfo(hwnd, SB_HORZ, &si, 1);
   si.nMax = maxY-curdim.bottom;
   SetScrollInfo(hwnd, SB_VERT, &si, 1);

   /* create a virtual window */
   hdc = GetDC(hwnd);
   memdc = CreateCompatibleDC(hdc);
   hbit = CreateCompatibleBitmap(hdc, maxX, maxY);
   SelectObject(memdc, hbit);
   hbrush = GetStockObject(WHITE_BRUSH);
   SelectObject(memdc, hbrush);
   PatBlt(memdc, 0, 0, maxX, maxY, PATCOPY);

   /* get text metrics */
   GetTextMetrics(hdc, &tm);

   for(i=0; i<100; i++) {
     strcpy(str,
            "Supercharged Repaints Using a Virtual Window");
     sprintf(str2, " -- This is one line %d.", i+1);
     strcat(str, str2);

     TextOut(memdc, X, Y, str, strlen(str)); /* output to memory */
     TextOut(hdc, X, Y, str, strlen(str)); /* output to window */
     /* advance to next line */
     Y = Y + tm.tmHeight + tm.tmExternalLeading;
   }

   ReleaseDC(hwnd, hdc);

   break;
 case WM_PAINT: /* process a repaint request */
   hdc = BeginPaint(hwnd, &ps); /* get DC */

   /* copy virtual window onto screen */
   BitBlt(hdc, ps.rcPaint.left, ps.rcPaint.top,
```

```
                ps.rcPaint.right-ps.rcPaint.left, /* width */
                ps.rcPaint.bottom-ps.rcPaint.top, /* height */
                memdc,
                ps.rcPaint.left+orgX, ps.rcPaint.top+orgY,
                SRCCOPY);

    EndPaint(hwnd, &ps); /* release DC */
    break;
  case WM_HSCROLL:
    switch(LOWORD(wParam)) {
      case SB_THUMBTRACK:
        orgX = HIWORD(wParam);
        break;
      case SB_LINERIGHT:
        if(orgX < maxX-curdim.right) orgX++;
        break;
      case SB_LINELEFT:
        if(orgX > 0) orgX--;
        break;
      case SB_PAGERIGHT:
        if(orgX+5 < maxX-curdim.right) orgX += 5;
        break;
      case SB_PAGELEFT:
        if(orgX-5 > 0) orgX -= 5;
        break;
    }
    si.fMask = SIF_POS;
    si.nPos = orgX;
    SetScrollInfo(hwnd, SB_HORZ, &si, 1);
    InvalidateRect(hwnd, NULL, 0);
    break;
  case WM_VSCROLL:
    switch(LOWORD(wParam)) {
      case SB_THUMBTRACK:
        orgY = HIWORD(wParam);
        break;
      case SB_LINEDOWN:
        if(orgY < maxY-curdim.bottom) orgY++;
        break;
      case SB_LINEUP:
        if(orgY > 0) orgY--;
        break;
      case SB_PAGEDOWN:
```

```
        if(orgY+5 < maxY-curdim.bottom) orgY += 5;
        break;
      case SB_PAGEUP:
        if(orgY-5 > 0) orgY -= 5;
        break;
    }
    si.fMask = SIF_POS;
    si.nPos = orgY;
    SetScrollInfo(hwnd, SB_VERT, &si, 1);
    InvalidateRect(hwnd, NULL, 0);
    break;
  case WM_SIZE:
    /* store current window extents */
    curdim.right = LOWORD(lParam);
    curdim.bottom = HIWORD(lParam);

    /* reinitialize scroll bar ranges */
    si.cbSize = sizeof(SCROLLINFO);
    si.fMask = SIF_RANGE;
    si.nMin = 0; si.nMax = maxX-curdim.right;
    SetScrollInfo(hwnd, SB_HORZ, &si, 1);
    si.nMax = maxY-curdim.bottom;
    SetScrollInfo(hwnd, SB_VERT, &si, 1);
    break;
  case WM_DESTROY: /* terminate the program */
    DeleteDC(memdc); /* delete the memory device context */
    PostQuitMessage(0);
    break;
  default:
    return DefWindowProc(hwnd, message, wParam, lParam);
  }
  return 0;
}
```

Let's take a closer look at the important parts of this program.

Notice that the window styles WS_HSCROLL and WS_VSCROLL have been added to the window style parameter in the call to **CreateWindow( )**. This causes the standard horizontal and vertical scroll bars to be included in the window.

Next, inside **WM_CREATE**, the dimensions of the client area are obtained and then used to set the range of the scroll bars. Notice that both **si** and **curdim** are declared as **static**. This is necessary because they must hold their values between calls to **WindowFunc( )**. They could also be made into global variables, if such a change better suits your application. For demonstration purposes, the virtual window is constructed to be twice as large as the physical dimensions of the screen. This is, of course, an arbitrary

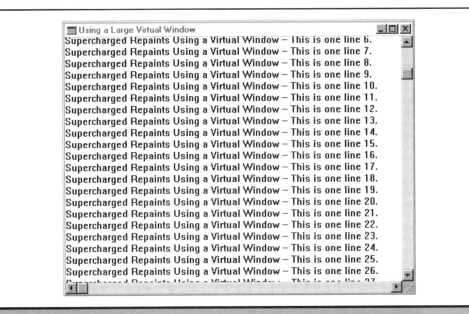

Figure 6-3. Sample output from the scrollable virtual window program

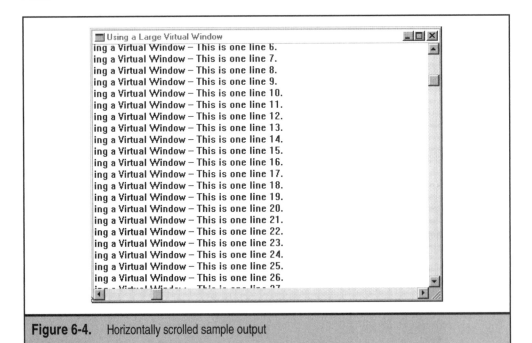

Figure 6-4. Horizontally scrolled sample output

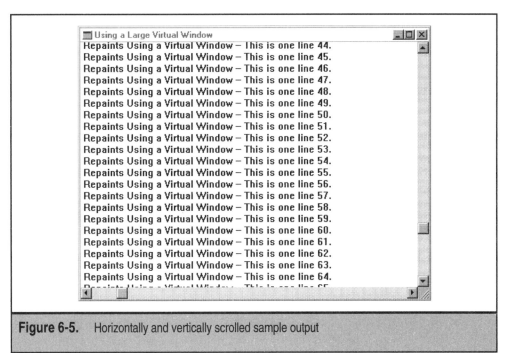

Figure 6-5.   Horizontally and vertically scrolled sample output

change that illustrates the use of a large workspace. Unless you need such a large workspace, you will not generally want to create such a large virtual window.

Inside **WM_CREATE**, 100 lines of text are output. This is actually more text than will fit into either window. But it ensures that the virtual window is filled. In this example, output is sent to both the virtual window and to the physical window. As mentioned, as long as the virtual window contains an exact copy of whatever is displayed in the physical window, there is no reason that output cannot be directly written to the physical window when this makes sense. In some situations, this approach will improve the performance of your program.

The only change to **WM_PAINT** is that the variables **orgX** and **orgY** are used to translate the current position within the virtual window into the coordinate system of the physical window. At the start, both **orgX** and **orgY** are zero. Each time a scroll bar is moved, their values are updated appropriately.

The scroll bar handling code within **WM_HSCROLL** and **WM_VSCROLL** is straightforward. Each time a scroll bar is accessed, either **orgX** or **orgY** is updated. Notice that a scroll bar cannot be moved beyond a certain point. For example, for the horizontal scroll bar, **orgX** will not be incremented past **maxX** (the rightmost extent of the virtual window) minus the width of the physical window. This mechanism ensures that no part of the physical window is ever moved beyond the edge of the virtual window.

Finally, each time a **WM_SIZE** message is received, the scroll bar ranges are reset accordingly.

DYNAMICALLY ADDING SCROLL BARS

To conclude this chapter, we will look at one other repaint-related optimization that you will want to add to your programs: *dynamic scroll bars*. One of the hallmarks of a professionally written program is that scroll bars automatically appear and disappear, as needed. For example, when you're displaying information in a window, scroll bars are displayed when the length of that information exceeds the current size of the client area. They are removed when the information can fit within the window's current size. As you will see, the virtual window technology makes using dynamic scroll bars straightforward.

Showing and Hiding Scroll Bars

It is quite easy to show or hide a scroll bar. Simply call the **ShowScrollBar( )** API function, whose prototype is shown here:

```
BOOL ShowScrollBar(HWND hwnd,
                   int Which,
                   BOOL display);
```

For standard scroll bars, *hwnd* specifies the handle of their window. For scroll bar controls, *hwnd* specifies the handle of the scroll bar control, itself. The value of *Which* determines which scroll bar is affected. To show or hide the vertical window scroll bar, then *Which* must be SB_VERT. To show or hide the horizontal window scroll bar, *Which* must be SB_HORZ. To affect both, specify SB_BOTH. To set a scroll bar control, *Which* must be SB_CTL. If *display* is TRUE, then the scroll bar is displayed. If it is FALSE, the bar is hidden. The function returns nonzero if successful and zero on failure.

Managing Dynamic Scroll Bars

To use dynamic scroll bars, your program must do the following:

1. Keep track of both the vertical and horizontal length of the information to be displayed.
2. Add code to show or hide the scroll bars inside the **WM_PAINT** handler.
3. Add code to show or hide the scroll bars inside the **WM_SIZE** handler.

Let's look at what each of these steps entails.

Your program must maintain variables that hold the maximum width and length of the information that is to be displayed in the window. The reason is easy to understand: your program must know the maximum dimensions of the information in order for it to know whether the current window size is sufficient to display it. If the window is too small, then one or both scroll bars will be needed.

Inside **WM_PAINT**, you will need to check the current size of the information against the current size of the window. If the window is too narrow to fully display the information, the horizontal scroll bar is activated. If the window is too short, the vertical scroll bar is activated. Otherwise, the scroll bars are hidden. The code inside **WM_PAINT** handles the cases in which information in a window is updated by your program. As long as you route all output through **WM_PAINT**, then the scroll bars can be displayed or hidden automatically, as needed, when new information is displayed.

You will also have to check the current size of the information against the current size of the window each time the window is resized (that is, each time a **WM_SIZE** message is received). If the new size of the window is too narrow to fully display the information, the horizontal scroll bar is activated. If the new size of the window is too short, the vertical scroll bar is activated. Otherwise, the scroll bars are hidden.

Demonstrating Dynamic Scroll Bars

The following program enhances the preceding program by adding dynamic scroll bars. When you run the program, first try resizing the window, watching how the scroll bars appear and disappear as needed. Next, press a key. This causes more information to be displayed. When the information exceeds what the window can hold, the appropriate scroll bar or bars are automatically activated. Sample output is shown in Figures 6-6 through 6-8.

```
/* Using Dynamic Scroll Bars */
#include <windows.h>
#include <string.h>
#include <stdio.h>

LRESULT CALLBACK WindowFunc(HWND, UINT, WPARAM, LPARAM);

char szWinName[] = "MyWin"; /* name of window class */

int X=0, Y=0; /* current output location */
int maxX, maxY; /* screen dimensions */
int orgX=0, orgY=0;

HDC memdc; /* store the virtual device handle */
HBITMAP hbit; /* store the virtual bitmap */
HBRUSH hbrush; /* store the brush handle */

int WINAPI WinMain(HINSTANCE hThisInst, HINSTANCE hPrevInst,
                   LPSTR lpszArgs, int nWinMode)
{
```

```
HWND hwnd;
MSG msg;
WNDCLASSEX wcl;

/* Define a window class. */
wcl.hInstance = hThisInst; /* handle to this instance */
wcl.lpszClassName = szWinName; /* window class name */
wcl.lpfnWndProc = WindowFunc; /* window function */
wcl.style = 0; /* default style */

wcl.cbSize = sizeof(WNDCLASSEX); /* set size of WNDCLASSEX */
wcl.hIcon = LoadIcon(NULL, IDI_APPLICATION); /* standard icon */
wcl.hIconSm = LoadIcon(NULL, IDI_APPLICATION); /* small icon */
wcl.hCursor = LoadCursor(NULL, IDC_ARROW); /* cursor style */
wcl.lpszMenuName = NULL; /* no main menu */
wcl.cbClsExtra = 0;
wcl.cbWndExtra = 0;

/* Use white background. */
wcl.hbrBackground = GetStockObject(WHITE_BRUSH);

/* Register the window class. */
if(!RegisterClassEx(&wcl)) return 0;

/* Now that a window class has been registered, a window
   can be created. */
hwnd = CreateWindow(
  szWinName, /* name of window class */
  "Using Dynamic Scroll Bars", /* title */
  WS_OVERLAPPEDWINDOW | WS_HSCROLL | WS_VSCROLL,
  CW_USEDEFAULT, /* X coordinate - let Windows decide */
  CW_USEDEFAULT, /* Y coordinate - let Windows decide */
  CW_USEDEFAULT, /* width - let Windows decide */
  CW_USEDEFAULT, /* height - let Windows decide */
  HWND_DESKTOP, /* no parent window */
  NULL, /* no override of class menu */
  hThisInst, /* handle of this instance of the program */
  NULL /* no additional arguments */
);

/* Display the window. */
ShowWindow(hwnd, nWinMode);
UpdateWindow(hwnd);
```

```
  /* Create the message loop. */
  while(GetMessage(&msg, NULL, 0, 0))
  {
    TranslateMessage(&msg); /* translate keyboard messages */
    DispatchMessage(&msg); /* return control to Windows */
  }
  return msg.wParam;
}

/* Window Procedure */
LRESULT CALLBACK WindowFunc(HWND hwnd, UINT message,
                           WPARAM wParam, LPARAM lParam)
{
  HDC hdc;
  PAINTSTRUCT ps;

  TEXTMETRIC tm;
  char str[256];
  int i;
  static SCROLLINFO si; /* scroll bar info */

  static RECT curdim;
  SIZE size;
  static int maxwidth=0, maxheight=0;

  switch(message) {
    case WM_CREATE:
      /* get screen coordinates */
      maxX = GetSystemMetrics(SM_CXSCREEN);
      maxY = GetSystemMetrics(SM_CYSCREEN);

      /* create virtual window that is twice as large */
      maxX += maxX;
      maxY += maxY;

      /* initialize scroll bar ranges */
      GetClientRect(hwnd, &curdim);

      si.cbSize = sizeof(SCROLLINFO);
      si.fMask = SIF_RANGE;
      si.nMin = 0; si.nMax = maxX-curdim.right;
      SetScrollInfo(hwnd, SB_HORZ, &si, 1);
      si.nMax = maxY-curdim.bottom;
      SetScrollInfo(hwnd, SB_VERT, &si, 1);
```

```
          /* create a virtual window */
          hdc = GetDC(hwnd);
          memdc = CreateCompatibleDC(hdc);
          hbit = CreateCompatibleBitmap(hdc, maxX, maxY);
          SelectObject(memdc, hbit);
          hbrush = GetStockObject(WHITE_BRUSH);
          SelectObject(memdc, hbrush);
          PatBlt(memdc, 0, 0, maxX, maxY, PATCOPY);

          /* get text metrics */
          GetTextMetrics(hdc, &tm);


          for(i=0; i<10; i++) {
            strcpy(str, "Dynamic scroll bars.  Press a key.");

            TextOut(memdc, X, Y, str, strlen(str)); /* output to memory */
            TextOut(hdc, X, Y, str, strlen(str)); /* output to window */
            /* advance to next line */
            Y = Y + tm.tmHeight + tm.tmExternalLeading;

            /* store maximum height */
            if(Y>maxheight) maxheight = Y;

            /* store maximum width */
            GetTextExtentPoint32(memdc, str, strlen(str), &size);
            if(size.cx>maxwidth) maxwidth = size.cx;
          }
          ReleaseDC(hwnd, hdc);
          break;
        case WM_PAINT: /* process a repaint request */
          hdc = BeginPaint(hwnd, &ps); /* get DC */

          GetClientRect(hwnd, &curdim);

          /* show or hide scroll bars */
          if(curdim.right < maxwidth)
            ShowScrollBar(hwnd, SB_HORZ, 1);
          else
            ShowScrollBar(hwnd, SB_HORZ, 0);

          if(curdim.bottom < maxheight)
            ShowScrollBar(hwnd, SB_VERT, 1);
```

```
    else
      ShowScrollBar(hwnd, SB_VERT, 0);

  /* copy virtual window onto screen */
  BitBlt(hdc, ps.rcPaint.left, ps.rcPaint.top,
         ps.rcPaint.right-ps.rcPaint.left, /* width */
         ps.rcPaint.bottom-ps.rcPaint.top, /* height */
         memdc,
         ps.rcPaint.left+orgX, ps.rcPaint.top+orgY,
         SRCCOPY);

  EndPaint(hwnd, &ps); /* release DC */
  break;
case WM_HSCROLL:
  switch(LOWORD(wParam)) {
    case SB_THUMBTRACK:
      orgX = HIWORD(wParam);
      break;
    case SB_LINERIGHT:
      if(orgX < maxX-curdim.right) orgX++;
      break;
    case SB_LINELEFT:
      if(orgX > 0) orgX--;
      break;
    case SB_PAGERIGHT:
      if(orgX+5 < maxX-curdim.right) orgX += 5;
      break;
    case SB_PAGELEFT:
      if(orgX-5 > 0) orgX -= 5;
      break;
  }
  si.fMask = SIF_POS;
  si.nPos = orgX;
  SetScrollInfo(hwnd, SB_HORZ, &si, 1);
  InvalidateRect(hwnd, NULL, 0);
  break;
case WM_VSCROLL:
  switch(LOWORD(wParam)) {
    case SB_THUMBTRACK:
      orgY = HIWORD(wParam);
      break;
    case SB_LINEDOWN:
      if(orgY < maxY-curdim.bottom) orgY++;
      break;
```

```
      case SB_LINEUP:
        if(orgY > 0) orgY--;
        break;
      case SB_PAGEDOWN:
        if(orgY+5 < maxY-curdim.bottom) orgY += 5;
        break;
      case SB_PAGEUP:
        if(orgY-5 > 0) orgY -= 5;
        break;
    }
    si.fMask = SIF_POS;
    si.nPos = orgY;
    SetScrollInfo(hwnd, SB_VERT, &si, 1);
    InvalidateRect(hwnd, NULL, 0);
    break;
  case WM_SIZE:
    /* store current window extents */
    curdim.right = LOWORD(lParam);
    curdim.bottom = HIWORD(lParam);

    /* reinitialize scroll bar ranges */
    si.cbSize = sizeof(SCROLLINFO);
    si.fMask = SIF_RANGE;
    si.nMin = 0;

    /* show or hide scroll bars */
    if(LOWORD(lParam) < maxwidth) {
      si.nMax = maxX-curdim.right;
      ShowScrollBar(hwnd, SB_HORZ, 1);
      SetScrollInfo(hwnd, SB_HORZ, &si, 1);
    } else
      ShowScrollBar(hwnd, SB_HORZ, 0);

    if(HIWORD(lParam) < maxheight) {
      si.nMax = maxY-curdim.bottom;
      ShowScrollBar(hwnd, SB_VERT, 1);
      SetScrollInfo(hwnd, SB_VERT, &si, 1);
    } else
      ShowScrollBar(hwnd, SB_VERT, 0);

    break;
  case WM_CHAR:
    /* add output to the window */
```

```
        GetTextMetrics(memdc, &tm);
        strcpy(str,

              "When the information exceeds the current size");
        strcat(str, " of the window, show the scroll bar.");

        for(i=0; i<10; i++) {
          TextOut(memdc, X, Y, str, strlen(str)); /* output to memory */
          /* advance to next line */
          Y = Y + tm.tmHeight + tm.tmExternalLeading;

          /* store maximum height */
          if(Y>maxheight) maxheight = Y;

          /* store maximum width */
          GetTextExtentPoint32(memdc, str, strlen(str), &size);
          if(size.cx>maxwidth) maxwidth = size.cx;
        }
        InvalidateRect(hwnd, NULL, 0);
        break;
      case WM_DESTROY: /* terminate the program */
        DeleteDC(memdc); /* delete the memory device context */
        PostQuitMessage(0);
        break;
      default:
        return DefWindowProc(hwnd, message, wParam, lParam);
    }
    return 0;
}
```

A Closer Look at the Dynamic Scroll Bars Program

The dynamic scroll bars program enhances the preceding program that scrolls through a virtual window. Inside **WindowFunc( )** it adds the following variables:

```
SIZE size;
static int maxwidth=0, maxheight=0;
```

In the program, **size** is used in a call to **GetTextExtentPoint32( )** to obtain the length of a string in logical units. The variables **maxwidth** and **maxheight** hold the maximum extents of the information displayed in the window in the horizontal and vertical directions, respectively. These variables must be updated whenever information is output to the window.

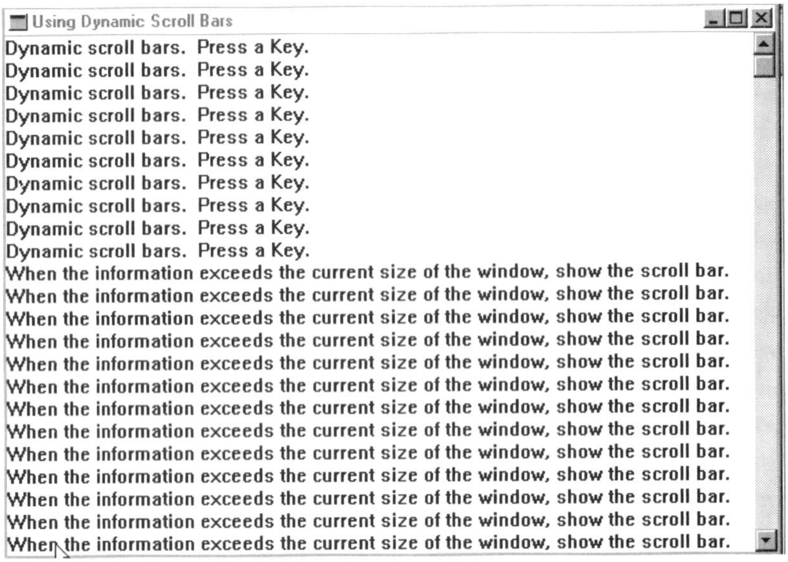

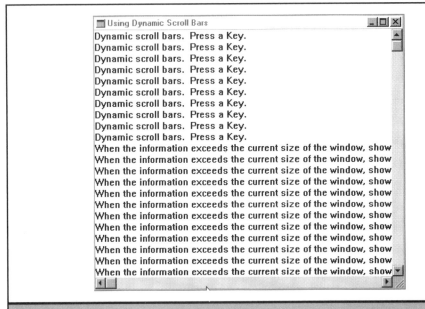

Figure 6-6.   Sample output from the dynamic scroll bars program without horizontal scroll bar

Figure 6-7.   Sample output with horizontal scroll bar

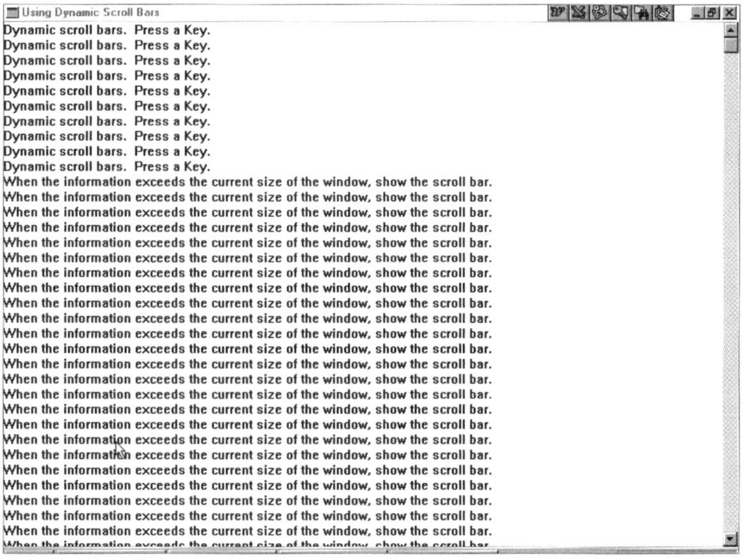

Figure 6-8. Sample output without horizontal scroll bar (when window is maximized)

Inside the **WM_PAINT** handler, the following code is added:

```
GetClientRect(hwnd, &curdim);

/* show or hide scroll bars */
if(curdim.right < maxwidth)
  ShowScrollBar(hwnd, SB_HORZ, 1);
else
  ShowScrollBar(hwnd, SB_HORZ, 0);

if(curdim.bottom < maxheight)
  ShowScrollBar(hwnd, SB_VERT, 1);
else
  ShowScrollBar(hwnd, SB_VERT, 0);
```

First, the current size of the window's client area is obtained by calling **GetClientRect( )**. The code then shows or hides the scroll bars based on the current size of the window and the maximum extents of the information to be displayed.

The additional code within the **WM_SIZE** handler is shown here:

```
/* show or hide scroll bars */
if(LOWORD(lParam) < maxwidth) {
  si.nMax = maxX-curdim.right;
  ShowScrollBar(hwnd, SB_HORZ, 1);
  SetScrollInfo(hwnd, SB_HORZ, &si, 1);
} else
  ShowScrollBar(hwnd, SB_HORZ, 0);

if(HIWORD(lParam) < maxheight) {
  si.nMax = maxY-curdim.bottom;
  ShowScrollBar(hwnd, SB_VERT, 1);
  SetScrollInfo(hwnd, SB_VERT, &si, 1);
} else
  ShowScrollBar(hwnd, SB_VERT, 0);
```

Each time the window is resized, the new dimensions (which are found in the high- and low-order words of *lParam*) are tested against the size of the information to be displayed. If the information can no longer fit, the appropriate scroll bar or bars are shown.

One last point: because window repainting is being performed using the virtual window technology discussed earlier, it is quite easy to add and use dynamic scroll bars. Once again, the virtual window approach to window repainting has made other aspects of managing output to a window easier.

CONCLUSION

In this chapter we looked at two issues every business programmer is likely to face when programming user interfaces—how to accelerate window repainting and how to handle screen output that doesn't fit in the client area.

As an advanced Windows NT programmer, you should know programming using both Win32 APIs and the MFC library. In view of this, while most of the examples in the other chapters of the book use the MFC library, this chapter shows examples using the APIs.

In the next chapter, we cover another important topic related to user interface programming—using common controls. The term "common" is somewhat of a misnomer, as you will see that the common controls are anything but common. In fact, the other controls that existed prior to the common controls were called *standard,* so the common controls are more aptly called *advanced* controls.

CHAPTER 7

Advanced Controls

Chapter 2 covered some of the basics of programming for the Windows user interface. We looked at the menu, the dialog box, the message box, the scroll bar, and so on. In this chapter we will take a look at some *advanced* controls (also called *common* controls), such as the Animation control and HotKey control. Use of the advanced controls gives you the same benefits as using the standard (or basic) controls—it gives your program's user interface a consistent look, and you get a lot of built-in code that makes your programming task easier. Advanced controls also add pizzazz to your user interface. They give your user interface a professional look.

ADVANCED CONTROLS

Although advanced controls have been around since Windows NT 3.51, these controls have become really popular since Windows NT 4.0 got the Windows 95 user interface. Now you can develop an application using advanced controls that will work with both operating systems. Maybe the commonality between Windows 95 and Windows NT led to the term "common" in "common controls," but the advanced controls are anything but standard or ordinary. In this chapter we will use the term "advanced controls" instead of "common controls." Programs developed using advanced controls will work only with Windows 95 or Windows NT. Windows NT provides a number of advanced controls. These controls, their function description, and the associated class are summarized in Table 7-1.

Control	Function Description	Associated MFC Class
Animation control	Displays an audio video interleaved (AVI) file, without the sound	CAnimateCtrl
Drag list box	Allows dragging of items in a list box	*See List View control*
Header control	Displays column headings	CHeaderCtrl
HotKey control	Supports user-created hot keys	CHotKeyCtrl
Image list	Displays a list of graphical images	CImageList

Table 7-1. Windows NT Advanced Controls, Function Descriptions, and Associated Classes

Control	Function Description	Associated MFC Class
List View control	Displays a list of icons and labels	CListCtrl
Progress control (also called *progress bar*)	Displays a visual indicator used to indicate the progress of a task	CProgressCtrl
Property Sheet	Displays properties dialog box	CPropertySheet, CPropertyPage
Rich Edit control	Displays an advanced Edit box	CRichEditCtrl
Slider control (also called *trackbar*)	Displays a slider-based control	CSliderCtrl
Spin control	Displays a combination Edit box and Up-Down control	CSpinButtonCtrl
Status window	Displays a horizontal bar that displays an application's status information	CStatusBarCtrl
Tab control	Displays a menu with tabs that can be selected	CTabCtrl
Toolbar control	Displays a menu of buttons that the user can select by clicking	CToolBarCtrl
Tooltip	Displays small pop-up windows that have text describing toolbar buttons	CToolTipCtrl
Tree View control	Displays a list of items in the form of a tree hierarchy	CTreeCtrl
Up-Down control	Displays up and down arrows (like a scroll bar without the middle portion—just the end arrows)	*See Spin control*

Table 7-1. Windows NT Advanced Controls, Function Descriptions, and Associated Classes (*continued*)

It is beyond the scope of this book to discuss all the advanced controls. We will cover some of the important ones—Animation, HotKey, Spin, Progress, and Slider controls—in detail with programming examples. We will briefly cover the characteristics of some of the other advanced controls. The techniques you gather from the controls discussed here should enable you to program all the advanced controls.

Advanced controls are child windows, so the programming considerations of using child windows apply to advanced controls. Advanced controls are implemented as a controls library and supplied with Windows NT as a DLL that you invoke. The DLL has the definitions of window classes and the window procedures that handle the window classes. The window procedures handle the control's details, such as the properties, appearance, and behavior of the control. You can vary the appearance and behavior of a control by the use of control styles included in the DLL.

PROGRAMMING ADVANCED CONTROLS USING APIs

You need to follow the steps listed here to include advanced controls in your program:

▼ Include the standard header file *Commctrl.h* in your program.

■ Link the advanced controls library to your program. For Microsoft Visual C++, the advanced controls library is called *Comctl32.lib*. For other vendor compilers, check the vendor documentation. You may need to link this library manually once if it is not automatically linked.

■ Call **InitCommonControls** to load the advanced controls library DLL.

■ Create an advanced control by passing the name of the control's window class as a parameter to the **CreateWindow** or **CreateWindowEx** function. You can also specify the control's window class name in a dialog box template or call a control-specific API. The advantage of using **CreateWindowEx** is that it permits the use of extended style attributes listed in Table 7-2. Keep in mind that not all of these styles apply to all the controls—some of these are default values for the controls, and use of some styles may override the use of other styles. (All styles listed here apply to header controls, toolbar controls, and status windows.)

■ Process messages from the controls such as **WM_COMMAND** or **WM_NOTIFY**.

▲ Sends messages to the controls using **SendMessage**.

The advanced control examples in this chapter use the MFC library. For advanced controls programming examples using APIs, see *Windows NT Programming from the Ground Up,* by Herbert Schildt, published by Osborne/McGraw-Hill.

Control Style	Description
CCS_ADJUSTABLE	This enables a toolbar's built-in customization features. The features include dragging buttons to move them to a new position or removing them from the toolbar. The features also include displaying the Customize Toolbar dialog box when the toolbar is double-clicked.
CCS_BOTTOM	This positions the control at the bottom of the client area of the parent window. The control's width is set to be the same as the parent window's width. Status windows have this style by default.
CCS_NODIVIDER	This prevents the drawing of a divider (two-pixel highlight) at the top of the control.
CCS_NOHILITE	This prevents the drawing of a highlight (one-pixel highlight) at the top of the control.
CCS_NOMOVEY	This prevents vertical movement of the control (the control can still be moved horizontally). The control is moved by a WM_SIZE message. Control movements are possible with this style only if CCS_NORESIZE is not used. Header windows include this style by default.
CCS_NOPARENTALIGN	This causes the control to be in its position even if the parent window is resized. If CCS_TOP or CCS_BOTTOM is also used, the height is adjusted to the default, but the position and width are unchanged.
CCS_NORESIZE	This causes the control to use the width and height specified in the control creation or sizing request, and to override the default width and height settings.
CCS_TOP	This positions the control at the top of the client area of the parent window. The control's width is set to be the same as the parent window's width. Toolbars include this style by default.

Table 7-2. Control Styles and Their Descriptions

PROGRAMMING ADVANCED CONTROLS USING THE MFC LIBRARY

You can include advanced controls in your MFC program by following these steps:

1. Create the control. You can do this by using the dialog editor or (in some cases) by hand.

2. Add a variable representing the control to the dialog class. Declare additional variables for handling I/O with the control as needed.

3. Initialize the control by use of **OnInitDialog** or dialog data exchange (DDX).

4. Send and receive messages from the control.

5. Perform cleanup activities such as destroying unnecessary objects and disposing of unwanted memory allocations (if needed).

This is the general sequence of steps. Let's look at some of the controls in detail. Keep in mind that the controls are not mutually exclusive, and you typically will use a combination of these controls to implement your user interface. The programming example that we will cover later in the chapter combines a Spin control, a Slider, and a progress bar in a dialog box as shown in Figure 7-1.

At times you will also find that the functions of the controls complement each other, and you can combine the working of the controls to make the user interface more intuitive. For example, the Edit box is typically combined with an *Up-Down control*. This is also called a *Spin control* and is covered later in the section on the Spin control. You can also combine a slider with an Up-Down control, and this is covered in the section on the Slider control.

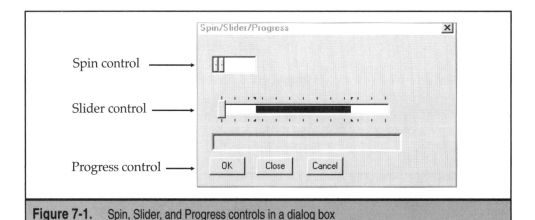

Figure 7-1. Spin, Slider, and Progress controls in a dialog box

ANIMATION CONTROL

An *Animation control* is a rectangular window that displays a video clip in audio video interleaved (AVI) format. AVI is the standard Windows video/audio format. An AVI clip is a series of bitmap frames. The Animation control displays the series of bitmap frames, adjusting the timing and position on the display. This creates an animation effect.

Use the Animation control when you are performing a lengthy operation and you want the user to see something other than an hourglass icon. You can also use the progress bar for this purpose. Examples of using the Animation control in Windows include when you copy a big file using the Explorer or when you do a search in Visual C++ and you see a rotating magnifying glass.

The Animation control does not support all the capabilities of the AVI format. Some of the capabilities of AVI that are not supported by the Animation control include the following:

▼ Animation control does not support the audio stream in AVI.

■ There must be only one video stream with at least one frame.

■ There can be at most two streams in the file (normally a video and an audio stream, although the audio is not used).

■ The clip must either be uncompressed or compressed with RLE8 compression.

▲ The video stream cannot have only one palette.

The typical sequence of an Animation control execution is as follows. First you create the Animation control using a dialog box template or the **Create** member function. Load the AVI clip by using the **Open** member function or **OnInitDialog**. Play the AVI clip using the **Play** member function. Alternatively, you can use the **OnInitDialog** for this purpose, or use the ACS_AUTOPLAY style for automatic playing of the animation. You can then use the **Close** member function, if required. Besides the ACS_AUTOPLAY style, the other styles you can use are ACS_CENTER, to center the control within the window, and ACS_TRANSPARENT, to use a transparent background instead of the background that is present in the AVI clip. The styles you can use with the Animation control are summarized in Table 7-3.

You can play all the frames in the AVI clip, or you can specify the number of frames you want the Animation control to play. You can also specify if you want to replay the animation and the number of times you want to replay. One useful variation is to set the number of times to replay as –1, which replays the AVI clip forever. This feature is useful if you want an unattended demo of the Animation control—in a conference or before a presentation.

The AVI clip you want to animate can be included as a dialog resource by use of the dialog editor. If you are importing the AVI clip from another source, you can leave the AVI clip in its own file. You can create AVI files using the Aviedit sample application included with the Win32 SDK. The Aviedit application is rather rudimentary. If you have

Style	Description
ACS_AUTOPLAY	This automatically starts playing as soon as the animation clip is opened.
ACS_CENTER	This centers the animation in the Animation control's window.
ACS_TIMER	This plays the clip without creating a thread (default is to create a separate thread to play the AVI clip). To synchronize playback internally, the control uses a Win32 timer.
ACS_TRANSPARENT	This uses a transparent background rather than the background color in the animation clip.

Table 7-3.   Animation Control Styles and Description

to program a lot with animations, then try a third-party tool such as Digital Video Producer to create AVI files.

Execution of the Animation control is asynchronous. When you can call the Animation control, Windows NT creates a separate thread, and your thread can perform other functions while the Animation control thread displays the animation.

When using **CAnimateCtrl**, you may have to ensure that you don't have memory leaks. A **CAnimateCtrl** object you create within a dialog box or from a dialog resource is automatically destroyed when the dialog box is closed. It is also automatically destroyed if you create the **CAnimateCtrl** object on the stack. If you create the **CAnimateCtrl** object on the heap by using the new function or if you derive a new class from **CAnimateCtrl** and allocate any memory in that class, then you have to manually destroy the **CAnimateCtrl** object and/or dispose of the memory allocations.

Animation Control Programming Example

The *Animate* sample program shows how to use the Animation control by use of the **CAnimateCtrl** MFC library class. The sample when run displays a window with a menu. Figures 7-2 through 7-4 show the AVI clip as it is being displayed. If Animate is selected from the File menu, a dialog panel with Animation control is displayed. The AVI clip file is loaded and can be played by selecting the Play button. Selecting the Autoplay check box will make the AVI clip play automatically and continuously. This play can be stopped by clicking the Stop button. Choosing the Transparent check box will make the Animation control transparent. Clicking the Cancel button will close the dialog panel. The AVI file used in Figures 7-2 through 7-4 is the *dillo.avi* included with Visual C++. You can use other AVI files as well.

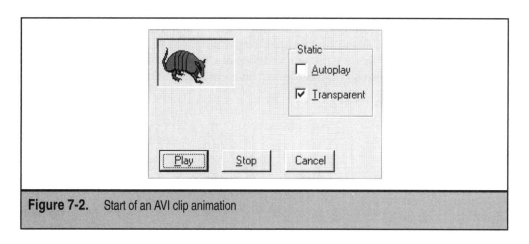

Figure 7-2.   Start of an AVI clip animation

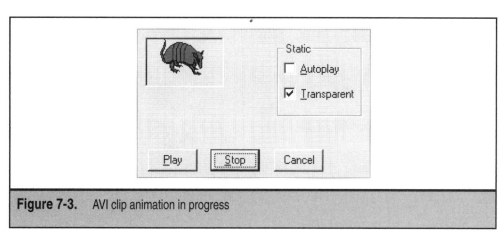

Figure 7-3.   AVI clip animation in progress

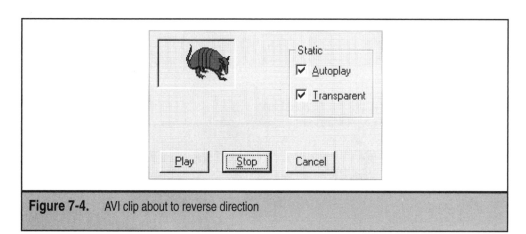

Figure 7-4.   AVI clip about to reverse direction

This sample extends the *Font* sample program in Chapter 5. The main application code is almost the same as the *Font* sample. This example has a few additional lines of code to handle the new menu item for the dialog box that would display the animation inside an Animation control. These additional lines are shown in boldface. For the sample a simple animation file is used.

```cpp
#include <afxwin.h>
#include <afxdlgs.h>
#include <afxcmn.h>              // Header file for Advanced controls
#include <strstrea.h>
#include "FontDlg.h"
#include "AnimateDlg.h"
#include "resource.h"

// Define the application object class
class CApp : public CWinApp
{
public:
        virtual BOOL InitInstance ();
};

// Define the window class
class CWindow : public CFrameWnd
{
public:
    CWindow();
    afx_msg void OnAppAbout();
    afx_msg void OnFontDlg();
    afx_msg void OnAnimateDlg();
    afx_msg void OnExit();
    DECLARE_MESSAGE_MAP()
};

/////////////////////////////////////////////////////////////////////////////
// CWindow

BEGIN_MESSAGE_MAP(CWindow, CFrameWnd)
        ON_COMMAND(ID_APP_ABOUT, OnAppAbout)
        ON_COMMAND(ID_FONTDLG, OnFontDlg)
        ON_COMMAND(ID_ANIMATEDLG, OnAnimateDlg)
        ON_COMMAND(ID_APP_EXIT, OnExit)
END_MESSAGE_MAP()
```

```
//////////////////////////////////////////////////////////////////////
// CWindow construction

CWindow::CWindow()
{
      Create( NULL, "Control Sample",
      WS_OVERLAPPEDWINDOW,
      rectDefault, NULL, MAKEINTRESOURCE(IDR_MAINFRAME) );
}


//////////////////////////////////////////////////////////////////////
// The one and only CApp object

CApp theApp;

//////////////////////////////////////////////////////////////////////
// CApp initialization

BOOL CApp::InitInstance()
{
      m_pMainWnd = new CWindow();
      m_pMainWnd -> ShowWindow( m_nCmdShow );
      m_pMainWnd -> UpdateWindow();
      return TRUE;
}


//////////////////////////////////////////////////////////////////////
// CAboutDlg dialog used for App About

class CAboutDlg : public CDialog
{
public:
      CAboutDlg();
      enum { IDD = IDD_ABOUTBOX };
      protected:

};

CAboutDlg::CAboutDlg() : CDialog(CAboutDlg::IDD)
{
}

// App command to run the dialog
```

```
void CWindow::OnAppAbout()
{
        CAboutDlg aboutDlg;
        aboutDlg.DoModal();
}


//////////////////////////////////////////////////////////////////////////////
// CWindow commands
// App command to run the dialog

// Font Dialog selected
void CWindow::OnFontDlg()
{
        CFontDlg fontDlg(this);
        fontDlg.DoModal();
}

// Animate Dialog selected
void CWindow::OnAnimateDlg()
{
        CAnimateDlg animateDlg(this);
        animateDlg.DoModal();
}

// On Exit handles the void
void CWindow::OnExit()
{
        DestroyWindow();
}
```

Before we look into the source code that deals with the Animation control dialog box, the dialog resource is shown:

```
IDD_ANIMATEDLG DIALOG DISCARDABLE  0, 0, 166, 95
STYLE DS_MODALFRAME | WS_POPUP | WS_CAPTION | WS_SYSMENU
CAPTION "Animate Control"
FONT 8, "MS Sans Serif"
BEGIN
    CONTROL         "Animate1",IDC_ANIMATE1,"SysAnimate32",WS_BORDER |
                    WS_TABSTOP,5,5,87,54
    CONTROL         "&Autoplay",IDC_AUTOPLAY,"Button",BS_AUTOCHECKBOX |
                    WS_TABSTOP,104,20,43,10
    CONTROL         "&Transparent",IDC_TRANSPARENT,"Button",BS_AUTOCHECKBOX |
                    WS_TABSTOP,104,36,54,10
```

```
    GROUPBOX            "Static",IDC_STATIC,99,8,61,48
    DEFPUSHBUTTON       "&Play",IDC_PLAY,7,77,35,14
    PUSHBUTTON          "Cancel",IDCANCEL,97,77,35,14
    PUSHBUTTON          "&Stop",IDC_STOP,52,77,35,14
END
```

The dialog box basically has an Animation control that in this case uses all the default styles for the Animation control. It has two check boxes, which are used to manipulate the style of the Animation control dynamically. It also has push buttons, one of which stops the animation. The resource file in addition has resource entries for menu items, icons, and so on.

Let's look at the dialog panel class code that handles the Animation control dialog box. As with many other sample programs, the template code was generated by use of the ClassWizard of Visual C++. There are advantages in doing this—not the least of which is that code generation through this method does not require you to memorize or refer to the manual for function prototypes.

```
// AnimateDlg.h : header file


/////////////////////////////////////////////////////////////////////////////
// CAnimateDlg dialog

class CAnimateDlg : public CDialog
{
private:
        CAnimateCtrl animateCtrl;
// Construction
public:
        CAnimateDlg(CWnd* pParent = NULL)
                : CDialog(IDD_ANIMATEDLG, pParent)
                                {}
// Implementation
protected:
        // Generated message map functions
        //{{AFX_MSG(CAnimateDlg)
        afx_msg void OnStop();
        afx_msg void OnPlay();
        afx_msg void OnAutoPlay();
        afx_msg void OnTransparent();
        virtual BOOL OnInitDialog();
        virtual void DoDataExchange(CDataExchange* pDX);        // DDX/DDV
        //}}AFX_MSG
        DECLARE_MESSAGE_MAP()
};
```

The **CAnimateDlg** class constructor constructs the Animate dialog box. A set of message map functions is also declared. The code for the class is discussed next.

```
// AnimateDlg.cpp : implementation file
//
#include <afxwin.h>
#include <afxdlgs.h>
#include <afxcmn.h>
#include "resource.h"
#include "AnimateDlg.h"
```

Note the inclusion of the advanced control header file *Afxcmn.h* and the **CAnimateDlg** class header file *AnimateDlg.h*.

```
BEGIN_MESSAGE_MAP(CAnimateDlg, CDialog)
        //{{AFX_MSG_MAP(CAnimateDlg)
        ON_BN_CLICKED(IDC_STOP, OnStop)
        ON_BN_CLICKED(IDC_PLAY, OnPlay)
        ON_BN_CLICKED(IDC_AUTOPLAY, OnAutoPlay)
        ON_BN_CLICKED(IDC_TRANSPARENT, OnTransparent)
        //}}AFX_MSG_MAP
END_MESSAGE_MAP()
```

The message map indicates that when the Stop button is clicked, the **OnStop** function is called; when the Play button is clicked, the **OnPlay** function is called; when the Autoplay check box is checked, the **OnAutoPlay** function is called; and when the Transparent check box is selected, the **OnTransparent** function is called.

```
/////////////////////////////////////////////////////////////////////
// CAnimateDlg message handlers

void CAnimateDlg::DoDataExchange(CDataExchange* pDX)
{
        CDialog::DoDataExchange(pDX);
        DDX_Control(pDX, IDC_ANIMATE1, animateCtrl);
}
```

The standard data exchange function called for the **CAnimateCtrl** class member animateCtrl.

```
BOOL CAnimateDlg::OnInitDialog()
{
```

```
        // TODO: Add extra initialization here
        CDialog::OnInitDialog();
        animateCtrl.Open("sample.avi");
        return TRUE;  // return TRUE unless you set the focus to a control
                      // EXCEPTION: OCX Property Pages should return FALSE
}
```

After initializing the dialog box, an AVI file is opened by use of the **Open** member function of the **CAnimateCtrl**. This opens the AVI file and displays the first frame. Notice that in the resource file we did not specify any style for the Animation control. Showing the first frame is the default behavior of this control. If ACS_AUTOPLAY style was set during creation of the Animation control or specified in the resource file, then opening the AVI file will automatically start playing the AVI clip. You may change the resource file to include ACS_AUTOPLAY style in the Animation control and try this out.

```
void CAnimateDlg::OnStop()
{
        // TODO: Add your control notification handler code here
        animateCtrl.Stop();
}
```

When the Stop button is clicked, the **OnStop** function is called, and it calls the **Stop** member function of the **CAnimateCtrl**.

```
void CAnimateDlg::OnPlay()
{
        animateCtrl.Play(0, (UINT)-1, (UINT)1);
}
```

When the Play button is clicked, the **OnPlay** function is called, and it calls the **Play** member function of the **CAnimateCtrl**. Here it specifies the control to play from frame 0 to –1, where –1 indicates the last frame. If a different number were specified, the control would have played until that frame. The third parameter indicates the replay count, and here the control is requested to play once. A value of –1 would tell it to play indefinitely.

```
void CAnimateDlg::OnAutoPlay()
{
        DWORD    dwStyle;
        animateCtrl.Stop();
        animateCtrl.Close();
        dwStyle = animateCtrl.GetStyle();        // Get the current style
```

```
    if(dwStyle & ACS_AUTOPLAY) // Check current style and toggle it
        dwStyle &= ~ACS_AUTOPLAY;
    else
        dwStyle |= ACS_AUTOPLAY;
    SetWindowLong(animateCtrl.GetSafeHwnd(), GWL_STYLE, dwStyle);
    animateCtrl.Open("sample.avi");
}
```

When the Autoplay check box is clicked, the **OnAutoPlay** function is called. Here it stops the control in case the AVI clip is playing, gets the control's current style, toggles the style, and sets the style again. It then reopens the AVI clip. A similar style change is made when the Transparent check box is clicked. The code is shown next:

```
void CAnimateDlg::OnTransparent()
{
    DWORD   dwStyle;
    dwStyle = animateCtrl.GetStyle();         // Get the current
style
    if(dwStyle & ACS_TRANSPARENT) // Check current style and
toggle it
        dwStyle &= ~ACS_TRANSPARENT;
    else
        dwStyle |= ACS_TRANSPARENT;
    SetWindowLong(animateCtrl.GetSafeHwnd(), GWL_STYLE, dwStyle);
    animateCtrl.Open("sample.avi");
}
```

SPIN CONTROL

A Spin control is actually the combination of two controls—an Up-Down control and another control (usually an Edit control). An Up-Down control consists of two arrows pointing in opposite directions. One way to visualize an Up-Down control is to think of a scroll bar with just the arrows and no bar connecting them (see Figure 7-5).

Figure 7-5.   An Up-Down control

Figure 7-6.   Spin control

Although you can use an Up-Down control in a stand-alone manner, the more common use is with another control such as an Edit box. The Edit box is called the Up-Down control's *buddy window.* As mentioned, the combination of an Up-Down control and an Edit box is called a Spin control (see Figure 7-6).

The Edit box contains a value, and clicking on the arrows of the associated Up-Down control increments and decrements the value in the Edit box. Figure 7-7 shows the results after the up arrow has been clicked and the Edit box has counted up to 45.

While the name suggests a vertical orientation for the Up-Down control, you can in fact have a horizontal orientation for the Up-Down control. In addition, you can position the Up-Down control to the left of the Edit box if you choose. Figure 7-8 shows the Up-Down control oriented horizontally and positioned to the left of the Edit box.

You can use the MFC class **CSpinButtonCtrl** to program a Spin control. **CSpinButtonCtrl** has several member functions that you can use to change the attributes of the Spin control. The attributes, their descriptions, and the member functions you can use to set the attributes are summarized in Table 7-4.

TIP: The default behavior of the Spin control is counterintuitive. The default maximum is 0, and the minimum is 100. Clicking the up arrow decreases the Edit box value, while clicking the down arrow increases it. You can change the range limits by using **SetRange** and **GetRange** member functions.

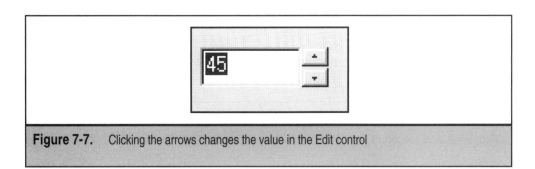

Figure 7-7.   Clicking the arrows changes the value in the Edit control

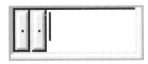

Figure 7-8. Horizontal Up-Down control to the left of the Edit box

You can also use styles to set the properties for a Spin control using the Styles tab of the Spin Properties dialog box in the dialog editor. The styles you can set and their descriptions are summarized in Table 7-5.

TIP: The AUTOBUDDY style automatically selects the previous window in Z order. So the order in which you specify the windows is important. Refer to the example for illustration of this point.

Attribute	Description	Member Functions
Acceleration	This adjusts the rate at which the position changes when the user holds down the arrow button.	SetAccel and GetAccel
Base	This changes the base to 10 or 16. Base is used to display the position in the caption of the buddy window.	GetBase and SetBase
Buddy Window	This dynamically queries or sets the buddy window.	GetBuddy and SetBuddy
Position	This queries and changes the position.	GetPos and SetPos
Range	This changes the maximum and minimum positions for the Spin control.	SetRange and GetRange

Table 7-4. Spin Control Attributes, Descriptions, and Associated Member Functions

Property	Meaning
Orientation	This sets the orientation of the control to be horizontal or vertical. Up-Down controls are vertical by default.
Alignment	This aligns the Up-Down control to the left or right of its buddy window. The width of the buddy window is adjusted to fit the Up-Down control.
Auto Buddy	This makes the buddy window the previous window in Z order.
No Thousands	This does not use the thousands separator (usually the comma) for buddy window displays.
Arrow Keys	This increments or decrements the Spin control value when the up arrow or down arrow key is pressed.
Set Buddy Integer	This automatically maintains synchronization between the value in the buddy window and the current position of the Up-Down control.
Wrap	This causes the position of the Up-Down control to "wrap around" when moved past an end. The default is to stop at the end.

Table 7-5.   Spin Control Properties and Description

Spin Control Programming Example

The *SpSlProg* sample program shows how to use the Spin Button control. If Spin Slider Progress is selected from the File menu, a dialog panel with a Spin control attached to an Edit control is displayed. Clicking the Spin control increments the count in the Edit control.

The main application code is still functionally minimal, with code added to handle the new menu item that will bring up the Spin Slider Progress dialog panel. These additional lines are shown in boldface. Although the code illustrates Slider and Progress controls, just look at the Spin control portions for this example. We will look at the other controls in the next two sections.

```
// Controls.CPP
#include <afxwin.h>
#include <afxdlgs.h>
```

```cpp
#include <afxcmn.h>              // Header file for Advanced controls
#include <strstrea.h>
#include "FontDlg.h"
#include "AnimateDlg.h"
#include "HotKeyDlg.h"
#include "SpSlProgDlg.h"
#include "resource.h"

// Define the application object class
class CApp : public CWinApp
{
public:
        virtual BOOL InitInstance ();
};


// Define the window class
class CWindow : public CFrameWnd
{
public:
    CWindow();
    afx_msg void OnAppAbout();
    afx_msg void OnFontDlg();
    afx_msg void OnAnimateDlg();
    afx_msg void OnHotKeyDlg();
    afx_msg void OnSpSlProgDlg();
    afx_msg void OnExit();
    afx_msg void OnSysCommand(UINT nID, LPARAM lParam); // To Process the Hot Key
    DECLARE_MESSAGE_MAP()
};

/////////////////////////////////////////////////////////////////////////////
// CWindow
BEGIN_MESSAGE_MAP(CWindow, CFrameWnd)
        ON_COMMAND(ID_APP_ABOUT, OnAppAbout)
        ON_COMMAND(ID_FONTDLG, OnFontDlg)
        ON_COMMAND(ID_ANIMATEDLG, OnAnimateDlg)
        ON_COMMAND(ID_HOTKEYDLG, OnHotKeyDlg)
        ON_COMMAND(ID_SPSLPROGDLG, OnSpSlProgDlg)
        ON_COMMAND(ID_APP_EXIT, OnExit)
        ON_WM_SYSCOMMAND()
END_MESSAGE_MAP()

/////////////////////////////////////////////////////////////////////////////
// CWindow construction
```

```
CWindow::CWindow()
{
    LoadAccelTable(MAKEINTRESOURCE(IDR_MAINFRAME));
    Create( NULL, "Control Sample",
    WS_OVERLAPPEDWINDOW,
    rectDefault, NULL, MAKEINTRESOURCE(IDR_MAINFRAME) );
}


/////////////////////////////////////////////////////////////////////////
// The one and only CApp object
CApp theApp;
/////////////////////////////////////////////////////////////////////////
// CApp initialization
BOOL CApp::InitInstance()
{
        m_pMainWnd = new CWindow();
        m_pMainWnd -> ShowWindow( m_nCmdShow );
        m_pMainWnd -> UpdateWindow();
        return TRUE;
}
/////////////////////////////////////////////////////////////////////////
// CAboutDlg dialog used for App About
class CAboutDlg : public CDialog
{
public:
        CAboutDlg();
        enum { IDD = IDD_ABOUTBOX };
        protected:
};

CAboutDlg::CAboutDlg() : CDialog(CAboutDlg::IDD)
{
}

// App command to run the dialog
void CWindow::OnAppAbout()
{
        CAboutDlg aboutDlg;
        aboutDlg.DoModal();
}


/////////////////////////////////////////////////////////////////////
// CWindow commands
// App command to run the dialog
```

```
// Font Dialog selected

void CWindow::OnFontDlg()
{
        CFontDlg fontDlg(this);
        fontDlg.DoModal();
}
// Animate Dialog selected
void CWindow::OnAnimateDlg()
{
        CAnimateDlg animateDlg(this);
        animateDlg.DoModal();
}
// HotKey Dialog selected
void CWindow::OnHotKeyDlg()
{
        CHotKeyDlg hotkeyDlg(this);
        hotkeyDlg.DoModal();
}
// Spin Slider Progress Dialog selected
void CWindow::OnSpSlProgDlg()
{
        CSpSlProgDlg spslprogDlg(this);
        spslprogDlg.DoModal();
}
// On Exit handles the void
void CWindow::OnExit()
{
        DestroyWindow();
}
void CWindow::OnSysCommand(UINT nID, LPARAM lParam)
{
    if (nID == SC_HOTKEY)
    {
        DestroyWindow();
    }
    else
    {   // Pass on all other messages to be processed.
        CWnd::OnSysCommand(nID, lParam);
    }
}
```

The dialog resource file for this sample is shown next. The style for the Spin control is set to be UDS_AUTOBUDDY. This will automatically select the previous window in the Z order as the control's buddy window. In the case of the dialog resource, it is the control that precedes the spin button in the tab order. So the position of the Edit control and the Spin control in the dialog resource is important. The other styles tell to wrap the position beyond the ending or beginning of the range (UDS_WRAP), not to inset thousand separators (UDS_NOTHOUSANDS), to set the text of the Edit control, and to enable UP and DOWN ARROW keys to increment and decrement the spin position. The style for the Slider control is set to TBS_AUTOTICKS to display tick marks in the Slider control.

```
IDD_SPSLPROG  DIALOG DISCARDABLE  0, 0, 201, 118
STYLE DS_MODALFRAME | WS_POPUP | WS_CAPTION | WS_SYSMENU
CAPTION "Spin/Slider/Progress"
FONT 8, "MS Sans Serif"
BEGIN
/* Since we are using AUTOBUDDY for the spin control the order   */
/* of the next two controls is essential. The AUTOBUDDY style    */
/* automatically selects the previous window in Z_order. In the  */
/* case of dialog template it is the control which precedes the  */
/* spin button in the tab order.                                 */
    EDITTEXT        IDC_EDIT,12,16,40,14,ES_AUTOHSCROLL
    CONTROL         "Spin2",IDC_SPIN,"msctls_updown32",UDS_WRAP |
UDS_NOTHOUSANDS | UDS_SETBUDDYINT | UDS_AUTOBUDDY |
UDS_ARROWKEYS,52,16,10,14
    CONTROL
"Slider1",IDC_SLIDER,"msctls_trackbar32",TBS_AUTOTICKS |
                WS_TABSTOP,12,45,162,17
    CONTROL
"Progress1",IDC_PROGRESS,"msctls_progress32",WS_BORDER,
                12,77,167,14,WS_EX_RTLREADING
    DEFPUSHBUTTON   "OK",IDOK,10,96,32,14
    PUSHBUTTON      "Close",IDC_CLOSE,52,96,32,14
    PUSHBUTTON      "Cancel",IDCANCEL,96,96,32,14
END
```

The class created for this dialog is shown next. It has three members, which correspond to **CSpinButtonCtrl**, **CSliderCtrl**, and **CProgressCtrl**. For the Edit control a **CString** member data is declared. It also declares the member functions **OnInitDialog**, which is called when the dialog panel is initialized; **OnChangeEdit**, which is called when the text in the Edit control changes; and **OnClose**, which is called when the Close button is clicked. Since the Edit control is set as the buddy to the Spin control, its value in the Edit control changes every time the Spin control is operated. This in turn will invoke the **OnChangeEdit** function.

```
// SpSlProgDlg.h : header file
//////////////////////////////////////////////////////////////////////
```

```
  // CSpSlProgDlg dialog
class CSpSlProgDlg : public CDialog
{
// Construction
public:
        CSpSlProgDlg(CWnd* pParent = NULL);        // standard constructor
// Dialog Data
        //{{AFX_DATA(CSpSlProgDlg)
        CSpinButtonCtrl m_spin;
        CSliderCtrl     m_slider;
        CProgressCtrl   m_progress;
        CString m_buddyedit;
        //}}AFX_DATA

        // ClassWizard generated virtual function overrides
        //{{AFX_VIRTUAL(CSpSlProgDlg)
        protected:
        virtual void DoDataExchange(CDataExchange* pDX);        // DDX/DDV support
        //}}AFX_VIRTUAL


// Implementation
protected:
        // Generated message map functions
        //{{AFX_MSG(CSpSlProgDlg)
        virtual BOOL OnInitDialog();
        afx_msg void OnChangeEdit();
        afx_msg void OnClose();
        //}}AFX_MSG
        DECLARE_MESSAGE_MAP()
};
```

The implementation code for the dialog panel class discussed earlier follows:

```
// SpSlProgDlg.cpp : implementation file
//
#include <afxwin.h>
#include <afxdlgs.h>
#include <afxcmn.h>
#include "resource.h"
#include "SpSlProgDlg.h"
/////////////////////////////////////////////////////////////////////////////
// CSpSlProgDlg dialog

CSpSlProgDlg::CSpSlProgDlg(CWnd* pParent /*=NULL*/)
        : CDialog(IDD_SPSLPROG, pParent)
```

```
{
    //{{AFX_DATA_INIT(CSpSlProgDlg)
    m_buddyedit = _T("");
    //}}AFX_DATA_INIT
}

void CSpSlProgDlg::DoDataExchange(CDataExchange* pDX)
{
        CDialog::DoDataExchange(pDX);
        //{{AFX_DATA_MAP(CSpSlProgDlg)
        DDX_Control(pDX, IDC_SPIN, m_spin);
        DDX_Control(pDX, IDC_SLIDER, m_slider);
        DDX_Control(pDX, IDC_PROGRESS, m_progress);
        DDX_Text(pDX, IDC_EDIT, m_buddyedit);
        //}}AFX_DATA_MAP
}
```

Notice that the data exchange between the Edit control and the member variable is done at the text level here.

```
BEGIN_MESSAGE_MAP(CSpSlProgDlg, CDialog)
        //{{AFX_MSG_MAP(CSpSlProgDlg)
        ON_EN_CHANGE(IDC_EDIT, OnChangeEdit)
        ON_BN_CLICKED(IDC_CLOSE, OnClose)
        //}}AFX_MSG_MAP
END_MESSAGE_MAP()
```

The message map specifies that the **OnChangeEdit** function be called when the text in the Edit control changes, and that the **OnClose** function be called when the Close button is clicked.

```
/////////////////////////////////////////////////////////////////////
// CSpSlProgDlg message handlers

BOOL CSpSlProgDlg::OnInitDialog()
{
    CDialog::OnInitDialog();
    // TODO: Add extra initialization here
    // Modify the default Spin button control range from 0-100 to 0-120
    // The rate at which the button spins can also be controlled by SetAccel method
    // When running this sample, keep the spin button pressed and notice the slider
    // control's speed increasing after a few seconds.
```

```
    m_spin.SetRange(0, 120);     // Just set the range.
    m_slider.SetRange(0, 120, TRUE); // Set the slider range
    m_slider.SetTicFreq(10);     // Put a tick mark at every 10 ticks

    m_progress.SetRange(0, 100);     // Range of the Progress indicator.
    m_progress.SetPos(100);          // Set the initial position.
    m_progress.SetStep(-1);          // Step increment every time StepIt is called.
    return TRUE;   // return TRUE unless you set the focus to a control
}
```

During initialization the default Spin button control range is changed from 0–100 to 0–120.

One of the interesting member functions that the Spin control provides is **SetAccel**. This function allows the user to set the rate of change at which the Spin control spins. This sample uses the default value. If the Spin control is kept selected when you're running the sample, the entry in the Edit control changes. This triggers the **OnChangeEdit** function, which reads the Spin control's position and sets the slider to reflect the position. As the Spin control is kept selected, the slider starts accelerating after a few seconds. This acceleration can be controlled by the **SetAccel** method of **CSpinButtonCtrl**.

```
void CSpSlProgDlg::OnChangeEdit()
{
    // TODO: Add your control notification handler code here
    int iCurrentPos;
    if (m_spin && m_slider) // Do not process before getting valid
objects.
    {
        iCurrentPos = m_spin.GetPos();
        m_slider.SetPos(iCurrentPos);
    }
}


void CSpSlProgDlg::OnClose()
{
    // TODO: Add your control notification handler code here
    AfxMessageBox("Watch the Progress Control.\nIn ten seconds this
Spin/Slider/Progress dialog will close");
    for (int i = 0; i < 100; i++)
    {
        Sleep(100);
        m_progress.StepIt();
    }
    EndDialog(1);
}
```

SLIDER CONTROL

The *Slider control,* also called a *trackbar,* is a window that contains a slider and a track along which the slider can be dragged. You can click on the slider indicator and drag it to set its position. Figure 7-9 shows a Slider control. A Slider control can also be associated with an Up-Down control, and the position of the slider can be controlled by use of the up and down arrows of the Up-Down control. Figures 7-10 through 7-12 show the position of the slider as it moves in relation to the Up-Down control. By default, the size of the slider is automatically determined by the system scroll bar width and is also limited by the size of the control.

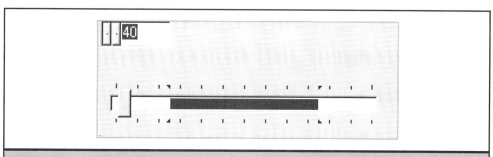

Figure 7-9. Slider control

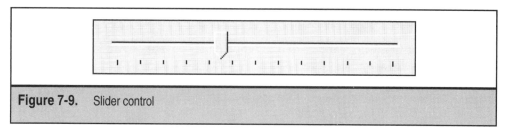

Figure 7-10. Slider at the left position when the Up-Down control is set to a small value

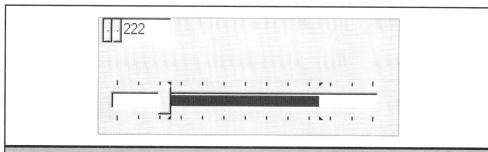

Figure 7-11. Slider advances in response to changes in the Up-Down control

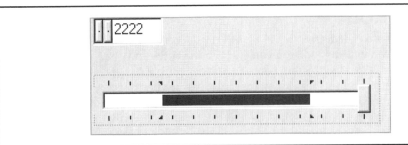

Figure 7-12.   Slider at the rightmost position when the Up-Down control is set to a large value

You can control the appearance of a slider using styles. The common styles you can use with sliders are described in Table 7-6.

The Slider controls shown in Figures 7-10 through 7-13 have the selection range enabled. Note that the tick marks that correspond to the ends of the selection range

Slider Control Style	Description
TBS_HORZ	Slider is oriented horizontally (default).
TBS_VERT	Slider is oriented vertically.
TBS_AUTOTICKS	This automatically creates a slider with a tick mark for each increment in the slider's range of values (you can change the tick frequency with the TBM_SETTICFREQ message).
TBS_NOTICKS	Slider does not display tick marks.
TBS_BOTTOM or TBS_TOP	This displays the tick marks at the bottom or top of the slider (for horizontal orientation).
TBS_RIGHT or TBS_LEFT	This displays the tick marks at the left or right sides of the slider (for vertical orientation).
TBS_BOTH	This displays tick marks on both sides of the slider (for any orientation).
TBS_ENABLESELRANGE	This displays a selection range within the slider. Range is set by use of TBM_SETSEL message.

Table 7-6.   Slider Control Styles

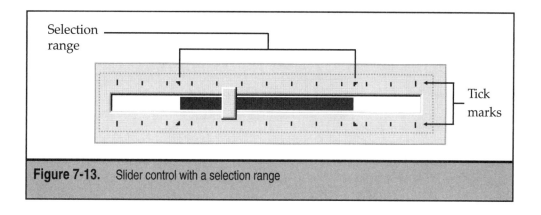

Figure 7-13.   Slider control with a selection range

change to triangles. This selection range-enabled slider is illustrated in the example that follows.

Slider Control Programming Example

The *SpSlProg* sample program also shows how to use the Slider control. When run, the sample displays a window with a menu. If Spin Slider Progress is selected from the File menu, a dialog panel with a Slider control is displayed. Clicking the Spin control arrows not only increments the count in the Edit control, but it also increments the Slider control.

The main application code is still functionally minimal, with code added to handle the new menu item that will bring up the Spin Slider Progress dialog panel. These additional lines are shown in boldface.

```
// Controls.CPP
#include <afxwin.h>
#include <afxdlgs.h>
#include <afxcmn.h>                    // Header file for Advanced controls
#include <strstrea.h>
#include "FontDlg.h"
#include "AnimateDlg.h"
#include "HotKeyDlg.h"
#include "SpSlProgDlg.h"
#include "resource.h"


// Define the application object class
class CApp : public CWinApp
{
public:
        virtual BOOL InitInstance ();
};
```

```
// Define the window class
class CWindow : public CFrameWnd
{
public:
    CWindow();
    afx_msg void OnAppAbout();
    afx_msg void OnFontDlg();
    afx_msg void OnAnimateDlg();
    afx_msg void OnHotKeyDlg();
    afx_msg void OnSpSlProgDlg();
    afx_msg void OnExit();
    afx_msg void OnSysCommand(UINT nID, LPARAM lParam); // To Process the Hot Key
    DECLARE_MESSAGE_MAP()
};

////////////////////////////////////////////////////////////////////
/////
// CWindow
BEGIN_MESSAGE_MAP(CWindow, CFrameWnd)
        ON_COMMAND(ID_APP_ABOUT, OnAppAbout)
        ON_COMMAND(ID_FONTDLG, OnFontDlg)
        ON_COMMAND(ID_ANIMATEDLG, OnAnimateDlg)
        ON_COMMAND(ID_HOTKEYDLG, OnHotKeyDlg)
        ON_COMMAND(ID_SPSLPROGDLG, OnSpSlProgDlg)
        ON_COMMAND(ID_APP_EXIT, OnExit)
        ON_WM_SYSCOMMAND()
END_MESSAGE_MAP()

////////////////////////////////////////////////////////////////////
// CWindow construction
CWindow::CWindow()
{
    LoadAccelTable(MAKEINTRESOURCE(IDR_MAINFRAME));
    Create( NULL, "Control Sample",
    WS_OVERLAPPEDWINDOW,
    rectDefault, NULL, MAKEINTRESOURCE(IDR_MAINFRAME) );
}

////////////////////////////////////////////////////////////////////
// The one and only CApp object
CApp theApp;
////////////////////////////////////////////////////////////////////
// CApp initialization
```

```
BOOL CApp::InitInstance()
{
        m_pMainWnd = new CWindow();
        m_pMainWnd -> ShowWindow( m_nCmdShow );
        m_pMainWnd -> UpdateWindow();
        return TRUE;
}
/////////////////////////////////////////////////////////////////////////////
// CAboutDlg dialog used for App About
class CAboutDlg : public CDialog
{
public:
        CAboutDlg();
        enum { IDD = IDD_ABOUTBOX };
        protected:
};

CAboutDlg::CAboutDlg() : CDialog(CAboutDlg::IDD)
{
}


// App command to run the dialog
void CWindow::OnAppAbout()

{
        CAboutDlg aboutDlg;
        aboutDlg.DoModal();
}


/////////////////////////////////////////////////////////////////////////////
// CWindow commands
// App command to run the dialog

// Font Dialog selected

void CWindow::OnFontDlg()
{
        CFontDlg fontDlg(this);
        fontDlg.DoModal();
}
// Animate Dialog selected
void CWindow::OnAnimateDlg()
{
        CAnimateDlg animateDlg(this);
        animateDlg.DoModal();
```

```
}
// HotKey Dialog selected
void CWindow::OnHotKeyDlg()
{
        CHotKeyDlg hotkeyDlg(this);
        hotkeyDlg.DoModal();
}
// Spin Slider Progress Dialog selected
void CWindow::OnSpSlProgDlg()
{
        CSpSlProgDlg spslprogDlg(this);
        spslprogDlg.DoModal();
}
// On Exit handles the void
void CWindow::OnExit()
{
        DestroyWindow();
}
void CWindow::OnSysCommand(UINT nID, LPARAM lParam)
{
    if (nID == SC_HOTKEY)
    {
        DestroyWindow();
    }
    else
    {   // Pass on all other messages to be processed.
        CWnd::OnSysCommand(nID, lParam);
    }
}
```

The dialog resource file for this sample is shown next. The style for the Spin control is set to be UDS_AUTOBUDDY. This will automatically select the previous window in the Z order as the control's buddy window. In the case of the dialog resource, it is the control that precedes the spin button in the tab order. Thus, the position of the Edit control and the Spin control in the dialog resource is important. The other styles specify to wrap the position beyond the ending or beginning of the range (UDS_WRAP), not to inset thousand separators (UDS_NOTHOUSANDS), to set the text of the Edit control (UDS_AUTOBUDDY), and to enable UP and DOWN ARROW keys to increment and decrement the spin position (UDS_ARROWKEYS). The style for the Slider control is set to TBS_AUTOTICKS to display tick marks in the Slider control.

```
IDD_SPSLPROG  DIALOG DISCARDABLE  0, 0, 201, 118
STYLE DS_MODALFRAME | WS_POPUP | WS_CAPTION | WS_SYSMENU
```

```
CAPTION "Spin/Slider/Progress"
FONT 8, "MS Sans Serif"
BEGIN
/* Since we are using AUTOBUDDY for the spin control the order    */
/* of the next two controls is essential. The AUTOBUDDY style     */
/* automatically selects the previous window in Z_order. In the   */
/* case of dialog template it is the control which precedes the   */
/* spin button in the tab order.                                  */
    EDITTEXT          IDC_EDIT,12,16,40,14,ES_AUTOHSCROLL
    CONTROL           "Spin2",IDC_SPIN,"msctls_updown32",UDS_WRAP |
UDS_NOTHOUSANDS | UDS_SETBUDDYINT | UDS_AUTOBUDDY | UDS_ARROWKEYS,52,16,10,14
    CONTROL           "Slider1",IDC_SLIDER,"msctls_trackbar32",TBS_AUTOTICKS |
                      WS_TABSTOP,12,45,162,17
    CONTROL           "Progress1",IDC_PROGRESS,"msctls_progress32",WS_BORDER,
                      12,77,167,14,WS_EX_RTLREADING
    DEFPUSHBUTTON     "OK",IDOK,10,96,32,14
    PUSHBUTTON        "Close",IDC_CLOSE,52,96,32,14
    PUSHBUTTON        "Cancel",IDCANCEL,96,96,32,14
END
```

The class created for this dialog is shown next. It has three members, one each corresponding to **CSpinButtonCtrl**, **CSliderCtrl**, and **CProgressCtrl**. It also declares the member functions **OnInitDialog,** which is called when the dialog panel is initialized; **OnChangeEdit**, which is called when the text in the Edit control changes; and **OnClose,** which is called when the Close button is clicked.

```
// SpSlProgDlg.h : header file
//////////////////////////////////////////////////////////////////////
// CSpSlProgDlg dialog
class CSpSlProgDlg : public CDialog
{
// Construction
public:
        CSpSlProgDlg(CWnd* pParent = NULL);        // standard
constructor
// Dialog Data
        //{{AFX_DATA(CSpSlProgDlg)
        CSpinButtonCtrl m_spin;
        CSliderCtrl     m_slider;
        CProgressCtrl   m_progress;
        CString m_buddyedit;
        //}}AFX_DATA

        // ClassWizard generated virtual function overrides
```

```
        //{{AFX_VIRTUAL(CSpSlProgDlg)
        protected:
        virtual void DoDataExchange(CDataExchange* pDX);          //
DDX/DDV support
        //}}AFX_VIRTUAL

// Implementation
protected:
        // Generated message map functions
        //{{AFX_MSG(CSpSlProgDlg)
        virtual BOOL OnInitDialog();
        afx_msg void OnChangeEdit();
        afx_msg void OnClose();
        //}}AFX_MSG
        DECLARE_MESSAGE_MAP()
};
```

The implementation code for the dialog panel class discussed earlier follows:

```
// SpSlProgDlg.cpp : implementation file
//
#include <afxwin.h>
#include <afxdlgs.h>
#include <afxcmn.h>
#include "resource.h"
#include "SpSlProgDlg.h"
/////////////////////////////////////////////////////////////////////////////
// CSpSlProgDlg dialog

CSpSlProgDlg::CSpSlProgDlg(CWnd* pParent /*=NULL*/)
        : CDialog(IDD_SPSLPROG, pParent)
{
    //{{AFX_DATA_INIT(CSpSlProgDlg)
    m_buddyedit = _T("");
    //}}AFX_DATA_INIT
}

void CSpSlProgDlg::DoDataExchange(CDataExchange* pDX)
{
        CDialog::DoDataExchange(pDX);
        //{{AFX_DATA_MAP(CSpSlProgDlg)
        DDX_Control(pDX, IDC_SPIN, m_spin);
        DDX_Control(pDX, IDC_SLIDER, m_slider);
        DDX_Control(pDX, IDC_PROGRESS, m_progress);
```

```
        DDX_Text(pDX, IDC_EDIT, m_buddyedit);
        //}}AFX_DATA_MAP
}
```

Notice that the data exchange between the Edit control and the member variable is done at the text level here.

```
BEGIN_MESSAGE_MAP(CSpSlProgDlg, CDialog)
        //{{AFX_MSG_MAP(CSpSlProgDlg)
        ON_EN_CHANGE(IDC_EDIT, OnChangeEdit)
        ON_BN_CLICKED(IDC_CLOSE, OnClose)
        //}}AFX_MSG_MAP
END_MESSAGE_MAP()
```

The message map specifies that the **OnChangeEdit** function should be called when the text in the Edit control changes, and that the **OnClose** function should be called when the Close button is clicked.

```
//////////////////////////////////////////////////////////////////////
// CSpSlProgDlg message handlers

BOOL CSpSlProgDlg::OnInitDialog()
{
    CDialog::OnInitDialog();
    // TODO: Add extra initialization here
    // Modify the default Spin button control range from 0-100 to 0-120
    // The rate at which the button spins can also be controlled by
SetAccel method
    // When running this sample, keep the spin button pressed and
notice the slider
    // control's speed increasing after a few seconds.
    m_spin.SetRange(0, 120);    // Just set the range.
    m_slider.SetRange(0, 120, TRUE); // Set the slider range
    m_slider.SetTicFreq(10);    // Put a tick mark at every 10 ticks

    m_progress.SetRange(0, 100);    // Range of the Progress indicator.
    m_progress.SetPos(100);         // Set the initial position.
    m_progress.SetStep(-1);         // Step increment every time StepIt
is called.
    return TRUE;  // return TRUE unless you set the focus to a control
}
```

During initialization the slider range is also set to 0–120.

```
void CSpSlProgDlg::OnChangeEdit()
{
    // TODO: Add your control notification handler code here
    int iCurrentPos;
    if (m_spin && m_slider) // Do not process before getting valid
objects.
    {
        iCurrentPos = m_spin.GetPos();
        m_slider.SetPos(iCurrentPos);
    }
}

void CSpSlProgDlg::OnClose()
{
    // TODO: Add your control notification handler code here
    AfxMessageBox("Watch the Progress Control.\nIn ten seconds this
Spin/Slider/Progress dialog will close");
    for (int i = 0; i < 100; i++)
    {
        Sleep(100);
        m_progress.StepIt();
    }
    EndDialog(1);
}
```

When the Close button is clicked, a message box is displayed to notify the user of the pending action, which in this case is the closure of the dialog panel.

PROGRESS CONTROL

The *Progress control* is used to indicate the progress of a long operation where the user has to wait. It consists of a rectangle that is gradually filled, from left to right or right to left, with the system highlight color as the operation progresses. Figures 7-14 and 7-15 show the progress bar progressing from left to right. Figures 7-16 and 7-17 show a progress bar progressing from right to left. You can control the progress direction, as the example program illustrates. Keep in mind that with snapshots, it is difficult to show the progress direction. Execute the programs to see the progress direction.

The operation could be copying a big file or a computation-intensive function. You see this control a lot when you install software. The user gets a much better feeling watching a progress bar compared with staring at an hourglass icon for a long time. The control also assures the user that the operation has not gone into a loop.

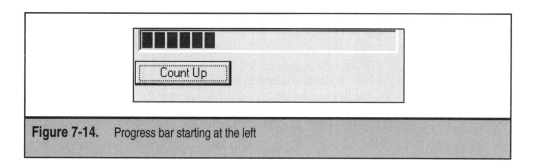

Figure 7-14.   Progress bar starting at the left

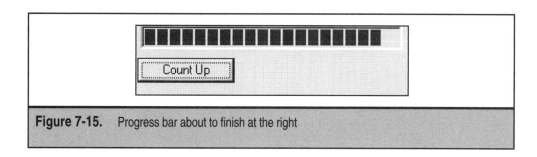

Figure 7-15.   Progress bar about to finish at the right

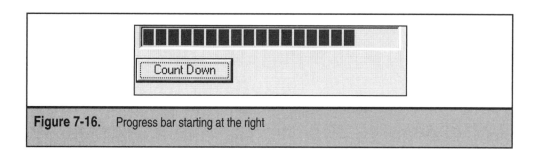

Figure 7-16.   Progress bar starting at the right

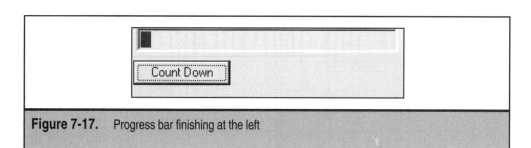

Figure 7-17.   Progress bar finishing at the left

Progress Control Programming Example

The *SpSlProg* sample program shows how to use the Progress control. The sample when run displays a window with a menu. If Spin Slider Progress is selected from the File menu, a dialog panel with a Progress control is displayed. Selecting the Close button displays a message box and starts countdown to close the dialog panel. As it counts down, the progress indicator is updated.

The main application code is still functionally minimal, with code added to handle the new menu item that will bring up the Spin Slider Progress dialog panel. These additional lines are shown in boldface.

```cpp
// Controls.CPP
#include <afxwin.h>
#include <afxdlgs.h>
#include <afxcmn.h>                      // Header file for Common Controls
#include <strstrea.h>
#include "FontDlg.h"
#include "AnimateDlg.h"
#include "HotKeyDlg.h"
#include "SpSlProgDlg.h"
#include "resource.h"

// Define the application object class
class CApp : public CWinApp
{
public:
        virtual BOOL InitInstance ();
};


// Define the window class
class CWindow : public CFrameWnd
{
public:
    CWindow();
    afx_msg void OnAppAbout();
    afx_msg void OnFontDlg();
    afx_msg void OnAnimateDlg();
    afx_msg void OnHotKeyDlg();
    afx_msg void OnSpSlProgDlg();
    afx_msg void OnExit();
    afx_msg void OnSysCommand(UINT nID, LPARAM lParam); // To Process the Hot Key
    DECLARE_MESSAGE_MAP()
};
```

```cpp
/////////////////////////////////////////////////////////////////////
// CWindow
BEGIN_MESSAGE_MAP(CWindow, CFrameWnd)
        ON_COMMAND(ID_APP_ABOUT, OnAppAbout)
        ON_COMMAND(ID_FONTDLG, OnFontDlg)
        ON_COMMAND(ID_ANIMATEDLG, OnAnimateDlg)
        ON_COMMAND(ID_HOTKEYDLG, OnHotKeyDlg)
        ON_COMMAND(ID_SPSLPROGDLG, OnSpSlProgDlg)
        ON_COMMAND(ID_APP_EXIT, OnExit)
        ON_WM_SYSCOMMAND()
END_MESSAGE_MAP()


/////////////////////////////////////////////////////////////////////
// CWindow construction
CWindow::CWindow()
{
    LoadAccelTable(MAKEINTRESOURCE(IDR_MAINFRAME));
    Create( NULL, "Control Sample",
    WS_OVERLAPPEDWINDOW,
    rectDefault, NULL, MAKEINTRESOURCE(IDR_MAINFRAME) );
}


/////////////////////////////////////////////////////////////////////
// The one and only CApp object
CApp theApp;
/////////////////////////////////////////////////////////////////////
// CApp initialization
BOOL CApp::InitInstance()
{
        m_pMainWnd = new CWindow();
        m_pMainWnd -> ShowWindow( m_nCmdShow );
        m_pMainWnd -> UpdateWindow();
        return TRUE;
}
/////////////////////////////////////////////////////////////////////
// CAboutDlg dialog used for App About
class CAboutDlg : public CDialog
{
public:
        CAboutDlg();
        enum { IDD = IDD_ABOUTBOX };
        protected:
};
```

```
CAboutDlg::CAboutDlg() : CDialog(CAboutDlg::IDD)
{
}

// App command to run the dialog
void CWindow::OnAppAbout()
{
        CAboutDlg aboutDlg;
        aboutDlg.DoModal();
}


//////////////////////////////////////////////////////////////////////
// CWindow commands
// App command to run the dialog

// Font Dialog selected

void CWindow::OnFontDlg()
{
        CFontDlg fontDlg(this);
        fontDlg.DoModal();
}
// Animate Dialog selected
void CWindow::OnAnimateDlg()
{
        CAnimateDlg animateDlg(this);
        animateDlg.DoModal();
}
// HotKey Dialog selected
void CWindow::OnHotKeyDlg()
{
        CHotKeyDlg hotkeyDlg(this);
        hotkeyDlg.DoModal();
}
// Spin Slider Progress Dialog selected
void CWindow::OnSpSlProgDlg()
{
        CSpSlProgDlg spslprogDlg(this);
        spslprogDlg.DoModal();
}
// On Exit handles the void
void CWindow::OnExit()
{
```

```
            DestroyWindow();
}
void CWindow::OnSysCommand(UINT nID, LPARAM lParam)
{
    if (nID == SC_HOTKEY)
    {
        DestroyWindow();
    }
    else
    {  // Pass on all other messages to be processed.
        CWnd::OnSysCommand(nID, lParam);
    }
}
```

The dialog resource file for this sample is shown next. The style for the Spin control is set to be UDS_AUTOBUDDY. This will automatically select the previous window in the Z order as the control's buddy window. In the case of the dialog resource, it is the control that precedes the spin button in the tab order. Thus, the position of the Edit control and the Spin control in the dialog resource is important. The other styles specify to wrap the position beyond the ending or beginning of the range (UDS_WRAP), not to inset the thousand separators (UDS_NOTHOUSANDS), to set the text of the Edit control (USA_AUTOBUDDY), and to enable UP and DOWN ARROW keys to increment and decrement the spin position (UDS_ARROWKEYS). The style for the Slider control is set to TBS_AUTOTICKS to display tick marks in the Slider control.

```
IDD_SPSLPROG  DIALOG DISCARDABLE  0, 0, 201, 118
STYLE DS_MODALFRAME | WS_POPUP | WS_CAPTION | WS_SYSMENU
CAPTION "Spin/Slider/Progress"
FONT 8, "MS Sans Serif"
BEGIN
/* Since we are using AUTOBUDDY for the spin control the order   */
/* of the next two controls is essential. The AUTOBUDDY style    */
/* automatically selects the previous window in Z_order. In the  */
/* case of dialog template it is the control which precedes the  */
/* spin button in the tab order.                                 */
    EDITTEXT          IDC_EDIT,12,16,40,14,ES_AUTOHSCROLL
    CONTROL           "Spin2",IDC_SPIN,"msctls_updown32",UDS_WRAP |
UDS_NOTHOUSANDS | UDS_SETBUDDYINT | UDS_AUTOBUDDY | UDS_ARROWKEYS,52,16,10,14
    CONTROL           "Slider1",IDC_SLIDER,"msctls_trackbar32",TBS_AUTOTICKS |
                      WS_TABSTOP,12,45,162,17
    CONTROL           "Progress1",IDC_PROGRESS,"msctls_progress32",WS_BORDER,
                      12,77,167,14,WS_EX_RTLREADING
    DEFPUSHBUTTON     "OK",IDOK,10,96,32,14
    PUSHBUTTON        "Close",IDC_CLOSE,52,96,32,14
```

```
     PUSHBUTTON      "Cancel",IDCANCEL,96,96,32,14
END
```

The class created for this dialog is shown next. It has three members, one each corresponding to **CSpinButtonCtrl**, **CSliderCtrl**, and **CProgressCtrl**. It also declares the member functions **OnInitDialog,** which is called when the dialog panel is initialized; **OnChangeEdit**, which is called when the text in the Edit control changes; and **OnClose,** which is called when the Close button is clicked.

```cpp
// SpSlProgDlg.h : header file
//////////////////////////////////////////////////////////////////////////////
// CSpSlProgDlg dialog
class CSpSlProgDlg : public CDialog
{
// Construction
public:
        CSpSlProgDlg(CWnd* pParent = NULL);        // standard constructor
// Dialog Data
        //{{AFX_DATA(CSpSlProgDlg)
        CSpinButtonCtrl m_spin;
        CSliderCtrl     m_slider;
        CProgressCtrl   m_progress;
        CString m_buddyedit;
        //}}AFX_DATA

        // ClassWizard generated virtual function overrides
        //{{AFX_VIRTUAL(CSpSlProgDlg)
        protected:
        virtual void DoDataExchange(CDataExchange* pDX);        // DDX/DDV support
        //}}AFX_VIRTUAL

// Implementation
protected:
        // Generated message map functions
        //{{AFX_MSG(CSpSlProgDlg)
        virtual BOOL OnInitDialog();
        afx_msg void OnChangeEdit();
        afx_msg void OnClose();
        //}}AFX_MSG
        DECLARE_MESSAGE_MAP()
};
```

The implementation code for the dialog panel class discussed earlier follows:

```
// SpSlProgDlg.cpp : implementation file
//
#include <afxwin.h>
#include <afxdlgs.h>
#include <afxcmn.h>
#include "resource.h"
#include "SpSlProgDlg.h"
/////////////////////////////////////////////////////////////////////////
// CSpSlProgDlg dialog

CSpSlProgDlg::CSpSlProgDlg(CWnd* pParent /*=NULL*/)
        : CDialog(IDD_SPSLPROG, pParent)
{
    //{{AFX_DATA_INIT(CSpSlProgDlg)
    m_buddyedit = _T("");
    //}}AFX_DATA_INIT
}

void CSpSlProgDlg::DoDataExchange(CDataExchange* pDX)
{
        CDialog::DoDataExchange(pDX);
        //{{AFX_DATA_MAP(CSpSlProgDlg)
        DDX_Control(pDX, IDC_SPIN, m_spin);
        DDX_Control(pDX, IDC_SLIDER, m_slider);
        DDX_Control(pDX, IDC_PROGRESS, m_progress);
        DDX_Text(pDX, IDC_EDIT, m_buddyedit);
        //}}AFX_DATA_MAP
}
```

Notice that the data exchange between the Edit control and the member variable is done at the text level here.

```
BEGIN_MESSAGE_MAP(CSpSlProgDlg, CDialog)
        //{{AFX_MSG_MAP(CSpSlProgDlg)
        ON_EN_CHANGE(IDC_EDIT, OnChangeEdit)
        ON_BN_CLICKED(IDC_CLOSE, OnClose)
        //}}AFX_MSG_MAP
END_MESSAGE_MAP()
```

The message map specifies that the **OnChangeEdit** function should be called when the text in the Edit control changes. In addition, it specifies that the **OnClose** function should be called when the Close button is clicked.

```
////////////////////////////////////////////////////////////////////////
// CSpSlProgDlg message handlers

BOOL CSpSlProgDlg::OnInitDialog()
{
    CDialog::OnInitDialog();
    // TODO: Add extra initialization here
    // Modify the default Spin button control range from 0-100 to 0-120
    // The rate at which the button spins can also be controlled by SetAccel method
    // When running this sample, keep the spin button pressed and notice the slider
    // control's speed increasing after a few seconds.
    m_spin.SetRange(0, 120);      // Just set the range.
    m_slider.SetRange(0, 120, TRUE); // Set the slider range
    m_slider.SetTicFreq(10);      // Put a tick mark at every 10 ticks

    m_progress.SetRange(0, 100);     // Range of the Progress indicator.
    m_progress.SetPos(100);          // Set the initial position.
    m_progress.SetStep(-1);          // Step increment every time StepIt is called.
    return TRUE;  // return TRUE unless you set the focus to a control
}
```

During initialization the initial position for the Progress control is set to 100, which is the maximum, and the step increment is set to –1. This would mean that the progress indicator will drop by 1 every time the Progress control is asked to step. It is being set to a negative range since the objective of the progress indicator is to visually show the countdown.

```
void CSpSlProgDlg::OnChangeEdit()
{
    // TODO: Add your control notification handler code here
    int iCurrentPos;
    if (m_spin && m_slider) // Do not process before getting valid
objects.
    {
        iCurrentPos = m_spin.GetPos();
        m_slider.SetPos(iCurrentPos);
    }
}
```

```
void CSpSlProgDlg::OnClose()
{
    // TODO: Add your control notification handler code here
    AfxMessageBox("Watch the Progress Control.\nIn ten seconds this
Spin/Slider/Progress dialog will close");
    for (int i = 0; i < 100; i++)
    {
        Sleep(100);
        m_progress.StepIt();
    }
    EndDialog(1);
}
```

When the Close button is clicked, a message box is displayed to notify the user of the pending action—which in this case is the closure of the dialog panel—and the progress indicator is stepped down after every 100 milliseconds. Notice that the progress indicator slides down because a negative value was set as the step value.

HOTKEY CONTROL

Hot keys are key combinations that let the user bypass menus and directly invoke a window or function. A *HotKey control* aids in the setting up of hot keys. A HotKey control is a window that displays a text representation of the key combination the user types, such as SHIFT-CTRL-ALT. Figure 7-18 shows setting a hot key dialog box.

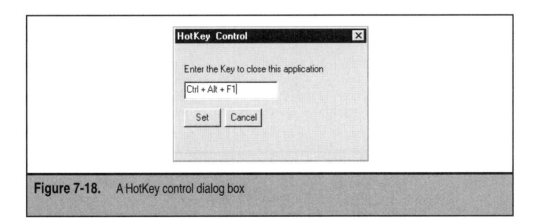

Figure 7-18.   A HotKey control dialog box

The control internally maintains the virtual key code for the hot key and a set of flags that represent the shift state. The HotKey control passes the key combination to your program so that you can set it. The scope of the hot key could be global or it can be thread specific.

The typical sequence of a HotKey control execution is as follows. The control is created by use of a dialog box template (with **CHotKeyCtrl** in your dialog class) or by use of the **Create** member function to create the control as a child window. You can set a default value by calling the **SetHotKey** member function. You can prohibit certain shift states by calling **SetRules**. The user interacts with the HotKey control and selects a hot key combination. Use the **GetHotKey** member function to retrieve the virtual key and shift state values when your program is notified that the user has selected a hotkey. You then set the hot key as a global hot key by sending a **WM_SETHOTKEY** message, or a thread-specific hot key by calling the Windows function **RegisterHotKey**. You then terminate the dialog box with the user and perform any cleanups, such as destroying the HotKey control and associated object.

TIP: The HotKey control facilitates setting up the hot key, but does not actually set the hot key. You have to programmatically set the hot key.

HotKey Control Progamming Example

The HotKey sample program shows how to use the HotKey control by use of the MFC library class **CHotKeyCtrl**. The sample when run displays a window with a menu. If the HotKey menu item is selected from the File menu, a dialog panel with a HotKey control is displayed. A hot key combination can be entered in the HotKey control. Clicking the Set button will set this hot key as the global hot key. The panel allows you to reset the hot key until the Cancel button is clicked. If the hot key is pressed after dismissing the panel, the application terminates.

The main application code is still the same, with code added to handle the new menu item that will bring up the HotKey control dialog panel. The sample program shows the setting of a global hot key. When the hot key is pressed, the specified window, which in this case is the main window, receives a **WM_SYSCOMMAND** that specifies SC_HOTKEY as the type of command. Code is added in the main application code to handle this message. These additional lines are shown in boldface.

```
// Controls.CPP
#include <afxwin.h>
#include <afxdlgs.h>
#include <afxcmn.h>              // Header file for Advanced controls
#include <strstrea.h>
#include "FontDlg.h"
#include "AnimateDlg.h"
#include "HotKeyDlg.h"
```

```
#include "resource.h"

// Define the application object class
class CApp : public CWinApp
{
public:
        virtual BOOL InitInstance ();
};

// Define the window class
class CWindow : public CFrameWnd
{
public:
    CWindow();
    afx_msg void OnAppAbout();
    afx_msg void OnFontDlg();
    afx_msg void OnAnimateDlg();
    afx_msg void OnHotKeyDlg();
    afx_msg void OnExit();
    afx_msg void OnSysCommand(UINT nID, LPARAM lParam); // To Process the Hot Key
    DECLARE_MESSAGE_MAP()
};

//////////////////////////////////////////////////////////////////////
// CWindow

BEGIN_MESSAGE_MAP(CWindow, CFrameWnd)
        ON_COMMAND(ID_APP_ABOUT, OnAppAbout)
        ON_COMMAND(ID_FONTDLG, OnFontDlg)
        ON_COMMAND(ID_ANIMATEDLG, OnAnimateDlg)
        ON_COMMAND(ID_HOTKEYDLG, OnHotKeyDlg)
        ON_COMMAND(ID_APP_EXIT, OnExit)
        ON_WM_SYSCOMMAND()
END_MESSAGE_MAP()

//////////////////////////////////////////////////////////////////////
// CWindow construction

CWindow::CWindow()
{
    LoadAccelTable(MAKEINTRESOURCE(IDR_MAINFRAME));
    Create( NULL, "Control Sample",
    WS_OVERLAPPEDWINDOW,
    rectDefault, NULL, MAKEINTRESOURCE(IDR_MAINFRAME) );
```

```
}

/////////////////////////////////////////////////////////////////////////
// The one and only CApp object

CApp theApp;

/////////////////////////////////////////////////////////////////////////
// CApp initialization
BOOL CApp::InitInstance()
{
        m_pMainWnd = new CWindow();
        m_pMainWnd -> ShowWindow( m_nCmdShow );
        m_pMainWnd -> UpdateWindow();
        return TRUE;
}

/////////////////////////////////////////////////////////////////////////
// CAboutDlg dialog used for App About

class CAboutDlg : public CDialog
{
public:
        CAboutDlg();

        enum { IDD = IDD_ABOUTBOX };

        protected:

};

CAboutDlg::CAboutDlg() : CDialog(CAboutDlg::IDD)
{
}


// App command to run the dialog
void CWindow::OnAppAbout()
{
        CAboutDlg aboutDlg;
        aboutDlg.DoModal();
}

/////////////////////////////////////////////////////////////////////////
```

```
// CWindow commands
// App command to run the dialog

// Font Dialog selected
void CWindow::OnFontDlg()
{
        CFontDlg fontDlg(this);
        fontDlg.DoModal();
}
// Animate Dialog selected
void CWindow::OnAnimateDlg()
{
        CAnimateDlg animateDlg(this);
        animateDlg.DoModal();
}
// HotKey Dialog selected

void CWindow::OnHotKeyDlg()
{
        CHotKeyDlg hotkeyDlg(this);
        hotkeyDlg.DoModal();
}
// On Exit handles the void
void CWindow::OnExit()
{
        DestroyWindow();
}


void CWindow::OnSysCommand(UINT nID, LPARAM lParam)
{
    if (nID == SC_HOTKEY)
    {
        DestroyWindow();
    }
    else
    {  // Pass on all other messages to be processed.
        CWnd::OnSysCommand(nID, lParam);
    }
}
```

When the window receives a **WM_SYSCOMMAND** message, the **OnSysCommand** member function is called. If the command is SC_HOTKEY, it terminates the application. If needed, any other action could have been performed here. The dialog resource for the

HotKey dialog panel is given next. No special style has been included for the HotKey control.

```
IDD_HOTKEYDLG  DIALOG DISCARDABLE  0, 0, 162, 88
STYLE DS_MODALFRAME | WS_POPUP | WS_CAPTION | WS_SYSMENU
CAPTION "Hot Key Control"
FONT 8, "MS Sans Serif"
BEGIN
    LTEXT       "Enter the Key to close this application",IDC_STATIC,7,15,135,8
    CONTROL         "Hotkey1",IDC_HOTKEY,"msctls_hotkey32",WS_BORDER |
                    WS_TABSTOP,7,28,80,14
    PUSHBUTTON      "Set",IDC_SETHOTKEY,7,49,31,14
    PUSHBUTTON      "Cancel",IDCANCEL,42,49,31,14
END
```

The dialog panel class maintains a pointer to the parent window's class handle, which is passed to the class during construction. This is used to send the **WM_SETHOTKEY**, which should be sent to the main window. It also has a **CHotKeyCtrl** member that corresponds to the HotKey control in the dialog box. The inline constructor code takes the parent window pointer and initializes the local member. It also declares the member functions **OnInitDialog** and **OnSet**. **OnInitDialog** is called when the dialog is initialized. The **OnSet** function is called when the Set button in the dialog panel is clicked.

```
// HotKeyDlg.h : header file
//
/////////////////////////////////////////////////////////////////////
//
// CHotKeyDlg dialog
class CHotKeyDlg : public CDialog
{
private:
        CWnd          *m_parent;
        CHotKeyCtrl hotkeyCtrl;

// Construction
public:
        CHotKeyDlg(CWnd* pParent = NULL)
                : CDialog(IDD_HOTKEYDLG, pParent)
                        {m_parent = pParent;}
        virtual void DoDataExchange(CDataExchange* pDX);        // DDX/DDV
// Implementation
protected:
        // Generated message map functions
        //{{AFX_MSG(CHotKeyDlg)
```

```
            afx_msg void OnSet();
            virtual BOOL OnInitDialog();
            //}}AFX_MSG
            DECLARE_MESSAGE_MAP()
};

// AnimateDlg.cpp : implementation file
//
#include <afxwin.h>
#include <afxdlgs.h>
#include <afxcmn.h>
#include "resource.h"
#include "HotKeyDlg.h"

BEGIN_MESSAGE_MAP(CHotKeyDlg, CDialog)
        //{{AFX_MSG_MAP(CHotKeyDlg)
        ON_BN_CLICKED(IDC_SETHOTKEY, OnSet)
        //}}AFX_MSG_MAP
END_MESSAGE_MAP()
```

The message map specifies that the **OnSet** function should be called when the Set button is clicked. Next follows the standard data exchange function:

```
/////////////////////////////////////////////////////////////////////////
// CHotKeyDlg message handlers
void CHotKeyDlg::DoDataExchange(CDataExchange* pDX)
{
        CDialog::DoDataExchange(pDX);
        DDX_Control(pDX, IDC_HOTKEY, hotkeyCtrl);
}


BOOL CHotKeyDlg::OnInitDialog()
{
    CDialog::OnInitDialog();
     // Make Alt+ key combination invalid. Modify Alt+ to Ctrl+ hot key.
    hotkeyCtrl.SetRules((WORD)(HKCOMB_A),
                        (WORD)(HKCOMB_C));
    return TRUE;  // return TRUE unless you set the focus to a control
                        // EXCEPTION: OCX Property Pages should return FALSE
}
```

The HotKey control enables you to specify invalid key combinations. It can be a combination of ALT, CTRL, CTRL-ALT, SHIFT, SHIFT-ALT, SHIFT-CTRL, or SHIFT-CTRL-ALT. It also allows you to specify the key combination to use when the user enters an invalid combination. During initialization the ALT key is defined to be invalid and is modified by the CTRL key. When a user enters an invalid key combination as defined in this function, the system uses the OR operator to combine the keys entered by the user with the flags specified as the second parameter here.

```
void CHotKeyDlg::OnSet()
{
        // TODO: Add your control notification handler code here
    WORD wKeyAndShift;
    // Get the hot key set in the HotKey control
    wKeyAndShift = (WORD)hotkeyCtrl.GetHotKey();
    // Set the hot key. It should be set to a nonchild window.
    // In our case it is being set to the main window.
    m_parent->SendMessage (WM_SETHOTKEY, wKeyAndShift);
}
```

When the user clicks the Set button, this function is called. It gets the hot key from the HotKey control and gives it to the main window by sending the **WM_SETHOTKEY** message. This hot key should be given to a nonchild window. In this case it is given to the main window.

TOOLBAR CONTROL

A *toolbar* is a bar that contains icons representing menu choices that the user can select by clicking on the icon. Using the toolbar to perform a menu selection is faster than navigating through layers of menus. In addition, it is easier for most users to recognize an icon than to remember the name of the menu selection, or on what menu or submenu the selection is listed. Typically the toolbar appears just below an application's menu bar, although the toolbar can be free-floating as well. An application can support multiple toolbars. Microsoft Office products such as Word and PowerPoint and developer products such as the Developer Studio support multiple toolbars and provide functions to let the user customize the toolbars. The user can select which toolbars he or she wants displayed. The user can also select the icons for each of the toolbars. In your program, you have to decide to what extent you want to provide customization features. The buttons on a toolbar can display a bitmap, a string, or both. A toolbar's height is determined by the height of the buttons, and its width is adjusted to be the same as that of the parent window's client area by default.

The MFC library provides two classes to create toolbars—**CToolBar** and **CToolBarCtrl**. **CToolBar** is a superset of **CToolBarCtrl**. However, if you don't need the added functionality of **CToolBar**, then **CToolBarCtrl** is preferable, as it results in a smaller executable. **CToolBarCtrl** objects use multiple data structures, and you must set up the following data structures before invoking **CToolBarCtrl**:

▼ A list of button image bitmaps

- A list of strings for button labels
- ▲ A list of **TBBUTTON** structures to associate an image bitmap and/or a label with the position, style, state, and command ID of the button

TIP: Remember that when you access the individual elements in these data structures, the index starts with zero. For example, in the bitmaps data structure, the first bitmap has an index of zero, the second bitmap has an index of one, and so on.

One way you can create a bitmap is by using the Image Editor in the Developer Studio. All the buttons you want on the toolbar are contained in the bitmap. Figure 7-19 shows a toolbar with icons. Figure 7-20 shows the same toolbar with icons and text and Reflect selected. Figure 7-21 shows the same toolbar with icons and text and Shear selected.

Toolbar Control Programming Example

The sample program shown next takes the *WrldXForm* sample from Chapter 5 and extends it to have a toolbar by use of the **CToolBarCtrl** MFC library class. **CToolBarCtrl** provides the functionality of NT's toolbar common control. The *WrldXForm* sample

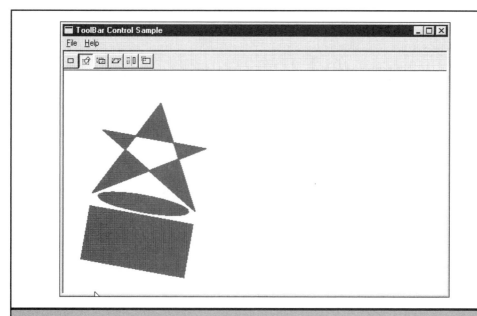

Figure 7-19. Toolbar with icons and no text

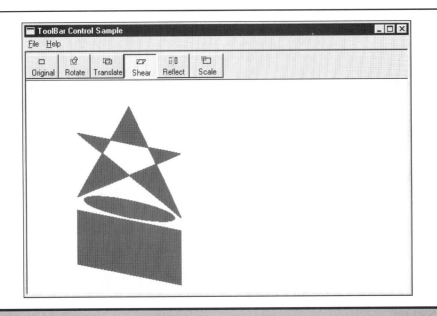

Figure 7-20. Toolbar with icons and text

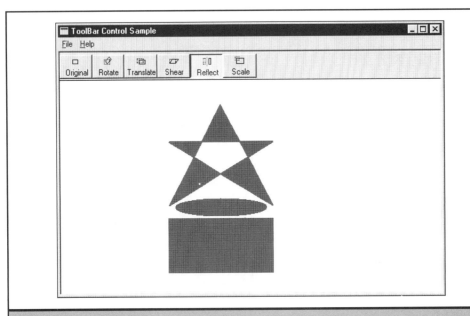

Figure 7-21. Toolbar with icons and text indicating a different selection

draws a graphic object and allows the user to choose from a menu of transforms. This sample extends that same functionality to the toolbar.

A command toolbar class, **CCmdToolBar**, is derived from **CToolBarCtrl**. The class header file is shown next. The number of buttons in the toolbar and the pointer to the toolbar button structure are declared as private members. Since additional initialization and termination need to be done during the creation and destruction of the toolbar control, the **Create** method is overridden and a destructor is defined.

```
// CmdToolBar.h : header file
class CCmdToolBar : public CToolBarCtrl
{
private:
    int       m_nButtonCount;
    TBBUTTON  *m_pTBButtons;

// Construction
public:
    CCmdToolBar();

// ClassWizard generated virtual function overrides
//{{AFX_VIRTUAL(CCmdToolBar)
public:
    virtual BOOL Create( DWORD dwStyle, const RECT& rect, CWnd* pParentWnd, UINT nID);
    //}}AFX_VIRTUAL
// Implementation
public:
    ~CCmdToolBar();
protected:
    DECLARE_MESSAGE_MAP()
};
```

The implementation file for the **CCmdToolBarCtrl** class is shown next. By design the sample application needs a toolbar with six buttons, one for each transform. A bitmap for this toolbar is created. An easy way to create this toolbar bitmap is through Visual C++ Developer Studio. This toolbar bitmap resource is added to the resource file. During the creation of the toolbar control, the toolbar bitmap is added by calling the **AddBitmap** function, and six toolbar button structures are allocated. For each toolbar button the state, style, bitmap, and command are initialized. The state of the button is set to be enabled, which would activate the button for user action. While the enabled state might be a logical state in this application, other applications may not need to enable the buttons. A typical example is the initial state of the Paste toolbar button, which will not be enabled if the Clipboard is empty. The state of the button can be queried by calling the **GetState** function, and changed by calling the **SetState** function. The style of the button is set to TBSTYLE_BUTTON, TBSTYLE_CHECK, and TBSTYLE_CHECKGROUP.

TBSTYLE_BUTTON creates a standard push button. TBSTYLE_CHECK creates the button that toggles between the pressed and unpressed states each time the user clicks it. Since only one transform can be active at a given time, all the buttons are given the TBSTYLE_CHECKGROUP style, which will release a button when another button gets pressed in the group. The command ID for each button is set to the command that the button would generate when it is pressed. The bitmap for the button is determined using the index of the bitmap in the toolbar bitmap, that was added to the control earlier. After the toolbar button structures are created, they are added to the control by calling the **AddButtons** function. This would take the number of buttons to be added and the button structure.

```cpp
// CmdToolBar.cpp : implementation file
#include <afxcmn.h>
#include <afxpriv.h>
#include "Resource.h"
#include "CmdToolBar.h"
/////////////////////////////////////////////////////////////////////////////
// CCmdToolBar

CCmdToolBar::CCmdToolBar() : m_pTBButtons(NULL)
{
}


CCmdToolBar::~CCmdToolBar()
{
    if (m_pTBButtons)
        delete []m_pTBButtons;
}

BEGIN_MESSAGE_MAP(CCmdToolBar, CToolBarCtrl)
    //{{AFX_MSG_MAP(CCmdToolBar)
    //}}AFX_MSG_MAP
END_MESSAGE_MAP()

BOOL CCmdToolBar::Create(DWORD dwStyle, const RECT& rect, CWnd* pParentWnd,
                        UINT nID )
{
    BOOL bRet = CToolBarCtrl::Create(dwStyle, rect, pParentWnd, nID);
    m_nButtonCount = 6;
    AddBitmap(m_nButtonCount, IDR_CMDTOOLBAR);
    m_pTBButtons = new TBBUTTON[m_nButtonCount];

    for (int i = 0; i < m_nButtonCount; i++)
    {
```

```
            m_pTBButtons[i].fsState  =  TBSTATE_ENABLED;
         m_pTBButtons[i].fsStyle = TBSTYLE_BUTTON | TBSTYLE_CHECK |
                                   TBSTYLE_CHECKGROUP;
         m_pTBButtons[i].dwData = 0;
         m_pTBButtons[i].iBitmap = i;
         m_pTBButtons[i].idCommand = i + IDM_ORIGINAL;
      }
    AddButtons(m_nButtonCount,&m_pTBButtons[0]);
    return bRet;
}
```

The main application code is shown next. This code is similar to that discussed earlier for *Wrldxform.cpp*. Some of the unchanged code has not been shown here. The changes made in order to add the toolbar are highlighted. As was done for other common controls, the *Afxcmn.h* header file is included along with the *Cmdtoolbar.h*, which has the **CCmdToolBar** class definitions. A private member data to correspond to the toolbar control is added in the **CWindow** class.

```
// WRLDXFORM.CPP
#include <afxwin.h>
#include <afxdlgs.h>
#include <afxcmn.h>
#include <math.h>
#include "Resource.h"
#include "CmdToolBar.h"

#define ORIGINAL    1
#define ROTATE      2
#define TRANSLATE   3
#define SHEAR       4
#define REFLECT     5
#define SCALE       6


XFORM    xForm;
int      iCurrentTransform;
int      iPreviousTransform;
short    sAngle;

// Define the application object class
class CApp : public CWinApp
{
public:
    virtual BOOL InitInstance ();
};
```

```cpp
// Define the window class
class CWindow : public CFrameWnd
{
private:
    CCmdToolBar m_cmdtoolbar;
public:
    CWindow();
    afx_msg void OnPaint();
    afx_msg void OnSize(UINT, INT, INT);
    afx_msg void OnKeyUp(UINT, UINT, UINT);
    afx_msg void OnAppAbout();
    afx_msg void OnOriginal();
    afx_msg void OnRotate();
    afx_msg void OnTranslate();
    afx_msg void OnShear();
    afx_msg void OnReflect();
    afx_msg void OnScale();
    afx_msg void OnExit();
    void UncheckMenu();
    void CheckMenu();
    DECLARE_MESSAGE_MAP()
};

/////////////////////////////////////////////////////////////////////////////
// CWindow

BEGIN_MESSAGE_MAP(CWindow, CFrameWnd)
    ON_WM_PAINT()
    ON_WM_SIZE()
    ON_WM_KEYUP()
    ON_COMMAND(ID_APP_ABOUT, OnAppAbout)
    ON_COMMAND(IDM_ORIGINAL, OnOriginal)
    ON_COMMAND(IDM_ROTATE, OnRotate)
    ON_COMMAND(IDM_TRANSLATE, OnTranslate)
    ON_COMMAND(IDM_SHEAR, OnShear)
    ON_COMMAND(IDM_REFLECT, OnReflect)
    ON_COMMAND(IDM_SCALE, OnScale)
    ON_COMMAND(ID_APP_EXIT, OnExit)
END_MESSAGE_MAP()

/////////////////////////////////////////////////////////////////////////////
// CWindow construction

CWindow::CWindow()
```

```
{
    LoadAccelTable(MAKEINTRESOURCE(IDR_MAINFRAME));
    Create( NULL, "ToolBar Control Sample",
    WS_OVERLAPPEDWINDOW,
    rectDefault, NULL, MAKEINTRESOURCE(IDR_MAINFRAME) );
    xForm.eM11 = 1.0;
    xForm.eM12 = 0.0;
    xForm.eM21 = 0.0;
    xForm.eM22 = 1.0;
    xForm.eDx  = 0.0;
    xForm.eDy  = 0.0;
    iCurrentTransform = ORIGINAL;
    iPreviousTransform = ORIGINAL;
```

The toolbar control is created by calling the **Create** method and passing the style, position, parent, and control ID. The toolbar control automatically sets the size and position of the toolbar window. The height is based on the height of the buttons in the toolbar. The width is the same as the width of the parent window's client area. Where the toolbar control is positioned is determined by the style CCS_TOP or CCS_BOTTOM, which places the control either at the top or bottom of the client area, respectively.

```
    m_cmdtoolbar.Create(WS_BORDER | WS_VISIBLE | WS_CHILD
            | CCS_TOP, CRect(0,0,0,0),this, IDR_CMDTOOLBAR);
    m_cmdtoolbar.AutoSize();
}


CApp theApp;

BOOL CApp::InitInstance()
{
    m_pMainWnd = new CWindow();
    m_pMainWnd -> ShowWindow( m_nCmdShow );
    m_pMainWnd -> UpdateWindow();
    return TRUE;
}


// Paint the window
void CWindow::OnPaint()
{
    CPaintDC dc(this);
    // Change the pen and the brush
    CPen pen(PS_SOLID, 2, RGB(255,0,0));
    CBrush brush(RGB(255,0,0));
    dc.SelectObject(&pen);
```

```
dc.SelectObject(&brush);

SetGraphicsMode(dc.GetSafeHdc(), GM_ADVANCED);
SetWorldTransform(dc.GetSafeHdc(), &xForm);
// Create the polygon

CPoint a[5];
a[0] = CPoint(80,200);
a[1] = CPoint(160,50);
a[2] = CPoint(240,200);
a[3] = CPoint(80,105);
a[4] = CPoint(240,105);
dc.SetPolyFillMode(ALTERNATE);
dc.Polygon(a, 5);
dc.Rectangle(80,220,240,300);
dc.Ellipse(90,190,230,215);

}
```

Whenever the window is resized, the toolbar should also be resized. To react to the change in size, the **WM_SIZE** message is handled through the **OnSize** function. The message map indicates this with the ON_WM_SIZE macro. This function checks to see that the window is minimized and resets the size of the toolbar control to fit to the new window size by calling the **AutoSize** method.

```
void CWindow::OnSize(UINT Type, INT x, INT y )
{
    if (Type != SIZE_MINIMIZED)
        m_cmdtoolbar.AutoSize();
}
```

The application allows you to select the transformation by means of a menu, an accelerator key, or the toolbar button. When the selection is made through the toolbar control button, the selection is depicted by a pressed button. To simulate this when the selection is made through the menu, the **CheckButton** function is called when processing the appropriate menu command. The command identifier and the checked state (TRUE) are passed to the **CheckButton** function.

```
void CWindow::OnOriginal()
{
    sAngle = 0;
    xForm.eM11 = 1.0;
    xForm.eM12 = 0.0;
    xForm.eM21 = 0.0;
```

```
    xForm.eM22 = 1.0;
    xForm.eDx   = 0.0;
    xForm.eDy   = 0.0;
    iPreviousTransform = iCurrentTransform;
    iCurrentTransform = ORIGINAL;
    UncheckMenu();
    CheckMenu();
    m_cmdtoolbar.CheckButton(IDM_ORIGINAL, TRUE);
    Invalidate(TRUE);
}
void CWindow::OnRotate()
{
    iPreviousTransform = iCurrentTransform;
    iCurrentTransform = ROTATE;
    UncheckMenu();
    CheckMenu();
    m_cmdtoolbar.CheckButton(IDM_ROTATE, TRUE);
}
```

Sometimes it is clearer to show text below the toolbar buttons (called *button labels*), particularly when the meaning of the bitmaps is not obvious. This text can easily be added by providing the text to appear below the bitmap in the toolbar button structure. Do not confuse button labels with tooltips. Button labels, when included, are always present. Tooltips are shown only when the mouse pointer pauses over the button bitmap. Also, the available space for button labels is somewhat restricted compared to tooltips. The **Create** function is modified to add this feature, and the change is highlighted below. An array of character buffer, which has the text that appears underneath the toolbar bitmap, is declared. The address of this string is given to **AddStrings**, which returns an integer that is given to the toolbar button structure.

```
BOOL CCmdToolBar::Create(DWORD dwStyle, const RECT& rect, CWnd* pParentWnd,
                         UINT nID )
{
    char ToolBarText[6][12] = {"Original\0", "Rotate\0", "Translate\0",
                               "Shear\0", "Reflect\0", "Scale\0"};
    BOOL bRet = CToolBarCtrl::Create(dwStyle, rect, pParentWnd, nID);
    m_nButtonCount = 6;
    AddBitmap(m_nButtonCount,IDR_CMDTOOLBAR);
    m_pTBButtons = new TBBUTTON[m_nButtonCount];

    for (int i = 0; i < m_nButtonCount; i++)
    {
```

```
        m_pTBButtons[i].iString = AddStrings(ToolBarText[i]);
        m_pTBButtons[i].fsState = TBSTATE_ENABLED;
        m_pTBButtons[i].fsStyle = TBSTYLE_BUTTON | TBSTYLE_CHECK |
                                  TBSTYLE_CHECKGROUP;
        m_pTBButtons[i].dwData = 0;
        m_pTBButtons[i].iBitmap = i;
        m_pTBButtons[i].idCommand = i + IDM_ORIGINAL;
    }
    AddButtons(m_nButtonCount,&m_pTBButtons[0]);
    return bRet;
}
```

Tooltips

A *tooltip* is a small text window that pops up when the mouse pointer pauses for about a second on a toolbar button (unless the mouse pointer was moved directly after displaying the tooltip of another button). The tooltip disappears when the mouse pointer is moved off the button. The text window typically displays a short description of the button. Tooltips enhance the user friendliness of your program, particularly if you opt to use a lot of icons that the users of your program may be unfamiliar with. To be consistent with Windows programming style, you may not want to wait for one second in your program, if the cursor was moved directly after displaying the tooltip of another button in the toolbar.

Tooltips can display static text windows, or you can dynamically change the text in the tooltip window based on the cursor position or selection. Figure 7-22 shows an example of a tooltip with static text. Figures 7-23 and 7-24 show examples of a tooltip where the text changes dynamically based on the cursor position or selection.

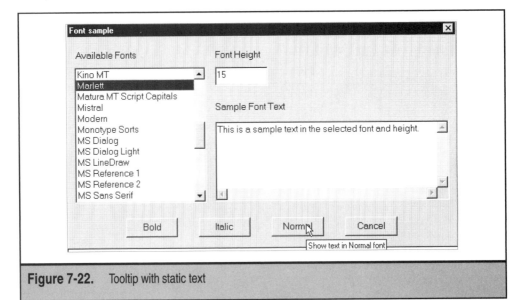

Figure 7-22. Tooltip with static text

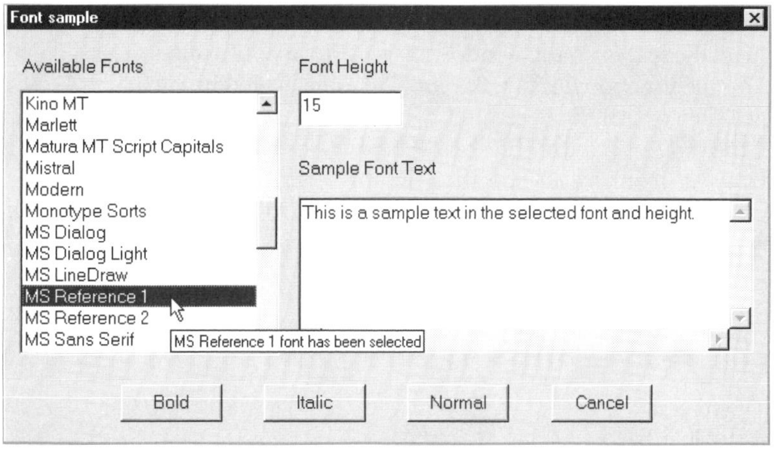

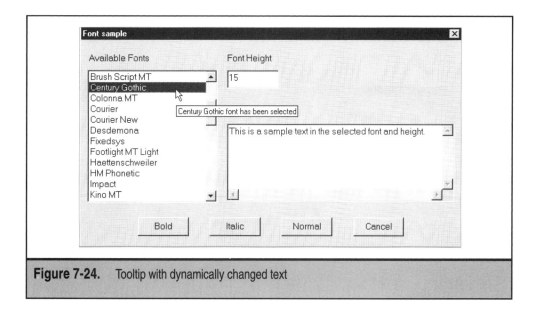

Figure 7-23. Tooltip with dynamically changing text

Tooltips for the buttons in the toolbar control can be added as follows. The toolbar control is created with the TBSTYLE_TOOLTIPS style. This style lets the toolbar create and manage a tooltip control. After specifying this style, the window should handle the tooltip notification message. The ON_NOTIFY_RANGE message macro is used to

Figure 7-24. Tooltip with dynamically changed text

process the tooltip notification. The TTN_NEEDTEXT notification code is associated with the **WM_NOTIFY** message. Thus, when the tooltip control needs to display a tooltip, it would request the text from the window by sending a notification message. This message is handled by the function **OnToolBarToolTip** as indicated in the ON_NOTIFY_RANGE macro. Since the control ID generated by the notification message is not guaranteed to be unique, the range of control ID should be set to between zero and the toolbar control ID. Based on the control ID specified in the notification message header structure **NMHDR**, the tooltip text is given to the tooltip control, which then displays it. Sections of the code added in *Wrldxform.cpp* to handle tooltips are highlighted next.

```cpp
// Define the window class
class CWindow : public CFrameWnd
{
private:
        CCmdToolBar m_cmdtoolbar;
public:
    CWindow();
    afx_msg void OnPaint();
    afx_msg void OnSize(UINT, INT, INT);
    afx_msg void OnKeyUp(UINT, UINT, UINT);
    afx_msg void OnAppAbout();
    afx_msg void OnOriginal();
    afx_msg void OnRotate();
    afx_msg void OnTranslate();
    afx_msg void OnShear();
    afx_msg void OnReflect();
    afx_msg void OnScale();
    afx_msg void OnToolBarToolTip(UINT nID, NMHDR * pNotifyStruct,
                                  LRESULT * lResult);
    afx_msg void OnExit();
    void UncheckMenu();
    void CheckMenu();
    DECLARE_MESSAGE_MAP()
};

// CWindow
BEGIN_MESSAGE_MAP(CWindow, CFrameWnd)
    ON_WM_PAINT()
    ON_WM_SIZE()
    ON_WM_KEYUP()
    ON_COMMAND(ID_APP_ABOUT, OnAppAbout)
```

```
    ON_COMMAND(IDM_ORIGINAL, OnOriginal)
    ON_COMMAND(IDM_ROTATE, OnRotate)
    ON_COMMAND(IDM_TRANSLATE, OnTranslate)
    ON_COMMAND(IDM_SHEAR, OnShear)
    ON_COMMAND(IDM_REFLECT, OnReflect)
    ON_COMMAND(IDM_SCALE, OnScale)
    ON_COMMAND(ID_APP_EXIT, OnExit)
    ON_NOTIFY_RANGE( TTN_NEEDTEXT, 0, IDR_CMDTOOLBAR, OnToolBarToolTip)
END_MESSAGE_MAP()


/////////////////////////////////////////////////////////////////////////////
// CWindow construction
CWindow::CWindow()
{
    LoadAccelTable(MAKEINTRESOURCE(IDR_MAINFRAME));
    Create( NULL, "ToolBar Control Sample",
    WS_OVERLAPPEDWINDOW,
    rectDefault, NULL, MAKEINTRESOURCE(IDR_MAINFRAME) );
    xForm.eM11 = 1.0;
    xForm.eM12 = 0.0;
    xForm.eM21 = 0.0;
    xForm.eM22 = 1.0;
    xForm.eDx  = 0.0;
    xForm.eDy  = 0.0;
    iCurrentTransform = ORIGINAL;
    iPreviousTransform = ORIGINAL;

        m_cmdtoolbar.Create(WS_BORDER | WS_VISIBLE | WS_CHILD
                        | CCS_TOP | CCS_ADJUSTABLE | TBSTYLE_TOOLTIPS,
                CRect(0,0,0,0),this, IDR_CMDTOOLBAR);
        m_cmdtoolbar.AutoSize();

}


void CWindow::OnToolBarToolTip(UINT nID, NMHDR * pNotifyStruct,
                               LRESULT * lResult )
{
    switch (pNotifyStruct->idFrom)
    {
    case IDM_ORIGINAL:
        ((TOOLTIPTEXT *)pNotifyStruct)->lpszText = "Original - Return to initial
```

```
                                                    settings";
            break;
        case IDM_ROTATE:
            ((TOOLTIPTEXT *)pNotifyStruct)->lpszText = "Rotate - Use Up/Down arrow
                                                        keys to rotate";
            break;
        case IDM_TRANSLATE:
            ((TOOLTIPTEXT *)pNotifyStruct)->lpszText = "Translate - Use
                                                        Up/Down/Left/Right arrow
                                                        keys to translate";
            break;
        case IDM_SHEAR:
            ((TOOLTIPTEXT *)pNotifyStruct)->lpszText = "Shear - Use
                                                        Up/Down/Left/Right arrow
                                                        keys to shear";
            break;
        case IDM_REFLECT:
            ((TOOLTIPTEXT *)pNotifyStruct)->lpszText = "Refelect - Use
                                                        Up/Down/Left/Right arrow
                                                        keys to reflect";
            break;
        case IDM_SCALE:
            ((TOOLTIPTEXT *)pNotifyStruct)->lpszText = "Scale - Use
                                                        Up/Down/Left/Right arrow
                                                        keys to scale";
            break;
    }

}
```

PROPERTY SHEETS

A *property sheet* allows the user to view and update properties associated with an item. A property sheet is used when an item's properties won't fit in one dialog box. In this case, you can use a series of dialog boxes, with each dialog box containing logically related properties. Each dialog box is a page or sheet of the item's properties and is identified and selected by a tab associated with it. A sample property sheet is shown in Figure 7-25.

You can consider a property sheet as being a collection of one or more child windows, each window being a modeless dialog box. That is, each page in a property sheet is defined by a dialog box template, and interaction with the page is handled by a dialog function. Each dialog box template is specified in your application's resource file.

All property sheets contain the OK and Cancel buttons at a minimum. Usually a third button, Apply, is also included. Depending on your application, a Help button may also

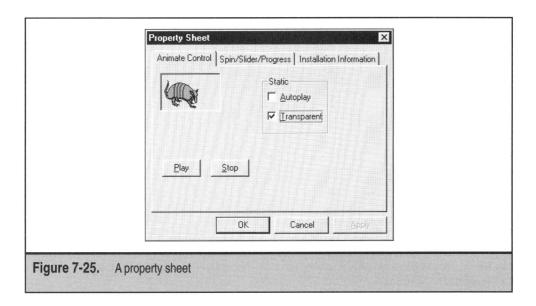

Figure 7-25.   A property sheet

be included. Keep in mind that the individual pages are just part of the overall property sheet. Items in one page of the property sheet may be related to items on another page, and the item settings on one page may affect another. Thus, you use the OK, Cancel, and Apply buttons at the overall property sheet level and not at the individual page level.

The dialog boxes that constitute the property sheet pages are part of the Property Sheet control. The Property Sheet control manages interaction with and between the individual pages. As a general rule, each dialog box function responds to its own controls in the normal fashion. That is, the individual controls that make up each page are handled in the standard way by the page's dialog box function. However, each page must also respond to messages generated by the enclosing property sheet.

A Property Sheet Programming Example

The *PropSheet* sample program shows how to use the property sheet by use of the **CPropertySheet** and **CPropertyPage** MFC library classes. The sample also shows how easy it is to convert a set of individual dialog boxes into property pages in a property sheet dialog box. To this end it takes the samples discussed earlier, *Animate* and *SpSlProg*, and a third dialog box as pages in a property sheet dialog box. When the program is run and the Property Sheet menu item is selected from the File menu, the property sheet dialog box with three tabs is displayed. When the information in the third dialog box is changed, the Apply button is enabled. When the OK button is clicked, a message box is displayed indicating the selection made in the third page.

The main program closely follows the structure discussed in earlier examples. Shown next is the code in the main section that is executed when the Property Sheet menu item is selected.

```
//////////////////////////////////////////////////////////////////
// CWindow commands
// App command to run the dialog

// Property Sheet Dialog selected
void CWindow::OnPropShDlg()
{
        CPropShDlg propshDlg("Property Sheet", this);
        propshDlg.DoModal();
}
```

Some trivial changes have been made to the *Animate* and *SpSlProg* dialog resources to suit this example. A third dialog box resource has been added, and this resource is shown next. This dialog box will form the third and last page of the property sheet. This page is a simple page which obtains path, drive, and version information selected by means of radio buttons.

```
IDD_INSTALLINFO DIALOG DISCARDABLE 0, 0, 185, 92
STYLE DS_MODALFRAME | WS_POPUP | WS_VISIBLE | WS_CAPTION | WS_SYSMENU
CAPTION "Installation Information"
FONT 8, "MS Sans Serif"
BEGIN
    LTEXT     "Path",IDC_STATIC,7,16,16,8
    LTEXT     "Drive",IDC_STATIC,7,32,18,8
    EDITTEXT  IDC_PATH,35,13,40,14,ES_AUTOHSCROLL
    EDITTEXT  IDC_DRIVE,36,31,40,14,ES_AUTOHSCROLL
    GROUPBOX  "Version",IDC_STATIC,93,7,64,54
    CONTROL   "Win95",IDC_95,"Button",BS_AUTORADIOBUTTON,102,18,39,10
    CONTROL   "Win NT",IDC_NT,"Button",BS_AUTORADIOBUTTON,102,30,41,10
END
```

The dialog captions appear as the default tab text for individual tabs. The code for the individual property page is very similar to the dialog box code that was discussed earlier. The difference is that instead of deriving the dialog from the **CDialog class**, the property pages are derived from **CPropertyPage**. The code for the last property page is shown next. As before, this code was generated with the aid of ClassWizard. The only thing to note here is that **CInstalInfoDlg** is derived from **CPropertyPage** instead of the usual **CDialog**.

```
// InstalInfoDlg.h : header file
//
// CInstalInfoDlg dialog
class CInstalInfoDlg : public CPropertyPage
```

```
{
        DECLARE_DYNCREATE(CInstalInfoDlg)
// Construction
public:
        CInstalInfoDlg();
        ~CInstalInfoDlg();

// Dialog Data
        //{{AFX_DATA(CInstalInfoDlg)
        enum { IDD = IDD_INSTALLINFO };
        CString m_drive;
        CString m_path;
        int     m_version;          // 0-Win95, 1 = WinNT
        //}}AFX_DATA
// Overrides
        // ClassWizard generate virtual function overrides
        //{{AFX_VIRTUAL(CInstalInfoDlg)
        public:
        virtual BOOL OnApply();
        protected:
        virtual void DoDataExchange(CDataExchange* pDX);// DDX/DDV
support
        //}}AFX_VIRTUAL

// Implementation
protected:
        // Generated message map functions
        //{{AFX_MSG(CInstalInfoDlg)
        afx_msg void OnPathChange();
        afx_msg void OnNt();
        afx_msg void On95();
        //}}AFX_MSG
        DECLARE_MESSAGE_MAP()
};
```

The code that implements the **CInstalInfoDlg** class is shown next:

```
// InstalInfoDlg.cpp : implementation file
//
#include <afxwin.h>
#include <afxdlgs.h>
#include <afxcmn.h>
#include "resource.h"
#include "InstalInfoDlg.h"
```

```
////
// CInstalInfoDlg property page

IMPLEMENT_DYNCREATE(CInstalInfoDlg, CPropertyPage)

CInstalInfoDlg::CInstalInfoDlg() : CPropertyPage(CInstalInfoDlg::IDD)
{
        //{{AFX_DATA_INIT(CInstalInfoDlg)
        m_drive = _T("");
        m_path = _T("");
        m_version = 0;
        //}}AFX_DATA_INIT
}
```

Apart from loading the resource, the constructor does some initialization of the member variables.

```
CInstalInfoDlg::~CInstalInfoDlg()
{
}


void CInstalInfoDlg::DoDataExchange(CDataExchange* pDX)
{
        CPropertyPage::DoDataExchange(pDX);
        //{{AFX_DATA_MAP(CInstalInfoDlg)
        DDX_Text(pDX, IDC_DRIVE, m_drive);
        DDV_MaxChars(pDX, m_drive, 1);
        DDX_Text(pDX, IDC_PATH, m_path);
        DDV_MaxChars(pDX, m_path, 32);
        //}}AFX_DATA_MAP
}
```

Unlike earlier samples, the dialog data exchange is done at the text level, and dialog data validation is done for both Edit controls for the number of characters that can be entered. Here the Drive Edit control is set to accept only one character, and the Path Edit control is set to accept 32 characters.

```
BEGIN_MESSAGE_MAP(CInstalInfoDlg, CPropertyPage)
        //{{AFX_MSG_MAP(CInstalInfoDlg)
        ON_EN_CHANGE(IDC_PATH, OnPathChange)
        ON_BN_CLICKED(IDC_NT, OnNt)
```

```
        ON_BN_CLICKED(IDC_95, On95)
        //}}AFX_MSG_MAP
END_MESSAGE_MAP()
//////////////////////////////////////////////////////////////////////
// CInstalInfoDlg message handlers

void CInstalInfoDlg::OnPathChange()
{
        // TODO: Add your control notification handler code here
        SetModified(TRUE);      // This page has been modified
}

void CInstalInfoDlg::OnNt()
{
        // TODO: Add your control notification handler code here
        m_version = 1;
        SetModified(TRUE);      // This page has been modified
}

void CInstalInfoDlg::On95()
{
        // TODO: Add your control notification handler code here
        m_version = 0;
        SetModified(TRUE);      // This page has been modified
}
```

The property sheet has OK, Cancel, and Apply buttons. It is the responsibility of the individual property page to inform the property sheet whether data inside the page has changed. When a property page becomes "dirty" (the user has made changes to the property page), it can indicate this fact to the property sheet by calling the **SetModified** member function and passing a value of TRUE. In the code earlier, whenever the Path, Drive, or Version radio buttons are changed, it indicates that the page has become dirty by calling **SetModified**.

The **OnApply** member function, which is overridden here, is called by the framework when the user chooses the OK or the Apply button. When these buttons are clicked, the **OnApply** method is called only for those pages that are dirty. Again a page can indicate that it is dirty by calling the **SetModified** member function and passing a value of TRUE. In the code next, it displays a message box indicating the selection made in the page and resets the dirty page by calling **SetModified** and passing a value of FALSE. It also returns TRUE to accept changes. Return FALSE to prevent changes from taking effect.

```
BOOL CInstalInfoDlg::OnApply()
{
        // TODO: Add your specialized code here and/or call the base class
        // UpdateData() would have been called automatically by the framework
        CString     message;
        message = m_drive + ":\\" + m_path;
        if (m_version == 1)
        {
            message = "NT Version to be installed at " + message;
        }
        else
        {
            message = "Win95 Version to be installed at " + message;
        }
        AfxMessageBox(message);
        SetModified(FALSE);
        return CPropertyPage::OnApply();
}
```

So far the property page has been discussed. Shown next is the code for the Property Sheet dialog box, which derives from **CPropertySheet**. For each page in the property sheet a member variable is defined that corresponds to the respective dialog class.

```
//////////////////////////////////////////////////////////////////////
// CPropShDlg

#include "AnimateDlg.h"
#include "SpSlProgDlg.h"
#include "InstalInfoDlg.h"

class CPropShDlg : public CPropertySheet
{
        DECLARE_DYNAMIC(CPropShDlg)

// Construction
public:
        CPropShDlg(LPCTSTR pszCaption, CWnd* pParentWnd = NULL, UINT iSelectPage = 0);

// Attributes
public:

        CAnimateDlg        m_animatedlg;
        CSpSlProgDlg       m_spslprogdlg;
```

```
        CInstalInfoDlg     m_installinfodlg;

// Operations
public:

// Overrides
        // ClassWizard generated virtual function overrides
        //{{AFX_VIRTUAL(CPropShDlg)
        //}}AFX_VIRTUAL

// Implementation
public:
        virtual ~CPropShDlg();
        virtual BOOL OnInitDialog();
        virtual void OnOK();

// Generated message map functions
protected:

        DECLARE_MESSAGE_MAP()
};
```

The code that implements this class is shown next. During construction of the class, the three pages are added to the property sheet by use of the **AddPage** method. Though it is defaulted here to the first page, the property sheet can be initialized such that any page is seen on top when the property sheet is shown.

```
// PropShDlg.cpp : implementation file
//
#include <afxwin.h>
#include <afxdlgs.h>
#include <afxcmn.h>
#include "resource.h"
#include "PropShDlg.h"


/////////////////////////////////////////////////////////////////////
// CPropShDlg

IMPLEMENT_DYNAMIC(CPropShDlg, CPropertySheet)

CPropShDlg::CPropShDlg(LPCTSTR pszCaption, CWnd* pParentWnd, UINT iSelectPage)
        :CPropertySheet(pszCaption, pParentWnd, iSelectPage)
{
        AddPage(&m_animatedlg);
```

```
                AddPage(&m_spslprogdlg);
                AddPage(&m_installinfodlg);
}


CPropShDlg::~CPropShDlg()
{
}


BEGIN_MESSAGE_MAP(CPropShDlg,        CPropertySheet)
           //{{AFX_MSG_MAP(CPropShDlg)
           //}}AFX_MSG_MAP
END_MESSAGE_MAP()


////////////////////////////////////////////////////////////////////
/////
//  CPropShDlg  message  handlers

BOOL    CPropShDlg::OnInitDialog()
{
           return  CPropertySheet::OnInitDialog();
}


void    CPropShDlg::OnOK()
{
     AfxMessageBox("The  results  are  ");
}
```

Many of the software installation programs display a series of dialog panels one after the other within the same dialog frame, giving the user the ability to go to a previous page or to proceed to the next page. This is accomplished through the Property Sheet dialog box by setting it to wizard mode. Call **SetWizardMode** before calling **DoModal**. The buttons that appear can also be customized by calling **SetWizardButtons**. Notice that when running in wizard mode, **DoModal** will return ID_WIZFINISH if the user closes with the Finish button or IDCANCEL.

TREE VIEW CONTROL

Tree View controls use a tree structure to display information. For example, the file list used by Windows NT's Explorer is an example of a Tree View control. Because trees imply a hierarchy, Tree View controls are typically used to display hierarchical information. Tree View controls support a large number of different options. Each item in the tree can have associated images (bitmaps) or text that is displayed to the user when the Tree View control is displayed (see Figure 7-26).

The Tree View control uses the **TV_INSERTSTRUCT** and **TV_ITEM** data structures shown next. These structures are used in the example.

```
typedef struct _TV_INSERTSTRUCT {   HTREEITEM hParent;
                                    HTREEITEM hInsertAfter;
                                    TV_ITEM item;

} TV_INSERTSTRUCT;

typedef struct _TV_ITEM {
  UINT mask;
  HTREEITEM hItem;
  UINT state;
  UINT stateMask;
  LPSTR pszText;
  int cchTextMax;
  int iImage;
  int iSelectedImage;
  int cChildren;
  LPARAM lParam;
} TV_ITEM;
```

Here, the values in *mask* determine which of the other members of **TV_ITEM** contain valid data when this structure receives information from the Tree View control.

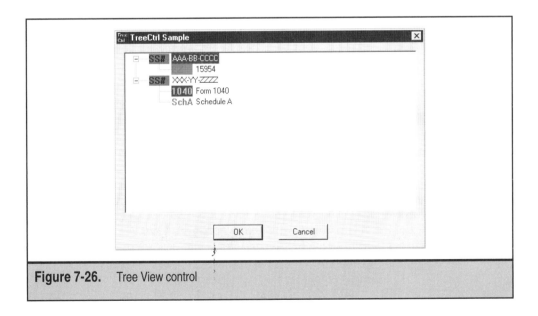

Figure 7-26. Tree View control

The values that it may contain are shown here:

Mask Value	Meaning
TVIF_HANDLE	*hItem* contains data
TVIF_STATE	*state* and *stateMask* contain data
TVIF_TEXT	*pszText* and *cchTextMax* contain data
TVIF_IMAGE	*iImage* contains data
TVIF_SELECTEDIMAGE	*iSelectedImage* contains data
TVIF_CHILDREN	*cChildren* contains data
TVIF_LPARAM	*lParam* contains data

The *state* member contains the state of the Tree View control. Here are some common tree *state* values:

State Value	Meaning
TVIS_DROPHILITED	The item is highlighted as the target of drag/drop operation.
TVIS_EXPANDED	The branch descending from the item is fully expanded (applies to parent items only).
TVIS_EXPANDEDONCE	The branch descending from the item is expanded one (or more) levels (applies to parent items only).
TVIS_SELECTED	The item is selected.

The *stateMask* variable determines which tab state to set or obtain. It will also be one or more of the preceding values.

When an item is being inserted into the tree, *pszText* points to the string that will be displayed in the tree. When information about an item is being obtained, *pszText* must point to an array that will receive its text. In this case, the value of *cchTextMax* specifies the size of the array pointed to by *pszText*. Otherwise, *cchTextMax* is ignored.

If there is an image list associated with the Tree View control, then *iImage* will contain the index of the image associated with the item when it is not selected. *iImageSelected* contains the index of the image used by the item when it is selected.

cChildren will contain 1 if the item has child items and zero if it does not.

lParam contains application-defined data.

A Tree View Control Programming Example

The TreeCtrl sample program shows how to use the Tree View control by use of the **CTreeCtrl** MFC library class. The sample is a dialog-based application that displays a dialog box with a Tree View control inside. It takes a tax filing example, where it displays two tax filers—one filing a 1040EZ and the other filing the long form 1040 and a Schedule A form. Each person is identified by his or her social security number. When the application starts, it displays two icons—one for each taxpayer. They are identified by their social security number. When these icons are expanded by clicking on them, they show their respective tax returns. These icons can also be opened by double-clicking, which then displays the details of the icons selected. For example, if the 1040EZ icon were opened, it would show the details of the 1040EZ form, and so on. Changes could be made to the forms and saved.

This hierarchical structure exists in many business applications. For instance, it could be employed in user administration in a LAN environment, where users and groups could be represented this way, or an organization chart could be represented this way.

The template code for this sample was generated by use of AppWizard and ClassWizard. The main application code is slightly different from the earlier samples that we saw. Here the dialog box containing the Tree View control is created and assigned as the main window for the application. The main application class header file and the class implementation code are shown next. You can ignore some of the details that were added by the AppWizard.

```
// TreeCtrl.h : main header file for the TREECTRL application
//
#ifndef __AFXWIN_H__
    #error include 'stdafx.h' before including this file for PCH
#endif
#include "resource.h"        // main symbols
/////////////////////////////////////////////////////////////////////////
// CApp:
// See TreeCtrl.cpp for the implementation of this class
//
class CApp : public CWinApp
{
public:
    CApp();
// Overrides
    // ClassWizard generated virtual function overrides
    //{{AFX_VIRTUAL(CApp)
    public:
    virtual BOOL InitInstance();
    //}}AFX_VIRTUAL
// Implementation
```

```cpp
    //{{AFX_MSG(CApp)
        // NOTE-the ClassWizard will add and remove member functions here.
        //      DO NOT EDIT what you see in these blocks of generated code!
    //}}AFX_MSG
    DECLARE_MESSAGE_MAP()
};

// TreeCtrl.cpp : Defines the class behaviors for the application.
//
#include "stdafx.h"
#include "TreeCtrl.h"
#include "TreeCtrlDlg.h"

#ifdef _DEBUG
#define new DEBUG_NEW
#undef THIS_FILE
static char THIS_FILE[] = __FILE__;
#endif

/////////////////////////////////////////////////////////////////////////////
// CApp

BEGIN_MESSAGE_MAP(CApp, CWinApp)
    //{{AFX_MSG_MAP(CApp)
        // NOTE-the ClassWizard will add and remove mapping macros here.
        //      DO NOT EDIT what you see in these blocks of generated code!
    //}}AFX_MSG
    ON_COMMAND(ID_HELP, CWinApp::OnHelp)
END_MESSAGE_MAP()

/////////////////////////////////////////////////////////////////////////////
// CApp construction

CApp::CApp()
{
    // TODO: add construction code here,
    // Place all significant initialization in InitInstance
}

/////////////////////////////////////////////////////////////////////////////
// The one and only CApp object

CApp theApp;
```

```
///////////////////////////////////////////////////////////////////////////
// CApp initialization

BOOL CApp::InitInstance()
{
    // Standard initialization
    // If you are not using these features and wish to reduce the size
    //  of your final executable, you should remove from the following
    //  the specific initialization routines you do not need.

#ifdef _AFXDLL
    Enable3dControls();              // Call this when using MFC in a shared DLL
#else
    Enable3dControlsStatic();     // Call this when linking to MFC statically
#endif

    CTreeCtrlDlg dlg;
    m_pMainWnd = &dlg;
    int nResponse = dlg.DoModal();
```

The code creates the Tree View control dialog box and assigns it as the application's main window. It then runs the dialog modally. In this sample it does not do much when the dialog box is closed. But if, for example, the data were loaded from a database, then you may want to commit the data to the database, depending on what the user selected in the dialog box.

```
if (nResponse == IDOK)
    {
        // TODO: Place code here to handle when the dialog is
        //  dismissed with OK
    }
    else if (nResponse == IDCANCEL)
    {
        // TODO: Place code here to handle when the dialog is
        //  dismissed with Cancel
    }

    // Since the dialog has been closed, return FALSE so that we exit the
    //  application, rather than start the application's message pump.
    return FALSE;
}
```

The dialog resource for the dialog box is given next. Notice that the style of the Tree View control is specified right in the resource. It indicates that the Tree View control has lines linking the child items to the parent items, has lines linking child items to the root of the hierarchy, and adds a button to the left of each parent item. These styles can be modified and rebuilt. These styles can also be set dynamically.

```
IDD_TREECTRL_DIALOG DIALOGEX 0, 0, 311, 185
STYLE DS_MODALFRAME | WS_POPUP | WS_VISIBLE | WS_CAPTION | WS_SYSMENU
EXSTYLE WS_EX_APPWINDOW
CAPTION "TreeCtrl Sample"
FONT 8, "MS Sans Serif", 0, 0, 0x1
BEGIN
    DEFPUSHBUTTON    "OK",IDOK,97,164,50,14
    PUSHBUTTON       "Cancel",IDCANCEL,163,164,50,14
    CONTROL          "Tree1",IDC_TREE,"SysTreeView32",WS_BORDER | WS_TABSTOP |
                     TVS_HASLINES | TVS_LINESATROOT | TVS_HASBUTTONS |
                     TVS_DISABLEDRAGDROP, 7,7,297,147
END
```

The **CTreeCtrlDlg** class declaration is shown next. This is similar to samples that were seen earlier.

```
// TreeCtrlDlg.h : header file
//
/////////////////////////////////////////////////////////////////////////////
// CTreeCtrlDlg dialog
class CTreeCtrlDlg : public CDialog
{
// Construction
public:
    CTreeCtrlDlg(CWnd* pParent = NULL);    // standard constructor

// Dialog Data
    //{{AFX_DATA(CTreeCtrlDlg)
    enum { IDD = IDD_TREECTRL_DIALOG };
    CTreeCtrl    m_treectrl;
    //}}AFX_DATA

    // ClassWizard generated virtual function overrides
    //{{AFX_VIRTUAL(CTreeCtrlDlg)
    protected:
    virtual void DoDataExchange(CDataExchange* pDX);    // DDX/DDV support
    //}}AFX_VIRTUAL

// Implementation
protected:
```

```
    HICON m_hIcon;

    // Generated message map functions
    //{{AFX_MSG(CTreeCtrlDlg)
    virtual BOOL OnInitDialog();
    afx_msg void OnSysCommand(UINT nID, LPARAM lParam);
    afx_msg void OnPaint();
    afx_msg HCURSOR OnQueryDragIcon();
    afx_msg void OnDblclkTree(NMHDR* pNMHDR, LRESULT* pResult);
    afx_msg void OnDestroy();
    void FreeItem(HTREEITEM hTVItem);
    //}}AFX_MSG
    DECLARE_MESSAGE_MAP()
private:
    void AddDataToTree(HTREEITEM hParent, int iType, char * pszText,
    LPARAM lpItemData, HTREEITEM *it);
};
```

The code for the **CTreeCtrlDlg** is shown next. The initial section of the code deals with information needed in the rest of the code like the **#define**s, the processing of the About box, and so on.

```
// TreeCtrlDlg.cpp : implementation file
//
#include "stdafx.h"
#include "TreeCtrl.h"
#include "TreeCtrlDlg.h"
#include "resource.h"
#include "TaxData.h"
#include "TaxPayer.h"
#include "Tax1040.h"
#include "EZ1040.h"
#include "SchA.h"


#ifdef _DEBUG
#define new DEBUG_NEW
#undef THIS_FILE
static char THIS_FILE[] = __FILE__;
#endif


#define BASE_BITMAP_ID  IDB_BITMAP1
#define TAXPAYER     0
#define FORMSTD      1
```

```
#define FORMSCHA      2
#define FORMEZ        3


/////////////////////////////////////////////////////////////////////
/////
// CAboutDlg dialog used for App About

class CAboutDlg : public CDialog
{
public:
        CAboutDlg();

// Dialog Data
        //{{AFX_DATA(CAboutDlg)
        enum { IDD = IDD_ABOUTBOX };
        //}}AFX_DATA

          // ClassWizard generated virtual function overrides
          //{{AFX_VIRTUAL(CAboutDlg)
        protected:
          virtual void DoDataExchange(CDataExchange* pDX);      // DDX/DDV
support
        //}}AFX_VIRTUAL

//   Implementation
protected:
        //{{AFX_MSG(CAboutDlg)
        //}}AFX_MSG
        DECLARE_MESSAGE_MAP()
};

CAboutDlg::CAboutDlg()    :    CDialog(CAboutDlg::IDD)
{
        //{{AFX_DATA_INIT(CAboutDlg)
        //}}AFX_DATA_INIT
}


void   CAboutDlg::DoDataExchange(CDataExchange*   pDX)
{
        CDialog::DoDataExchange(pDX);
      //{{AFX_DATA_MAP(CAboutDlg)
      //}}AFX_DATA_MAP
}
```

```
BEGIN_MESSAGE_MAP(CAboutDlg, CDialog)
        //{{AFX_MSG_MAP(CAboutDlg)
                // No message handlers
        //}}AFX_MSG_MAP
END_MESSAGE_MAP()


/////////////////////////////////////////////////////////////////////////////
// CTreeCtrlDlg dialog

CTreeCtrlDlg::CTreeCtrlDlg(CWnd* pParent /*=NULL*/)
        : CDialog(CTreeCtrlDlg::IDD, pParent)
{
        //{{AFX_DATA_INIT(CTreeCtrlDlg)
        // NOTE: the ClassWizard will add member initialization here
        //}}AFX_DATA_INIT
        // Note that LoadIcon does not require a subsequent
        // DestroyIcon in Win32
        m_hIcon = AfxGetApp()->LoadIcon(IDR_MAINFRAME);
}



void CTreeCtrlDlg::DoDataExchange(CDataExchange* pDX)
{
        CDialog::DoDataExchange(pDX);
        //{{AFX_DATA_MAP(CTreeCtrlDlg)
        DDX_Control(pDX, IDC_TREE, m_treectrl);
        //}}AFX_DATA_MAP
}


BEGIN_MESSAGE_MAP(CTreeCtrlDlg, CDialog)
        //{{AFX_MSG_MAP(CTreeCtrlDlg)
        ON_WM_SYSCOMMAND()
        ON_WM_PAINT()
        ON_WM_QUERYDRAGICON()
        ON_NOTIFY(NM_DBLCLK, IDC_TREE, OnDblclkTree)
        ON_WM_DESTROY()
    //}}AFX_MSG_MAP
END_MESSAGE_MAP()


/////////////////////////////////////////////////////////////////////////////
// CTreeCtrlDlg message handlers
```

The code that follows does the initialization on the **CTreeCtrlDlg** dialog box. Since this sample is a dialog-based application, the About menu item is added to the system menu. The advantage of code generation by use of AppWizard is that the code is automatically generated for the user.

During initialization the program creates various objects that are to be placed in the Tree View control. In this sample these objects are created and given to the Tree View control. In practical applications these objects would likely be queried from a database and created. Five objects of four kinds are created and their data is initialized.

```
BOOL CTreeCtrlDlg::OnInitDialog()
{
        CDialog::OnInitDialog();

        // Add "About..." menu item to system menu.
        // IDM_ABOUTBOX must be in the system command range.
        ASSERT((IDM_ABOUTBOX & 0xFFF0) == IDM_ABOUTBOX);
        ASSERT(IDM_ABOUTBOX < 0xF000);

        CMenu* pSysMenu = GetSystemMenu(FALSE);
        CString strAboutMenu;
        strAboutMenu.LoadString(IDS_ABOUTBOX);
        if (!strAboutMenu.IsEmpty())
        {
                pSysMenu->AppendMenu(MF_SEPARATOR);
                pSysMenu->AppendMenu(MF_STRING, IDM_ABOUTBOX, strAboutMenu);
        }

        // Set the icon for this dialog.  The framework does this automatically
        //  when the application's main window is not a dialog
        SetIcon(m_hIcon, TRUE);                    // Set big icon
        SetIcon(m_hIcon, FALSE);                   // Set small icon

        // TODO: Add extra initialization here
```

This program defines a set of structures to maintain the information about individual taxpayers and individual forms. **TaxPayerStruct** has information about the taxpayer's name and social security number. **EZStruct** has information filed in the 1040EZ form, **StdStruct** has information filed in the standard 1040 tax form, and **SchAStruct** has information filed in the Schedule A form.

```
        // Set up taxpayers data.
        PTaxPayerStruct pJohn, pKate;
        PEZStruct        pJohnEZ;
```

```
PStdStruct          pKateStd;
PSchAStruct         pKateSchA;

pJohn = new TaxPayerStruct;
pKate = new TaxPayerStruct;
pJohnEZ = new EZStruct;
pKateStd = new StdStruct;
pKateSchA = new SchAStruct;

strcpy(pJohn->szName, "John");
strcpy(pJohn->szSSN, "AAA-BB-CCCC");
strcpy(pJohnEZ->szTotalIncome, "49875");
strcpy(pJohnEZ->szTotalTax, "15954");
strcpy(pKate->szName, "Kate");
strcpy(pKate->szSSN, "XXX-YY-ZZZZ");
strcpy(pKateStd->szTotalIncome, "64851");
strcpy(pKateStd->szTotalDeduction, "14175");
strcpy(pKateStd->szTotalTax, "13169");
strcpy(pKateSchA->szRealEstateDeduction, "9175");
strcpy(pKateSchA->szOtherDeductions, "5000");
```

Every tree view item can be associated with two images, one for the selected state and the other for the regular state. These images are loaded, added to an image list, and the image list is given to the Tree View control. The indices of the images in this image list can later be referenced when a tree view item is inserted into the Tree View control. In this sample the same image is used for both selected state and regular state. The tree view items are added to the Tree View control by use of the **AddDataToTree( )** function. The individual tax returns are added as children of the respective taxpayer.

```
// Set up the Tree View control related data
CImageList       *pImageList;
CBitmap          bitmap;
pImageList = new CImageList();
pImageList->Create(32, 16, TRUE, 4, 2);
// Load the bitmaps into the imagelist.
for (int  i = 0; i<4; i++)
{
        bitmap.LoadBitmap(BASE_BITMAP_ID + i);
        pImageList->Add(&bitmap, (COLORREF)0xFFFFFF);
        bitmap.DeleteObject();
}
m_treectrl.SetImageList(pImageList, TVSIL_NORMAL);
```

```
// Start inserting the taxpayers and their info in the Tree View control.
        HTREEITEM hTreeItem, hParentItem;
```

To each tree view item, 32-bit application-defined data can be attached inside the tree view item's attribute structure **TV_ITEM**. This data can be used by the application for its own advantage. In this sample the data associated with each object is in a structure, and a pointer to this structure, essentially data associated with an individual tree view item, is stored in the 32-bit application-defined data. This 32-bit data will be retrieved later by getting the item's attribute and then used to get information about the object itself.

```
        AddDataToTree(NULL, TAXPAYER, pJohn->szSSN, (LPARAM)pJohn, &hTreeItem);
        hParentItem = hTreeItem;
        AddDataToTree(hParentItem, FORMEZ, pJohnEZ->szTotalTax, (LPARAM)pJohnEZ,
                &hTreeItem);
        AddDataToTree(NULL, TAXPAYER, pKate->szSSN, (LPARAM)pKate, &hTreeItem);
        hParentItem = hTreeItem;
        AddDataToTree(hParentItem, FORMSTD, "Form 1040", (LPARAM)pKateStd,
                &hTreeItem);
        AddDataToTree(hParentItem, FORMSCHA, "Schedule A", (LPARAM)pKateSchA,
                &hTreeItem);
        return TRUE; // return TRUE unless you set the focus to a control
}


void CTreeCtrlDlg::OnSysCommand(UINT nID, LPARAM lParam)
{
        if ((nID & 0xFFF0) == IDM_ABOUTBOX)
        {
                CAboutDlg dlgAbout;
                dlgAbout.DoModal();
        }
        else
        {
                CDialog::OnSysCommand(nID, lParam);
        }
}


// If you add a minimize button to your dialog, you will need the code below
//  to draw the icon.  For MFC applications using the document/view model,
//  this is automatically done for you by the framework.

void CTreeCtrlDlg::OnPaint()
```

```
{
        if (IsIconic())
        {
                CPaintDC dc(this); // device context for painting

                SendMessage(WM_ICONERASEBKGND, (WPARAM) dc.GetSafeHdc(), 0);

                // Center icon in client rectangle
                int cxIcon = GetSystemMetrics(SM_CXICON);
                int cyIcon = GetSystemMetrics(SM_CYICON);
                CRect rect;
                GetClientRect(&rect);
                int x = (rect.Width()-cxIcon + 1) / 2;
                int y = (rect.Height()-cyIcon + 1) / 2;

                // Draw the icon
                dc.DrawIcon(x, y, m_hIcon);
        }
        else
        {
                CDialog::OnPaint();
        }
}


// The system calls this to obtain the cursor to display while the user drags
//   the minimized window.
HCURSOR CTreeCtrlDlg::OnQueryDragIcon()
{
        return (HCURSOR) m_hIcon;
}
```

The functions **OnSysCommand**, **OnPaint**, and **OnQueryDragIcon** are generated by the AppWizard and would meet the needs of this sample. When the user double-clicks on the tree view item, the details of the item are displayed in a dialog box. The dialog box allows the user to change the information and save it. The double-click is processed by the following section of code. The selected Tree View item is queried, and based on its image information, the type of item is identified. From the Tree View item's attribute the application data is retrieved and passed on to the respective dialog boxes. The code dealing with these dialog boxes shows how this data is used.

```
void CTreeCtrlDlg::OnDblclkTree(NMHDR* pNMHDR, LRESULT* pResult)
{
        // TODO: Add your control notification handler code here
        HTREEITEM    hSelectedItem;
```

```
      hSelectedItem = m_treectrl.GetSelectedItem();

TV_ITEM    tvItem;
tvItem.hItem = hSelectedItem;
tvItem.mask = TVIF_HANDLE | TVIF_IMAGE | TVIF_PARAM;
m_treectrl.GetItem(&tvItem);

switch (tvItem.iImage)
{
case TAXPAYER:
    {
        // Do other processing if needed.
        PTaxPayerStruct pTaxPayer = (PTaxPayerStruct) tvItem.lParam;
        TaxPayer    tp(NULL, pTaxPayer);
```

The dialog box is created and is run modally. When the dialog box terminates, the information on the screen is updated to reflect any change that the user would have made. Similar processing is done for all the other types of tree view items.

```
        if(tp.DoModal() == IDOK)
         {
            m_treectrl.SetItem(hSelectedItem, TVIF_TEXT,
                               pTaxPayer->szSSN,0,0,0,0,0);
         }
    }
    break;

case FORMSTD:
    {
        // Do other processing if needed.
        PStdStruct pStd = (PStdStruct) tvItem.lParam;
        Tax1040    tp(NULL, pStd);
        tp.DoModal();
    }
    break;

case FORMSCHA:
    {
        // Do other processing if needed.
        PSchAStruct pSchA = (PSchAStruct) tvItem.lParam;
        SchA    tp(NULL, pSchA);
        tp.DoModal();
    }
    break;
```

```
      case FORMEZ:
          {
              // Do other processing if needed.
              PEZStruct pEZ = (PEZStruct) tvItem.lParam;
              EZ1040    tp(NULL, pEZ);
              tp.DoModal();
          }
          break;

      }

      *pResult = 1;
}
```

Notice that the value pointed to by **pResult** is set to 1. This specifies to the MFC library class that the message has been processed and nothing else needs to be done. Returning a zero will cause the MFC library class to process the message, yielding a result similar to that obtained by clicking on the buttons on the left of the root items.

To add an item to a Tree View control, a **TV_INSERTSTRUCT** is created and the three pieces of information that it needs—the parent to this item, order of insertion, and the item's attribute in **TV_ITEM**—are supplied. Based on the item type, the image for the item and its image when selected are set. In this case both are assumed to be the same image. The parent for this item is set, and the order of insertion is indicated to be TVI_SORT, sorted order. Other possible orders are TVI_FIRST, which inserts the item at the beginning of the list, and TVI_LAST, which inserts the item at the end of the list. The item's attribute should be set in a **TV_ITEM** structure. The text to appear at the bottom of the item image and application specific data are set. The **InsertItem** method inserts the tree view item into the Tree View control.

```
void CTreeCtrlDlg::AddDataToTree(HTREEITEM hParent, int iType, char *
pszText, LPARAM lpItemData, HTREEITEM *it)
{
    TV_INSERTSTRUCT tvistruct;
    if (iType == TAXPAYER)
    {
        tvistruct.item.iImage = 0;
        tvistruct.item.iSelectedImage = 0;
    }
    else if (iType == FORMSTD)
    {
        tvistruct.item.iImage = 1;
        tvistruct.item.iSelectedImage = 1;
    }
```

```
    else if (iType == FORMSCHA)
    {
        tvistruct.item.iImage = 2;
        tvistruct.item.iSelectedImage = 2;
    }
    else if (iType == FORMEZ)
    {
        tvistruct.item.iImage = 3;
        tvistruct.item.iSelectedImage = 3;
    }
    tvistruct.hParent = hParent;
    tvistruct.hInsertAfter = TVI_SORT;
    tvistruct.item.pszText = pszText;
    tvistruct.item.mask = TVIF_IMAGE | TVIF_SELECTEDIMAGE | TVIF_TEXT |
                          TVIF_PARAM;
    tvistruct.item.lParam = lpItemData;
    *it = m_treectrl.InsertItem (&tvistruct);
}


void CTreeCtrlDlg::OnDestroy()
{
    CDialog::OnDestroy();

    // TODO: Add your message handler code here
    CImageList    *pImageList;
    pImageList = m_treectrl.GetImageList(TVSIL_NORMAL);
    delete pImageList;
    HTREEITEM    hTVItemRoot, hTVItemChild;
    hTVItemRoot = m_treectrl.GetRootItem();

    do
    {
        FreeItem(hTVItemRoot);
        if (m_treectrl.ItemHasChildren(hTVItemRoot))
        {
            hTVItemChild = m_treectrl.GetChildItem(hTVItemRoot);
            do
            {
                FreeItem(hTVItemChild);
            } while(hTVItemChild = m_treectrl.GetNextSiblingItem(hTVItemChild));
        }
    } while (hTVItemRoot = m_treectrl.GetNextSiblingItem(hTVItemRoot));

}
```

Notice that during creation of tree view items, memory was allocated to hold information about the taxpayer and the individual tax forms. We also allocated resources for the bitmap. These resources have to be freed when the application terminates. This is done when the **CTreeCtrlDlg** class is destroyed. The code starts from the root, and for every item at the root level, it frees the resources associated with the root item and proceeds until all the resources for all its second-level children are freed. It assumes that there are only two levels. It uses the FreeItem member functions to free a given Tree View item.

```cpp
void CTreeCtrlDlg::FreeItem (HTREEITEM hTVItem)
{
    TV_ITEM    tvItem;
    tvItem.hItem = hTVItem;
    tvItem.mask = TVIF_HANDLE | TVIF_IMAGE | TVIF_PARAM;
    m_treectrl.GetItem(&tvItem);
    switch (tvItem.iImage)
    {
    case TAXPAYER:
        {
            // Do other processing if needed.
            PTaxPayerStruct pTaxPayer = (PTaxPayerStruct) tvItem.lParam;
            delete pTaxPayer;
        }
        break;

    case FORMSTD:
        {
            // Do other processing if needed.
            PStdStruct pStd = (PStdStruct) tvItem.lParam;
            delete pStd;
        }
        break;
    case FORMSCHA:
        {
            // Do other processing if needed.
            PSchAStruct pSchA = (PSchAStruct) tvItem.lParam;
            delete pSchA;
        }
        break;
    case FORMEZ:
        {
            // Do other processing if needed.
            PEZStruct pEZ = (PEZStruct) tvItem.lParam;
```

```
            delete pEZ;
        }
        break;
    }


}
```

The code that actually processes the dialog box when the user double-clicks on the taxpayer item is shown next. This is standard dialog box processing, except that during construction of the dialog, the information associated with the item is passed and is saved in a private member data. The relevant information here is in boldface. The code for processing the 1040, EZ, and SchA items is similar to this.

```
#if
!defined(AFX_TAXPAYER_H__16A0A280_B455_11D0_9768_0004ACB5DCC1__INCLUDED_)
#define AFX_TAXPAYER_H__16A0A280_B455_11D0_9768_0004ACB5DCC1__INCLUDED_

#if _MSC_VER >= 1000
#pragma once
#endif // _MSC_VER >= 1000
// TaxPayer.h : header file
//


/////////////////////////////////////////////////////////////////////////////
// TaxPayer dialog

class TaxPayer : public CDialog
{
// Construction
public:
        TaxPayer(CWnd* pParent = NULL, PTaxPayerStruct pData = NULL);
// standard constructor

// Dialog Data
        //{{AFX_DATA(TaxPayer)
        enum { IDD = IDD_TAXPAYER };
        CEdit   m_ssno;
        CEdit   m_name;
        //}}AFX_DATA

// Overrides
        // ClassWizard generated virtual function overrides
        //{{AFX_VIRTUAL(TaxPayer)
```

```
        protected:
        virtual void DoDataExchange(CDataExchange* pDX);      // DDX/DDV support
        //}}AFX_VIRTUAL

// Implementation
protected:

        // Generated message map functions
        //{{AFX_MSG(TaxPayer)
        virtual BOOL OnInitDialog();
        virtual void OnOK();
        //}}AFX_MSG
        DECLARE_MESSAGE_MAP()
private:
        PTaxPayerStruct pTaxPayerData;
};


//{{AFX_INSERT_LOCATION}}

#endif //

// TaxPayer.cpp : implementation file
//

#include "stdafx.h"
#include "treectrl.h"
#include "TaxData.h"
#include "TaxPayer.h"

#ifdef _DEBUG
#define new DEBUG_NEW
#undef THIS_FILE
static char THIS_FILE[] = __FILE__;
#endif

/////////////////////////////////////////////////////////////////////////////
// TaxPayer dialog

TaxPayer::TaxPayer(CWnd* pParent /*=NULL*/, PTaxPayerStruct pData)
        : CDialog(TaxPayer::IDD, pParent)
{
        //{{AFX_DATA_INIT(TaxPayer)
        //}}AFX_DATA_INIT
        pTaxPayerData = pData;
```

```
}

void  TaxPayer::DoDataExchange(CDataExchange*  pDX)
{
        CDialog::DoDataExchange(pDX);
        //{{AFX_DATA_MAP(TaxPayer)
        DDX_Control(pDX, IDC_SSNO, m_ssno);
        DDX_Control(pDX, IDC_NAME, m_name);
        //}}AFX_DATA_MAP
}


BEGIN_MESSAGE_MAP(TaxPayer,  CDialog)
        //{{AFX_MSG_MAP(TaxPayer)
        //}}AFX_MSG_MAP
END_MESSAGE_MAP()

//////////////////////////////////////////////////////////////////////
// TaxPayer message handlers

BOOL TaxPayer::OnInitDialog()
{
      CDialog::OnInitDialog();

      // TODO: Add extra initialization here
      m_ssno.SetWindowText(pTaxPayerData->szSSN);
      m_name.SetWindowText(pTaxPayerData->szName);
      return TRUE;  // return TRUE unless you set the focus to a control
                    // EXCEPTION: OCX Property Pages should return FALSE
}

void TaxPayer::OnOK()
{
      // TODO: Add extra validation here
      CDialog::OnOK();
      m_name.GetWindowText(pTaxPayerData->szName, 16+1);
      m_ssno.GetWindowText(pTaxPayerData->szSSN, 11+1);


}
```

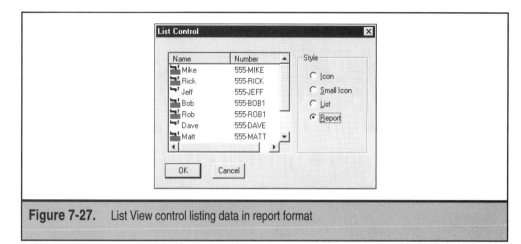

Figure 7-27.   List View control listing data in report format

LIST VIEW CONTROL

List View control lets you show a list of items in different ways, such as using small icons, large icons, lists, and so on, as shown in Figures 7-27 through 7-30.

The List View control uses a number of data structures, but two of the important ones are the **LV_COLUMN** structure and the **LV_ITEM** structure. These structures are used in the example program. Let's look at these data structures.

The **LV_COLUMN** structure contains information about a column in a List View control. This structure is also used to receive information about a column.

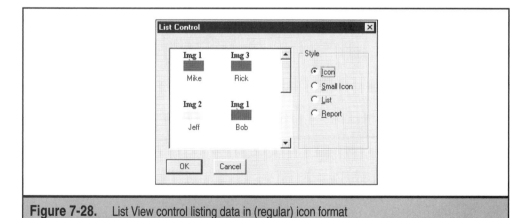

Figure 7-28.   List View control listing data in (regular) icon format

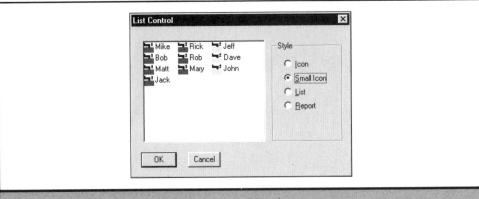

Figure 7-29. List View control listing data in small icon format

```
typedef struct _LV_COLUMN { UINT mask;
    int fmt;
    int cx;
    LPTSTR pszText;
    int cchTextMax;
    int iSubItem;
} LV_COLUMN;
```

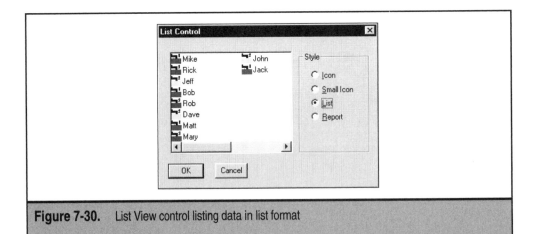

Figure 7-30. List View control listing data in list format

mask specifies which members of this structure contain valid information as shown in the table that follows:

Mask Value	Description
LVCF_FMT	The *fmt* member is valid.
LVCF_SUBITEM	The *iSubItem* member is valid.
LVCF_TEXT	The *pszText* member is valid.
LVCF_WIDTH	The *cx* member is valid.

fmt specifies the alignment of the column heading and the subitem text in all columns except the leftmost column in a List View control, which must be left aligned. The values and description for *fmt* are as follows:

Fmt Value	Description
LVCFMT_CENTER	Text is centered.
LVCFMT_LEFT	Text is left-aligned.
LVCFMT_RIGHT	Text is right-aligned.

cx specifies the width, in pixels, of the column.

pszText is a pointer to the column heading if the structure contains information about a column. If the structure is receiving information about a column, this member specifies the address of the buffer that receives the column heading.

cchTextMax specifies the size, in characters, of the buffer pointed to by the *pszText* member. If the structure is not receiving information about a column, this member is ignored.

iSubItem specifies the index of the subitem associated with a column.

List View Control programming example

The *ListCtrl* sample program shows how to use the List View control by use of the MFC library class **CListCtrl**. When the sample is run, it displays a window with a menu. If List Control is selected from the File menu, a dialog box with the list control is displayed. The list control has two columns and displays ten different entries. The style of the List View control can be changed by selecting various radio buttons shown in the Style Group box.

This sample extends the Spin/Slider/Progress control sample. The main application code is shown next. It is similar to the earlier samples, and it would suffice to look at the boldface code.

```
//*****************************************************************
// This sample demonstrates the class/functions related to
```

```
// Advanced controls.
//****************************************************************
// Controls.CPP

#include <afxwin.h>
#include <afxdlgs.h>
#include <afxcmn.h>                      // Header file for Advanced controls
#include <strstrea.h>
#include "FontDlg.h"
#include "AnimateDlg.h"
#include "HotKeyDlg.h"
#include "SpSlProgDlg.h"
#include "ListCtrlDlg.h"
#include "resource.h"

// Define the application object class
class CApp : public CWinApp
{
public:
        virtual BOOL InitInstance ();
};
// Define the window class
class CWindow : public CFrameWnd
{
public:
    CWindow();
    afx_msg void OnAppAbout();
    afx_msg void OnFontDlg();
    afx_msg void OnAnimateDlg();
    afx_msg void OnHotKeyDlg();
    afx_msg void OnSpSlProgDlg();
    afx_msg void OnListCtrlDlg();
    afx_msg void OnExit();
    afx_msg void OnSysCommand(UINT nID, LPARAM lParam); // Process the Hot Key
    DECLARE_MESSAGE_MAP()
};
/////////////////////////////////////////////////////////////////////
// CWindow
BEGIN_MESSAGE_MAP(CWindow, CFrameWnd)
        ON_COMMAND(ID_APP_ABOUT, OnAppAbout)
        ON_COMMAND(ID_FONTDLG, OnFontDlg)
        ON_COMMAND(ID_ANIMATEDLG, OnAnimateDlg)
        ON_COMMAND(ID_HOTKEYDLG, OnHotKeyDlg)
        ON_COMMAND(ID_SPSLPROGDLG, OnSpSlProgDlg)
```

```
            ON_COMMAND(ID_LISTCTRLDLG, OnListCtrlDlg)
            ON_COMMAND(ID_APP_EXIT, OnExit)
            ON_WM_SYSCOMMAND()
END_MESSAGE_MAP()
//////////////////////////////////////////////////////////////////////
// CWindow construction
CWindow::CWindow()
{
    LoadAccelTable(MAKEINTRESOURCE(IDR_MAINFRAME));
    Create( NULL, "Control Sample",
    WS_OVERLAPPEDWINDOW,
    rectDefault, NULL, MAKEINTRESOURCE(IDR_MAINFRAME) );
}
//////////////////////////////////////////////////////////////////////
// The one and only CApp object

CApp theApp;

//////////////////////////////////////////////////////////////////////
// CApp initialization

BOOL CApp::InitInstance()
{
        m_pMainWnd = new CWindow();
        m_pMainWnd -> ShowWindow( m_nCmdShow );
        m_pMainWnd -> UpdateWindow();
        return TRUE;
}


//////////////////////////////////////////////////////////////////////
/////
// CAboutDlg dialog used for App About

class CAboutDlg : public CDialog
{
public:
        CAboutDlg();
        enum { IDD = IDD_ABOUTBOX };
        protected:
};

CAboutDlg::CAboutDlg() : CDialog(CAboutDlg::IDD)
{
}
```

```
// App command to run the dialog
void CWindow::OnAppAbout()
{
        CAboutDlg aboutDlg;
        aboutDlg.DoModal();
}
// Code to process other menu items...

// ListControl Dialog selected

void CWindow::OnListCtrlDlg()
{
        CListCtrlDlg listctrlDlg(this);
        listctrlDlg.DoModal();
}

// On Exit handles the void
void CWindow::OnExit()
{
        DestroyWindow();
}
```

The items shown inside the List View control have icons associated with them. These icons and the resource for the List Control dialog box are shown next. Three icons are defined and these icons will be reused for the items inserted into the List View control. The style LVS_REPORT specifies a report view for the List View control, and the style LVS_AUTOARRANGE specifies that the icons are automatically kept arranged in icon and small icon view. Some of the other styles will be dynamically changed.

```
LANGUAGE LANG_NEUTRAL, SUBLANG_NEUTRAL
/////////////////////////////////////////////////////////////////////////////
// Icon
// Icon with lowest ID value placed first to ensure application icon
// remains consistent on all systems.
IDR_MAINFRAME           ICON    DISCARDABLE     "Control.ico"

IDI_IMG1                ICON    DISCARDABLE     "Img1.ico"
IDI_IMG2                ICON    DISCARDABLE     "Img2.ico"
IDI_IMG3                ICON    DISCARDABLE     "Img3.ico"

IDD_LISTCTRLDLG DIALOG DISCARDABLE  0, 0, 229, 140
STYLE DS_MODALFRAME | WS_POPUP | WS_CAPTION | WS_SYSMENU
CAPTION "List Control"
```

```
FONT 8, "MS Sans Serif"
BEGIN
    CONTROL         "List1",IDC_LISTCTRL,"SysListView32",LVS_REPORT |
                    LVS_AUTOARRANGE | WS_BORDER | WS_TABSTOP,12,13,129,96
    GROUPBOX        "Static",IDC_STATIC,148,14,74,95
    CONTROL         "&Icon",IDC_ICONVIEW,"Button",BS_AUTORADIOBUTTON,160,31,
                    47,10
    CONTROL         "&Small Icon",IDC_SMALLICON,"Button",BS_AUTORADIOBUTTON,
                    160,44,47,10
    CONTROL         "&List",IDC_LIST,"Button",BS_AUTORADIOBUTTON,160,57,47,
                    10
    CONTROL         "&Report",IDC_REPORT,"Button",BS_AUTORADIOBUTTON,160,70,
                    47,10
    DEFPUSHBUTTON   "OK",IDOK,9,118,38,14
    PUSHBUTTON      "Cancel",IDCANCEL,59,118,34,14
END
```

The **CListCtrlDlg** class declaration is shown next. A **CListCtrl** member is defined for the list control in the dialog box. Pointers to two **CImageListobjects** are also defined. The image list for the full-sized icons and a separate image list contain smaller versions of the same icons for use in other views. Member functions **OnInitDialog**, **OnIconView**, **OnSmallIconView**, **OnListView**, and **OnReportView** are declared. These functions are tied to the button-click event on the radio button through the message map. A private function, **InsertOneItem**, which is used to add one item at a time to the List View control, is also declared. A destructor is also defined, since the resource allocated for the image list should be released. This image list resource is freed in the destructor.

```
// ListCtrlDlg.h : header file
/////////////////////////////////////////////////////////////////////////
// CListCtrlDlg dialog

class CListCtrlDlg : public CDialog
{
// Construction
public:
        CListCtrlDlg(CWnd* pParent = NULL);   // standard constructor
        ~CListCtrlDlg();
// Dialog Data
        //{{AFX_DATA(CListCtrlDlg)
        enum { IDD = IDD_LISTCTRLDLG };
        CListCtrl       m_listctrl;
        CImageList      *m_pimagelist;
        CImageList      *m_psmallimagelist;
```

```
            //}}AFX_DATA
// Overrides
        // ClassWizard generated virtual function overrides
        //{{AFX_VIRTUAL(CListCtrlDlg)
        protected:
        virtual void DoDataExchange(CDataExchange* pDX);    // DDX/DDV support
        //}}AFX_VIRTUAL
// Implementation
protected:
        // Generated message map functions
        //{{AFX_MSG(CListCtrlDlg)
        virtual BOOL OnInitDialog();
        afx_msg void OnIconView();
        afx_msg void OnSmallIconView();
        afx_msg void OnListView();
        afx_msg void OnReportView();
        //}}AFX_MSG
        DECLARE_MESSAGE_MAP()
private:
        void InsertOneItem(short sItemNumber, char *szName, char *szNumber,
                        short sImage);
};
```

The code that implements the **CListCtrlDlg** is shown next. The class constructor just initializes the member variables. The DDX is used to update the data between the control and the **CListCtrl** member variable in the class. The message map specifies what function is to be called when the radio buttons are clicked.

```
// ListCtrlDlg.cpp : implementation file
//
#include <afxwin.h>
#include <afxdlgs.h>
#include <afxcmn.h>
#include "resource.h"
#include "ListCtrlDlg.h"
////////////////////////////////////////////////////////////////////////////
// CListCtrlDlg dialog
CListCtrlDlg::CListCtrlDlg(CWnd* pParent /*=NULL*/)
        : CDialog(CListCtrlDlg::IDD, pParent)
{
        //{{AFX_DATA_INIT(CListCtrlDlg)
                // NOTE: the ClassWizard will add member initialization here
        //}}AFX_DATA_INIT
        m_pimagelist = NULL;
```

```
                m_psmallimagelist = NULL;
}
void CListCtrlDlg::DoDataExchange(CDataExchange* pDX)
{
        CDialog::DoDataExchange(pDX);
        //{{AFX_DATA_MAP(CListCtrlDlg)
        DDX_Control(pDX, IDC_LISTCTRL, m_listctrl);
        //}}AFX_DATA_MAP
}
BEGIN_MESSAGE_MAP(CListCtrlDlg, CDialog)
        //{{AFX_MSG_MAP(CListCtrlDlg)
        ON_BN_CLICKED(IDC_ICONVIEW, OnIconView)
        ON_BN_CLICKED(IDC_SMALLICON, OnSmallIconView)
        ON_BN_CLICKED(IDC_LIST, OnListView)
        ON_BN_CLICKED(IDC_REPORT, OnReportView)
        //}}AFX_MSG_MAP
END_MESSAGE_MAP()
```

During the dialog box initialization, the List View control is populated with items. For this sample ten items are inserted. In a real application the data to be inserted inside the List View control can be queried during this initialization process and inserted. Before inserting the items, two image lists are created and assigned to the List View control by use of the **SetImageList** function. The List View control displays names and phone numbers. Therefore two columns are needed. To insert a column, a **LV_COLUMN** structure is created. The width of each column is half the size of the control. The columns are headed "Name" and "Number." **InsertColumn** inserts the column.

```
///////////////////////////////////////////////////////////////////////////
// CListCtrlDlg message handlers
BOOL CListCtrlDlg::OnInitDialog()
{
        CWinApp *pApp;
        LV_COLUMN lvcolumn;
        CDialog::OnInitDialog();

        char Name[10][10] = {"Jack", "John", "Mary", "Matt", "Dave", "Rob",
                             "Bob", "Jeff", "Rick", "Mike"};
        char Number[10][10] = {"555-JACK", "555-JOHN","555-MARY",
                               "555-MATT","555-DAVE", "555-ROB1",
                               "555-BOB1", "555-JEFF","555-RICK", "555-MIKE"};
        // TODO: Add extra initialization here
        pApp = (CWinApp *)AfxGetApp();
        m_pimagelist = new CImageList();
        m_psmallimagelist = new CImageList();
```

```
    m_pimagelist->Create(32, 32, TRUE, 3, 3);
m_psmallimagelist->Create(16, 16, TRUE, 3, 3);
m_pimagelist->Add(pApp->LoadIcon(IDI_IMG1));
m_pimagelist->Add(pApp->LoadIcon(IDI_IMG2));
m_pimagelist->Add(pApp->LoadIcon(IDI_IMG3));
m_psmallimagelist->Add(pApp->LoadIcon(IDI_IMG1));
m_psmallimagelist->Add(pApp->LoadIcon(IDI_IMG2));
m_psmallimagelist->Add(pApp->LoadIcon(IDI_IMG3));

m_listctrl.SetImageList(m_pimagelist, LVSIL_NORMAL);
m_listctrl.SetImageList(m_psmallimagelist, LVSIL_SMALL);

CRect rect;
m_listctrl.GetWindowRect(&rect);  // Get the size of the List control

// Create two columns.

lcolumn.mask = LVCF_FMT | LVCF_SUBITEM | LVCF_TEXT | LVCF_WIDTH;
lvcolumn.fmt = LVCFMT_LEFT; // Other possible formats are LVCFMT_CENTER
// & LVCFMT_RIGHT
lvcolumn.cx = rect.Width()/2;  // Occupy half the width

lvcolumn.pszText = "Name";
lvcolumn.iSubItem = 1;
m_listctrl.InsertColumn(1, &lvcolumn);

lvcolumn.pszText = "Number";
lvcolumn.iSubItem = 2;
m_listctrl.InsertColumn(2, &lvcolumn);


for (int j = 0; j < 10; j++)
{
    InsertOneItem(j, Name[j], Number[j], j%3);
}

return TRUE;  // return TRUE unless you set the focus to a control
              // EXCEPTION: OCX Property Pages should return FALSE
}
```

The resource allocated for the **CImageList** is released when the **CListCtrlDlg** class is destroyed.

```
CListCtrlDlg::~CListCtrlDlg()
{
        // Delete the memory allocated
        delete m_pimagelist;
        delete m_psmallimagelist;
}
```

The next four member functions modify the style of the List View control when the user changes the styles by clicking on the radio button. The list control style is stored in a 32-bit value at a specified offset into the extra window memory of the window. This is retrieved by calling **GetWindowLong**. The least significant two bits store the style, which specifies whether the style of the List View control is icon, small icon, list, or report. The current style of the List View control is checked to make sure that the styles setting is not set redundantly. If style needs to be set, the appropriate bit is set and the style is updated by calling **SetWindowLong**.

```
void CListCtrlDlg::OnIconView()
{
    long        lStyle;
    short       sStyle;

    lStyle = GetWindowLong(m_listctrl.m_hWnd, GWL_STYLE);
    sStyle = lStyle & LVS_TYPEMASK;
    if (!(sStyle == LVS_ICON))
    {
        lStyle &= ~0x00000003;      //Reset the view mode bits
        lStyle |= LVS_ICON;         //Set the new view mode
    }
    SetWindowLong(m_listctrl.m_hWnd, GWL_STYLE, lStyle);

}
void CListCtrlDlg::OnSmallIconView()
{
    long        lStyle;
    short       sStyle;

    lStyle = GetWindowLong(m_listctrl.m_hWnd, GWL_STYLE);
    sStyle = lStyle & LVS_TYPEMASK;
    if (!(sStyle == LVS_SMALLICON))
    {
        lStyle &= ~0x00000003;//Reset the view mode bits
        lStyle |= LVS_SMALLICON;            // Set the new view mode
    }
```

```
        SetWindowLong(m_listctrl.m_hWnd, GWL_STYLE, lStyle);

}
void CListCtrlDlg::OnListView()
{
    long     lStyle;
    short    sStyle;

    lStyle = GetWindowLong(m_listctrl.m_hWnd, GWL_STYLE);
    sStyle = lStyle & LVS_TYPEMASK;
    if (!(sStyle == LVS_LIST))
    {
        lStyle &= ~0x00000003;     //Reset the view mode bits
        lStyle |= LVS_LIST;        //Set the new view mode
    }
    SetWindowLong(m_listctrl.m_hWnd, GWL_STYLE, lStyle);

}
void CListCtrlDlg::OnReportView()
{
    long     lStyle;
    short    sStyle;

    lStyle = GetWindowLong(m_listctrl.m_hWnd, GWL_STYLE);
    sStyle = lStyle & LVS_TYPEMASK;
    if (!(sStyle == LVS_REPORT))
    {
        lStyle &= ~0x00000003;     //Reset the view mode bits
        lStyle |= LVS_REPORT;      //Set the new view mode
    }
    SetWindowLong(m_listctrl.m_hWnd, GWL_STYLE, lStyle);

}
```

The next function is a helper function that inserts one item into the List View control.

```
void CListCtrlDlg::InsertOneItem(short sItemNumber, char *szName, char
*szNumber, short sImage)
{
        int inewitem;
        LV_ITEM lvitem;

        lvitem.mask = LVIF_TEXT|LVIF_IMAGE;
        lvitem.iItem =  0;
```

```
        lvitem.iSubItem = 0;
        lvitem.pszText = szName;
        lvitem.iImage = sImage;
        inewitem = m_listctrl.InsertItem(&lvitem);

        lvitem.mask = LVIF_TEXT;
        lvitem.iItem =  0;
        lvitem.iSubItem = 1;
        lvitem.pszText = szNumber;
        m_listctrl.SetItem(&lvitem);

}
```

CONCLUSION

We examined advanced (also called common) controls. Advanced controls make your user interface look professional, and you will most certainly be using advanced controls in your business applications. We looked at programming examples of the Animation control, HotKey control, Spin control, Slider control, Progress control, List View control, and Tree View control. As mentioned earlier, it is not possible to cover all the advanced controls here. But using the examples shown, you should be able to use the other advanced controls.

So far in this part, we have looked at graphics programming, how to speed up repainting and set up automatic scrolling, perform animation programmatically, and use advanced controls. These user interface topics give you a good set of programs and techniques to use in your own user interface programming. Next, let's look at animation using bitmaps.

CHAPTER 8

Animation Using Bitmaps

M ore and more, animation is becoming part of top-quality, professionally written Windows NT programs. Whether you are using animation to guide the user through a complex sequence of selections, to prompt for input, or simply to spice up your application, it is very likely that some form of animation will be part of your future Windows NT applications.

There are two general ways in which you can display motion under Windows NT. The first way is to animate bitmapped images. *Bitmap-level animation* is generally used to move relatively small objects over a fixed background. This is the type of animation discussed in this chapter. The second way is to display an AVI (audio video interleaved) file by use of an animation control. AVI files are generally used to display full-motion video. The animation control is described in Chapter 7.

While bitmap-based animation is conceptually simple, in practice it requires the application of several advanced techniques, including various bitmap manipulations, timers, and making use of the idle time in an application. This chapter contains a number of examples of bitmap-based animation, beginning with a simple banner program, a program that displays a moving message. It then explains how to animate a sprite (a bitmapped object). Finally, it concludes with a discussion of foregrounds and backgrounds.

ANIMATION FUNDAMENTALS

As you likely know, animation is accomplished by drawing, erasing, and redrawing an object. Between the two drawings, the object is either moved, changed, or both. If this process is performed fast enough, the object appears to be moving and animation is achieved. While this general process is easy to understand, it may not be completely clear how animation is actually programmed under Windows NT.

To begin, let's define two terms. The draw, erase, redraw sequence completes one *animation cycle.* At the end of each cycle, a new *frame* has been produced. The rapid sequencing of frames produces the illusion of motion.

In the most general sense, animation is achieved on a computer by use of *bit manipulations.* For example, a screen image can be moved left by left-shifting the bits that make up that image. Animation can also be produced by rapidly erasing and redrawing an object by use of a *bit-block transfer.*

One of the greatest problems with computer animation is *flicker.* Flicker is produced when one or both of the following conditions occur:

▼ The drawing, erasing, and redrawing sequence is performed too slowly.

▲ The animation process is performed incorrectly.

Fortunately, Windows NT provides the means by which images can be rapidly drawn, and you will soon see that it is relatively easy to correctly animate an image.

Animation makes extensive use of bitmaps and memory device contexts. In fact, all the examples in this chapter use the virtual window technology developed in Chapter 6.

If you haven't yet read Chapter 6, you will want to at least skim through it so that its basic concepts are familiar. (Pay special attention to the description of the **BitBlt( )** function. It is used extensively in this chapter.)

Before we begin our exploration of animation, one small but important side issue must be discussed.

DRIVING THE ANIMATION

Because animation requires that the draw, erase, redraw cycle be repeated evenly and regularly, there must be some way to drive this process. That is, your program must provide a mechanism that repeatedly causes the next cycle to take place in a regular fashion. At first you might think that this is a trivial problem. However, that is not the case. The reason is that a Windows NT application program is *message driven*. This means that, in general, your program is active only when it is responding to a message. Put differently, a Windows NT program cannot enter a "mode" of operation. For example, a Windows NT program cannot simply enter a loop that draws, erases, and redraws images. Instead, it must return control to Windows NT as soon as it has finished processing a message. The question then becomes "How do I force each animation cycle to occur?" There are three ways in which this can be done. The first way is to use a *timer*. In this way, each time the timer goes off, your program performs one animation cycle. The second way is to take advantage of the *idle time* that occurs when your program is not processing any other messages. The third way is to use *multithreaded multitasking*, with each animated object driven by its own thread of execution. In this chapter, the first two ways are examined. Multithreading is explored in Chapter 10.

The first animation example will use the timer. In case you are not familiar with setting a timer and responding to timer messages, they are described next.

Using a Timer

Using Windows NT, you can establish a timer that will interrupt your program at periodic intervals. Each time the timer goes off, Windows NT sends a **WM_TIMER** message to your program. Using a timer is a good way to "wake up" your program every so often. This is particularly useful when your program is running as a background task.

To start a timer, use the **SetTimer( )** API function, whose prototype is shown here:

```
UINT SetTimer(HWND hwnd,
              UINT nID,
              UINT wLength,
              TIMERPROC lpTFunc);
```

Here, *hwnd* is the handle of the window that uses the timer. Generally, this window will be either your program's main window or a dialog box window. The value of *nID* specifies a value that will be associated with this timer. (More than one timer can be active.) The value of *wLength* specifies the length of the period in milliseconds. That is, *wLength* specifies how much time there is between interrupts. The function pointed to by *lpTFunc* is the timer function that will be called when the timer goes off. However, if the value of *lpTFunc* is NULL, then the window function associated with the window specified by *hwnd* is called and there is no need to specify a separate timer function. In this case, each time the timer goes off, a **WM_TIMER** message is put into the message queue for your program and processed like any other message. This is the approach used by the example that follows. The **SetTimer( )** function returns *nID* if successful. If the timer cannot be allocated, zero is returned.

If you wish to define a separate timer function, it must be a callback function that has the following prototype (of course, the name of the function may be different):

```
VOID CALLBACK TFunc(HWND hwnd,
                    UINT msg,
                    UINT TimerID,
                    DWORD SysTime);
```

Here, *hwnd* will contain the handle of the timer window, *msg* will contain the message **WM_TIMER**, *TimerID* will contain the ID of the timer that went off, and *SysTime* will contain the current system time.

Once a timer has been started, it continues to interrupt your program until either you terminate the application or your program executes a call to the **KillTimer( )** API function, whose prototype is shown here:

```
BOOL KillTimer(HWND hwnd,
               UINT nID);
```

Here, *hwnd* is the window that contains the timer, and *nID* is the value that identifies that particular timer. The function returns nonzero if successful and zero on failure.

Each time a **WM_TIMER** message is generated, the value of *wParam* contains the ID of the timer and *lParam* contains the address of the timer callback function (if specified). For the example that follows, *lParam* will be NULL.

ANIMATING TEXT: A BANNER PROGRAM

Let's begin our examination of animation with a simple but useful program. This program will animate a line of text from right to left. That is, the program will display a moving banner. As the text moves off the left end, it wraps around to the right end. Although this example is quite simple, it introduces all of the basic elements found in any animation situation. In the first version of the program, the animation is driven by the timer.

To begin, here is the entire animated banner program. Sample output is shown in Figures 8-1 through 8-3. The banner starts at the right edge of the window and moves to the left.

```
/* A simple animated banner that is driven by a timer. */
#include <windows.h>
#include <string.h>
#include <stdio.h>

LRESULT CALLBACK WindowFunc(HWND, UINT, WPARAM, LPARAM);

char szWinName[] = "MyWin"; /* name of window class */

int X=0, Y=20; /* current output location */
int maxX, maxY; /* screen dimensions */
TEXTMETRIC tm; /* font information */
RECT animdim; /* size of area to animate */

HDC memdc; /* store the virtual device handle */
HBITMAP hbit; /* store the virtual bitmap handle */
HBRUSH hbrush; /* store the brush handle */

int WINAPI WinMain(HINSTANCE hThisInst, HINSTANCE hPrevInst,
                   LPSTR lpszArgs, int nWinMode)
{
  HWND hwnd;
  MSG msg;
  WNDCLASSEX wcl;

  /* Define a window class. */
  wcl.hInstance = hThisInst; /* handle to this instance */
  wcl.lpszClassName = szWinName; /* window class name */
  wcl.lpfnWndProc = WindowFunc; /* window function */
  wcl.style = 0; /* default style */

  wcl.cbSize = sizeof(WNDCLASSEX); /* set size of WNDCLASSEX */

  wcl.hIcon = LoadIcon(NULL, IDI_APPLICATION); /* standard icon */
  wcl.hIconSm = LoadIcon(NULL, IDI_APPLICATION); /* small icon */
  wcl.hCursor = LoadCursor(NULL, IDC_ARROW); /* cursor style */

  wcl.lpszMenuName = NULL; /* no main menu */
  wcl.cbClsExtra = 0; /* no extra */
  wcl.cbWndExtra = 0; /* information needed */

  /* Use white background. */
  wcl.hbrBackground = GetStockObject(WHITE_BRUSH);
```

```
/* Register the window class. */
if(!RegisterClassEx(&wcl)) return 0;

/* Create the window. */
hwnd = CreateWindow(
  szWinName, /* name of window class */
  "Animating a Message", /* title */
  WS_OVERLAPPEDWINDOW, /* standard window */
  CW_USEDEFAULT, /* X coordinate - let Windows decide */
  CW_USEDEFAULT, /* Y coordinate - let Windows decide */
  CW_USEDEFAULT, /* width - let Windows decide */
  CW_USEDEFAULT, /* height - let Windows decide */
  HWND_DESKTOP, /* no parent window */
  NULL, /* no override of class menu */
  hThisInst, /* handle of this instance of the program */
  NULL /* no additional arguments */
);

/* Display the window. */
ShowWindow(hwnd, nWinMode);
UpdateWindow(hwnd);

/* Create the message loop. */
while(GetMessage(&msg, NULL, 0, 0))
{
  TranslateMessage(&msg); /* translate keyboard messages */
  DispatchMessage(&msg); /* return control to Windows */
}
return msg.wParam;
}

/* Window Procedure */
LRESULT CALLBACK WindowFunc(HWND hwnd, UINT message,
                            WPARAM wParam, LPARAM lParam)
{
  HDC hdc;
  PAINTSTRUCT ps;

  char str[] = "This is an animated message.";

  switch(message) {
    case WM_CREATE:
      /* start a timer */
```

```
      if(!SetTimer(hwnd, 1, 50, NULL))
        MessageBox(hwnd, "Timer Error", "Error", MB_OK);

      /* get screen coordinates */
      maxX = GetSystemMetrics(SM_CXSCREEN);
      maxY = GetSystemMetrics(SM_CYSCREEN);

      /* create a compatible bitmap */
      hdc = GetDC(hwnd);
      memdc = CreateCompatibleDC(hdc);
      hbit = CreateCompatibleBitmap(hdc, maxX, maxY);
      SelectObject(memdc, hbit);
      hbrush = GetStockObject(WHITE_BRUSH);
      SelectObject(memdc, hbrush);
      PatBlt(memdc, 0, 0, maxX, maxY, PATCOPY);

      /* get text metrics */
      GetTextMetrics(hdc, &tm);

      animdim.left = X; animdim.top = Y;
      animdim.right = maxX + X;
      animdim.bottom = tm.tmHeight + Y;

      TextOut(memdc, X, Y, str, strlen(str)); /* output to memory */

      ReleaseDC(hwnd, hdc);
      InvalidateRect(hwnd, NULL, 1);
      break;
    case WM_PAINT: /* process a repaint request */
      hdc = BeginPaint(hwnd, &ps); /* get DC */

      /* copy virtual window onto screen */
      BitBlt(hdc, ps.rcPaint.left, ps.rcPaint.top,
             ps.rcPaint.right-ps.rcPaint.left, /* width */
             ps.rcPaint.bottom-ps.rcPaint.top, /* height */
             memdc,
             ps.rcPaint.left, ps.rcPaint.top,
             SRCCOPY);

      EndPaint(hwnd, &ps); /* release DC */
      break;
    case WM_TIMER: /* timer went off - update display */
      /* move left edge to the right end */
      BitBlt(memdc, maxX-1, Y, 1, tm.tmHeight,
```

```
                        memdc, 0, Y, SRCCOPY);

        /* move remaining image left */
        BitBlt(memdc, 0, Y, maxX-1, tm.tmHeight,
                memdc, 1, Y, SRCCOPY);

        /* update */
        InvalidateRect(hwnd, &animdim, 0);
        break;
      case WM_DESTROY: /* terminate the program */
        DeleteDC(memdc);
        PostQuitMessage(0);
        break;
      default:
        return DefWindowProc(hwnd, message, wParam, lParam);
  }
  return 0;
}
```

Let's take a closer look at the animated banner program.

Figure 8-1.   Banner starting at the right edge of the window

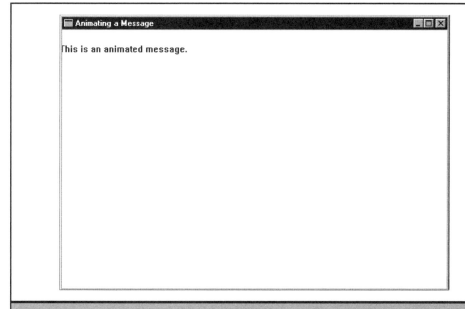

Figure 8-2. Banner in the middle of the window

Figure 8-3. Banner at the left edge of the window

As you can see, this program contains relatively little code. It uses the virtual window mechanism described in Chapter 6. In this case, the virtual window is used for two purposes: to refresh the window when a **WM_PAINT** message is received and to prepare the next frame for animation.

Inside **WM_CREATE** the timer is started. The length of the timer period determines how fast the message is scrolled across the screen. Next, the virtual window is created, and information about the text font is obtained. The height of the font is used to initialize the **animdim** structure. This structure defines the size of the area that contains the text that will be scrolled across the screen. It will be used in calls to **InvalidateRect( )** when the text is moved. Next, the string to be animated is output to the virtual window. Finally, the first frame is output to the screen via a call to **InvalidateRect( )**.

The most interesting parts of the program are found under the **WM_TIMER** message. Each time the timer goes off, a two-step process occurs. First, the leftmost bits of the text region are moved to the far right side. Next, the remaining portion of the text region is moved left one position. This process is repeated and this produces the effect of moving the text region as shown in Figure 8-2 and Figure 8-3.

When you run this program, you will notice that the message scrolls rather slowly. This is not because Windows NT is slow. It is caused by inherent limitations in how fast timer messages can be produced and processed through the system. However, in the next section, you will see how your animations can be driven substantially faster.

USING IDLE CYCLES FOR ANIMATION

While using the timer to drive animation will work for some applications, it is far too slow for many others. Most animation applications require that the animation take place at rates approximating real-time activities. To accomplish this, you need a way to "nudge" the animation subsystem as frequently as possible. One way is to take advantage of idle time. In most Windows NT applications, idle time occurs frequently. Consider the following message loop common to all Windows NT applications:

```
while(GetMessage(&msg, NULL, 0, 0))
{
  TranslateMessage(&msg);
  DispatchMessage(&msg);
}
```

This piece of code repeatedly obtains and dispatches messages. When your application is not processing a message in its window procedure, it is running this message loop. Put differently, this loop is running whenever your application is idle. By adding code to the message loop that cycles the animation system, you can achieve fast motion. The following version of the preceding moving banner program implements such a scheme.

```
/* An animated banner that runs during idle cycles. */
#include <windows.h>
#include <string.h>
#include <stdio.h>

void run(HWND hwnd, HDC memdc);

LRESULT CALLBACK WindowFunc(HWND, UINT, WPARAM, LPARAM);

char szWinName[] = "MyWin"; /* name of window class */

int X=0, Y=20; /* current output location */
int maxX, maxY; /* screen dimensions */
RECT animdim; /* size of area to animate */
TEXTMETRIC tm;

HDC memdc; /* store the virtual device handle */
HBITMAP hbit; /* store the virtual bitmap handle */
HBRUSH hbrush; /* store the brush handle */

int WINAPI WinMain(HINSTANCE hThisInst, HINSTANCE hPrevInst,
                   LPSTR lpszArgs, int nWinMode)
{
  HWND hwnd;
  MSG msg;
  WNDCLASSEX wcl;

  /* Define a window class. */
  wcl.hInstance = hThisInst; /* handle to this instance */
  wcl.lpszClassName = szWinName; /* window class name */
  wcl.lpfnWndProc = WindowFunc; /* window function */
  wcl.style = 0; /* default style */

  wcl.cbSize = sizeof(WNDCLASSEX); /* set size of WNDCLASSEX */

  wcl.hIcon = LoadIcon(NULL, IDI_APPLICATION); /* standard icon */
  wcl.hIconSm = LoadIcon(NULL, IDI_APPLICATION); /* small icon */
  wcl.hCursor = LoadCursor(NULL, IDC_ARROW); /* cursor style */

  wcl.lpszMenuName = NULL; /* no main menu */
  wcl.cbClsExtra = 0; /* no extra */
  wcl.cbWndExtra = 0; /* information needed */
```

```
/* Use white background. */
wcl.hbrBackground = GetStockObject(WHITE_BRUSH);

/* Register the window class. */
if(!RegisterClassEx(&wcl)) return 0;

/* Create the window. */
hwnd = CreateWindow(
  szWinName, /* name of window class */
  "Animating a Message", /* title */
  WS_OVERLAPPEDWINDOW, /* standard window */
  CW_USEDEFAULT, /* X coordinate - let Windows decide */
  CW_USEDEFAULT, /* Y coordinate - let Windows decide */
  CW_USEDEFAULT, /* width - let Windows decide */
  CW_USEDEFAULT, /* height - let Windows decide */
  HWND_DESKTOP, /* no parent window */
  NULL, /* no override of class menu */
  hThisInst, /* handle of this instance of the program */
  NULL /* no additional arguments */
);

/* Display the window. */
ShowWindow(hwnd, nWinMode);
UpdateWindow(hwnd);

/* Create the message loop. */
while(GetMessage(&msg, NULL, 0, 0))
{
  TranslateMessage(&msg); /* translate keyboard messages */
  DispatchMessage(&msg); /* return control to Windows */
  run(hwnd, memdc); /* cycle the animation */
}
return msg.wParam;
}

/* Window Procedure */
LRESULT CALLBACK WindowFunc(HWND hwnd, UINT message,
                            WPARAM wParam, LPARAM lParam)
{
  HDC hdc;
  PAINTSTRUCT ps;

  char str[] = "This is an animated message.";
```

```
switch(message) {
  case WM_CREATE:
    /* get screen coordinates */
    maxX = GetSystemMetrics(SM_CXSCREEN);
    maxY = GetSystemMetrics(SM_CYSCREEN);

    /* create a compatible bitmap */
    hdc = GetDC(hwnd);
    memdc = CreateCompatibleDC(hdc);
    hbit = CreateCompatibleBitmap(hdc, maxX, maxY);
    SelectObject(memdc, hbit);
    hbrush = GetStockObject(WHITE_BRUSH);
    SelectObject(memdc, hbrush);
    PatBlt(memdc, 0, 0, maxX, maxY, PATCOPY);

    /* get text metrics */
    GetTextMetrics(hdc, &tm);

    animdim.left = X; animdim.top = Y;
    animdim.right = maxX + X;
    animdim.bottom = tm.tmHeight + Y;

    TextOut(memdc, X, Y, str, strlen(str)); /* output to memory */

    ReleaseDC(hwnd, hdc);
    InvalidateRect(hwnd, NULL, 1);
    break;
  case WM_PAINT: /* process a repaint request */
    hdc = BeginPaint(hwnd, &ps); /* get DC */

    /* copy virtual window onto screen */
    BitBlt(hdc, ps.rcPaint.left, ps.rcPaint.top,
           ps.rcPaint.right-ps.rcPaint.left, /* width */
           ps.rcPaint.bottom-ps.rcPaint.top, /* height */
           memdc,
           ps.rcPaint.left, ps.rcPaint.top,
           SRCCOPY);

    EndPaint(hwnd, &ps); /* release DC */
    break;
  case WM_DESTROY: /* terminate the program */
    DeleteDC(memdc);
```

```
      PostQuitMessage(0);
      break;
    default:
      return DefWindowProc(hwnd, message, wParam, lParam);
  }
  return 0;
}

/* Animate the banner during idle time. */
void run(HWND hwnd, HDC memdc)
{
  Sleep(10); // slow down the banner

  /* move left edge to the right end */
  BitBlt(memdc, maxX-1, Y, 1, tm.tmHeight,
         memdc, 0, Y, SRCCOPY);

  /* move remaining image left */
  BitBlt(memdc, 0, Y, maxX-1, tm.tmHeight,
         memdc, 1, Y, SRCCOPY);
  InvalidateRect(hwnd, &animdim, 0);
}
```

In this version, pay special attention to the function called **run( )**. This function cycles the animation system and then calls **InvalidateRect( )** to update the screen. Notice how the function is called within the program's message loop. When you try this version of the program, you will see a remarkable improvement in speed. In fact, it may run too fast. If it does, simply increase the magnitude of the argument to **Sleep( )**. **Sleep( )** causes execution to suspend for the specified number of milliseconds.

Since the use of idle time produces much faster animation, it will be used by the subsequent examples in this chapter.

ANIMATING SPRITES

A *sprite* is a small, animated object. Usually, a sprite is a bitmapped image, but it could be any animated object no matter how it is drawn. For the purposes of this chapter, all sprites are bitmapped images. As you will see, the general method used to animate a sprite is straightforward. Of course, complexity increases as your animated landscape grows.

The remainder of this chapter develops three sample programs that animate bitmaps. The first presents the easiest animation case: a single bitmap is moved over a solid background. The second animates three slightly different versions of the bitmap, enhancing the illusion of movement. The third creates a foreground and background aspect.

Let's start by creating a bitmapped sprite.

Creating a Sprite

Although the techniques developed in this chapter can be used to animate any size bitmap, the examples use bitmaps that are 64×64 pixels square. To create the bitmaps required by the examples, you will need to use an image editor. One will typically be supplied with your compiler. For the first example, you will need one bitmap. Call this bitmap *Bp1.bmp.* The one used by the first example is the train engine shown in Figure 8-4 as it is being edited. (Of course, you can draw any object you like. Just be consistent.)

After you have created the first bitmap, you will need to create the following resource file. This file will be used by the example programs.

```
MYBP1 BITMAP BP1.BMP
```

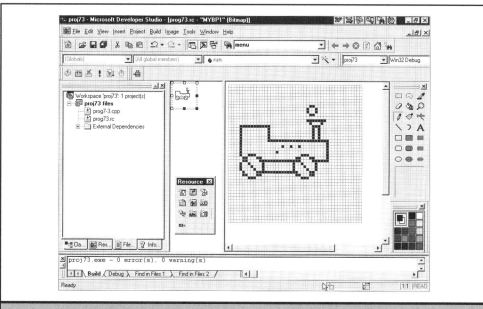

Figure 8-4.   Bitmap of a train engine used in the animation example

This tells the resource compiler to add the bitmap defined in BP1.BMP to your program, calling it MYBP1.

A SIMPLE EXAMPLE OF SPRITE ANIMATION

The simplest case of sprite animation occurs when the following two conditions are met:

1. The bitmap is moved over a solid background.

2. The bitmap contains a border that is at least one pixel thick and is the same color as the background color.

Figures 8-5 through 8-7 show the output of the following example as the train engine moves from left to right on the screen.

In this case, all you have to do is repeatedly redraw the image. As each new image is drawn, it overwrites the old image. Because the background colors are the same, there is no need for an explicit erase operation. Of course, using this scheme, you must not move the sprite farther than the width of its border in any single animation cycle. While this

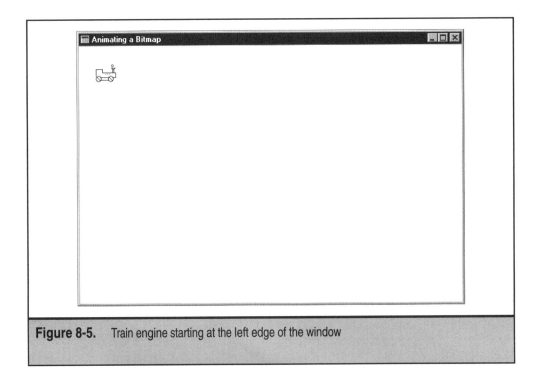

Figure 8-5.   Train engine starting at the left edge of the window

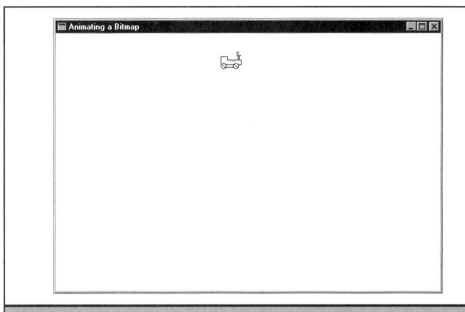

Figure 8-6. Train engine in the middle of the window

Figure 8-7. Train engine at the right edge of the window

approach may at first seem limiting, it is actually quite useful in a variety of situations and is very efficient. The following program implements this approach.

```c
/* Animating a bitmapped sprite. */
#include <windows.h>
#include <string.h>
#include <stdio.h>

#define BITMAPSIZE 64

void run(HWND hwnd, HDC memdc);

LRESULT CALLBACK WindowFunc(HWND, UINT, WPARAM, LPARAM);

char szWinName[] = "MyWin"; /* name of window class */

int X=0, Y=20; /* current output location */
int maxX, maxY; /* screen dimensions */
RECT animdim; /* size of area to animate */

HDC memdc; /* store the virtual device handle */
HDC bmpdc; /* store bitmap device handle */
HBITMAP hbit; /* store the virtual bitmap handle */
HBITMAP hAnBit1; /* store the animation bitmap */
HBRUSH hbrush; /* store the brush handle */

int WINAPI WinMain(HINSTANCE hThisInst, HINSTANCE hPrevInst,
                   LPSTR lpszArgs, int nWinMode)
{
  HWND hwnd;
  MSG msg;
  WNDCLASSEX wcl;

  /* Define a window class. */
  wcl.hInstance = hThisInst; /* handle to this instance */
  wcl.lpszClassName = szWinName; /* window class name */
  wcl.lpfnWndProc = WindowFunc; /* window function */
  wcl.style = 0; /* default style */

  wcl.cbSize = sizeof(WNDCLASSEX); /* set size of WNDCLASSEX */

  wcl.hIcon = LoadIcon(NULL, IDI_APPLICATION); /* standard icon */
```

```
wcl.hIconSm = LoadIcon(NULL, IDI_APPLICATION); /* small icon */
wcl.hCursor = LoadCursor(NULL, IDC_ARROW); /* cursor style */

wcl.lpszMenuName = NULL; /* no main menu */
wcl.cbClsExtra = 0; /* no extra */
wcl.cbWndExtra = 0; /* information needed */

/* Use white background. */
wcl.hbrBackground = GetStockObject(WHITE_BRUSH);

/* Register the window class. */
if(!RegisterClassEx(&wcl)) return 0;

/* load the bitmap */
hAnBit1 = LoadBitmap(hThisInst, "MYBP1"); /* load bitmap */

/* Create the window. */
hwnd = CreateWindow(
  szWinName, /* name of window class */
  "Animating a Bitmap", /* title */
  WS_OVERLAPPEDWINDOW, /* standard window */
  CW_USEDEFAULT, /* X coordinate - let Windows decide */
  CW_USEDEFAULT, /* Y coordinate - let Windows decide */
  CW_USEDEFAULT, /* width - let Windows decide */
  CW_USEDEFAULT, /* height - let Windows decide */
  HWND_DESKTOP, /* no parent window */
  NULL, /* no override of class menu */
  hThisInst, /* handle of this instance of the program */
  NULL /* no additional arguments */
);

/* Display the window. */
ShowWindow(hwnd, nWinMode);
UpdateWindow(hwnd);

/* Create the message loop. */
while(GetMessage(&msg, NULL, 0, 0))
{
  TranslateMessage(&msg); /* translate keyboard messages */
  DispatchMessage(&msg); /* return control to Windows */
  run(hwnd, memdc); /* cycle the animation */
```

```
    }
  return msg.wParam;
}


/* Window Procedure */
LRESULT CALLBACK WindowFunc(HWND hwnd, UINT message,
                              WPARAM wParam, LPARAM lParam)
{
  HDC hdc;
  PAINTSTRUCT ps;

  switch(message) {
    case WM_CREATE:
      /* get screen coordinates */
      maxX = GetSystemMetrics(SM_CXSCREEN);
      maxY = GetSystemMetrics(SM_CYSCREEN);

      /* create a virtual window */
      hdc = GetDC(hwnd);
      memdc = CreateCompatibleDC(hdc);
      hbit = CreateCompatibleBitmap(hdc, maxX, maxY);
      SelectObject(memdc, hbit);
      hbrush = GetStockObject(WHITE_BRUSH);
      SelectObject(memdc, hbrush);
      PatBlt(memdc, 0, 0, maxX, maxY, PATCOPY);

      animdim.left = X; animdim.top = Y;
      animdim.right = X + BITMAPSIZE;
      animdim.bottom = Y + BITMAPSIZE;

      bmpdc = CreateCompatibleDC(hdc);

      SelectObject(bmpdc, hAnBit1);
      /* copy bitmap to virtual window */
      BitBlt(memdc, X, Y, BITMAPSIZE, BITMAPSIZE,
             bmpdc, 0, 0, SRCCOPY);

      ReleaseDC(hwnd, hdc);
      InvalidateRect(hwnd, NULL, 1);
      break;
    case WM_PAINT: /* process a repaint request */
      hdc = BeginPaint(hwnd, &ps); /* get DC */
```

```
      /* copy virtual window onto screen */
      BitBlt(hdc, ps.rcPaint.left, ps.rcPaint.top,
             ps.rcPaint.right-ps.rcPaint.left, /* width */
             ps.rcPaint.bottom-ps.rcPaint.top, /* height */
             memdc,
             ps.rcPaint.left, ps.rcPaint.top,
             SRCCOPY);

      EndPaint(hwnd, &ps); /* release DC */
      break;
    case WM_DESTROY: /* terminate the program */
      DeleteDC(memdc);
      DeleteDC(bmpdc);
      PostQuitMessage(0);
      break;
    default:
      return DefWindowProc(hwnd, message, wParam, lParam);
  }
  return 0;
}

/* Animate during idle time. */
void run(HWND hwnd, HDC memdc)
{
  RECT r;

  Sleep(10); // slow down animation

  X++;

  /* get size of client area */
  GetClientRect(hwnd, &r);
  if(X+1 > r.right) X = 0;

  /* copy bitmap to virtual window */
  BitBlt(memdc, X, Y, BITMAPSIZE, BITMAPSIZE,
         bmpdc, 0, 0, SRCCOPY);

  animdim.left = X;
  animdim.top = Y;
  animdim.right = X + BITMAPSIZE;
  animdim.bottom = Y + BITMAPSIZE;
  InvalidateRect(hwnd, &animdim, 0);
}
```

When the program begins, it loads the sprite bitmap and puts its handle into **hAnBit1**. Inside **WM_CREATE** a compatible DC is created, and the sprite bitmap is selected into this device context. Next, the bitmap is initially drawn to the screen.

The most important part of this program is contained in the **run( )** function. In this and subsequent examples, the sprite is repeatedly moved across the window, left to right. To accomplish this, **X** is incremented. When the rightmost extent is reached, **X** is reset to 0. However, since the size of the window may change, the first thing that **run( )** does is obtain the current dimensions of the client area. This provides the current rightmost coordinate no matter what size the window is. After the coordinates have been updated, the next image is copied into the virtual window specified by **memdc**, and then **InvalidateRect( )** is called to actually update the screen. To see the effect of this, try maximizing the animation window size when the program is running. The train engine will now move to the edge of the maximized window.

As mentioned, this approach to animation is limited for two reasons. First, it moves only a single bitmap. Second, it will work only with a solid background. In the next two sections, these two limitations will be removed.

SPRITE-LEVEL ANIMATION

If you think about it, there are really two types of animation. The first is *screen* based. This is the type of animation implemented by the preceding program. In screen-based animation, a fixed object is moved about the screen. But, the object is unchanging. The second type of animation is *sprite* based. In this case, the sprite changes form as it is animated. For example, to effectively animate an image of an engine moving, you will need to move the entire engine, but you will need to show its wheels turning and its smoke billowing, too. The movement of the wheels and smoke occurs within the sprite. To achieve life-like animation, both screen-level and sprite-level animation are required. In this section, you will see how to create sprite-level animation.

There are various ways to perform sprite-level animation. One of the easiest is to simply create multiple sprites, each slightly different from the next. When the sprite is animated, the images are sequenced with each animation cycle. This is the method of sprite-level animation used by the following example.

To try the program, you will need to create two additional 64×64 pixel sprites and save them into files called *Bp2.bmp* and *Bp3.bmp*. You will also need to create a resource file that contains the following:

```
MYBP1 BITMAP BP1.BMP
MYBP2 BITMAP BP2.BMP
MYBP3 BITMAP BP3.BMP
```

The two sprites used by the example program are shown (while being edited) in Figure 8-8 and Figure 8-9.

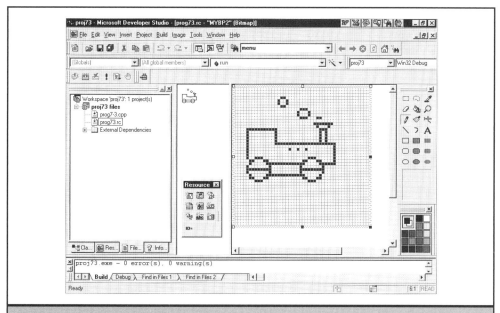

Figure 8-8. First additional sprite required for sprite-level animation example

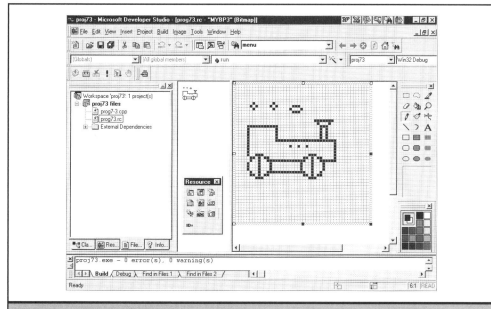

Figure 8-9. Second additional sprite required for sprite-level animation example

The output from the program is shown in Figures 8-10 and 8-11. Note the difference in the smoke shown in these figures and that shown in Figures 8-5 through 8-7.

Here is the entire program that performs both screen-level and sprite-level animation.

```c
/* Adding sprite-level animation. */
#include <windows.h>
#include <string.h>
#include <stdio.h>

#define BITMAPSIZE 64

void run(HWND hwnd, HDC memdc);

LRESULT CALLBACK WindowFunc(HWND, UINT, WPARAM, LPARAM);

char szWinName[] = "MyWin"; /* name of window class */

int X=0, Y=20; /* current output location */
int maxX, maxY; /* screen dimensions */
RECT animdim; /* size of area to animate */

HDC memdc; /* store the virtual device handle */
HDC bmpdc; /* store the bitmap device handle */
HBITMAP hbit; /* store the virtual bitmap handle */
HBITMAP hAnBit1, hAnBit2, hAnBit3; /* animation bitmaps */
HBRUSH hbrush; /* store the brush handle */

int WINAPI WinMain(HINSTANCE hThisInst, HINSTANCE hPrevInst,
                   LPSTR lpszArgs, int nWinMode)
{
  HWND hwnd;
  MSG msg;
  WNDCLASSEX wcl;

  /* Define a window class. */
  wcl.hInstance = hThisInst; /* handle to this instance */
  wcl.lpszClassName = szWinName; /* window class name */
  wcl.lpfnWndProc = WindowFunc; /* window function */
  wcl.style = 0; /* default style */

  wcl.cbSize = sizeof(WNDCLASSEX); /* set size of WNDCLASSEX */

  wcl.hIcon = LoadIcon(NULL, IDI_APPLICATION); /* standard icon */
  wcl.hIconSm = LoadIcon(NULL, IDI_APPLICATION); /* small icon */
  wcl.hCursor = LoadCursor(NULL, IDC_ARROW); /* cursor style */
```

```
wcl.lpszMenuName = NULL; /* no main menu */
wcl.cbClsExtra = 0; /* no extra */
wcl.cbWndExtra = 0; /* information needed */

/* Use white background. */
wcl.hbrBackground = GetStockObject(WHITE_BRUSH);

/* Register the window class. */
if(!RegisterClassEx(&wcl)) return 0;

/* load the bitmap */
hAnBit1 = LoadBitmap(hThisInst, "MYBP1"); /* load bitmap */
hAnBit2 = LoadBitmap(hThisInst, "MYBP2"); /* load bitmap */
hAnBit3 = LoadBitmap(hThisInst, "MYBP3"); /* load bitmap */

/* Create the window. */
hwnd = CreateWindow(
  szWinName, /* name of window class */
  "Animating Multiple Bitmaps", /* title */
  WS_OVERLAPPEDWINDOW, /* standard window */
  CW_USEDEFAULT, /* X coordinate - let Windows decide */
  CW_USEDEFAULT, /* Y coordinate - let Windows decide */
  CW_USEDEFAULT, /* width - let Windows decide */
  CW_USEDEFAULT, /* height - let Windows decide */
  HWND_DESKTOP, /* no parent window */
  NULL, /* no override of class menu */
  hThisInst, /* handle of this instance of the program */
  NULL /* no additional arguments */
);

/* Display the window. */
ShowWindow(hwnd, nWinMode);
UpdateWindow(hwnd);

/* Create the message loop. */
while(GetMessage(&msg, NULL, 0, 0))
{
  TranslateMessage(&msg); /* translate keyboard messages */
  DispatchMessage(&msg); /* return control to Windows */
  run(hwnd, memdc); /* cycle the animation */
}
return msg.wParam;
}
```

```
/* Window Procedure */
LRESULT CALLBACK WindowFunc(HWND hwnd, UINT message,
                            WPARAM wParam, LPARAM lParam)
{
  HDC hdc;
  PAINTSTRUCT ps;

  switch(message) {
    case WM_CREATE:
      /* get screen coordinates */
      maxX = GetSystemMetrics(SM_CXSCREEN);
      maxY = GetSystemMetrics(SM_CYSCREEN);

      /* create a virtual window */
      hdc = GetDC(hwnd);
      memdc = CreateCompatibleDC(hdc);
      hbit = CreateCompatibleBitmap(hdc, maxX, maxY);
      SelectObject(memdc, hbit);
      hbrush = GetStockObject(WHITE_BRUSH);
      SelectObject(memdc, hbrush);
      PatBlt(memdc, 0, 0, maxX, maxY, PATCOPY);

      animdim.left = X; animdim.top = Y;
      animdim.right = X + BITMAPSIZE;
      animdim.bottom = Y + BITMAPSIZE;

      bmpdc = CreateCompatibleDC(hdc);
      /* select and copy first bitmap to virtual window */
      SelectObject(bmpdc, hAnBit1);
      BitBlt(memdc, X, Y, BITMAPSIZE, BITMAPSIZE,
             bmpdc, 0, 0, SRCCOPY);

      ReleaseDC(hwnd, hdc);
      InvalidateRect(hwnd, NULL, 1);
      break;
    case WM_PAINT: /* process a repaint request */
      hdc = BeginPaint(hwnd, &ps); /* get DC */

      /* copy virtual window onto screen */
      BitBlt(hdc, ps.rcPaint.left, ps.rcPaint.top,
             ps.rcPaint.right-ps.rcPaint.left, /* width */
             ps.rcPaint.bottom-ps.rcPaint.top, /* height */
             memdc,
```

```
                ps.rcPaint.left, ps.rcPaint.top,
                SRCCOPY);

      EndPaint(hwnd, &ps); /* release DC */
      break;
    case WM_DESTROY: /* terminate the program */
      DeleteDC(memdc);
      DeleteDC(bmpdc);
      PostQuitMessage(0);
      break;
    default:
      return DefWindowProc(hwnd, message, wParam, lParam);
  }
  return 0;
}

/* Animate during idle time. */
void run(HWND hwnd, HDC memdc)
{
  RECT r;

  static int map = 0;

  Sleep(10); // slow down animation

  X++;

  /* get size of client area */
  GetClientRect(hwnd, &r);
  if(X+1 > r.right) X = 0;

  map++;
  if(map>2) map = 0;

  /* switch between sprites */
  switch(map) {
    case 0:
      SelectObject(bmpdc, hAnBit1);
      BitBlt(memdc, X, Y, BITMAPSIZE, BITMAPSIZE,
            bmpdc, 0, 0, SRCCOPY);
      break;
    case 1:
      SelectObject(bmpdc, hAnBit2);
      BitBlt(memdc, X, Y, BITMAPSIZE, BITMAPSIZE,
```

```
                 bmpdc, 0, 0, SRCCOPY);
      break;
    case 2:
      SelectObject(bmpdc, hAnBit3);
      BitBlt(memdc, X, Y, BITMAPSIZE, BITMAPSIZE,
                 bmpdc, 0, 0, SRCCOPY);
      break;
  }

  animdim.left = X;
  animdim.top = Y;
  animdim.right = X + BITMAPSIZE;
  animdim.bottom = Y + BITMAPSIZE;
  InvalidateRect(hwnd, &animdim, 0);
}
```

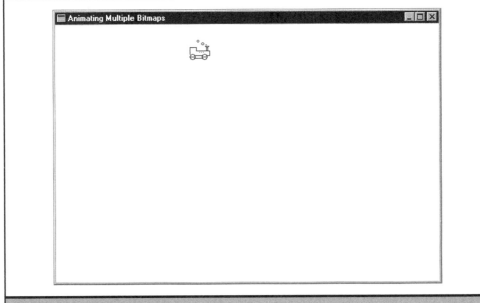

Figure 8-10.   Sprite-level animation (1 of 2)

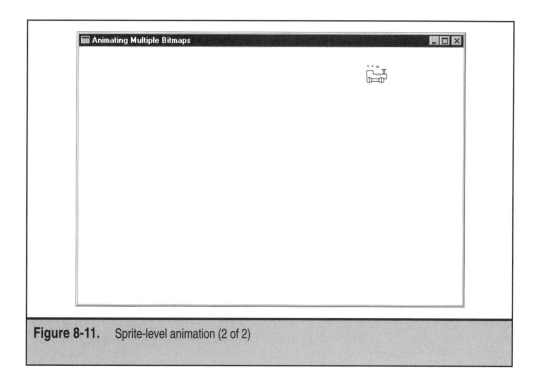

Figure 8-11.   Sprite-level animation (2 of 2)

Again, the major changes to this program are found in the **run( )** function. Notice that in this version each animation cycle displays a different bitmap. This causes the wheels and smoke from the engine to move as it runs across the window.

WORKING WITH FOREGROUNDS AND BACKGROUNDS

Up to this point, all animation has taken place against a solid background. However, for more sophisticated animation, you will be animating a sprite against some sort of background or foreground scene. Working with foregrounds and backgrounds adds complexity and overhead to any animation system. However, this is the price that must be paid for more lifelike animation.

When you're working against a background scene, another step is added to the animation cycle, because the background must be preserved. Thus, each time an animation cycle occurs, the following two steps must be taken:

1. The background of the region currently occupied by the sprite must be restored, erasing the sprite in the process.

2. The sprite must be redrawn in its new location, preserving any part of the background that is not part of the sprite.

Step 2 is potentially complicated. If the sprite is contained in a bitmap, then some means of drawing the sprite needs to be worked out so that only those portions of the background that are actually covered by the sprite are overwritten.

Typically, the background is held in its own bitmap, which means that another bitmap will be added to the animation program. It is important to understand that only those parts of the background that need to be restored should be restored. The reason for this is to increase speed. It takes much less time to restore a small region than it does to restore the entire screen.

Handling the Transparency Problem

When you're working with a foreground and a background, the most troubling problem is the issue of *transparency*. For example, if you want to animate the engine running down a track and the engine is contained in a bitmap, then when the engine bitmap is copied on the background, you want only the engine—not the entire rectangular region—to appear in the final scene. How this is done will depend on what effect you are trying to achieve. For example, if you can color-code your background and foreground so that both use different color sets, then you can write very fast animation code. However, it is also possible to write "generic" code that will allow you to add a sprite over any background. This method is described here and used in the example at the end of this section.

To begin, let's restate the problem a bit more formally. As you know, in Windows NT, bitmaps are rectangular objects. That is, it is not possible to create an irregularly shaped bitmap. Most often, the sprite is contained within the confines of its bitmap, but does not utilize every pixel in the map. The engine shown in Figure 8-4 is an example. The engine occupies a relatively small portion of the entire map. The remainder of the map is unused. In the preceding examples, this situation did not cause a problem because the background of the screen was the same solid color as that of the background of the bitmap. However, when you want to animate a bitmapped sprite over a background scene containing several different shapes and colors, there must be some mechanism to prevent the unused portions of the bitmap from overwriting the background. Put differently, when you animate a sprite over a background scene, you want to see only the sprite, not the entire rectangular bitmap. Thus, there must be some means by which the unused background surrounding the sprite is rendered transparent.

The most general method to get the desired result is through the use of a sequence of logical bitwise operations using the **BitBlt( )** function. In basic terms, here is what will occur. First, you need to decide upon a transparent color. For the purposes of this chapter, white is used. Next, a monochrome (that is, black and white) image of each sprite in the animation sequence must be generated. These monochrome images will serve as masking bitmaps. Construct each mask so that the entire sprite is black on a white background. Once you have created each mask, the following steps are required to transparently write a sprite over an existing background scene:

1. Redraw the background, if necessary—that is, start with an untouched background.

2. AND the mask onto the background. This causes the area that will be occupied by the sprite to be cut out of the scene. (It will look like a sprite-shaped cookie-cutter was used.)

3. Invert the mask. This produces a negative (black and white reversed) image of the mask.

4. AND the inverted mask with the sprite and save the result.

5. Invert the mask a second time to restore it to its original appearance so that it is ready for the next animation cycle.

6. OR the result of step 4 onto the background created in step 2.

After you follow these steps, the sprite portion of the bitmap will have been copied to the screen, but the surrounding background will have been left as is. This process is depicted in Figure 8-12.

Now that the general method has been explained, let's see what it takes to implement it. In the process, we will modify the preceding program so that the engine runs down a track.

Creating the Masks

To begin, you must create the three masks that correspond to the three versions of the engine sprites. The easiest way to do this is to simply create exact monochrome versions of each sprite. Save these masks in the files *Bp4.bmp*, *Bp5.bmp*, and *Bp6.bmp*. You will also need to change the resource file so that it looks like this:

```
MYBP1 BITMAP BP1.BMP
MYBP2 BITMAP BP2.BMP
MYBP3 BITMAP BP3.BMP
MASKBIT1 BITMAP BP4.BMP
MASKBIT2 BITMAP BP5.BMP
MASKBIT3 BITMAP BP6.BMP
```

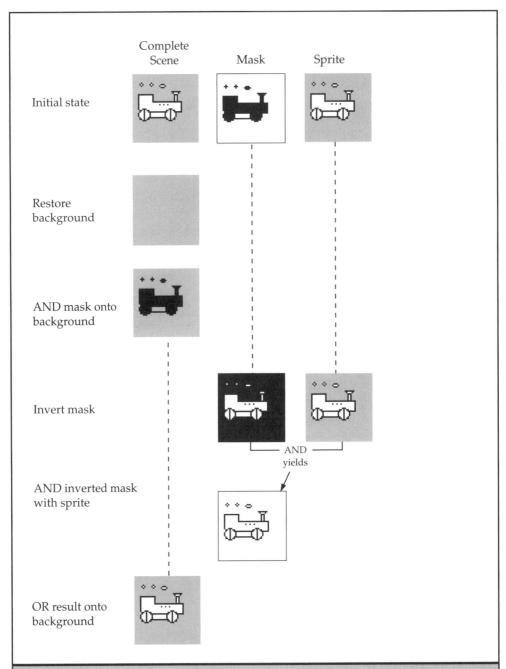

Figure 8-12.   Transparently drawing a sprite over a background scene

The Entire Background/Foreground Example

Here is the complete program that illustrates animating a sprite against a background. Sample output is shown in Figures 8-13 and 8-14.

```
/* Working with foregrounds and backgrounds. */
#include <windows.h>
#include <string.h>
#include <stdio.h>

#define BITMAPSIZE 64

void run(HWND hwnd, HDC memdc);

LRESULT CALLBACK WindowFunc(HWND, UINT, WPARAM, LPARAM);

char szWinName[] = "MyWin"; /* name of window class */

int X=0, Y=18; /* current output location */
int maxX, maxY; /* screen dimensions */
RECT animdim; /* size of area to animate */

HDC memdc; /* virtual window DC */
HDC backgroundDC; /* background DC */
HDC bmpdc; /* bitmap DC */
HDC tempdc1, tempdc2;
HBITMAP hbit, hbit2, hbittemp1, hbittemp2;  /* bitmap handles */
HBITMAP hAnBit1, hAnBit2, hAnBit3; /* animation bitmaps */
HBITMAP hmaskbit1, hmaskbit2, hmaskbit3; /* masks */
HBRUSH hbrush; /* store the brush handle */

int WINAPI WinMain(HINSTANCE hThisInst, HINSTANCE hPrevInst,
                   LPSTR lpszArgs, int nWinMode)
{
  HWND hwnd;
  MSG msg;
  WNDCLASSEX wcl;

  /* Define a window class. */
  wcl.hInstance = hThisInst; /* handle to this instance */
  wcl.lpszClassName = szWinName; /* window class name */
  wcl.lpfnWndProc = WindowFunc; /* window function */
  wcl.style = 0; /* default style */

  wcl.cbSize = sizeof(WNDCLASSEX); /* set size of WNDCLASSEX */
```

```
wcl.hIcon = LoadIcon(NULL, IDI_APPLICATION); /* standard icon */
wcl.hIconSm = LoadIcon(NULL, IDI_APPLICATION); /* small icon */
wcl.hCursor = LoadCursor(NULL, IDC_ARROW); /* cursor style */

wcl.lpszMenuName = NULL; /* no main menu */
wcl.cbClsExtra = 0; /* no extra */
wcl.cbWndExtra = 0; /* information needed */

/* Use white window. */
wcl.hbrBackground = GetStockObject(WHITE_BRUSH);

/* Register the window class. */
if(!RegisterClassEx(&wcl)) return 0;

/* load the bitmaps */
hAnBit1 = LoadBitmap(hThisInst, "MYBP1"); /* load bitmap */
hAnBit2 = LoadBitmap(hThisInst, "MYBP2"); /* load bitmap */
hAnBit3 = LoadBitmap(hThisInst, "MYBP3"); /* load bitmap */

/* load the masks */
hmaskbit1 = LoadBitmap(hThisInst, "MASKBIT1");
hmaskbit2 = LoadBitmap(hThisInst, "MASKBIT2");
hmaskbit3 = LoadBitmap(hThisInst, "MASKBIT3");

/* Create window. */
hwnd = CreateWindow(
  szWinName, /* name of window class */
  "Working with Foregrounds and Backgrounds", /* title */
  WS_OVERLAPPEDWINDOW, /* standard window */
  CW_USEDEFAULT, /* X coordinate - let Windows decide */
  CW_USEDEFAULT, /* Y coordinate - let Windows decide */
  CW_USEDEFAULT, /* width - let Windows decide */
  CW_USEDEFAULT, /* height - let Windows decide */
  HWND_DESKTOP, /* no parent window */
  NULL, /* no menu */
  hThisInst, /* handle of this instance of the program */
  NULL /* no additional arguments */
);

/* Display the window. */
ShowWindow(hwnd, nWinMode);
UpdateWindow(hwnd);
```

```
  /* Create the message loop. */
  while(GetMessage(&msg, NULL, 0, 0))
  {
    TranslateMessage(&msg); /* translate keyboard messages */
    DispatchMessage(&msg); /* return control to Windows */
    run(hwnd, memdc); /* cycle the animation */
  }
  return msg.wParam;
}

/* Window Procedure */
LRESULT CALLBACK WindowFunc(HWND hwnd, UINT message,
                            WPARAM wParam, LPARAM lParam)
{
  HDC hdc;
  PAINTSTRUCT ps;

  int i;

  switch(message) {
    case WM_CREATE:
      /* get screen coordinates */
      maxX = GetSystemMetrics(SM_CXSCREEN);
      maxY = GetSystemMetrics(SM_CYSCREEN);

      /* create a virtual window */
      hdc = GetDC(hwnd);
      memdc = CreateCompatibleDC(hdc);
      hbit = CreateCompatibleBitmap(hdc, maxX, maxY);
      SelectObject(memdc, hbit);
      hbrush = GetStockObject(WHITE_BRUSH);
      SelectObject(memdc, hbrush);
      PatBlt(memdc, 0, 0, maxX, maxY, PATCOPY);

      /* create the background DC */
      backgroundDC = CreateCompatibleDC(hdc);
      hbit2 = CreateCompatibleBitmap(hdc, maxX, maxY);
      SelectObject(backgroundDC, hbit2);
      SelectObject(backgroundDC, hbrush);
      PatBlt(backgroundDC, 0, 0, maxX, maxY, PATCOPY);

      tempdc1 = CreateCompatibleDC(hdc);
      tempdc2 = CreateCompatibleDC(hdc);
```

```
      hbittemp2 = CreateCompatibleBitmap(hdc, BITMAPSIZE, BITMAPSIZE);
      SelectObject(tempdc2, hbittemp2);

      /* draw background */
      for(i=40; i<60; i += 10) {
        MoveToEx(backgroundDC, 0, i, NULL);
        LineTo(backgroundDC, maxX, i);
      }
      for(i=10; i<maxX; i += 10) {
        MoveToEx(backgroundDC, i, 35, NULL);
        LineTo(backgroundDC, i, 56);
      }

      BitBlt(memdc, 0, 0, maxX, maxY,
             backgroundDC, 0, 0, SRCCOPY); /* copy background */

      animdim.left = X; animdim.top = Y;
      animdim.right = X + BITMAPSIZE;
      animdim.bottom = Y + BITMAPSIZE;

      bmpdc = CreateCompatibleDC(hdc);

      ReleaseDC(hwnd, hdc);
      InvalidateRect(hwnd, NULL, 1);
      break;
    case WM_PAINT: /* process a repaint request */
      hdc = BeginPaint(hwnd, &ps); /* get DC */

     /* copy virtual window onto screen */
      BitBlt(hdc, ps.rcPaint.left, ps.rcPaint.top,
             ps.rcPaint.right-ps.rcPaint.left, /* width */
             ps.rcPaint.bottom-ps.rcPaint.top, /* height */
             memdc,
             ps.rcPaint.left, ps.rcPaint.top,
             SRCCOPY);

      EndPaint(hwnd, &ps); /* release DC */
      break;
    case WM_DESTROY: /* terminate the program */
      DeleteDC(memdc);
      DeleteDC(bmpdc);
      DeleteDC(backgroundDC);
      DeleteDC(tempdc1);
      DeleteDC(tempdc2);
```

```
      PostQuitMessage(0);
      break;
    default:
      return DefWindowProc(hwnd, message, wParam, lParam);
  }
  return 0;
}

/* Animate during idle time. */
void run(HWND hwnd, HDC memdc)
{
  RECT r;

  static int map = 0;

  Sleep(10); // slow down animation

  /* restore the background */
  BitBlt(memdc, X, Y, BITMAPSIZE, BITMAPSIZE,
         backgroundDC, X, Y, SRCCOPY);

  X++;

  /* get size of client area */
  GetClientRect(hwnd, &r);
  if(X+1 > r.right) X = 0;

  map++;
  if(map>2) map = 0;

  switch(map) {
    case 0:
      SelectObject(bmpdc, hAnBit1);
      SelectObject(tempdc1, hmaskbit1);
      break;
    case 1:
      SelectObject(bmpdc, hAnBit2);
      SelectObject(tempdc1, hmaskbit2);
      break;
    case 2:
      SelectObject(bmpdc, hAnBit3);
      SelectObject(tempdc1, hmaskbit3);
      break;
```

```
}

/* AND masking image on background */
BitBlt(memdc, X, Y, BITMAPSIZE, BITMAPSIZE,
       tempdc1, 0, 0, SRCAND);

/* invert mask */
BitBlt(tempdc1, 0, 0, BITMAPSIZE, BITMAPSIZE,
       tempdc1, 0, 0, DSTINVERT);
/* copy sprite to work area */
BitBlt(tempdc2, 0, 0, BITMAPSIZE, BITMAPSIZE,
       bmpdc, 0, 0, SRCCOPY);
/* AND sprite with inverted mask */
BitBlt(tempdc2, 0, 0, BITMAPSIZE, BITMAPSIZE,
       tempdc1, 0, 0, SRCAND);
/* restore mask */
BitBlt(tempdc1, 0, 0, BITMAPSIZE, BITMAPSIZE,
       tempdc1, 0, 0, DSTINVERT);

/* OR resulting image onto background */
BitBlt(memdc, X, Y, BITMAPSIZE, BITMAPSIZE,
       tempdc2, 0, 0, SRCPAINT);

animdim.left = X;
animdim.top = Y;
animdim.right = X + BITMAPSIZE;
animdim.bottom = Y + BITMAPSIZE;

InvalidateRect(hwnd, &animdim, 0);
}
```

As you can see, this program is substantially more complex than the others in this chapter. This is because of all the extra bit manipulations needed to handle the foreground and background. For example, the program requires the use of two bitmaps that will act simply as scratch work areas. The handles to these areas are specified by **hbittemp1** and **hbittemp2**. The device contexts used by the scratch bitmaps are **tempdc1** and **tempdc2**. The handles to the masking bitmaps are held in **hmaskbit1**, **hmaskbit2**, and **hmaskbit3**. The background scene is held in the bitmap whose handle is **hbit2** and whose device context is specified by **backgroundDC**. Inside **WM_CREATE** the various device contexts and bitmaps are created. Also, the track is drawn onto the background bitmap. Inside **run( )**, the various bit manipulations implement the general technique described earlier. You should be able to follow all the bit manipulations if you work through the code carefully.

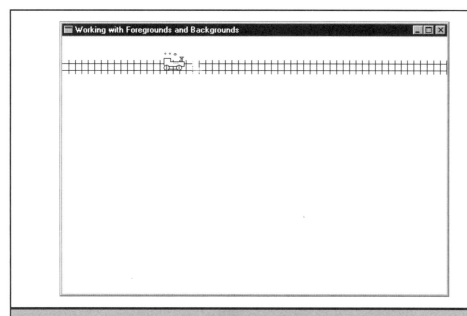

Figure 8-13. First sample output from the Foreground/Background program

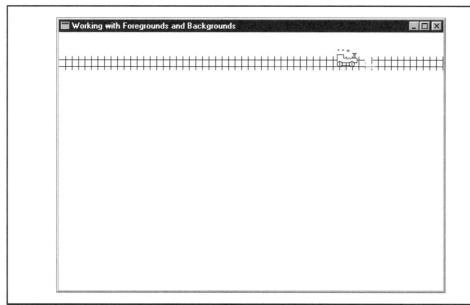

Figure 8-14. Second sample output from the Foreground/Background program

CONCLUSION

We have been covering advanced GUI. A picture is worth a thousand words, and you convey a lot about your program with your program's user interface. How do you improve what you convey with your picture? You add motion or action to it.

As mentioned in the beginning of this chapter, there are two general ways in which you can display motion under Windows NT. The first way is to animate bitmapped images. Bitmap-level animation is generally used to move relatively small objects over a fixed background. This type of animation was discussed and illustrated with examples in this chapter. The second way is to display an AVI (audio video interleaved) file by use of an animation control, which was described in Chapter 7. AVI files are generally used to display full-motion video.

CHAPTER 9

NT Dynamic Link Libraries (DLLs)

A *dynamic link library* is a library of functions or resources. The process of creating the DLL is very similar to that of creating a Windows application. The functions are invoked by applications or other DLLs. DLLs are an integral part of Windows NT programming, and using DLLs is an important tool in the repertoire of Windows NT programmers. DLLs have been available in prior versions of Windows—you may have programmed DLLs with Win16. But don't skip this chapter based on the 16-bit DLL experience, since there are significant differences between Win32 DLLs and Win16 DLLs. We will cover the differences in this chapter.

We will start with the need for DLLs and compare the development of DLLs and of applications. Developing DLLs is very similar to developing applications, with minor differences in linking and execution. You can invoke a DLL for execution in two ways. We will see how you can make functions in a DLL available for invocation by applications. We will explore the concept of DLL versions and how you can use versions to ensure that the right version of the DLL is loaded.

Note for UNIX Programmers

If you have used shared libraries that support dynamic linking/loading, then Windows NT DLLs are conceptually the same.

WHY DLLs

If you are developing a Windows application, then using DLLs is not mandatory, although you are likely to find that any nontrivial system using Windows applications will use DLLs. There are good reasons to use DLLs. Windows NT itself uses a large number of DLLs internally. You may be familiar with many of these DLLs. Table 9-1 lists some of these DLLs and the functions performed by them.

One of the advantages of using DLLs is that DLLs enable you to group commonly used functions into a unit that can be invoked by a number of different applications. In the course of developing a large software system, after high-level design and before coding, you will allocate the overall system functions into code modules. During this allocation, you will identify a number of common functions that are useful throughout the overall system. DLLs are a handy way to group these functions. You will typically end up with a number of DLLs, with each DLL containing related functions, data, and/or resources. Any application in the system can invoke the functionality in the DLL and thus does not have to repeat the DLL functionality. Allocating the common functions to DLLs also helps to contain any changes required in the common functions to the DLLs, and to ensure that the rest of the applications in the system are not affected. For example, in a financial system, calculating interest needs to be performed in different parts of the system. Isolating the interest calculation code to a DLL makes it easy to compute interest differently (for example, to use a different compounding method). Later in this chapter we will look at an example where calculating interest is one of the functions in a DLL.

DLL	Function
KERNEL32.DLL	Kernel functions, such as functions for managing processes, memory, and so on
GDI32.DLL	Graphics functions, such as drawing geometrical shapes, filling the shapes, and so on
OLESVR32.DLL	OLE server functions (32 bit)
SHELL32.DLL	Shell functions supporting 32-bit shell APIs
USER32.DLL	User interface functions, such as managing windows and handling messages

Table 9-1.   Windows NT DLLs and Their Functions

Another advantage of DLLs is in software packaging and distribution. In software development, you will invariably have portions of the overall software that are applicable only to certain customers. Thus, it is beneficial to isolate the portions that are customer specific to DLLs, and to organize the rest of the system as one or more EXEs applicable to all customers. Appendix A contains a simple example that lets users key in their name and then redisplay the name keyed in. The example is designed to let users using different languages, such as French and German, see dialog boxes that are in their own language. The names are input with keyboards supporting their language. In this case, there is one EXE and the language-specific resources are contained within DLLs. Such an approach permits shipping the main EXE and appropriate language-specific DLLs to each country. If you want to add an additional language, you just add the DLLs for it (which does not affect the existing users). The same is true if you want to drop the support for a language. Thus, you can add new resources, functions, and so on, to a DLL, and the new DLLs will work with the existing applications so long as the EXE-to-DLL interface does not change.

Yet another advantage of DLLs is run-time memory savings. Once a DLL has been loaded, further requests to load the DLL by other threads in the same process do not cause additional copies of the DLL to be loaded. Windows recognizes that the DLL has already been loaded and keeps a count of the number of threads using the DLL by means of a *usage count.* Loading a DLL only once saves memory. In addition, the DLL can be loaded when needed. The initial memory to be allocated to the EXE that invokes the DLL is less than the memory that would need to be allocated if the DLL were part of the EXE.

Finally, splitting the overall system functions into EXEs and DLLs permits simultaneous development of DLLs and the EXEs.

The benefits of using DLLs are not free. Once you split the functions that are in an EXE into an EXE and a DLL, you have introduced an interface (that between the EXE and the DLL). Interfaces between applications are one of the trouble spots in a software system. Any large software system is like a chain of links. The individual programs make up the software system chain, and the adage "A chain is as strong as its weakest link" translates into "The software system is as error free as its interfaces." Quite often the individual programs that make up a software system work fine, but the system as a whole does not. Invariably the first set of error reports from a system test almost exclusively contains interface errors.

A related problem with DLLs is one of version control. DLLs can be changed without changing the invoking EXE or DLL. This is true only as long as the interface does not change. If the interface changes and the invoking EXE or DLL has to change, we may have situations where the invoking EXE or DLL will work correctly only if the correct version of the DLL is available (and not any older version). If you are in programming, you are bound to come across "Murphy's law." In this case, Murphy's law states that the EXE will somehow find the wrong versions of the DLL. One of the most common questions support teams and help desks face deals with versions. It is not uncommon in many development efforts to repeat program builds because the wrong version was picked up during the build. Software configuration control systems try to maintain version control. You can also use the version feature of DLLs to keep track of DLL versions. This is covered in an example later in this chapter.

Another simple problem is that although you can create a DLL with Visual C++, you can create the EXE with another tool, for example, a regular C compiler. In this case, you have to watch out for name mangling. *Name mangling* refers to the fact that C++ compilers alter the names of functions they export, and as a result a calling application using an unmangled name may not be able to find the function in the DLL. Name mangling is covered later in this chapter.

COMPARING DLL AND APPLICATION DEVELOPMENT

The development of DLLs up to the compilation stage is the same as that of a Windows application. You write the DLL code and compile the code just as you would with any Windows application.

At the linking stage, you have to indicate to the linkage editor that you are link editing a DLL and not an application. The typical linkage editor options for a DLL are /dll, /nologo, and /subsystem:windows. The "/dll" indicates to the linkage editor that you are linkage editing a DLL. You can also check the Win32 DLL box in the Developer Studio as a type of application.

In the execution stage you manually start an application for execution by double-clicking an icon associated with the application's EXE file (you can also key in the application's name at a command prompt). The DLL does not execute in a stand-alone manner, unlike the application. Instead it is invoked for execution by an application or by another DLL. DLLs can be specified to be invoked during link-edit time or at run time. Invoking DLLs is covered later in the chapter.

Typically DLLs do not handle end-user interfaces. One of the consequences is that DLLs cannot use the About option under Help to display information about the DLL itself. EXEs that handle end-user interfaces use the About option under Help to display messages about the EXE itself, such as its version information, copyright information, and so on. However, you can use a DLL's version-control resource file for this purpose, and this is illustrated in an example later in this chapter.

WIN16 AND WIN32 DLL DIFFERENCES

As mentioned in the beginning of the chapter, there are significant differences between Win16 DLLs and Win32 DLLs. These differences are summarized in Table 9-2.

If you are migrating old 16-bit DLLs to 32-bit DLLs in Windows NT, then you have to take care of references to **LibMain**, **WEP**, **GetModuleUsage**, and so on by replacing obsolete references with equivalent current ones.

Win16 DLL	Win32 DLL
Once loaded, all executing applications can access all functions in the DLL.	The DLL is process specific, and only the threads of the process that loads the DLL can access the DLL functions by default.
The DLL allocates and uses its own memory.	The DLL allocates from the memory space of the process.
GetModuleUsage provides the current usage count for the DLL.	GetModuleUsage is not supported. You can check if a DLL is loaded using GetModuleHandle.
The return value when a DLL is not loaded is a number that indicates the reason for the error.	The return value is NULL. Use GET_LAST_ERROR to find the reason.
LibMain is called when a DLL is initialized.	DllMain is called as the entry and exit routine.
There is no concept of threads in Win16.	DllMain is called for the process loading the DLL as well as when individual threads are created in the process after the DLL is loaded.

Table 9-2.   Comparison of Win16 DLLs and Win32 DLLs

INVOKING AND FREEING DLLs

As mentioned earlier, DLLs can be specified to be invoked during link-edit time or at run time. Let's look at each of the methods in detail.

At link-edit time, you specify the DLL functions that an application can call in the DLL's LIB file that is passed to the linkage editor. The linkage editor includes the name of the DLL in the calling application's EXE file. At run time, Windows looks for the required DLLs when it loads the application's EXE file and performs a number of steps related to the invocation of the DLL as shown under "Steps in Invoking a DLL." The usage count of a DLL included at link-edit time is automatically set to 1 at run time. In addition, if the same DLL is loaded again at run time by another thread in the process then the usage count is incremented.

Alternatively, you can invoke a DLL at run time by using **LoadLibrary** or **LoadLibraryEx**. Both specify the name of the DLL to be loaded. **LoadLibraryEx** supports two additional parameters, one of which (see the HANDLE *hFl* parameter in the prototype next) must be NULL. The other parameter (*dwFlgs*) lets you include some options to override the default Windows behavior as mentioned under "Steps in Invoking a DLL." If the *dwFlgs* parameter is zero, **LoadLibrary** and **LoadLibraryEx** behave identically. We will cover these options in this section. The prototype for **LoadLibraryEx** is shown here:

```
HINSTANCE LoadLibraryEx( LPCTSTR lpLibFlNam,
                         HANDLE hFl,
                         DWORD dwFlgs
 );
```

where *lpLibFlNam* is a pointer to a string that contains the filename of an executable module. The executable module can be either a DLL file or an EXE file. The filename can be just the filename, or it can include a path name. If the path name is specified and the LOAD_WITH_ALTERED_SEARCH_PATH value is specified for *dwFlgs*, then Windows tries to load the executable using the path name. If the executable is not found in the directory pointed to by the path name or in one of the other directories Windows uses to locate a DLL (see "Library Search Order" next), **LoadLibraryEx** returns NULL.

If the path name is not specified and the filename does not have an extension, then ".DLL" is automatically appended to the filename (unless the filename ends with a period).

If the path name is not specified or the LOAD_WITH_ALTERED_SEARCH_PATH value is not specified for *dwFlgs*, then Windows NT uses a specific search order (see "Library Search Order" next).

hFl is reserved and must be NULL.

dwFlgs can contain valid combinations of LOAD_LIBRARY_AS_DATAFILE, LOAD_WITH_ALTERED_SEARCH_PATH, and DONT_RESOLVE_DLL_REFERENCES.

LOAD_LIBRARY_AS_DATAFILE, as its name implies, just causes Windows NT to load the DLL as a data file and not perform some of the steps that are normally done when a DLL is loaded (see steps 4 through 6 in "Steps in Invoking a DLL" later in this chapter). This option is normally used to load a DLL to access resources and messages from the DLL (but not functions).

DONT_RESOLVE_DLL_REFERENCES is similar to LOAD_LIBRARY_AS_DATAFILE in that it also causes Windows NT to just load the DLL and not perform other steps (see steps 4 through 6 in "Steps in Invoking a DLL" later in this chapter) that Windows NT normally performs. In particular, Windows NT does not call the entry point function which performs initialization steps associated with the DLL.

Both **LoadLibrary** and **LoadLibraryEx** return the handle to the loaded DLL if successful and NULL otherwise.

You can free a DLL you invoked by using **FreeLibrary**, whose prototype is shown next:

```
BOOL FreeLibrary( HMODULE hLibMod
    );
```

where *hLibMod* contains the handle that was returned by **LoadLibrary** or **LoadLibraryEx**.

FreeLibrary returns nonzero if successful, and zero otherwise.

Windows NT decrements the usage count in response to the **FreeLibrary** call. If the usage count is zero, then the DLL is unmapped from the process' address space. Windows NT also invokes your DLL exit routine.

In instances when you create a thread within the invoked DLL and want to unload the DLL and terminate the thread, you must use the **FreeLibraryAndExitThread** function instead of **FreeLibrary**. This is because when you call **FreeLibrary** in the DLL, the DLL immediately gets unmapped and the rest of the DLL code (including the **ExitThread**) is no longer available. **FreeLibraryAndExitThread** also decrements the usage count and has no return values. (The only real exception you can have is that the handle of the DLL you passed is invalid and **FreeLibraryAndExitThread** ignores invalid handles—you are freeing the DLL anyway and an invalid handle suggests that the DLL is probably already free.)

Library Search Order

Windows searches various libraries in the following sequence to locate the DLL to load:

1. The directory that contains the EXE file of the application (which is loading the DLL) or the directory specified in the *lpLibFlNam* parameter (you must also specify LOAD_WITH_ALTERED_SEARCH_PATH for *dwFlgs*).

2. The current directory of the process.

3. The 32-bit Windows System Directory, which is SYSTEM32 by default. (The user can override the default. You can obtain the current Windows System Directory by using the **GetSystemDirectory** function.)

4. The 16-bit Windows System Directory (which is SYSTEM by default).

    5. The Windows Directory.

    6. The directories contained in the PATH environment variable.

STEPS IN INVOKING A DLL

When you invoke a DLL, Windows, by default, performs the following steps. (You can change some of this behavior by using the options for the *dwFlgs* parameter as mentioned earlier.)

1. Windows checks to see if the DLL has already been loaded or mapped into the address space of the process.

2. If the DLL is not currently loaded, Windows loads the DLL into the address space of the invoking process and sets the usage count to 1.

3. If the DLL is currently loaded, then Windows does not load the DLL again. Windows just increments the usage count for the DLL by 1 (see Tip that follows). The rest of the steps listed apply only when a DLL is being loaded for the first time.

4. Windows also checks to see if additional DLLs are invoked by the DLL being loaded and recursively invokes the other DLLs as well.

5. Windows prepares the DLL for execution by performing such functions as assigning page attributes.

6. Windows calls the entry point function to initialize the DLL. DLL entry and exit functions are covered in more detail in the next section.

TIP: Keep in mind that in Windows NT, DLLs are process specific. If process X and process Y invoke the same DLL, two usage counts are established—one for process X, and one for process Y. Incrementing and decrementing are on a per-process basis. Thus, if the usage count for the DLL goes to zero in Process X, the DLL will be unmapped for the address space of Process X, but this has no effect on the DDL or its usage count in Process Y.

DLL ENTRY/EXIT FUNCTIONS

You can have an entry/exit function for your DLL, although it is not mandatory. (There is a default entry/exit routine that just returns TRUE regardless of the purpose for which it is called.) It is one function that is called for both entry and exit. The entry/exit function is called when the DLL is being mapped and unmapped to a process. The entry/exit function also is called when a thread is created or terminated. The entry/exit function is typically made up of different parts, each of which handles one reason for which the entry/exit function is called. The entry/exit function could use the following prototype:

```
BOOL WINAPI DllMain(
HANDLE hinst,
DWORD dwcallpurpose,
LPVOID lpvResvd,
);
```

where *hinst* is the handle to the DLL's instance and *lpvResvd* is reserved.

dwcallpurpose identifies the purpose of the call to the function. The valid values for *dwcallpurpose* and their description are summarized as follows:

DLL_PROCESS_ATTACH	The DLL is being mapped to the current process address space. This call is made only when the usage count is 1. You can use the part of the entry/exit function dealing with DLL_PROCESS_ATTACH to perform process-specific DLL initialization, such as allocating heap memory, and so on.
DLL_THREAD_ATTACH	The entry/exit function is called because the process is creating a new thread (after the DLL has already been mapped into the process' address space). Windows creates a primary thread when it creates the process. During the process creation, the entry/exit function was called with DLL_PROCESS_ATTACH. The entry/exit function is not called again for the primary thread with DLL_THREAD_ATTACH. In addition, Windows NT does not retroactively call the entry/exit function for threads that may already be running when the DLL is mapped (using LoadLibrary). You can use the part of the entry/exit routine dealing with DLL_THREAD_ATTACH to perform thread-specific initialization, such as allocating memory a thread local storage (TLS) slot.
DLL_THREAD_DETACH	The entry/exit function is called as a result of a thread terminating. You can use the part of the entry/exit routine to perform thread-relative cleanup functions, such as freeing memory allocated to a TLS slot.
DLL_PROCESS_DETACH	The DLL is being unmapped from the address space of the calling process. You can use the part of the entry/exit routine dealing with DLL_PROCESS_DETACH to perform process-relative cleanup functions such as freeing heap memory, and so on.

TIP: Although it appears that there is a sequence (Attach Process, Attach Thread, Detach Thread, Detach Process) for calling the entry/exit routine, do not count on this sequence to happen all the time. One reason is that if there is only one thread (a very common situation), the entry/exit routine will not be called with DLL_THREAD_ATTACH. Another reason is that if any thread calls Terminate_thread, or worse yet, calls Terminate_process, the entry/exit function is not called. Finally, the timing of starting the thread and loading the DLL is important. The entry/exit routines are not called for the threads that have already started when the DLL is loaded.

EXPORTING AND IMPORTING FUNCTIONS AND VARIABLES WITH DLLs

While the purpose of creating DLLs is to provide a common library of functions, resources, and data variables, you still have to perform work in addition to invoking the DLL. This is because none of the functions, data variables, and so on, within a DLL is available to a calling EXE or another DLL by default. The functions and data variables have to be exported from the DLL. You can then specify (as shown in the example that follows) how to "import" the exported functions and data in an EXE or DLL. You can export functions and data using module definition files or by using **dllexport**. Using **dllexport** is a newer and better method, and this is the method used in the following example. You can import functions and data using **dllimport** or you can use the C **extern** keyword. The example uses **dllimport**.

TIP: You have to watch out for name mangling when you export a DLL created with a Visual C++ compiler and try to use a function in the DLL from an EXE created using non-C++ compilers or C++ compilers from other vendors. When a function is exported, Visual C++ mangles the name by prefixing the function name with an underscore (_) and suffixing the function name with the @ symbol and a number that represents the total number of bytes of the function's parameters. One way of taking care of name mangling is by using a module definition file with an EXPORTS section.

DLL PROGRAMMING EXAMPLE FOR EXPORT/IMPORT

Exporting a function and a variable in a DLL, and importing a function and a variable in an EXE are shown in the following example. The example consists of a DLL that has a function which calculates simple interest given the principal and the period. The interest rate is initialized during DLL initialization. The function and the interest rate variable are exported. An EXE prompts the user for the principal and period, and calculates the interest rate. After two iterations, it prompts for a new interest rate and modifies the interest rate stored in the interest rate variable, which is also exported.

The symbols that need to be exported can be exported by use of a module definition file. Using a module definition file, or DEF file, can be cumbersome. Newer compilers provide a better means of exporting symbols. Visual C++ and Borland C++ compilers have defined **dllexport** and **dllimport** as extended keywords. These keywords are combined with another keyword, **__declspec**, to export or import symbols. The sample uses this method. The header file for the DLL is shown next:

```
// CalcInterest.h
#ifdef __cplusplus
extern "C" {
#endif

#ifdef DLLBUILD
// export the function
float __declspec(dllexport) CalcInterest(float flPrincipal, int iYear);
#else
// import the function
float __declspec(dllimport) CalcInterest(float flPrincipal, int iYear);
#endif

#ifdef __cplusplus
}
#endif
```

As the same header file is used in both the DLL and the EXE, conditional compile is done for DLL and EXE. Using the "C" linkage specification prevents the name mangling of the symbol. The DLL code is shown next:

```
//CalcInterest.c
#define DLLBUILD     // Trigger for dll export in the header file
#include "CalcInterest.h"

float __declspec(dllexport) flInterestRate;

BOOL WINAPI DllMain(HINSTANCE hInstance, DWORD dwReason, LPVOID lpReserved)
{
    if (dwReason == DLL_PROCESS_ATTACH)
    {
        flInterestRate = 5.0;
    }
    else if (dwReason == DLL_PROCESS_DETACH)
    {
        flInterestRate = 0.0;
    }
    else if (dwReason == DLL_THREAD_DETACH)
    {
    }
    else if (dwReason == DLL_THREAD_DETACH)
```

```
    {
    }
    return 1;    // Return TRUE if successful
}


float CalcInterest(float flPrincipal, int iYear)
{
    return ((float)((flPrincipal * (float)iYear * flInterestRate)/ 100.0));
}
```

The program that uses this DLL is shown next. Notice that after two iterations the interest rate is changed, and the rest of the interest calculation will be based on the new interest rate.

```
Interest.CPP
#include <iostream.h>
#include "CalcInterest.h"
extern "C" {
extern float __declspec(dllimport) flInterestRate;
}
void main ()
{
    float   flP;
    int     iY;
    float   flInterest;

    for (int i =0; i<4; i++)
    {
        cout << "Enter the Principal: ";
        cin >> flP;
        cout << "Enter number of years: ";
        cin >> iY;

        cout << "Interest Rate is " << flInterestRate << endl;
        flInterest = CalcInterest(flP, iY);

        cout << "The interest is: " << flInterest << endl;

        if (i == 1)
        {
            cout << "Now change the interest rate. Enter the new interest rate:";
            cin >> flInterestRate;
        }
    }
}
```

The program that follows changes the interest rate that is stored in the DLL. While running the preceding program, notice that the change in the interest rate by this program has no effect on the other program. This is because the DLL is loaded in the address space of the calling process instead of in a global address space.

```
//  ChangeInt.CPP
#include <iostream.h>
#include "CalcInterest.h"
extern "C" {
extern float __declspec(dllimport) flInterestRate;
}
void main ()

{
    char c;
    cout << "The interest rate will be changed in the DLL.\n";
    cout << "But this will not affect the other executable using
            the CalcIntDll.dll.\n";
    cout << "\nEnter the new interest rate: ";
    cin >> flInterestRate;
    cout << "The interest rate has been changed.\n";
    cout << "Type any character and press ENTER to continue.";
    cin >> c;
}
```

DLL PROGRAMMING EXAMPLE TO LOAD A DLL

As mentioned earlier in the chapter, you can specify that a DLL is to be loaded either at link-edit time or at run time. The following example shows how the same DLL that was loaded at link-edit time can be loaded at run time.

In the previous example the function that calculates the interest was *linked* to the executable by use of the DLL's export library. When the executable is loaded, the system also loads the DLL that this executable uses. This is called *load-time dynamic linking*. It is also possible to defer this DLL loading at load time by use of *run-time dynamic loading*. The next sample performs the same function as earlier, but loads the DLL dynamically, uses the function, and frees the DLL.

This is achieved by the **LoadLibrary**, **GetProcAddress**, and **FreeLibrary** APIs. The DLL name is provided to the **LoadLibrary** API, which loads the DLL and returns a handle to the library. The address of the function, **CalcInterest**, that is needed from the library can then be retrieved by providing the library handle and the function name to the **GetProcAddress** API. Note that the function name is case sensitive, and only functions that are exported can be retrieved. The library is finally freed by calling the **FreeLibrary** API and passing in the library handle.

```
#include <iostream.h>
#include <windows.h>
#include "CalcInterest.h"

void main ()
{
    float    flP;
    int      iY;
    float    flInterest;

    HMODULE hLoadLib;
    float (*CalcIntFunc)(float, int);

    hLoadLib = LoadLibrary("CalcIntDll.dll");
    if (!hLoadLib)
    {
        cout << "Cannot load CalcIntDll.dll";
        return;
    }
    CalcIntFunc = (float (*)(float, int)) GetProcAddress(hLoadLib,
                                    "CalcInterest");
    cout << "Enter the Principal: ";
    cin >> flP;
    cout << "Enter number of years: ";
    cin >> iY;

    flInterest = (*CalcIntFunc) (flP, iY);

    cout << "The interest is: " << flInterest << endl;

    FreeLibrary(hLoadLib);
}
```

The next sample shows a DLL exporting a class:

```
//  CalcIntClass.H
#ifdef DLLBUILD
#define DLLClass __declspec(dllexport)
#else
#define DLLClass __declspec(dllimport)
#endif

class DLLClass CCalcInterest
```

```
{
private:
    float    flInterestRate;

public:
    CCalcInterest();
    float getInterestRate();
    float getInterest(float flP, int iY);


};

//  CalcIntClass.CPP
#define DLLBUILD    // trigger class export
#include <iostream.h>
#include "CalcIntClass.h"

CCalcInterest::CCalcInterest()
{
    flInterestRate = 5.0;
}

float CCalcInterest::getInterestRate()
{
return (flInterestRate);
}

float CCalcInterest::getInterest(float flPrincipal, int iYear)
{
return ((float)((flPrincipal * (float)iYear * flInterestRate)/100.0));
}

// CLASSCALCINT.CPP
#include <iostream.h>
#include "CalcIntClass.h"
void main ()
{
    CCalcInterest    intCalc;
    float    flP;
    float    flI;
    int      iY;
    cout << "Enter the Principal: ";
    cin >> flP;
    cout << "Enter number of years: ";
    cin >> iY;
```

```
    cout << "Interest Rate is " << intCalc.getInterestRate() << endl;
    flI = intCalc.getInterest(flP, iY);
    cout << "The interest is: " << flI << endl;
}
```

DLL VERSION CONTROL

As mentioned earlier in the chapter, one of the disadvantages of DLLs is that you have to ensure that the correct version of the DLL is used when an EXE or DLL invokes a DLL. Version information could be a hierarchy that includes a company name, product name, the specific version and/or release of the product, and so on. Windows NT lets you attach a version resource to an executable or DLL. You can use the built-in functions in Microsoft Developer Studio to attach a version resource. Windows NT also provides functions to query the version-control information. The following example illustrates DLL version control.

DLL PROGRAMMING EXAMPLE FOR VERSION CONTROL

One of the resources that can be attached to a dynamic link library or an executable is a version resource. Information like the company name, product name, version, and so on, can be specified in the version resource. These version-control resources can be queried by use of version-control functions provided by Windows NT. The sample checks if the DLL is of the correct version and if it's not, it terminates. An easy way to add the version-control resource is through Developer Studio. However, the version-control information can also be created with an editor and linked to the DLL or EXE. The DLL code is shown next:

```
// CALCINTEREST.C
#define DLLBUILD    // Trigger for dll export in the header file
#include "CalcInterest.h"
float __declspec(dllexport) flInterestRate = 5.0;
float CalcInterest(float flPrincipal, int iYear)
{
    return ((float)((flPrincipal * (float)iYear * flInterestRate)/100.0));
}


// CALCINTEREST.H
#ifdef __cplusplus
extern "C" {
#endif

#ifdef DLLBUILD
// export the function
float __declspec(dllexport) CalcInterest(float flPrincipal, int iYear);
```

```
#else
// import the function
float __declspec(dllimport) CalcInterest(float flPrincipal, int iYear);
#endif


#ifdef __cplusplus
}
#endif
```

The version-control resource file for this DLL is shown next. This file was generated by use of the Visual C++ Developer Studio. Product version is set to 2, 1, 2, 3. Other information like file version, operating system, file type (application, dll, device driver, font), and type of build (debug or nondebug, prerelease, special build) can also be specified. This can be a good place to put the copyright information, company information, and product name.

```
// CALCINTEREST.RC
/////////////////////////////////////////////////////////////////////
//
// Version
//

VS_VERSION_INFO VERSIONINFO
 FILEVERSION 1,2,3,4
 PRODUCTVERSION 2,1,2,3
 FILEFLAGSMASK 0x3fL
#ifdef _DEBUG
 FILEFLAGS 0x21L
#else
 FILEFLAGS 0x20L
#endif
 FILEOS 0x40004L
 FILETYPE 0x2L
 FILESUBTYPE 0x0L
BEGIN
    BLOCK "StringFileInfo"
    BEGIN
        BLOCK "040904b0"
        BEGIN
            VALUE "CompanyName", "Osborne\0"
            VALUE "FileDescription", "Interest Calculator DLL\0"
            VALUE "FileVersion", "1, 2, 3, 4\0"
            VALUE "InternalName", "CalcInterest\0"
```

```
                    VALUE "LegalCopyright", "Copyright © 1997\0"
                    VALUE "OriginalFilename", "CalcInterest.dll\0"
                    VALUE "ProductName", "Osborne Interest Calculator\0"
                    VALUE "ProductVersion", "2, 1, 2, 3\0"
                    VALUE "SpecialBuild", "7525\0"
                END
            END
        BLOCK "VarFileInfo"
        BEGIN
            VALUE "Translation", 0x409, 1200
        END
END
```

The code that reads this version-control information is shown next. First, the program checks if the version information of the DLL can be queried, and if available, the size in bytes of version information. This is done by calling the **GetFileVersionInfoSize** function. The DLL name is given to the function, and if version information is available, it returns the size in bytes of that information. A buffer to retrieve the version information is allocated, and the information is retrieved by calling the **GetFileVersionInfo** function. By use of this information in the buffer, various individual information is queried by calling the **VerQueryValue** function. The \StringFile Info\040904b0 signifies the block that needs to be read. The value 040904b0 is essentially the hex representation of sublanguage, language, and code page information. "04" is the SUBLANG_ENGLISH_USA, "09" is the LANG_ENGLISH, and the rest is the code page information. The program checks if the DLL version is 2, 1, 2, 3 and if it's not, it terminates. This version-related library is available in the *Version.lib* library.

```cpp
// INTEREST.CPP
#include <iostream.h>
#include <windows.h>
#include "CalcInterest.h"

extern "C" {
extern float __declspec(dllimport) flInterestRate;
}

void main ()

{
    float   flP;
    int     iY;
    float   flInterest;

    DWORD   dwVersionInfoLen;
```

```
LPSTR    lpVersion;
DWORD    dwVersionHandle;
UINT     uVersionLen;
BOOL     bRetCode;
char     szDLLName[20];

strcpy(szDLLName, "CalcInterestDLL.dll");

dwVersionInfoLen = GetFileVersionInfoSize(szDLLName, &dwVersionHandle);
if (dwVersionInfoLen)
{
    LPSTR    lpstrVersionInfo;
    lpstrVersionInfo = (LPSTR)new char[dwVersionInfoLen];
    GetFileVersionInfo(szDLLName, dwVersionHandle, dwVersionInfoLen,
                    lpstrVersionInfo);

    bRetCode = VerQueryValue((LPVOID)lpstrVersionInfo,
                    TEXT("\\StringFileInfo\\040904b0\\ProductVersion"),
                    (LPVOID *)&lpVersion, &uVersionLen);

    if(bRetCode && !strcmp(lpVersion, "2, 1, 2, 3"))
    {
        for (int i =0; i<4; i++)
        {
            cout << "Enter the Principal: ";
            cin >> flP;
            cout << "Enter number of years: ";
            cin >> iY;

            cout << "Interest Rate is " << flInterestRate << endl;
            flInterest = CalcInterest(flP, iY);

            cout << "The interest is: " << flInterest << endl;

            if (i == 1)
            {
                cout << "Now change the interest rate.  Enter the new
                        interest rate: ";
                cin >> flInterestRate;
            }
        }
    }
    else
```

```
        {
            cout << "Incorrect DLL. Program terminated.\n";
        }

        delete [] lpstrVersionInfo;
    }
    else
    {
        cout << "Incorrect DLL. Program terminated.\n";
    }
}
```

CONCLUSION

In this chapter, we looked at an important tool for Windows NT programmers—using a DLL. We looked at the need for using DLLs as well as the advantages and disadvantages of using DLLs. We compared DLLs and applications. We examined examples of exporting functions from a DLL and importing them into other executables. We also looked at the two ways of invoking a DLL and looked at a sample that illustrated them. Finally, we looked at how to use the version-control information with a DLL.

In the next chapter, we will continue our discussion of OS services and look at threads, interprocess communication mechanisms, and so on.

CHAPTER 10

Advanced
OS Services

As a Windows programmer, you would have already used basic operating system services such as memory allocation, message processing, and so on. While these services are common in all Windows environments, Windows NT also includes some advanced services such as multithreading and communication between threads. As an advanced Windows NT programmer, you should be aware of these important programming tools, which are covered in this chapter.

We will start with how to create and terminate processes. Next we will look at one of the important programming tools that Windows NT provides—threads. We will discuss how and when to create threads, and the safe and not so safe ways of terminating threads. Then we will cover how thread priorities work and how you can adjust them. Next we will discuss guidelines on when to use a thread. We will also cover thread local storage and end the chapter by covering the different communication mechanisms available for communicating between threads.

Before we begin, let's clarify what the different "multi" things in Windows NT are, since we will be discussing one of them here. Windows NT is a multitasking, multithreading operating system that supports symmetric multiprocessing (SMP) on multiple processors, but is not a multiuser operating system (at least not the way UNIX and mainframe operating systems are).

Multitasking is the ability to run more than one program (or task) at the same time by sharing the CPU among the different tasks. This feature has been part of Windows since its first release. Multitasking is also sometimes referred to as "multiprocessing" (the "process" in multiprocessing refers to a program process and not a CPU processor).

A *process* is an executing instance of a program. This doesn't mean that the process actually executes, as we will see later. It just means that compared with your application that was residing on the disk, there is now an instance of the application that is known to the operating system and has resources allocated to it. A process is made up of at least one thread called the *primary* or *main thread.* A process (the primary thread) or a thread created by the primary thread can create more threads. There is no hierarchy among threads as there is between a process and its threads. (Terminating a process terminates the threads of that process, whereas terminating a thread does not terminate the threads created by that thread.) In Windows NT, it is the threads of a process that are executed. A multithreading operating system is one that supports a process having multiple threads. Windows NT is a multitasking, multithreading operating system. By contrast, Windows 3.1 is a multitasking but not a multithreading operating system.

An operating system can also recognize and take advantage of multiple CPUs that may be present on a machine. It can treat all installed processors the same (*symmetric multiprocessing*) or reserve one for the operating system itself and use other CPUs for application programs (*asymmetric multiprocessing*). Again, Windows NT supports SMP, and Windows 95 does not.

There is one important difference between Windows NT and operating systems such as UNIX and mainframe operating systems. The difference is the concept of who a user is. In UNIX and mainframe operating systems, the user is typically the human being who can log in from a *terminal.* The operating system maintains a list of valid users and logs in valid users to let them use the system. Windows NT is a client/server operating system. To such an operating system, the users are clients requesting services from the operating system. The fact that a client may be a computer with a human being as its user is incidental to the operating system itself. In this sense, Windows NT is not a "multiuser" system. Citrix systems licensed Windows NT source code and added multiuser features to enable Windows NT to perform multiuser functions the way other operating systems do. Microsoft recently licensed these multiuser enhancements from Citrix and may provide the multiuser capabilities in future versions of Windows NT.

CREATING AND TERMINATING PROCESSES

As mentioned earlier, even though Windows NT executes threads, threads belong to a process. Let's start with processes. Here "process" refers to the program process. As mentioned earlier, a process is an executing instance of an application program. An executing instance has memory and other resources assigned to it. You can start a process either manually or programmatically. You manually start a process when you start an application in Windows NT. There are different ways to start an application. You can start an application by double-clicking the program entry in Windows NT Explorer or (if you have included it) from the Start menu or the program's icon on the desktop. You can also use the DOS method of keying in the program name at the command prompt. Regardless of how you start an application, Windows NT creates a process for your application. A process has its own 4Gb address space.

Note for UNIX Programmers

Creating a process from another process is conceptually similar between UNIX and Windows NT, although there are a lot of detail differences. To create a process, you *fork* and *exec* in UNIX, while you **CreateProcess** in Windows NT. However, Windows NT does not automatically establish a parent-child relationship, unlike UNIX. There are also differences about what is passed to the created processes between UNIX and Windows NT.

You can programmatically create a process using **CreateProcess**, whose prototype is as follows:

```
BOOL CreateProcess( LPCTSTR lpAppNam,
                    LPTSTR lpCmdLine,
                    LPSECURITY_ATTRIBUTES lpProcAttr,
                    LPSECURITY_ATTRIBUTES lpThreadAttr,
                    BOOL bInhHandls,
                    DWORD dwCreatFlgs,
                    LPVOID lpEnv,
```

```
                        LPCTSTR lpCurrDir,
                        LPSTARTUPINFO lpStrtInfo,
                        LPPROCESS_INFORMATION lpProcInfo
);
```

where the parameters are as follows:

lpAppNam points to the program to be executed and contains the full or partially qualified path name of the executable. You can specify this parameter as NULL, in which case the *lpCmdLine* parameter must contain the name of the program. For 16-bit applications, you *should* specify the program name in *lpCmdLine* and specify NULL for *lpAppNam*. If you want to pass parameters to the program through the command line (which can retrieve the passed parameters using **GetCommandLine** or argc/argv), specify the program name in *lpAppNam* and the command-line parameters in *lpCmdLine*. If you do not specify a fully qualified path name, Windows NT searches for the program to be executed in different directories in the following order:

1. The directory where your application resides

2. The directory of the parent process

3. The 32-bit Windows system directory (which typically is SYSTEM32)

4. The 16-bit Windows system directory (which typically is SYSTEM)

5. The Windows directory

6. The directories listed in the PATH environment variable

lpProcAttr points to a **SECURITY_ATTRIBUTES** structure. You can use the structure to specify security attributes (such as whether another child process can inherit object handles). If *lpProcAttr* is NULL, a default security descriptor is used.

lpThreadAttr is exactly similar to *lpProcAttr*, except that it deals with thread security instead of process security. *lpThreadAttr* points to a **SECURITY_ATTRIBUTES** structure. You can use the structure to specify security attributes (such as whether another child process can inherit object handles). If *lpThreadAttr* is NULL, a default security descriptor is used.

bInhHandls is a Boolean parameter to specify whether the new process being created can inherit handles of the calling process.

dwCreatFlgs specifies flags relating to the priority of the process being created, as shown in the table that follows.

Flag Value	Description
CREATE_DEFAULT _ERROR_MODE	This flag overrides the default of the newly created process inheriting the error mode of the calling process.

Flag Value	Description
CREATE_NEW _CONSOLE	This flag, which is mutually exclusive with the DETACHED_PROCESS flag, lets the newly created process have its own console, instead of inheriting the console of the calling process.
CREATE_NEW _PROCESS_GROUP	The newly created process is the root process of a new process group.
CREATE_SEPARATE _WOW_VDM	Processes of 16-bit Windows-based applications run in their own private virtual DOS machine (VDM). This overrides the default of a shared VDM.
CREATE_SHARED _WOW_VDM	This flag overrides the DefaultSeparateVDM switch (which runs applications in separate VDMs) and runs the new process in the shared virtual DOS machine.
CREATE _SUSPENDED	The primary thread of the new process is created in a suspended state (and is not scheduled for execution until a ResumeThread is issued—see ResumeThread discussion in the section "Thread Priority Classes and Levels" later in this chapter).
CREATE_UNICODE _ENVIRONMENT	The environment block uses Unicode characters (if set) and ANSI characters otherwise.
DEBUG_PROCESS	The calling process is notified of all debug events in the created process.
DEBUG_ONLY_THIS _PROCESS	This is set to debug the calling process using the created process' debugger.
DETACHED _PROCESS	The newly created process does not get the default console and has to allocate one if it needs a console. This flag is mutually exclusive with the CREATE_ NEW_CONSOLE flag.

You can also set the priority class for the newly created process using dwCreation Flags. The priority class can be one of the values shown in Table 10-1. The priority class determines a range of priority levels. For example, for the NORMAL_PRIORITY_CLASS, the priority for a "lowest" level thread is 6. The highest priority for a "highest" level thread is 10 (for an average value of 8). Thread priority levels are covered in the section "Thread Priority Classes and Levels" later in this chapter.

lpEnv is a pointer to an environment block. Specifying NULL for this parameter causes the new process to use the environment of the calling process.

Priority Class	Description
HIGH_PRIORITY_CLASS	This is used for tasks that require real high priority, such as tasks that handle user interfaces. The average priority level is 13.
IDLE_PRIORITY_CLASS	This is used for low-priority tasks that need to run only when the system is idle (for example, screen-savers). The average priority level is 4. This priority class is assigned to the created process if the calling process has this priority class.
NORMAL_PRIORITY _CLASS	This is used normally for most tasks. The average priority level is 8.
REALTIME_PRIORITY _CLASS	This is used for tasks that need the highest possible priority. Be careful with this, since a thread with this priority class is scheduled for execution even ahead of Windows NT's own tasks. The average priority level is 24.

Table 10-1.   Priority Classes and Descriptions

lpCurrDir is a pointer to a string that specifies the current drive and directory for the newly created process. Specifying NULL for this parameter causes the newly created process to have the same current drive and directory as that of the calling process.

lpStrtInfo is a pointer to a **STARTUPINFO** structure. The **STARTUPINFO** structure specifies the properties of the main window for a GUI process such as the window title, or the console for a Console process.

lpProcInfo is a pointer to a **PROCESS_INFORMATION** structure. Windows NT fills the **PROCESS_INFORMATION** structure with information such as handle and ID for a newly created process and its primary thread.

CreateProcess returns nonzero if successful and zero otherwise.

You can use **CreateProcess** to invoke another application if the functions you want already exist in the other application. If you are developing a new application and you want split functions, you can use threads.

You can terminate a process in three ways.

First, you can call **ExitProcess**, whose prototype is shown here:

```
VOID ExitProcess( UINT uExitCode
);
```

ExitProcess is a clean way to terminate a process and all the threads of the process and is the preferred way to terminate a process. Windows NT performs the following cleanup actions in response to **ExitProcess**:

▼ The entry-point function of all attached dynamic link libraries (DLLs) is called with an indication that the process is detaching.

■ Object handles opened by the process are closed.

■ The threads in the process are terminated.

■ Threads waiting for this process or any of its threads to terminate are released (the state of the process and all its threads are set to the Signaled state).

▲ Process termination status changes from STILL_ACTIVE to the exit value.

Secondly, a process can also be terminated by calling **TerminateProcess**, whose prototype is shown here:

```
BOOL TerminateProcess( HANDLE hProcess,
                       UINT uExitCd
);
```

where *hProcess* is the process handle, and *uExitCd* is the process' exit code. **TerminateProcess** returns nonzero when successful and zero otherwise.

Unlike **ExitProcess**, **TerminateProcess** does not call the entry-point function of attached DLLs. So the processing in the entry point functions is skipped, and this in turn may lead to unpredictable consequences and loss of data integrity.

A third way that processes are terminated is when all the threads in a process are terminated. The threads in a process could be terminated by **ExitThread** or **TerminateThread**. Terminating threads is covered in the section "Thread Programming with Win32 API" later in this chapter.

Before we move on to threads and how to write multithreaded programs, let's examine the need for multithreading. If your application has only one thread and that thread has to wait for an event such as an I/O completion, then your thread will not execute until the event it is waiting for has completed. On the other hand, if your application has more than one thread, then there is a chance that when one of your application's threads is waiting, other threads of your application can execute. Thus, developing your application as a multithreaded application improves the overall throughput of your applications besides potentially improving processor utilization. The results will be even more significant when there is more than one processor on the system. In this case, two or more threads of your application could actually be executing in parallel.

This does not mean that you should divide your application into a large number of threads. Having multiple threads means that your application may need more communication between threads that you need to take care of, so the complexity increases. In addition, Windows NT has to keep track of more threads, and more threads need more system resources. Thus, deciding how many threads to have and what the threads will do is as much an art as it is a science. You need to balance the cost of having additional threads with the potential benefits. There is no set formula that will specify if, when, and how many threads should be used in a given situation.

TIP: Do not conclude that you should think of multithreading your application only if you are running your application on systems with multiple processors. If your application would benefit from multithreading, go ahead with multithreading. There will be some benefits even on single-processor systems. With the falling prices of processors, multiprocessor systems are becoming more common, and your application will transparently be able to take advantage of multiple processors if it is multithreaded and runs on a system with multiple processors.

THREAD BASICS

As mentioned earlier, a process is made up of one or more threads. In Windows NT a process has memory and other resources, but it does not execute by itself. Rather, it is the threads in the process that are scheduled for execution. A process must have at least one thread. When you create a process, one thread is also created for the process. This thread is called the primary thread. The primary thread can create other threads. Threads created by the *primary thread* can also create threads.

Windows NT schedules threads for execution using the priority of threads. Each thread has a *priority class*. A priority class has multiple priority levels within it. Thread priority is covered later in the section "Thread Priority Classes and Levels." When Windows NT wants to schedule a thread for execution, it schedules the next highest-priority thread that is ready for execution (that is, the thread is in a ready state—thread states are covered later). If there are multiple threads available with the same priority, Windows NT schedules the threads with the same priority in a round-robin fashion. In addition, when a low-priority thread is executing and a higher-priority thread becomes ready for execution, Windows NT preempts the low-priority thread and schedules the higher-priority thread. You may wonder if a low-priority thread will ever be executed if there are always higher-priority threads around. Windows NT ensures that low-priority threads are executed by incrementing the priority of low-priority threads if the threads have not executed in a while.

A thread that is ready to be executed is in a *ready state*. The different states a thread can be in are summarized in Table 10-2.

Actually, there is another state value that happens rarely. The state value is 7 and the state is Unknown.

The life of a thread in the system starts with Initialized and ends at Terminated. In the interim, it goes through repetitive cycles of the Ready, Standby, Running, Waiting, and/or Transition states.

Thread State Value	Description	Comment
0	Initialized	The thread is now a valid thread in the system.
1	Ready	The thread is ready for execution (usually when what the thread was waiting for is now available).
2	Running	The thread is currently executing in a processor.
3	Standby	The thread is about to start execution in a processor.
4	Terminated	The thread has completed execution.
5	Waiting	The thread is waiting for events such as I/O completion.
6	Transition	The thread is waiting for resources (other than the processor).

Table 10-2.   Thread State Values and Description

You have three options if you want to work with threads in Microsoft Windows NT:

1. You can use C library multithreading functions.
2. You can use Win32 APIs such as **CreateThread**.
3. You can use MFC classes such as **CWinThread**.

We will not cover option 1 in this chapter. We will cover option 2 briefly, including the relevant APIs. We also will cover option 3 and include code samples using it.

THREAD PROGRAMMING WITH WIN32 API

We will look at the Win32 API method in this section. For creating and terminating threads using MFC, see the next section, "Thread Programming with MFC." You can create a thread using the **CreateThread** API, whose prototype is shown here:

```
HANDLE CreateThread( LPSECURITY_ATTRIBUTES lpThreadAttr,
                     DWORD dwStakSz,
                     LPTHREAD_START_ROUTINE lpStrtAddr,
                     LPVOID lpParm,
                     DWORD dwCreatFlgs,
                     LPDWORD lpThreadId
);
```

where the parameters are as follows:

lpThreadAttr points to a **SECURITY_ATTRIBUTES** structure. Specifying NULL for this parameter causes a default security descriptor to be used.

dwStakSz is the thread stack size in bytes. The thread stack is part of the process address space. Specifying zero causes the thread stack size to be the same as that of the primary thread of the process.

lpStrtAddr is the starting address of the new thread.

lpParm is a parameter that can be passed to the thread.

dwCreatFlgs is a flag to specify if the thread is to be created in a suspended state or whether it can execute right after creation.

lpThreadId is a pointer to the thread identifier that is returned when the thread is successfully created.

CreateThread returns the handle to the created thread when successful and NULL otherwise.

As with processes, you can terminate threads in three ways.

First, you can call **ExitThread**, whose prototype is shown here:

```
VOID ExitThread (DWORD dwExitCd
);
```

where *dwExitCd* is the thread's exit code (which can be retrieved using the **GetExit CodeThread** function). **ExitThread** does not return a value. Windows NT performs the following cleanup actions in response to **ExitThread**:

▼ The thread's stack is deallocated.

■ The entry-point function of all attached dynamic link libraries (DLLs) is called with an indication that the thread is detaching.

■ The process that created the thread is terminated if the current thread is the last thread of the process.

■ Threads waiting for this thread to terminate are released (the state of the thread is changed to Signaled).

▲ Thread termination status changes from STILL_ACTIVE to the exit code.

Second, you can call **TerminateThread**, whose prototype is shown here:

```
BOOL TerminateThread( HANDLE hThread,
                      DWORD dwExitCd
);
```

where *hThread* is the thread handle, and *dwExitCd* is the thread's exit code (which can be retrieved using the **GetExitCodeThread** function). **TerminateThread** returns nonzero when successful and zero otherwise.

Unlike **ExitThread**, **TerminateThread** does not deallocate the thread's stack and does not call the entry-point function of attached DLLs. So the processing in the entry-point functions is skipped, and this may lead to unpredictable consequences and loss of data integrity.

Third, a thread (actually all the threads of a process) is terminated if the process is terminated.

> *TIP:*   You can also use C run-time functions for thread management. Don't mix and match C functions and Win32 functions. For example, don't try to terminate a thread using **ExitThread** if you are using C functions such as **_beginthread.**

THREAD PROGRAMMING WITH MFC

Threads in MFC applications are represented by **CWinThread** objects. You can call **AfxBeginThread** to create **CWinThread** objects. Creating and managing threads through Win32 APIs are relatively simpler than through **CWinThread** objects. The sample that follows creates threads using the **CWinThread** method by calling the **AfxBeginThread** API. In MFC applications all threads should be created through the **CWinThread** method to make your application MFC thread safe. The thread local data that is used by the framework to maintain thread-specific information is managed by **CWinThread** objects. Since **CWinThread** handles the thread local data, any thread that uses the MFC must be created by the MFC through the **CWinThread** method. This may sound complicated, but it is straightforward to do this in most cases. All that has to be done in an MFC application is to create threads by calling **AfxBeginThread**.

Though threads are not distinguished at the Win32 API level, they are distinguished at the MFC level. MFC distinguishes two types of threads. Threads that generally handle user input and respond to events and user-generated messages are called *user-interface* threads, and those that do not have any interaction with the user interface are called *worker* threads. User-interface threads handle *message pumps* (a message pump is a program loop that retrieves messages from a thread's message queue, translates them, and dispatches them), while worker threads do not handle message pumps. The primary thread that is automatically created when you start an MFC application is a user-interface thread. You create user-interface and worker threads using **AfxBeginThread**. This is illustrated in the example that follows. The prototype for **AfxBeginThread** is shown here:

```
CWinThread *AfxBeginThread (AFX_THREADPROC ThreadProc,
                            LPVOID Parm,
                            int Prty = THREAD_PRIORITY_LOWEST,
                            UINT StakSz = 0,
                            DWORD CreatFlgs = 0,
                            LPSECURITY_ATTRIBUTES
                            SecAttr = NULL );
```

where the parameters are defined as follows:

ThreadProc is a thread function that has the prototype

```
UINT ThreadProc(LPVOID tpparm)
```

A thread starts and terminates its execution in the thread function. The thread function is defined in the process that is creating the thread.

Parm is a parameter you can pass to the thread function.

Prty is the priority level you want for the thread being created and must be one of the values listed in Table 10-3. You can specify zero for this parameter, in which case the priority of the created thread becomes the same as that of the creating thread.

StakSz is the stack size in bytes for the thread being created. The thread stack is part of the process address space. You can specify zero for this parameter, in which case the stack size of the created thread becomes the same as that of the creating thread.

CreatFlgs specifies if the thread is to be created in a suspended state (use CREATE_SUSPEND) or whether it can execute right after creation (use zero).

SecAttr points to a **SECURITY_ATTRIBUTES** structure. Specifying NULL for this parameter causes the security attributes of the created thread to be the same as that of the creating thread.

AfxBeginThread returns a pointer to the newly created thread if successful and zero otherwise. You will use this pointer for subsequent processing involving the newly created thread.

The thread terminates in one of two ways. The thread automatically terminates when *ThreadProc* completes. At times, you may know within the thread that you can terminate

Priority Level	Priority Calculation
THREAD_PRIORITY_IDLE	15 for REALTIME_PRIORITY class, 1 for all other classes
THREAD_PRIORITY_LOWEST	Average class priority –2
THREAD_PRIORITY_BELOW_NORMAL	Average class priority –1
THREAD_PRIORITY_NORMAL	Average class priority
THREAD_PRIORITY_ABOVE_NORMAL	Average class priority + 1
THREAD_PRIORITY_HIGHEST	Average class priority + 2
THREAD_PRIORITY_TIME_CRITICAL	31 for REALTIME_PRIORITY class, 16 for all other classes

Table 10-3.   Priority Levels

the thread processing. At any point, a thread can terminate itself by calling **AfxEndThread**. The prototype of **AfxEndThread** is shown here:

```
void AfxEndThread( UINT ExitCd );
```

where *ExitCd* is the exit code.

PROGRAMMING EXAMPLE FOR CREATING THREADS

The Threads sample program demonstrates the creation of threads using the **AfxBeginThread** API. When run, the program will display a window, and a new thread can be created by selecting New Thread from the File menu. This will create a thread that will run a color ribbon across the window. Notice that while one ribbon runs across the window, more threads can be created.

The code for the *Thread* sample is shown next. The main application class is similar to other samples discussed earlier. The frame window class is derived from **CFrameWnd**. The method that is used to draw the ribbon will draw it in a compatible device context and then **BitBlt** while processing the **WM_PAINT** message. Appropriate members are defined in the frame window class. When the user selects New Thread from the File menu, **OnNewThread** is called. It creates the thread by calling **AfxBeginThread** and passing the controlling function for the worker thread.

```
#include <afxwin.h>
#include "Resource.h"

UINT RibbonThread(LPVOID);
COLORREF GetRibbonColor(int);

#define RIBBONWIDTH        50
#define RIBBONSEPARATION   10
COLORREF GetRibbonColor(int);

int iWidth, iHeight;    // Screen size
int iThreadInstance;    // Instance of the thread
// Define the application object class
class CApp : public CWinApp
{
public:
    virtual BOOL InitInstance ();
};
```

The frame window class definition and the message map follow.

```
// The frame window class
class CThreadWindow : public CFrameWnd
{
public:
    CDC m_memDC;
    CBitmap m_bmp;
    CBrush m_bkbrush;

    CThreadWindow();
    afx_msg void OnAppAbout();
    afx_msg void OnPaint();
    afx_msg void OnNewThread();
    afx_msg void OnExit();
    DECLARE_MESSAGE_MAP()
};


//////////////////////////////////////////////////////////////////////
// CThreadWindow

BEGIN_MESSAGE_MAP(CThreadWindow, CFrameWnd)
    ON_WM_PAINT()
    ON_COMMAND(ID_APP_ABOUT, OnAppAbout)
    ON_COMMAND(IDM_NEWTHREAD, OnNewThread)
    ON_COMMAND(ID_APP_EXIT, OnExit)
END_MESSAGE_MAP()


//////////////////////////////////////////////////////////////////////
// CThreadWindow construction

CThreadWindow::CThreadWindow()
{
    LoadAccelTable(MAKEINTRESOURCE(IDR_MAINFRAME));
    Create( NULL, "Threads Sample",
            WS_OVERLAPPEDWINDOW,
            rectDefault, NULL, MAKEINTRESOURCE(IDR_MAINFRAME) );

    iWidth = GetSystemMetrics(SM_CXSCREEN);
    iHeight = GetSystemMetrics(SM_CYSCREEN);
```

The thread that draws the ribbon does so indirectly. The ribbon is first drawn in a memory device context. Then it is bit-block transferred by the main application thread when processing the paint message. To achieve this, a compatible device context and compatible bitmap are created, selected, and cleared.

```
    // create a compatible background window for the thread
    // and clear the background to white.
    CClientDC  DC(this);
    m_memDC.CreateCompatibleDC(&DC);
    m_bmp.CreateCompatibleBitmap(&DC, iWidth, iHeight);
    m_memDC.SelectObject(&m_bmp);
    m_bkbrush.CreateStockObject(WHITE_BRUSH);
    m_memDC.SelectObject(&m_bkbrush);
    m_memDC.PatBlt(0, 0, iWidth, iHeight, PATCOPY);
}


///////////////////////////////////////////////////////////////////
// The CApp object

CApp theApp;

///////////////////////////////////////////////////////////////////
// CApp initialization

BOOL CApp::InitInstance()
{
    m_pMainWnd = new CThreadWindow();
    m_pMainWnd -> ShowWindow( m_nCmdShow );
    m_pMainWnd -> UpdateWindow();
    return TRUE;
}


///////////////////////////////////////////////////////////////////
// CAboutDlg dialog used for App About

class CAboutDlg : public CDialog
{
public:
    CAboutDlg();

    enum { IDD = IDD_ABOUTBOX };
};

CAboutDlg::CAboutDlg() : CDialog(CAboutDlg::IDD)
{
}
```

```
// App command to run the dialog
void CThreadWindow::OnAppAbout()
{
    CAboutDlg aboutDlg;
    aboutDlg.DoModal();
}


// Handle exposures
void CThreadWindow::OnPaint()
{
    CPaintDC dc(this);
    dc.BitBlt(0, 0, iWidth, iHeight, &m_memDC, 0, 0, SRCCOPY);
}


void CThreadWindow::OnNewThread()
{
    AfxBeginThread(RibbonThread, this);
}

// On Exit processing
void CThreadWindow::OnExit()
{
    DestroyWindow();
}
```

Shown next is the thread function of the worker thread that was created earlier. When the thread was created, a pointer to the frame window object was passed. This pointer is passed to the function as a parameter. Though the MFC objects created by one thread cannot be used by another thread, in general it is okay to call the inline functions in the MFC objects. The color of the ribbon is decided, and a small filled rectangle is drawn. The drawing of the rectangle proceeds in a loop, sleeping a fixed amount of time at the beginning of each loop.

```
UINT RibbonThread(LPVOID ThreadWindow)
{
    int iX1, iY1, iX2, iY2;
    int yOffset;
    COLORREF  c;
    RECT  rect;

    iThreadInstance++;
    CThreadWindow *pTW = (CThreadWindow *) ThreadWindow;
    iX1= iY1 = iX2 = iY2 = 0;
```

```
        yOffset = (iThreadInstance-1)*(RIBBONWIDTH+RIBBONSEPARATION);
        c = GetRibbonColor(iThreadInstance);
        CBrush Brush(c);
        for(int i=1; i<500; i++)
        {
            Sleep(50);
            iX1 = (i-1)*2;
            iY1 = yOffset;
            iX2 = i*2;
            iY2 = iY1+RIBBONWIDTH;

            rect.left = (long) iX1;
            rect.top = (long) iY1;
            rect.right = (long) iX2;
            rect.bottom = (long) iY2;

            pTW->m_memDC.FillRect(&rect, &Brush);
            pTW->InvalidateRect(&rect);
        }
    return 0;
}


COLORREF GetRibbonColor(int i)
{
    COLORREF c;
    switch(i%8)
    {
    case 0:
        c = RGB(0xFF, 0, 0);
        break;
    case 1:
        c = RGB(0, 0xFF, 0);
        break;
    case 2:
        c = RGB(0,0,0xFF);
        break;
    case 3:
        c = RGB(0xFF, 0xFF, 0);
        break;
    case 4:
        c = RGB(0xFF, 0, 0xFF);
        break;
    case 5:
```

```
        c = RGB(0x77, 0x77, 0x77);
        break;
    case 6:
        c = RGB(0xFF, 0x77, 0);
        break;
    case 7:
        c = RGB(0, 0xFF, 0x77);
        break;
    }
    return (c);
}
```

The sleep time can be increased to make the ribbon run slower. While running the program, notice that the menu bar and the rest of the application window are active and respond to user interaction. If, instead of the creating thread, the **RibbonThread** function were directly called, the whole application would hang without responding to the user action until the entire loop completed. More than one thread can be started, and all the ribbons are drawn simultaneously. As each thread gets a slice of CPU time, a section of the ribbon is drawn.

THREAD PRIORITY CLASSES AND LEVELS

As mentioned earlier, each thread has a priority class. Priority classes are subdivided into priority levels. There are four priority classes: HIGH_PRIORITY, IDLE_PRIORITY, NORMAL_PRIORITY, and REALTIME_PRIORITY. For a description of these priority classes and the average priority value for each class, see Table 10-1. Within each priority class, there are seven levels. When a thread is initialized, it is given a *base priority* based on its priority class and priority level as shown in Table 10-3.

For example, if you have a thread whose priority class is NORMAL_PRIORITY _CLASS (the average priority value is 8), and the priority level is THREAD_PRIORITY _ABOVE_NORMAL, then the base priority for the thread is calculated as 8 + 1 = 9. Thus, any thread will have a base priority from 1 through 31. The higher the number, the bigger the priority. Even when priorities are changed automatically by Windows NT, the 1 through 31 range still holds.

You can use the **GetPriorityClass** function to get the current priority class of the process. You can use the **SetPriorityClass** function to set the priority class of a process. You can use the **GetThreadPriority** function to get the current priority level of a thread. You can use the **SetThreadPriority** function to set the priority level of a thread.

The prototype for **GetPriorityClass** is

```
DWORD GetPriorityClass(HANDLE hProcess);
```

and the prototype for **SetPriorityClass** is

```
BOOL SetPriorityClass( HANDLE hProcess,
                       DWORD dwPrtyCls
);
```

The priority class returned by **GetPriorityClass** and the priority specified in *dwPrtyCls* for **SetPriorityClass** is one of the values listed in Table 10-1. *hProcess* is the process' handle.

The prototype for **GetThreadPriority** is

```
int GetThreadPriority( );
```

and the prototype for **SetThreadPriority** is

```
BOOL SetThreadPriority( int nPrty );
```

The priority level returned by **GetThreadPriority** and the priority level specified in *nPrty* for **SetThreadPriority** are values from Table 10-3. Unlike **GetPriorityClass** and **SetPriorityClass**, which are API functions and need a handle, **GetThreadPriority** and **SetThreadPriority** are **CWinThread** member functions.

TIP: Remember, there is no free lunch here. The benefits of executing with increased priority for your thread(s) comes at the expense of the other applications' threads. If users notice a significant performance degradation in other applications after they install your application, they are not likely to accept your application.

Besides using the priority-related functions in the preceding paragraph, you can also suspend and resume the execution of a thread using the **SuspendThread** and **ResumeThread** member functions.

Each thread has a count used with these functions. **SuspendThread** increments the count, while **ResumeThread** decrements the count. The count is zero, by default, when the thread is created (unless the thread was created with the CREATE_SUSPENDED flag). When the thread's count is zero and you call **SuspendThread**, Windows NT increments the count to 1 and suspends the thread. Subsequently when you call **ResumeThread**, the count goes back to zero and the thread resumes. The thread will not be scheduled for execution as long as the count is nonzero.

The prototype for **SuspendThread** is

```
DWORD SuspendThread( );
```

and the prototype for **ResumeThread** is

```
DWORD ResumeThread( );
```

Both **ResumeThread** and **SuspendThread** return the thread's previous suspend count if successful and –1 otherwise.

For a programming example using thread priority, see the example under "Critical Sections," later in this chapter.

TIP: Keep in mind that when a thread resumes as a result of **ResumeThread**, it resumes at the starting point of its code, although it may have been at another point in the code when it was suspended (by use of **SuspendThread**).

STATIC AND DYNAMIC THREAD LOCAL STORAGE

Thread local storage (*TLS*) is a mechanism to allocate memory for storing thread-specific data. Only the thread that owns the TLS can access the data in the TLS. You can allocate and use TLS dynamically using APIs such as **TlsAlloc**, **TlsGetValue**, **TlsSetValue**, and **TlsFree**. The TLS APIs and their descriptions are summarized in Table 10-4.

TLS API	Description
TlsAlloc	Allocates a TLS index that is used on subsequent TLS-related calls
TlsGetValue	Retrieves the TLS slot data given a TLS index
TlsSetValue	Stores TLS slot data for a given TLS index
TlsFree	Frees a TLS index

You can also allocate and use TLS in a static manner using an extended storage class modifier called *thread* as shown in the following example:

```
typedef _declspec (thread) TLStor;
TLStor char x;
```

You can have both dynamic and static TLS allocated to your application.

PROCESS AND THREAD SYNCHRONIZATION

While multithreading solves some issues and improves some aspects of your application, it also introduces new issues that you need to handle in your program.

Let's first understand the need for synchronization using a real-life example. There are many bridges where the number of lanes on the bridge is less than the number of lanes leading up to it. In a very simple example, there may be only one lane on the bridge, while there may be multiple lanes leading up to the bridge. Signals are typically used to ensure that only the automobiles on one lane at a time are allowed access to the bridge. Automobiles in other lanes wait for access to the bridge if they arrive when the bridge is already being used. In a computer version of this example, the bridge is a resource. The automobiles are threads. The signals are synchronization objects. When one of your application threads wants to use a resource, it must synchronize its access with other threads using synchronization objects.

Since all the threads of your application work together in performing the functions in your application, quite often there is a need for the threads to synchronize their actions. Windows NT provides a number of *synchronization objects* such as semaphores, mutexes, and critical sections, and these are summarized in Table 10-4.

Note for UNIX Programmers

Most UNIX systems provide synchronization mechanisms similar to the ones provided by Windows NT. If you have programmed using these mechanisms, the concepts and semantics are the same. Of course, there are syntax differences.

Synchronization Object	Description
Event	One or more threads can wait for an event object. An event object notifies waiting threads when the event occurs.
Mutex	This enables threads to take turns by forcing each thread to own the mutex object. The mutex object can be owned by only one thread at a time.
Semaphore	This restricts the number of threads that can access a shared resource.
Timer	This waits for a specific time and notifies waiting threads.
Critical section	This allows only one thread at a time to access a resource such as common data or a section of code.

Table 10-4. Synchronization Objects and Description

Critical Sections

Critical sections serialize the access of multiple threads to a common resource or to a portion of code by allowing access to only one thread at a time. Critical sections are fast relative to other synchronization objects such as mutexes, but a critical section can be used only for the threads within a process. You can use a critical section by creating a variable of type **CSingleLock** or **CMultiLock** in your resource's access member function. You then call the lock object's **Lock** member function. If the resource is not being used, your thread gains access. If the resource is being used, your thread waits (until it either gains access or it times out). You unlock (and release the resource if you gained access) using the **Unlock** member function. The APIs you can use with critical sections are summarized in the following table:

Critical Section APIs	Description
InitializeCriticalSection	This initializes a critical section object prior to using other critical section APIs listed in this table.
EnterCriticalSection	This causes the calling thread to wait for owning the critical section object and returns when the calling thread gets ownership.
TryEnterCriticalSection	This is the same as EnterCriticalSection, except that this API does not wait.
DeleteCriticalSection	This releases the system resources used by a critical section object. The critical section object should not be owned by any thread.
LeaveCriticalSection	This releases ownership of a critical section object.

In addition to the APIs just listed, there are two other critical section APIs: **InitializeCriticalSectionAndSpinCount**, which initializes a critical section object and sets its spin count, and **SetCriticalSectionSpinCount**, which sets the spin count for an existing critical section that may be provided in a future release of Windows NT.

A programming sample illustrating thread priority and the use of critical sections is shown here. This sample shows how to suspend, resume, and change the priority of a thread. This sample and the next two samples use trains as an example. When the threads are started, two small rectangular blocks (representing two trains traveling), each in a different color, travel across the screen from left to right. Through menu pull-downs or accelerator keys these trains could be stopped or resumed or their speed could be altered. This is achieved by changing the priority of the threads or suspending and resuming the threads that draw the train. Figure 10-1 shows the trains starting. Figure 10-2 shows the top train (thread) suspended. Figure 10-3 shows the top train moving slower compared to the bottom train due to reduced thread priority.

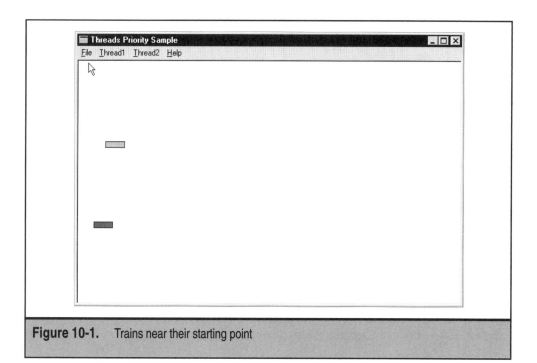

Figure 10-1. Trains near their starting point

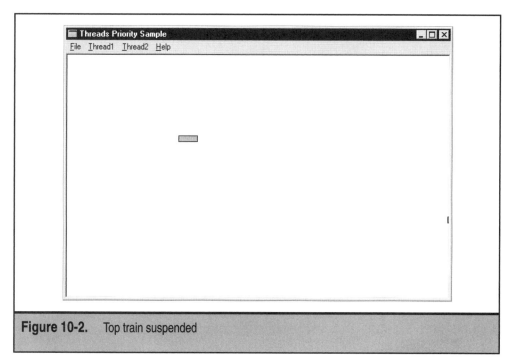

Figure 10-2. Top train suspended

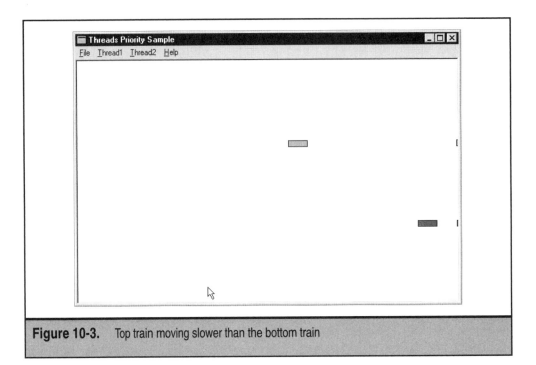

Figure 10-3. Top train moving slower than the bottom train

Unlike the earlier sample, the trains are user-interface threads that are derived from
CWinThread, and they serialize drawing the train by using critical sections. The sample
is made up of two C++ modules—one the main application processing the user
commands and the other dealing with the user-interface thread. The main module that
handles the user command is shown next. This is very similar to other samples discussed
earlier. The pointers to the two thread objects that represent the trains are held globally
for simplicity. The message map shows the functions called for various menu selections.

```
#include <afxwin.h>
#include "Resource.h"
#include "TrainThread.h"

CTrainThread  *Thread1;    // Pointer to two threads
CTrainThread  *Thread2;

// Define the application object class
class CApp : public CWinApp
{
public:
    virtual BOOL InitInstance ();
```

```
        virtual BOOL ExitInstance ();
};
// The frame window class
class CThreadWindow : public CFrameWnd
{
public:
    CClientDC    *m_pDC;
public:
    CThreadWindow();
    ~CThreadWindow();
    afx_msg void OnAppAbout();
    afx_msg void OnNewThread();
    afx_msg void OnT1Suspend();
    afx_msg void OnT1Resume();
    afx_msg void OnT1TimeCritical();
    afx_msg void OnT1Highest();
    afx_msg void OnT1AboveNormal();
    afx_msg void OnT1Normal();
    afx_msg void OnT1BelowNormal();
    afx_msg void OnT1Lowest();
    afx_msg void OnT1Idle();
    afx_msg void OnT2Suspend();
    afx_msg void OnT2Resume();
    afx_msg void OnT2TimeCritical();
    afx_msg void OnT2Highest();
    afx_msg void OnT2AboveNormal();
    afx_msg void OnT2Normal();
    afx_msg void OnT2BelowNormal();
    afx_msg void OnT2Lowest();
    afx_msg void OnT2Idle();
    afx_msg void OnExit();
    DECLARE_MESSAGE_MAP()
};

// CThreadWindow message map
BEGIN_MESSAGE_MAP(CThreadWindow, CFrameWnd)
    ON_COMMAND(ID_APP_ABOUT, OnAppAbout)
    ON_COMMAND(IDM_NEWTHREAD,                 OnNewThread)
    ON_COMMAND(IDM_T1_SUSPEND,                OnT1Suspend)
    ON_COMMAND(IDM_T1_RESUME,                 OnT1Resume)
    ON_COMMAND(IDM_T1_PRIORITY_CRITICAL,      OnT1TimeCritical)
    ON_COMMAND(IDM_T1_PRIORITY_HIGHEST,       OnT1Highest)
    ON_COMMAND(IDM_T1_PRIORITY_ABOVENORMAL,OnT1AboveNormal)
    ON_COMMAND(IDM_T1_PRIORITY_NORMAL,        OnT1Normal)
```

```
    ON_COMMAND(IDM_T1_PRIORITY_BELOWNORMAL,OnT1BelowNormal)
    ON_COMMAND(IDM_T1_PRIORITY_LOWEST,      OnT1Lowest)
    ON_COMMAND(IDM_T1_PRIORITY_IDLE,        OnT1Idle)
    ON_COMMAND(IDM_T2_SUSPEND,              OnT2Suspend)
    ON_COMMAND(IDM_T2_RESUME,               OnT2Resume)
    ON_COMMAND(IDM_T2_PRIORITY_CRITICAL,    OnT2TimeCritical)
    ON_COMMAND(IDM_T2_PRIORITY_HIGHEST,     OnT2Highest)
    ON_COMMAND(IDM_T2_PRIORITY_ABOVENORMAL,OnT2AboveNormal)
    ON_COMMAND(IDM_T2_PRIORITY_NORMAL,      OnT2Normal)
    ON_COMMAND(IDM_T2_PRIORITY_BELOWNORMAL,OnT2BelowNormal)
    ON_COMMAND(IDM_T2_PRIORITY_LOWEST,      OnT2Lowest)
    ON_COMMAND(IDM_T2_PRIORITY_IDLE,        OnT2Idle)
    ON_COMMAND(ID_APP_EXIT, OnExit)
END_MESSAGE_MAP()

// CThreadWindow constructor
CThreadWindow::CThreadWindow()
{
    LoadAccelTable(MAKEINTRESOURCE(IDR_MAINFRAME));
    Create( NULL, "Threads Priority Sample",
            WS_OVERLAPPEDWINDOW,
            rectDefault, NULL, MAKEINTRESOURCE(IDR_MAINFRAME) );
    m_pDC = new CClientDC(this);
    Thread2 = NULL;
    Thread1 = NULL;
}
```

The resource associated with the thread objects, if they exist, are freed when the user-interface thread is deleted.

```
CThreadWindow::~CThreadWindow()
{
    //  free the thread resource.
    if (Thread2)
    {
        delete Thread2;
    }
    if (Thread1)
    {
        delete Thread1;
    }
```

```
    delete m_pDC;
}


// The Main appplication CApp object

CApp theApp;
```

When the threads are created, they use the same device context to render the train. Since they share the same device context, this resource should be serialized. A critical section object is used to serialize the access to the device context while rendering. This critical section object should be initialized before using it. Once initialized, the threads of the process can **EnterCriticalSection** and **LeaveCriticalSection** using that object. The initialization of the critical section object is done when the application is started, and it is deleted when the application exits.

```
// The Main application class initialization
BOOL CApp::InitInstance()
{
    InitializeCriticalSection(&CTrainThread::m_cs);
    m_pMainWnd = new CThreadWindow();
    m_pMainWnd -> ShowWindow( m_nCmdShow );
    m_pMainWnd -> UpdateWindow();
    return TRUE;
}


int CApp::ExitInstance()
{
    DeleteCriticalSection(&CTrainThread::m_cs);
    return CWinApp::ExitInstance();
}


// CAboutDlg dialog used for App About
class CAboutDlg : public CDialog
{
public:
    CAboutDlg();
    enum { IDD = IDD_ABOUTBOX };
};


CAboutDlg::CAboutDlg() : CDialog(CAboutDlg::IDD)
{
}
```

```
// App command to run the dialog
void CThreadWindow::OnAppAbout()
{
    CAboutDlg aboutDlg;
    aboutDlg.DoModal();
}
```

When the user starts the new threads, the old thread objects are deleted if they exist, new thread objects are allocated, and threads are created. The constructor of the thread takes the pointer to the frame window object and the handle to the device context, and tracks where the train runs. MFC maintains a list of all GDI objects on a per-thread basis. Thus, the CDC object in the main application thread cannot be directly used. Instead the handle to the device context is passed, which can then be converted to an MFC object. This is done in the code that handles the train thread and will be seen later.

```
void CThreadWindow::OnNewThread()
{
    if (Thread2)
    {
        delete Thread2;
    }
    if (Thread1)
    {
        delete Thread1;
    }
    Thread1 = new CTrainThread(this, m_pDC->GetSafeHdc(), UPPER_TRAIN);
    Thread2 = new CTrainThread(this, m_pDC->GetSafeHdc(), LOWER_TRAIN);

    Thread1->CreateThread();
    Thread2->CreateThread();
}

// On Exit handles the void
void CThreadWindow::OnExit()
{
    DestroyWindow();
}
```

The rest of the code deals with processing user commands for suspending, resuming, and altering the priorities of the threads. These are done by use of the **SuspendThread**, **ResumeThread**, and **SetThreadPriority** member functions of **CWinThread**.

```
void CThreadWindow::OnT1Suspend()
{
  Thread1->SuspendThread();
}
void CThreadWindow::OnT1Resume()
{
  Thread1->ResumeThread();
}
void CThreadWindow::OnT1TimeCritical()
{
  Thread1->SetThreadPriority(THREAD_PRIORITY_TIME_CRITICAL);
  Beep(300,30);
}
void CThreadWindow::OnT1Highest()
{
  Thread1->SetThreadPriority(THREAD_PRIORITY_HIGHEST);
  Beep(300,30);
}
void CThreadWindow::OnT1AboveNormal()
{
  Thread1->SetThreadPriority(THREAD_PRIORITY_ABOVE_NORMAL);
  Beep(300,30);
}
void CThreadWindow::OnT1Normal()
{
  Thread1->SetThreadPriority(THREAD_PRIORITY_NORMAL);
  Beep(300,30);
}
void CThreadWindow::OnT1BelowNormal()
{
  Thread1->SetThreadPriority(THREAD_PRIORITY_BELOW_NORMAL);
  Beep(300,30);
}
void CThreadWindow::OnT1Lowest()
{
  Thread1->SetThreadPriority(THREAD_PRIORITY_LOWEST);
  Beep(300,30);
}
void CThreadWindow::OnT1Idle()
{
```

```cpp
  Thread1->SetThreadPriority(THREAD_PRIORITY_IDLE);
  Beep(300,30);
}
void CThreadWindow::OnT2Suspend()
{
  Thread2->SuspendThread();
}
void CThreadWindow::OnT2Resume()
{
  Thread2->ResumeThread();
}
void CThreadWindow::OnT2TimeCritical()
{
  Thread2->SetThreadPriority(THREAD_PRIORITY_TIME_CRITICAL);
  Beep(300,30);
}
void CThreadWindow::OnT2Highest()
{
  Thread2->SetThreadPriority(THREAD_PRIORITY_HIGHEST);
  Beep(300,30);
}
void CThreadWindow::OnT2AboveNormal()
{
  Thread2->SetThreadPriority(THREAD_PRIORITY_ABOVE_NORMAL);
  Beep(300,30);
}
void CThreadWindow::OnT2Normal()
{
  Thread2->SetThreadPriority(THREAD_PRIORITY_NORMAL);
  Beep(300,30);
}
void CThreadWindow::OnT2BelowNormal()
{
  Thread2->SetThreadPriority(THREAD_PRIORITY_BELOW_NORMAL);
  Beep(300,30);
}
void CThreadWindow::OnT2Lowest()
{
  Thread2->SetThreadPriority(THREAD_PRIORITY_LOWEST);
  Beep(300,30);
}
void CThreadWindow::OnT2Idle()
{
```

```
   Thread2->SetThreadPriority(THREAD_PRIORITY_IDLE);
   Beep(300,30);
}
```

The resource file for this sample is shown next.

```
//Microsoft Developer Studio generated resource script.
//
#include "afxres.h"
#include "resource.h"
LANGUAGE LANG_NEUTRAL, SUBLANG_NEUTRAL
/////////////////////////////////////////////////////////////////////////////
//
// Icon
//

// Icon with lowest ID value placed first to ensure application icon
// remains consistent on all systems.
IDR_MAINFRAME           ICON    DISCARDABLE     "Threads.ico"


/////////////////////////////////////////////////////////////////////////////
//
// Menu
//

IDR_MAINFRAME MENU PRELOAD DISCARDABLE
BEGIN
    POPUP "&File"
    BEGIN
        MENUITEM "&New Threads\tCtrl+T",        IDM_NEWTHREAD
        MENUITEM SEPARATOR
        MENUITEM "E&xit",                       ID_APP_EXIT
    END
    POPUP "&Thread1"
    BEGIN
        MENUITEM "&Suspend\tCtrl+S",            IDM_T1_SUSPEND
        MENUITEM "&Resume\tCtrl+R",             IDM_T1_RESUME
        POPUP "&Priority"
        BEGIN
            MENUITEM "&Time Critical\tCtrl+1",  IDM_T1_PRIORITY_CRITICAL
            MENUITEM "&Highest\tCtrl+2",        IDM_T1_PRIORITY_HIGHEST
            MENUITEM "&Above Normal\tCtrl+3",   IDM_T1_PRIORITY_ABOVENORMAL
```

```
                    MENUITEM "&Normal\tCtrl+4",            IDM_T1_PRIORITY_NORMAL
                    MENUITEM "&Below Normal\tCtrl+5",    IDM_T1_PRIORITY_BELOWNORMAL
                    MENUITEM "&Lowest\tCtrl+6",            IDM_T1_PRIORITY_LOWEST
                    MENUITEM "&Idle\tCtrl+7",              IDM_T1_PRIORITY_IDLE
                END
            END
            POPUP "&Thread2"
            BEGIN
                MENUITEM "&Suspend\tAlt+S",                IDM_T2_SUSPEND
                MENUITEM "&Resume\tAlt+R",                 IDM_T2_RESUME
                POPUP "&Priority"
                BEGIN
                    MENUITEM "&Time Critical\tAlt+1",    IDM_T2_PRIORITY_CRITICAL
                    MENUITEM "&Highest\tAlt+2",            IDM_T2_PRIORITY_HIGHEST
                    MENUITEM "&Above Normal\tAlt+3",    IDM_T2_PRIORITY_ABOVENORMAL
                    MENUITEM "&Normal\tAlt+4",             IDM_T2_PRIORITY_NORMAL
                    MENUITEM "&Below Normal\tAlt+5",    IDM_T2_PRIORITY_BELOWNORMAL
                    MENUITEM "&Lowest\tAlt+6",             IDM_T2_PRIORITY_LOWEST
                    MENUITEM "&Idle\tAlt+7",               IDM_T2_PRIORITY_IDLE
                END
            END
            POPUP "&Help"
            BEGIN
                MENUITEM "&About...",                      ID_APP_ABOUT
            END
END


/////////////////////////////////////////////////////////////////////
//
// Accelerator
//

IDR_MAINFRAME ACCELERATORS PRELOAD MOVEABLE PURE
BEGIN
    "T",            IDM_NEWTHREAD,                  VIRTKEY, CONTROL
    "S",            IDM_T1_SUSPEND,                 VIRTKEY, CONTROL
    "R",            IDM_T1_RESUME,                  VIRTKEY, CONTROL
    "1",            IDM_T1_PRIORITY_CRITICAL,       VIRTKEY, CONTROL

    "2",            IDM_T1_PRIORITY_HIGHEST,        VIRTKEY, CONTROL
    "3",            IDM_T1_PRIORITY_ABOVENORMAL,    VIRTKEY, CONTROL
```

```
      "4",              IDM_T1_PRIORITY_NORMAL,        VIRTKEY, CONTROL
      "5",              IDM_T1_PRIORITY_BELOWNORMAL,   VIRTKEY, CONTROL
      "6",              IDM_T1_PRIORITY_LOWEST,        VIRTKEY, CONTROL
      "7",              IDM_T1_PRIORITY_IDLE,          VIRTKEY, CONTROL
      "S",              IDM_T2_SUSPEND,                VIRTKEY, ALT
      "R",              IDM_T2_RESUME,                 VIRTKEY, ALT
      "1",              IDM_T2_PRIORITY_CRITICAL,      VIRTKEY, ALT
      "2",              IDM_T2_PRIORITY_HIGHEST,       VIRTKEY, ALT
      "3",              IDM_T2_PRIORITY_ABOVENORMAL,   VIRTKEY, ALT
      "4",              IDM_T2_PRIORITY_NORMAL,        VIRTKEY, ALT
      "5",              IDM_T2_PRIORITY_BELOWNORMAL,   VIRTKEY, ALT
      "6",              IDM_T2_PRIORITY_LOWEST,        VIRTKEY, ALT
      "7",              IDM_T2_PRIORITY_IDLE,          VIRTKEY, ALT
END


/////////////////////////////////////////////////////////////////////
//
// Dialog
//

IDD_ABOUTBOX DIALOG DISCARDABLE  0, 0, 217, 55
STYLE DS_MODALFRAME | WS_POPUP | WS_CAPTION | WS_SYSMENU
CAPTION "About Threads"
FONT 8, "MS Sans Serif"
BEGIN
    ICON            IDR_MAINFRAME,IDC_STATIC,11,17,21,20
    LTEXT           "Threads-Priority sample",IDC_STATIC,40,10,119,8,SS_NOPREFIX
    LTEXT           "Copyright © 1997",IDC_STATIC,40,25,119,8
    DEFPUSHBUTTON   "OK",IDOK,178,7,32,14,WS_GROUP
END
```

The header file and implementation file for the **CTrainThread** user-interface thread is shown next. A user-interface thread is commonly used to handle user input and respond to user events independent of other threads that might be running in the current process. All user-interface threads are derived from **CWinThread** and must declare and implement this class using the DECLARE_DYNCREATE and IMPLEMENT _DYNCREATE macros. The classes derived from **CWinThread** must override the **InitInstance** method and may optionally override other methods. In this sample the **InitInstance** method and the **ExitInstance** methods are overridden.

```
class CTrainThread : public CWinThread
{
```

```
public:
   DECLARE_DYNAMIC(CTrainThread)
   CTrainThread(CWnd* pWnd, HDC hDC, short sDirection);
public:
   short    m_position;
   short    m_trainmoves;
   HDC m_hDC;
   HBRUSH m_hBrush;
   HBRUSH m_hWbrush;
   CDC m_dc;
   CBrush m_brush;
   CBrush m_wbrush;
   CRect m_clientsize;
   CRect m_rectPosition;

   static CRITICAL_SECTION m_csGDILock;

public:
   void MoveTrain();

protected:
   virtual BOOL InitInstance();
   virtual int ExitInstance();
   DECLARE_MESSAGE_MAP()
};
```

The implementation file for the **CTrainThread** is shown next.

```
#include <afxwin.h>
#include "TrainThread.h"

#define TRAINLENGTH      30
#define TRAINWIDTH       10
#define TRAINSTEPSIZE     3


// CTrainThread—Implementation file
CRITICAL_SECTION CTrainThread::m_cs;
IMPLEMENT_DYNAMIC(CTrainThread, CWinThread)
BEGIN_MESSAGE_MAP(CTrainThread, CWinThread)
       //{{AFX_MSG_MAP(CTrainThread)
              // NOTE-the ClassWizard will add and remove mapping macros here.
       //}}AFX_MSG_MAP
END_MESSAGE_MAP()
```

As mentioned earlier, the GDI objects cannot be passed between threads, so the handle to the device context is passed to the thread during thread creation. This is maintained as a member variable and is later used in **InitInstance** to attach to a CDC object. When the thread is created, the color and the location of the thread are initialized based on the position of the train. The width of the screen is determined to calculate the position of the train and the number of moves it has to make to go across the window.

```
CTrainThread::CTrainThread(CWnd* pWnd, HDC hDC, short sPosition)
{
    CBrush  brush;
    CBrush  Whitebrush;

    m_bAutoDelete = FALSE;
    m_pMainWnd = pWnd;
    m_pMainWnd->GetClientRect(&m_clientsize);
    m_hDC = hDC;
    m_position = sPosition;

    Whitebrush.CreateSolidBrush(RGB(0xFF, 0xFF,0xFF));
    m_hWbrush = (HBRUSH)Whitebrush.Detach();

    if (m_position == UPPER_TRAIN)
    {
        brush.CreateSolidBrush(RGB(0x00, 0xFF,0x00));
        m_rectPosition.SetRect(0, m_clientsize.Height()/3,
                               0+TRAINLENGTH,
                               (m_clientsize.Height()/3)+TRAINWIDTH);
    }
    else
    {
        brush.CreateSolidBrush(RGB(0xFF, 0x00,0x00));
        m_rectPosition.SetRect(0, m_clientsize.Height()*2/3,
                               0+TRAINLENGTH,
                               (m_clientsize.Height()*2/3)+TRAINWIDTH);
    }
    m_trainmoves = (short)(m_clientsize.Width()/TRAINSTEPSIZE);
    m_hBrush = (HBRUSH)brush.Detach();
}

BOOL CTrainThread::InitInstance()
{
    m_wbrush.Attach(m_hWbrush);
    m_brush.Attach(m_hBrush);
```

```
    m_dc.Attach(m_hDC);
    for (int j = 0; j<m_trainmoves; j++)
    {
        for (unsigned int k =0; k<200000;k++);
        MoveTrain();
    }
    // Destination reached.  Beep
    Beep(1000,200);
    // thread cleanup
    m_dc.Detach();
    return FALSE;
}

int CTrainThread::ExitInstance()
{
    return (0);
}
```

The **MoveTrain** method moves the rectangular color block by redrawing one new color block and clearing the old color block. This simulates the train movement. The same device context is used by both threads for rendering. The thread currently rendering in the device context enters a critical section to prevent the other thread from rendering.

```
void CTrainThread::MoveTrain()
{

    CRect OldRect;
    OldRect = m_rectPosition;

    m_rectPosition.OffsetRect(TRAINSTEPSIZE,0);
    EnterCriticalSection(&CTrainThread::m_cs);
    {
        CBrush* oldbrush;
        CPen*   oldPen;
    // Draw the new position of the train
        oldbrush = m_dc.SelectObject(&m_brush);
        m_dc.Rectangle(m_rectPosition);
        m_dc.SelectObject(oldbrush);

    // Clear the old position of the train
        oldbrush = m_dc.SelectObject(&m_wbrush);
        oldPen = (CPen*) m_dc.SelectStockObject(WHITE_PEN);
        OldRect.OffsetRect(TRAINSTEPSIZE-TRAINLENGTH, 0);
        m_dc.Rectangle(OldRect);
```

```
        m_dc.SelectObject(oldbrush);
        m_dc.SelectObject(oldPen);
        GdiFlush();
    }
    LeaveCriticalSection(&CTrainThread::m_cs);
}
```

When you're trying the example, it is better to create a debug version of the program, since the looping that simulates the work in the thread will be more manageable. Also try it with the window maximized to give more room for the train movement. After you start the trains, the priority of the train, actually the thread, can be altered and the change observed. The trains can be suspended and resumed. Notice that if the train is suspended twice, then it has to be resumed twice before it starts moving again. This is because each thread has a suspend count, and if the suspend count is greater than zero, the thread is suspended. Every time **SuspendThread** is called, the suspend count is incremented once, and every time **ResumeThread** is called, the suspend thread count is decremented once.

 TIP: MFC maintains a list of all GDI objects on a per-thread basis.

Mutexes

A *mutex* is very similar to a critical section, except that a mutex can be used across processes. One way in which you can use a mutex is by creating a variable of type **CSingleLock** or **CMultiLock** in your resource's access member function. You then call the lock object's **Lock** member function. If the resource is not being used, your thread gains access. If the resource is being used, your thread waits (until it either gains access or it times out). You unlock (and release the resource if you gained access) using the **Unlock** member function. The APIs you can use with mutex objects are summarized in the following table:

Mutex APIs	Description
ReleaseMutex	This releases ownership of the specified mutex object. It is used when the owning thread has finished using the resource controlled by the mutex.
CreateMutex	This creates a mutex object.
OpenMutex	This enables synchronization across multiple processes by returning the handle of a mutex object that has already been created (using CreateMutex).

As an exercise try rewriting the critical section example using a mutex.

Events

An *event* is a synchronization object, which (like other synchronization objects) has two states, signaled and nonsignaled. Events are typically used to synchronize thread execution. When Thread A has to wait for Thread B, it waits for Thread B to signal an event. Windows NT does not schedule Thread A for execution until Thread B signals the event and changes the state of the event to Signaled. Windows NT now schedules Thread A for execution. The APIs you can use with event objects are summarized in the table here:

Event APIs	Description
SetEvent	This sets the state of the event object to Signaled.
CreateEvent	This creates an event object.
ResetEvent	This resets the state of the event object to nonsignaled.
OpenEvent	This enables multiple processes to use an event object by returning the handle of an existing event object.
PulseEvent	This sets the state of the specified event object to Signaled and then resets it to Nonsignaled. It is used for releasing waiting threads.

The *ThreadEvent* sample takes the Thread Priority sample and uses Event to synchronize the two threads. In the *ThreadPriority* sample the two trains were running from left to right across the screen. In this sample one train runs from west to east, and the other train runs from north to south of the screen. When the train running from north to south (NSTrain) comes to the center of the screen, it waits for the other train to cross. The west to east train (WETrain) signals the NSTrain after it crosses the center of the screen. After receiving the signal, the NSTrain proceeds south. The NSTrain does not wait indefinitely. If for some reason the WETrain gets stuck before reaching the center, the NSTrain will still proceed south after waiting for a while. Synchronization, in this example, is implemented using threads and events. Most of the code is the same or similar to the Thread Priority sample, and the differences are highlighted and discussed next. The screen shots you get when the event sample program is executed are shown in Figures 10-4 through 10-6. Figure 10-4 shows the two trains close to their starting positions. Figure 10-5 shows the trains about to cross each other. Figure 10-6 shows the trains after they have crossed each other.

The *Threads.Cpp* code is shown next. An event handle is defined in the global space, and the event is created when the frame window is created by calling the **CreateEvent** API. This event is closed when the frame window is destroyed by calling the **CloseHandle** API. When the threads are created, the event is reset by calling **ResetEvent** API. Thus, any thread waiting for this event would be blocked until the event is set. The rest of the code that deals with this event is in the *TrainThread.Cpp* module. Notice that the priority of the threads can be altered, or the threads can be suspended and resumed

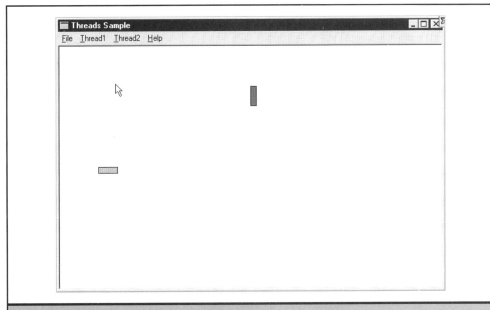

Figure 10-4.   Trains near the starting point

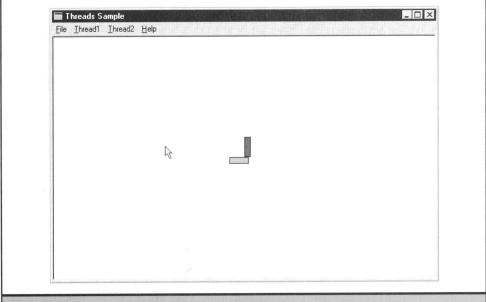

Figure 10-5.   Trains waiting to cross at intersection

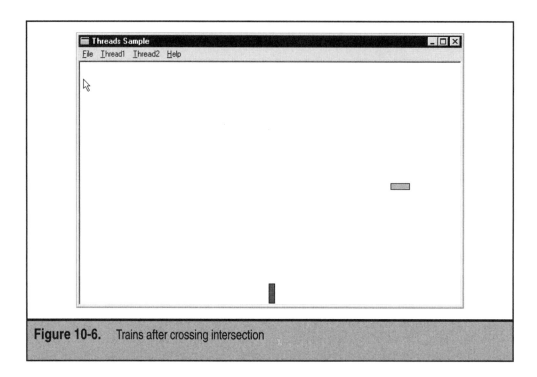

Figure 10-6.   Trains after crossing intersection

as in the *ThreadPriority* example. The rest of the code has no significant changes. The resource file is not shown here, since it changes very little.

```
#include <afxwin.h>
#include "Resource.h"
#include "TrainThread.h"


CTrainThread  *ThreadWE;    // Pointer to two threads
CTrainThread  *ThreadNS;
HANDLE  hEventGreenLight;   // Signal light event handle

// Define the application object class
class CApp : public CWinApp
{
public:
    virtual BOOL InitInstance ();
    virtual BOOL ExitInstance ();
};
// The frame window class
class CThreadWindow : public CFrameWnd
```

```
{

public:
    CClientDC    *m_pDC;
public:
    CThreadWindow();
    ~CThreadWindow();
    afx_msg void OnAppAbout();
    afx_msg void OnNewThread();
    afx_msg void OnT1Suspend();
    afx_msg void OnT1Resume();
    afx_msg void OnT1TimeCritical();
    afx_msg void OnT1Highest();
    afx_msg void OnT1AboveNormal();
    afx_msg void OnT1Normal();
    afx_msg void OnT1BelowNormal();
    afx_msg void OnT1Lowest();
    afx_msg void OnT1Idle();
    afx_msg void OnT2Suspend();
    afx_msg void OnT2Resume();
    afx_msg void OnT2TimeCritical();
    afx_msg void OnT2Highest();
    afx_msg void OnT2AboveNormal();
    afx_msg void OnT2Normal();
    afx_msg void OnT2BelowNormal();
    afx_msg void OnT2Lowest();
    afx_msg void OnT2Idle();
    afx_msg void OnExit();
    DECLARE_MESSAGE_MAP()
};

// CThreadWindow

BEGIN_MESSAGE_MAP(CThreadWindow, CFrameWnd)
    ON_COMMAND(ID_APP_ABOUT, OnAppAbout)
    ON_COMMAND(IDM_NEWTHREAD,                 OnNewThread)
    ON_COMMAND(IDM_T1_SUSPEND,                OnT1Suspend)
    ON_COMMAND(IDM_T1_RESUME,                 OnT1Resume)
    ON_COMMAND(IDM_T1_PRIORITY_CRITICAL,      OnT1TimeCritical)
    ON_COMMAND(IDM_T1_PRIORITY_HIGHEST,       OnT1Highest)
    ON_COMMAND(IDM_T1_PRIORITY_ABOVENORMAL,OnT1AboveNormal)

    ON_COMMAND(IDM_T1_PRIORITY_NORMAL,        OnT1Normal)
    ON_COMMAND(IDM_T1_PRIORITY_BELOWNORMAL,OnT1BelowNormal)
```

```
    ON_COMMAND(IDM_T1_PRIORITY_LOWEST,      OnT1Lowest)
    ON_COMMAND(IDM_T1_PRIORITY_IDLE,        OnT1Idle)
    ON_COMMAND(IDM_T2_SUSPEND,              OnT2Suspend)
    ON_COMMAND(IDM_T2_RESUME,               OnT2Resume)
    ON_COMMAND(IDM_T2_PRIORITY_CRITICAL,    OnT2TimeCritical)
    ON_COMMAND(IDM_T2_PRIORITY_HIGHEST,     OnT2Highest)
    ON_COMMAND(IDM_T2_PRIORITY_ABOVENORMAL, OnT2AboveNormal)
    ON_COMMAND(IDM_T2_PRIORITY_NORMAL,      OnT2Normal)
    ON_COMMAND(IDM_T2_PRIORITY_BELOWNORMAL, OnT2BelowNormal)
    ON_COMMAND(IDM_T2_PRIORITY_LOWEST,      OnT2Lowest)
    ON_COMMAND(IDM_T2_PRIORITY_IDLE,        OnT2Idle)
    ON_COMMAND(ID_APP_EXIT, OnExit)
END_MESSAGE_MAP()

// CThreadWindow constructor and destructor

CThreadWindow::CThreadWindow()
{
    LoadAccelTable(MAKEINTRESOURCE(IDR_MAINFRAME));
    Create( NULL, "Threads—Event Sample",
            WS_OVERLAPPEDWINDOW,
            rectDefault, NULL, MAKEINTRESOURCE(IDR_MAINFRAME) );

    m_pDC = new CClientDC(this);
    hEventGreenLight = CreateEvent(NULL, TRUE, FALSE, NULL);
    ThreadNS = NULL;
    ThreadWE = NULL;
}


CThreadWindow::~CThreadWindow()
{
    // Close the handle and free the thread resource.
    CloseHandle(hEventGreenLight);
    if (ThreadNS)
    {
        delete ThreadNS;
    }
    if (ThreadWE)
    {

        delete ThreadWE;
    }

    delete m_pDC;
```

```
}

// The CApp object

CApp theApp;

// CApp initialization

BOOL CApp::InitInstance()
{
    InitializeCriticalSection(&CTrainThread::m_cs);
    m_pMainWnd = new CThreadWindow();
    m_pMainWnd -> ShowWindow( m_nCmdShow );
    m_pMainWnd -> UpdateWindow();
    return TRUE;
}

int CApp::ExitInstance()
{
    DeleteCriticalSection(&CTrainThread::m_cs);

        return CWinApp::ExitInstance();
}

// CAboutDlg dialog used for App About box
class CAboutDlg : public CDialog
{
public:
    CAboutDlg();
    enum { IDD = IDD_ABOUTBOX };
};

CAboutDlg::CAboutDlg() : CDialog(CAboutDlg::IDD)
{
}

// App command to run the dialog
void CThreadWindow::OnAppAbout()
{

    CAboutDlg aboutDlg;
    aboutDlg.DoModal();
}
```

```
void CThreadWindow::OnNewThread()
{
    if (ThreadNS)
    {
        delete ThreadNS;
    }
    if (ThreadWE)
    {
        delete ThreadWE;
    }

    ResetEvent(hEventGreenLight);

    ThreadWE = new CTrainThread(this, m_pDC->GetSafeHdc(),
                             DIRECTION_WEST_TO_EAST);
    ThreadNS = new CTrainThread(this, m_pDC->GetSafeHdc(),
                             DIRECTION_NORTH_TO_SOUTH);
    ThreadWE->CreateThread();
    ThreadNS->CreateThread();
}



// On Exit handling function
void CThreadWindow::OnExit()
{
    DestroyWindow();
}
```

The **CTrainThread** class header file is shown next. There is no significant change here when compared with the *ThreadPriority* sample.

```
// TrainThread.h : The Train thread header file for
// the Threads-Event sample application

#define DIRECTION_WEST_TO_EAST 1
#define DIRECTION_NORTH_TO_SOUTH 2

class CTrainThread : public CWinThread
{
public:
    DECLARE_DYNAMIC(CTrainThread)
    CTrainThread(CWnd* pWnd, HDC hDC, short sDirection);
```

```
// Attributes
public:
    short    m_direction;      // W-E or N-S train direction
    short    m_trainmoves;
    HDC m_hDC;
    HBRUSH m_hBrush;
    HBRUSH m_hWbrush;
    CDC m_dc;
    CBrush m_brush;
    CBrush m_wbrush;
    CRect m_clientsize;
    CRect m_rectPosition;

    static CRITICAL_SECTION m_cs;

public:
    virtual ~CTrainThread();
    void MoveTrain();

protected:
    virtual BOOL InitInstance();
    DECLARE_MESSAGE_MAP()
};
```

The code that handles the execution of the thread is shown next. The significant code is in the **InitInstance** section of the code.

```
#include <afxwin.h>
#include "TrainThread.h"


#define TRAINLENGTH      30
#define TRAINWIDTH       10
#define TRAINSTEPSIZE    30
#define SLEEPTIME        200


// CTrainThread—Implementation file

CRITICAL_SECTION CTrainThread::m_cs;

IMPLEMENT_DYNAMIC(CTrainThread, CWinThread)

BEGIN_MESSAGE_MAP(CTrainThread, CWinThread)
```

```
        //{{AFX_MSG_MAP(CTrainThread)
        // NOTE-the ClassWizard will add and remove mapping macros here.
        //}}AFX_MSG_MAP
END_MESSAGE_MAP()

CTrainThread::CTrainThread(CWnd* pWnd, HDC hDC, short sDirection)
{
    CBrush  brush;
    CBrush  Whitebrush;

    m_bAutoDelete = FALSE;
    m_pMainWnd = pWnd;
    m_pMainWnd->GetClientRect(&m_clientsize);
    m_hDC = hDC;
    m_direction = sDirection;

    Whitebrush.CreateSolidBrush(RGB(0xFF, 0xFF,0xFF));
    m_hWbrush = (HBRUSH)Whitebrush.Detach();

    if (m_direction == DIRECTION_WEST_TO_EAST)
    {
        brush.CreateSolidBrush(RGB(0x00, 0xFF,0x00));
        m_rectPosition.SetRect(0, m_clientsize.Height()/2,
                            0+TRAINLENGTH,
                            (m_clientsize.Height()/2)+TRAINWIDTH);

        m_trainmoves = (short)(m_clientsize.Width()/TRAINLENGTH);
    }
    else
    {
        brush.CreateSolidBrush(RGB(0xFF, 0x00,0x00));
        m_rectPosition.SetRect((m_clientsize.Width()/2),0,
                            (m_clientsize.Width()/2)+TRAINWIDTH,
                            0+TRAINLENGTH);
        m_trainmoves = (short)(m_clientsize.Height()/TRAINLENGTH);
    }

    m_hBrush = (HBRUSH)brush.Detach();
}
```

When the thread is executed, the thread that represents NSTrain moves just before the center of the screen and then waits for the event by calling the **WaitForSingleObject**

API. However, it does not wait indefinitely. It waits for the amount of time it would take for the other train to go across the screen. The thread representing the WETrain signals the event just after passing the center of the screen. It beeps after setting the signal. When WETrain signals, this will trigger the NSTrain, which will be waiting to proceed. When the sample is run, the trains can be seen going from north to south and west to east. The NSTrain will wait for a beep and then proceed south. If the WETrain is suspended, the NSTrain, which is waiting, will proceed after a while.

```
BOOL CTrainThread::InitInstance()
{

    extern HANDLE    hEventGreenLight;
    m_wbrush.Attach(m_hWbrush);
    m_brush.Attach(m_hBrush);
    m_dc.Attach(m_hDC);


    // Move the train until it reaches the signal light
    for (int j = 0; j<m_trainmoves; j++)
    {
        Sleep(SLEEPTIME);
        if ((m_direction == DIRECTION_NORTH_TO_SOUTH) &&
            (j == (m_trainmoves/2-1)) )
        {   // North South train waits at the center till the West East train
            // passes OR times out.
            WaitForSingleObject(hEventGreenLight, SLEEPTIME*m_trainmoves);
        }


        if ((m_direction == DIRECTION_WEST_TO_EAST) &&
            (j == (m_trainmoves/2 + 1)) )
        {   // West East train signals the North South train after it passes the
            // center
            Beep(1000,70);
            SetEvent(hEventGreenLight);
        }
          MoveTrain();
    }
        // Destination reached.  Beep
    Beep(1000,200);
    // thread cleanup
    m_dc.Detach();
```

```
// avoid entering standard message loop by returning FALSE
    return FALSE;
}


CTrainThread::~CTrainThread()
{
}


void CTrainThread::MoveTrain()
{

    CRect OldRect;
    OldRect = m_rectPosition;

    if (m_direction == DIRECTION_WEST_TO_EAST)
    {
        m_rectPosition.OffsetRect(TRAINSTEPSIZE,0);
    }
    else
    {
        m_rectPosition.OffsetRect(0,TRAINSTEPSIZE);
    }

    EnterCriticalSection(&CTrainThread::m_cs);
    {
        CBrush* oldbrush;

        CPen*   oldPen;
    // Draw the new position of the train
        oldbrush = m_dc.SelectObject(&m_brush);
        m_dc.Rectangle(m_rectPosition);
        m_dc.SelectObject(oldbrush);

    // Clear the old position of the train
        oldbrush = m_dc.SelectObject(&m_wbrush);
        oldPen = (CPen*) m_dc.SelectStockObject(WHITE_PEN);
        m_dc.Rectangle(OldRect);
        m_dc.SelectObject(oldbrush);
        m_dc.SelectObject(oldPen);

        GdiFlush();
    }
    LeaveCriticalSection(&CTrainThread::m_cs);
}
```

Semaphores

Semaphores are used to control access to a resource by a certain number of threads (as opposed to critical sections, which let only one thread access a resource or section of code). A semaphore has a *resource counter*. Every thread that wants to access the resource controlled by the semaphore waits for the semaphore, and the resource counter is decremented by 1. If the counter is zero, then there are no more resources, and future requests to access the resource wait. When a thread finishes using the resource, it releases the semaphore, which increments the resource counter. The following APIs are used with semaphores:

Semaphore-Related APIs	Description
CreateSemaphore	Creates a semaphore and sets its resource count
ReleaseSemaphore	Releases a semaphore and increments its resource count
WaitForSingleObject	Waits for a semaphore (or any object)
CloseHandle	Closes handle and releases resources

The *ThreadSem* sample shows the use of semaphores by simulating two trains traveling in different directions competing for a single track on a bridge. There are two train tracks running left to right, with a bridge one-third the way through. Though there is one track for each direction, there is only one track for both directions on the bridge. Trains crossing the bridge share this one track resource on the bridge. The train coming to the bridge first uses the track on the bridge, while the train coming later waits until the track is available. To implement this scenario, the program uses threads for each train, and the single-track bridge is protected by a semaphore. When the program is run and the threads are started, two trains can be seen, one moving left to right on the upper track, and the other moving right to left on the lower track. When they each travel one-third the way, the train coming first uses the bridge, while the other train waits on the other side of the bridge. After the first train crosses over the bridge, the next train uses the bridge. The priority of each train can be controlled as before, and the trains can be suspended and resumed. The screen shots of the trains as they start, as they are waiting to cross each other at a bridge, and after they cross are shown in Figures 10-7, 10-8, and 10-9, respectively. The bridge is not shown in the figure, but when you execute the program, you will see that the trains come close to each other and then move apart.

The main application code is shown next, and it is similar to the code discussed earlier. The changes made are in the semaphore area and are highlighted. A semaphore handle is defined in the global space, and the semaphore is created during the creation of the application frame window by calling the **CreateSemaphore** API. Since there is only one resource to control (one track on the bridge), the maximum resource count is set to 1. The track is available, so the initial count is also set to 1. When the application is closed,

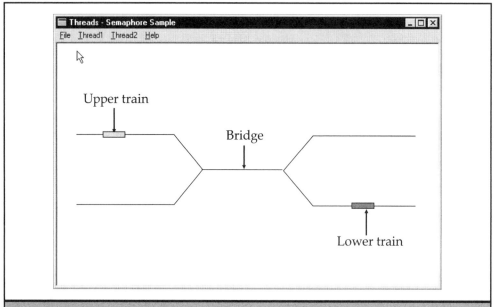

Figure 10-7.   Trains near their starting point

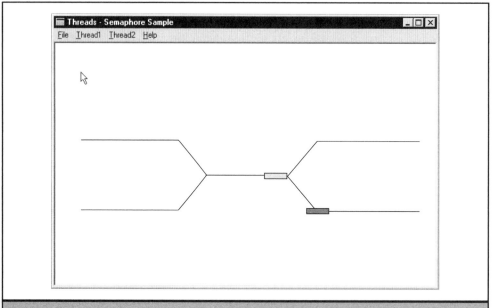

Figure 10-8.   Trains passing each other at a bridge

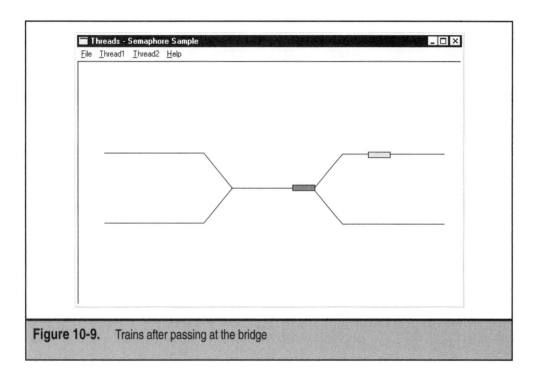

Figure 10-9. Trains after passing at the bridge

the semaphore is also closed by calling the **CloseHandle** API. The rest of the code and the resource file have little significant change.

```
#include <afxwin.h>
#include "Resource.h"
#include "TrainThread.h"

CTrainThread  *TrainThread1;    // Pointer to two threads
CTrainThread  *TrainThread2;
HANDLE  hSemaphore;            // Train track availability semaphore.

// Define the application object class
class CApp : public CWinApp
{
public:
    virtual BOOL InitInstance ();
    virtual BOOL ExitInstance ();
};

// The window class
```

```
class CThreadWindow : public CFrameWnd
{
public:
    CClientDC   *m_pDC;
public:
    CThreadWindow();
    ~CThreadWindow();
    afx_msg void OnAppAbout();
    afx_msg void OnNewThread();
    afx_msg void OnT1Suspend();
    afx_msg void OnT1Resume();
    afx_msg void OnT1TimeCritical();
    afx_msg void OnT1Highest();
    afx_msg void OnT1AboveNormal();
    afx_msg void OnT1Normal();
    afx_msg void OnT1BelowNormal();
    afx_msg void OnT1Lowest();
    afx_msg void OnT1Idle();
    afx_msg void OnT2Suspend();
    afx_msg void OnT2Resume();
    afx_msg void OnT2TimeCritical();
    afx_msg void OnT2Highest();
    afx_msg void OnT2AboveNormal();
    afx_msg void OnT2Normal();
    afx_msg void OnT2BelowNormal();
    afx_msg void OnT2Lowest();
    afx_msg void OnT2Idle();
    afx_msg void OnExit();
    DECLARE_MESSAGE_MAP()
};


// CThreadWindow

BEGIN_MESSAGE_MAP(CThreadWindow, CFrameWnd)
    ON_COMMAND(ID_APP_ABOUT, OnAppAbout)
    ON_COMMAND(IDM_NEWTHREAD,                 OnNewThread)
    ON_COMMAND(IDM_T1_SUSPEND,                OnT1Suspend)
    ON_COMMAND(IDM_T1_RESUME,                 OnT1Resume)
    ON_COMMAND(IDM_T1_PRIORITY_CRITICAL,      OnT1TimeCritical)
    ON_COMMAND(IDM_T1_PRIORITY_HIGHEST,       OnT1Highest)
    ON_COMMAND(IDM_T1_PRIORITY_ABOVENORMAL,OnT1AboveNormal)
    ON_COMMAND(IDM_T1_PRIORITY_NORMAL,        OnT1Normal)
    ON_COMMAND(IDM_T1_PRIORITY_BELOWNORMAL,OnT1BelowNormal)
```

```
    ON_COMMAND(IDM_T1_PRIORITY_LOWEST,      OnT1Lowest)
    ON_COMMAND(IDM_T1_PRIORITY_IDLE,        OnT1Idle)
    ON_COMMAND(IDM_T2_SUSPEND,              OnT2Suspend)
    ON_COMMAND(IDM_T2_RESUME,               OnT2Resume)
    ON_COMMAND(IDM_T2_PRIORITY_CRITICAL,    OnT2TimeCritical)
    ON_COMMAND(IDM_T2_PRIORITY_HIGHEST,     OnT2Highest)
    ON_COMMAND(IDM_T2_PRIORITY_ABOVENORMAL, OnT2AboveNormal)
    ON_COMMAND(IDM_T2_PRIORITY_NORMAL,      OnT2Normal)
    ON_COMMAND(IDM_T2_PRIORITY_BELOWNORMAL, OnT2BelowNormal)
    ON_COMMAND(IDM_T2_PRIORITY_LQWEST,      OnT2Lowest)
    ON_COMMAND(IDM_T2_PRIORITY_IDLE,        OnT2Idle)
    ON_COMMAND(ID_APP_EXIT, OnExit)
END_MESSAGE_MAP()

// CThreadWindow constructor and destructor
CThreadWindow::CThreadWindow()
{
    LoadAccelTable(MAKEINTRESOURCE(IDR_MAINFRAME));
    Create( NULL, "Threads-Semaphore Sample",
            WS_OVERLAPPEDWINDOW,
            rectDefault, NULL, MAKEINTRESOURCE(IDR_MAINFRAME) );
    m_pDC = new CClientDC(this);
    hSemaphore = CreateSemaphore(NULL, 1, 1, NULL);
    TrainThread2 = NULL;
    TrainThread1 = NULL;
}
CThreadWindow::~CThreadWindow()
{
    // Close the handle and free the thread resource.

    CloseHandle(hSemaphore);
    if (TrainThread2)
    {
        delete TrainThread2;
    }
    if (TrainThread1)
    {
        delete TrainThread1;
    }
    delete m_pDC;
}
// The CApp object
CApp theApp;
```

```
BOOL CApp::InitInstance()
{
    InitializeCriticalSection(&CTrainThread::m_csGDILock);
    m_pMainWnd = new CThreadWindow();
    m_pMainWnd -> ShowWindow( m_nCmdShow );
    m_pMainWnd -> UpdateWindow();
    return TRUE;
}
int CApp::ExitInstance()
{
    DeleteCriticalSection(&CTrainThread::m_csGDILock);
    return CWinApp::ExitInstance();
}
// CAboutDlg dialog used for Application About box
class CAboutDlg : public CDialog
{
public:
    CAboutDlg();
    enum { IDD = IDD_ABOUTBOX };
};

CAboutDlg::CAboutDlg() : CDialog(CAboutDlg::IDD)
{
}

// App command to run the dialog
void CThreadWindow::OnAppAbout()
{
    CAboutDlg aboutDlg;
    aboutDlg.DoModal();
}
void CThreadWindow::OnNewThread()
{
    if (TrainThread2)
    {
        delete TrainThread2;
    }
    if (TrainThread1)
    {
        delete TrainThread1;
    }
    TrainThread1 = new CTrainThread(this, m_pDC->GetSafeHdc(), TRAIN_NO_1);
    TrainThread2 = new CTrainThread(this, m_pDC->GetSafeHdc(), TRAIN_NO_2);
```

```
    TrainThread1->CreateThread();
    TrainThread2->CreateThread();
}

// OnExit handles Exit command
void CThreadWindow::OnExit()
{
    DestroyWindow();
}
```

The *TrainThread* header file is shown next and has no significant change.

```
#define TRAIN_NO_1   1
#define TRAIN_NO_2   2
class CTrainThread : public CWinThread
{
public:
    DECLARE_DYNAMIC(CTrainThread)
    CTrainThread(CWnd* pWnd, HDC hDC, short sTrainNo);

// Attributes
public:
    short    m_train;
    short    m_trainmoves;
    HDC      m_hDC;
    HBRUSH   m_hBrush;
    HBRUSH   m_hWbrush;
    CDC      m_dc;
    CBrush   m_brush;
    CBrush   m_wbrush;
    CRect    m_clientsize;
    CRect    m_rectPosition;
    CRect    m_oldRect;

    static CRITICAL_SECTION m_csGDILock;
public:
    virtual ~CTrainThread();
    void MoveTrain(short);

protected:
    virtual BOOL InitInstance();
    DECLARE_MESSAGE_MAP()
};
```

The thread function is shown next.

```
#include <afxwin.h>
#include "TrainThread.h"


#define TRAINLENGTH       30
#define TRAINWIDTH        10
#define TRAINSTEPSIZE     30
#define SLEEPTIME         200
#define SINGLETRACKSECTION     2
#define MULTITRACKSECTION      1
// CTrainThread-Implementation file

CRITICAL_SECTION CTrainThread::m_csGDILock;
IMPLEMENT_DYNAMIC(CTrainThread, CWinThread)
BEGIN_MESSAGE_MAP(CTrainThread, CWinThread)
    //{{AFX_MSG_MAP(CTrainThread)
    // NOTE—the ClassWizard will add and remove mapping macros here.
    //}}AFX_MSG_MAP
END_MESSAGE_MAP()

CTrainThread::CTrainThread(CWnd* pWnd, HDC hDC, short sTrainNo)
{
    CBrush  brush;
    CBrush  Whitebrush;

    m_bAutoDelete = FALSE;
    m_pMainWnd = pWnd;
    m_pMainWnd->GetClientRect(&m_clientsize);
    m_hDC = hDC;
    m_train = sTrainNo;

    Whitebrush.CreateSolidBrush(RGB(0xFF, 0xFF,0xFF));
    m_hWbrush = (HBRUSH)Whitebrush.Detach();

    if (m_train == TRAIN_NO_1)
    {
        brush.CreateSolidBrush(RGB(0x00, 0xFF,0x00));
        m_rectPosition.SetRect(0, m_clientsize.Height()/3,
                            0+TRAINLENGTH,
                            (m_clientsize.Height()/3)+TRAINWIDTH);
    }
    else
```

```
    {
        brush.CreateSolidBrush(RGB(0xFF, 0x00,0x00));
        m_rectPosition.SetRect(m_clientsize.Width(),
m_clientsize.Height()*2/3,
                                 m_clientsize.Width()-TRAINLENGTH,
                                 (m_clientsize.Height()*2/3)+TRAINWIDTH);
    }

    m_trainmoves = (short)(m_clientsize.Width()/TRAINLENGTH);
    m_hBrush = (HBRUSH)brush.Detach();
}
```

The **InitInstance** function controls the movement of the thread. When the train has moved one-third the way, it would have reached the bridge. The thread (and hence the train) waits for the semaphore using the **WaitForSingelObject** API and proceeds when the semaphore is acquired. Notice that it waits indefinitely, as makes sense in this situation. After crossing the bridge it releases the semaphore by calling the **ReleaseSemaphore** API, thereby indicating the release of the resource. Since only one count of the resource was released, the release count is set to 1 in the **ReleaseSemaphore** API. Waiting for a semaphore indefinitely is the common cause of deadlocks in multithreading programs. You can simulate this deadlock situation by suspending the thread whose train is on the bridge.

```
BOOL CTrainThread::InitInstance()
{
    extern HANDLE    hSemaphore;
    m_wbrush.Attach(m_hWbrush);
    m_brush.Attach(m_hBrush);
    m_dc.Attach(m_hDC);

    // Move the train until it reaches the single track section which is 1/3
    // way through
    for (int j = 0; j<m_trainmoves/3; j++)
    {
        Sleep(SLEEPTIME);
        MoveTrain(MULTITRACKSECTION);
        m_oldRect = m_rectPosition;
    }
    WaitForSingleObject(hSemaphore, INFINITE);
    // Move the train in the single track section
    if(m_train == TRAIN_NO_1)
    {
```

```
            m_rectPosition.OffsetRect(TRAINSTEPSIZE,m_clientsize.Height()/6);
    }
    else
    {
        m_rectPosition.OffsetRect(TRAINSTEPSIZE,-m_clientsize.Height()/6);
    }
    for (j = 0; j<m_trainmoves/3; j++)
    {
        Sleep(SLEEPTIME);
        MoveTrain(SINGLETRACKSECTION);
        m_oldRect = m_rectPosition;
    }

            // Off the single track section. Release the Semaphore and put back in
            // the original track
    ReleaseSemaphore(hSemaphore, 1, NULL);
    if(m_train == TRAIN_NO_1)
    {
        m_rectPosition.OffsetRect(TRAINSTEPSIZE,-m_clientsize.Height()/6);
    }
    else
    {
        m_rectPosition.OffsetRect(TRAINSTEPSIZE, m_clientsize.Height()/6);
    }
    for (j = 0; j<m_trainmoves/3; j++)
    {
        Sleep(SLEEPTIME);
        MoveTrain(MULTITRACKSECTION);
        m_oldRect = m_rectPosition;
    }
    // Destination reached.  Beep
    Beep(1000,200);
    // thread cleanup
    m_dc.Detach();

    return FALSE;    // return false to prevent entering the message loop
}


CTrainThread::~CTrainThread()
{
}


void CTrainThread::MoveTrain(short Track)
{
```

```
if (m_train == TRAIN_NO_1)
{
    m_rectPosition.OffsetRect(TRAINSTEPSIZE,0);
}
else
{
    m_rectPosition.OffsetRect(-TRAINSTEPSIZE,0);
}

EnterCriticalSection(&CTrainThread::m_csGDILock);
{
    CBrush* oldbrush;
    CPen*   oldPen;
// Draw the new position of the train
    oldbrush = m_dc.SelectObject(&m_brush);
    m_dc.Rectangle(m_rectPosition);
    m_dc.SelectObject(oldbrush);

// Clear the old position of the train
    oldbrush = m_dc.SelectObject(&m_wbrush);
    oldPen = (CPen*) m_dc.SelectStockObject(WHITE_PEN);
    m_dc.Rectangle(m_oldRect);
    m_dc.SelectObject(oldbrush);
    m_dc.SelectObject(oldPen);

    GdiFlush();
}
    LeaveCriticalSection(&CTrainThread::m_csGDILock);
}
```

Assume that there are more than two tracks on either side of the bridge and that there are two tracks on the bridge. This sample can be easily modified to simulate such a situation. When creating the semaphore, the maximum count will be set to 2, and the initial count will also be set to 2. The graphic rendering of the train should also be adjusted for additional tracks.

Waitable Timers

There are many events that happen according to time of day. Customer service lines typically start at a given time. When a number of activities have to be started in a synchronous manner based on a single occurrence such as a specific time of day, a *waitable timer* could be used. You can start a waitable timer thread, which will use a timer to release all the other threads. The APIs you can use with a waitable timer are summarized in the table that follows. The sample uses all of these APIs except **OpenWaitableTimer**.

Waitable Timer APIs	Description
CancelWaitableTimer	This cancels the request to the waitable timer and sets the timer to the inactive state.
CreateWaitableTimer	This creates a waitable timer.
SetWaitableTimer	This sets the waitable timer by specifying the time at which the timer will be activated (or set to Signaled state).
OpenWaitableTimer	This enables multiple processes to wait for the same waitable timer. One process uses CreateWaitableTimer, and the other processes get a handle to the waitable timer using OpenWaitableTimer.

The *Remind* sample program is a simple reminder that accepts a notification time and a message. When the time comes, it displays a message box with the given message. After setting the reminder, it minimizes itself and also allows the user to cancel the reminder. For simplicity the reminder can be set for the given day. However, it can be modified to accommodate future dates.

The following figures illustrate this example. Figure 10-10 shows the initial menu that lets you specify the time when you want to be reminded and a brief description. Figure 10-11 shows the message box displayed when the timer goes off. Figure 10-12 shows how you can cancel the timer that has been set. Note that the Cancel Timer button, which was grayed out in Figure 10-10, is now enabled. The Set Timer button, which was enabled in Figure 10-10, is now grayed out.

This sample uses the waitable timer available in Windows NT 4 to set the timer. A separate thread sets the timer and waits for its expiration. Once the timer has expired, the waitable timer posts a message to the main program to display a message. The various APIs used are **CreateWaitableTimer**, **SetWaitableTimer**, and **CancelWaitableTimer**.

The sample is a dialog-based application and was created using the Visual C++ App Wizard. The **CRemindDlg** class is shown next; there is nothing unusual in the class.

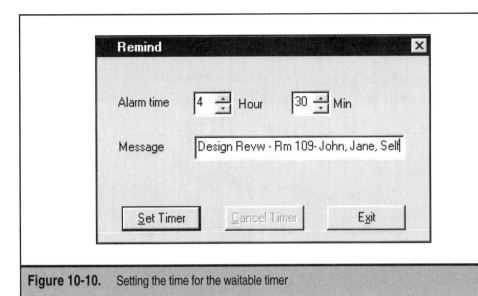

Figure 10-10.   Setting the time for the waitable timer

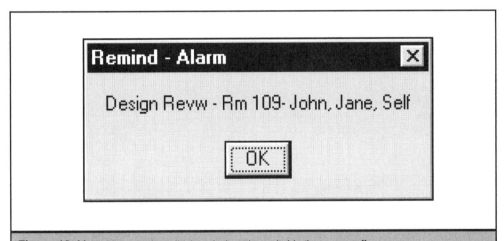

Figure 10-11.   Message box displayed when the waitable timer goes off

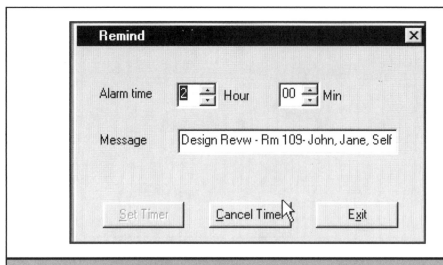

Figure 10-12. Canceling a waitable timer request

```
#if !defined(AFX_REMINDDLG_H__68C4EAF6_E1DA_11D0_977C_0004ACB5DCC1__INCLUDED_)
#define AFX_REMINDDLG_H__68C4EAF6_E1DA_11D0_977C_0004ACB5DCC1__INCLUDED_

#if _MSC_VER >= 1000
#pragma once
#endif // _MSC_VER >= 1000

/////////////////////////////////////////////////////////////////////////

// CRemindDlg dialog

class CRemindDlg : public CDialog
{
// Construction
public:
    CRemindDlg(CWnd* pParent = NULL);   // standard constructor

// Dialog Data
    //{{AFX_DATA(CRemindDlg)
    enum { IDD = IDD_REMIND_DIALOG };
    CSpinButtonCtrl     m_spinmin;
    CSpinButtonCtrl     m_spinhour;
```

```
    CString      m_edithour;
    CString      m_editmin;
    CString      m_message;
    //}}AFX_DATA

    // ClassWizard generated virtual function overrides
    //{{AFX_VIRTUAL(CRemindDlg)
    protected:
    virtual void DoDataExchange(CDataExchange* pDX);     // DDX/DDV support
    //}}AFX_VIRTUAL

// Implementation
protected:
    HICON m_hIcon;

    // Generated message map functions
    //{{AFX_MSG(CRemindDlg)
    virtual BOOL OnInitDialog();
    afx_msg void OnSysCommand(UINT nID, LPARAM lParam);
    afx_msg void OnPaint();
    afx_msg HCURSOR OnQueryDragIcon();
    afx_msg void OnSetTimer();
    afx_msg void OnCancelTimer();
    afx_msg void OnExit();
    afx_msg void OnAlarm();
    //}}AFX_MSG
    DECLARE_MESSAGE_MAP()
};


//{{AFX_INSERT_LOCATION}}


#endif //
!defined(AFX_REMINDDLG_H__68C4EAF6_E1DA_11D0_977C_0004ACB5DCC1__INCLUDED_)
```

The **RemindDlg** class implementation file is shown next. Note the definition of _WIN32_WINNT_, which is required to include appropriate header files dealing with waitable timer APIs. A user-defined message is defined to communicate between the waitable timer thread and the application. The **TIMERINFO** structure is defined and used to pass information from the main thread to the timer thread. The due time and the application dialog window handle are passed to the thread through the **TIMERINFO** structure. For simplicity the handles to the waitable timer, to the timer thread, and to the message to display when the alarm goes off are defined in the global space. The message map indicates the functions to be called for various messages. The relevant code is highlighted for quick browsing.

```cpp
// RemindDlg.cpp : implementation file
//
#define _WIN32_WINNT 0x400

#include "stdafx.h"
#include "Remind.h"
#include "RemindDlg.h"// RemindDlg.h : header file
//

#ifdef _DEBUG
#define new DEBUG_NEW
#undef THIS_FILE
static char THIS_FILE[] = __FILE__;
#endif


#define WM_USER_ALARM    WM_USER+200
UINT TimerThread(LPVOID);

typedef struct _TIMERINFO {
    HWND      hDialogHandle;
    LARGE_INTEGER    li;
} TIMERINFO;

HANDLE   hWaitableTimer;
CString AlarmMessage;
HANDLE   hTimerThread;
TIMERINFO    *ptinfo;
BOOL     bTimerExists;
/////////////////////////////////////////////////////////////////////////
// CAboutDlg dialog used for App About

class CAboutDlg : public CDialog
{
public:

        CAboutDlg();

// Dialog Data
        //{{AFX_DATA(CAboutDlg)
        enum { IDD = IDD_ABOUTBOX };
        //}}AFX_DATA
```

```cpp
        // ClassWizard generated virtual function overrides
        //{{AFX_VIRTUAL(CAboutDlg)
        protected:
        virtual void DoDataExchange(CDataExchange* pDX);     // DDX/DDV support
        //}}AFX_VIRTUAL

// Implementation
protected:
        //{{AFX_MSG(CAboutDlg)
        //}}AFX_MSG
        DECLARE_MESSAGE_MAP()
};

CAboutDlg::CAboutDlg() : CDialog(CAboutDlg::IDD)
{
        //{{AFX_DATA_INIT(CAboutDlg)
        //}}AFX_DATA_INIT
}

void CAboutDlg::DoDataExchange(CDataExchange* pDX)
{
        CDialog::DoDataExchange(pDX);
        //{{AFX_DATA_MAP(CAboutDlg)
        //}}AFX_DATA_MAP
}

BEGIN_MESSAGE_MAP(CAboutDlg, CDialog)
        //{{AFX_MSG_MAP(CAboutDlg)
                // No message handlers
        //}}AFX_MSG_MAP
END_MESSAGE_MAP()

/////////////////////////////////////////////////////////////////////
// CRemindDlg dialog

CRemindDlg::CRemindDlg(CWnd* pParent /*=NULL*/)

        : CDialog(CRemindDlg::IDD, pParent)
{
        //{{AFX_DATA_INIT(CRemindDlg)
        m_edithour = _T("");
        m_editmin = _T("");
        m_message = _T("");
        //}}AFX_DATA_INIT
```

```
                // Note that LoadIcon does not require a subsequent DestroyIcon in Win32
                m_hIcon = AfxGetApp()->LoadIcon(IDR_MAINFRAME);
}


void CRemindDlg::DoDataExchange(CDataExchange* pDX)
{
        CDialog::DoDataExchange(pDX);
        //{{AFX_DATA_MAP(CRemindDlg)
        DDX_Control(pDX, IDC_SPINMINUTE, m_spinmin);
        DDX_Control(pDX, IDC_SPINHOUR, m_spinhour);
        DDX_Text(pDX, IDC_HOUR, m_edithour);
        DDX_Text(pDX, IDC_MINUTE, m_editmin);
        DDX_Text(pDX, IDC_MESSAGE, m_message);
        //}}AFX_DATA_MAP
}


BEGIN_MESSAGE_MAP(CRemindDlg, CDialog)
        //{{AFX_MSG_MAP(CRemindDlg)
        ON_WM_SYSCOMMAND()
        ON_WM_PAINT()
        ON_WM_QUERYDRAGICON()
        ON_BN_CLICKED(IDOK, OnSetTimer)
        ON_BN_CLICKED(IDCANCEL, OnExit)
        ON_BN_CLICKED(IDC_CANCEL_TIMER, OnCancelTimer)
        ON_MESSAGE(WM_USER_ALARM, OnAlarm)
        //}}AFX_MSG_MAP
END_MESSAGE_MAP()
```

When the dialog box is initialized, the spin controls are initialized with the relevant range of hour and minute. The hour is set from the current hour onward. The waitable timer is created by calling the **CreateWaitableTimer** API, and the handle is stored for future use. Since the timer is a local timer, a NULL is passed as the name of the timer. This sample conveniently leaves the responsibility of closing the waitable timer handle to the system. The system closes the handle when the program terminates. The Cancel Timer button is grayed, since it is not valid to operate yet.

```
//////////////////////////////////////////////////////////////////////
// CRemindDlg message handlers

BOOL CRemindDlg::OnInitDialog()
{
    CDialog::OnInitDialog();

    // Add "About..." menu item to system menu.
```

```
    // IDM_ABOUTBOX must be in the system command range.
    ASSERT((IDM_ABOUTBOX & 0xFFF0) == IDM_ABOUTBOX);
    ASSERT(IDM_ABOUTBOX < 0xF000);

    CMenu* pSysMenu = GetSystemMenu(FALSE);
    if (pSysMenu != NULL)
    {
        CString strAboutMenu;
        strAboutMenu.LoadString(IDS_ABOUTBOX);
        if (!strAboutMenu.IsEmpty())
        {
            pSysMenu->AppendMenu(MF_SEPARATOR);
            pSysMenu->AppendMenu(MF_STRING, IDM_ABOUTBOX, strAboutMenu);
        }
    }

    // Set the icon for this dialog.  The framework does this automatically
    //  when the application's main window is not a dialog
    SetIcon(m_hIcon, TRUE);                 // Set big icon
    SetIcon(m_hIcon, FALSE);                // Set small icon

    // TODO: Add extra initialization here
    SYSTEMTIME  systemTime;
    GetLocalTime(&systemTime);
    m_spinhour.SetRange(systemTime.wHour, 23);  // Hour range : Current hour-23
    m_spinmin.SetRange(0, 59);   // Min 0—59
    hWaitableTimer = CreateWaitableTimer(NULL, 1, NULL);

    // Gray the Cancel Timer button
    GetDlgItem(IDC_CANCEL_TIMER)->EnableWindow(FALSE);
    return TRUE;  // return TRUE unless you set the focus to a control
}

void CRemindDlg::OnSysCommand(UINT nID, LPARAM lParam)
{
    if ((nID & 0xFFF0) == IDM_ABOUTBOX)
    {
        CAboutDlg dlgAbout;
        dlgAbout.DoModal();
    }
    else
    {
        CDialog::OnSysCommand(nID, lParam);
```

```
        }
}

// If you add a minimize button to your dialog, you will need the code below
//   to draw the icon. For MFC applications using the document/view model,
//   this is automatically done for you by the framework.

void CRemindDlg::OnPaint()

{
    if (IsIconic())
    {
        CPaintDC dc(this); // device context for painting

        SendMessage(WM_ICONERASEBKGND, (WPARAM) dc.GetSafeHdc(), 0);

        // Center icon in client rectangle
        int cxIcon = GetSystemMetrics(SM_CXICON);
        int cyIcon = GetSystemMetrics(SM_CYICON);
        CRect rect;
        GetClientRect(&rect);
        int x = (rect.Width()-cxIcon + 1) / 2;
        int y = (rect.Height()-cyIcon + 1) / 2;

        // Draw the icon
        dc.DrawIcon(x, y, m_hIcon);
    }
    else
    {
        CDialog::OnPaint();
    }
}

// The system calls this to obtain the cursor to display while the user drags
//   the minimized window.
HCURSOR CRemindDlg::OnQueryDragIcon()
{
    return (HCURSOR) m_hIcon;
}
```

When the user sets the timer, the local time is queried and the local time (hour and minute) is overlaid on the system time. When the waitable timer is set, the time when the timer is to be set to the Signaled state (or in other words, the *due time*), is given in a LARGE_INTEGER format. To convert to this format, the local time is first converted to

FILETIME format by calling the **SystemTimeToFileTime** API. Since the due time given to the **SetWaitableTimer** function is based on the system time, the local time in the FILETIME format is converted to the system time in FILETIME format by calling the **LocalFileTimeToFileTime** API. The resulting FILETIME is then copied to the LARGE_INTERGER format. The due time and the dialog window handle are then moved to the **TIMERINFO** structure. A worker thread is created, and the data is passed to the thread. The thread function will be seen later. The Cancel Timer button is enabled, the Set Timer button is disabled, and the dialog window is minimized.

```cpp
void CRemindDlg::OnSetTimer()
{
        // TODO: Add your control notification handler code here
    int iHour;
    int iMin;
    SYSTEMTIME   systemTime;
    FILETIME     localfileTime;
    FILETIME     duefileTime;
    LARGE_INTEGER   largeInt;

    UpdateData();

    ptinfo = new TIMERINFO;
    iHour = m_spinhour.GetPos();
    iMin = m_spinmin.GetPos();
    AlarmMessage = m_message;

    GetLocalTime(&systemTime);
    systemTime.wSecond = 0;      // On the second
    systemTime.wMilliseconds = 0;  // On the millisec
    systemTime.wMinute = iMin;   // At the given minute
    systemTime.wHour = iHour;    // At the given hour

    SystemTimeToFileTime(&systemTime, &localfileTime);
    LocalFileTimeToFileTime(&localfileTime, &duefileTime);
    largeInt.LowPart = duefileTime.dwLowDateTime;
    largeInt.HighPart = duefileTime.dwHighDateTime;

    ptinfo->li = largeInt;
    ptinfo->hDialogHandle = GetSafeHwnd();
    hTimerThread = AfxBeginThread(TimerThread, ptinfo);

    // Gray the Set Time button and enable the Cancel Timer button
    GetDlgItem(IDOK)->EnableWindow(FALSE);
    GetDlgItem(IDC_CANCEL_TIMER)->EnableWindow(TRUE);
```

```
    ShowWindow(SW_MINIMIZE);
}
```

When the user cancels the pending reminder, the **CancelWaitableTimer** API is called to cancel the timer. The **CancelWaitableTimer** function sets the specified waitable timer to the inactive state. Note that the function does not change the signaled state of the timer. Thus, the thread that will be waiting for this timer will wait forever, or until the timer is activated and its state is set to Signaled state. In this sample the thread is terminated by calling **TerminateThread** API, and the memory allocated for the information passed to the thread is freed.

```
void CRemindDlg::OnCancelTimer()
{
        // TODO: Add your control notification handler code here
    if (bTimerExists)
    {   // Clean up allocated data and thread
        CancelWaitableTimer(hWaitableTimer);
        TerminateThread(hTimerThread, 0);
        delete ptinfo;
        ptinfo = NULL;
        bTimerExists = FALSE;

        // Gray the Cancel Time button and enable the Set Timer button
        GetDlgItem(IDOK)->EnableWindow(TRUE);
        GetDlgItem(IDC_CANCEL_TIMER)->EnableWindow(FALSE);
    }
}

void CRemindDlg::OnExit()
{
        // TODO: Add extra cleanup here
    if (ptinfo)
    {
        delete ptinfo;
    }
    CDialog::OnCancel();
}
```

When the timer goes off, the timer thread that was created sends a user message to the application. The application beeps and puts a message box with the reminder message text. To improve this sample, a WAV file may be played here and some animation may be shown.

```
void CRemindDlg::OnAlarm()
{

        // TODO: Add your control notification handler code here
    ShowWindow(SW_RESTORE);
    // include your own music here
    Beep(300,70);
    Sleep(100);
    Beep(300,70);
    Sleep(100);
    Beep(300,70);
    Sleep(100);
    Beep(300,500);
    MessageBox(AlarmMessage, "Remind—Alarm");

    // Gray the Cancel Time button and enable the Set Timer button
    GetDlgItem(IDOK)->EnableWindow(TRUE);
    GetDlgItem(IDC_CANCEL_TIMER)->EnableWindow(FALSE);
    if (ptinfo) // Free memory
    {
        delete ptinfo;
        ptinfo = NULL;
    }
}
```

The thread function is shown next. It receives the due time parameter passed to the thread when the thread is started. This due time is used to call the **SetWaitableTimer** API. This sample does not use the periodic timer and completion routine. The sample can be extended to provide a snooze facility, in which case a value can be specified for the periodic timer. Note that if a completion routine is provided, then the thread should be in an alertable state. If the thread is not in an alertable state, the completion routine is skipped. The thread in the sample is not in an alertable state. APIs such as **WaitForSingleObjectEx** can be used instead.

```
UINT TimerThread(LPVOID alarmTime)
{
    TIMERINFO       *ptinfo;
    ptinfo = (TIMERINFO *)alarmTime;
    bTimerExists = SetWaitableTimer (hWaitableTimer, &ptinfo->li, 0 , NULL,
                            NULL, 0);
    if (WaitForSingleObject(hWaitableTimer, INFINITE) == WAIT_TIMEOUT)
    {
```

```
            // You may change INFINITE to a value and
            // optionally act when it times out.
            // Since the wait is currently INFINITE no need for any action.
      }
      else
      {
         PostMessage(ptinfo->hDialogHandle, WM_USER_ALARM, 0 ,0); // Post Message
      }
      bTimerExists = FALSE;
      return 0;
}
```

The resource file that is relevant to the sample is shown next.

```
IDD_REMIND_DIALOG DIALOGEX 0, 0, 212, 105
STYLE DS_MODALFRAME | WS_POPUP | WS_VISIBLE | WS_CAPTION | WS_SYSMENU
EXSTYLE WS_EX_APPWINDOW
CAPTION "Remind"
FONT 8, "MS Sans Serif"
BEGIN
    LTEXT           "Alarm time",IDC_STATIC,14,21,44,8
    EDITTEXT        IDC_HOUR,61,19,25,14,ES_AUTOHSCROLL
    CONTROL         "Spin1",IDC_SPINHOUR,"msctls_updown32",UDS_WRAP |
                    UDS_SETBUDDYINT | UDS_ALIGNRIGHT | UDS_AUTOBUDDY |
                    UDS_ARROWKEYS,86,19,10,14
    LTEXT           "Hour",IDC_STATIC,90,22,16,8
    EDITTEXT        IDC_MINUTE,123,19,25,14,ES_AUTOHSCROLL
    CONTROL         "Spin2",IDC_SPINMINUTE,"msctls_updown32",UDS_WRAP |
                    UDS_SETBUDDYINT | UDS_ALIGNRIGHT | UDS_AUTOBUDDY |
                    UDS_ARROWKEYS,147,19,10,14
    LTEXT           "Min",IDC_STATIC,150,22,12,8
    LTEXT           "Message",IDC_STATIC,14,46,44,8
    EDITTEXT        IDC_MESSAGE,62,44,134,14,ES_AUTOHSCROLL
    DEFPUSHBUTTON   "&Set Timer",IDOK,16,84,50,14
    PUSHBUTTON      "&Cancel Timer",IDC_CANCEL_TIMER,81,84,50,14
    PUSHBUTTON      "E&xit",IDCANCEL,146,84,50,14
END
```

For an example of using critical sections, please refer to the earlier example on thread priority in the "Critical Sections" section.

Note that there are other means of synchronizing threads. For example, you can use **SuspendThread** and **ResumeThread** as a synchronization mechanism. You can start worker threads using the CREATE_SUSPENDED flag in your primary user-interface thread, and you can **ResumeThread** for the worker threads when appropriate. You may want to start multiple worker threads for different distinct functions using this technique. Based on user input you can adjust the thread attributes such as priority when starting the worker threads.

You can also use the **Sleep/SleepEx** and **SwitchToThread** functions. You can think of **Sleep/SleepEx** as a way for a thread to synchronize with itself after an elapsed time interval. **Sleep/SleepEx** and **SwitchToThread** give up the use of the processor.

CONCLUSION

In this chapter we looked at how to create and terminate processes. Then we looked at one of the important programming tools that Windows NT provides to improve the efficiency of your application as well as processor usage—threads. We discussed how and when to create threads and the safe (and not so safe) ways of terminating threads. We covered how thread priorities work and how you can adjust them. We covered guidelines on when to use a thread. We covered thread local storage and the different communication mechanisms available for communicating between threads.

In the next chapter we'll look at the nervous system connecting Windows applications and the operating system—the message subsystem—and look at how you can intercept the message subsystem using message hooks.

WINDOWS NT
Professional
Library

CHAPTER 11

Recording Messages and Using Hooks

If you have ever wanted to create an automated demo for a program, add a macro facility to your application, or keep a record of program events, then this chapter is for you. What these items have in common is the recording and playing back of messages. This chapter shows various ways to accomplish this useful task. In the process, it describes one of Windows NT's more interesting and sophisticated API subsystems: *hooks*.

The recording and replaying of messages requires some careful thought and planning, because it involves intercepting and manipulating the message stream. And messages are, of course, at the very core of Windows. Fortunately, Windows NT provides substantial support for this activity, and because of Windows NT's 32-bit, thread-based architecture, one solution to this problem has become substantially easier.

There are many reasons why you might want to monitor, record, or play back a series of window messages. First, recording messages is one way to implement a macro facility in your application program. For example, to create a *macro*, you simply turn on the recorder, manually perform the procedure, and then stop the recorder. To use the macro, simply play back the prerecorded messages. A second reason for recording messages is to allow them to be examined, possibly during *debugging*. A third reason is to create and maintain a *journal* of program activity. Such a journal could be used to analyze and optimize your program's input features. It could also be used to maintain a log to help detect unauthorized accesses. A fourth reason for recording messages is to allow the creation of automated program *demos*. Finally, you might want to monitor the message stream so that a new hardware device can be *tested*.

In this chapter, three sample programs are developed that monitor, record, and play back messages. Each implements a different strategy. The first simply records messages received by the program. The second intercepts messages using a hook function. The third implements a systemwide message journal using two hook functions. Depending upon your need, you will find that one of these approaches will satisfy most message monitoring, recording, or playback needs.

RECORDING AND REPLAYING APPLICATION MESSAGES

In this section you will see the easiest way to record and replay messages. As you know, Windows NT communicates with your program by sending messages to its main window function (and to any other child windows created by the program). Therefore, it is a relatively easy task to save each message that your program receives. Once a sequence of messages has been recorded, the messages can be replayed by sending them, in sequence, to your program by use of the **SendMessage( )** function.

While the approach to recording and replaying messages described in this section is the easiest to implement, it is also the most limited, because it will only record messages that are dispatched by your program's main message loop. It cannot be used to record messages sent to message boxes or to modal dialog boxes. The reason is that these objects maintain their own message loops, which are beyond the control of your program. Later in this chapter, you will see one way around this restriction.

Since messages and the **SendMessage( )** function are fundamental to the implementation of the message recorder, let's review them now.

The MSG Structure

As you know, Windows NT communicates with your program by sending it messages. All messages sent to your program are stored in its *message queue* until they can be processed. When your program is ready to process another message, it retrieves it from the message queue and takes appropriate action. To accomplish this, your program uses a message loop, similar to the one shown here:

```
while(GetMessage(&msg, NULL, 0, 0))
{
  if(!TranslateAccelerator(hwnd, hAccel, &msg)) {
    TranslateMessage(&msg);
    DispatchMessage(&msg);
  }
}
```

Each time **GetMessage( )** is called, it retrieves another message from your application's message queue. It puts this message into the structure pointed to by **msg**. All messages are structures of type **MSG**, which is defined like this:

```
typedef struct tagMSG {
  HWND hwnd; /* handle of window */
  UINT message; /* message, itself */
  WPARAM wParam; /* message-specific info */
  LPARAM lParam; /* message-specific info */
  DWORD time; /* time message posted */
  POINT pt; /* position of mouse when message posted */
} MSG
```

Here, *hwnd* is the handle of the window receiving the message. The actual message is contained in *message*. *wParam* and *lParam* contain any extra information associated with the message. The time the message was posted is contained in *time*, and the coordinates of the mouse when the message was posted are in *pt*. For our purposes, only the first four fields (*hwnd, message, wParam,* and *lParam*) are of interest.

After a message is retrieved, accelerator keys and virtual keys are processed, if necessary. Then the message is dispatched to the appropriate window by use of **DispatchMessage( )**. As you know, when a message is sent to one of your program's windows, it is passed to its *window function* (also referred to as its *window procedure*). The window function receives only the first four members of the **MSG** structure.

The SendMessage( ) Function

SendMessage( ) is used to send a message to a window. You are probably familiar with **SendMessage( )** from your previous Windows programming experience. However, since it forms a crucial part of the message recorder, its use is summarized here. **SendMessage( )** has this prototype:

```
LRESULT SendMessage(HWND hwnd,
                    UINT msg,
                    WPARAM wParam,
                    LPARAM lParam);
```

Here, *hwnd* is the handle of the window that will receive the message. *msg* is the message, itself. *wParam* and *lParam* contain any other values required by the message. Notice that the parameters to **SendMessage( )** are the same as the first four members of the **MSG** structure obtained by **GetMessage( )**.

The value returned by **SendMessage( )** is the result generated by the message that it sends.

Using **SendMessage( )**, you can send a message to any window in your program. Thus, if you have a sequence of prerecorded messages, you can replay that sequence by sending each message to your program's main window using the **SendMessage( )** function.

Recording and Replaying Application Messages

The easiest way to record application messages is to add a step to your program's message loop. This extra step will record each message sent to your program. Keep in mind that this extra step will add overhead to your application. However, such overhead is unavoidable, because it is part of the recording process.

As each message is received, it must be stored. For simple applications (such as the examples in this chapter), which will not be recording many messages, each message can be stored in an array. For the example program that follows, messages will be stored in the following structure array:

```
struct messages {
  UINT msg;
  WPARAM wParam;
  LPARAM lParam;
  HWND hwnd;
} MsgArray[MAXMESS];
```

For more demanding applications, you will either need to allocate space for each message dynamically or to use a disk file for message storage.

When you're recording messages, it is important to understand that a Windows program receives a large number of messages. For example, every time you move the mouse, a message is sent. Not every message will be of interest to your program. Unwanted messages do not need to be recorded. Since you need to set aside storage for the messages that you record, recording only those of interest to your application helps reduce the amount of space you need when recording.

Once you have recorded a message sequence, it can be replayed by sending each message, in the order in which it was received, to the appropriate window. Since your program is in control during replay, prerecorded messages can be played back at varying speeds or, possibly, even in a different order than they were recorded.

A SIMPLE MESSAGE RECORDER

The following program puts into practice the preceding discussion. It allows you to record and play back mouse, keyboard, and command messages that are received by the program's main window. In the program, recording and playback is controlled by the Record menu. To use the program, first select Start to begin recording messages. To stop recording, select Stop. To replay the sequence, select Run. You can replay the sequence as many times as you like. To record a new sequence, first select Reset and then select Start to record the new sequence.

The Options menu lets you clear the screen. It also lets you activate a slow play mode. As you will see, being able to slowly replay messages is useful in a variety of situations, including debugging and demonstrations. Slow play mode can also prevent the message queue of your program from being overrun.

Here is the complete program listing. It uses the virtual window technique described in Chapter 6 to handle **WM_PAINT** requests. Sample output is shown in Figure 11-1.

The sample output shows the window when the left mouse button and the right mouse button are alternately clicked on different parts of the screen. It also shows that the letters "asdf" were typed.

```
/* A simple message recorder. */
#include <windows.h>
#include <string.h>
#include <stdio.h>
#include "rec.h"

#define MAXMESS 1000
#define ON 1
#define OFF 0
#define DELAY 200

LRESULT CALLBACK WindowFunc(HWND, UINT, WPARAM, LPARAM);

char szWinName[] = "MyWin"; /* name of window class */

struct messages {
```

```
  UINT msg;
  WPARAM wParam;
  LPARAM lParam;
  HWND hwnd;
} MsgArray[MAXMESS];

int lastmess = 0;

HINSTANCE hInst;

int record = OFF;
int delay = 0;

int X=0, Y=0; /* current output location */
int maxX, maxY; /* screen dimensions */

HDC memdc; /* store the virtual device handle */
HBITMAP hbit; /* store the virtual bitmap */
HBRUSH hbrush; /* store the brush handle */

HMENU hMenu;

int WINAPI WinMain(HINSTANCE hThisInst, HINSTANCE hPrevInst,
                   LPSTR lpszArgs, int nWinMode)
{
  HWND hwnd;
  MSG msg;
  WNDCLASSEX wcl;
  HANDLE hAccel;

  /* Define a window class. */
  wcl.hInstance = hThisInst; /* handle to this instance */
  wcl.lpszClassName = szWinName; /* window class name */
  wcl.lpfnWndProc = WindowFunc; /* window function */
  wcl.style = 0; /* default style */

  wcl.cbSize = sizeof(WNDCLASSEX); /* set size of WNDCLASSEX */

  wcl.hIcon = LoadIcon(NULL, IDI_APPLICATION); /* standard icon */
  wcl.hIconSm = LoadIcon(NULL, IDI_APPLICATION); /* small icon */
  wcl.hCursor = LoadCursor(NULL, IDC_ARROW); /* cursor style */
  wcl.lpszMenuName = "MYMENU";

  wcl.cbClsExtra = 0; /* no extra */
```

```
wcl.cbWndExtra = 0; /* information needed */

/* Use white background. */
wcl.hbrBackground = GetStockObject(WHITE_BRUSH);

/* Register the window class. */
if(!RegisterClassEx(&wcl)) return 0;

/* Create Window. */
hwnd = CreateWindow(
  szWinName, /* name of window class */
  "A Simple Event Recorder", /* title */
  WS_OVERLAPPEDWINDOW, /* Standard Window */
  CW_USEDEFAULT, /* X coordinate - let Windows decide */
  CW_USEDEFAULT, /* Y coordinate - let Windows decide */
  CW_USEDEFAULT, /* width - let Windows decide */
  CW_USEDEFAULT, /* height - let Windows decide */
  HWND_DESKTOP, /* no parent window */
  NULL, /* no override of class menu */
  hThisInst, /* handle of this instance of the program */
  NULL /* no additional arguments */
);

hInst = hThisInst;

hAccel = LoadAccelerators(hThisInst, "MYMENU");

hMenu = GetMenu(hwnd); /* get handle to main menu */

/* Display the window. */
ShowWindow(hwnd, nWinMode);
UpdateWindow(hwnd);

/* Create the message loop. */
while(GetMessage(&msg, NULL, 0, 0))
{
  if(record)
    switch(msg.message) { /* filter messages */
      case WM_CHAR:
      case WM_LBUTTONDOWN:
      case WM_RBUTTONDOWN:
      case WM_COMMAND:
        MsgArray[lastmess].hwnd = msg.hwnd;
        MsgArray[lastmess].msg = msg.message;
        MsgArray[lastmess].lParam = msg.lParam;
```

```
          MsgArray[lastmess].wParam = msg.wParam;
          lastmess++;
          if(lastmess == MAXMESS)
            MessageBox(hwnd, "Too Many Messages",
                    "Recorder Error", MB_OK);
        }
    if(!TranslateAccelerator(hwnd, hAccel, &msg)) {
      TranslateMessage(&msg); /* translate keyboard messages */
      DispatchMessage(&msg); /* return control to Windows */
    }
  }
  return msg.wParam;
}

/* Window procedure */
LRESULT CALLBACK WindowFunc(HWND hwnd, UINT message,
                            WPARAM wParam, LPARAM lParam)
{
  HDC hdc;
  PAINTSTRUCT ps;

  int i, response;
  static unsigned j=0;
  char str[255];
  TEXTMETRIC tm;
  SIZE size;

  switch(message) {
    case WM_CREATE:
      /* get screen coordinates */
      maxX = GetSystemMetrics(SM_CXSCREEN);
      maxY = GetSystemMetrics(SM_CYSCREEN);

      /* create a virtual window */
      hdc = GetDC(hwnd);
      memdc = CreateCompatibleDC(hdc);
      hbit = CreateCompatibleBitmap(hdc, maxX, maxY);
      SelectObject(memdc, hbit);
      hbrush = GetStockObject(WHITE_BRUSH);
      SelectObject(memdc, hbrush);
      PatBlt(memdc, 0, 0, maxX, maxY, PATCOPY);

      ReleaseDC(hwnd, hdc);
      break;
```

```
case WM_COMMAND:
  switch(LOWORD(wParam)) {
    case IDM_START:
      lastmess = 0;
      record = ON;
      SetWindowText(hwnd, "Recording");
      EnableMenuItem(hMenu, IDM_START, MF_GRAYED);
      EnableMenuItem(hMenu, IDM_RESET, MF_GRAYED);
      EnableMenuItem(hMenu, IDM_RUN, MF_GRAYED);
      EnableMenuItem(hMenu, IDM_EXIT, MF_GRAYED);
      break;
    case IDM_STOP:
      record = OFF;
      SetWindowText(hwnd, "A Simple Event Recorder");
      EnableMenuItem(hMenu, IDM_START, MF_ENABLED);
      EnableMenuItem(hMenu, IDM_RESET, MF_ENABLED);
      EnableMenuItem(hMenu, IDM_RUN, MF_ENABLED);
      EnableMenuItem(hMenu, IDM_EXIT, MF_ENABLED);
      break;
    case IDM_RESET:
      lastmess = 0;
      record = OFF;
      X = Y = 0;
      EnableMenuItem(hMenu, IDM_RUN, MF_GRAYED);
      break;
    case IDM_RUN:
      SetWindowText(hwnd, "Replaying");
      X = Y = 0;
      for(i=0; i<lastmess; i++) {
        SendMessage(MsgArray[i].hwnd,
                    MsgArray[i].msg,
                    MsgArray[i].wParam,
                    MsgArray[i].lParam);
        Sleep(delay);
      }
      SetWindowText(hwnd, "A Simple Event Recorder");
      break;
    case IDM_CLEAR:
      hdc = GetDC(hwnd);
      hbrush = GetStockObject(WHITE_BRUSH);
      SelectObject(memdc, hbrush);
      PatBlt(memdc, 0, 0, maxX, maxY, PATCOPY);
      SelectObject(hdc, hbrush);
      PatBlt(hdc, 0, 0, maxX, maxY, PATCOPY);
```

```
            ReleaseDC(hwnd, hdc);
            break;
          case IDM_SLOW:
            if(!delay) {
              CheckMenuItem(hMenu, IDM_SLOW, MF_CHECKED);
              delay = DELAY;
            }
            else {
              CheckMenuItem(hMenu, IDM_SLOW, MF_UNCHECKED);
              delay = 0;
            }
            break;
          case IDM_EXIT:
            response = MessageBox(hwnd, "Quit the Program?",
                                  "Exit", MB_YESNO);
            if(response == IDYES) PostQuitMessage(0);
            break;
          case IDM_HELP:
            MessageBox(hwnd, "Help", "Help", MB_OK);
            break;
        }
        break;
      case WM_CHAR:
        hdc = GetDC(hwnd);

        /* get text metrics */
        GetTextMetrics(hdc, &tm);

        sprintf(str, "%c", (char) wParam); /* stringize character */

        /* output a carriage return, linefeed sequence */
        if((char)wParam == '\r') {
          Y = Y + tm.tmHeight + tm.tmExternalLeading;
          X = 0; /* reset to start of line */
        }
        else {
          TextOut(memdc, X, Y, str, 1); /* output to memory */
          TextOut(hdc, X, Y, str, 1); /* output to screen */
          /* compute length of character */
          GetTextExtentPoint32(memdc, str, strlen(str), &size);
          X += size.cx; /* advance to end of character */
        }
```

```
          ReleaseDC(hwnd, hdc);
          break;
        case WM_LBUTTONDOWN:
          hdc = GetDC(hwnd);
          strcpy(str, "Left Button Down");
          TextOut(memdc, LOWORD(lParam), HIWORD(lParam),
                  str, strlen(str));
          TextOut(hdc, LOWORD(lParam), HIWORD(lParam),
                  str, strlen(str));
          ReleaseDC(hwnd, hdc);
          break;
        case WM_RBUTTONDOWN:
          hdc = GetDC(hwnd);
          strcpy(str, "Right Button Down");
          TextOut(memdc, LOWORD(lParam), HIWORD(lParam),
                  str, strlen(str));
          TextOut(hdc, LOWORD(lParam), HIWORD(lParam),
                  str, strlen(str));
          ReleaseDC(hwnd, hdc);
          break;
        case WM_PAINT: /* process a repaint request */
          hdc = BeginPaint(hwnd, &ps); /* get DC */

          /* copy virtual window onto screen */
          BitBlt(hdc, ps.rcPaint.left, ps.rcPaint.top,
                  ps.rcPaint.right-ps.rcPaint.left, /* width */
                  ps.rcPaint.bottom-ps.rcPaint.top, /* height */
                  memdc,
                  ps.rcPaint.left, ps.rcPaint.top,
                  SRCCOPY);

          EndPaint(hwnd, &ps); /* release DC */
          break;
        case WM_DESTROY: /* terminate the program */
          DeleteDC(memdc); /* delete the memory device */
          PostQuitMessage(0);
          break;
        default:
          return DefWindowProc(hwnd, message, wParam, lParam);
      }
      return 0;
    }
```

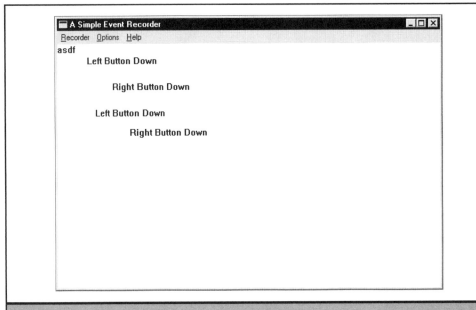

Figure 11-1. Sample output from the simple recorder program

The program requires the following resource file:

```
// Event recorder resource file.
#include <windows.h>
#include "rec.h"

MYMENU MENU
{
  POPUP "&Recorder"
  {
    MENUITEM "&Start\tF2", IDM_START
    MENUITEM "Sto&p\tF3", IDM_STOP
    MENUITEM "Rese&t\tF4", IDM_RESET
    MENUITEM "&Run\tF5", IDM_RUN, GRAYED
    MENUITEM "&Exit\tF9", IDM_EXIT
  }
  POPUP "&Options"
  {
    MENUITEM "&Clear Window\tF6", IDM_CLEAR
    MENUITEM "&Slow Motion\tF7", IDM_SLOW
```

```
    }
    MENUITEM "&Help", IDM_HELP
}

MYMENU ACCELERATORS
{
    VK_F2, IDM_START, VIRTKEY
    VK_F3, IDM_STOP, VIRTKEY
    VK_F4, IDM_RESET, VIRTKEY
    VK_F5, IDM_RUN, VIRTKEY
    VK_F6, IDM_CLEAR, VIRTKEY
    VK_F7, IDM_SLOW, VIRTKEY
    VK_F9, IDM_EXIT, VIRTKEY
    VK_F1, IDM_HELP, VIRTKEY
}
```

The header file Rec.h is shown here:

```
#define IDM_EXIT     101
#define IDM_HELP     102
#define IDM_START    103
#define IDM_STOP     104
#define IDM_RESET    105
#define IDM_RUN      106
#define IDM_CLEAR    107
#define IDM_SLOW     108
```

A Closer Look at the First Recorder Program

As mentioned earlier, to record messages, you must add a step to your program's message loop that records each message. The message loop for the example program is shown here, for your convenience:

```
while(GetMessage(&msg, NULL, 0, 0))
{
    if(record)
        switch(msg.message) { /* filter messages */
            case WM_CHAR:
            case WM_LBUTTONDOWN:
            case WM_RBUTTONDOWN:
            case WM_COMMAND:
                MsgArray[lastmess].hwnd = msg.hwnd;
                MsgArray[lastmess].msg = msg.message;
```

```
      MsgArray[lastmess].lParam = msg.lParam;
      MsgArray[lastmess].wParam = msg.wParam;
      lastmess++;
      if(lastmess == MAXMESS)
        MessageBox(hwnd, "Too Many Messages",
                   "Recorder Error", MB_OK);
    }
  if(!TranslateAccelerator(hwnd, hAccel, &msg)) {
    TranslateMessage(&msg); /* translate keyboard messages */
    DispatchMessage(&msg); /* return control to Windows */
  }
}
```

The program only records four types of message: keyboard, left and right mouse button presses, and **WM_COMMAND** messages. Recall that **WM_COMMAND** messages are generated by such things as menu selections and dialog box actions. Of course, in your own application you can record all messages or any other set of messages that you desire. The global variable **record** governs the recording of messages. At the beginning of the program, it is set to OFF (zero). When Start is selected, it is set to ON (1). When Stop is selected, it is reset to OFF.

The length of the sequence is stored in **lastmess**. This variable is incremented each time another message is recorded. The value of **lastmess** is also used when a prerecorded sequence is replayed.

After a message sequence has been recorded, it can be replayed by selecting Run. When this is done, the following code sequence is executed.

```
case IDM_RUN:
  SetWindowText(hwnd, "Replaying");
  X = Y = 0;
  for(i=0; i<lastmess; i++) {
    SendMessage(MsgArray[i].hwnd,
                MsgArray[i].msg,
                MsgArray[i].wParam,
                MsgArray[i].lParam);
    Sleep(delay);
  }
  SetWindowText(hwnd, "A Simple Event Recorder");
  break;
```

Notice that after each call to **SendMessage( )**, **Sleep( )** is called. If **delay** is zero, then no delay takes place. Otherwise, the program will suspend for the specified number of milliseconds. Initially, **delay** is zero. However, if you have selected Slow in the Options menu, then a 200-millisecond delay will occur between each message.

When you're recording, the title of the window is changed to Recording and all but the Stop selection in the Record menu are disabled. During playback, the window title is changed to Replaying.

You will want to experiment with this program before moving on. For example, start recording and then select the Help main menu option. You will receive the Help message box. Select OK. Then stop recording. When you play this sequence back, you will notice that the replay "hangs" when the Help message box is displayed and you must manually select OK. The reason is easy to understand: a message box (or a modal dialog box) creates its own message loop. Thus, events that occur within the message box are not sent to your program's main message loop and are, therefore, not recorded. In many situations, this is what you want to occur. That is, a message box is usually activated because user input is, indeed, required. (For example, a serious error may have occurred.) On the other hand, if this is not what you desire, then there are various ways around this problem. For example, during replay, you could simply not activate the message box. Another solution is presented later in this chapter, when a message journal is created.

HOOK FUNCTIONS

While there is nothing technically wrong with the preceding program, it is not generally the best way to implement a message recorder. First, most programmers will find the extra code inside the message loop to be unsettling. It is also potentially inefficient. For example, if you only want to record or monitor certain messages, you will be adding significant overhead to all messages—whether or not they are recorded. Fortunately, there is another method by which your program can tap into the message stream, and this approach is built into Windows NT itself. The mechanism that allows this is the *hook function*. Hook functions allow you to "hook into" the message stream and monitor the flow of messages. Since hook functions operate under Windows NT's control and execute (more or less) at the operating system level, they provide a better approach to monitoring the message stream. They also provide capabilities beyond those available within the application program.

Before you can use a hook function to monitor and record messages, you will need to understand their theory of operation and learn about the API functions that support them.

NOTE: You may be familiar with hook functions from your previous programming experience. However, if you understand hook functions from the point of view of Windows 3.1, you will find that some changes have taken place which, in some cases, make them substantially easier to use under Windows NT.

Hook Theory

When you create a hook function, you are inserting a function into Windows NT's message handling chain. Once installed, the hook function can monitor messages. In some cases, it can even alter messages. The hook function is depicted in Figure 11-2.

There are two general types of hook functions: *systemwide* and *application-specific*. Using a systemwide hook function, you can intercept all messages that enter the system. Using an application-specific hook function, you can intercept only those messages directed at a specified window or application. Moreover, an application-specific hook will only monitor messages associated with a specific thread. This means that multithreaded programs may need to install additional hooks if each thread creates a window that must be monitored. (This differs from Windows 3.1 in which each application consists of only one thread.)

When you're using an application-specific hook, it is possible to select various categories of messages that the hook will receive. For example, it is possible to insert a hook that receives only keyboard messages. Another can receive only mouse messages. Since each hook affects system performance, the ability to narrow the scope of a hook will be important in some applications. Of course, it is also possible to receive all messages associated with an application.

Windows NT implements hooks by maintaining a pointer to each hook function that has been installed in the system. Each hook function is called automatically by Windows NT when a message relating to that hook occurs in the input stream.

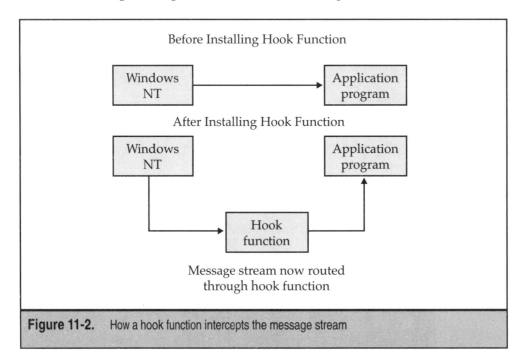

Figure 11-2. How a hook function intercepts the message stream

The General Form of a Hook Function

All hook functions have the following prototype:

```
LRESULT CALLBACK Hook(int code,
                      WPARAM wParam,
                      LPARAM lParam);
```

As you can see, all hooks are callback functions. The reason for this is obvious: they are called by Windows NT and not by your program. Here, **Hook** is the name of the hook function, which can be anything you like. Each time the hook function is called, the value of *code* determines what type of information is in the remaining two parameters and what action, if any, the hook function must take. The exact value of *code* depends upon the type of hook and what type of action has taken place. The values of *wParam* and *lParam* also vary, depending upon the type of the hook, but usually *lParam* points to an object that describes the message. The return value of a hook function depends upon the nature of the hook and what action has occurred.

Installing a Hook Function

To install a hook function, you must use **SetWindowsHookEx( )**. Its prototype is shown here:

```
HHOOK SetWindowsHookEx(int type,
                       HOOKPROC HookFunc,
                       HINSTANCE hInst,
                       DWORD ThreadId);
```

If successful, the function returns a handle to the hook, or NULL if an error occurs. The type of hook being installed is specified by *type*. It must be one of these values:

Hook Type	Purpose
WH_CALLWNDPROC	Monitors messages sent to your program's window procedure
WH_CALLWNDPROCRET	Monitors messages after your program's window procedure has handled them
WH_CBT	Monitors computer-based training commands
WH_DEBUG	Monitors all messages—used for debugging
WH_GETMESSAGE	Monitors messages obtained by GetMessage( ) or examined by PeekMessage( )
WH_JOURNALPLAYBACK	Plays back mouse or keyboard messages

Hook Type	Purpose
WH_JOURNALRECORD	Records mouse or keyboard messages
WH_KEYBOARD	Monitors keyboard messages
WH_MOUSE	Monitors mouse messages
WH_MSGFILTER	Monitors dialog, menu, scroll bar, or message box messages
WH_SHELL	Monitors shell-related messages
WH_SYSMSGFILTER	A global (systemwide) version of WH_MSGFILTER

Of these, the WH_JOURNALRECORD, WH_JOURNALPLAYBACK, and WH_ SYSMSGFILTER are always global. The others may be global or local to a specific thread.

HookFunc is a pointer to the hook function that will be installed. The instance handle of the module in which the hook function is defined is passed in *hInst*. However, if the hook function is defined within the current process and is monitoring a thread created by that process, then *hInst* must be NULL.

ThreadId is the ID of the thread being monitored. You can specify zero for *ThreadId* to monitor all threads.

Removing a Hook Function

Since hook functions negatively affect system performance, they should be removed as soon as they are no longer needed. To do this, call the **UnhookWindowsHookEx( )** function. Its prototype is shown here:

```
BOOL UnhookWindowsHookEx(HHOOK HookFunc);
```

Here, *HookFunc* is the handle of the hook function being removed. The function returns nonzero if successful and zero on failure.

Calling the Next Hook Function

In some cases a hook function must ignore a message and simply pass it along to the next hook function. It does this by calling the **CallNextHookEx( )** function, shown here:

```
LRESULT CallNextHookEx(HHOOK CurHook,
                       int code,
                       WPARAM wParam,
                       LPARAM lParam);
```

Here, *CurHook* is the handle of the currently executing hook. The values of *code*, *wParam*, and *lParam* must be those that are passed to the calling hook function. That is, the current hook function simply passes along the value of its parameters.

USING A HOOK FUNCTION TO RECORD MESSAGES

Now that you understand the theory behind hooks and the functions required to support them, we can use a hook to improve the message recorder presented earlier. To do this, the program will install a **WM_GETMESSAGE** hook. This hook is called whenever the application calls **GetMessage( )** or **PeekMessage( )**. Let's begin by examining what a **WM_GETMESSAGE** hook must do each time it is called.

Using the WM_GETMESSAGE Hook

When a **WM_GETMESSAGE** hook function is called, the value of *code* determines what action the hook function must perform. If *code* is negative, then the function must immediately pass the message along to the next hook function by calling **CallNextHookEx( )** and return its result. If *code* is HC_ACTION, the function must handle the message. After processing the message, the hook function must return zero.

The value of *wParam* indicates whether the message has been removed from the message queue by a call to **GetMessage( )** or has only been examined because of a call to **PeekMessage( )**. If the message has been removed, *wParam* will contain PM_REMOVE. If it is still in the queue, *wParam* will contain PM_NOREMOVE. For the example in this book, the value of *wParam* can be ignored, because all messages will be obtained by calling **GetMessage( )**.

The value of *lParam* points to a **MSG** structure that contains the message.

The Complete Message Recorder Using a Hook

Here is the reworked message recorder program shown earlier. This version uses a **WM_GETMESSAGE** hook function to monitor messages. It uses the same header and resource files as the previous version of the program.

```
/* Using a message hook function. */
#include <windows.h>
#include <string.h>
#include <stdio.h>
#include "rec.h"

#define MAXMESS 1000
#define ON 1
```

```
#define OFF 0
#define DELAY 200

LRESULT CALLBACK WindowFunc(HWND, UINT, WPARAM, LPARAM);

LRESULT CALLBACK MsgHook(int code, WPARAM wParam,
                        LPARAM lParam);

char szWinName[] = "MyWin"; /* name of window class */

struct messages {
  UINT msg;
  WPARAM wParam;
  LPARAM lParam;
  HWND hwnd;
} MsgArray[MAXMESS];

int lastmess = 0;

HINSTANCE hInst;

int record = OFF;
int delay = 0;

int X=0, Y=0; /* current output location */
int maxX, maxY; /* screen dimensions */

HDC memdc; /* store the virtual device handle */
HBITMAP hbit; /* store the virtual bitmap */
HBRUSH hbrush; /* store the brush handle */

HMENU hMenu;

HHOOK hHook; /* message hook handle */

HWND hwndglobal;

int WINAPI WinMain(HINSTANCE hThisInst, HINSTANCE hPrevInst,
                   LPSTR lpszArgs, int nWinMode)
{
  HWND hwnd;
  MSG msg;
  WNDCLASSEX wcl;
  HANDLE hAccel;
```

```
/* Define a window class. */
wcl.hInstance = hThisInst; /* handle to this instance */
wcl.lpszClassName = szWinName; /* window class name */
wcl.lpfnWndProc = WindowFunc; /* window function */
wcl.style = 0; /* default style */

wcl.cbSize = sizeof(WNDCLASSEX); /* set size of WNDCLASSEX */

wcl.hIcon = LoadIcon(NULL, IDI_APPLICATION); /* standard icon */
wcl.hIconSm = LoadIcon(NULL, IDI_APPLICATION); /* small icon */
wcl.hCursor = LoadCursor(NULL, IDC_ARROW); /* cursor style */
wcl.lpszMenuName = "MYMENU";

wcl.cbClsExtra = 0; /* no extra */
wcl.cbWndExtra = 0; /* information needed */

/* Use white background. */
wcl.hbrBackground = GetStockObject(WHITE_BRUSH);

/* Register the window class. */
if(!RegisterClassEx(&wcl)) return 0;

/* Create window. */
hwnd = CreateWindow(
  szWinName, /* name of window class */
  "Using a Message Hook", /* title */
  WS_OVERLAPPEDWINDOW, /* Standard Window */
  CW_USEDEFAULT, /* X coordinate - let Windows decide */
  CW_USEDEFAULT, /* Y coordinate - let Windows decide */
  CW_USEDEFAULT, /* width - let Windows decide */
  CW_USEDEFAULT, /* height - let Windows decide */
  HWND_DESKTOP, /* no parent window */
  NULL, /* no override of class menu */
  hThisInst, /* handle of this instance of the program */
  NULL /* no additional arguments */
);

hInst = hThisInst;

hAccel = LoadAccelerators(hThisInst, "MYMENU");

hMenu = GetMenu(hwnd); /* get handle to main menu */
```

```
    hwndglobal = hwnd;

    /* Display the window. */
    ShowWindow(hwnd, nWinMode);
    UpdateWindow(hwnd);

    /* Create the message loop. */
    while(GetMessage(&msg, NULL, 0, 0))
    {
      if(!TranslateAccelerator(hwnd, hAccel, &msg)) {
        TranslateMessage(&msg); /* translate keyboard messages */
        DispatchMessage(&msg); /* return control to Windows */
      }
    }
    return msg.wParam;
}

/* Window Procedure */
LRESULT CALLBACK WindowFunc(HWND hwnd, UINT message,
                            WPARAM wParam, LPARAM lParam)
{
  HDC hdc;
  PAINTSTRUCT ps;

  int i, response;
  static unsigned j=0;
  char str[255];
  TEXTMETRIC tm;
  SIZE size;

  switch(message) {
    case WM_CREATE:
      hHook = SetWindowsHookEx(WH_GETMESSAGE, (HOOKPROC) MsgHook,
                      NULL, GetCurrentThreadId());

      /* get screen coordinates */
      maxX = GetSystemMetrics(SM_CXSCREEN);
      maxY = GetSystemMetrics(SM_CYSCREEN);

      /* create a virtual window */
      hdc = GetDC(hwnd);
      memdc = CreateCompatibleDC(hdc);
      hbit = CreateCompatibleBitmap(hdc, maxX, maxY);
      SelectObject(memdc, hbit);
```

```
    hbrush = GetStockObject(WHITE_BRUSH);
    SelectObject(memdc, hbrush);
    PatBlt(memdc, 0, 0, maxX, maxY, PATCOPY);

    ReleaseDC(hwnd, hdc);
    break;
  case WM_COMMAND:
    switch(LOWORD(wParam)) {
      case IDM_START:
        lastmess = 0;
        record = ON;
        SetWindowText(hwnd, "Recording");
        EnableMenuItem(hMenu, IDM_START, MF_GRAYED);
        EnableMenuItem(hMenu, IDM_RESET, MF_GRAYED);
        EnableMenuItem(hMenu, IDM_RUN, MF_GRAYED);
        EnableMenuItem(hMenu, IDM_EXIT, MF_GRAYED);
        break;
      case IDM_STOP:
        record = OFF;
        SetWindowText(hwnd, "Using a Message Hook");
        EnableMenuItem(hMenu, IDM_START, MF_ENABLED);
        EnableMenuItem(hMenu, IDM_RESET, MF_ENABLED);
        EnableMenuItem(hMenu, IDM_RUN, MF_ENABLED);
        EnableMenuItem(hMenu, IDM_EXIT, MF_ENABLED);
        break;
      case IDM_RESET:
        lastmess = 0;
        record = OFF;
        X = Y = 0;
        EnableMenuItem(hMenu, IDM_RUN, MF_GRAYED);
        break;
      case IDM_RUN:
        SetWindowText(hwnd, "Replaying");
        X = Y = 0;
        for(i=0; i<lastmess; i++) {
          SendMessage(MsgArray[i].hwnd,
                      MsgArray[i].msg,
                      MsgArray[i].wParam,
                      MsgArray[i].lParam);
          Sleep(delay);
        }
        SetWindowText(hwnd, "Using a Message Hook");
        break;
      case IDM_CLEAR:
```

```
      hdc = GetDC(hwnd);
      hbrush = GetStockObject(WHITE_BRUSH);
      SelectObject(memdc, hbrush);
      PatBlt(memdc, 0, 0, maxX, maxY, PATCOPY);
      SelectObject(hdc, hbrush);
      PatBlt(hdc, 0, 0, maxX, maxY, PATCOPY);
      ReleaseDC(hwnd, hdc);
      break;
    case IDM_SLOW:
      if(!delay) {
        CheckMenuItem(hMenu, IDM_SLOW, MF_CHECKED);
        delay = DELAY;
      }
      else {
        CheckMenuItem(hMenu, IDM_SLOW, MF_UNCHECKED);
        delay = 0;
      }
      break;
    case IDM_EXIT:
      response = MessageBox(hwnd, "Quit the Program?",
                            "Exit", MB_YESNO);
      if(response == IDYES) PostQuitMessage(0);
      break;
    case IDM_HELP:
      MessageBox(hwnd, "Help", "Help", MB_OK);
      break;
  }
  break;
case WM_CHAR:
  hdc = GetDC(hwnd);

  /* get text metrics */
  GetTextMetrics(hdc, &tm);

  sprintf(str, "%c", (char) wParam); /* stringize character */

  /* output a carriage return, linefeed sequence */
  if((char)wParam == '\r') {
    Y = Y + tm.tmHeight + tm.tmExternalLeading;
    X = 0; /* reset to start of line */
  }
  else {
    TextOut(memdc, X, Y, str, 1); /* output to memory */
    TextOut(hdc, X, Y, str, 1); /* output to screen */
```

```c
      /* compute length of character */
      GetTextExtentPoint32(memdc, str, strlen(str), &size);
      X += size.cx; /* advance to end of character */
    }
    ReleaseDC(hwnd, hdc);
    break;
  case WM_LBUTTONDOWN:
    hdc = GetDC(hwnd);
    strcpy(str, "Left Button Down");
    TextOut(memdc, LOWORD(lParam), HIWORD(lParam),
            str, strlen(str));
    TextOut(hdc, LOWORD(lParam), HIWORD(lParam),
            str, strlen(str));
    ReleaseDC(hwnd, hdc);
    break;
  case WM_RBUTTONDOWN:
    hdc = GetDC(hwnd);
    strcpy(str, "Right Button Down");
    TextOut(memdc, LOWORD(lParam), HIWORD(lParam),
            str, strlen(str));
    TextOut(hdc, LOWORD(lParam), HIWORD(lParam),
            str, strlen(str));
    ReleaseDC(hwnd, hdc);
    break;
  case WM_PAINT: /* process a repaint request */
    hdc = BeginPaint(hwnd, &ps); /* get DC */

    /* copy virtual window onto screen */
    BitBlt(hdc, ps.rcPaint.left, ps.rcPaint.top,
           ps.rcPaint.right-ps.rcPaint.left, /* width */
           ps.rcPaint.bottom-ps.rcPaint.top, /* height */
           memdc,
           ps.rcPaint.left, ps.rcPaint.top,
           SRCCOPY);

    EndPaint(hwnd, &ps); /* release DC */
    break;
  case WM_DESTROY: /* terminate the program */
    UnhookWindowsHookEx(hHook);
    DeleteDC(memdc); /* delete the memory device */
    PostQuitMessage(0);
    break;
  default:
    return DefWindowProc(hwnd, message, wParam, lParam);
```

```
  }
  return 0;
}


/* A WM_GETMESSAGE hook function. */
LRESULT CALLBACK MsgHook(int code, WPARAM wParam, LPARAM lParam)
{
  MSG *msg;

  msg = (MSG *) lParam;

  if(code < 0)
    return CallNextHookEx(hHook, code, wParam, lParam);
  else {
    if(record) {
      switch(msg->message) {
        case WM_CHAR:
        case WM_LBUTTONDOWN:
        case WM_RBUTTONDOWN:
        case WM_COMMAND:
          MsgArray[lastmess].hwnd = msg->hwnd;
          MsgArray[lastmess].msg = msg->message;
          MsgArray[lastmess].lParam = msg->lParam;
          MsgArray[lastmess].wParam = msg->wParam;
          lastmess++;
          if(lastmess == MAXMESS)
            MessageBox(hwndglobal, "Too Many Messages",
                       "Recorder Error", MB_OK);
      }
    }
  }
  return 0;
}
```

KEEPING A SYSTEMWIDE MESSAGE JOURNAL

The preceding two example programs only recorded a few specific messages. Further, they only recorded messages associated with the main window (or any child windows) of the application. As mentioned, this means that they did not keep a record of events that occur within message boxes or modal dialog boxes. However, what if you want to keep a record of all messages that occur within the system, no matter what window generates them or what window they are for? At first, you might think that this is a difficult task. However, as you will see, support for such a job is built into Windows NT.

The facility that allows you to monitor, record, and replay systemwide messages is Windows NT's journal hooks. Windows NT supports two special hook functions which are specified by WH_JOURNALRECORD and WH_JOURNALPLAYBACK when **SetWindowsHookEx( )** is called. Using these hooks, you can maintain a systemwide journal of message activity and, if you choose, replay those messages later.

Under older versions of Windows (specifically, Windows 3.1) the journal hook had to reside in a DLL. However, because of Windows NT's 32-bit architecture and thread-based multitasking, this is no longer the case. Instead, a journal hook can be part of the application program that utilizes the journal. Needless to say, this substantially simplifies the use of message journals.

Before a systemwide journal can be created, you need to understand how to create the necessary record and playback hooks. Although they have the same general form as all other hook functions, they require some special handling on your part.

Creating a Journal Record Hook

Each time a WH_JOURNALRECORD hook is called, its *code* parameter determines what course of action the hook must follow. If *code* is negative, then the hook must simply pass the message along to the next hook function. It does so by calling **CallNextHookEx( )** and returning the result of this call. Otherwise, if *code* is HC_ACTION, the hook must record the message. Two other values may be contained in *code:* HC_SYSMODALON and HC_SYSMODALOFF. These values indicate that a system-modal dialog box was created or destroyed, respectively. Your hook function should not record messages that occur when a system-modal dialog box is active.

wParam is always NULL and unused. *lParam* points to an **EVENTMSG** structure, which is defined like this:

```
typedef struct tagEVENTMSG {
  UINT message;
  UINT paramL;
  UINT paramH;
  DWORD time;
  HWND hwnd;
} EVENTMSG;
```

Each time your journal recorder function receives a message, it must store it. That is, your program must sequentially store all messages received by the recorder function. If you will be recording just a few messages, then you can use an array of type **EVENTMSG** for this purpose. Otherwise, you will either need to dynamically allocate storage or to utilize a file for this purpose. It is important, however, that you store every message, because all will be needed to ensure an accurate playback.

Except when *code* is negative, your record hook function must return zero.

Since a journal records virtually all input events, a special means of signaling your program to stop the recording of journal entries is needed. To solve this problem, the key combination CTRL-BREAK is reserved as a stop signal during the recording process. Pressing this key combination generates a **WM_KEYDOWN** message with the VK_CANCEL key code contained within the *wParam* parameter. Your program must watch for this code and stop recording when it is received. Depending upon your application, you may or may not want to record the stop signal. If you do, then it can also be used to signal the end of a playback sequence. This is the approach used by the journal example that follows.

A WH_JOURNALRECORD hook begins receiving messages as soon as it is installed. Therefore, you will not want to install one until it is needed. Also, you will want to remove the hook as soon as you are done recording.

Creating a Journal Playback Function

Each time a WH_JOURNALPLAYBACK hook is called, its *code* parameter determines what course of action the hook must follow. If *code* is negative, then the hook must simply pass the message along to the next hook function. It does so by calling **CallNextHookEx( )** and returning the result of this call. If *code* is HC_GETNEXT, the hook must obtain the next message and copy it to the **EVENTMSG** structure pointed to by *lParam*. If *code* is HC_SKIP, the hook must prepare for the next HC_GETNEXT request. Thus, when HC_GETNEXT is received, your hook function copies the current message to the object pointed to by *lParam,* but it does *not* advance to the next message. The only time your hook function advances to the next message is when HC_SKIP is received. Therefore, two HC_GETNEXT requests without an intervening HC_SKIP request must return the same message.

The values HC_SYSMODALON and HC_SYSMODALOFF may also be contained in *code.* These values indicate that a system-modal dialog box was created or destroyed, respectively. Your hook function should not play back messages when a system-modal dialog box is active.

The return value of a playback hook is ignored unless *code* contains HC_GETNEXT. In this case, the return value indicates a delay interval that will be observed before the next message is processed. If the hook returns zero, the message is processed immediately. Otherwise, the specified delay will occur. The delay period is specified in terms of system clock ticks. You can use the delay feature to replay events at a faster or slower speed than the one at which they were recorded. It is also valuable as a means of preventing the input queue from being overrun. Remember, your program can replay input events far faster than you can enter them manually. Thus, it is possible to overrun the input queue during playback if too many messages are dispatched.

To play back the journal recorded by a WH_JOURNALRECORD hook, you simply install a WH_JOURNALPLAYBACK hook. Once installed, it will automatically begin being called by Windows NT to obtain messages. That is, immediately upon its installation, the message stream will switch from your input to that produced by the WH_JOURNALPLAYBACK hook. In fact, while the journal playback hook is installed, mouse and keyboard input are disabled—except for a few special key combinations, such as CTRL-ALT-DEL. Therefore, before installing a playback hook, make sure that it is ready to provide messages. Also, you must remove the hook as soon as it has reached the end of the journal. Failure to do so will almost certainly lead to disaster.

Journals Are Systemwide Resources

As mentioned earlier, a journal is a systemwide feature. Thus, it will record events that happen in any active window. For example, by using a journal, you can also record input events that occur within message boxes, modal dialog boxes, and even other programs.

Since a journal places itself into the systemwide message system, you must exercise care with its use. First, it will degrade the performance of all tasks because there are more messages that need to be handled in the systemwide message system. Second, you may create unforeseen side effects when a complex series of commands is replayed. For example, if you alter the shape or position of a window while recording and then play back those events without first returning the window to its former size and appearance, spurious messages may be sent to other applications that were previously under the original window. Sometimes playing back a journal will not produce the precise results that you expect. Be careful.

There are three key combinations that cannot be recorded because they cancel journal hook functions. They are CTRL-ESC, ALT-ESC, and CTRL-ALT-DEL. These keys are especially useful if your application becomes "stuck" during record or playback. Pressing any of these keys will cancel the journal hooks.

A Complete Journal Example

The following program implements a systemwide journal. You should have no trouble understanding its operation. It works much like the two preceding examples, except that it will record all input events that occur within the system. Therefore, use it with care. Remember, to stop recording, press CTRL-BREAK. Sample output is shown in Figure 11-3.

```c
/* Using a system journal. */
#include <windows.h>
#include <string.h>
#include <stdio.h>
#include "rec.h"

#define MAXMESS 2000
#define ON 1
#define OFF 0
#define DELAY 200

LRESULT CALLBACK WindowFunc(HWND, UINT, WPARAM, LPARAM);
LRESULT CALLBACK RecHook(int, WPARAM, LPARAM);
LRESULT CALLBACK PlayHook(int, WPARAM, LPARAM);
```

```
char szWinName[] = "MyWin"; /* name of window class */

EVENTMSG MsgArray[MAXMESS];

int lastmess = 0;
int curmess = 0;
int delay = 1;

HINSTANCE hInst;

int record = OFF;

int X=0, Y=0; /* current output location */
int maxX, maxY; /* screen dimensions */

HDC memdc; /* store the virtual device handle */
HBITMAP hbit; /* store the virtual bitmap */
HBRUSH hbrush; /* store the brush handle */

HHOOK hRecHook, hPlayHook;

HMENU hMenu;

HWND hwndglobal;

int WINAPI WinMain(HINSTANCE hThisInst, HINSTANCE hPrevInst,
                   LPSTR lpszArgs, int nWinMode)
{
  HWND hwnd;
  MSG msg;
  WNDCLASSEX wcl;
  HANDLE hAccel;

  /* Define a window class. */
  wcl.hInstance = hThisInst; /* handle to this instance */
  wcl.lpszClassName = szWinName; /* window class name */
  wcl.lpfnWndProc = WindowFunc; /* window function */
  wcl.style = 0; /* default style */

  wcl.cbSize = sizeof(WNDCLASSEX); /* set size of WNDCLASSEX */

  wcl.hIcon = LoadIcon(NULL, IDI_APPLICATION); /* standard icon */
  wcl.hIconSm = LoadIcon(NULL, IDI_APPLICATION); /* small icon */
  wcl.hCursor = LoadCursor(NULL, IDC_ARROW); /* cursor style */
```

```
wcl.lpszMenuName = "MYMENU";

wcl.cbClsExtra = 0; /* no extra */
wcl.cbWndExtra = 0; /* information needed */

/* Use white background. */
wcl.hbrBackground = GetStockObject(WHITE_BRUSH);

/* Register the window class. */
if(!RegisterClassEx(&wcl)) return 0;

/* Create Window */
hwnd = CreateWindow(
  szWinName, /* name of window class */
  "Using a Journal", /* title */
  WS_OVERLAPPEDWINDOW, /* Standard Window */
  CW_USEDEFAULT, /* X coordinate - let Windows decide */
  CW_USEDEFAULT, /* Y coordinate - let Windows decide */
  CW_USEDEFAULT, /* width - let Windows decide */
  CW_USEDEFAULT, /* height - let Windows decide */
  HWND_DESKTOP, /* no parent window */
  NULL, /* no override of class menu */
  hThisInst, /* handle of this instance of the program */
  NULL /* no additional arguments */
);

hInst = hThisInst;
hwndglobal = hwnd;

hAccel = LoadAccelerators(hThisInst, "MYMENU");

hMenu = GetMenu(hwnd); /* get handle to main menu */

/* Display the window. */
ShowWindow(hwnd, nWinMode);
UpdateWindow(hwnd);

/* Create the message loop. */
while(GetMessage(&msg, NULL, 0, 0))
{
  if(!TranslateAccelerator(hwnd, hAccel, &msg)) {
    TranslateMessage(&msg); /* translate keyboard messages */
    DispatchMessage(&msg); /* return control to Windows */
  }
```

```
    }
  return msg.wParam;
}


/* Window Procedure */
LRESULT CALLBACK WindowFunc(HWND hwnd, UINT message,
                            WPARAM wParam, LPARAM lParam)
{
  HDC hdc;
  PAINTSTRUCT ps;

  int response;
  char str[255];
  TEXTMETRIC tm;
  SIZE size;

  switch(message) {
    case WM_CREATE:
      /* get screen coordinates */
      maxX = GetSystemMetrics(SM_CXSCREEN);
      maxY = GetSystemMetrics(SM_CYSCREEN);

      /* create a virtual window */
      hdc = GetDC(hwnd);
      memdc = CreateCompatibleDC(hdc);
      hbit = CreateCompatibleBitmap(hdc, maxX, maxY);
      SelectObject(memdc, hbit);
      hbrush = GetStockObject(WHITE_BRUSH);
      SelectObject(memdc, hbrush);
      PatBlt(memdc, 0, 0, maxX, maxY, PATCOPY);

      ReleaseDC(hwnd, hdc);
      break;
    case WM_COMMAND:
      switch(LOWORD(wParam)) {
        case IDM_START:
          lastmess = 0;
          record = ON;
          EnableMenuItem(hMenu, IDM_START, MF_GRAYED);
          EnableMenuItem(hMenu, IDM_RESET, MF_GRAYED);
          EnableMenuItem(hMenu, IDM_RUN, MF_GRAYED);
```

```
      EnableMenuItem(hMenu, IDM_EXIT, MF_GRAYED);
      SetWindowText(hwnd, "Recording -- Ctrl-Break to Stop");

      hRecHook =SetWindowsHookEx(WH_JOURNALRECORD,
                                 (HOOKPROC) RecHook, hInst, 0);
      break;
    case IDM_RESET:
      X = Y = 0;
      lastmess = 0;
      curmess = 0;
      record = OFF;
      EnableMenuItem(hMenu, IDM_RUN, MF_GRAYED);
      break;
    case IDM_RUN:
      X = Y = 0;
      curmess = 0;
      SetWindowText(hwnd, "Replaying");
      hPlayHook = SetWindowsHookEx(WH_JOURNALPLAYBACK,
                                   (HOOKPROC) PlayHook, hInst, 0);
      break;
    case IDM_CLEAR:
      hdc = GetDC(hwnd);
      hbrush = GetStockObject(WHITE_BRUSH);
      SelectObject(memdc, hbrush);
      PatBlt(memdc, 0, 0, maxX, maxY, PATCOPY);
      SelectObject(hdc, hbrush);
      PatBlt(hdc, 0, 0, maxX, maxY, PATCOPY);
      ReleaseDC(hwnd, hdc);
      break;
    case IDM_SLOW:
      if(delay==1) {
        CheckMenuItem(hMenu, IDM_SLOW, MF_CHECKED);
        delay = DELAY;
      }
      else {
        CheckMenuItem(hMenu, IDM_SLOW, MF_UNCHECKED);
        delay = 1;
      }
      break;
    case IDM_EXIT:
      response = MessageBox(hwnd, "Quit the Program?",
                            "Exit", MB_YESNO);
```

```
      if(response == IDYES) PostQuitMessage(0);
        break;
      case IDM_HELP:
        MessageBox(hwnd, "Help", "Help", MB_OK);
        break;
    }
    break;
  case WM_KEYDOWN: /* check for VK_CANCEL */
    if(wParam == VK_CANCEL && record) {
      /* stop recording */
      UnhookWindowsHookEx(hRecHook);
      record = OFF;
      SetWindowText(hwnd, "Using a Journal");
      EnableMenuItem(hMenu, IDM_START, MF_ENABLED);
      EnableMenuItem(hMenu, IDM_RESET, MF_ENABLED);
      EnableMenuItem(hMenu, IDM_RUN, MF_ENABLED);
      EnableMenuItem(hMenu, IDM_EXIT, MF_ENABLED);
    }
    else if(wParam == VK_CANCEL && !record) {
      /* stop playback */
      UnhookWindowsHookEx(hPlayHook);
      record = OFF;
      SetWindowText(hwnd, "Using a Journal");
    }
    break;
  case WM_CHAR: /* process keystroke */
    hdc = GetDC(hwnd);

    /* get text metrics */
    GetTextMetrics(hdc, &tm);

    sprintf(str, "%c", (char) wParam); /* stringize character */

    /* output a carriage return, linefeed sequence */
    if((char)wParam == '\r') {
      Y = Y + tm.tmHeight + tm.tmExternalLeading;
      X = 0; /* reset to start of line */
    }
    else {
      TextOut(memdc, X, Y, str, 1); /* output to memory */
      TextOut(hdc, X, Y, str, 1); /* output to memory */
      /* compute length of character */
      GetTextExtentPoint32(memdc, str, strlen(str), &size);
```

```
        X += size.cx; /* advance to end of character */
      }
      ReleaseDC(hwnd, hdc);
      break;
    case WM_LBUTTONDOWN:
      hdc = GetDC(hwnd);
      strcpy(str, "Left Button Down");
      TextOut(memdc, LOWORD(lParam), HIWORD(lParam),
              str, strlen(str));
      TextOut(hdc, LOWORD(lParam), HIWORD(lParam),
              str, strlen(str));
      ReleaseDC(hwnd, hdc);
      break;
    case WM_RBUTTONDOWN:
      hdc = GetDC(hwnd);
      strcpy(str, "Right Button Down");
      TextOut(memdc, LOWORD(lParam), HIWORD(lParam),
              str, strlen(str));
      TextOut(hdc, LOWORD(lParam), HIWORD(lParam),
              str, strlen(str));
      ReleaseDC(hwnd, hdc);
      break;
    case WM_PAINT: /* process a repaint request */
      hdc = BeginPaint(hwnd, &ps); /* get DC */

      /* copy virtual window onto screen */
      BitBlt(hdc, ps.rcPaint.left, ps.rcPaint.top,
             ps.rcPaint.right-ps.rcPaint.left, /* width */
             ps.rcPaint.bottom-ps.rcPaint.top, /* height */
             memdc,
             ps.rcPaint.left, ps.rcPaint.top,
             SRCCOPY);

      EndPaint(hwnd, &ps); /* release DC */
      break;
    case WM_DESTROY: /* terminate the program */
      DeleteDC(memdc); /* delete the memory device */
      PostQuitMessage(0);
      break;
    default:
      return DefWindowProc(hwnd, message, wParam, lParam);
  }
  return 0;
}
```

```c
/* Journal record hook. */
LRESULT CALLBACK RecHook(int code, WPARAM wParam, LPARAM lParam)
{
  static int recOK = 1;

  if(code < 0)
    return CallNextHookEx(hRecHook, code, wParam, lParam);
  else if(code == HC_SYSMODALON)
    recOK = 0;
  else if(code == HC_SYSMODALOFF)
    recOK = 1;
  else if(recOK && record && (code == HC_ACTION)) {
    MsgArray[lastmess] = * (EVENTMSG *) lParam;
    lastmess++;
    if(lastmess == MAXMESS)
      MessageBox(hwndglobal, "Too Many Messages",
                 "Recorder Error", MB_OK);
  }
  return 0;
}

/* Journal playback hook. */
LRESULT CALLBACK PlayHook(int code, WPARAM wParam, LPARAM lParam)
{
  static s = 0;
  static playOK = 1;

  if(code < 0)
    return CallNextHookEx(hPlayHook, code, wParam, lParam);
  else if(code == HC_SYSMODALON)
    playOK = 0;
  else if(code == HC_SYSMODALOFF)
    playOK = 1;
  else if(playOK && (code == HC_GETNEXT)) {
    s = !s;
    if(s) return delay;
    * (EVENTMSG *)lParam = MsgArray[curmess];
  }
  else if(playOK && (code == HC_SKIP)) curmess++;

  return 0;
}
```

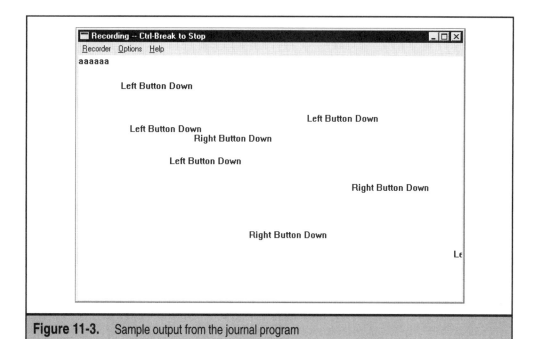

Figure 11-3.   Sample output from the journal program

The program uses the following resource file:

```
// Event recorder resource file.
#include <windows.h>
#include "rec.h"

MYMENU MENU
{
  POPUP "&Recorder"
  {
    MENUITEM "&Start\tF2", IDM_START
    MENUITEM "Rese&t\tF3", IDM_RESET
    MENUITEM "&Run\tF4", IDM_RUN, GRAYED
    MENUITEM "&Exit\tF9", IDM_EXIT
  }
  POPUP "&Options"
  {
    MENUITEM "&Clear Window\tF5", IDM_CLEAR
    MENUITEM "&Slow Motion\tF6", IDM_SLOW
  }
```

```
    MENUITEM "&Help", IDM_HELP
}

MYMENU ACCELERATORS
{
  VK_F2, IDM_START, VIRTKEY
  VK_F3, IDM_RESET, VIRTKEY
  VK_F4, IDM_RUN, VIRTKEY
  VK_F5, IDM_CLEAR, VIRTKEY
  VK_F6, IDM_SLOW, VIRTKEY
  VK_F9, IDM_EXIT, VIRTKEY
  VK_F1, IDM_HELP, VIRTKEY
}
```

The header file *Rec.h* is the same as that used by the preceding programs.

CONCLUSION

We saw how to record and play back keystrokes, mouse movements, and so on. This could be handy when you are unit testing your program. But what is also significant is that you tapped into the nervous system of windows programming—message handling. Windows programming is not the straight line, step-by-step programming common in many other environments. When your program starts, it doesn't cause a sequence of things to happen. It waits for, receives, and processes messages. This is illustrated well in this program, and you had a chance to work first hand with Windows message processing.

Processing messages makes a fitting ending to Part 2, where we looked at advanced user interface functions such as GDI, advanced controls, animation, and OS services such as multithreading. In Part 3, we will cover communications-related programming for Windows NT, including important topics that you are likely to use a lot, such as OLE and ActiveX.

WINDOWS
NT
Professional
Library

PART III

NT Communications Programming

CHAPTER 12

Introduction to OLE and ActiveX

Continuing our communications focus, let's look at an important Windows technology—OLE (object linking and embedding). OLE is based on the Component Object Model (COM). One important aspect of OLE, OLE custom controls, has advanced significantly since the introduction of OLE and is now called ActiveX controls. As an advanced Windows NT programmer, you can expect to spend a lot of your programming effort in OLE and ActiveX. The interest in these COM-based technologies has grown, partly because Microsoft is facing intense competition in this area and is aggressively trying to establish OLE, ActiveX, and COM. HP and DEC are among the vendors who plan to include support for COM in their own operating systems. Once you master COM and COM-based technologies, you may be able to develop applications in other environments besides Windows NT.

The primary significance of COM and the technologies based on it, OLE and ActiveX, is not the features, such as including a spreadsheet in a Word document transparently or the ability to download and execute a control in a browser. The more important underlying phenomenon is the transition of Windows from an API-driven operating system (from an application development perspective) to an object-oriented operating system. Windows programming can be viewed as a three-step evolution—API, MFC, and OLE/ActiveX. The MFC library was a small step over APIs, but the programming benefits of masking the details and programming at a higher level are already apparent in the MFC library. OLE and ActiveX are a much bigger step and take programming to a still higher level. The transition is by no means complete. But the trend is evident.

In this chapter, we will briefly review the basics of OLE and ActiveX and the programming aspects of OLE and ActiveX controls. We will look at how OLE 2 attempts to address the problems of OLE 1. In the next two chapters, we will cover programming examples involving OLE and ActiveX.

OLE 2 BASICS

OLE started with the need to create documents that matched the real world. Within the computer world we make a distinction between a word processing document, a spreadsheet, a graphic, or a multimedia object and have separate applications to deal with them. But more often than not, all the objects coexist as part of regular business communications. The term *compound document* denotes this coexistence of objects, and OLE started as the means for the different applications to individually deal with portions of the compound document. OLE performed this through object linking or object embedding. We will not go into the basics of OLE 1.0 here. Chapter 1 has a brief review of OLE. This chapter also presumes that you are familiar with OLE terminology such as an OLE *item* or *object* (a graphic, spreadsheet, and so on), an OLE *container* (the client that contains the different objects), an OLE *miniserver* (edits only embedded items), an OLE *full server* (edits embedded and linked items), and an OLE *automation server* (see "OLE

Automation" later in this chapter). What we will note here are some of the limitations of OLE 1.0 and how these are addressed in OLE 2.0.

The primary advantage of object linking is that changes to the linked object are automatically reflected in the compound document that the object belongs to. The primary problem is that links get broken. Embedding an object ensures that the object cannot get lost, but in the process sacrifices the advantage of automatic updates. Another problem with OLE 1.0 relates to the end-user interface. When the user edits a linked or embedded object, the corresponding application takes over the existing user interface including the menus, toolbars, and so on, and in the process takes a long time (in most environments).

OLE 2.0 has attempted to provide solutions to the problems of OLE 1.0, but it has also expanded beyond compound documents. It has become the basis for component software-based Windows programming and includes features such as reusable custom controls, in-place activation, OLE automation, enhanced linking, and drag-and-drop. Let's briefly review these concepts. Of these, two features are probably the most significant. One that has taken on a life of its own is the custom controls (ActiveX controls), and this is covered starting with the section "ActiveX Basics" later in this chapter. The other is OLE automation, which is covered starting with the section "OLE Automation" also later in this chapter.

In-Place Activation or Visual Editing

When you edit an embedded object, the complete application associated with the object is loaded and control is transferred to the application to edit the embedded object. This has two problems. The first is that it takes a long time to load the application and the whole object. This problem is somewhat alleviated by use of *structured storage* which allows an application to read and write portions of an object instead of the whole object (see "Structured Storage" later in this chapter). Secondly, the user does not get the feeling that he or she is editing one document using one editor. The user is very aware that the application has been switched. For example, Figure 12-1 shows that when you want to insert a PowerPoint slide in a Word document, the PowerPoint application is started with its own window, menu, and toolbars. The heading for the slide is "Slide in Document3."

In-place activation addresses this problem. When an embedded object is edited, the application that handles the embedded object is activated in-place (rather than in a separate window), and most of the user interface elements of the original application (such as menus, toolbars, and palettes) are supplanted by those of the application handling the embedded object. Figure 12-2 shows that when you insert an Excel worksheet, a separate window is not created (actually the OLE 2 specification gives a choice between in-place activation and opening a separate window). Instead, the Excel menu and toolbars supplant Word's menu and toolbars, and the heading is still the Word heading "Document2." In addition, in-place activation also ensures that depending on where the cursor is in the compound document, the appropriate pop-up menu will be displayed.

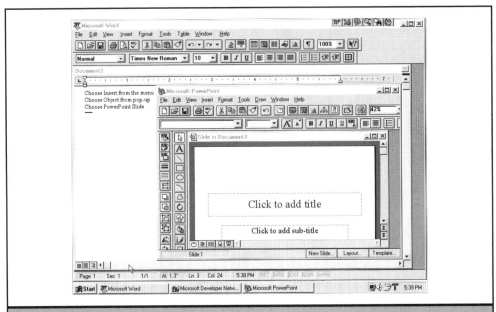

Figure 12-1. Editing an OLE object without in-place activation

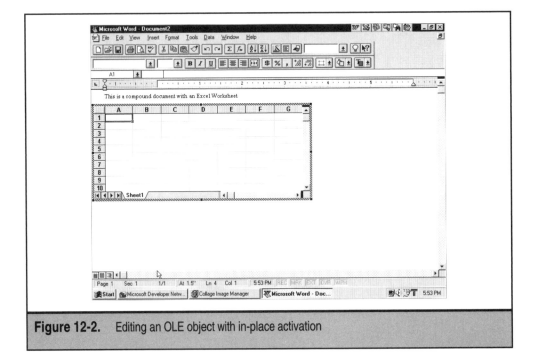

Figure 12-2. Editing an OLE object with in-place activation

Structured Storage

As mentioned earlier, when you double-click an OLE object in a container, the OLE server for the object and the entire object are loaded, which takes considerable time. The entire object is also saved when changes are made to the object.

To understand some of the persistent storage features supported by COM, let's start with a word processor. A word processor like Word will store the changes you make to the word processing document separate from the document itself. This makes it easy for Word to support functions such as Undo, and it is also easy to support the option of letting the user discard all changes to a document in an editing session. Applying this analogy, COM makes it easy for your OLE application to store updates separate from the object (and thus save time compared with updating the whole object). OLE provides structured storage called *compound files*. Compound files support storage and stream objects.

> **TIP:** Do not confuse "compound files" with the similar sounding "compound documents." Compound documents contain types of objects, while compound files are one way of storing compound documents.

Storage and stream objects are conceptually equivalent to directories and files, respectively. *Storage objects,* like directories, contain other (child) storage objects and stream objects. *Stream objects* store your application's data.

You can perform updates to the storage/stream objects in one of two modes—direct or transaction mode. In *transaction mode,* updates are buffered until they are committed or reverted. You can use transaction mode to provide your user the option to cancel all updates and revert the object to its original state. Updates in *direct mode* are immediately applied to the object being updated.

The storage and stream objects are accessed by use of the **IStorage** and **IStream** interfaces, respectively. The **IStorage** interface creates and manages structured storage objects. The **IStorage** interface contains root storage objects, child storage objects, and stream objects and methods for managing these objects. These methods provide functions to create, open, copy, move, rename, and so on, the objects contained in the storage object. **IStorage** interface methods are summarized in Table 12-1.

IStorage Method	Description
CreateStream	This creates/opens a stream object within the storage object. You can replace an existing stream by another with the same name using this method.

Table 12-1. IStorage Methods

IStorage Method	Description
OpenStream	This opens an existing stream object within the storage object. You can specify permissions of the stream object which are constrained by that of the storage object that the stream belongs to.
CreateStorage	This creates/opens a storage object within another storage object. The new storage object is nested within the other storage object.
OpenStorage	This opens an existing storage object.
CopyTo	This copies the contents of one storage object into another. Nested objects within the storage object are also copied. Contents of stream objects are replaced while copying, whereas contents of storage objects are added to.
MoveElementTo	This moves a substorage or stream from this storage object to another storage object. You can set a flag value in this method to copy instead of move. You can also rename an element.
Commit	This commits known changes for a transacted storage object to the next higher level. If the commit is done at the root storage object level, the changes are committed at the device level. Changes in currently opened nested elements are not committed. For a direct mode root storage object, changes in memory buffers are flushed.
Revert	This discards uncommitted changes to a transacted storage object. Committed changes from nested elements that have not been propagated to the next higher level are also discarded. If this method is used for a root storage object without a prior commit, then all changes by the object and nested elements are discarded, and the object reverts to its former state before the transaction. This method has no effect on directed mode storage objects.

Table 12-1. IStorage Methods (*continued*)

IStorage Method	Description
EnumElements	This returns a handle to an enumerator object that implements the standard IEnumSTATSTG interface. Use this method to enumerate the storage and stream objects within this storage object.
DestroyElement	This deletes a substorage or stream element. Call the Commit method after a call to this method for a transacted object to commit the change.
RenameElement	This renames a substorage or stream object. The substorage or stream object cannot be open. Call the Commit method after a call to this method for a transacted object to commit the change.
SetElementTimes	This sets time statistics such as modification, access, and creation times of a storage element. A statistic is set only if supported by the underlying file system and is ignored otherwise. Specify NULL if you do not want to change an existing value.
SetClass	This assigns a class identifier (CLSID) to this storage object. A CLSID is a unique global 128-bit identifier.
SetStateBits	This is reserved (stores up to 32 bits of storage object state information).
Stat	This retrieves the STATSTG structure, which contains statistical information about the current storage. It is used in conjunction with EnumElements (see EnumElements in this table).

Table 12-1.   IStorage Methods (*continued*)

You release the **IStorage** pointers when processing is complete to deallocate memory used by the storage object. At times, you may need to serialize the access to a storage object. You can serialize access using the **IPersistStorage** interface. The methods of the **IStorage** interface handle the management of objects. The methods to actually read and write data are part of the **IStream** interface.

The **IStream** interface contains methods for seeking, reading, and writing data as summarized in Table 12-2.

IStream Method	Description
Read	This reads a specified number of bytes from the stream object into memory starting at the current seek pointer and increments the seek pointer. You can get the actual number of bytes read (the actual bytes read may be different from the requested number, in case there is not enough data left in the stream, or if there is an error).
Write	This writes a specified number of bytes into the stream object starting at the current seek pointer and increments the seek pointer. It optionally returns the actual number of bytes written (which may be zero if the data couldn't be written for any reason). If the amount of data to be written exceeds the available space in the stream, the stream is automatically extended.
Seek	This changes the seek pointer to a new location or returns the current location of the seek pointer. The new location can be specified as an offset relative to the beginning of the stream, the end of the stream, or the current seek pointer. You will get an error for seeking before the start of the stream but not after the end (the position beyond the end will be used to extend the stream for write requests with data that exceeds the available space in the stream).
SetSize	This allocates contiguous space for stream objects. For a new stream object, the space is allocated. For an existing stream object, the current size is truncated or extended to match the specified size. The seek pointer is unaffected.
CopyTo	This copies the data from a portion of a stream or the complete stream to another stream and adjusts the seek pointers in both streams.
Commit	This commits changes to a stream object opened in transacted mode to the next higher level. Note: OLE compound file implementation does not support transacted mode processing of streams.

Table 12-2. IStream Methods

IStream Method	Description
Revert	This discards uncommitted changes to a transacted mode stream (changes since the last commit). This method has no effect on directed mode streams or on OLE compound file implementation (since commits are not supported, there is nothing to revert).
LockRegion	This restricts access to a specified range of bytes in the stream for read, write, or exclusive access. The locked region must be unlocked (see UnlockRegion next) before releasing the stream. This method depends on the underlying file system for support. Compound files do not support this method.
Unlock Region	This unlocks the range of bytes locked by LockRegion. Compound files do not support this method.
Stat	This retrieves the STATSTG structure, which contains statistical information about the current stream. This is used in conjunction with EnumElements (see the EnumElements method in Table 12-1).
Clone	This clones an existing stream object (creates a new stream object that references the same data as the existing stream). The cloned stream object has a new seek pointer (separate from the pointer of the existing stream) whose initial setting is the value of the seek pointer of the existing stream at cloning time.

Table 12-2. IStream Methods (*continued*)

An important feature of storage and stream objects is that they are sharable across processes (an **IStorage** or **IStream** instance pointer can be marshaled to another process). Nested objects (for example, an Excel worksheet within a PowerPoint slide within a Word document) are easily implemented as nested storage objects.

Moniker

Another problem with OLE 1 is that of broken links. In OLE 1, when an OLE container links to another object, the linked-to object resides outside the OLE container in its own file. The filename of the object (including the path) is the link to the object. Thus, if the file is moved to another directory or to another computer, the link is broken.

OLE 2 attempts to solve this problem (to a large extent) through a *moniker*. Moniker is a referencing mechanism to locate objects. OLE 2 stores the absolute path as in OLE 1, but also stores a relative path. The *relative path* of an object is the path as it relates to the current location of the container and is typically the difference in the path (as opposed to the *absolute path,* which starts with a drive letter and has all the directories leading up to the object). The relative path is searched first, and if the link could not be established, the absolute path is searched. When an OLE object and its container are moved to another subdirectory or another drive (even a network drive) while maintaining the relative path, the link will break in OLE 1, but not in OLE 2. When the container is moved, the relative path may change, but the linked object can still be found if its absolute path is not changed. Thus, the addition of the relative path in OLE 2 significantly reduced the possibility of broken links. Note, however, that a link may still be broken if the *linked object* is moved, and its relative path with the container is also changed. So far in this discussion monikers were used in the context of identifying any object that is stored in its own file. Such a moniker is called a *file moniker.* But there are other types of monikers such as *item moniker* (a moniker used to identify an object contained in another object), *composite moniker* (a moniker that is a composite of other monikers), and so on.

Drag-and-Drop

Your OLE application can be made really user friendly by providing support for OLE drag-and-drop functionality. OLE drag-and-drop is conceptually similar to transferring data between documents (or even within the same document) using the cut and paste functions and the Clipboard. However, OLE drag-and-drop is faster and easier because the menu bar is not used. In OLE drag-and-drop, you highlight the drag-and-drop source (the portion of the document you want to copy) and while keeping the left mouse button pressed, drag the highlighted selection to the drag-and-drop target and release the left mouse button. Both the source and target must be open and visible (at least partially) on the desktop for the drag-and-drop operation to be successful. The actual data transfer mechanism used by OLE is called *uniform data transfer.*

The source of drag-and-drop could be non-OLE applications. You can get source data from applications that do not support compound documents (or customize standard OLE drag-and-drop behavior). The programming details for implementing drag-and-drop are similar for both container and server applications. In most cases OLE takes care of deleting the data involved in the drag-and-drop operation after the drag-and-drop operation is complete. OLE drag-and-drop is covered in more detail in Chapter 13.

Binding

OLE 1 supported only one form of binding, called the VTable binding. OLE 2 supports additional forms of binding such as

▼ Early binding

■ Late binding

▲ ID binding

Early binding, also called *VTable (or VTBL) binding,* allows an ActiveX client to call a method or property access function directly. This binding tends to be faster than the other two forms of binding. Early binding does not require the object whose methods are being accessed to implement the **IDispatch** interface. Early binding also does not use dispatch identifiers (DISPIDs) and generates code to call the object's methods or properties through the object's VTable.

Late binding is performed by use of the **IDispatch** interface. The methods of the **IDispatch** interface are summarized in Table 12-3. This is the slowest of the three options. Typically, two calls are made at run time. The first call is used to find the DISPID (see **GetIDsOfNames** in Table 12-3), and the second call invokes the method using the DISPID. No compile-time checks are made, and there is no need for type libraries. Of course, besides the process being slow, you may get run-time errors, for example, if the name is not found.

ID binding established the DISPID-name equivalence at compile time by use of a type library. As a result, at run time you need only one call (invoke) instead of the two calls required for late binding. Thus, ID binding is faster compared with late binding, and name-not-found errors are caught at compile time rather than at run time.

IDispatch Member Function	Description
GetIDsOfNames	This maps method, property, and parameter names into a corresponding set of integer dispatch identifiers (DISPIDs). The DISPIDs are used by the Invoke member function.
GetTypeInfo	This retrieves the type information for interfaces supported by an OLE server.
GetTypeInfoCount	This retrieves the number of type information interfaces that an OLE server supports. The returned value is 1 if the server supports a type information interface and zero otherwise. However, the OLE server may still be programmable through IDispatch without the type information.
Invoke	This provides access to properties and methods exposed by an object. As an alternative, you may use the CreateStdDispatch and DispInvoke functions.

Table 12-3. IDispatch Member Functions

Besides the previous enhancements, OLE 2 also removes the restriction that an embedded or linked object must fit in one contiguous region. Instead the embedded object can occupy noncontiguous regions within the container. OLE 2 also allows embedded text to be searched and edited by the container application.

OLE AUTOMATION

Another important programming concept associated with OLE that you should be familiar with is OLE Automation (or simply automation). *OLE Automation* is the mechanism by which one application (an OLE Automation client or automation controller) can invoke programmable objects of another application (an OLE Automation server). This process involves the application that owns the programmable objects to expose the programming objects (properties and methods), it is designed to expose to client applications.

You can create a skeleton OLE Automation Server using the AppWizard, and enhance it to suit your needs. Before an Automation client can invoke the Automation Server, the Automation Server must be registered in the system Registry. (OLE uses the information in the Registry to present the user with a list of OLE objects that can be inserted when the user wants to insert a new object.)

The principal communication mechanism between an OLE client and an OLE automation server is the **IDispatch** interface. Access using **IDispatch** is a *late binding* access, since the connection between the OLE client and the OLE Automation Server occurs at run time (not when the OLE client is link edited). OLE 2 also supports calling an object's methods using a table (early binding). The member functions of the **IDispatch** interface and their descriptions are summarized in Table 12-3.

TIP: An OLE Automation Server need not necessarily be an OLE object server as well, although it is possible to make the same application an OLE Automation Server and an OLE object server.

OLE PROGRAMMING ASPECTS

As mentioned earlier, OLE is based on COM, and this means that an OLE-compatible application should follow the COM rules for functions and interfaces. There are many interfaces that are available for OLE applications, and many OLE applications use only a small subset of the interfaces. The one interface all OLE applications should implement is the **IUnknown** interface, which is like an entry point for all other interfaces. In fact, it includes the **QueryInterface** function that provides the list of the other interfaces available.

OLE and MFC

The MFC library provides classes to support OLE. These classes can be classified by the type of OLE component (such as Base, Client, Server, and so on) the class supports. Table 12-4 summarizes the common OLE MFC library classes and their types.

Class Name	Class Type	Description
COleDocument	Base	This is the base class for OLE documents. This class is derived from CDocument.
COleLinkingDoc	Base	This is the base class for OLE documents that support linking to the embedded items.
CDocItem	Base	This is the base class for OLE document items. Multiple CDocItems are treated as representations of OLE items by COleDocument.
COleClientItem	Client	This class defines the container interface to OLE items.
COleObjectFactory	Server	This class implements the OLE object factory. This class creates OLE objects such as server documents and OLE automation objects.
COleServerDoc	Server	This is the base class for OLE server documents. An OLE server document contains COleServerItem objects.
COleServerItem	Server	This class provides the server interface to OLE items.
COleTemplate Server	Server	This class is typically used to implement an OLE full server. Your application needs one COleTemplateServer object for each type of server document (spreadsheet, database, and so on) it supports.

Table 12-4.   MFC OLE Classes and Types

Class Name	Class Type	Description
COleIPFrameWnd	In-place Frame Window	This class handles control bars within the container application's window to support in-place editing.
COleException	Exception	This class has a data member that has a status code from operations. Typically AfxThrowOleException is called to create a COleException object and throw an exception.
COleDataSource	Data	This class is used as a data source by an application to provide data for Clipboard and drag-and-drop operations. COleClientItem and COleServerItem classes also create OLE data sources implicitly.
COleDataObject	Data	This class is used to retrieve data filled by other applications using data sources (for example retrieving data from a clipboard).
COleStreamFile	Data	This class is derived from CFile. An object of this class represents a stream of compound file data. This class enables MFC serialization to use OLE structured storage.

Table 12-4.   MFC OLE Classes and Types (*continued*)

There are also portions of OLE that are not partially or fully supported by the MFC library. For example, the MFC library implements only creation support for compound files and does not provide mechanisms for the programmer to invoke interfaces such as IMoniker using the MFC library.

TIP: It is important to distinguish between MFC library classes and OLE interfaces. COM defines a base class, the **IUnknown**, from which all COM-compatible classes are derived. In OLE, all classes derived from **IUnknown** are interfaces, which are just protocol definitions without any implementation. While sometimes the **IUnknown** interface is referred to as a C++ class, it is important to note that COM is not language specific. The "I" in **IUnknown** or **IDispatch** stands for "Interface."

ACTIVEX BASICS

ActiveX controls are an outgrowth of OLE custom controls. An ActiveX control is a COM object, the same as an OLE control. The primary difference, though, is that an ActiveX control is required to implement only the **IUnknown** interface, whereas an OLE control is required to implement a lot more interfaces. Although ActiveX controls typically implement more than just the **IUnknown** interface, removing mandatory support makes it possible to create ActiveX controls that are relatively small.

While it is common for an ActiveX control to have its own window, it is possible to have windowless ActiveX controls. You can make your ActiveX control use windowless activation, by including the windowless Activate flag in **COleControl::GetControlFlags**. A windowless control uses the window services of its container. An ActiveX control is in either an active state or an inactive state. Controls in the active state typically have a window, and controls in the inactive state do not have a window. Even if a control has a window, you can cause a control to remain inactive until it needs to be activated (for example, when the user tabs to the control)—omit the control's OLEMISC_ACTIVATEWHENVISIBLE flag (this is automatic if you use the ControlWizard to create the ActiveX control with the Activate When Visible option turned off). An inactive control can be the target of an OLE drag-and-drop operation. You can subclass a common control to create an ActiveX control. Common controls are covered in Chapter 7.

In-Process and Out-of-Process Servers

In-process servers are servers where the server code executes in the same process address space as that of the client that invoked the server. By contrast, servers are *out-of-process* when the server code executes in a process address space other than the client. This process address space could be on the same computer or on another computer. Sometimes the out-of-process server is also called a local server or a remote server, depending on whether the server executes on the same computer where the client code executes (in a different process space) or on a remote computer. In-process servers are typically implemented as DLLs, while local servers are commonly implemented as EXEs. Remote servers can either be EXEs or DLLs.

ActiveX controls are usually in-process servers. This is primarily because you can create one entity that handles user interface and additional server logic in-process, which makes it easy for distribution and licensing. In addition, an in-process server loads faster than an out-of-process server implemented as an EXE. The major downside to an in-process server is that it is a DLL and has the problems of DLLs, such as message handling. DLLs are covered in Chapter 9. Also, the code that contains the in-process server as an embedded DLL is usually longer than code that uses out-of-process servers.

Location Transparency

One of the benefits of the COM is that whether the servers are in-process or out-of-process, the interface to the COM object remains the same. If you are writing client code, then your calls interface with the actual COM object if in-process or to a *proxy object* if out-of-process. If you are writing server code, then the interface is likewise to the actual object if in-process or to a *stub object*. COM provides RPC mechanisms for the stub object and proxy object to communicate. This communication is transparent to your application. Thus, the location of the object is transparent to your application. For performance reasons, it is possible to override the default behavior by use of custom marshaling (custom marshaling refers to the overriding of the internal Imarshal interface used by COM when an object does not provide an Imarshal interface).

ActiveX Controls As Connectable Objects

Most ActiveX controls are connectable objects. A *connectable object* is one that supports outgoing interfaces (an *outgoing interface* is the opposite of the traditional incoming interface, where a client invokes an OLE server through one of its incoming interfaces). For the OLE server object to have an outgoing interface to the client, the client uses a *sink object* (the sink object's members are called by the OLE server), and it is the pointer to the sink that is used for the outgoing interface. The connectable object-related interfaces and their methods are summarized in Table 12-5.

The common methods used by the connection point interfaces listed in Table 12-5 are summarized in Table 12-6.

ActiveX Control Properties and Methods

An ActiveX control communicates with its container using events. An ActiveX control container interacts with the control using properties and methods. The methods can be stock methods or custom methods. Stock methods are similar to OLE automation methods. The properties associated with ActiveX controls are summarized in Table 12-7.

Connectable Object Interface	Description
IConnectionPoint	Supports connection points for connectable objects
IConnectionPointContainer	Indicates the existence of the outgoing interfaces
IEnumConnectionPoints	Enumerates connection points
IEnumConnections	Enumerates all the supported connections for each outgoing interface

Table 12-5. Connectable Object Interfaces

Connection Point Interface Methods	Description
GetConnectionInterface	Retrieves the IID (globally unique identifier) of the connection point interface
GetConnectionPointContainer	Retrieves an interface pointer to the connectable object
Advise	Establishes a connection between the connection point and the caller's sink
unAdvise	Terminates a connection previously established by Advise
EnumConnections	Creates an enumerator object to loop through the current connections for a connection point
FindConnectionPoint	Retrieves an interface pointer to the connection point supporting the specified IID

Table 12-6. Common Connection Point Interface Methods

PROGRAMMING ACTIVEX CLIENTS

You can use the **IDispatch** interface discussed earlier in this chapter to create ActiveX clients as illustrated by the following steps:

1. Initialize OLE. You can do this using the **OleInitialize** API function.

2. Create an instance of the object you want to access using **CoCreateInstance**. The object's ActiveX component creates the object. **CoCreateInstance** creates an instance of the class represented by the specified CLSID and returns a pointer to the object's **IUnknown** interface. **CoCreateInstance** is a component object API function.

3. You can check if the object has implemented the **IDispatch** interface and get a pointer to the interface using the **IUnknown** interface's **QueryInterface**, which checks whether **IDispatch** has been implemented for the object. If so, it returns a pointer to the **IDispatch** implementation.

4. You can access and use the methods and properties of the object being accessed in one of three ways—early binding, late binding, or ID binding. (See "Binding" earlier in this chapter.)

5. Terminate the object by invoking the appropriate method in its **IDispatch** interface, or by releasing all references to the object. You can use **IUnknown's Release** method to decrement the reference count for the **IUnknown** or **IDispatch** object.

6. Uninitialize OLE using the OLE API function **OleUninitialize**.

As mentioned earlier, an ActiveX control is required to support only the **IUnknown** interface. Removing mandatory support makes it possible to create ActiveX controls that are relatively small. This opens up a particularly interesting possibility, where you can download an ActiveX control to enhance the functionality of a web page. The relatively small size of an ActiveX control is an important factor here.

This functionality of ActiveX controls resembles that of Java applets for Java-enabled web browsers. As is to be expected, there is a lot of competition in this area.

CONCLUSION

In this chapter, we reviewed the basics of OLE and ActiveX and the programming aspects of OLE and ActiveX controls. We looked at how OLE 2 attempts to address the problems of OLE 1. In the next two chapters, we will cover programming examples involving OLE and ActiveX.

Properties	Description
Stock	These are properties that have already been implemented and are ready to use, such as the control's foreground and background colors, caption, and so on.
Ambient	These are properties of the container that a control can use to make the control's appearance the same as that of the container. For example, a control can display text using the same font as that of the container.
Custom	These are properties you develop that are unique for each application.
Extended	These are properties implemented by the container on behalf of the control at run time, such as the control's position.
Advanced	These are properties with advanced functions related to properties, such as making properties read-only or write-only.

Table 12-7. ActiveX Control Properties

CHAPTER 13

Using OLE

Let's build on the introduction to OLE in the previous chapter and look at some programming examples. We will look at OLE Automation Servers and illustrate developing an OLE Automation Server using a programming example. In the example, we will also discuss how to make an OLE Automation Server a stand-alone application. Next we will look at OLE Automation clients and illustrate developing an OLE Automation client using a programming example. This example will access the OLE Automation Server mentioned in Chapter 12. Finally we will take a closer look at a significant OLE user interface enhancement—OLE drag-and-drop—including a programming example that illustrates OLE drag-and-drop.

OLE AUTOMATION

OLE Automation is a mechanism for one application to implement a functionality and to let other applications use that functionality. For example, let's say that you want to write an application that includes these steps: access some data from a database, create a spreadsheet using the data, create a graph with the output of the spreadsheet, and include the graph in a report and print it. You can, of course, do all these steps manually using the set of office products from Microsoft such as Microsoft Access, Microsoft Excel, and so on, or use other vendors' equivalent products.

If you want to perform these steps to be implemented within an application, then you can do it in two ways. You can write the application from scratch and write all the code for extracting the data, performing the spreadsheet manipulation, and so on. But wouldn't it be a lot simpler if you could access the necessary functionality of the other applications, and all you had to do was to invoke these functionalities? That is the idea behind OLE Automation. Automation is not restricted to shrink-wrapped applications such as Microsoft Word or Excel. When you develop your business applications, you can make them OLE Automation Servers and make some functionality available for other applications to invoke. Thus, an organization can significantly enhance code reuse and cut down new development by using OLE Automation. The application that provides the functionality for other applications to invoke is called the *OLE Automation Server*, and the application that invokes the functionality is typically the *OLE Automation client*.

OLE Automation Server

The client and the server can be on the same machine or on different machines connected by a network. When the client and the server are on the same machine, the server could be *in-process*, if the server is implemented as a DLL that runs in the client's address space, or *out-of-process*, if the server executes in an address space different from that of the client. Should you set up your OLE Automation in-process or out-of-process?

If your OLE Automation client is using products such as Word or Excel, then you do not have a choice and the server is out-of-process. If you are developing an OLE automation server, keep the following in mind in choosing between in-process and out-of-process servers. It is faster to pass parameters between an OLE Automation client and an in-process server compared with an out-of-process server. However, each client of an in-process server has a copy of the server in its address space, whereas only one copy is kept in memory for an out-of-process server.

OLE Automation Server and Client Communication

Communication between OLE Automation Server and client is implemented according to whether the server is an in-process server or an out-of-process server.

In an in-process server, since the OLE Automation Server and client share an address space, the in-process server can directly access reference parameters passed by the client, and the server's methods can use the client's stack.

In an out-of-process server, but within the same computer, the previously mentioned direct access facilitated by the client memory space is not feasible. In this case, OLE copies the data for passed parameters into the out-of-process OLE server's address space and makes a copy of the pointer to the original data. The OLE server method uses the copy pointer to modify the data in the server's address space. When the method ends, the modified data that needs to be copied back is copied back into the OLE client's address space. This method of parameter data transfer is called *marshaling.* The copying and passing of data is accomplished automatically and transparently by OLE using a *proxy* in the client process and a *stub* in the server process. The proxy and stub handle the marshaling and unmarshaling of parameters.

In an out-of-process server on a different computer than the client's computer, marshaling and unmarshaling is accomplished by use of an extended proxy/stub mechanism that uses remote procedure calls (RPCs) for communication between the proxy and the stub, and another OLE component called the Automation Manager is used. The proxy in the client process uses RPC to communicate with a stub in the Automation Manager, and a proxy within the Automation Manager communicates with the stub in the server.

GUIDs

Code reuse facilitated by automation is good, but there are some problems that must be solved. Within an organization, it may be possible to have unique names for classes and interfaces. But there is no simple way to achieve uniqueness across different vendor products. If two vendors come up with the same names for classes/interfaces, there should be a way to let both vendor implementations coexist. The way is to assign a *globally unique identifier* (*GUID*) to classes and interfaces. Microsoft includes utilities such as *UUIDGEN,* which generates a unique identifier that, practically, will not be duplicated. Although it is theoretically possible to produce duplicate IDs, inclusion of the time and the address of the machine (the address of the machine's network interface card) as part of the ID ensures nonduplication of IDs (including those produced on the same machine at different times or different machines at the same time).

PROGRAMMING EXAMPLE FOR AN OLE AUTOMATION SERVER

The sample program shown here is an OLE Automation Server program. It is a simple mortgage calculator that is created as a stand-alone application and to which OLE Automation is added later. Since the program is a stand-alone application, loan details, such as the loan amount, interest rate, and period of loan, can be given by selecting a menu item. The monthly payment can be computed and displayed by selecting another menu item. Later a set of properties and methods is added to the program to make it an OLE Automation Server. This server will then be used by an OLE Automation client that will be created as part of the next sample program.

The simplest way to create the OLE Automation Server and client is by using MFC AppWizard. The steps to create the Automation Server application using MFC AppWizard are detailed next:

1. A new MFC AppWizard (exe) project is created by selecting New from the File menu.

2. The project name is given as **MortCalc**.

3. In MFC AppWizard—Step 1, Single Document is selected.

4. The Next button is clicked in the dialog box, and defaults are accepted in the Step 2 dialog box.

5. In the Step 3 dialog box, the Automation check box is checked.

6. In the Step 4 dialog box, the Advanced button is selected to specify advanced options.

7. The default **MortCa** is changed to **MortCalc** in File New Name and File Type Name. The name given as the File Type Name (MortCalc Document) is used as the long name of the Automation object when used in the Automation client.

8. Default values are accepted in the next two steps, and the Finish button followed by the OK button are clicked to create all the necessary files and open the project.

The information related to the mortgage calculation is stored in the **CMortCalcDoc** class. Thus, the loan amount (*flLoan*), interest rate (*flRate*), loan period in months (*iNumofPayments*), and monthly payments (*flMonthlyPayment*) are declared as protected member variables in the *Mortcalcdoc.h* header file. Also declared are three member functions: **SetLoanData**, to set the loan amount, interest rate, and number of years to repay the loan; **Compute**, to calculate the monthly payment; and **GetLoanData**, to return all information about the loan, like the loan amount, rate, period, and monthly payment.

For this application to be a stand-alone application, there must be a way to input the loan details. This is done by use of a dialog box. So the next step is to create a dialog box to enter loan details. Figure 13-1 shows the initial dialog box displayed when the application is started.

The ResourceView tab in the workspace window is selected, and the dialog box is inserted by clicking the right mouse button on the dialog folder and selecting Insert Dialog. A dialog box is created with three static fields and three entry fields, one set each for loan amount, interest rate, and period. The entry field IDs are respectively IDC_AMOUNT, IDC_RATE, and IDC_PERIOD. The OK button is renamed to Set Data. Figure 13-2 shows this dialog box. Figure 13-3 shows the mortgage calculation results when a loan amount, rate, and period are entered.

Start the ClassWizard by double-clicking the dialog box while holding down the CTRL key. Since a class does not exist yet, select Create A New Class in the Adding A Class dialog box. OK is clicked to bring the New Class dialog box. The class name is specified as **CSetLoanDlg**, and the automation is left as none. OK is clicked to return to the MFC ClassWizard dialog box. Three member variables are added in the Member Variables page. The details of each member variable are as follows: IDC_AMOUNT, m_amount, value, float; IDC_RATE, m_rate, value, float; and IDC_YEARS, m_years, value, int. The

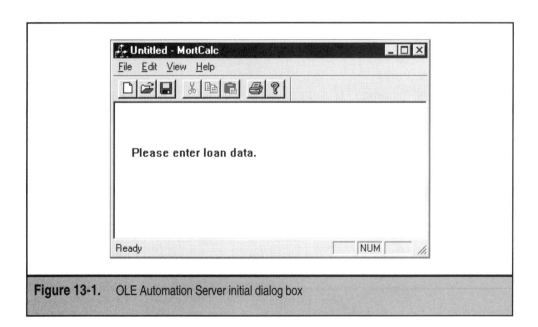

Figure 13-1.   OLE Automation Server initial dialog box

ClassWizard is closed by selecting OK, and this will generate the **CSetLoanDlg** class. Shown next are the header file and implementation file for the **CSetLoanDlg** class.

```cpp
#if !defined(AFX_SETLOANDLG_H)
#define AFX_SETLOANDLG_H

#if _MSC_VER >= 1000
#pragma once
#endif // _MSC_VER >= 1000
// SetLoanDlg.h : header file

// CSetLoanDlg dialog

class CSetLoanDlg : public CDialog
{
// Construction
public:
    CSetLoanDlg(CWnd* pParent = NULL); // standard constructor

// Dialog Data
    //{{AFX_DATA(CSetLoanDlg)
    enum { IDD = IDD_SETLOANDATA };
    float       m_amount;
    float       m_rate;
    int         m_years;
    //}}AFX_DATA


// Overrides
    // ClassWizard generated virtual function overrides
    //{{AFX_VIRTUAL(CSetLoanDlg)
    protected:
    virtual void DoDataExchange(CDataExchange* pDX);
 //}}AFX_VIRTUAL

// Implementation
protected:

    // Generated message map functions
    //{{AFX_MSG(CSetLoanDlg)
    // NOTE: the ClassWizard will add member functions here
    //}}AFX_MSG
    DECLARE_MESSAGE_MAP()
};
//{{AFX_INSERT_LOCATION}}
#endif
```

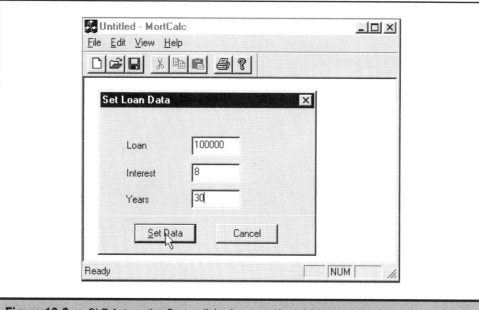

Figure 13-2. OLE Automation Server dialog box to set loan data

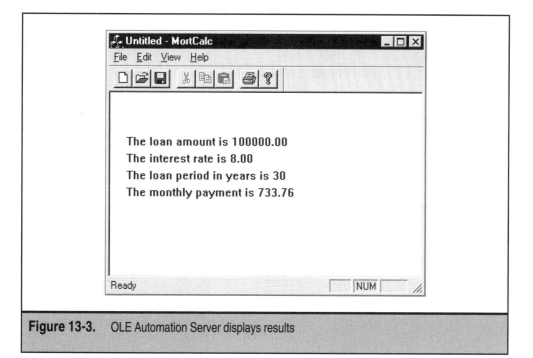

Figure 13-3. OLE Automation Server displays results

The implementation file for the dialog class is shown next. Since the data is exchanged automatically by calling the **DoDataExchange** function, there is no custom code in this class.

```cpp
// SetLoanDlg.cpp : implementation file

#include "stdafx.h"
#include "MortCalc.h"
#include "SetLoanDlg.h"

#ifdef _DEBUG
#define new DEBUG_NEW
#undef THIS_FILE
static char THIS_FILE[] = __FILE__;
#endif

// CSetLoanDlg dialog


CSetLoanDlg::CSetLoanDlg(CWnd* pParent /*=NULL*/)
    : CDialog(CSetLoanDlg::IDD, pParent)
{
    //{{AFX_DATA_INIT(CSetLoanDlg)
    m_amount = 0.0f;
    m_rate = 0.0f;
    m_years = 0;
    //}}AFX_DATA_INIT
}


void CSetLoanDlg::DoDataExchange(CDataExchange* pDX)
{
    CDialog::DoDataExchange(pDX);
    //{{AFX_DATA_MAP(CSetLoanDlg)
    DDX_Text(pDX, IDC_AMOUNT, m_amount);
    DDX_Text(pDX, IDC_RATE, m_rate);
    DDX_Text(pDX, IDC_YEARS, m_years);
    //}}AFX_DATA_MAP
}

BEGIN_MESSAGE_MAP(CSetLoanDlg, CDialog)
    //{{AFX_MSG_MAP(CSetLoanDlg)
    // NOTE: the ClassWizard will add message map macros here
    //}}AFX_MSG_MAP
END_MESSAGE_MAP()

// CSetLoanDlg message handlers
```

Next the interface to invoke the previously discussed dialog box is added. Two menu items are added to the Edit menu: one to set the loan data through the dialog box discussed earlier and the other to calculate the monthly mortgage payment. From ResourceView the Menu folder is selected, and the IDR_MAINFRAME menu is opened. Under the Edit menu two menu items are added with the following IDs and caption: IDM_SETLOAN/&Set Loan Data and IDM_PAYMENT/&Monthly Payment. The ClassWizard is brought up, and in the Message Maps tab the **CMortCalcView** class is selected. For the IDM_SETLOAN object ID the **COMMAND** message is double-clicked, and the default function name in the Add Member Function dialog box is accepted. The same is done for the IDM_PAYMENT object ID.

The next step is to add the OLE Automation feature for the application. To do this, the Automation tab is selected in the ClassWizard dialog box. The **CMortCalcDoc** document class is selected for the name, and the Add Property button is clicked. This brings up the Add Property dialog box. The **Get/Set** methods implementation is selected. For the loan amount property, the external name is given as Principal, the type is specified as float, and the default **Get** function name is accepted. Since there is no need for a **Set** function, it is omitted. No parameters are needed for this function, so none is selected. Three more properties are added for interest rate (Rate/float/GetRate), period of loan (Period/long/GetPeriod), and monthly payment (Payment/float/GetPayment). This OLE Automation Server exposes two methods: one to reset the data and the other to set the loan data. They are added by selecting the Add Methods button and specifying details in the Add Method dialog box. The external and internal name for the first method is **Reset**, and its return type is void. It takes no parameters. The external and internal name for the second method is **SetLoanInfo**, and its return type is void. It takes three parameters whose name/type are Principal/float, Rate/float, and Period/long. Click on OK in the ClassWizard, and the application is enabled to act as an OLE Automation Server. Of course, code has to be plugged into the respective empty member functions. The code is shown next.

The **CMortCalcDoc** class, which is the engine for this OLE Automation Server, is shown next. Shown first is the header file. Notice the highlighted code, which shows the member variables and member functions that were added and the OLE-related functions that were added by use of ClassWizard. Notice that there is no individual **Set** function, but instead one **SetLoanInfo** function that sets the loan information. Also, the **Compute** function is not an OLE Automation method, so the OLE Automation clients cannot call **Compute** directly.

```
// MortCalcDoc.h : interface of the CMortCalcDoc class
//

#if !defined(AFX_MORTCALCDOC_H)
#define AFX_MORTCALCDOC_H

#if _MSC_VER >= 1000
#pragma once
```

```cpp
#endif // _MSC_VER >= 1000


class CMortCalcDoc : public CDocument
{
protected: // create from serialization only
    CMortCalcDoc();
    DECLARE_DYNCREATE(CMortCalcDoc)

// Attributes
public:

// Operations
public:
    void    SetLoanData(float amount, float rate, int years);
    void    Compute();
    void    GetLoanData(float *P, float *R, int *Y, float *M);

// Overrides
    // ClassWizard generated virtual function overrides
    //{{AFX_VIRTUAL(CMortCalcDoc)
    public:
    virtual BOOL OnNewDocument();
    virtual void Serialize(CArchive& ar);
    //}}AFX_VIRTUAL

// Implementation
public:
    virtual ~CMortCalcDoc();
#ifdef _DEBUG
    virtual void AssertValid() const;
    virtual void Dump(CDumpContext& dc) const;
#endif

protected:
    float   flLoan;
    float   flRate;
    int     iNumofPayments;
    float   flMonthlyPayment;

// Generated message map functions
protected:
    DECLARE_MESSAGE_MAP()
    // Generated OLE dispatch map functions
```

```
    //{{AFX_DISPATCH(CMortCalcDoc)
    afx_msg float GetPrincipal();
    afx_msg float GetRate();
    afx_msg long GetPeriod();
    afx_msg float GetPayment();
    afx_msg void Reset();
    afx_msg void SetLoanInfo(float Principal,
                             float Rate, long Period);
    //}}AFX_DISPATCH
    DECLARE_DISPATCH_MAP()
    DECLARE_INTERFACE_MAP()
};


//{{AFX_INSERT_LOCATION}}

#endif
```

The implementation file is shown next. Looking at the MFC class hierarchy, you can see that **CMortCalcDoc** class indirectly derives from **CCmdTarget**. To be exposed through Automation, the **CCmdTarget** derived class, **CMortCalcDoc** in this case, should call the **EnableAutomation** member function during construction of the class object, and should also include a dispatch map. Since the Automation was exposed by use of AppWizard, the ClassWizard automatically adds the code. The class should also call **AfxOleLockApp** and **AfxOleUnlockApp** to increment and decrement the global count of active objects maintained by the framework. This prevents the user from closing the application that still has active objects. If there are still active objects, the framework hides the application instead of completely shutting it down. Thus, during construction **AfxOleLockApp** is called, and during destruction **AfxOleUnlockApp** is called. The DISP_PROPERTY_EX macro defines the OLE Automation property by its external name, the accessing functions (in this sample the **Set** function is not supported), and the properties type. The DISP_FUNCTION macro defines the OLE Automation methods by its external name, member function name, return type, and parameters type (in this case, since there are multiple parameters, they are separated by space).

```
// MortCalcDoc.cpp:implementation of the CMortCalcDoc class
#include "stdafx.h"
#include "MortCalc.h"

#include "MortCalcDoc.h"

#ifdef _DEBUG
#define new DEBUG_NEW
#undef THIS_FILE
```

```
static char THIS_FILE[] = __FILE__;
#endif

// CMortCalcDoc

IMPLEMENT_DYNCREATE(CMortCalcDoc, CDocument)

BEGIN_MESSAGE_MAP(CMortCalcDoc, CDocument)
END_MESSAGE_MAP()

BEGIN_DISPATCH_MAP(CMortCalcDoc, CDocument)
    //{{AFX_DISPATCH_MAP(CMortCalcDoc)
    DISP_PROPERTY_EX(CMortCalcDoc, "Principal",
                     GetPrincipal, SetNotSupported, VT_R4)
    DISP_PROPERTY_EX(CMortCalcDoc, "Rate", GetRate,
                     SetNotSupported, VT_R4)
    DISP_PROPERTY_EX(CMortCalcDoc, "Period", GetPeriod,
                     SetNotSupported, VT_I4)
    DISP_PROPERTY_EX(CMortCalcDoc, "Payment", GetPayment,
                     SetNotSupported, VT_R4)
    DISP_FUNCTION(CMortCalcDoc, "Reset", Reset,
                  VT_EMPTY, VTS_NONE)
    DISP_FUNCTION(CMortCalcDoc, "SetLoanInfo", SetLoanInfo,
                  VT_EMPTY, VTS_R4 VTS_R4 VTS_I4)
    //}}AFX_DISPATCH_MAP
END_DISPATCH_MAP()
```

All OLE Automation Servers and ActiveX control servers require a unique class ID, which is defined here.

```
// Note: we add support for IID_IMortCalc to support
// typesafe binding from VBA.  This IID must match the GUID
// that is attached to the dispinterface in the .ODL file.

// {0109A0D5-1969-11D1-97B2-000000000000}
static const IID IID_IMortCalc =
{ 0x109a0d5, 0x1969, 0x11d1,
 { 0x97, 0xb2, 0x0, 0x0, 0x0, 0x0, 0x0, 0x0 } };

BEGIN_INTERFACE_MAP(CMortCalcDoc, CDocument)
    INTERFACE_PART(CMortCalcDoc, IID_IMortCalc, Dispatch)
END_INTERFACE_MAP()
```

```
// CMortCalcDoc construction/destruction

CMortCalcDoc::CMortCalcDoc()
{
    // TODO: add one-time construction code here

    EnableAutomation();
    AfxOleLockApp();

    flLoan = 0.0;
    flRate = 0.0;
    iNumofPayments = 0;
    flMonthlyPayment = 0.0;
}

CMortCalcDoc::~CMortCalcDoc()
{
    AfxOleUnlockApp();
}

BOOL CMortCalcDoc::OnNewDocument()
{
    if (!CDocument::OnNewDocument())
        return FALSE;

    // TODO: add reinitialization code here
    // (SDI documents will reuse this document)

    return TRUE;
}

// CMortCalcDoc serialization
void CMortCalcDoc::Serialize(CArchive& ar)
{
    if (ar.IsStoring())
    {
        // TODO: add storing code here
    }
    else
    {
        // TODO: add loading code here
    }
}
```

```
// CMortCalcDoc diagnostics
#ifdef _DEBUG
void CMortCalcDoc::AssertValid() const
{
    CDocument::AssertValid();
}

void CMortCalcDoc::Dump(CDumpContext& dc) const
{
    CDocument::Dump(dc);
}
#endif //_DEBUG
```

The next three functions are member functions of the **CMortCalcDoc** class. They set the loan data (notice that the year is converted to months, assuming monthly payment), compute the monthly payment, and return the loan data, including monthly payment.

```
// CMortCalcDoc commands
void CMortCalcDoc::SetLoanData(float amount,
                               float rate, int years)
{
    flLoan = amount;
    flRate = rate;
    iNumofPayments = years*12;
}

void CMortCalcDoc::Compute()
{
// P = principal, I = interest rate, l = years.
// J = I/(12*100)
// N = L*12 - number payments
// Monthly payment = P * (J/(1-(1+J)** -N))

    double J = flRate/(1200.0);
    double OnePlusJPowerMinusN = pow ((double)(1.0 + J),
                             (double)-iNumofPayments);
    flMonthlyPayment = flLoan *
                    (float)(J/(1.0-OnePlusJPowerMinusN));
}

void CMortCalcDoc::GetLoanData(float *P, float *R,
                               int *Y, float *M)
{
```

```
    *P = flLoan;
    *R = flRate;
    *Y = iNumofPayments/12;
    *M = flMonthlyPayment;
}
```

The next six functions implement the OLE Automation properties and methods exposed by this MortCalc application. Since a method to compute the monthly payment is not exposed, the **SetLoanInfo** method during its processing sets the loan data and calls the **Compute** function.

```
float CMortCalcDoc::GetPrincipal()
{
    // TODO: Add your property handler here
    return flLoan;
}

float CMortCalcDoc::GetRate()
{
    // TODO: Add your property handler here
    return flRate;
}

long CMortCalcDoc::GetPeriod()
{
    // TODO: Add your property handler here
    return iNumofPayments/12;
}

float CMortCalcDoc::GetPayment()
{
    // TODO: Add your property handler here
    return flMonthlyPayment;
}

void CMortCalcDoc::Reset()
{
    // TODO: Add your dispatch handler code here
    flLoan = 0.0;
    flRate = 0.0;
    iNumofPayments = 0;
    flMonthlyPayment = 0.0;
}
```

```
void CMortCalcDoc::SetLoanInfo(float Principal,
                                float Rate, long Period)
{
    // TODO: Add your dispatch handler code here
    flLoan = Principal;
    flRate = Rate;
    iNumofPayments = Period*12;
    Compute();
}
```

As mentioned earlier this OLE Automation Server application can also be a stand-alone application. The code in the **CMortCalcView** class provides an interface to the user to enter loan data, calculate the monthly payment, and display the results on the screen. The header file is shown, followed by the implementation file. The relevant code is highlighted.

```
// MortCalcView.h : interface of the CMortCalcView class

#if !defined(AFX_MORTCALCVIEW_H)
#define AFX_MORTCALCVIEW_H

#if _MSC_VER >= 1000
#pragma once
#endif // _MSC_VER >= 1000

class CMortCalcView : public CView
{
protected: // create from serialization only
    CMortCalcView();
    DECLARE_DYNCREATE(CMortCalcView)
// Attributes
public:
    CMortCalcDoc* GetDocument();
// Operations
public:
// Overrides
    // ClassWizard generated virtual function overrides
    //{{AFX_VIRTUAL(CMortCalcView)
    public:
    virtual void OnDraw(CDC* pDC);  // overridden to draw this view
    virtual BOOL PreCreateWindow(CREATESTRUCT& cs);
    protected:
    virtual BOOL OnPreparePrinting(CPrintInfo* pInfo);
    virtual void OnBeginPrinting(CDC* pDC, CPrintInfo* pInfo);
```

```
        virtual void OnEndPrinting(CDC* pDC, CPrintInfo* pInfo);
        //}}AFX_VIRTUAL

// Implementation
public:
        virtual ~CMortCalcView();
#ifdef _DEBUG
        virtual void AssertValid() const;
        virtual void Dump(CDumpContext& dc) const;
#endif

protected:

// Generated message map functions
protected:
        //{{AFX_MSG(CMortCalcView)
        afx_msg void OnPayment();
        afx_msg void OnSetloan();
        //}}AFX_MSG
        DECLARE_MESSAGE_MAP()
};

#ifndef _DEBUG  // debug version in MortCalcView.cpp
inline CMortCalcDoc* CMortCalcView::GetDocument()
        { return (CMortCalcDoc*)m_pDocument; }
#endif
//{{AFX_INSERT_LOCATION}}
#endif


// MortCalcView.cpp : implementation of the CMortCalcView class
//
#include "stdafx.h"
#include "MortCalc.h"

#include "MortCalcDoc.h"
#include "MortCalcView.h"
#include "SetLoanDlg.h"

#ifdef _DEBUG
#define new DEBUG_NEW
#undef THIS_FILE
static char THIS_FILE[] = __FILE__;
#endif
```

```
// CMortCalcView

IMPLEMENT_DYNCREATE(CMortCalcView, CView)

BEGIN_MESSAGE_MAP(CMortCalcView, CView)
    //{{AFX_MSG_MAP(CMortCalcView)
    ON_COMMAND(IDM_PAYMENT, OnPayment)
    ON_COMMAND(IDM_SETLOAN, OnSetloan)
    //}}AFX_MSG_MAP
    // Standard printing commands
    ON_COMMANDID_FILE_PRINT,CView::OnFilePrint)
    ON_COMMANDID_FILE_PRINT_DIRECT,CView::OnFilePrint)
    ON_COMMANDID_FILE_PRINT_PREVIEW,CView::OnFilePrintPreview)
END_MESSAGE_MAP()

// CMortCalcView construction/destruction

CMortCalcView::CMortCalcView()
{
    // TODO: add construction code here
}


CMortCalcView::~CMortCalcView()
{
}


BOOL CMortCalcView::PreCreateWindow(CREATESTRUCT& cs)
{
  // TODO: Modify the Window class or styles here by modifying
  //   the CREATESTRUCT cs
    return CView::PreCreateWindow(cs);
}

// CMortCalcView drawing

void CMortCalcView::OnDraw(CDC* pDC)
{
    CMortCalcDoc* pDoc = GetDocument();
    ASSERT_VALID(pDoc);

    // TODO: add draw code for native data here
    float P, R, M;
    int Y;
```

```
    char    szBuffer[256];
    pDoc->GetLoanData(&P, &R, &Y, &M);
    if (M == 0.0)
    {
        strcpy (szBuffer, "Please enter loan data.");
        pDC->TextOut(20, 50, szBuffer);
    }
    else
    {
        sprintf (szBuffer, "The loan amount is %.2f", P);
        pDC->TextOut(20, 50, szBuffer);
        sprintf (szBuffer, "The interest rate is %.2f", R);
        pDC->TextOut(20, 70, szBuffer);
        sprintf (szBuffer, "The loan period in years is %d",
                Y);
        pDC->TextOut(20, 90, szBuffer);
        sprintf (szBuffer, "The monthly payment is %.2f", M);
        pDC->TextOut(20, 110, szBuffer);
    }
}


// CMortCalcView printing

BOOL CMortCalcView::OnPreparePrinting(CPrintInfo* pInfo)
{
    // default preparation
    return DoPreparePrinting(pInfo);
}

void CMortCalcView::OnBeginPrinting
                    (CDC* /*pDC*/, CPrintInfo* /*pInfo*/)
{
    // TODO: add extra initialization before printing
}

void CMortCalcView::OnEndPrinting
                    (CDC* /*pDC*/, CPrintInfo* /*pInfo*/)
{
    // TODO: add cleanup after printing
}

// CMortCalcView diagnostics

#ifdef _DEBUG
```

```
void CMortCalcView::AssertValid() const
{
    CView::AssertValid();
}

void CMortCalcView::Dump(CDumpContext& dc) const
{
    CView::Dump(dc);
}

CMortCalcDoc* CMortCalcView::GetDocument()
{
  ASSERT(m_pDocument->IsKindOf(RUNTIME_CLASS(CMortCalcDoc)));
  return (CMortCalcDoc*)m_pDocument;
}
#endif //_DEBUG

// CMortCalcView message handlers
void CMortCalcView::OnPayment()
{
    // TODO: Add your command handler code here
    CMortCalcDoc     *pDoc = GetDocument();
    ASSERT_VALID(pDoc);
    pDoc->Compute();
    Invalidate();
}

void CMortCalcView::OnSetloan()
{
    // TODO: Add your command handler code here
    CSetLoanDlg dbSetLoanDlg;

    if (dbSetLoanDlg.DoModal() == IDOK)
    {
        CMortCalcDoc     *pDoc = GetDocument();
        ASSERT_VALID(pDoc);
        pDoc->SetLoanData(dbSetLoanDlg.m_amount,
                          dbSetLoanDlg.m_rate,
                          dbSetLoanDlg.m_years);
    }
}
```

The main application class, **CMortCalcApp**, is shown next. The code related to the About dialog box is omitted. This code is automatically generated by the AppWizard, and it is worth looking at the OLE-related code.

```
// MortCalc.h : main header file for the MORTCALC application
//

#if !defined(AFX_MORTCALC_H)
#define AFX_MORTCALC_H

#if _MSC_VER >= 1000
#pragma once
#endif // _MSC_VER >= 1000

#ifndef __AFXWIN_H__
  #error include 'stdafx.h' before including this file for PCH
#endif

#include "resource.h"
// CMortCalcApp:
// See MortCalc.cpp for the implementation of this class

class CMortCalcApp : public CWinApp
{
public:
    CMortCalcApp();

// Overrides
    // ClassWizard generated virtual function overrides
    //{{AFX_VIRTUAL(CMortCalcApp)
    public:
    virtual BOOL InitInstance();
    //}}AFX_VIRTUAL

// Implementation
    COleTemplateServer m_server;
        // Server object for document creation
    //{{AFX_MSG(CMortCalcApp)
    afx_msg void OnAppAbout();
    DECLARE_MESSAGE_MAP()
};
```

```
#endif

// MortCalc.cpp

#include "stdafx.h"
#include "MortCalc.h"

#include "MainFrm.h"
#include "MortCalcDoc.h"
#include "MortCalcView.h"

#ifdef _DEBUG
#define new DEBUG_NEW
#undef THIS_FILE
static char THIS_FILE[] = __FILE__;
#endif

// CMortCalcApp

BEGIN_MESSAGE_MAP(CMortCalcApp, CWinApp)
    //{{AFX_MSG_MAP(CMortCalcApp)
    ON_COMMAND(ID_APP_ABOUT, OnAppAbout)
    // Standard file based document commands
    ON_COMMAND(ID_FILE_NEW, CWinApp::OnFileNew)
    ON_COMMAND(ID_FILE_OPEN, CWinApp::OnFileOpen)
    // Standard print setup command
    ON_COMMAND(ID_FILE_PRINT_SETUP, CWinApp::OnFilePrintSetup)
END_MESSAGE_MAP()

// CMortCalcApp construction
CMortCalcApp::CMortCalcApp()
{
    // TODO: add construction code here
    // Place all significant initialization in InitInstance
}

// The one and only CMortCalcApp object

CMortCalcApp theApp;

// {0109A0D3-1969-11D1-97B2-000000000000}
static const CLSID clsid =
{ 0x109a0d3, 0x1969, 0x11d1,
  { 0x97, 0xb2, 0x0, 0x0, 0x0, 0x0, 0x0, 0x0 } };
```

During initialization of the application, OLE DLLs are initialized by calling the **AfxOleInit** function. The call to **ConnectTemplate** registers this application's class ID in the Registry. The class ID shown earlier that is generated by the AppWizard is random and is statistically guaranteed to be unique. A regeneration of this application will produce a different class ID altogether.

```
// CMortCalcApp initialization
BOOL CMortCalcApp::InitInstance()
{
    // Initialize OLE libraries
    if (!AfxOleInit())
    {
        AfxMessageBox(IDP_OLE_INIT_FAILED);
        return FALSE;
    }

#ifdef _AFXDLL
    Enable3dControls();
#else
    Enable3dControlsStatic();
#endif

    // Change the registry key under which our settings
    // are stored. You should modify this string to be
    // something appropriate such as the name of your
    // company or organization.
    SetRegistryKey(_T("Local AppWizard-Generated Applications"));
    LoadStdProfileSettings();

    // Register the application's document templates.
    // Document templates serve as the connection
    // between documents, frame windows and views.

    CSingleDocTemplate* pDocTemplate;
    pDocTemplate = new CSingleDocTemplate(
        IDR_MAINFRAME,
        RUNTIME_CLASS(CMortCalcDoc),
        RUNTIME_CLASS(CMainFrame),
        RUNTIME_CLASS(CMortCalcView));
    AddDocTemplate(pDocTemplate);

    // Connect the COleTemplateServer to the document template.
    //  The COleTemplateServer creates new documents on behalf
    //  of requesting OLE containers by using information
```

```
    //  specified in the document template.
    m_server.ConnectTemplate(clsid, pDocTemplate, TRUE);
    // Note: SDI applications register server objects
    // only if /Embedding or /Automation is present
    // on the command line.

    // Parse command line for standard shell commands,
    // DDE, file open
    CCommandLineInfo cmdInfo;
    ParseCommandLine(cmdInfo);

    // Check to see if launched as OLE server
    if (cmdInfo.m_bRunEmbedded || cmdInfo.m_bRunAutomated)
    {
        // Register all OLE server (factories) as running.
        // This enables the OLE libraries to create objects
        // from other applications.
        COleTemplateServer::RegisterAll();

        // Application was run with /Embedding
        // or /Automation.  Don't show the
        //  main window in this case.
        return TRUE;
    }

    // When a server application is launched stand-alone,
    // it is a good idea to update the system registry
    // in case it has been damaged.
    m_server.UpdateRegistry(OAT_DISPATCH_OBJECT);
    COleObjectFactory::UpdateRegistryAll();

    // Dispatch commands specified on the command line
    if (!ProcessShellCommand(cmdInfo))
        return FALSE;

    // The one and only window has been initialized,
    // so show and update it.
    m_pMainWnd->ShowWindow(SW_SHOW);
    m_pMainWnd->UpdateWindow();

    return TRUE;
}
```

After building this OLE server application, you need to register it with Windows. AppWizard creates a registry text file that can be imported into the Registry. To import the registry file, start REGEDIT and select Import Registry File from the File menu. In the file selection dialog box, navigate through the directory structure and select the *MortCalc.reg* file. REGEDIT imports the registry file and displays an informational message. For convenience the executable is also copied to a directory that is in the PATH statement.

OLE AUTOMATION CLIENTS

Next let's look at OLE Automation clients. OLE Automation clients include the functionality provided by OLE Automation Servers. One OLE Automation client can include the functionality provided by many OLE Automation Servers as part of the same application.

There are two types of OLE Automation clients:

▼ Clients that obtain information about the methods and properties of the server at run time using the **IDispatch** interface.

▲ Clients that include information about the methods and properties of the server at compile time and use the **COleDispatchDriver** class and the ClassWizard. You can specify the type-library file describing the properties and functions of the server application's object. ClassWizard reads this file and creates the **COleDispatchDriver**-derived class, with member functions that your application can call to access the server application's objects.

PROGRAMMING EXAMPLE FOR AN OLE AUTOMATION CLIENT

The next sample discussed here is an Automation client application that drives the *MORTCALC* sample application developed earlier. When run, it displays a dialog box with entry fields to enter the loan details, such as the loan amount, interest rate, and period of loan, as shown in Figure 13-4.

When the Calculate button in the dialog box is clicked, it invokes the Automation Server method, which calculates the monthly payments. The application then retrieves the monthly payment property and displays in the dialog box as shown in Figure 13-5.

This dialog-based application is created by use of the AppWizard, and the steps to create the application are discussed here. A new MFC AppWizard (exe) project is created with the project name MortDriv. In the MFC AppWizard—Step 1 dialog box, the application type is set to Dialog Based Application Type. In MFC AppWizard—Step 2—the ActiveX check box is unchecked, and Mortgage Driver Program is specified as the program heading. The rest of the information is defaulted, and the Finish button is

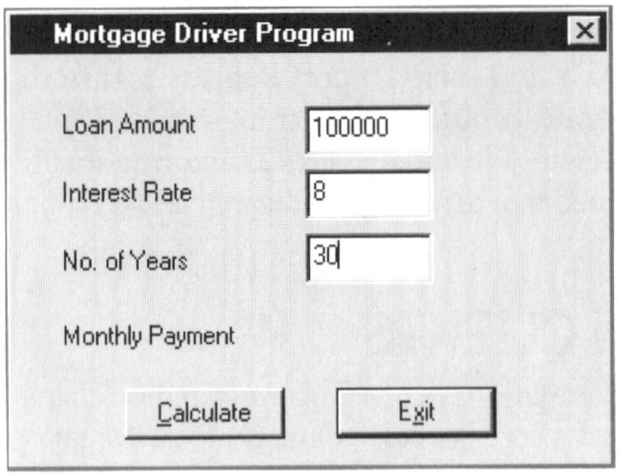

Figure 13-4. OLE Automation client initial dialog box

clicked. OK is clicked in the New Project Information dialog box. This creates all the necessary files for this project.

The main dialog box is created by selecting the ResourceView tab in the Workspace window, opening the Dialog folder, and double-clicking on IDD_MORTDRIV_DIALOG. This brings up the dialog editor. Three sets of static text and entry fields are created—one each for Loan Amount, Interest Rate, and No. of Years. The entry field IDs are respectively IDC_PRINCIPAL, IDC_RATE, and IDC_PERIOD. After the monthly mortgage payment is calculated, the result is shown as static text in the dialog box. To do this, two more static

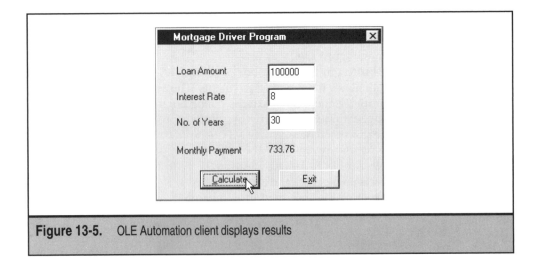

Figure 13-5. OLE Automation client displays results

fields—one for prompt text (Monthly Payment) and the other for actual monthly payment—are created. The ID for the static text that displays actual monthly payment is specified as IDC_PAYMENT. A control ID is specified since this static text needs to be altered every time the monthly payment is calculated.

The Automation server MortCalc is accessed by the client through a proxy class that encapsulates the server. The ClassWizard provides an easy means for generating this proxy class from the Automation Server application's type library. To generate the proxy class, the ClassWizard is brought up and the Add Class button is clicked. From the pull-down menu the From A Type Library option is selected. The Import From Type Library dialog box is displayed, and the Automation Server type library is selected by navigating through the directory structure and selecting the *MortCalc.tlb* file. In the Confirm Class dialog box the class name is changed from **IMortCalc** to **CMortCalc** just to match the rest of the class names. The rest of the module names are accepted as suggested by the panel. Selecting OK will generate the proxy class. An object of this proxy class is added as a protected member variable of the application dialog class, as will be seen later.

The rest of the client application functionality is completed by adding member variables for each of the modifiable fields in the dialog box, namely, IDC_PRINCIPAL, IDC_RATE, IDC_PERIOD, and IDC_PAYMENT. The member variable name, category, and variable type for these are respectively m_principal/value/float, m_rate/value/float, m_period/value/int, and m_payment/value/CString.

In the Message Maps tab the processing of the **BN_CLICKED** message for the IDC_CALCULATE button is set to the function **OnCalculate**. Selecting OK in the ClassWizard dialog box would create the boilerplate code for the dialog box. The dialog class header file and the implementation file are shown next. This is a standard dialog class. The noticeable difference is the addition of a **CMortCalc** object, m_mortcalc. **CMortCalc**, it may be recalled, is the wrapper class for the Automation Server. An object of the Automation Server wrapper class, m_mortcalc is added as a protected member variable. The methods and properties of the Automation Server are accessed by use of this Automation Server object.

```
// MortDrivDlg.h : header file
//
#if !defined(AFX_MORTDRIVDLG_H)
#define AFX_MORTDRIVDLG_H

#if _MSC_VER >= 1000
#pragma once
#endif // _MSC_VER >= 1000

// CMortDrivDlg dialog
class CMortDrivDlg : public CDialog
{
```

```
// Construction
public:
    CMortDrivDlg(CWnd* pParent = NULL);

// Dialog Data
    //{{AFX_DATA(CMortDrivDlg)
    enum { IDD = IDD_MORTDRIV_DIALOG };
    CString     m_payment;
    int         m_period;
    float       m_principal;
    float       m_rate;
    //}}AFX_DATA

    // ClassWizard generated virtual function overrides
    //{{AFX_VIRTUAL(CMortDrivDlg)
    protected:
    virtual void DoDataExchange(CDataExchange* pDX);
    //}}AFX_VIRTUAL

// Implementation
protected:
    HICON m_hIcon;
    CMortCalc   m_mortcalc;

    // Generated message map functions
    //{{AFX_MSG(CMortDrivDlg)
    virtual BOOL OnInitDialog();
    afx_msg void OnSysCommand(UINT nID, LPARAM lParam);
    afx_msg void OnPaint();
    afx_msg HCURSOR OnQueryDragIcon();
    afx_msg void OnCalculate();
    afx_msg int OnCreate(LPCREATESTRUCT lpCreateStruct);
    //}}AFX_MSG
    DECLARE_MESSAGE_MAP()
};
#endif
```

The implementation file is shown next. The code relating to the About dialog box processing is not shown. In the **OnCreate** function the **IDispatch** object is created by calling the **CreateDispatch** member function. This creates the **IDispatch** object and attaches it to the **COleDispatchDriver** object. A pointer to the programmatic identifier to the Automation object, **MortCalc.Document** in this case, is passed. The only other function of interest is the button command processing for the Calculate button.

```
// MortDrivDlg.cpp : implementation file
//

#include "stdafx.h"
#include "MortDriv.h"
#include "MortCalc.h"
#include "MortDrivDlg.h"

#ifdef _DEBUG
#define new DEBUG_NEW
#undef THIS_FILE
static char THIS_FILE[] = __FILE__;
#endif

// CMortDrivDlg dialog

CMortDrivDlg::CMortDrivDlg(CWnd* pParent /*=NULL*/)
    : CDialog(CMortDrivDlg::IDD, pParent)
{
    //{{AFX_DATA_INIT(CMortDrivDlg)
    m_payment = _T("");
    m_period = 0;
    m_principal = 0.0f;
    m_rate = 0.0f;
    //}}AFX_DATA_INIT
    m_hIcon = AfxGetApp()->LoadIcon(IDR_MAINFRAME);
}

void CMortDrivDlg::DoDataExchange(CDataExchange* pDX)
{
    CDialog::DoDataExchange(pDX);
    //{{AFX_DATA_MAP(CMortDrivDlg)
    DDX_Text(pDX, IDC_PAYMENT, m_payment);
    DDX_Text(pDX, IDC_PERIOD, m_period);
    DDX_Text(pDX, IDC_PRINCIPAL, m_principal);
    DDX_Text(pDX, IDC_RATE, m_rate);
    //}}AFX_DATA_MAP
}

BEGIN_MESSAGE_MAP(CMortDrivDlg, CDialog)
    //{{AFX_MSG_MAP(CMortDrivDlg)
    ON_WM_SYSCOMMAND()
    ON_WM_PAINT()
```

```
        ON_WM_QUERYDRAGICON()
        ON_BN_CLICKED(IDC_CALCULATE, OnCalculate)
        ON_WM_CREATE()
        //}}AFX_MSG_MAP
END_MESSAGE_MAP()


// CMortDrivDlg message handlers

int CMortDrivDlg::OnCreate(LPCREATESTRUCT lpCreateStruct)
{
    if (CDialog::OnCreate(lpCreateStruct) == -1)
        return -1;
    // TODO: Add your specialized creation code here
    if (!m_mortcalc.CreateDispatch(_T("MortCalc.Document")))
    {
        AfxMessageBox("MortCalc Missing");
        return -1;
    }
    return 0;
}



BOOL CMortDrivDlg::OnInitDialog()
{
    CDialog::OnInitDialog();

    // Add "About..." menu item to system menu.

    // IDM_ABOUTBOX must be in the system command range.
    ASSERT((IDM_ABOUTBOX & 0xFFF0) == IDM_ABOUTBOX);
    ASSERT(IDM_ABOUTBOX < 0xF000);

    CMenu* pSysMenu = GetSystemMenu(FALSE);
    if (pSysMenu != NULL)
    {
        CString strAboutMenu;
        strAboutMenu.LoadString(IDS_ABOUTBOX);
        if (!strAboutMenu.IsEmpty())
        {
            pSysMenu->AppendMenu(MF_SEPARATOR);
            pSysMenu->AppendMenu(MF_STRING,
                                        IDM_ABOUTBOX,
                                        strAboutMenu);
        }
```

```
    }

    // Set the icon for this dialog.
    // The framework does this automatically
    //  when the application's main window is not a dialog
    SetIcon(m_hIcon, TRUE);              // Set big icon
    SetIcon(m_hIcon, FALSE);          // Set small icon

    // TODO: Add extra initialization here
    return TRUE;
}

void CMortDrivDlg::OnSysCommand(UINT nID, LPARAM lParam)
{
    if ((nID & 0xFFF0) == IDM_ABOUTBOX)
    {
        CAboutDlg dlgAbout;
        dlgAbout.DoModal();
    }
    else
    {
        CDialog::OnSysCommand(nID, lParam);
    }
}

void CMortDrivDlg::OnPaint()
{
    if (IsIconic())
    {
        CPaintDC dc(this); // device context for painting

        SendMessage(WM_ICONERASEBKGND,
                    (WPARAM) dc.GetSafeHdc(), 0);

        // Center icon in client rectangle
        int cxIcon = GetSystemMetrics(SM_CXICON);
        int cyIcon = GetSystemMetrics(SM_CYICON);
        CRect rect;
        GetClientRect(&rect);
        int x = (rect.Width() - cxIcon + 1) / 2;
        int y = (rect.Height() - cyIcon + 1) / 2;

        // Draw the icon
        dc.DrawIcon(x, y, m_hIcon);
```

```
    }
    else
    {
        CDialog::OnPaint();
    }
}


// The system calls this to obtain the cursor to
// display while the user drags
// the minimized window.
HCURSOR CMortDrivDlg::OnQueryDragIcon()
{
    return (HCURSOR) m_hIcon;
}
```

When the Calculate button is clicked, the data from the dialog box is updated and the **SetLoanInfo** method of the Automation Server is called to set the loan data. This would not only set the loan information, but also compute the monthly payment. The Payment property is queried and displayed in the dialog box.

```
void CMortDrivDlg::OnCalculate()
{
    float    flPayment;
    char     szPayment[32];

    UpdateData(TRUE);

    m_mortcalc.SetLoanInfo(m_principal, m_rate, m_period);
    flPayment = m_mortcalc.GetPayment();
    sprintf(szPayment, "%.2f", flPayment);
    m_payment = szPayment;
    UpdateData (FALSE);
}
```

It is not shown here, but the OLE-related DLLs are initialized during the **InitInstance** processing of the application in *Mortdriv.cpp*.

Shown next is the ClassWizard-generated proxy class for the Automation Server.

```
// Machine generated IDispatch wrapper class(es)
// created with ClassWizard
// CMortCalc wrapper class

class CMortCalc : public COleDispatchDriver
{
```

```
public:
    CMortCalc() {}
    CMortCalc(LPDISPATCH pDispatch) :
        COleDispatchDriver(pDispatch) {}
    CMortCalc(const CMortCalc& dispatchSrc) :
        COleDispatchDriver(dispatchSrc) {}

// Attributes
public:
    float GetPrincipal();
    void SetPrincipal(float);
    float GetRate();
    void SetRate(float);
    long GetPeriod();
    void SetPeriod(long);
    float GetPayment();
    void SetPayment(float);

// Operations
public:
    void Reset();
    void SetLoanInfo(float Principal,float Rate,long Period);
};
```

The ClassWizard-generated implementation module follows:

```
// Machine generated IDispatch wrapper class(es)
// created with ClassWizard

#include "stdafx.h"
#include "mortcalc.h"

#ifdef _DEBUG
#define new DEBUG_NEW
#undef THIS_FILE
static char THIS_FILE[] = __FILE__;
#endif

// CMortCalc properties

float CMortCalc::GetPrincipal()
{
    float result;
    GetProperty(0x1, VT_R4, (void*)&result);
```

```
        return result;
    }

void CMortCalc::SetPrincipal(float propVal)
    {
        SetProperty(0x1, VT_R4, propVal);
    }

float CMortCalc::GetRate()
    {
        float result;
        GetProperty(0x2, VT_R4, (void*)&result);
        return result;
    }

void CMortCalc::SetRate(float propVal)
    {
        SetProperty(0x2, VT_R4, propVal);
    }

long CMortCalc::GetPeriod()
    {
        long result;
        GetProperty(0x3, VT_I4, (void*)&result);
        return result;
    }

void CMortCalc::SetPeriod(long propVal)
    {
        SetProperty(0x3, VT_I4, propVal);
    }

float CMortCalc::GetPayment()
    {
        float result;
        GetProperty(0x4, VT_R4, (void*)&result);
        return result;
    }

void CMortCalc::SetPayment(float propVal)
    {
        SetProperty(0x4, VT_R4, propVal);
    }
```

```
// CMortCalc operations

void CMortCalc::Reset()
{
    InvokeHelper(0x5, DISPATCH_METHOD, VT_EMPTY, NULL, NULL);
}

void CMortCalc::SetLoanInfo(float Principal,
                           float Rate,
                           long Period)
{
    static BYTE parms[] =
        VTS_R4 VTS_R4 VTS_I4;
    InvokeHelper(0x6, DISPATCH_METHOD, VT_EMPTY, NULL, parms,
        Principal, Rate, Period);
}
```

OLE DRAG-AND-DROP

The concept of drag-and-drop is not unique to OLE. You can drag and drop a file in Windows Explorer if you want to copy a file, for example. OLE drag-and-drop is a more generalized drag-and-drop. Unlike the Explorer, which deals primarily with files in its drag-and-drop operations, OLE drag-and-drop, like a Clipboard, can handle a wide variety of data, and the user interface mechanism is a lot simpler compared with the keystroke/mouse clicks required to copy data using the Clipboard.

By use of OLE drag-and-drop, the data transfer could be from one location to another within the same document, or between different documents, or even between different applications. The source and target for the drag-and-drop must be open and must be at least partially visible on the screen.

There are a number of functions and methods available for you to program the OLE drag-and-drop capability, and these are summarized in Table 13-1.

The source of drag-and-drop may be non-OLE applications. You can get source data from applications that do not support compound documents (or customize standard OLE drag-and-drop behavior) by creating a **COleDataSource** object and calling the **DoDragDrop** function from this object when the user starts a drag-and-drop operation. Similarly, the target for drag-and-drop could be non-OLE applications as well as OLE applications. You enable drop support in your OLE (or non-OLE) application by adding a member variable of type **COleDropTarget** (or a class derived from it) to each view in the application that you want to be a drop target, and calling the new member variable's **Register** member function from the view class' function that handles the **WM_CREATE** message. You may override functions such as **OnDragEnter**, **OnDragLeave**, and so on. The programming details for implementing drag-and-drop mentioned earlier apply to

Function/Methods	Description
RegisterDragDrop	This registers the specified window as a potential target of an OLE drag-and-drop operation. This function calls the IUnknown::AddRef method.
RevokeDragDrop	This revokes the registration of the specified application window. This function calls the IUnknown::Release method.
DoDragDrop	This invokes different methods in IDropSource and IDropTarget interfaces and carries out a drag-and-drop operation.
IUnknown::AddRef	This increments the reference count for the calling interface on an object and is called for every new copy of a pointer to an interface on a given object.
IUnknown::Release	This decrements the reference count for the calling interface on an object. The memory allocated to the object is freed if the reference count for the object falls to zero.

Table 13-1.   Functions and Methods Used in OLE Drag-and-Drop

both container and server applications. In most cases OLE takes care of deleting the data involved in the drag-and-drop operation after the drag-and-drop operation is complete.

PROGRAMMING EXAMPLE FOR OLE DRAG-AND-DROP

The next sample shows how to implement a simple drag-and-drop by providing OLE's **IDropTarget** interface. It is a dialog-based application that has two buttons and a status window. The dialog box is shown in Figure 13-6.

One of the buttons allows the user to enable the application for drag-and-drop, and the other button exits the application. When enabled for drag-and-drop, the status window displays the status of drag-and-drop activities. When text is dropped, it displays the dropped text. To run the application, start it and click on the Enable D'ND button to enable the application for drag-and-drop. The dialog box in Figure 13-7 appears.

Using the WordPad application, mark some text and then drag and drop it on this application. Notice the status window, which shows the drag-and-drop activities; when the text is dropped, it is displayed in the status window. Figure 13-8 shows the status when you attempt an invalid drag-and-drop operation, while Figure 13-9 shows the

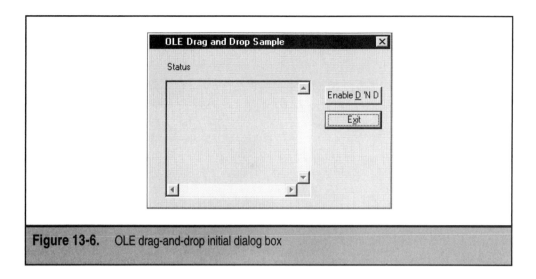

Figure 13-6.   OLE drag-and-drop initial dialog box

status for a valid drag-and-drop operation. The text in the WordPad application that is the source of the drag-and-drop is shown in Figure 13-10.

Two sets of code are shown here. One is the code related to the dialog box, which for the most part is very typical; the second is the implementation of the **IDropTarget** interface. The application dialog box–related code is shown next, starting with the header file and followed by the implementation code. The code of interest is highlighted. The About dialog box processing is not shown, for brevity.

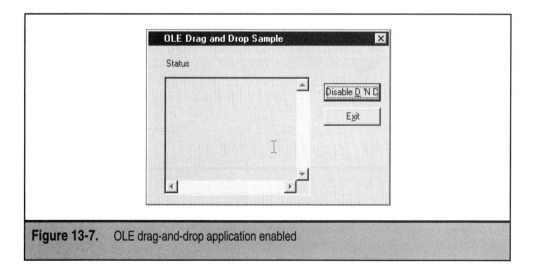

Figure 13-7.   OLE drag-and-drop application enabled

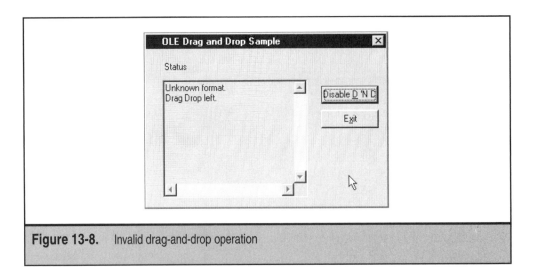

Figure 13-8. Invalid drag-and-drop operation

A means to display text in the status window is provided by public method **SetStatus**. Since the implementation of **IDropTarget** displays the activities of drag-and-drop and there will be many calls to **DragOver**, the status window will be cluttered with **DragOver** activity information. To prevent this, only the first **DragOver** activity is displayed. To achieve this, a flag is maintained as a member variable, and the member functions are provided to set and query the status of the flag. Since the application allows the user to enable and disable drag-and-drop, a pointer to the **IDropTarget** object is maintained

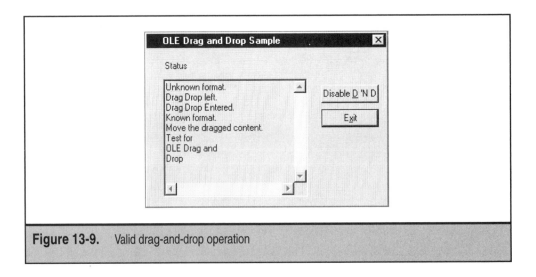

Figure 13-9. Valid drag-and-drop operation

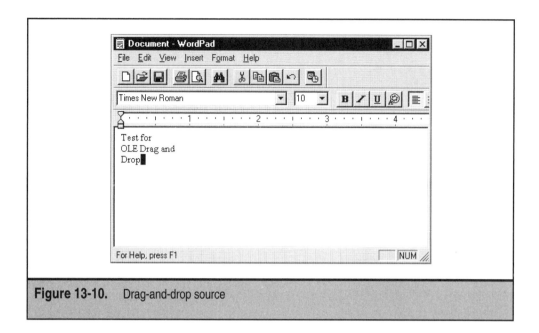

Figure 13-10. Drag-and-drop source

where the pointer to the constructed object is saved. The **OnDragdrop** function handles the drag-and-drop button in the dialog box.

```
// DragDropDlg.h : header file
//
#if !defined(AFX_DRAGDROPDLG_H)
#define AFX_DRAGDROPDLG_H

#if _MSC_VER >= 1000
#pragma once
#endif // _MSC_VER >= 1000

// CDragDropDlg dialog

class CDragDropTarget;
class CDragDropDlg : public CDialog
{
// Construction
public:
    CDragDropDlg(CWnd* pParent = NULL);
    void SetStatus(char *);
    void SetMoveFlag(BOOL);
    BOOL GetMoveFlag();
```

```
// Dialog Data
    //{{AFX_DATA(CDragDropDlg)
    enum { IDD = IDD_DRAGDROP_DIALOG };
    CEdit    m_status;
    //}}AFX_DATA

    // ClassWizard generated virtual function overrides
    //{{AFX_VIRTUAL(CDragDropDlg)
    protected:
    virtual void DoDataExchange(CDataExchange* pDX);
    //}}AFX_VIRTUAL

// Implementation
protected:
    HICON    m_hIcon;
    BOOL     fDragDropEnabled;
    BOOL     fMoveMsgDisplayed;
    CDragDropTarget *pCDDTarget;

    // Generated message map functions
    //{{AFX_MSG(CDragDropDlg)
    virtual BOOL OnInitDialog();
    afx_msg void OnSysCommand(UINT nID, LPARAM lParam);
    afx_msg void OnPaint();
    afx_msg HCURSOR OnQueryDragIcon();
    afx_msg void OnDragdrop();
    //}}AFX_MSG
    DECLARE_MESSAGE_MAP()
};
#endif
```

Shown next is the implementation file for the **CDragDropDlg** class. The About dialog box processing is not shown. The code of interest is highlighted.

```
// DragDropDlg.cpp : implementation file
//

#include "stdafx.h"
#include "DragDrop.h"
#include "DragDropDlg.h"
#include "DragDropTarget.h"

#ifdef _DEBUG
#define new DEBUG_NEW
#undef THIS_FILE
```

```
static char THIS_FILE[] = __FILE__;
#endif

// CDragDropDlg dialog

CDragDropDlg::CDragDropDlg(CWnd* pParent /*=NULL*/)
    : CDialog(CDragDropDlg::IDD, pParent)
{
    //{{AFX_DATA_INIT(CDragDropDlg)
    //}}AFX_DATA_INIT
    m_hIcon = AfxGetApp()->LoadIcon(IDR_MAINFRAME);

    fDragDropEnabled = FALSE;
}

void CDragDropDlg::DoDataExchange(CDataExchange* pDX)
{
    CDialog::DoDataExchange(pDX);
    //{{AFX_DATA_MAP(CDragDropDlg)
    DDX_Control(pDX, IDC_STATUS, m_status);
    //}}AFX_DATA_MAP
}

BEGIN_MESSAGE_MAP(CDragDropDlg, CDialog)
    //{{AFX_MSG_MAP(CDragDropDlg)
    ON_WM_SYSCOMMAND()
    ON_WM_PAINT()
    ON_WM_QUERYDRAGICON()
    ON_BN_CLICKED(IDC_DRAGDROP, OnDragdrop)
    //}}AFX_MSG_MAP
END_MESSAGE_MAP()

// CDragDropDlg message handlers

BOOL CDragDropDlg::OnInitDialog()
{
    CDialog::OnInitDialog();

    // Add "About..." menu item to system menu.
    // IDM_ABOUTBOX must be in the system command range.
    ASSERT((IDM_ABOUTBOX & 0xFFF0) == IDM_ABOUTBOX);
    ASSERT(IDM_ABOUTBOX < 0xF000);

    CMenu* pSysMenu = GetSystemMenu(FALSE);
    if (pSysMenu != NULL)
```

```
    {
        CString strAboutMenu;
        strAboutMenu.LoadString(IDS_ABOUTBOX);
        if (!strAboutMenu.IsEmpty())
        {
            pSysMenu->AppendMenu(MF_SEPARATOR);
            pSysMenu->AppendMenu(MF_STRING,
                                 IDM_ABOUTBOX,
                                 strAboutMenu);
        }
    }

    // Set the icon for this dialog.
    // The framework does this automatically
    //  when the application's main window is not a dialog
    SetIcon(m_hIcon, TRUE);            // Set big icon
    SetIcon(m_hIcon, FALSE);        // Set small icon

    // TODO: Add extra initialization here

    return TRUE;
}

void CDragDropDlg::OnSysCommand(UINT nID, LPARAM lParam)
{
    if ((nID & 0xFFF0) == IDM_ABOUTBOX)
    {
        CAboutDlg dlgAbout;
        dlgAbout.DoModal();
    }
    else
    {
        CDialog::OnSysCommand(nID, lParam);
    }
}

void CDragDropDlg::OnPaint()
{
    if (IsIconic())
    {
        CPaintDC dc(this); // device context for painting

        SendMessage(WM_ICONERASEBKGND,
                    (WPARAM)dc.GetSafeHdc(),0);
```

```
        // Center icon in client rectangle
        int cxIcon = GetSystemMetrics(SM_CXICON);
        int cyIcon = GetSystemMetrics(SM_CYICON);
        CRect rect;
        GetClientRect(&rect);
        int x = (rect.Width() - cxIcon + 1) / 2;
        int y = (rect.Height() - cyIcon + 1) / 2;

        // Draw the icon
        dc.DrawIcon(x, y, m_hIcon);
    }
    else
    {
        CDialog::OnPaint();
    }
}


// The system calls this to obtain the cursor
// to display while the user drags
//  the minimized window.
HCURSOR CDragDropDlg::OnQueryDragIcon()
{
    return (HCURSOR) m_hIcon;
}
```

To enable the application for OLE's drag-and-drop, an object derived from **IDropTarget** should be created and given to the operating system. After creating the object, the reference count is incremented and the **CoLockObjectExternal** is called to lock the object and to make sure that it stays in memory. Notice that this call must be made in the process in which the object actually resides. After locking the object in memory, the application informs the operating system that the specified window (in this case the dialog window) can be the target of an OLE drag-and-drop operation. This is done by calling the **RegisterDragDrop** function and giving the window handle of the window that can be the target for the drag-and-drop operation and the pointer to the **IDropTarget** object. This registration must be done whenever any window in the application is available as a drop target. However, in this application there is only one window, and it does not have to bother about it. To stop the window from being a target of an OLE drag-and-drop, the **RevokeDragDrop** function is called and given the handle of the window handle that should not be the target. This is followed by unlocking the lock placed on the **IDropTarget** object by calling **CoLockObjectExternal** and then **Release**. You will see later that the **Release** function actually discards the object when it's no longer referenced. The code here toggles the action of the button and changes the name of the button to show what action will be performed when it is clicked.

```
void CDragDropDlg::OnDragdrop()
{
    CButton *pButton;

    pButton = (CButton *)GetDlgItem(IDC_DRAGDROP);

    // TODO: Add your control notification handler code here
    if (fDragDropEnabled)
    {
        // Disable drag drop
        RevokeDragDrop(m_hWnd);
        CoLockObjectExternal(pCDDTarget, FALSE, TRUE);
        pCDDTarget->Release();

        fDragDropEnabled = FALSE;
        pButton->SetWindowText("Enable &D 'N D");

    }
    else
    {
        // Enable Drag drop
        pCDDTarget = new CDragDropTarget(this);
        pCDDTarget->AddRef();
        CoLockObjectExternal(pCDDTarget, TRUE, FALSE);
        RegisterDragDrop(m_hWnd, pCDDTarget);


        fDragDropEnabled = TRUE;
        pButton->SetWindowText("Disable &D 'N D");
    }
}
```

The next three member functions are helper functions that display text in the status window and provide the status of the state flag indicating whether the first **DragOver** message has been displayed in the status window.

```
void CDragDropDlg::SetStatus(char *pszStatus)
{
    m_status.SetSel(-1,0);
    m_status.ReplaceSel(pszStatus);
}


BOOL CDragDropDlg::GetMoveFlag()
```

```
{
    return(fMoveMsgDisplayed);
}

void CDragDropDlg::SetMoveFlag(BOOL f)
{
    fMoveMsgDisplayed = f;
}
```

Shown next is the implementation of the **Drop** target class that supports the OLE's **IDropTarget** interface. When implementing in C++, this **Drop** target class is derived from **IDropTarget** class, and all the virtual methods of **IDropTarget** class are implemented. To display status in the status area, a pointer to the dialog class is provided when the class is constructed. A member variable for keeping track of the reference count is maintained. Note that this class must also implement the **IUnknown** interfaces.

```
#if !defined(CDRAGDROPTARGET_H)
#define CDRAGDROPTARGET_H

class CDragDropDlg;
class CDragDropTarget : public IDropTarget
{
protected:
    ULONG    m_ReferenceCount;
    BOOL     fKnownFormat;
    CDragDropDlg    *pDDDlg;

public:
    CDragDropTarget(CDragDropDlg *);
    ~CDragDropTarget();

    // IUnknown interface members

    STDMETHODIMP_(ULONG) AddRef();
    STDMETHODIMP_(ULONG) Release();
    STDMETHODIMP QueryInterface(REFIID , LPVOID* );

    // IDropTarget interface members

    STDMETHODIMP DragEnter(IDataObject *, DWORD,
                        POINTL, DWORD *);
    STDMETHODIMP DragOver(DWORD, POINTL, DWORD *);
    STDMETHODIMP DragLeave();
    STDMETHODIMP Drop(IDataObject *, DWORD,
```

```
                        POINTL, DWORD *);


};
#endif
```

The implementation of the **Drop** target class derived from **IDropTarget** is shown next. Notice the inclusion of *Oleidl.h,* which has the definitions needed. All COM interfaces are derived from the **IUnknown** interface. So is this class and it implements the methods of the **IUnknown** interface, which are **AddRef**, **QueryInterface**, and **Release**.

```
#include "stdafx.h"
#include <oleidl.h>
#include "DragDrop.h"
#include "DragDropDlg.h"
#include "DragDropTarget.h"

CDragDropTarget::CDragDropTarget(CDragDropDlg *pDlg)
{
  pDDDlg = pDlg;
  fKnownFormat = FALSE;
  m_ReferenceCount = 0;
}


CDragDropTarget::~CDragDropTarget()
{
}
```

AddRef increments the object's reference count by 1 when an interface or another application binds itself to the object. This reference count is maintained in the protected member variable, **m_ReferenceCount**.

```
STDMETHODIMP_(ULONG) CDragDropTarget::AddRef()
{
    m_ReferenceCount += 1;
    return (m_ReferenceCount);
}
```

QueryInterface queries the object about the features it supports by requesting pointers to a specific interface. Thus, if the ID of the requested interface is either **IUnknown** or **IDropTarget**, a pointer to this object is returned.

```
STDMETHODIMP CDragDropTarget::QueryInterface(
    REFIID iid, LPVOID* ppvObj)
{
```

```
    if (IsEqualIID(iid, IID_IUnknown) ||
        IsEqualIID(iid, IID_IDropTarget))
    {
        *ppvObj = this;
        AddRef();
        return S_OK;
    }


    return E_NOINTERFACE;
}
```

Release decrements the object's reference count by 1, and when there are no more references to the object, it is deleted.

```
STDMETHODIMP_(ULONG) CDragDropTarget::Release()
{
    m_ReferenceCount -= 1;
    if (m_ReferenceCount < 1)
    {
        delete this;
        return 0;
    }
    return m_ReferenceCount;
}
```

When the user drags the mouse the first time into the window that is registered for a drop target, the system calls **DragEnter**. The system provides a pointer to the source data object, keyboard modifier, pointer location, and a pointer to the effect of the drag-drop operation. In response the application must check whether it can use the data provided by checking the format and media of the data object and the state of the modifier keys, and update the value of the effect pointed to by *pdwEffect*. If the application cannot handle the data, it updates the effect to DROPEFFECT_NONE. If it can handle the data, the effect is set to other DROPEFFECT values. The system in turn calls the drop source to show the visual feedback by displaying the appropriate pointer. In this sample it checks whether the format is text.

```
STDMETHODIMP CDragDropTarget::DragEnter(
                            IDataObject *pDataObject,
                            DWORD grfKeyState,
                            POINTL pt,
                            DWORD *pdwEffect)
{
    FORMATETC   format;
```

```
        pDDDlg->SetMoveFlag(FALSE);

        format.cfFormat = CF_TEXT ;
        format.ptd = NULL ;
        format.dwAspect = DVASPECT_CONTENT ;
        format.lindex = -1 ;
        format.tymed = TYMED_HGLOBAL ;

        if (pDataObject->QueryGetData (&format) == S_OK)
        {
            fKnownFormat = TRUE;
            pDDDlg->SetStatus("Drag Drop Entered.\r\n");
            pDDDlg->SetStatus("Known format.\r\n");
                DragOver(grfKeyState, pt, pdwEffect) ;
        }
        else
        {
                *pdwEffect = DROPEFFECT_NONE ;
        }
        return S_OK ;
}
```

When the user moves the mouse across the target window, the system calls the **DragOver** method. The processing of this method is generally similar to that of **DragEnter**. Note that the system calls this function frequently and it should be optimized. In this sample the status window is updated only once, and for all future calls it is not updated.

```
STDMETHODIMP CDragDropTarget::DragOver(DWORD grfKeyState,
                                        POINTL pt,
                                        DWORD *pdwEffect)
{
    char    *pszStatus;
    if (!fKnownFormat)
    {
        *pdwEffect = DROPEFFECT_NONE;
        pszStatus = "Unknown format.\r\n";
    }
    else if ((grfKeyState & MK_CONTROL) &&
            (grfKeyState & MK_SHIFT))
    {
        *pdwEffect = DROPEFFECT_LINK;
        pszStatus = "Link the dragged content.\r\n";
    }
```

```
    else if (grfKeyState & MK_CONTROL)
    {
        *pdwEffect = DROPEFFECT_COPY;
        pszStatus = "Copy the dragged content.\r\n";
    }
    else
    {
        *pdwEffect = DROPEFFECT_MOVE;
        pszStatus = "Move the dragged content.\r\n";
    }

    if (!pDDDlg->GetMoveFlag())
    {
        pDDDlg->SetStatus(pszStatus);
        pDDDlg->SetMoveFlag(TRUE);
    }
    return S_OK;
}
```

DragLeave is called by the system when the user moves the mouse out of the target window that is enabled for the drop target, or if the user cancels the current drag-and-drop operation. In response to this, the application may remove any visual feedback that it provides to the user or release any reference to the data transfer object. In this sample it displays information in the status window and resets some state flags.

```
STDMETHODIMP CDragDropTarget::DragLeave()
{
    fKnownFormat = FALSE;
    pDDDlg->SetStatus("Drag Drop left.\r\n");
    pDDDlg->SetMoveFlag(FALSE);
    return S_OK;
}
```

The **Drop** function is called by the system when the user completes the drag-and-drop operation. In turn the target application should incorporate the data based on the modifier keys such as CTRL and SHIFT. In this sample the data is obtained by calling the **GetData** method of the data object and providing the format and a storage medium structure. The data is pointed by a global memory handle whose actual pointer is requested by locking the handle. The data is displayed in the status window, and the storage medium is freed by calling **ReleaseStgMedium**. Apart from this, the effect is updated, in this case by calling **DragOver**, such that the source application can do any necessary cleanup. Any visual effect that the target application provided should also be removed, and any reference to the data object is released. This application does not provide any visual feedback.

```
STDMETHODIMP CDragDropTarget::Drop(IDataObject *pDataObject,
                                   DWORD grfKeyState,
                                   POINTL pt,
                                   DWORD *pdwEffect)
{
    STGMEDIUM    Stg;
    FORMATETC    format;
    char         *pDDData;

    format.cfFormat = CF_TEXT ;
    format.ptd = NULL ;
    format.dwAspect = DVASPECT_CONTENT ;
    format.lindex = -1 ;
    format.tymed = TYMED_HGLOBAL ;

    pDataObject->GetData(&format, &Stg);
    pDDData = (char *)GlobalLock(Stg.hGlobal);

    pDDDlg->SetStatus(pDDData);
    pDDDlg->SetStatus("\r\n");

    ReleaseStgMedium(&Stg);
    DragOver(grfKeyState, pt, pdwEffect) ;
    return S_OK;
}
```

Conclusion

In this chapter, we looked at OLE Automation Servers and at an OLE Automation Server programming example. In the example, we also discussed how to make an OLE Automation Server a stand-alone application. Next we looked at OLE Automation clients and an OLE Automation client programming example. This client example accessed the OLE Automation Server mentioned earlier. Finally we took a closer look at a significant OLE user interface enhancement—OLE drag-and-drop—including a programming example that illustrated OLE drag-and-drop.

Chapter 14 covers another very important Windows NT programming topic—ActiveX.

CHAPTER 14

Using ActiveX

ctiveX is one of the hot programming technologies of Windows NT. With the increased use of the Web and intranets for business programming, you are likely to use ActiveX controls and containers because ActiveX controls enable you to include dynamic content. For instance, you might create an onscreen stock ticker where the stock prices are changing dynamically; this is only one example of the potential of ActiveX controls.

We covered ActiveX briefly in Chapter 12 and noted that ActiveX controls are an outgrowth of what used to be OLE custom controls. We will build upon ActiveX controls including properties, methods, and events in this chapter. We will look at a programming example where we create an ActiveX control. We will also examine containers and a container programming example. Since an ActiveX control you develop may access the local resources, such as the file system on the local computer to which it has been downloaded, you have to take extra precautions to ensure that the control does not cause any damage. You should also know whether ActiveX controls you download to your computer are safe to use. There are ways, such as signing and marking ActiveX controls, that help improve the security aspects of using ActiveX controls. We will look at signing and marking ActiveX controls and at a related programming example.

ACTIVEX CONTROL AND CONTAINER COMMUNICATION

An ActiveX control inherits all the features of an MFC window object as it is derived from the base class, **COleControl**. This means that besides features such as firing events, the ActiveX control also inherits advanced features such as in-place activation, automation, and windowless controls.

The ActiveX control communicates with the container by firing *events*. The container operates an ActiveX control using the control's *properties* and *methods*. We looked at properties, methods, and events briefly in Chapter 12. Let's look at these in more detail here.

ActiveX Control Properties, Methods, and Events

Events are notifications from the control to the container of significant happenings in the control. Events can have associated parameters that provide additional data to the container. Some common events are mouse clicks on the control or the entry of keyboard data. There are two types of events—stock events and custom events. *Stock* events, such as single and double mouse clicks, are those for which there is built-in support in **COleControl**. *Custom* events are events, such as the receipt of a specific window message, for which there is no built-in support in **COleControl**, and for which you have to provide your own implementation. Your control class must map each event of the control to a member function that is called when the event occurs. Custom events can have the same name as stock events so long as you don't try to use both implementations in the same control. While containers normally are programmed to respond to events, keep in mind that the container can choose not to act on the events.

Properties are control attributes, such as the appearance of the control, that can be modified by a container or by a user of the control. Properties are similar to C++ class member variables and are data members of the ActiveX control. There are two types of properties—stock properties and custom properties. *Stock* properties, such as a control's caption, are those for which there is built-in support in **COleControl**. *Custom* properties are properties such as the appearance and state of a control, for which there is no built-in support in **COleControl**, and for which you have to provide your own implementation. Properties can have associated parameters to provide additional data. You can override the built-in notification functions of most stock properties. There are four ways of implementing custom properties, each with its own dispatch map macro (see the dispatch map later in this section), as shown in Table 14-1.

Sometimes it is useful to be able to set a property to be read-only or write-only. If you are creating a new control, you can designate the ActiveX control to be read-only or write-only using the ClassWizard, which inserts the function **SetNotSupported** or **GetNotSupported** in the dispatch map. If you want to change an existing property to be read-only or write-only unconditionally, you can manually edit the dispatch map and remove the existing **Set**/**Get** functions. If you want to change an existing property to be read-only or write-only based on your application logic, then provide your implementation for the **Get**/**Set** functions and call **SetNotSupported** or **GetNotSupported** where appropriate. You can indicate that an error occurred in a method using the **ThrowError** member function of **COleControl**.

Sometimes you may want to ensure that your ActiveX control fits seamlessly within its container by matching the container's characteristics such as fonts, background color, and so on. You can be notified and take action when the container's ambient property changes by overriding the **OnAmbientPropertyChanged** function and get information about the container's ambient properties using the **GetAmbientProperty** function of **COleControl**.

The properties of an ActiveX control can be viewed and changed through a control properties dialog box. The properties dialog box can be displayed either by invoking the control's properties verb or by the container. It is possible to have a control with more than one property page, and you can add property pages to an existing control. You can allow the user to change the font of any text that may be present in your control by changing the font property. You can let the user choose from stock fonts, or you can include custom fonts.

Just as properties are similar to C++ class member variables, methods are similar to C++ class member functions and provide interfaces that are exposed to the container (and other applications). As with events and properties, there are two types of methods—stock methods and custom methods. *Stock* methods are those for which there is built-in support in **COleControl** (for example the **Refresh** method). *Custom* methods are methods for which there is no built-in support in **COleControl** and for which you have to provide your own implementation. You can indicate that an error occurred in a method by using the **ThrowError** member function of **COleControl**.

Properties and methods are exposed by use of a *dispatch map*. A dispatch map is a set of macros that expands into the declarations and calls needed to expose methods and

Custom Property Implementation	Description	Dispatch Map Macro
Member variable implementation	The property's state is represented as a variable in the control class. No notification is made when the property value changes. This implementation creates the least amount of support code.	DISP_PROPERTY
Member variable with notification implementation	This implementation adds a notification function to the member variable implementation, which automatically is called when the property value changes.	DISP_PROPERTY_ NOTIFY
Get/Set methods implementation	This implementation uses a Get member function that is called when the control user retrieves the current property value and uses a Set member function when the control user wants to change the property value. You can use the Get/Set member functions to validate a user's input or to dynamically derive a property value. You can also use the Get/Set member functions to implement a read-only or write-only property.	DISP_PROPERTY_ EX
Parameterized implementation	This implementation lets you use a single property in your control to represent a homogenous set of property values (also called a property array).	DISP_PROPERTY_ PARAM

Table 14-1. Custom Property Implementation

properties. The dispatch map designates the internal and external names of object functions and properties, as well as the data types of the function arguments and properties. A dispatch map is analogous to a message map that maps functions to Windows message IDs, except that a dispatch map maps virtual member functions.

CREATING AN ACTIVEX CONTROL

Your ActiveX control must satisfy some basic requirements. It must

▼ Be a COM object

■ Export the **DLLRegisterServer** function

■ Export the **DLLUnRegisterServer** function

▲ Implement the **IUnknown** interface

You can create ActiveX controls using the Visual C++ ControlWizard. You can also create ActiveX controls using the ActiveX Template Library (ATL). The examples in this chapter will use the MFC method. The steps involved in creating an ActiveX control are summarized here:

1. Use the Visual C++ ControlWizard to create an ActiveX control shell.

2. Add stock and custom properties using ClassWizard.

3. Add stock and custom methods using ClassWizard.

4. Add stock and custom events using ClassWizard.

5. Create property pages.

6. Associate controls and the property pages using ClassWizard.

7. Add application-specific code where appropriate.

8. Compile and build the ActiveX control.

9. Register the ActiveX control.

10. Test your ActiveX control. You can use the Test container Microsoft provides. If you are using the ActiveX control with a web page, you have to make up an object tag and specify the complete filename of your control in the *CODEBASE* parameter.

The following example expands on each of the preceding steps.

PROGRAMMING EXAMPLE TO ILLUSTRATE CREATING AN ACTIVEX CONTROL

In the next sample, an ActiveX control is created that maintains a list of addresses. The control has two property pages—one page containing custom properties such as Name, Address, and Remark—and the other page containing stock properties, foreground color, and background color. The control will have four methods: to add an address to the list, to view an address, to reset the address list, and to get the count of the number of addresses in the list. The control will also fire three events, one for each of the field changes.

One of the ways to create an ActiveX control is to use the Visual C++ ControlWizard. When you use the ControlWizard, it will create the shell required for the ActiveX control. This sample uses the ControlWizard to create all the necessary files in the project as follows:

1. A new project is created by clicking on the New menu item in the File menu.
2. In the Projects tab, MFC ActiveX ControlWizard is selected, and the project name and location are given.
3. **Rec_ax** is used as the sample project name.
4. Clicking on OK brings up the MFC ActiveX ControlWizard—Step 1 of 2 dialog box. Information that appears as default is used here.
5. Clicking on the Next> button will bring the Step 2 of 2 dialog box.
6. The class and filename automatically generated by the ControlWizard can be changed. To change them, the Edit Names button is clicked and the name of the Control's and Property Page's class name, header file, type name, implementation file, and type ID are changed by replacing "Rec_ax" with "Records."
7. The steps are completed by selecting the Finish button.
8. Clicking on OK in the New Project Information dialog box will create all the necessary files for the project.

This project can now be compiled, and an ActiveX control can be built. This, of course, does not yet have any functionality. The next step is to add functionality.

To add properties:

1. ClassWizard from the View menu is selected.
2. On the Automation tab **CRecordsCtrl** class name is selected.
3. The Add Properties… button is clicked to bring up the Add Property dialog box. The control needs three custom properties: **Name**, **Address**, and **Remarks**. These are entered and for each property, **CString** is selected as the type.
4. The generated variable name is accepted and implemented as a member variable by selecting the Member Variable radio button.
5. Clicking on OK creates this property.

6. Steps 3–5 are repeated for the other two custom properties.

7. Two more stock properties—the foreground and background color properties—are also added. In the Add Property dialog box these stock properties are selected from the predefined list of the external names.

The next step is to add methods. The methods added are **View**, **Add**, **Reset**, and **GetCount**. All methods except **GetCount** have a return type of void, and **GetCount** returns a short. To add a method:

1. The Add Method… button is clicked. This brings up the Add Method dialog box.

2. The name of the method is entered in the External Name box.

3. The automatically generated Internal Name is accepted.

4. The return type is selected and OK is clicked.

Next the events are added. Three custom events are added to signal the change in the three properties. To add the events:

1. The ActiveX Events tab is clicked, and then the Add Event… button is pressed. This brings up the Add Event dialog box.

2. The external name is specified in the External Name field and OK is clicked. The three external names entered are **NameChanged**, **AddressChanged**, and **RemarksChanged**.

Next the property page dialog box is created as follows:

1. The ResourceView is selected, the Rec_ax resources folder is expanded, and then the Dialog folder is expanded.

2. Double-clicking on IDD_PROPPAGE_REC_AX will bring the default dialog box.

3. The default control is deleted and three sets of controls—one each for **Name**, **Address**, **Remarks**—are created.

4. Each set has a static control and an edit box control. The edit box control IDs are specified as **IDC_NAME**, **IDC_ADDR**, and **IDC_REM**. Note that the size of the property page should be limited to either 250×62 dialog units or 250×110 dialog units. The stock and color property pages are 250×62 dialog units, and the stock font property page is 250×110 dialog units.

Now that the property page has been created, these controls are tied to the properties, thereby enabling them to display and modify the properties. To do this:

1. The ClassWizard is invoked and the **CRecordsPropPage** class is selected. The list of control IDs earlier defined in the property page dialog box appears.

2. For each control ID a variable is added by clicking the Add Variable… button. The member variable names for the Name control, Address control, and Remarks control are, respectively, **m_Name**, **m_Addr**, and **m_Rem**. The Value category is selected, and the variable type of **CString** is selected for all three controls.

Earlier we talked about generating the ActiveX control code by use of ControlWizard. Shown next are the code that is generated and the code added to the ActiveX control files. Shown first is the entry module for the ActiveX control. The class that is derived from **COleControlModule** is the main entry point to the control. The AppWizard by default overrides the **InitInstance** and **ExitInstance** member functions in this class where the ActiveX control-related initialization and termination can be done. This application does not perform any special initialization and termination. Before an ActiveX control can be used, it should be registered with the control-related information in the Registry. The ActiveX control created using the ControlWizard automatically generates the code to register and unregister the control. These register and unregister entry points are exported (look in the module definition file), and applications that load these controls call these entry points to register or unregister. If the control is built by use of Visual C++, it automatically calls this function and registers the control. You can also manually register a control using the *Regsvr32.exe* program and passing the complete path and filename of the control. Alternately, you can write a separate setup program. The setup program could load the control DLL (using **LoadLibrary**), and call the **DllRegisterServer** function. If you install and register an ActiveX control, you should also register *Olepro32.dll* (unless *Olepro32.dll* is already installed). In addition, if your control uses stock property pages, you should register *Mfcx0.dll* as well.

```
#if !defined(AFX_REC_AX_H)
#define AFX_REC_AX_H

#if _MSC_VER >= 1000
#pragma once
#endif // _MSC_VER >= 1000

// rec_ax.h : main header file for REC_AX.DLL

#if !defined( __AFXCTL_H__ )
    #error include 'afxctl.h' before including this file
#endif

#include "resource.h"        // main symbols

/////////////////////////////////////////////////
// CRec_axApp : See rec_ax.cpp for implementation.
```

```
class CRec_axApp : public COleControlModule
{
public:
    BOOL InitInstance();
    int ExitInstance();
};

extern const GUID CDECL _tlid;
extern const WORD _wVerMajor;
extern const WORD _wVerMinor;

//{{AFX_INSERT_LOCATION}}

#endif

// rec_ax.cpp : Implementation of CRec_axApp and DLL registration.

#include "stdafx.h"
#include "rec_ax.h"

#ifdef _DEBUG
#define new DEBUG_NEW
#undef THIS_FILE
static char THIS_FILE[] = __FILE__;
#endif


CRec_axApp NEAR theApp;

const GUID CDECL BASED_CODE _tlid =
    { 0xe150326c, 0xebda, 0x11d0,
      { 0xa9, 0xee, 0x9, 0x92, 0, 0x54, 0, 0x30 } };
const WORD _wVerMajor = 1;
const WORD _wVerMinor = 0;

/////////////////////////////////////////////////////
// CRec_axApp::InitInstance - DLL initialization
BOOL CRec_axApp::InitInstance()
{
    BOOL bInit = COleControlModule::InitInstance();
    if (bInit)
    {
```

```
        // TODO: Add your own module initialization code here.
    }
    return bInit;
}


/////////////////////////////////////////////////////
// CRec_axApp::ExitInstance - DLL termination
int CRec_axApp::ExitInstance()
{
    // TODO: Add your own module termination code here.
    return COleControlModule::ExitInstance();
}



/////////////////////////////////////////////////////
// DllRegisterServer - Adds entries to the system registry
STDAPI DllRegisterServer(void)
{
    AFX_MANAGE_STATE(_afxModuleAddrThis);

    if (!AfxOleRegisterTypeLib(AfxGetInstanceHandle(), _tlid))
        return ResultFromScode(SELFREG_E_TYPELIB);

    if (!COleObjectFactoryEx::UpdateRegistryAll(TRUE))
        return ResultFromScode(SELFREG_E_CLASS);

    return NOERROR;
}



/////////////////////////////////////////////////////
// DllUnregisterServer - Removes entries from the system registry
STDAPI DllUnregisterServer(void)
{
    AFX_MANAGE_STATE(_afxModuleAddrThis);

    if (!AfxOleUnregisterTypeLib(_tlid, _wVerMajor, _wVerMinor))
        return ResultFromScode(SELFREG_E_TYPELIB);

    if (!COleObjectFactoryEx::UpdateRegistryAll(FALSE))
        return ResultFromScode(SELFREG_E_CLASS);

    return NOERROR;
}
```

Shown next is the ActiveX control class derived from **COleControl**. This has both the automatically generated code and the code that was added later.

```
// RecordsCtl.cpp : Implementation of the CRecordsCtrl ActiveX
// Control class.

#include "stdafx.h"
#include "rec_ax.h"
#include "RecordsCtl.h"
#include "RecordsPpg.h"

#ifdef _DEBUG
#define new DEBUG_NEW
#undef THIS_FILE
static char THIS_FILE[] = __FILE__;
#endif

IMPLEMENT_DYNCREATE(CRecordsCtrl, COleControl)
```

The type of custom property that has been implemented here is the member variable with notification. The ClassWizard creates the necessary code in the dispatch map. The notification code is automatically called by the framework when the property value is changed. Each custom property that is added to the control has an entry in the dispatch map. The ClassWizard also adds these notification functions as member functions inside the class, as can be seen in the code that follows.

Also added in the dispatch map are the four methods that were added through the ClassWizard: **View**, **Reset**, **Add**, and **GetCount**. The two stock properties that were added are also included here. The ClassWizard also adds the stub code for the methods.

```
/////////////////////////////////////////////////
// Message map

BEGIN_MESSAGE_MAP(CRecordsCtrl, COleControl)
    //{{AFX_MSG_MAP(CRecordsCtrl)
    ON_WM_CREATE()
    //}}AFX_MSG_MAP
    ON_OLEVERB(AFX_IDS_VERB_PROPERTIES, OnProperties)
END_MESSAGE_MAP()


/////////////////////////////////////////////////
// Dispatch map
```

```
BEGIN_DISPATCH_MAP(CRecordsCtrl, COleControl)
    //{{AFX_DISPATCH_MAP(CRecordsCtrl)
    DISP_PROPERTY_NOTIFY(CRecordsCtrl, "Name", m_name,
                        OnNameChanged, VT_BSTR)
    DISP_PROPERTY_NOTIFY(CRecordsCtrl, "Address",
                        m_address, OnAddressChanged,
                        VT_BSTR)
    DISP_PROPERTY_NOTIFY(CRecordsCtrl, "Remarks",
                        m_remarks, OnRemarksChanged,
                        VT_BSTR)
    DISP_FUNCTION(CRecordsCtrl, "View", View, VT_EMPTY, VTS_I2)
    DISP_FUNCTION(CRecordsCtrl, "Reset", Reset, VT_EMPTY,
                VTS_NONE)
    DISP_FUNCTION(CRecordsCtrl, "Add", Add, VT_EMPTY, VTS_NONE)
    DISP_FUNCTION(CRecordsCtrl, "GetCount", GetCount, VT_I2,
                VTS_NONE)
    DISP_STOCKPROP_BACKCOLOR()
    DISP_STOCKPROP_FORECOLOR()
    //}}AFX_DISPATCH_MAP
    DISP_FUNCTION_ID(CRecordsCtrl, "AboutBox", DISPID_ABOUTBOX,
                    AboutBox, VT_EMPTY, VTS_NONE)
END_DISPATCH_MAP()
```

Seen next is the declaration of event maps. Recall that while creating the application, three custom events were created. Unlike the stock events, custom events should be handled by the control and are not automatically fired by the **COleControl** class. The event map entries for the custom events are represented by the EVENT_CUSTOM macro. When an event is created by use of the ClassWizard, it creates all the stub code necessary. Additional code should be written by the control developer to fire the event. The event map indicates to the user of this ActiveX control that this control is capable of firing these events. The events are fired by the function specified as the second parameter in the EVENT_CUSTOM macro.

```
/////////////////////////////////////////////////
// Event map

BEGIN_EVENT_MAP(CRecordsCtrl, COleControl)
    //{{AFX_EVENT_MAP(CRecordsCtrl)
    EVENT_CUSTOM("NameChanged", FireNameChanged, VTS_BSTR)
    EVENT_CUSTOM("AddressChanged", FireAddressChanged, VTS_BSTR)
    EVENT_CUSTOM("RemarksChanged", FireRemarksChanged, VTS_BSTR)
    //}}AFX_EVENT_MAP
END_EVENT_MAP()
```

The next section declares the property pages for the control. This control has one custom property page and has a second stock property page. The entry for the custom property page has been added by the ClassWizard. The second is a stock property page provided by MFC. Of the three stock property pages available (**CLSID_CColorPropPage**, **CLSID_CFontPropPage**, and **CLSID_CPicturePropPage**), the color property page is used here. Notice that as the generated comment reminds, the count should be increased every time a property page is added.

```
/////////////////////////////////////////////////////
// Property pages

// TODO: Add more property pages as needed.
//   Remember to increase the count!
BEGIN_PROPPAGEIDS(CRecordsCtrl, 2)
    PROPPAGEID(CRecordsPropPage::guid)
    PROPPAGEID(CLSID_CColorPropPage)
END_PROPPAGEIDS(CRecordsCtrl)
```

The next macro implements the control's class factory and the **GetClassID** function. This is followed by the IMPLEMENT_OLETYPELIB macro, which implements the **GetTypeLib** member function.

```
/////////////////////////////////////////////////////
// Initialize class factory and guid
IMPLEMENT_OLECREATE_EX(CRecordsCtrl, "RECAX.RecordsCtrl.1",
    0xe150326f, 0xebda, 0x11d0, 0xa9, 0xee, 0x9, 0x92, 0,
    0x54, 0, 0x30)


/////////////////////////////////////////////////////
// Type library ID and version
IMPLEMENT_OLETYPELIB(CRecordsCtrl, _tlid, _wVerMajor, _wVerMinor)


/////////////////////////////////////////////////////
// Interface IDs

const IID BASED_CODE IID_DRecords =
        { 0xe150326d, 0xebda, 0x11d0, { 0xa9, 0xee, 0x9, 0x92,
          0, 0x54, 0, 0x30 } };
const IID BASED_CODE IID_DRecordsEvents =
        { 0xe150326e, 0xebda, 0x11d0, { 0xa9, 0xee, 0x9, 0x92,
          0, 0x54, 0, 0x30 } };
```

```
/////////////////////////////////////////////////
// Control type information

static const DWORD BASED_CODE _dwRecordsOleMisc =
    OLEMISC_ACTIVATEWHENVISIBLE |
    OLEMISC_SETCLIENTSITEFIRST |
    OLEMISC_INSIDEOUT |
    OLEMISC_CANTLINKINSIDE |
    OLEMISC_RECOMPOSEONRESIZE;

IMPLEMENT_OLECTLTYPE(CRecordsCtrl, IDS_RECORDS, _dwRecordsOleMisc)


/////////////////////////////////////////////////
// CRecordsCtrl::CRecordsCtrlFactory::UpdateRegistry -
// Adds or removes system registry entries for CRecordsCtrl

BOOL CRecordsCtrl::CRecordsCtrlFactory::UpdateRegistry(BOOL bRegister)
{
    // TODO: Verify that your control follows apartment-model
    // threading rules.
    // Refer to MFC TechNote 64 for more information.
    // If your control does not conform to the apartment-model
    // rules, then you must modify the code below, changing the
    // 6th parameter from afxRegApartmentThreading to 0

    if (bRegister)
        return AfxOleRegisterControlClass(
            AfxGetInstanceHandle(),
            m_clsid,
            m_lpszProgID,
            IDS_RECORDS,
            IDB_RECORDS,
            afxRegApartmentThreading,
            _dwRecordsOleMisc,
            _tlid,
            _wVerMajor,
            _wVerMinor);
    else
        return AfxOleUnregisterClass(m_clsid, m_lpszProgID);

}
```

```
///////////////////////////////////////////////////
// CRecordsCtrl::CRecordsCtrl - Constructor

CRecordsCtrl::CRecordsCtrl()
{
    InitializeIIDs(&IID_DRecords, &IID_DRecordsEvents);

    // TODO: Initialize your control's instance data here.
}



///////////////////////////////////////////////////
// CRecordsCtrl::~CRecordsCtrl - Destructor

CRecordsCtrl::~CRecordsCtrl()
{
    // TODO: Clean up your control's instance data here.
}
```

The **OnDraw** member function stub is replaced with the control-specific drawing functions. Here it basically sets the background and foreground colors and displays the number of records in the address book:

```
///////////////////////////////////////////////////
// CRecordsCtrl::OnDraw - Drawing function

void CRecordsCtrl::OnDraw(
            CDC* pdc, const CRect& rcBounds, const CRect& rcInvalid)
{
    // TODO: Replace the following code with your own drawing code.
    OLE_COLOR oleclr = GetBackColor();
    COLORREF clr = TranslateColor( oleclr );
    CBrush brush( clr );
    pdc->FillRect(rcBounds, &brush);
    oleclr = GetForeColor();
    clr = TranslateColor( oleclr );
    pdc->SetBkMode( TRANSPARENT );
    pdc->SetTextColor( clr );
    CRect rect = rcBounds;
    char buf[81];
    sprintf( buf, "Total Records: %d", GetCount() );
    pdc->DrawText( buf, -1, rect,
        DT_LEFT | DT_WORDBREAK );
}
```

A control may wish to initialize the property when the control is loaded or may wish to save a persistent value of the property when it is stored. This can be handled in the **DoPropExchange** member function. This member function is called when the control is loaded and when the control is stored. Since in this example the control does not care for any persistent data, or in other words, does not stream the data, nothing is done. If the control needs to initialize or store the property, the **PX_** functions can be used.

```
/////////////////////////////////////////////////////
// CRecordsCtrl::DoPropExchange - Persistence support

void CRecordsCtrl::DoPropExchange(CPropExchange* pPX)
{
    ExchangeVersion(pPX, MAKELONG(_wVerMinor, _wVerMajor));
    COleControl::DoPropExchange(pPX);

// TODO: Call PX_ functions for each persistent custom property.

}



/////////////////////////////////////////////////////
// CRecordsCtrl::OnResetState - Reset control to default state

void CRecordsCtrl::OnResetState()
{
    // Resets defaults found in DoPropExchange
    COleControl::OnResetState();
    // TODO: Reset any other control state here.
    Reset();
}

/////////////////////////////////////////////////////
// CRecordsCtrl::AboutBox - Display an "About" box to the user

void CRecordsCtrl::AboutBox()
{
    CDialog dlgAbout(IDD_ABOUTBOX_RECORDS);
    dlgAbout.DoModal();
}
```

The preceding member function handles the AboutBox by displaying the About dialog box. The rest of the code deals with the properties change notification and the four methods defined by the control. In the case of the three notification member functions, additional code is added to fire the respective events signaling the respective property changes. These firing functions, **FireNameChanged**, **FireAddressChanged**, and **FireRemarksChanged**, are defined inline in the control's header file.

```
/////////////////////////////////////////////////////
// CRecordsCtrl message handlers

void CRecordsCtrl::OnNameChanged()
{
    // TODO: Add notification handler code
    SetModifiedFlag();
    FireNameChanged( m_name );
}

void CRecordsCtrl::OnAddressChanged()
{
    // TODO: Add notification handler code
    SetModifiedFlag();
    FireAddressChanged( m_address );
}

void CRecordsCtrl::OnRemarksChanged()
{
    // TODO: Add notification handler code
    SetModifiedFlag();
    FireRemarksChanged( m_remarks );
}
```

The control maintains the address list in three **CStringArray** classes that are created as private member variables in the control's **CRecordsCtrl** class. As addresses are added, they are stored in these **CStringArrays**, and if needed, they are retrieved.

The next four member functions implement the methods of the control: **View**, **Reset**, **Add**, and **GetCount**. In the case of **View**, after preliminary checks, it retrieves the selected record from the string array that is maintained for the list of addresses. In the case of **Reset**, it empties the address list, and in the case of **Add**, it adds the current data from the properties to the address list. **GetCount** returns the number of addresses maintained by the address list.

```
void CRecordsCtrl::View(short idx)
{
    // TODO: Add your dispatch handler code here
    ASSERT( m_AllNames.GetSize() == m_AllAddresses.GetSize() );
    ASSERT( m_AllNames.GetSize() == m_AllRemarks.GetSize() );
    int cnt = m_AllNames.GetSize();
```

```
    if ( idx<0 || idx>=cnt )
    {
        MessageBeep( MB_ICONHAND );
        return;
    }
    m_name = m_AllNames[idx];
    m_address = m_AllAddresses[idx];
    m_remarks = m_AllRemarks[idx];
}

void CRecordsCtrl::Reset()
{
    // TODO: Add your dispatch handler code here
    m_AllNames.RemoveAll();
    m_AllAddresses.RemoveAll();
    m_AllRemarks.RemoveAll();
    m_name.Empty();
    m_address.Empty();
    m_remarks.Empty();
    InvalidateControl( );
}

void CRecordsCtrl::Add()
{
    // TODO: Add your dispatch handler code here
    ASSERT( m_AllNames.GetSize() == m_AllAddresses.GetSize() );
    ASSERT( m_AllNames.GetSize() == m_AllRemarks.GetSize() );
    m_AllNames.Add( m_name );
    m_AllAddresses.Add( m_address );
    m_AllRemarks.Add( m_remarks );
    InvalidateControl( );
}

short CRecordsCtrl::GetCount()
{
    // TODO: Add your dispatch handler code here
    ASSERT( m_AllNames.GetSize() == m_AllAddresses.GetSize() );
    ASSERT( m_AllNames.GetSize() == m_AllRemarks.GetSize() );
    return (short)m_AllNames.GetSize();
}

int CRecordsCtrl::OnCreate(LPCREATESTRUCT lpCreateStruct)
{
    if (COleControl::OnCreate(lpCreateStruct) == -1)
```

```
    return -1;

  // TODO: Add your specialized creation code here

  return 0;
}
```

Earlier, after creating the property page, the controls in the property page were tied to the properties. When this was done, the ClassWizard generated the ActiveX control's property page class, which is derived from **COlePropertyPage**. The ClassWizard adds code to initialize the member variables and to handle the exchange of data between the dialog controls, member variables, and the properties.

```
// RecordsPpg.cpp : Implementation of the CRecordsPropPage
// property page class.

#include "stdafx.h"
#include "rec_ax.h"
#include "RecordsPpg.h"

#ifdef _DEBUG
#define new DEBUG_NEW
#undef THIS_FILE
static char THIS_FILE[] = __FILE__;
#endif

IMPLEMENT_DYNCREATE(CRecordsPropPage, COlePropertyPage)

/////////////////////////////////////////////////
// Message map
BEGIN_MESSAGE_MAP(CRecordsPropPage, COlePropertyPage)
    //{{AFX_MSG_MAP(CRecordsPropPage)
    //}}AFX_MSG_MAP
END_MESSAGE_MAP()

/////////////////////////////////////////////////
// Initialize class factory and guid

IMPLEMENT_OLECREATE_EX(CRecordsPropPage, "RECAX.RecordsPropPage.1",
    0xe1503270, 0xebda, 0x11d0, 0xa9, 0xee, 0x9, 0x92, 0,
    0x54, 0, 0x30)


/////////////////////////////////////////////////
```

```
// CRecordsPropPage::CRecordsPropPageFactory::UpdateRegistry -
// Adds or removes system registry entries for CRecordsPropPage

BOOL CRecordsPropPage::
    CRecordsPropPageFactory::UpdateRegistry(BOOL bRegister)
{
    if (bRegister)
        return AfxOleRegisterPropertyPageClass
                (AfxGetInstanceHandle(),
                 m_clsid, IDS_RECORDS_PPG);
    else
        return AfxOleUnregisterClass(m_clsid, NULL);
}


/////////////////////////////////////////////////
// CRecordsPropPage::CRecordsPropPage - Constructor

CRecordsPropPage::CRecordsPropPage() :
    COlePropertyPage(IDD, IDS_RECORDS_PPG_CAPTION)
{
    //{{AFX_DATA_INIT(CRecordsPropPage)
    m_Addr = _T("");
    m_Name = _T("");
    m_Rem = _T("");
    //}}AFX_DATA_INIT
}
```

In the preceding code the member variables are initialized during the construction of the property page. The next member function handles the exchange of data between the control, member variable, and the property. The **DDX_Text** macro is the same as has been discussed in earlier samples. It exchanges data between the controls on the property page dialog box and the member variables in the class. The **DDP_Text** macro exchanges data between the member variables and the specified properties.

```
/////////////////////////////////////////////////
// CRecordsPropPage::DoDataExchange
void CRecordsPropPage::DoDataExchange(CDataExchange* pDX)
{
    //{{AFX_DATA_MAP(CRecordsPropPage)
    DDP_Text(pDX, IDC_ADDR, m_Addr, _T("Address") );
    DDX_Text(pDX, IDC_ADDR, m_Addr);
    DDP_Text(pDX, IDC_NAME, m_Name, _T("Name") );
```

```
    DDX_Text(pDX, IDC_NAME, m_Name);
    DDP_Text(pDX, IDC_REM, m_Rem, _T("Remarks") );
    DDX_Text(pDX, IDC_REM, m_Rem);
    //}}AFX_DATA_MAP
    DDP_PostProcessing(pDX);
}


//////////////////////////////////////////////////
// CRecordsPropPage message handlers

BOOL CRecordsPropPage::OnInitDialog()
{
    COlePropertyPage::OnInitDialog();

    // TODO: Add extra initialization here

    return TRUE;
}
```

CREATING AN ACTIVEX CONTROL CONTAINER

An ActiveX control is an in-process server that can be used in any OLE container and is typically represented as a child window. Of course, the full functionality of the ActiveX control is available only if the container has been designed to take advantage of the ActiveX control. You can build your own container. Keep in mind that Microsoft Access (starting with version 2.0) and Microsoft Visual Basic (starting with version 4.0) are some of the products that fully support ActiveX controls.

The sequence of events that occurs at the control and the container when a user action triggers a **WM_PAINT** message depends on whether the control is in active or inactive state (see Chapter 12 for a discussion on active and inactive states of a control). For an *active* control, the control's base class handles **WM_PAINT** in its **OnPaint** function, which by default calls your control's **OnDraw** function. For an *inactive* control, which usually is marked by the absence of a visible window (and hence cannot process a paint message), the container calls your control's **OnDraw** function directly. You have to handle painting of the control in the **OnDraw** function, which receives the window rectangle corresponding to the control and a device context (DC). If the control is active, the DC is that of the control; if the control is inactive, the DC is that of the container. Keep in mind that, although normally the DC is that of a screen DC, the DC could correspond to a metafile DC for print and print preview operations.

You can create a container application using the MFC AppWizard, and the process of creating a container is basically the same as creating any other MFC-based application that we have been using throughout this book.

PROGRAMMING EXAMPLE TO ILLUSTRATE CREATING A CONTAINER APPLICATION

The next step after creating the ActiveX control is to see how the control can be inserted in a container. Here we'll create a container application that will use the ActiveX control created earlier. This application is basically an address list application with the core of the address list functionality done by the ActiveX control developed earlier. This application provides the front-end for accepting the data, inserting it, viewing particular data, and resetting the address book. It uses the methods that were shown in the earlier ActiveX control sample to provide these functionalities. It does not provide any interface to the end user to change the foreground and background colors, but it changes them every time an address is added to the list.

Figures 14-1 through 14-5 show what you will see when you run the sample. Figure 14-1 shows the first dialog box. It shows that there are no records currently present.

Figure 14-2 shows the dialog box after one record is added. Total Records now shows 1, and the background color has changed.

Figure 14-3 shows the dialog box after yet another record is added. Total Records now shows 2, and the background color has changed again.

Figure 14-4 shows the dialog box that appears when the View button is clicked. It provides an option to select a record by an index.

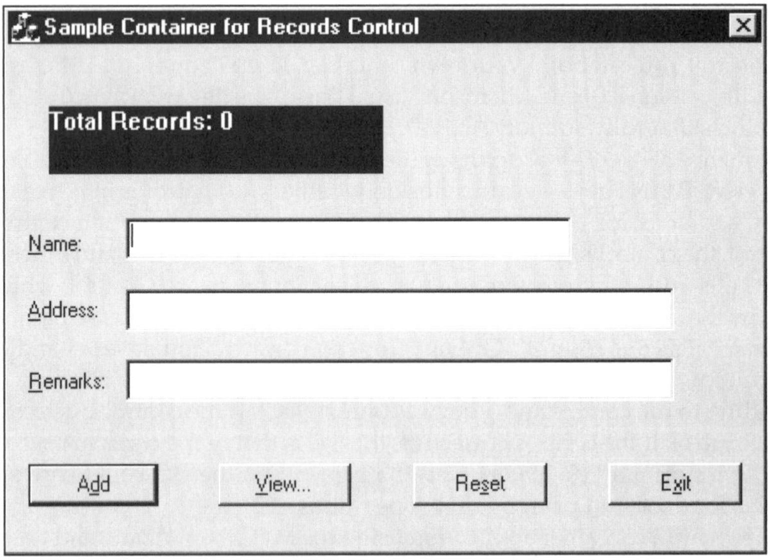

Figure 14-1.   Opening dialog of the ActiveX example

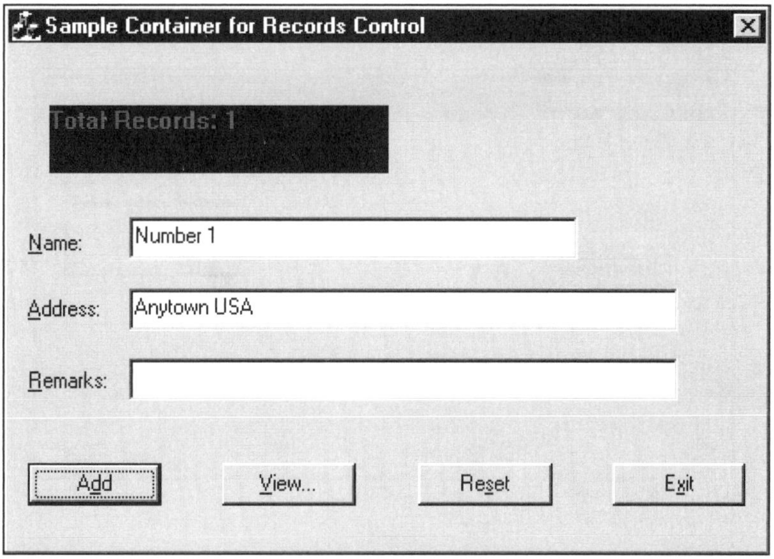

Figure 14-2. ActiveX control after adding one record

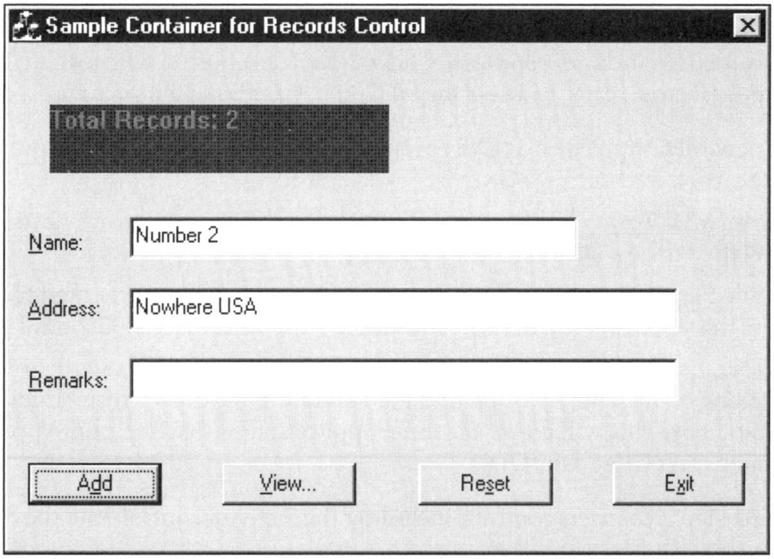

Figure 14-3. ActiveX control after adding second record

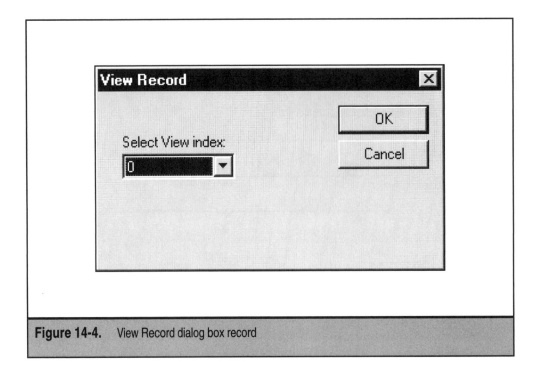

Figure 14-4. View Record dialog box record

Figure 14-5 shows the effect of clicking the Reset button. All the records are deleted (reset), and Total Records now shows 0. Clicking the View button will now have no effect. This application is created by use of the MFC AppWizard, and the steps are described here:

1. A new MFC AppWizard (EXE) project is created by specifying the project name (**Rec_cont**) and clicking OK.

2. In the MFC AppWizard—Step 1 dialog box—the type of the application is specified to be a Dialog Based Application.

3. In the Step 2 dialog box, the ActiveX Controls check box is checked to indicate that this application will need additional support for ActiveX controls.

4. The rest of the steps are defaulted, and the application framework is created by clicking on the Finish button and then on OK in the New Project Information dialog box. This will create the main application class **CRec_contApp** and a dialog class **CRec_contDlg**.

The next step is to insert controls, including the ActiveX control, into the dialog box:

1. The ResourceView tab is selected in the workspace window.

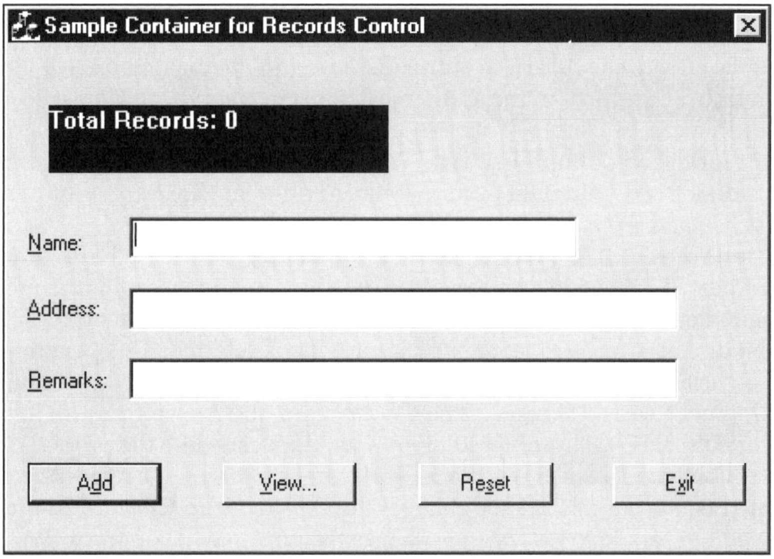

Figure 14-5.   Effect of resetting records

2. Expanding the resource tree, the IDD_REC_CONT_DIALOG dialog resource is double-clicked to open the dialog box.

3. The right mouse button is clicked on the dialog box to select the Insert ActiveX Control ("Insert OLE Control" in earlier versions of Visual C++) menu item. This will bring up the Insert ActiveX Control dialog box.

4. The Records Control ActiveX control is selected and OK is clicked. (Note if the ActiveX control developed earlier is not registered, then it will not appear in the list.) This will display the ActiveX control in the dialog box.

5. Three pairs of static and edit box controls, one each for Name, Address, and Remarks, are inserted in the dialog box. Four buttons—Add, View, Reset, and Exit—are also added.

When the container is operational, the user will be able to enter the name, address, and remark and click on the Add button to add the information to the address list. When information is added, the ActiveX control displayed in the dialog box will increment to show the number of records in the address list. If users want to view a particular record, the View button can be clicked. This will bring up a (yet to be defined) dialog box that will prompt for the record number. When a record number is specified, the control will update this dialog box with data from that record number. The Reset button will empty the address list, and the Exit button will close the application.

The ClassWizard is then invoked, and the type library of the ActiveX control created earlier is imported by clicking on the Add Class button and selecting the From A Type Library menu item. This brings up the Import From Type Library dialog box. Navigating through the directory, the *Rec_ax.tlb* type library file is selected. This generates the stub class or proxy class for the ActiveX control that is to be included in this container.

In the Member Variables page of the ClassWizard, the ActiveX control ID is selected to add a variable. MFC will prompt to insert a wrapper class into the project. When OK is selected, the Confirm Classes dialog box is displayed. The class name can be left alone to use the generated name, but this sample changes the class name to **CRecordControl**, changes the generated header file to *Recs.h*, and changes the implementation file to *Recs.cpp*. OK is selected. This will then bring up the Add Member Variable dialog box. The member variable is named **m_RecCtrl** and OK is selected. Member variables are also added for the Name, Address, and Remarks edit controls; for these the Control category is selected.

In the Message Maps tab of the ClassWizard dialog box, member functions are added for the BN_CLICKED message of the Add, View, and Reset buttons. The ActiveX control that was inserted into this dialog box can generate three messages (that were exposed when the control was created in the previous example). These messages are also handled. To do this, the ActiveX control ID is selected, and the individual messages are double-clicked. The ClassWizard brings up the Add Member Function panel with a suggested member function name. These suggested names are accepted.

The code related to this container application follows. Shown first is the main application class, **CRec_contApp**. There is nothing special in this code, and it is shown only for convenience. Notice the call to the **AfxEnableControlContainer** function in the application's **InitInstance** member function. This enables support to use ActiveX controls in the application.

```
// rec_cont.h : main header file for the REC_CONT application
//

#if !defined(AFX_REC_CONT_H)
#define AFX_REC_CONT_H

#if _MSC_VER >= 1000
#pragma once
#endif // _MSC_VER >= 1000
```

```
#ifndef __AFXWIN_H__
  #error include 'stdafx.h' before including this file for PCH
#endif

#include "resource.h"          // main symbols

/////////////////////////////////////////////////
// CRec_contApp:
// See rec_cont.cpp for the implementation of this class
//

class CRec_contApp : public CWinApp
{
public:
    CRec_contApp();

// Overrides
    // ClassWizard generated virtual function overrides
    //{{AFX_VIRTUAL(CRec_contApp)
    public:
    virtual BOOL InitInstance();
    //}}AFX_VIRTUAL

// Implementation

    //{{AFX_MSG(CRec_contApp)
    //}}AFX_MSG
    DECLARE_MESSAGE_MAP()
};


/////////////////////////////////////////////////

//{{AFX_INSERT_LOCATION}}

#endif

// rec_cont.cpp : Defines the class behaviors for the application.
//

#include "stdafx.h"
#include "rec_cont.h"
#include "rec_contDlg.h"
```

```
#ifdef _DEBUG
#define new DEBUG_NEW
#undef THIS_FILE
static char THIS_FILE[] = __FILE__;
#endif

/////////////////////////////////////////////////
// CRec_contApp

BEGIN_MESSAGE_MAP(CRec_contApp, CWinApp)
    //{{AFX_MSG_MAP(CRec_contApp)
    //}}AFX_MSG
    ON_COMMAND(ID_HELP, CWinApp::OnHelp)
END_MESSAGE_MAP()

/////////////////////////////////////////////////
// CRec_contApp construction

CRec_contApp::CRec_contApp()
{
    // TODO: add construction code here.
    // Place all significant initialization in InitInstance
}

/////////////////////////////////////////////////
// The one and only CRec_contApp object

CRec_contApp theApp;

/////////////////////////////////////////////////
// CRec_contApp initialization

BOOL CRec_contApp::InitInstance()
{
    AfxEnableControlContainer();


#ifdef _AFXDLL
    Enable3dControls();
#else
    Enable3dControlsStatic();
#endif
```

```
    CRec_contDlg dlg;
    m_pMainWnd = &dlg;
    int nResponse = dlg.DoModal();
    if (nResponse == IDOK)
    {
        // TODO: Place code here to handle when the dialog is
        //  dismissed with OK
    }
    else if (nResponse == IDCANCEL)
    {
        // TODO: Place code here to handle when the dialog is
        //  dismissed with Cancel
    }

// Since the dialog has been closed, return FALSE so that we exit the
//  application, rather than start the application's message pump.
    return FALSE;
}
```

Shown next is the code related to the main dialog box of the application. It contains both the code generated by the ClassWizard and the code added later to handle various user actions. The class header file is shown for completeness. Notice the inclusion of *Recs.h*, which has the wrapper class for the ActiveX control. The way MFC deals with the ActiveX control is to create an intermediate wrapper class; the interface to the ActiveX control is through this wrapper class. One added member function, **ChangeColor**, is used internally during the processing of other member functions.

```
// rec_contDlg.h : header file
//{{AFX_INCLUDES()
#include "recs.h"
//}}AFX_INCLUDES

#if !defined(AFX_REC_CONTDLG_H)
#define AFX_REC_CONTDLG_H

#if _MSC_VER >= 1000
#pragma once
#endif // _MSC_VER >= 1000


/////////////////////////////////////////////////
// CRec_contDlg dialog
class CRec_contDlg : public CDialog
{
// Construction
```

```
public:
        CRec_contDlg(CWnd* pParent = NULL);
// Dialog Data
        //{{AFX_DATA(CRec_contDlg)
        enum { IDD = IDD_REC_CONT_DIALOG };
        CEdit       m_Remarks;
        CEdit       m_Name;
        CEdit       m_Address;
        CRecordsControl        m_RecCtrl;
        //}}AFX_DATA

        // ClassWizard generated virtual function overrides
        //{{AFX_VIRTUAL(CRec_contDlg)
        protected:
        virtual void DoDataExchange(CDataExchange* pDX);
        //}}AFX_VIRTUAL

    void ChangeColor();

// Implementation
protected:
        HICON m_hIcon;

        // Generated message map functions
        //{{AFX_MSG(CRec_contDlg)
        virtual BOOL OnInitDialog();
        afx_msg void OnSysCommand(UINT nID, LPARAM lParam);
        afx_msg void OnPaint();
        afx_msg HCURSOR OnQueryDragIcon();
        afx_msg void OnBtnadd();
        afx_msg void OnBtnreset();
        afx_msg void OnBtnview();
        afx_msg void OnNameChangedRecordsctrl1
                        (LPCTSTR NewName);
        afx_msg void OnAddressChangedRecordsctrl1
                        (LPCTSTR NewAddress);
        afx_msg void OnRemarksChangedRecordsctrl1
                        (LPCTSTR NewRemarks);
        DECLARE_EVENTSINK_MAP()
        //}}AFX_MSG
        DECLARE_MESSAGE_MAP()
};
```

```
//{{AFX_INSERT_LOCATION}}
#endif //
```

The implementation file follows.

```
// rec_contDlg.cpp : implementation file
//
#include "stdafx.h"
#include "rec_cont.h"
#include "rec_contDlg.h"
#include "viewdlg.h"

#ifdef _DEBUG
#define new DEBUG_NEW
#undef THIS_FILE
static char THIS_FILE[] = __FILE__;
#endif

/////////////////////////////////////////////////
// CAboutDlg dialog used for App About

class CAboutDlg : public CDialog
{
public:
        CAboutDlg();

// Dialog Data
        //{{AFX_DATA(CAboutDlg)
        enum { IDD = IDD_ABOUTBOX };
        //}}AFX_DATA

        // ClassWizard generated virtual function overrides
        //{{AFX_VIRTUAL(CAboutDlg)
        protected:
        virtual void DoDataExchange(CDataExchange* pDX);
        //}}AFX_VIRTUAL

// Implementation
protected:
        //{{AFX_MSG(CAboutDlg)
        //}}AFX_MSG
```

```
                DECLARE_MESSAGE_MAP()
};

CAboutDlg::CAboutDlg() : CDialog(CAboutDlg::IDD)
{
        //{{AFX_DATA_INIT(CAboutDlg)
        //}}AFX_DATA_INIT
}

void CAboutDlg::DoDataExchange(CDataExchange* pDX)
{
        CDialog::DoDataExchange(pDX);
        //{{AFX_DATA_MAP(CAboutDlg)
        //}}AFX_DATA_MAP
}

BEGIN_MESSAGE_MAP(CAboutDlg, CDialog)
        //{{AFX_MSG_MAP(CAboutDlg)
                // No message handlers
        //}}AFX_MSG_MAP
END_MESSAGE_MAP()

/////////////////////////////////////////////////
// CRec_contDlg dialog

CRec_contDlg::CRec_contDlg(CWnd* pParent /*=NULL*/)
        : CDialog(CRec_contDlg::IDD, pParent)
{
        //{{AFX_DATA_INIT(CRec_contDlg)
        //}}AFX_DATA_INIT

        m_hIcon = AfxGetApp()->LoadIcon(IDR_MAINFRAME);
}

void CRec_contDlg::DoDataExchange(CDataExchange* pDX)
{
        CDialog::DoDataExchange(pDX);
        //{{AFX_DATA_MAP(CRec_contDlg)
        DDX_Control(pDX, IDC_EDITREMARKS, m_Remarks);
        DDX_Control(pDX, IDC_EDITNAME, m_Name);
        DDX_Control(pDX, IDC_EDITADDRESS, m_Address);
        DDX_Control(pDX, IDC_RECORDSCTRL1, m_RecCtrl);
        //}}AFX_DATA_MAP
}
```

```
BEGIN_MESSAGE_MAP(CRec_contDlg, CDialog)
        //{{AFX_MSG_MAP(CRec_contDlg)
        ON_WM_SYSCOMMAND()
        ON_WM_PAINT()
        ON_WM_QUERYDRAGICON()
        ON_BN_CLICKED(IDC_BTNADD, OnBtnadd)
        ON_BN_CLICKED(IDC_BTNRESET, OnBtnreset)
        ON_BN_CLICKED(IDC_BTNVIEW, OnBtnview)
        //}}AFX_MSG_MAP
END_MESSAGE_MAP()

/////////////////////////////////////////////////
// CRec_contDlg message handlers

BOOL CRec_contDlg::OnInitDialog()
{
        CDialog::OnInitDialog();

        // Add "About..." menu item to system menu.

        // IDM_ABOUTBOX must be in the system command range.
        ASSERT((IDM_ABOUTBOX & 0xFFF0) == IDM_ABOUTBOX);
        ASSERT(IDM_ABOUTBOX < 0xF000);

        CMenu* pSysMenu = GetSystemMenu(FALSE);
        if (pSysMenu != NULL)
        {
                CString strAboutMenu;
                strAboutMenu.LoadString(IDS_ABOUTBOX);
                if (!strAboutMenu.IsEmpty())
                {
                        pSysMenu->AppendMenu(MF_SEPARATOR);
                        pSysMenu->AppendMenu(MF_STRING, IDM_ABOUTBOX,
                                strAboutMenu);
                }
        }

        // Set the icon for this dialog.  The framework does this automatically
        //  when the application's main window is not a dialog
        SetIcon(m_hIcon, TRUE);
        SetIcon(m_hIcon, FALSE);
```

```
        // TODO: Add extra initialization here

        return TRUE;
}

void CRec_contDlg::OnSysCommand(UINT nID, LPARAM lParam)
{
        if ((nID & 0xFFF0) == IDM_ABOUTBOX)
        {
                CAboutDlg dlgAbout;
                dlgAbout.DoModal();
        }
        else
        {
            CDialog::OnSysCommand(nID, lParam);
    }
}


void CRec_contDlg::OnPaint()
{
    if (IsIconic())
    {
        CPaintDC dc(this); // device context for painting

        SendMessage(WM_ICONERASEBKGND, (WPARAM) dc.GetSafeHdc(), 0);

        // Center icon in client rectangle
        int cxIcon = GetSystemMetrics(SM_CXICON);
        int cyIcon = GetSystemMetrics(SM_CYICON);
        CRect rect;
        GetClientRect(&rect);
        int x = (rect.Width() - cxIcon + 1) / 2;
        int y = (rect.Height() - cyIcon + 1) / 2;

        // Draw the icon
        dc.DrawIcon(x, y, m_hIcon);
    }
    else
    {
        CDialog::OnPaint();
```

```
    }
}

// The system calls this to obtain the cursor to display while the
// user drags the minimized window.
HCURSOR CRec_contDlg::OnQueryDragIcon()
{
    return (HCURSOR) m_hIcon;
}
```

When the Add button is pressed, the message is processed by the **OnBtnadd** member function. During the processing, the name, address, and the remark are picked up from the dialog box and are passed on to the ActiveX control through the **SetName**, **SetAddress**, and **SetRemarks** member functions of the ActiveX control's wrapper class, which was generated by MFC. This wrapper class, as you may recall, is defined in the *Recs.h* and *Recs.cpp* modules. These **Set** functions set the properties of the control. Earlier, when the ActiveX control was created, it was created such that every time one of these properties was set, an event was fired. The firing, you may recall, was directed to be handled by **On*ChangedRecordsctrl1** functions (where * is either **Name**, **Address**, or **Remarks**) when the message map for the ActiveX control (IDC_RECORDSCTRL1) was defined. Notice in the code that the **On*ChangedRecordsctrl1** functions call the **ChangeColor** member function, which changes the foreground and the background stock property of this ActiveX control. Thus, for every addition of the record, the color stock property is changed thrice, once each for the Name, Address, and the Remarks. This is an overkill for this application, but shows the ability to handle the firing at the property level. With the change in the foreground and the background color, the ActiveX control will paint the text in two different colors.

```
void CRec_contDlg::OnBtnadd()
{
    // TODO: Add your control notification handler code here
    CString sName, sAddr, sRem;
    m_Name.GetWindowText(sName);
    m_Address.GetWindowText(sAddr);
    m_Remarks.GetWindowText(sRem);
    m_RecCtrl.SetName( sName );
    m_RecCtrl.SetAddress( sAddr );
    m_RecCtrl.SetRemarks( sRem );
    m_RecCtrl.Add();
}
Clicking on the Reset button invokes the Reset method of the ActiveX control.
```

```
void CRec_contDlg::OnBtnreset()
{
    // TODO: Add your control notification handler code here
    m_RecCtrl.Reset();
}
```

When the View button is clicked, the application should present the number of records available in the address list to the user in a combo box in a separate View dialog box. The user can then select the record number that the user wants to view. Upon return from the View dialog box, that record is presented to the user. This is handled by the **OnBtnview** member function.

The total number of records is queried by calling the **GetCount** method of the ActiveX control, and it is passed to the View dialog box. The user's selection is maintained in a member variable of the View class, which is used to get the data and display it in the dialog box.

```
void CRec_contDlg::OnBtnview()
{
    // TODO: Add your control notification handler code here
    int cnt = m_RecCtrl.GetCount();
    if ( cnt <= 0 )
       return;
    CViewDlg* pViewDlg = new CViewDlg( cnt-1, this );
     int nResponse = pViewDlg->DoModal();
     if (nResponse == IDOK)
     {
         m_RecCtrl.View( pViewDlg->m_ViewIdx );
       m_Name.SetWindowText(m_RecCtrl.GetName());
       m_Address.SetWindowText(m_RecCtrl.GetAddress());
       m_Remarks.SetWindowText(m_RecCtrl.GetRemarks());
     }
    delete pViewDlg;
}


BEGIN_EVENTSINK_MAP(CRec_contDlg, CDialog)
    //{{AFX_EVENTSINK_MAP(CRec_contDlg)
    ON_EVENT(CRec_contDlg, IDC_RECORDSCTRL1, 1 /* NameChanged */,
            OnNameChangedRecordsctrl1, VTS_BSTR)
    ON_EVENT(CRec_contDlg, IDC_RECORDSCTRL1, 2 /* AddressChanged */,
            OnAddressChangedRecordsctrl1, VTS_BSTR)
    ON_EVENT(CRec_contDlg, IDC_RECORDSCTRL1, 3 /* RemarksChanged */,
            OnRemarksChangedRecordsctrl1, VTS_BSTR)
    //}}AFX_EVENTSINK_MAP
END_EVENTSINK_MAP()
```

```
void CRec_contDlg::OnNameChangedRecordsctrl1(LPCTSTR NewName)
{
    // TODO: Add your control notification handler code here
    ChangeColor();
}

void CRec_contDlg::OnAddressChangedRecordsctrl1(LPCTSTR NewAddress)
{
    // TODO: Add your control notification handler code here
    ChangeColor();
}

void CRec_contDlg::OnRemarksChangedRecordsctrl1(LPCTSTR NewRemarks)
{
    // TODO: Add your control notification handler code here
    ChangeColor();
}
void CRec_contDlg::ChangeColor()
{
    static char i=0;
    if ( i )
    {
        m_RecCtrl.SetBackColor( RGB(0,100,0) );
        m_RecCtrl.SetForeColor( RGB(100,0,0) );
        i=0;
    }
    else
    {
        m_RecCtrl.SetBackColor( RGB(0,0,80) );
        m_RecCtrl.SetForeColor( RGB(120,120,0) );
        i=1;

    }
}
```

The code for the View dialog box is shown here. The constructor takes the number of records in the address list. A member variable, **m_ViewIdx**, is used to keep trace of the selection made by the user.

```
#if !defined(AFX_VIEWDLG_H)
#define AFX_VIEWDLG_H

#if _MSC_VER >= 1000
```

```
#pragma once
#endif // _MSC_VER >= 1000
// ViewDlg.h : header file
//

/////////////////////////////////////////////////////
// CViewDlg dialog

class CViewDlg : public CDialog
{
// Construction
public:
    CViewDlg(int MaxViewIdx, CWnd* pParent = NULL);

// Dialog Data
    //{{AFX_DATA(CViewDlg)
    enum { IDD = IDD_VIEWDLG };
    int       m_ViewIdx;
    //}}AFX_DATA


// Overrides
    // ClassWizard generated virtual function overrides
    //{{AFX_VIRTUAL(CViewDlg)
    protected:
    virtual void DoDataExchange(CDataExchange* pDX);
    //}}AFX_VIRTUAL

// Implementation
protected:

    // Generated message map functions
    //{{AFX_MSG(CViewDlg)
    virtual void OnOK();
    virtual void OnCancel();
    virtual BOOL OnInitDialog();
    //}}AFX_MSG
    DECLARE_MESSAGE_MAP()

private:
    int m_MaxViewIdx;
};

//{{AFX_INSERT_LOCATION}}
```

```
#endif //
```

The implementation file is shown next. The integer passed in the constructor is used to initialize the combo box list during the dialog initialization, **OnInitDialog**. The selection in the combo box is handled through **DDX_CBIndex**, which transfers the index to the member variable **m_ViewIdx**. Since the index is also the record number in the address list, this works well for this application.

```
// ViewDlg.cpp : implementation file
//

#include "stdafx.h"
#include "rec_cont.h"
#include "ViewDlg.h"

#ifdef _DEBUG
#define new DEBUG_NEW
#undef THIS_FILE
static char THIS_FILE[] = __FILE__;
#endif

/////////////////////////////////////////////////
// CViewDlg dialog


CViewDlg::CViewDlg(int MaxViewIdx, CWnd* pParent /*=NULL*/)
    : CDialog(CViewDlg::IDD, pParent)
{
    //{{AFX_DATA_INIT(CViewDlg)
    m_ViewIdx = -1;
    //}}AFX_DATA_INIT
    ASSERT( MaxViewIdx >= 0 );
    m_MaxViewIdx = MaxViewIdx;
}



void CViewDlg::DoDataExchange(CDataExchange* pDX)
{
    CDialog::DoDataExchange(pDX);
    //{{AFX_DATA_MAP(CViewDlg)
    DDX_CBIndex(pDX, IDC_VIEWIDX, m_ViewIdx);
    //}}AFX_DATA_MAP
```

```
}


BEGIN_MESSAGE_MAP(CViewDlg, CDialog)
    //{{AFX_MSG_MAP(CViewDlg)
    //}}AFX_MSG_MAP
END_MESSAGE_MAP()


/////////////////////////////////////////////////
// CViewDlg message handlers

void CViewDlg::OnOK()
{
    // TODO: Add extra validation here

    CDialog::OnOK();
}

void CViewDlg::OnCancel()
{
    // TODO: Add extra cleanup here

    CDialog::OnCancel();
}

BOOL CViewDlg::OnInitDialog()
{
    CDialog::OnInitDialog();

    // TODO: Add extra initialization here
    CComboBox* pCBox = (CComboBox*)GetDlgItem( IDC_VIEWIDX );
    int i;
    char buf[10];
    for (i=0; i<=m_MaxViewIdx; i++)
    {
        sprintf( buf, "%d", i );
        pCBox->AddString( buf );
    }
    pCBox->SetCurSel(0);

     return TRUE; }
```

ACTIVEX CONTROL SECURITY

As mentioned at the beginning of this chapter, an ActiveX control you develop may access the local resources such as the file system on the local computer to which it is downloaded. Similarly, an ActiveX control you download to your computer may access your computer's resources. Thus, there is a potential for damage in both situations, and you have to take extra precautions to ensure that the control does not create any damage. One of the obvious possibilities is that a virus could be passed in an ActiveX control. As an author of an ActiveX control, you can *sign* a control, which lets the users of your control know that the control was signed by use of a certificate dialog box when the control is downloaded. You can also *mark* your control. You can mark your control as safe for initializing. You can also mark your control as safe for scripting. Signing and marking are independent steps. As a user downloads an ActiveX control, a certificate dialog box assures that the control has been signed. A marked control implies that the author deems it is safe for initializing and/or scripting. Let's first look at signing and marking from a developer's perspective. Then we will look at signing and marking from a user's perspective.

Signing an ActiveX Control

An ActiveX control can be signed either individually (by the developer) or by a company. In either case, a *certificate* is required. A certificate can be obtained from a certificate authority such as VeriSign (you can find more details at **http://digitalid.verisign. com/codesign.htm**). VeriSign verifies data about the individual or corporation before issuing a certificate. Individuals are issued Class 2 certificates, and corporations are issued Class 3 certificates. There is a yearly fee associated with the certificates.

Once a certificate is obtained, you can sign a control using the SIGNCODE program included with the ActiveX SDK. Note that you have to sign a control every time you modify the control. You do not have to sign a control if your company handles this.

Signing is thus a way for a control user to trace back to the individual or corporation that developed or is responsible for the control.

Marking an ActiveX Control

As a developer you mark a control to let a user of your control know that your control can be safely initialized and/or scripted. There is no way to specify that your control is safe for specific environments such as specific web browsers. Once a control is marked safe, it is presumed safe in all environments in which the control could be used. This may require some extra testing and validation on your part before you can mark a control.

You can mark a control by adding entries to the Registry manually or by letting the control add the Registry entries when the control registers itself or by using the **IObjectSafety** OLE interface. For more details on how to mark a control using each of the preceding methods and for an overall description of signing and marking ActiveX controls, refer to an excellent article available from Microsoft at **http://www.microsoft. com/intdev/controls/signmark.htm**.

Using Signed and Marked ActiveX Controls

Now let's look at signing and marking from a user's perspective. We will take the example of an ActiveX control being downloaded using the Internet Explorer. Internet Explorer provides three security levels—high, medium, and none. High is the default. Table 14-2 summarizes the results when an ActiveX control with initialization and scripting is downloaded by Internet Explorer.

Internet Explorer Security Setting	Unsigned/ Unmarked	Signed, Not Marked	Signed and Marked
High	This downloads but does not display the control; it prevents the control from being used. This displays a dialog box asking the user to change security settings.	This downloads the control and displays a certificate. The control will run without initialization and without scripting.	This downloads the control and displays a certificate. The control will run with initialization and scripting.
Medium	This downloads and provides an option to the user to install the control.	This user is provided with separate options to accept the control without marking for initialization and scripting.	This control will run with initialization and scripting.
None	There is no warning dialog box. The control will run with initialization and scripting.		

Table 14-2.   ActiveX Controls and Internet Explorer

Now let's take a look at an ActiveX security programming example.

PROGRAMMING EXAMPLE TO ILLUSTRATE SIGNING AND MARKING ACTIVEX CONTROLS

The following code shows how to mark an ActiveX control. It takes the control developed earlier and adds code to mark the control during registration. The code that has been added to the control developed earlier is highlighted here. Part of the code that did not change is not shown here.

```
// RecordsCtl.cpp : Implementation of the
// CRecordsCtrl ActiveX Control class.

#include "stdafx.h"
#include "rec_ax.h"
#include "RecordsCtl.h"
#include "RecordsPpg.h"

#ifdef _DEBUG
#define new DEBUG_NEW
#undef THIS_FILE
static char THIS_FILE[] = __FILE__;
#endif


IMPLEMENT_DYNCREATE(CRecordsCtrl, COleControl)


/////////////////////////////////////////////////
// Message map

BEGIN_MESSAGE_MAP(CRecordsCtrl, COleControl)
    //{{AFX_MSG_MAP(CRecordsCtrl)
    ON_WM_CREATE()
    //}}AFX_MSG_MAP
    ON_OLEVERB(AFX_IDS_VERB_PROPERTIES, OnProperties)
END_MESSAGE_MAP()


/////////////////////////////////////////////////
// Dispatch map
```

```
BEGIN_DISPATCH_MAP(CRecordsCtrl, COleControl)
    //{{AFX_DISPATCH_MAP(CRecordsCtrl)
    DISP_PROPERTY_NOTIFY(CRecordsCtrl, "Name", m_name,
                        OnNameChanged, VT_BSTR)
    DISP_PROPERTY_NOTIFY(CRecordsCtrl, "Address", m_address,
                        OnAddressChanged, VT_BSTR)
    DISP_PROPERTY_NOTIFY(CRecordsCtrl, "Remarks", m_remarks,
                        OnRemarksChanged, VT_BSTR)
    DISP_FUNCTION(CRecordsCtrl, "View", View, VT_EMPTY, VTS_I2)
    DISP_FUNCTION(CRecordsCtrl, "Reset", Reset, VT_EMPTY,
                    VTS_NONE)
    DISP_FUNCTION(CRecordsCtrl, "Add", Add, VT_EMPTY, VTS_NONE)
    DISP_FUNCTION(CRecordsCtrl, "GetCount", GetCount, VT_I2,
                    VTS_NONE)
    DISP_STOCKPROP_BACKCOLOR()
    DISP_STOCKPROP_FORECOLOR()
    //}}AFX_DISPATCH_MAP
    DISP_FUNCTION_ID(CRecordsCtrl, "AboutBox", DISPID_ABOUTBOX,
                    AboutBox, VT_EMPTY, VTS_NONE)
END_DISPATCH_MAP()


/////////////////////////////////////////////////
// Event map

BEGIN_EVENT_MAP(CRecordsCtrl, COleControl)
    //{{AFX_EVENT_MAP(CRecordsCtrl)
    EVENT_CUSTOM("NameChanged", FireNameChanged, VTS_BSTR)
    EVENT_CUSTOM("AddressChanged", FireAddressChanged, VTS_BSTR)
    EVENT_CUSTOM("RemarksChanged", FireRemarksChanged, VTS_BSTR)
    //}}AFX_EVENT_MAP
END_EVENT_MAP()


/////////////////////////////////////////////////
// Property pages

// TODO: Add more property pages as needed.
//   Remember to increase the count!
BEGIN_PROPPAGEIDS(CRecordsCtrl, 2)
    PROPPAGEID(CRecordsPropPage::guid)
    PROPPAGEID(CLSID_CColorPropPage)
END_PROPPAGEIDS(CRecordsCtrl)
```

```
/////////////////////////////////////////////////
// Initialize class factory and guid

IMPLEMENT_OLECREATE_EX(CRecordsCtrl, "RECAX.RecordsCtrl.1",
  0xe150326f, 0xebda,0x11d0,0xa9,0xee,0x9,0x92,0,0x54,0,0x30)
```

Marking the ActiveX control is essentially adding entries in the Registry. When the control is registered, the following three keys are added to the Registry. Adding these keys to the Registry would indicate the control is marked and would suppress the security warnings that Microsoft Internet Explorer would prompt.

```
#define MARKINGKEY  \
"CLSID\\{E150326F-EBDA-11D0-A9EE-099200540030}\\Implemented Categories\\"
#define MARKSAFEINIT "{7DD95802-9882-11CF-9FA9-00AA006C42C4}"
#define MARKSAFESCRIPT "{7DD95801-9882-11CF-9FA9-00AA006C42C4}"
```

The CLSID of the ActiveX control may be obtained by the Registry using OLE/COM viewer (*Oleview.exe*). As part of the marking, a new key called *Implemented Categories* is created under the ActiveX control's CLSID. Under Implemented Categories two keys are created, one to mark the control as safe for data initialization, and the other to mark it as safe for scripting. These keys are defined in **MAKESAFEINIT** and **MAKESAFESCRIPT**, and they should be exactly as they appear.

```
// Type library ID and version

IMPLEMENT_OLETYPELIB(CRecordsCtrl, _tlid, _wVerMajor, _wVerMinor)

// Interface IDs
const IID BASED_CODE IID_DRecords =
        { 0xe150326d, 0xebda, 0x11d0, { 0xa9, 0xee,
          0x9, 0x92, 0, 0x54, 0, 0x30 } };
const IID BASED_CODE IID_DRecordsEvents =
        { 0xe150326e, 0xebda, 0x11d0, { 0xa9, 0xee,
          0x9, 0x92, 0, 0x54, 0, 0x30 } };


/////////////////////////////////////////////////
// Control type information

static const DWORD BASED_CODE _dwRecordsOleMisc =
    OLEMISC_ACTIVATEWHENVISIBLE |
    OLEMISC_SETCLIENTSITEFIRST |
    OLEMISC_INSIDEOUT |
```

```
        OLEMISC_CANTLINKINSIDE |
        OLEMISC_RECOMPOSEONRESIZE;

IMPLEMENT_OLECTLTYPE(CRecordsCtrl, IDS_RECORDS,
                    _dwRecordsOleMisc)


// CRecordsCtrl::CRecordsCtrlFactory::UpdateRegistry -
// Adds or removes system registry entries for CRecordsCtrl

BOOL CRecordsCtrl::CRecordsCtrlFactory::
                    UpdateRegistry(BOOL bRegister)
{
    if (bRegister)
    {
      BOOL brc =
          AfxOleRegisterControlClass(
            AfxGetInstanceHandle(),
            m_clsid,
            m_lpszProgID,
            IDS_RECORDS,
            IDB_RECORDS,
            afxRegApartmentThreading,
            _dwRecordsOleMisc,
            _tlid,
            _wVerMajor,
            _wVerMinor);

        // mark our ActiveX control as safe for MSIE
        /* Create or just open the key... */
        HKEY hRegistryKey;
        DWORD dwDisposition;
        CString sMarking = MARKINGKEY;
        sMarking += MARKSAFEINIT;
        long lRc = RegCreateKeyEx( HKEY_CLASSES_ROOT,
                        sMarking,
                        0L,
                        "",
                        REG_OPTION_NON_VOLATILE,
                        KEY_ALL_ACCESS,
                        NULL,
                        &hRegistryKey,
                        &dwDisposition  );
        if ( lRc != ERROR_SUCCESS )
```

```
   {
      AfxMessageBox( "Failed to register implemented categories"
                     " for safe initialization." );
   }
   else
      RegCloseKey( hRegistryKey );

   sMarking = MARKINGKEY;
   sMarking += MARKSAFESCRIPT;
   lRc = RegCreateKeyEx( HKEY_CLASSES_ROOT,
                         sMarking,
                         0L,
                         "",
                         REG_OPTION_NON_VOLATILE,
                         KEY_ALL_ACCESS,
                         NULL,
                         &hRegistryKey,
                         &dwDisposition  );
   if ( lRc != ERROR_SUCCESS )
   {
      AfxMessageBox( "Failed to register implemented categories"
                     " for safe scripting." );
   }
   else
      RegCloseKey( hRegistryKey );

   return brc;
}
 else
    return AfxOleUnregisterClass(m_clsid, m_lpszProgID);
}
```

The rest of the code remains unchanged and is not shown.

ACTIVEX CONTROL TIPS

Keep the following tips in mind when you are designing and developing ActiveX controls:

▼ Keep the buttons and other control elements as small as possible. This helps in faster downloading when your controls are used in web-based environments.

■ It is not always possible to restrict the ActiveX control to have just small control elements, and you will need to deal with BLOBs, such as bitmap images or AVI files. In such cases, structure the control and the container application so that the user does not have to wait for the complete downloading of images or video data, by incrementally retrieving the data and overlapping asynchronous data retrieval with user interaction. To download control properties asynchronously, you can click the Loads Properties Asynchronously button in the Advanced ActiveX Features dialog box of the ControlWizard.

■ For really large downloads, try to indicate the progress and expected completion time to the user.

■ Building and displaying a window is very time-consuming. Keep in mind that your ActiveX control does not need its own window. Your control can be set up for windowless activation. Your control can use the container's window services if appropriate.

■ Many times the control needs its own window. However, by default, the entire control area is painted. You can speed up repainting by repainting only what is required with the control's **OnDraw** function.

■ Quite often there is a requirement for the control to be drawn in both screen and metafile DCs. To facilitate the drawing in both DCs, make sure that you only use member functions supported in both DCs, and keep in mind that the coordinate system may not be using pixels.

■ You can make your ActiveX control user friendly by providing context-sensitive help for the control's property, event, and so on, by modifying the ODL file for the control.

▲ If your control is drawn exactly the same way when it is active or inactive, then you can eliminate the redrawing of the control at state transitions. This not only saves some processing and time, but it also avoids the flicker that accompanies redrawing the control. You can specify the Flicker-free Activation option in the Advanced ActiveX features page of ControlWizard or specify it programmatically by setting the noFlickerActivate flag in the flags returned by **GetControlFlags**.

Conclusion

In this chapter, we built upon ActiveX controls, introduced in Chapter 12. We discussed ActiveX control properties, methods, and events. We looked at a programming example where we created an ActiveX control. We also examined containers and a container programming example. We looked at ways to improve the security aspects of using ActiveX controls, such as signing and marking ActiveX controls, and discussed a related programming example.

In the next chapter, we will look at another common Windows NT communication mechanism—sockets.

WINDOWS
NT
Professional
Library

CHAPTER 15

Windows Sockets

ontinuing our communications focus, let's look at one of the most important communications programming mechanisms Windows NT provides—Windows Sockets (WinSock).

In this chapter, we will look at Windows Sockets programming using the WinSock APIs. We will also look at MFC library support for Windows Sockets. Sockets programming sometimes involves communicating between computers with different architectures, which introduces some unique issues. We will cover these issues. We will also look at a sample socket program using WinSock APIs. The CD accompanying this book has two additional socket examples based on MFC.

SOCKET BASICS

A *socket* is a communications endpoint. Since the typical communication is between a client and a server, there are two endpoints, one at the client end and the other at the server end. Correspondingly, there are two sockets and the two sockets make up a connection for two-way transfer of data between the client and the server.

We looked at the OSI 7 layer communications model in Chapter 3, in particular Figure 3-1, which shows how the communication functions in Windows NT map to the OSI model. Note that WinSock fits in at the session level. As specified in the model, each layer is built on top of the functions provided in the layers below it. The WinSock layer, for example, uses the transport layer protocols such as Transmission Control Protocol (TCP), which in turn uses network layer protocols such as Internet Protocol (IP). For simplicity, the protocols are combined and we specify that WinSock uses TCP/IP. TCP/IP is not the only protocol supported by Windows Sockets. Windows Sockets provides a communications programming mechanism that you can use to develop applications that are independent of network specifics such as protocols. In fact, Windows Sockets also supports Novell's IPX/SPX, Digital's DECnet, and other protocols besides TCP/IP.

There are basically two types of sockets—a stream socket and a datagram socket. *Stream sockets* are used for the bidirectional transmission of a large stream of data. The data stream could be record streams or byte streams, depending on the protocol. Streams are normally used for transmitting and receiving date that is *unduplicated* (packets are sent and received only once) and *sequenced* (the order in which the data packets are sent is preserved). Stream sockets guarantee data delivery. *Datagram sockets* are used primarily for broadcast functions.

Your socket application will use a *port* to communicate with another socket application. There could be multiple communication functions being carried on in different windows simultaneously. For example, the user may be performing FTP in one window while running your socket application or another communication program in another. A mechanism is necessary to ensure that data of your application is not mixed up with the data of the FTP application. The mechanism that ensures the separation is the port. Common communication functions such as FTP use a reserved port (reserved ports are listed in *Winsock2.h*). You can specify a port that is not a reserved port and is not being used, or you can let a port be assigned for you by passing zero as the port value.

Each socket also has a socket address, which typically is the IP address of the machine your application is running on (unless the machine your application is running on uses multiple network cards for connecting to different networks).

Each socket has a handle, and Windows defines a special data type—called SOCKET—for the handle. The SOCKET handle is conceptually the same as the HWND handle for a window. Each socket also operates in one of two modes—blocking mode or nonblocking mode. Blocking is discussed later in the section "Blocking."

As with many other areas of Windows programming, you can program Windows Sockets using APIs or the MFC library. The APIs used for programming Windows Sockets functions are collectively called the WinSock APIs.

WINSOCK APIs

Windows NT actually provides 44 socket-related API functions, which can be grouped into four categories as follows:

▼ Database functions

■ Socket functions

■ Conversion functions

▲ Extension functions

The socket APIs are implemented as DLLs. *Winsock.dll* is the 16-bit version, and *Wsock32.dll* is the 32-bit version used by Windows Sockets version 1.1 applications. *WS2_32.dll* is used by Sockets version 2 applications. Let's look at socket functions in greater detail.

Socket Database Functions

The socket database functions provide the ability for your socket application to retrieve information about a computer that you want to communicate with, a protocol (such as TCP or UDP), or a service.

Socket database functions are part of the so-called "getXbyY" function family (except **GetHostName**). You get information about X (which could be a host, protocol, or service)

Note for UNIX Programmers

Many UNIX systems support sockets. Windows Sockets is based on Berkeley Software Distribution (BSD) sockets. If you have programmed using sockets in the UNIX environment, the concepts are pretty much the same for Windows Sockets. There are differences in the detail, however. For example, in UNIX, socket descriptors are file descriptors, while Windows uses a special data type (SOCKETS). UNIX socket

by providing Y (which could be a name, address, port, and so on). Socket database functions are summarized in Table 15-1.

Socket Conversion Functions

When you write socket applications that communicate across machines with different architectures or where the byte order of the data in the network is different from that of the host computer your application is running on, you need conversion routines to convert data from host byte order to network byte order and vice versa. You can write your own conversion routines, but it is easier to use the built-in conversion functions. See the section "Byte Ordering" later in this chapter for more details about byte-order differences and a list of conversion functions.

Socket Database Function	Description
gethostbyaddr	This gets information about a host computer using its IP address. This function progressively checks the local computer, checks a HOSTS file, queries a DNS server, and tries NETBIOS name resolution to locate a host computer with the given address.
gethostbyname	This gets information about a host using its name. This function checks the local computer, checks a HOSTS file, queries a DNS server, and tries NETBIOS name resolution to locate a host computer with the given name.
gethostname	This gets the name of the local host computer.
getprotobyname	This gets information about a protocol using the name of the protocol.
getprotobynumber	This gets information about a protocol using the number or ID of the protocol.
getservbyname	This gets information about a service using the name of the service.
getservbyport	This gets information about a service using a port number.

Table 15-1. Socket Database Functions

Socket Extensions

When Microsoft developed its Windows Sockets based on BSD sockets, it added an important variation to handle asynchronous communication. Besides the GUI, one of the features that sets Windows apart from other operating systems is its message-driven architecture. Message handling is essentially asynchronous in nature. Your application, for example, has a message queue that gets messages posted asynchronously while some other part of your application is executing. Microsoft extended the asynchronous notion to sockets and defined a set of extension functions to sockets that provide asynchronous access to network events as well as provide overlapped I/O. These extension functions are summarized in Table 15-2.

Socket Extension Function	Description
WSAAccept	This is an extended version of the accept function.
WSAAsyncGetHostByAddr	This is an async version of GetHostByAddr. (Refer to the socket database functions for this and other "getXbyY" functions.)
WSAAsyncGetHostByName	This is an async version of GetHostByName.
WSAAsyncGetProtoByName	This is an async version of GetProtoByName.
WSAAsyncGetProtoByNumber	This is an async version of GetProtoByNumber.
WSAAsyncGetServByName	This is an async version of GetServByName.
WSAAsyncGetServByPort	This is an async version of GetServByPort.
WSAAsyncSelect	This is an async version of the select function.
WSACancelAsyncRequest	This cancels an outstanding WSAAsyncGetXByY function call.
WSACleanup	This ends the use of underlying DLL (*WS2_32.dll*).
WSACloseEvent	This closes an event object's handle.
WSAConnect	This is an extended version of the connect function. It establishes an active connection for stream sockets and establishes a default destination address for datagram sockets.

Table 15-2. Socket Extensions

Socket Extension Function	Description
WSACreateEvent	This creates an event object and gets its handle.
WSADuplicateSocket	This enables a socket to be shared between processes.
WSAEnumNetworkEvents	This discovers occurrences of network events for a socket since the previous invocation of WSAEnumNetworkEvents.
WSAEnumProtocols	This retrieves information about available protocols in the local computer.
WSAEventSelect	This associates network events with an event object. The event object is signaled when the network events occur.
WSAGetLastError	This gets the details of the error that occurred during the last socket operation. Do not use this function to check for an error on receipt of an asynchronous message (use the *lParam* field of the message instead).
WSAGetOverlappedResult	This gets the result of the last overlapped operation on the socket.
WSAGetQOSByName	This initializes quality of service (QOS) parameters based on a template.
WSAHtonl	This is an extended version of htonl; see Table 15-3 for a description of htonl.
WSAHtons	This is an extended version of htons; see Table 15-3 for a description of htons.
WSAIoctl	This is an extended version of ioctl capable of handling overlapped sockets.
WSAJoinLeaf	This joins a leaf node to a multipoint session.
WSANtohl	This is an extended version of ntohl; see Table 15-3 for a description of ntohl.

Table 15-2. Socket Extensions (*continued*)

Socket Extension Function	Description
WSANtohs	This is an extended version of ntohs; see Table 15-3 for a description of ntohs.
WSARecv	This is an extended version of **recv** that allows multiple buffers for scatter/gather I/O, supports overlapped sockets, and provides the flags parameter for both input and output.
WSARecvFrom	This is an extended version of RecvFrom that allows multiple buffers for scatter/gather I/O, supports overlapped sockets, and provides the flags parameter for both input and output.
WSAResetEvent	This resets an event object to not signaled.
WSASend	This is an extended version of the send function. that allows multiple buffers for scatter/gather I/O and supports overlapped sockets.
WSASendTo	This is an extended version of SendTo that allows multiple buffers for scatter/gather I/O and supports overlapped sockets.
WSASetEvent	This sets an event object to signaled.
WSASetLastError	This sets the error code. (The error code is returned by WSAGetLastError; see WSAGetLastError in this table.)
WSASocket	This is an extended version of the socket function. It supports overlapped sockets and allows the socket to create or join a socket group.
WSAStartup	This is the first sockets call your application issues to initialize the sockets DLL; you can specify the desired sockets version.
WSAWaitForMultipleEvents	This waits for multiple event objects to be signaled.

Table 15-2.   Socket Extensions (*continued*)

> ***TIP:***   Do not confuse WinSock APIs and WNet APIs. Although both APIs are for network-related functions, the WinSock family deals with socket connections, while the WNet family lets you programmatically list, connect, and disconnect network resources such as disks and printers.

COMMON SOCKET STRUCTURES

Common socket structures used by the WinSock functions mentioned earlier include **sockaddr_in**, **hostent**, **protoent**, and **servent**. The **sockaddr_in** and **hostent** structures are used in the programming example included later in this chapter. **sockaddr_in** is used for storing an IP port and address of a computer that is a socket endpoint. **sockaddr_in** is an Internet-specific format of the more general **sockaddr** structure. **hostent** is used for host information (including local host). **protoent** is used for protocol information. **servent** is used for service information. Let's look at each of these structures.

sockaddr_in

```
struct sockaddr_in{short sin_family;
                    unsigned short sin_port;
                    struct in_addr sin_addr;
                    char sin_zero[8];
};
```

where

>   *sin_family* is the address family and must be AF_INET
>   *sin_port* is the IP port
>   *sin_addr* is the IP address, which is of type **in_addr** (**in_addr** structure is defined in *Winsock2.h*)
>   *sin_zero* is padding to match the size of this structure to **sockaddr**

hostent

This structure returns host-related data such as the host name (and any aliases) and a list of addresses of the host. Windows NT allocates this structure and returns a pointer to the structure on host-related calls such as **GetHostByAddr**. Since your application did not allocate the structure, do not free the structure or any of its components. One copy of this structure is allocated per thread, and the structure is reused by Windows Sockets API calls. For example, if you follow one **GetHostByAddr** call with another, the host information of the second call will overlay the first. So if you want to save any data, you should store the information you need that is returned by the API call elsewhere before you issue another call. The **hostent** structure is shown here:

```
struct hostent { char FAR * h_nam;
                 char FAR * FAR * h_aliases;
                 short h_addrtype;
                 short h_len;
                 char FAR * FAR * h_addrlst ;
};
```

where

h_nam is the host name. The name that is returned depends on whether you use a
name-resolution system such as DNS. If you use DNS, the name returned is the
Fully Qualified Domain Name (FQDN). If you use a local *hosts* file, the name
returned is the first entry after the IP address.
h_aliases is an array of aliases
h_addrtype is the type of returned address
h_len is the address length in bytes
h_addrlst is a list of addresses for the host in network byte order

protoent

This structure returns protocol data for protocols used with sockets such as TCP or UDP.
The protocol data includes the protocol name, including aliases, and the protocol number
(in host byte order). The use of this structure is very similar to that of **hostent**. Windows
NT allocates **protoent** and returns a pointer to the structure on protocol-related calls such
as **GetProtoByName**. Since your application did not allocate the structure, do not free
the structure or any of its components. One copy of this structure is allocated per thread,
and the structure is reused by Windows Sockets API calls. For example, if you follow one
GetProtoByName call with another, the protocol information of the second call will
overlay the first. To save any data, you should store the information you need that is
returned by the API call elsewhere before you issue another call. The **protoent** structure
is shown here:

```
struct protoent { char FAR * p_nam;
                  char FAR * FAR * p_aliases;
                  short p_protno;
};
```

where

p_nam is the protocol name
p_aliases is an array of aliases
p_protno is the protocol number or ID (in host byte order)

servent

This structure returns service-related data such as the service name (and any aliases), a port number for contacting the service, and the protocol that can be used with the service.

```
struct servent { char FAR * s_nam;
                 char FAR * FAR * s_aliases;
                 short s_portno;
                 char FAR * s_protnam;
};
```

where

s_nam is the service name
s_aliases is an array of aliases
s_portno is the port number (in network byte order) for contacting the service
s_protnam is the protocol name to be used with the service

SOCKETS API PROGRAMMING

Having looked at available sockets API functions and the common data structures they use, let's take a look at how we can actually program using sockets. Socket communication typically has three phases. In the first phase, you commonly perform setup functions, such as creating and binding a socket and locating and establishing a socket connection with a remote compute. In the second phase, you send and receive data. If you are writing a service-type socket application, you can create a socket and listen for incoming socket connections from clients. If you have multiple clients trying to establish connections simultaneously, you can ask that the connection requests be backlogged. In the final phase, you perform cleanup functions, such as shutting down and closing the socket connection. Most of the APIs you would use for database socket functions are listed in Table 15-1. Table 15-2 lists the APIs for performing asynchronous communications using Windows socket extensions.

You can also perform a *broadcast* (also called a *multicast*) of a message to a list of IP addresses.

SOCKETS PROGRAMMING USING MFCs

MFC socket objects encapsulate Windows Sockets object handles and provide classes to perform operations on the encapsulated handle. You can use the MFC library classes **CSocket** and **CAsyncSocket** for sockets programming. **CAsyncSocket** is derived from the **CObject** class, and **CSocket** is derived from **CAsyncSocket**. **CAsyncSocket** is a lower-level class compared with **CSocket**. With **CAsyncSocket** you have to take care of some low-level network functions such as blocking, byte order differences (see the "Byte

Ordering" section), and so on. **CSocket** takes care of these functions for you. **CAsyncSocket** provides callbacks to notify you of network events. So if you want low-level control and efficiency, use **CAsyncSocket**. Otherwise, use the more general **CSocket**. **CSocket** handles the low-level details using a **CArchive** object (with an associated **CSocketFile** object).

You can derive your own classes from these two classes and override the member functions they contain such as **OnConnect**, **OnSend**, **OnAccept**, and so on.

The following are the major steps for stream socket communications using **CAsyncSocket** or **CSocket**:

1. Call the object's constructor. You can use either the stack or the heap for the object.

2. Call the **create** member function to create the socket. (This step is not required if you are not creating a socket but are accepting a socket connection.) The socket could be either a stream socket or a datagram socket (see the discussion on socket types in the "Socket Basics" section at the beginning of the chapter.) You can also specify a port for the socket. You normally would specify a port for server socket applications but accept the default for client socket applications.

3. Call the **connect** member function. (If you are writing a server socket application that will start and wait for clients to connect, then you would use the **listen** and **accept** member functions.)

4. Perform socket communication functions that are application dependent by use of member functions such as **send** and **receive**. You may also override notifications such as **OnSend**, and so on. If you are using **CSocket**, you will be using a **CArchive** object (with an associated **CSocketFile** object) for sending data and perhaps another **CArchive** for receiving data.

5. Destroy the socket object. If you used the heap in step 1, then you have to explicitly delete the object. If you used the stack in step 1, the destructor is called when the function goes out of scope. The destructor automatically calls the **close** member function.

ISSUES IN SOCKETS PROGRAMMING

There are special issues you may need to be aware of in sockets programming. Depending on the approach you take (MFC versus API, **CAsyncSocket** versus **CSocket**), some of the issues may be taken care of automatically. The issues in sockets programming include byte-order differences, blocking, and string conversion.

Byte Ordering

Bytes are stored (or ordered) within a word in two ways. You can have the *most* significant byte on the left end of a word (also called "big-endian"), or you can have the *least* significant byte on the left end of a word (also called "little-endian"). Computers using the Intel x86 architecture use the little-endian method, while computers using the

Motorola architecture (Macs) and computers using the RISC architecture (many UNIX systems) use the big-endian method. The common byte order on TCP/IP networks is also big-endian (also called "network byte order"). When you are developing a sockets application, you may be communicating from a computer using one of the methods for byte ordering to another computer using the other method. If you use **CArchive** (by using a **CSocket**), the conversion is automatically done for you. If not, you have to do the conversion in your application. Windows NT provides conversion functions summarized in Table 15-3.

Sockets version 2 includes functions such as **WSAHtonl**, **WSAHtons**, and so on, which are WinSock extension functions that perform the conversion of byte orders.

Blocking

As mentioned earlier, a socket can be in one of two modes—blocking mode or nonblocking mode. *Blocking mode* is synchronous. For example, if you call the **receive** function, your thread will not receive control until the receive is completed. If your socket is unable to receive data immediately, it waits (it is blocked) for the sending application to send the data if you use the blocking version of **CSocket** or **CAsyncSocket**. While most of the time the **receive** function should be able to receive the data, there is always the possibility that the receive may be significantly delayed if there are computer, network, or application problems. If you have users using your socket application, then you may not want them to wait on the blocked socket.

You can avoid users waiting on a blocked socket in one of two ways. First, you can use nonblocking versions of **CSocket** or **CAsyncSocket**. Alternatively, you can create a worker thread to handle socket communications including receive and send, and have the user interface thread interface with the user. The worker thread could be blocked, if necessary. For more details about user interface threads, worker threads, and multithreading, refer to Chapter 10.

Conversion Function	Description
htonl	Converts a 32-bit long number from host byte order to network byte order
htons	Converts a 16-bit short number from host byte order to network byte order
ntohl	Converts a 32-bit long number from network byte order to host byte order
ntohs	Converts a 16-bit short number from network byte order to host byte order

Table 15-3. Socket Conversion Functions

String Conversion

Just as you could be performing socket communications between computers whose architectures could be using different byte ordering, you could also be communicating across computers using different character sets such as ANSI, MBCS, and UNICODE. See Appendix A for more details about character sets. If you use **CAsyncSocket**, you must perform the string conversions in your application. If you use **CSocket**, then the associated **CArchive** object handles string conversion using the **CString** class.

PROGRAMMING EXAMPLE USING SOCKETS

The *Echocs* sample program shown next is a client/server program based on Windows Sockets. The client accepts a string from the user and sends that string to the server through a socket interface, and a thread listening at the echo port at the server sends back the same string to the client, which displays the string on the console. The sample is designed as a single executable which, based on the input parameters, behaves either as a server or a client. Starting the executable with the *-d* parameter will start the executable as a server, and starting it with the *-c* and *hostname* parameters will start it as a client where *hostname* is the name of the host where the server is running. Figures 15-1 through 15-5 show the startup and communication using sockets between the client and the server. The text typed in the client window is echoed at the server, and the same text is sent back to the client. Note that for this example, the client and the server were both the same

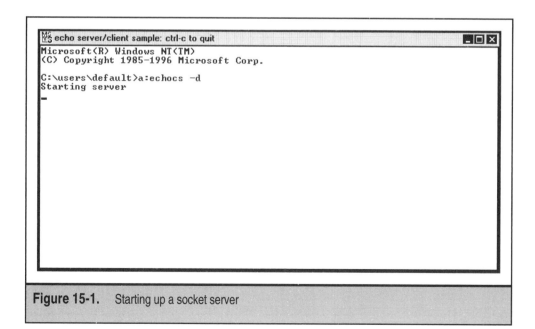

Figure 15-1.   Starting up a socket server

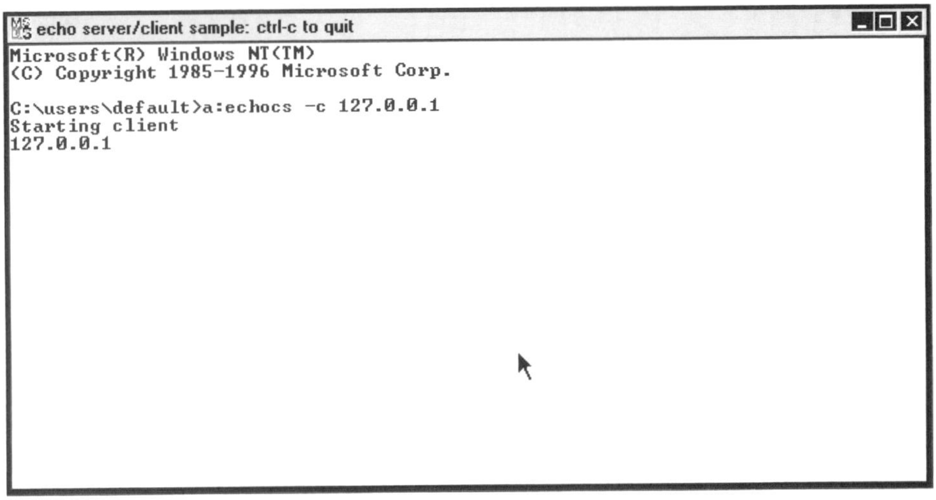

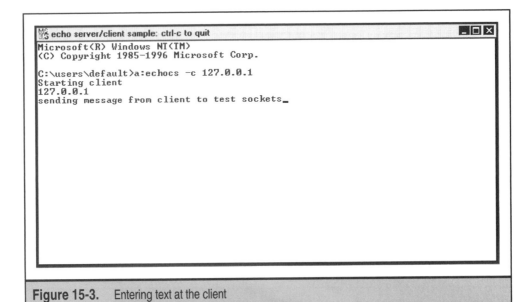

Figure 15-2. Starting up a socket client

Figure 15-3. Entering text at the client

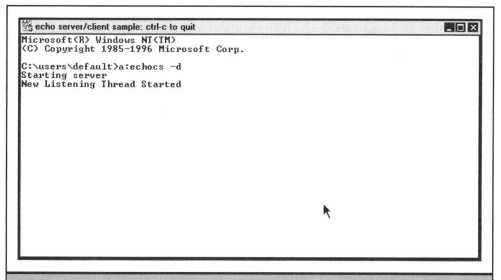

Figure 15-4. Server echoes client text

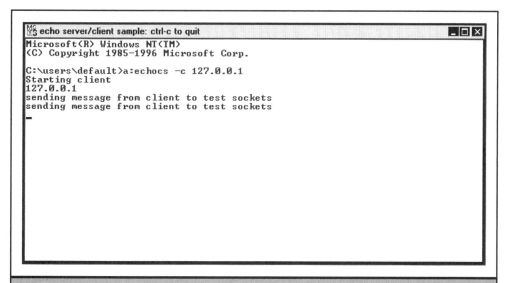

Figure 15-5. Client receives text back from server

machine. The server was started first with the command **echocs -d** at the command prompt. The client was started next with the command **echocs -c 127.0.0.1**. You can try this example on different machines by substituting the appropriate address for "127.0.0.1." Keep in mind though, that there may be problems in running this example if either the client or the server is behind a firewall that does not permit such functions.

To use Windows Sockets the *Winsock.h* header file is included. For simplicity the thread information and the socket handle are defined as global.

```
#include <stdio.h>
#include <stdlib.h>
#include <windows.h>
#include <winsock.h>

// Function declarations
BOOL InitWinSock( char *szError );
int RunServer();
SOCKET StartServer( UINT nPort, char *szError );
BOOL WINAPI ClientThread( LPVOID lp );
int RunClient( char *szHost );
SOCKET ConnectToServer(char *name, UINT nPort, char *szError);
BOOL  SendToSocket(SOCKET hSocket, char *buf, int nSize, char *szError);
int ReadFromSocket(SOCKET hSocket, char *szBuffer, UINT nLength,
                char *szError );
BOOL WINAPI ControlHandler(DWORD dwCtrlType);
void TerminateWinSock( SOCKET hSocket );

// thread structure
typedef struct
{
    SOCKET hSocket;
    BOOL bTerminate;
} ThreadStruct;

// global thread struct
ThreadStruct g_Info;
SOCKET g_hSocket = INVALID_SOCKET;      // global client/server socket
```

The main program checks the input parameters, initializes the sockets environment, and depending on the input parameter, either is run as a server or as a client. It also adds a console control handler to handle events generated by pressing CTRL-C or CTRL-BREAK, closing the console, logon, logoff, or shutdown. This is done to handle such events gracefully and close the application. When such an event occurs, the control of the program is transferred to the control handler function, which is **ControlHandler** in this sample.

```
int main( int argc, char *argv[] )
{
    BOOL bServer = TRUE;
    char *szHost;
    char szError[1024];

    if( argc == 3 )
    {
        if( !strcmp( argv[1], "-c") )
        {
            bServer = FALSE;
            szHost = argv[2];
        }
    }
    else if ( argc > 3 )
    {
        // invalid args.
        puts("For server: \n\tusage: echocs [-d]\nFor client:\n\tusage:\
            echocs -c host\n");
        return 1;
    }

    if( !InitWinSock( szError ) )
    {
        puts(szError);
        return 1;
    }
    // set control event handler and console title
    SetConsoleCtrlHandler( ControlHandler, TRUE );
    SetConsoleTitle("echo server/client sample: ctrl-c to quit");

    if( bServer )
    {
        // server
        return RunServer();
    }
    else
    {
        // client
        return RunClient( szHost );
    }
    return 0; // never reached
}
```

The next function, **InitWinSock**, initializes the Windows Sockets environment by calling **WSAStartup**. **WSAStartup** must be the first Windows Sockets function called by a WinSock application or DLL. This allows the application or DLL to specify the Windows Sockets version required and to retrieve the information of Windows Sockets as implemented in the current environment. This API checks the version requested by the application and returns "success" if the requested version is equal to or higher than the lowest version supported by the Windows Sockets implementation. It returns this version information in the **WSAData** structure passed in the API and expects the caller to look in the data and decide. This negotiation allows both the caller and the Windows Sockets DLL to support a range of Windows Sockets versions. In this sample, version 1.1 is requested. If the API returns "failure," the error is returned to the caller. It should be noted that the API returns the error code directly, and the standard mechanism of getting the error through **WSAGetLastError** cannot be used, since the Windows Sockets DLL may not have established the client data area where the last error is stored.

```
/////////////////////////////////////////////////////////////////////
// InitWinSock
//          starts up winsock.dll or wsock32.dll
BOOL InitWinSock( char *szError )
{
    WSAData wsData;
    int iRC;

    // change 1,1 to 2,0 if using 2.0
    WORD wVersion = MAKEWORD(1,1);  // winsock version

    if( (iRC = WSAStartup(wVersion, &wsData)) !=   0 )
    {
        if( szError )
        {
            sprintf(szError,"WSAStartup failed: WSA ERROR: %d\r\n",
                    iRC);
        }
        return FALSE;
    }
    return TRUE;
}
```

The main program calls the **RunServer** function shown next if the application is started as a server. This function calls the **StartServer** function, which creates a listening socket on the specified port and returns the listening socket. The listening socket is created by use of the **socket** function call. The address family is specified as AF_INET, and a stream socket type is specified. This function call allocates the socket descriptor and any related resources, and is bound to the specific transport service provider. The first available service provider that supports the requested combination of address family, socket type, and protocol is used. A socket of type SOCK_STREAM provides a full duplex connection and must be in a connected state before any data can be sent or received on it. A connection to another socket is created by use of the **connect** function call. After the connection, data can be transferred or received by use of **send** or **recv** function calls. After the socket is created, it is bound to associate a local address with the socket. When a socket is created by use of the **socket** function call, it exists in the address space without a name assigned to it. The **bind** function call establishes the local association of the socket by assigning a local name to an unnamed socket. The name is specified by use of the **SOCKADDR** structure. The **SOCKADDR** structure varies depending on the protocol selected. The **sockaddr_in** is used for TCP/IP. Note that except for the family field, all fields are expressed in network byte order. Helper functions **htonl** and **htons** are used to convert to network byte order. The **ZeroMemory** API is used to initialize the data structure.

After binding, the socket is placed in a listening state by use of the **listen** function call. This places the socket in a state where it is listening for incoming connections. To accept connections, the socket created earlier and a maximum backlog of incoming connections is given to the **listen** function call. If a connection request arrives and the queue is full, the client will receive an error. Though the backlog parameter is an *int*, the underlying service limits the backlog to a reasonable value. Even if the caller specifies an unreasonable value, it is replaced by the closest reasonable value.

The server then goes in a loop selecting the socket and accepting the connection. The **select** function call determines the status of the socket, waiting, if necessary, to perform synchronous I/O. The connection is accepted by use of the **accept** function call, and when the connection is accepted, a thread is started to handle the client connection. The **accept** function call extracts the first connection on the queue of pending connections on the given socket. It creates a new socket and returns the handle to the new socket. This newly created socket will handle the connection. The information about the socket is passed to the thread through the *thread* parameter.

```
/////////////////////////////////////////////////
// RunServer
//          Server stuff
int RunServer()
{
    char szError[1024];

    puts("Starting server");
    g_hSocket = StartServer( 7, szError ); // echo port is 7
    struct sockaddr_in client;
    if( g_hSocket == INVALID_SOCKET )
    {
        puts(szError);
        return 1;
    }
```

```
    // loop forever
    // pressing ctrl+c will call the control handler, which will


    // terminate the process.
    while ( TRUE )
    {
        int nLength = sizeof(client);
        DWORD dwThreadId;
        g_Info.bTerminate = FALSE;
        fd_set fds;
        int nError;
        struct timeval timeout;

        timeout.tv_sec = 1;      //  1 second timeout


        timeout.tv_usec = 0;

///////////////////////////////////////////////////////////////////
        // NOTE; we use select to avoid blocking on accept forever.
        //          It prevents Ctrl-C from calling the control handler.
        FD_ZERO(&fds);
        FD_SET( g_hSocket, &fds );
        nError = select( g_hSocket + 1, &fds, NULL, NULL, &timeout );

        if( nError == WSAEINTR )
            continue;  // interrupted: no harm done
        else if( nError < 0 )
        {
            // error:
            return 1;
        }

        if( FD_ISSET( g_hSocket, &fds ) )
        {
            // accept connection.
            if( (g_Info.hSocket = accept(g_hSocket,
                (struct sockaddr *)&client,
                &nLength)) < 0)
            {
                 puts("accept failed: exiting...");
                 return 1;
```

```
                    }
                     // start a thread to handle client connnection
                      if (NULL == CreateThread( (LPSECURITY_ATTRIBUTES) NULL,
                                          0,
                                             (LPTHREAD_START_ROUTINE)
ClientThread,
                                              (LPVOID)&g_Info,
                                          0,
                                           &dwThreadId ))
                    {
                           puts("can't create thread");
                            TerminateWinSock( g_hSocket );
                           return 1;
                    }
                  // wait 1 second for thread to initialize
                   Sleep(1000);
              }
      }
     return 0;
}


/////////////////////////////////////////////////////////////
// StartServer
//     creates a listening socket on the specified port.
//          returns the listening socket.
SOCKET StartServer( UINT nPort, char *szError )
{
    SOCKET hSocket;
    struct sockaddr_in server;
    if( (hSocket =  socket(AF_INET, SOCK_STREAM, 0)) < 0 )
    {
        sprintf(szError, "socket failed");
        return INVALID_SOCKET;
    }
    // fill in server structure
    ZeroMemory( (char *)&server, sizeof(server));
    server.sin_family = AF_INET;
    server.sin_addr.s_addr = htonl(INADDR_ANY);
    server.sin_port = htons(nPort);

    // bind address to socket
    if( bind( hSocket, (struct sockaddr *)&server, sizeof(server)) < 0 )
    {
        sprintf(szError, "bind failed");
```

```
            return INVALID_SOCKET;
    }

    if( listen(hSocket, 5) < 0 )
    {
        sprintf(szError, "listen failed");
        return INVALID_SOCKET;
    }
    return hSocket;
}
```

The thread function that handles the client connection is shown next. It basically does a select on the socket and then reads data from the socket by calling **ReadFromSocket**; if it reads data from the socket, it sends that data back to the client by calling **SendToSocket**. The socket is finally closed by use of the **closesocket** function call. This releases the socket descriptor so further reference to this socket will fail.

```
//////////////////////////////////////////////////////////////////////////
// ClientThread
//          A thread function to handle each client connection.
//
BOOL WINAPI ClientThread( LPVOID lp )
{
    ThreadStruct* pInfo = (ThreadStruct *)lp;
    SOCKET hSocket = pInfo->hSocket;
    char szBuffer[1024];
    char szError[1024];
    fd_set fds;
    int nError, nLength;
    struct timeval timeout;

    timeout.tv_sec = 1;     //  1 second timeout
    timeout.tv_usec = 0;

    while( ! pInfo->bTerminate )
    {
        ZeroMemory( szBuffer, 1024 );
        ZeroMemory( szError, 1024 );
        FD_ZERO(&fds);
        FD_SET( hSocket, &fds );
        nError = select( hSocket + 1, &fds, NULL, NULL, &timeout );
        if( nError == WSAEINTR )
            continue;  // interrupt
        else if( nError < 0 )
```

```
        {
            break;
        }
    if( FD_ISSET( hSocket, &fds) )
        {
            // read from client
            if((nLength = ReadFromSocket(hSocket, szBuffer, 1024, szError))>0)
            {
                // send whatever we just read: this is an echo server
                if( !SendToSocket(hSocket, szBuffer, nLength, szError) )
                {
                    puts(szError);
                    break;
                }
            }
            else
            {
                puts(szError);
                break;
            }
        }
    }

    // close connection and exit
    closesocket(hSocket);
    return TRUE;
}
```

Up to now we have seen the operation of the server side of the sample. The **RunClient** function is called when the sample is executed as a client. This function sets up a connection to the server by calling the **ConnectToServer** function. In **ConnectToServer** the server name, which is actually an input to the sample program when it is started, is verified if it is in the numeric dot format. If not, the address of the host is queried by use of the **GetHostByName** function call. The **sockaddr_in** structure is initialized with the information of the server. A stream socket is created by use of the **socket** function call, and the connection is established with the server by use of the **connect** function call. This call will initiate an active connection to the server, since the type of the socket is stream socket. After the completion of this call, the socket is ready to send and receive data to the server. This socket handle is then used to send data to the server using **SendToSocket** and to read data from the server using **ReadFromSocket**. If data is received, it is displayed on the console, else an error message is displayed. These functions are shown next.

```
// RunClient
int RunClient( char *szHost )
```

```c
{
    char szError[1024];
    char szBuffer[1024];
    // client
    puts("Starting client");
    puts(szHost);

    // connect to server
    g_hSocket = ConnectToServer( szHost, 7, szError );

    if( g_hSocket == INVALID_SOCKET )
    {
        puts(szError);
        return 1;
    }
    // loop forever
    while( TRUE )
    {
        ZeroMemory( szBuffer, 1024 );
        ZeroMemory( szError, 1024 );
        gets(szBuffer);
        if( SendToSocket(g_hSocket, szBuffer, strlen(szBuffer), szError) )
        {
            if( ReadFromSocket(g_hSocket, szBuffer, 1024, szError ) < 0 )
            {
                puts(szError);
                return 1;
            }
            puts(szBuffer);
        }
    }
  return 0;
}
// ConnectToServer:
//    connects to a server on a specified port number
//    returns the connected socket
SOCKET ConnectToServer(char *name, UINT nPort, char *szError)
{
  SOCKET hSocket;
  struct sockaddr_in server;
  struct hostent far *hp;
  if( !name || !*name )
        return INVALID_SOCKET;
```

```
if( isdigit(name[0]))
{
    ZeroMemory((char *) &server, sizeof(server));
    server.sin_family      = AF_INET;
    server.sin_addr.s_addr = inet_addr(name);
    server.sin_port     = htons(nPort);
}
else
{
  if ( (hp = (struct hostent far *) gethostbyname(name)) == NULL)
  {
      sprintf(szError,"Error: gethostbyname failed: %s.",name);
      return INVALID_SOCKET;
  }


  ZeroMemory((char *)&server, sizeof(server));
  CopyMemory((char *) &server.sin_addr,hp->h_addr,hp->h_length);
  server.sin_family = hp->h_addrtype;
  server.sin_port = htons(nPort);
}
/* create socket */
if( (hSocket = socket(AF_INET, SOCK_STREAM, 0)) < 1)
{
  sprintf(szError,"socket failed to create stream socket");
  return INVALID_SOCKET;
}

// connect to server.
if (connect(hSocket,(struct sockaddr *)&server, sizeof(server))< 0)
{
  sprintf(szError,"connect failed to connect to requested address.");
  return INVALID_SOCKET;
}
return hSocket;
}
```

The next two functions send and receive data to and from the server. The
SendToSocket function calls the **send** function to send data on a connected socket. If no
error occurs, the **send** function returns the total number of bytes sent, which can be less
than the number of bytes in the buffer. The **SendToSocket** function checks if all the bytes
are sent and if needed, repeats the send after adjusting the buffer and buffer length.

Though the **send** function may complete successfully, it does not mean that the data was successfully delivered.

Note that for message-oriented sockets, care must be taken not to exceed the maximum packet size of the underlying provider. This maximum size can be queried by use of the **GetSockOpt** function call.

```
// SendToSocket
//          sends a buffer (buf) of size nSize to the specified socket
//          returns TRUE or FALSE.
BOOL  SendToSocket(SOCKET hSocket, char *buf,
                   int nSize, char *szError)
{
  int    rv;
  /* write it all */
  while ((rv = send(hSocket, buf, nSize,0)) != nSize)
  {
    if (rv == -1)
    {
      sprintf(szError,"error sending to server. WSA ERROR: %d\r\n",
              WSAGetLastError());
      return FALSE;
    }

    if (rv == nSize)
      break;
    buf += rv;
    nSize -= rv;
  }
  return TRUE;
}
```

The **ReadFromSocket** function reads data from the socket by use of the **recv** function call. The **recv** function call receives data on a specified socket. The data is received in the given buffer, whose length is also specified. If the data or message available is larger than the buffer, then the behavior depends on the protocol. For reliable protocols, the buffer is filled with as much data as possible, and the **recv** function generates the **WSAEMSGSIZE** error. The data is retained until it is successfully read by calling the **recv** function with a large enough buffer. For unreliable protocols like UDP, the excess data is lost. The **recv** function call can be used to read data either on a connection-oriented socket or on a connectionless socket. If the socket is a connection-oriented socket, it must be connected before receiving data using the **recv** function. If the socket is a connectionless socket, the socket must be bound before receiving data using the **recv** function.

```
// ReadFromSocket
// Reads some bytes from the specified socket
// into szBuffer of size nLength.
//
int ReadFromSocket(SOCKET hSocket, char *szBuffer,
                   UINT nLength, char *szError )
{
    int rv = recv(hSocket, (LPSTR)szBuffer, nLength, 0);

    if( rv <= 0 )
        sprintf( szError, "recv failed");
    return rv;
}
```

The next function handles any control event generated by the user by pressing either CTRL-C or CTRL-BREAK, closing the console, logging off, or shutting down the system. Since a console control handler was set in the main program, the system will pass control to this function when a control event occurs. This function basically terminates the program gracefully by terminating the Windows Sockets and performing a cleanup function. The **TerminateWinSock** function cancels blocking calls by calling the **WSACancelBlockingCall** API. Note that this function has been removed from the Windows Sockets 2 specification. If the socket is active, it is closed and the use of Windows Sockets DLL is terminated by calling the **WSACleanup** API. The application must call **WSACleanup** to deregister itself from Windows Sockets and allow it to free any resources allocated on behalf of the application or DLL. When **WSACleanup** is called, any pending blocking or asynchronous calls issued by any thread in this process are canceled without posting any notification messages or signaling any event objects. Even if **CloseSocket** was not called, calling **WSACleanup** will reset and deallocate any open socket.

```
// ControlHandler
//      Control event handler: Ctrl-C, etc.
BOOL WINAPI ControlHandler(DWORD dwCtrlType)
{
  switch(dwCtrlType)
    {
    case CTRL_C_EVENT:              // Ctrl-C pressed
    case CTRL_BREAK_EVENT:          // ctrl+break pressed
    case CTRL_CLOSE_EVENT:          // window closing
    case CTRL_LOGOFF_EVENT:         // user logoff
    case CTRL_SHUTDOWN_EVENT:       // system shutdown
            TerminateWinSock( g_hSocket );  // unload winsock
        break;
  return(TRUE);
```

```
}


/////////////////////////////////////////////////////
// TerminateWinSock
// call this function with the current socket or INVALID_SOCKET
void TerminateWinSock( SOCKET hSocket )
{
    // cancel blocking calls, if any
    WSACancelBlockingCall();

    // close socket
    if( hSocket != INVALID_SOCKET )
        closesocket(hSocket);

    g_Info.bTerminate = TRUE;
    // allow threads to terminate, if any.
    Sleep(2000);
    Sleep(3000);

    // unload winsock
    WSACleanup();
}
```

CONCLUSION

In this chapter, we looked at Windows Sockets programming using the WinSock APIs. We also looked at MFC support for Windows Sockets. We covered unique issues related to sockets programming involving communicating between computers with different architectures. We also looked at a sample socket program using WinSock APIs. The CD accompanying this book has two additional socket examples based on MFC.

In the next chapter we will look at Internet-related programming using ISAPI.

CHAPTER 16

Internet Programming

Continuing our communications focus, let's take a look at Internet-related programming and Windows NT. With the advent of intranets and the continued popularity of web browsers, more and more corporate applications are being developed for a web-centric intranet environment. As a business programmer, you can expect to spend a lot of time developing intranet applications using the World Wide Web. There are two aspects of programming web applications—the client side and the server side.

In this chapter, we will take a look at the programming aspects of both server and client Internet programming in the Windows NT environment. We will start with a brief review of web and Internet Server API (ISAPI) basics, compare ISAPI and another method for Internet-related programming—Common Gateway Interface (CGI)—and look at the steps involved in developing the two types of ISAPI applications—filters and extensions. We will also discuss programming aspects at the client. In particular, we will look at the Windows Internet extensions and some examples of programming typical Internet functions such as FTP, Gopher, and HTTP.

WEB PROGRAMMING BASICS

There are two aspects of programming web applications—the client side and the server side. The typical environments used for client side programming include Java, ActiveX, VBScript, Win32 Internet Extensions (WinInet), and so on. Windows Internet extensions provide an alternative to programming using Windows Sockets (covered in Chapter 15) and TCP/IP. WinInet is covered in the section "Internet Client Programming" later in this chapter. ActiveX and programming examples using ActiveX are covered in Chapters 12 and 14. The typical environments for the server side include CGI, ISAPI, and so on. A simple interaction between a web client and a web server is shown in Figure 16-1.

The client could be a browser such as Netscape or Internet Explorer. It could also be stand-alone applications developed by use of languages such as Java/ActiveX, or it could be browsers with embedded Java applets/ActiveX controls. The client interacts with the user and sends a request to a web/Internet server such as Microsoft's Internet Information Server (IIS) or the Peer Web Server. This server is an add-on function on top of the base operating system such as Windows NT server and runs as a Windows NT service. The client/server communications typically use the HTTP protocol. The web server receives the client request and invokes an extension or filter function written by use of ISAPI. ISAPI extensions and filters are DLLs that are invoked just like any other DLLs. The extension uses MFC ODBC classes to access a database. (ODBC, which stands for Open Database Connectivity, is one of two common mechanisms for Windows applications to access databases, the other being Data Access Objects (DAO). ODBC is covered in detail in Chapter 20, and DAO is covered in Chapter 21.) The data from the database is passed from the database to the client through the ISAPI extension and the

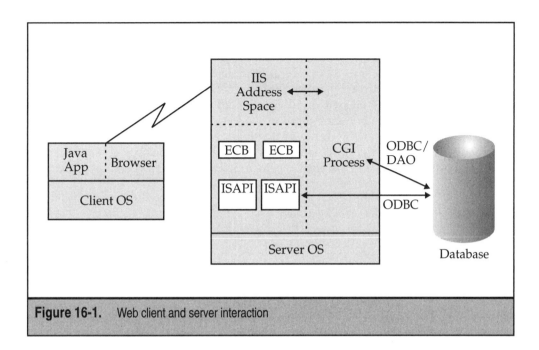

Figure 16-1.   Web client and server interaction

web server. IIS supports ISAPI on Windows NT Advanced Server starting with version 3.51. Peer Web Server supports ISAPI on Windows NT Workstation 4.0 and Windows 95. Most business Internet/intranet programming is likely to use IIS and Windows NT Advanced Server.

Other terms you should be familiar with in Windows NT Internet programming are *Active Server Pages (ASP)*, *cookies*, and *CGI*.

ASP provides server-side scripting capabilities (in the same way as *VBScript* provides client-side scripting). ASPs typically are in-process servers. ASP is attracting a lot of attention, but as an advanced Windows NT programmer, you should still be familiar with the ISAPI.

Cookies are mechanisms for data exchange between an Internet server and client. Cookies are typically used to contain client state data, which is used by the server to return appropriate data consistent with the client's state.

CGI has been used in UNIX systems for a while. Although IIS supports CGI, it is for compatibility purposes only. If you are developing web applications for the Windows environment, you are better off using ISAPI. See "ISAPI and CGI" for a comparison of ISAPI and CGI.

Now that we know where ISAPI fits in web programming, let's take a closer look at ISAPI.

ISAPI BASICS

ISAPI is part of the Win32 API family. It allows you to develop two types of applications that work in conjunction with IIS to extend IIS functionality—*extensions* and *filters*. An ISAPI *extension* is typically used to return a programmatically built HTML page (dynamic content) in response to a client request. The HTML page could contain data from a database accessed from within the extension. An ISAPI *filter* can be used to intercept the two-way data flow between the client and the server, and to select or modify the data for purposes such as authentication, compression, encryption, and so on. ISAPI applications are developed as DLLs that are invoked at run time by an Internet/web server to enhance the functionality of the Internet/web server.

ISAPI AND CGI

CGI and ISAPI provide somewhat equivalent functions, and the fact that you use CGI or ISAPI at the server side is transparent to the client (as it should be). Although Windows NT supports CGI, it is for compatibility purposes only.

Note for UNIX Programmers

Many UNIX systems support CGI. If you have CGI applications or if you want to develop Internet server-based applications that can execute across many Internet/web servers, then CGI is more portable than ISAPI. If you are programming essentially for the Windows environment, ISAPI can provide some advantages over CGI, such as improved performance. Programming for CGI and ISAPI are very similar, and you can convert CGI to ISAPI (see Table 16-1).

Table 16-1 shows the equivalence between CGI and ISAPI constructs.

TIP: While loading the ISAPI applications in the server process space improves performance, it also opens the possibility that the code you write in the DLL can cause problems such as memory/resource leaks, and so on, which could affect the server. Since the server may be up for an extended time, these problems could have cumulative effects. You should pay extra attention when developing ISAPI applications to avoid such problems.

Next, let's take a look at developing ISAPI applications.

DEVELOPING USING ISAPI

You would typically use Visual C++ and MFC to develop ISAPI extensions and filters. A simple way to develop an ISAPI extension or filter is to use the ISAPI extension wizard,

CGI Application	ISAPI Application
Each CGI application/script runs as a separate process.	ISAPI extensions and filters are DLLs and are loaded within the process of the web/Internet server.
Receives client data primarily through stdin.	Receives client data primarily through the lpbData member of Extension_Control_Block (ECB).
Accesses necessary variables such as the user ID using getenv C run-time function.	Accesses necessary variables through ECB or by calling GetServerVariable.
Sends data to client by writing to stdout.	Sends data to client using the WriteClient function.
Provides status information using stdout.	Provides status using WriteClient or ServerSupportFunction.
Client invocation reference for a CGI application is "http://.../cgi.exe?Param1+Param2".	Client invocation reference for an ISAPI application is "http://.../isapi.dll.exe?Param1+Param2".
The main entry point is main.	The main entry point is HttpExtensionProc or HttpFilterProc.

Table 16-1. Comparing CGI and ISAPI

which, like the application and class wizards, generates code that you can build on. The code generated by the ISAPI extension wizard is MFC compatible.

ISAPI Application Data Structures

To better understand the execution flow in an ISAPI application, we need to understand the data structures used in ISAPI applications. The primary data structure used in ISAPI is the **EXTENSION_CONTROL_BLOCK**.

The **EXTENSION_CONTROL_BLOCK** structure contains data members as well as function pointers as shown here:

```
typedef struct _EXTENSION_CONTROL_BLOCK {

    DWORD     cbSize;                        //IN
    DWORD     dwVersion                      //IN
    HCONN     ConnID;                        //IN
```

```
      DWORD      dwHttpStatusCode;                        //OUT
      CHAR       lpszLogData[HSE_LOG_BUFFER_LEN];         //OUT
      LPSTR      lpszMethod;                              //IN
      LPSTR      lpszQueryString;                         //IN
      LPSTR      lpszPathInfo;                            //IN
      LPSTR      lpszPathTranslated;                      //IN
      DWORD      cbTotalBytes;                            //IN
      DWORD      cbAvailable;                             //IN
      LPBYTE     lpbData;                                 //IN
      LPSTR      lpszContentType;                         //IN

      BOOL ( WINAPI * GetServerVariable )
           ( HCONN    hConn,
             LPSTR    lpszVariableName,
             LPVOID   lpvBuffer,
             LPDWORD  lpdwSize );

      BOOL ( WINAPI * WriteClient )
           ( HCONN    ConnID,
             LPVOID   Buffer,
             LPDWORD  lpdwBytes,
             DWORD    dwReserved );

      BOOL ( WINAPI * ReadClient )
           ( HCONN    ConnID,
             LPVOID   lpvBuffer,
             LPDWORD  lpdwSize );

      BOOL ( WINAPI * ServerSupportFunction )
           ( HCONN    hConn,
             DWORD    dwHSERRequest,
             LPVOID   lpvBuffer,
             LPDWORD  lpdwSize,
             LPDWORD  lpdwDataType );

} EXTENSION_CONTROL_BLOCK, *LPEXTENSION_CONTROL_BLOCK;
```

where

cbSize contains the size of the ECB structure.

dwVersion contains the version information (the HIWORD contains the major version number and the LOWORD contains the minor version number).

ConnID contains a unique number assigned to identify each connection by the HTTP server. You normally do not need to modify the *cbSize, dwVersion,* and *ConnID* fields.

dwHttpStatusCode contains the current transaction status when the request is complete. The value contained can be one of HTTP_STATUS_BAD_REQUEST, HTTP_STATUS_AUTH_REQUIRED, HTTP_STATUS_FORBIDDEN, HTTP_STATUS_NOT_FOUND, HTTP_STATUS_SERVER_ERROR, or HTTP_STATUS_NOT_IMPLEMENTED.

lpszLogData contains log information of the current transaction in a buffer of size HSE_LOG_BUFFER_LEN. This log information will be entered in the HTTP server log.

lpszMethod is the method with which the request was made. This is equivalent to the CGI variable **REQUEST_METHOD**.

lpszQueryString contains the query information.

lpszPathInfo contains client-provided path information.

lpszPathTranslated contains the translated path.

cbTotalBytes contains the total number of bytes to be received from the client. If the data to be received from the client is 4 gigabytes or more, use CHttpServerContext::ReadClient repeatedly until all the data from the client is read.

cbAvailable contains the available number of bytes. If *cbTotalBytes* is the same as *cbAvailable,* the buffer point to variable *lpbData* contains all the data sent by the client. Otherwise, use CHttpServerContext::ReadClient repeatedly until all the data from the client is read.

lpbData points to a buffer of size *cbAvailable* containing the data sent by the client.

lpszContentType contains the content type of the client data.

The functions in the ECB are summarized in the following table:

ECB	Description
GetServerVariable	Copies connection or server information
WriteClient	Sends information to the client
ReadClient	Reads information from the client
ServerSupportFunction	Provides server-specific and general-purpose functions

Your ISAPI application may also need environment data such as the user ID and the password of the current client request. Such data is available through server variables. For example, the user ID is available in **REMOTE_USER**, and the password is available in **HTTP_AUTHORIZATION** (in UUEncoded format). Windows NT basic authentication should be on for this data to be available.

Developing ISAPI Extensions

When you use the extension wizard, the skeleton extension it creates includes an APP variable to initialize MFC and an extension variable to initialize the ISAPI extension. You can build on the skeleton and add code to its three main important function entry points shown here:

1. **GetExtensionVersion**
2. **HttpExtensionProc**
3. **TerminateExtension**

The first two are mandatory and the third is optional.

GetExtensionVersion identifies the name and version of the extension. This function is the first one called (and is called only once) when the ISAPI extension is loaded. You would typically initialize variables with this function. You can also use the version information to ensure that a compatible version of the extension is loaded. **GetExtensionVersion** returns TRUE upon successful function execution and FALSE otherwise. Setting FALSE will cause the extension DLL not to be loaded.

HttpExtensionProc is used to process client requests and is called once for each client request. **HttpExtensionProc** uses callback functions to read client data. **HttpExtensionProc** uses the **EXTENSION_CONTROL_BLOCK** structure (this structure was described earlier under "ISAPI Application Data Structures").

TerminateExtension is used to perform cleanup activities. This function is the last one called (and is called only once) when the ISAPI extension is unloaded. One of the most common cleanup activities is to free memory and other resources. Using a flag passed to the function, you can decide if the extension must be unloaded or whether the unloading can be deferred. The flag HSE_TERM_ADVISORY_ UNLOAD provides an option for the extension to decide if it should be unloaded immediately. The extension returns TRUE to accept immediate unloading and FALSE to prevent immediate unloading. Deferred unloading may be useful if the extension wants to keep open connections it made (which are costly to break and reestablish), such as a database connection. The flag HSE_TERM_MUST_ UNLOAD doesn't provide an option and indicates that the extension will be immediately unloaded.

Developing ISAPI Filters

Developing ISAPI filters is very similar to developing ISAPI extensions. The two main functions of an ISAPI filter are **GetFilterVersion** and **HttpFilterProc**, which perform similar functions as **GetExtensionVersion** and **HttpExtensionProc** for ISAPI extensions. You can load ISAPI filters automatically when W3 service (W3SVC) starts by adding the full path name where the filter DLL resides to the registry key:

```
HKEY_LOCAL_MACHINES\System\CurrentControlSet\Services\W3SVC\Parameters\Filter DLLs
```

If you want to use multiple filters, separate the path names by a comma. When the Internet/web server starts up, it loads all the listed DLLs and calls **GetFilterVersion** for each filter DLL. The events for which the DLLs should be notified and the priority order of invoking the filter DLLs (when multiple filters are to be invoked for the same event) are established at this time.

When an event occurs, the server invokes **HttpFilterProc** for each filter registered for the event. The filter then performs the appropriate function (encryption, event logging, authentication, and so on).

Filter Enhancements in IIS 4.0

If you are programming for IIS 4.0 or later, note that the filter information is loaded from the Metabase (a new storage location introduced in IIS 4.0), rather than the Registry. The filter information in the Registry should be in the Metabase. Filters can also be applied either globally or to a particular web site. A new entry point function, **TerminateFilter**, has been introduced. IIS 4.0 also introduced new filter notifications, new server variables, new ServerSupportFunction commands, and new members in the **HTTP_FILTER_LOG** structure. For more details, refer to the latest Microsoft Developer Network information for IIS and ISAPI.

Cookie Programming with ISAPI

Cookies are sent as part of the HTTP header. Cookies are not normally persistent across browser sessions. However, the server can override this default behavior by specifying an expiration attribute that causes the browser to store the cookie across browser sessions until expiration. While the primary purpose of using cookies is to pass client-state data, there have been concerns expressed about cookies because the data transfer happens transparently to the user and cookies could be potentially used to pass non–state-related client data. These concerns have led some browsers to enable the user to disable cookie support. When you are programming with cookies, you need to account for the possibility that the client may not respond as anticipated. Cookies are typically transmitted in the clear (without encryption) between the client and the server, and are also not protected when stored at the client. You have to take this into account when you decide the type of data you want to pass using cookies and avoid passing sensitive information.

You can send and retrieve cookies in your ISAPI extension or filter DLL. The HTTP header cookie information is added (to be sent to the client) in an ISAPI application by use of the **AddResponseHeaders** member function (in the **HTTP_FILTER_CONTEXT** structure passed to the ISAPI application) or as an additional header in the call to **ServerSupportFunction**. A cookie sent by the client is retrieved by use of the **GetHeader** member function (in the **HTTP_FILTER_PREPROC_HEADERS** structure) or by use of the **GetServerVariable** member function (in the **HTTP_FILTER_CONTEXT** and **EXTENSION_CONTROL_BLOCK** structures).

ISAPI and Database Programming

As mentioned earlier, your ISAPI applications must be thread safe. Hence, if you need to perform database access from your ISAPI application, you can use ODBC, but not DAO. MFC DAO classes and the DAO SDK aren't thread safe. Alternately you can use the Internet Database Connector feature of the IIS or write a CGI application.

Additional ISAPI-Related Considerations

Since IIS runs as a service and ISAPI applications are DLLs, debugging your ISAPI application development becomes somewhat of a challenge. Some major challenges are the absence of a desktop (since the DLL is part of a service) and the fact that the DLL executes in the local system context. There are some tips you can use in developing and debugging your ISAPI applications. The following is an abbreviated summary of some points in Microsoft's Knowledge Base article Q152054. Refer to the article for more details.

▼ If you are developing ISAPI extensions, you are likely to make changes and create new versions of your extension code. The default behavior of IIS is to cache ISAPI extensions (to improve performance), which means you have to bring down IIS and bring it back up again to test your extension changes. A better solution is to force IIS to disable caching extensions. You can do this by setting the registry key

```
HKEY_LOCAL_MACHINE\System\CurrentControlSet\Services\
                W3SVC\Parameters\CacheExtensions
```

to zero. Remember to set it to 1 (enable caching) after development is done, as the overhead of loading and unloading extensions is significant. If you are debugging an ISAPI filter, you must stop the IIS service using the administration tool, overlay the old version of your filter with the new version, and restart the service.

■ Output debugging text using the **OutputDebugString** function, and view debug strings using the utility DBMON included with the Win32 SDK.

■ Log error messages or trace execution flow using the NT event log or your own log file. If you use your own log file and Win32 file functions, you have to ensure that for important messages, you can also use the message box. However, as mentioned earlier, there is no default desktop. To cause the message box to appear in the logged-in user's desktop, you need to specify MB_SERVICE_NOTIFICATION | MB_TOPMOST (refer to Win32 SDK's online help for message boxes).

▲ You can also debug by running IIS as a console application (rather than a service) and use the Visual C++ debugger.

If there are current applications written as OLE servers, the ActiveX SDK includes a sample application called OLE2ISAPI, which uses ISAPI to communicate with the web server and behaves like an OLE client to the OLE server application.

Another server programming technique that you should be aware of is *Server Side Includes (SSI)*. SSI is a set of HTML extensions that are in the form of directives to the web/Internet server. An example of an SSI directive is *#include,* which lets one HTML file reference another HTML file. When the client requests an HTML file that references another HTML file reference, the web/Internet server retrieves the original file and the reference. Although there are other directives, IIS 2.0 supports only the #include directive.

Before we look at Internet client-side programming, you should be aware of another server programming technique—Active Server Pages (ASP). ASP makes it possible to combine ActiveX scripts and ActiveX components to create dynamic content. ASP files have the *.asp* extension. ASP files consist of HTML tags, Script commands, and text. ASP files can be referenced as URLs from a browser. ASP scripting is handled by the Internet/web server, and an expanded HTML page is then sent to the client. Active Server pages can be used as components of an Advanced Data Connector application.

INTERNET CLIENT PROGRAMMING

There are several ways to program clients that use the Internet. If the primary end-user application is a browser, you can write add-on functions, such as Java applets or ActiveX controls, to work in conjunction with the browser. With more operating systems providing native Java support, you can write stand-alone programs using Java. You can also use Windows Sockets and TCP/IP. Windows Sockets is covered in Chapter 15. For programmers who want to perform simple Internet functions such as FTP, HTTP, and Gopher without knowing Sockets and TCP/IP, Microsoft also provides Windows Internet extensions (WinInet). WinInet lets the programmer access Internet resources in the same manner as accessing local resources such as hard drives. Some of the functions you can perform with WinInet include

▼ Upload or download files using FTP

■ Download HTML pages using HTTP

▲ Use Gopher to access Internet resources

Programming examples to perform each of the preceding functions are included in the "Internet Programming Examples" section below. The client programming is the same whether there is an external network connection between client and server (Internet) or whether the connection is through an internal network (intranet).

MFC WinInet Classes

You can write a WinInet client application by calling the Win32 functions directly or by using the MFC WinInet classes. MFC provides WinInet classes that encapsulate the underlying Win32 functions. There are also global "**Afx**" functions that are useful in Internet client programming. These classes/functions are summarized in Table 16-2.

In case you are wondering, there is no file find function for HTTP servers as there are for FTP and Gopher, because HTTP does not support direct file access and search.

Adding Security with WinInet

The ability to add security is of paramount importance for business applications using the Internet. You can also add security to your Internet clients using Secure HTTP as part of your WinInet application. Security in the current WinInet environment is provided by the *Schannel.dll*, which uses the SSL/PCT authentication protocol. With Windows NT 5.0, you may be able to choose Kerberos security as well. Using WinInet provides an easier way to implement security than using Security Support Provider Interface (SSPI) directly (WinInet invokes SSPI under the covers). You add security by calling the **InternetConnect** API with the INTERNET_FLAG_SECURE flag turned on. Some versions of Windows NT 3.51 and the Internet Information Server version 1.0 impose a restriction of 32K data size when communicating using the Secure Sockets Layer, which causes a problem with large HTML pages. If you encounter this problem, make sure you apply the appropriate service pack.

Internet Programming Examples

For those who always wanted to write an Internet client application but were afraid to learn sockets programming, MFC includes the Win32 Internet Extensions (WinInet) for creating FTP, HTTP, and other Internet client applications. WinInet classes encapsulate FTP, HTTP, and Gopher protocols, and provide a simple set of member functions that can be used to write powerful client applications to download files over the Internet. These applications can use the Win32 functions directly, or use the MFC WinInet classes.

FTP Sample

The sample program shown next is a very simple application that retrieves a file from an FTP site using FTP protocol. The size of the program shows the simplicity of using the

WinInet Class/ Global Function	Description
CInternetSession	This creates and initializes one or more simultaneous Internet sessions. This class can also be used to interface with a proxy server.
CInternetConnection	This manages an Internet server connection. This class is the base class for CFtpConnection, CHttpConnection, and CGopherConnection. You need a CInternetSession object and a CInternetConnection object to communicate with an Internet server.
CFtpConnection	This manages your application's FTP connection to an Internet server. This class lets your application access directories and files on the Internet server. A CFtpConnection object is created when you invoke CInternetSession::GetFtpConnection.
CHttpConnection	This manages your application's HTTP connection to an Internet server. This class lets your application communicate with the Internet server using the HTTP protocol and perform functions such as downloading HTML pages. A CHttpConnection object is created when you invoke CInternetSession::GetHttpConnection.
CGopherConnection	This manages your application's connection to a Gopher Internet server for Gopher functions. A CGopherConnection object is created when you invoke CInternetSession::GetGopherConnection.
CInternetFile	This provides a base class for the CHttpFile and CGopherFile file classes. This class (and the derived classes) provides access to remote files. A CInternetFile object is created when you invoke CGopherConnection::OpenFile or CHttpConnection::OpenRequest or CFtpConnection::OpenFile.
CHttpFile	This lets your application access and read files residing on an HTTP server.

Table 16-2. WinInet Classes and Global Functions

WinInet Class/ Global Function	Description
CGopherFile	This lets your application access and read files residing on a Gopher server.
CFtpFileFind	This is used in FTP server file searches. This class includes member functions to begin a search, locate files, and return the URLs/descriptive information about files.
CGopherFileFind	This is used in Gopher server file searches. This class includes member functions to begin a search, locate files, and return the URLs/descriptive information about files.
CGopherLocator	This gets a Gopher locator from a Gopher server, which is then used by CGopherFileFind. A Gopher locator contains attributes determining file/server types. You must get a Gopher server's locator before you can retrieve information from the Gopher server.
CInternetException	This object is used when you encounter an exception condition on an Internet operation. The CInternetException class includes a public data member that contains the exception's error code and another public data member that contains the context identifier of the Internet application associated with the exception.
AfxParseURL	This parses a URL string and returns the type of service and its components. The function returns a nonzero return code upon successful parsing and zero otherwise.
AfxGetInternetHandleType	This determines the type of an Internet handle, such as INTERNET_HANDLE_TYPE_INTERNET or INTERNET_HANDLE_TYPE_FTP_FIND. The complete list of types is defined in *Wininet.h*.
AfxThrowInternet Exception	This throws an Internet exception and specifies the context and the error associated with the exception.

Table 16-2. WinInet Classes and Global Functions (*continued*)

WinInet classes. When the sample is run, the FTP site and the file to be downloaded are given as parameters. The program FTPs to that site as an anonymous user and downloads that file. The program can be easily upgraded to log on with a given user ID and password.

After checking for the parameters, the program first creates and initializes an Internet session by creating a **CInternetSession** object. The session identifies itself as *FtpSample* to the server. Among other things that can be specified while creating an Internet session are a context identifier for the operation, the access type required, the name of a preferred proxy, a list of server addresses that may be bypassed when using proxy access cache, and asynchronous options. These options are defaulted here. Next the application connects to the FTP server by calling the **GetFtpConnection** member function and specifying the FTP server address. This establishes an FTP connection and returns a pointer to a **CFtpConnection** object. When you're establishing a connection to an FTP server, a logon user name and password can be specified by passing these parameters to **GetFtpConnection**. This function only establishes an FTP connection and does not perform any operation on the server. By default it uses "anonymous" as the user name and the user's e-mail name as the password. If this method fails, it throws an exception of object type **CInternetException**. The filename that needs to be retrieved from the FTP site is parsed and is passed to the **GetFile** member function of the **CFtpConnection**. This member function gets the file from the FTP server and stores it on the local machine. The default transfer type is binary. If the transfer mode is specified to be ASCII (FILE_TRANSFER_TYPE_ASCII), the translation of the file data also converts the control and formatting characters to Windows equivalents. The default context identifier can be overridden. Make sure that this sample is run outside of a firewall, because it does not handle firewalls. A sample parameter could be *ftp.microsoft.com dirmap.txt*, which downloads the directory map of the Microsoft's FTP site.

```
#include <afxinet.h>
#include <iostream.h>
#include <string.h>


int main(int argc, char **argv)
{
    CFtpConnection *pftpCon = NULL;
    if (argc!=3)
    {
        cerr << "usage: ftpsample <ftp server>\
                <remote file directory path>"
            << endl;
        exit(0);
    }
    try
    {
```

```
        CInternetSession session("FtpSample");

        pftpCon = session.GetFtpConnection(
                argv[1] // ftp server
                );

        char * pszLocalFile=strrchr(argv[2],'/');
        if (pszLocalFile==0)
        {
            pszLocalFile=argv[2];
        }
        else
        {
            pszLocalFile=pszLocalFile+1;
        }
        cout << "downloading "
            << argv[2]
            << " from  site(" << argv[1] << ")"
            << endl;

        BOOL bRetVal=pftpCon->GetFile(
            argv[2], // remote file path
            pszLocalFile // local file
            );
        if (bRetVal)
        {
            cout << "downloaded!" << endl;
        }
        else
        {
            cout << "download failed!!" << endl;
        }
    }
    catch (CInternetException *pEX)
    {
        cout << "Error : " << pEX->m_dwError
            << " Refer WININET.H" << endl;
    }
    if (pftpCon)
    {
        delete pftpCon;
    }
    return(0);
}
```

After the file is downloaded, the FTP connection is deleted, and the Internet session is closed by calling the **Close** member function. The **CFtpConnection** class has other useful member functions like **SetCurrentDirectory**, **GetCurrentDirectory**, **RemoveDirectory**, and **CreateDirectory**, which help to navigate through the directories at the FTP site and to manage directories. Files can also be placed at an FTP site by use of the **PutFile** member function.

There is another class that might be of interest when you're dealing with FTP. This is the **CFtpFileFind** class, which helps in Internet file searches at the FTP site, using its member functions **FileFind**, **FindNextFile**, and **GetFileURL**. This class derives from **CFileFind**.

HTTP Sample

The next sample is similar to the previous one, except that it retrieves a file using HTTP rather than FTP. This sample takes a URL and retrieves the top page from the HTTP server. It then prints the top page on the console. The output can be redirected to a file, and it can be viewed by use of a web browser. The program can be modified to retrieve a specific page. The code is shown next.

The code first checks for the parameters and initializes an Internet session by creating a **CInternetSession** object. The session identifies itself as HTTPSample to the HTTP server. As mentioned earlier, a context identifier for the operation, access type required, the name of a preferred proxy, a list of server addresses that may be bypassed when using proxy access and cache and asynchronous options can be specified during the creation of the Internet session. The default options are accepted in this sample. It then establishes an HTTP connection by calling the **GetHTTPConnection** member function and passing in the HTTP server name. This returns a pointer to a **CHttpConnection** object. Optionally, a user name and password can be specified while connecting to the HTTP server. This function only establishes a connection and does not perform any operation on the server. An HTTP connection is then opened by calling the **OpenRequest** member function, which returns a pointer to a **CHttpFile** object. The request type is set to the "GET" verb, and the top page is requested. The rest of the parameters are defaulted. A set of flags can also be specified to force a download on the requested object instead of getting it from a local cache (INTERNET_FLAG_RELOAD), not to cache the object (INTERNET_FLAG_DONT_CACHE), to add the object to the persistent cache (INTERNET_FLAG_MAKE_PERSISTENT), to use secure transaction semantics (INTERNET_FLAG_SECURE), and not to handle redirections automatically (INTERNET_FLAG_NO_AUTO_REDIRECT). The context identifier can also be overridden to identify this operation to the **OnStatusCallback** member function. The request is then sent to the HTTP server by calling the **SendRequest** member function, and the status of the request is queried by calling the **QueryInfoStatusCode** member function. If there are no errors, the file is read by calling the **ReadString** member function of the **CInternetFile** class from which **CHttpFile** is derived. The information is then displayed on the console. After the object is downloaded from the HTTP server, the file object is closed by calling **Close( )**, and the Internet session is also closed.

```
#include <afxinet.h>
#include <iostream.h>
```

```cpp
#include <string.h>

int main(int argc, char **argv)
{
    if (argc!=2)
    {
        cerr << "usage: httpsample <web server>" << endl;
        cerr<<"(example) httpsample www.microsoft.com"<<endl;
        exit(0);
    }
    CInternetSession session("HTTPSample");
    try
    {
        CHttpConnection *phttpCon=session.GetHttpConnection(argv[1]);

        CHttpFile *pFile=phttpCon->OpenRequest(
                        CHttpConnection::HTTP_VERB_GET,
                        "/", NULL, 1,
                         NULL, NULL,
                        INTERNET_FLAG_RELOAD);
        pFile->SendRequest();
        DWORD statusCode;
        if (pFile->QueryInfoStatusCode(statusCode)==0)
        {
            DWORD dRC=GetLastError();
            cout << "Error retrieving status."
                << "Error: " << dRC << endl;
        }
        else
        {
            if (statusCode==HTTP_STATUS_OK)
            {
                CString aLine;
                while (pFile->ReadString(aLine))
                {
                    cout << aLine << endl;
                }
            }
            else
            {
                cout << "Error occurred in the HTTP request."
                    << "Error number : "
```

```
                            << statusCode << endl
                            << "Program Terminating"
                            << endl;
                    char szError[512];
                    while (pFile->ReadString(szError, 511))
                    {
                        cout << szError;
                    }

                }

            pFile->Close();
            delete pFile;
            delete phttpCon;
            }
        }
    catch (CInternetException *pEX)
    {
        switch(pEX->m_dwError)
        {
            case ERROR_INTERNET_NAME_NOT_RESOLVED:
                {
                    cout << "Server name could not be resolved."
                        << endl;
                    break;
                }
            case ERROR_INTERNET_TIMEOUT:
                {
                    cout << "Connection timed out." << endl;
                    break;
                }
            default:
                {
                    cout << "Win Inet Error: " << pEX->m_dwError
                        << "Look in WININET.H" << endl;
                }
        }
    }
    session.Close();
    return(0);
}
```

Gopher Sample

The next sample deals with the Gopher protocol. To run the sample program, just start the program and provide two parameters on the command line: the Gopher site and the file to display. The program connects to the Gopher site, dumps all the screen names available, and then displays the requested file on the console. For example, to display the constitution of the United States of America, you can type **gopherapp wiretap.spies.com 0/Gov/World/usa.con**. This would display the screen names available at that Gopher site and then open the file and display it. With the popularity of the World Wide Web sites the importance of the Gopher sites has diminished.

The code for the preceding sample is shown next. As in other applications, an Internet session is first established, and a Gopher connection is created by calling the **GetGopherConnection** member function. A pointer to the Gopher server name is passed. A user name, password, and port number can also be optionally passed to the **GetGopherConnection** member function. This member function creates a Gopher connection and returns a pointer to the Gopher connection. A Gopher locator object is created by calling the **CreateLocator** member function of the **CGopherConnection** object. This gets a Gopher locator from the Gopher server, determines the locator's type, and makes the locator available to the **CGopherFileFind** class. A Gopher server's locator must be gotten before the application can retrieve information from the server. To get the screen names, a **CGopherFileFind** object is created by passing in the Gopher connection object to the **CGopherFileFind** constructor. The **FileFind** member function is used to find the first file. The **GetScreenName** member function gets the name of the Gopher screen that is printed until all of them are displayed. To retrieve a file, the Gopher locator created earlier with the filename is used to open the file using the **OpenFile** member function of the Gopher connector. This returns a pointer to a **CGopherFile** object, which is used to read the file and display it on the console.

```
#include <afxinet.h>
#include <iostream.h>
#include <string.h>

int main(int argc, char **argv)
  {
    if (argc < 3)
    {
        cerr << "Usage: gopherapp <gopher server> "
            << "<full file to display>"
            << endl
            << "Ex: gopherapp wiretap.spies.com 0/About_Gopher"
            << endl;
        exit(0);
    }
    CInternetSession session("GopherSample");
```

```
CGopherConnection *pgopherCon =
    session.GetGopherConnection(argv[1]);

CGopherLocator CGLocator = pgopherCon->CreateLocator(NULL,
                            argv[2], GOPHER_TYPE_TEXT_FILE);

CGopherFileFind *pFile=new CGopherFileFind(pgopherCon);

BOOL bRetVal=pFile->FindFile(argv[1]);

while (bRetVal)
{
    cout << pFile->GetScreenName() << endl;
    bRetVal=pFile->FindNextFile();
}

try
{
    CGopherFile *pCGFile = pgopherCon->OpenFile(CGLocator);
    CString aLine;
    while(pCGFile->ReadString(aLine))
    {
        cout << aLine << endl;
    }

}
catch(CInternetException *pEX)
{
    cout << "Error Win32 " << pEX->m_dwError << endl;
}
delete pFile;
delete pgopherCon;
session.Close();
return(0);
}
```

Notice the *Afxinet.h* file that has been included in all the applications. This header file has all the relevant information about the WinInet classes.

In general when an application performs a time-consuming task, it is good to show the progress to the user. This is particularly true in the case of Internet applications, where the tasks are relatively much slower than other applications. The MFC library classes that we used in the samples shown earlier provide a means to display status to the user. The next sample takes the HTTP sample program that was discussed earlier and extends it to show the progress as the activities of the program proceed. The changes made are highlighted.

An application can establish a callback function that the Internet session can call to notify the status. The **CInternetSession** class provides a member function, **EnableStatusCallback**, which can be used to establish a status callback routine. Once enabled for status callback, the Internet session calls the **OnStatusCallback** member function to indicate the status of the operation. To handle this, the **OnStatusCallback** member function should be overridden by deriving a class from the **CInternetSession**. In the sample that follows, the application's own **CMyHttpSession** class is derived from **CInternetSession**, and the **OnStatusCallback** member function is overridden. Whenever the **OnStatusCallback** member function is called, the Internet session passes the context for which this callback was called, the status, and some additional information related to the status. The context can be thought of as a token or identification of the operation. This context identifier is provided by the application when certain operations are performed. For example, a context can be passed when calling the **GetFile** member function of the **CFtpConnection** class, when calling the **OpenRequest** member function of the **CHttpConnection** class, or when calling the **OpenFile** member function of the **CGopherConnection** class. By default all these contexts are set to 1, and that default is used by this application. If the application performs multiple requests at the same time— for example, opening two requests on an HTTP connection—then each can have a different context identifying itself. When the **OnStatusCallback** function is called, the respective context identifies the respective operation. This is particularly useful in asynchronous operations.

This application displays the status information on the console as it arrives.

```
#include <afxinet.h>
#include <iostream.h>
#include <string.h>


// Create our own class derived from CInternetSession
// to handle OnStatusCallback.
class CMyHttpSession : public CInternetSession
{
public:
 CMyHttpSession(LPCTSTR pszAppName);
 virtual void OnStatusCallback(DWORD dwContext, DWORD dwInternetStatus,
 LPVOID lpvStatusInfomration,
 DWORD dwStatusInformationLen);
};

CMyHttpSession::CMyHttpSession(LPCTSTR pszAppName)
 : CInternetSession(pszAppName,1,INTERNET_OPEN_TYPE_PRECONFIG)
```

```
{
}

void CMyHttpSession::OnStatusCallback(DWORD dwContext, DWORD dwInternetStatus,
 LPVOID lpvStatusInformation, DWORD dwStatusInformationLen )
{
 if ((dwInternetStatus == INTERNET_STATUS_RESOLVING_NAME))
 {
 cerr << "Resolving server name." << endl;
 }
 else if ((dwInternetStatus == INTERNET_STATUS_NAME_RESOLVED))
 {
 cerr << "Server name resolved." << endl;
 }
 else if ((dwInternetStatus == INTERNET_STATUS_CONNECTING_TO_SERVER))
 {
 cerr << "Connecting to server." << endl;
 }
 else if ((dwInternetStatus == INTERNET_STATUS_CONNECTED_TO_SERVER))
 {
 cerr << "Connected to server." << endl;
 }
 else if ((dwInternetStatus == INTERNET_STATUS_SENDING_REQUEST))
 {
 cerr << "Sending request." << endl;
 }
 else if ((dwInternetStatus == INTERNET_STATUS_REQUEST_SENT))
 {
 cerr << "Request sent." << endl;
 }
 else if ((dwInternetStatus == INTERNET_STATUS_RECEIVING_RESPONSE))
 {
 cerr << "Response receiving." << endl;
 }
 else if ((dwInternetStatus == INTERNET_STATUS_RESPONSE_RECEIVED))
 {
 cerr << "Response received." << endl;
 }
 else if ((dwInternetStatus == INTERNET_STATUS_CLOSING_CONNECTION))
 {
 cerr << "Closing connection." << endl;
 }
```

```cpp
    else if ((dwInternetStatus == INTERNET_STATUS_CONNECTION_CLOSED))
    {
    cerr << "Connection closed." << endl;
    }
}

int main(int argc, char **argv)
{
 if (argc!=2)
 {
 cerr << "usage: httpsample <web server>" << endl;
 cerr << "(example) httpsample www.microsoft.com" << endl;
 exit(0);
 }
 CMyHttpSession session("HTTPSample");
 try
 {
 session.EnableStatusCallback(TRUE);
 CHttpConnection *phttpCon=session.GetHttpConnection(argv[1]);

 CHttpFile *pFile=phttpCon->OpenRequest(
 CHttpConnection::HTTP_VERB_GET,
 "/"
 );
 pFile->SendRequest();
 DWORD statusCode;
 if (pFile->QueryInfoStatusCode(statusCode)==0)
 {
 DWORD dRC=GetLastError();
 cout << "Error retrieving status."
 << "Error: " << dRC << endl;
 }
 else
 {
 if (statusCode==HTTP_STATUS_OK)
 {
 CString aLine;
 while (pFile->ReadString(aLine))
 {
 cout << aLine << endl;
 }
 }
```

```
    else
    {
cout << "Error occurred in the HTTP request. "
<< "Error number : "
<< statusCode << endl;
<< "Program Terminating"
<< endl;
char szError[512];
while (pFile->ReadString(szError, 511))
{
cout << szError;
}
}
pFile->Close();
delete pFile;
delete phttpCon;
}
}
catch (CInternetException *pEX)
{
switch(pEX->m_dwError)
{
case ERROR_INTERNET_NAME_NOT_RESOLVED:
{
cout << "Server name could not be resolved." << endl;
break;
}
case ERROR_INTERNET_TIMEOUT:
{
cout << "Connection timed out." << endl;
break;
}
default:
{
cout << "Win Inet Error: " << pEX->m_dwError
<< "Look in WININET.H" << endl;
}
}
}
session.Close();
return(0);
}
```

Conclusion

In this chapter, we looked at the programming aspects of both server and client Internet programming in the Windows NT environment. We started with a brief review of web and ISAPI basics, compared ISAPI and CGI, and looked at the steps involved in developing the two types of ISAPI applications—filters and extensions. We also discussed programming aspects at the client. In particular, we looked at the Windows Internet extensions and some examples of programming typical Internet functions such as FTP, Gopher, and HTTP.

WINDOWS
NT
Professional
Library

PART IV

NT Multimedia and Database Programming

WINDOWS NT
Professional Library

CHAPTER 17

Multimedia Programming

Now we'll cover some really exciting and useful topics. We will start with the exciting part, multimedia programming, where we will look at the different ways you can program audio and video. We will look at examples where you write your own audio CD player and video players. We will also look at using Telephony Application Programming Interface (TAPI) to write your own communication programs and how to use OpenGL sophisticated 3-D graphics programming. Then we will look at useful topics that you are most likely to use as a business programmer—accessing databases using Open Database Connectivity (ODBC) and Data Access Objects (DAO).

We will look at multimedia programming in this chapter. The term "multimedia" is a generic term, and as the name implies, deals with different media types. The two major categories of multimedia are audio and video. Windows NT provides a number of ways to incorporate audio and video support in your application.

We will start with a brief review of multimedia basics, including time formats. Then we will look at some audio programming methods—using the media control interface and MCIWnd. Next we will examine an audio programming example, a CD player. Then we will discuss video programming methods and look at a video programming example that plays AVI video clips.

There are numerous audio and video multimedia devices with varying functions and features. Windows NT attempts both to provide a common programming interface and to enable you to take advantage of device-specific functions by substituting default data structures with custom data structures. Your application can then use the additional fields in the structures to provide increased functionality.

MULTIMEDIA PROGRAMMING BASICS

Before we look at multimedia programming aspects, let's briefly review the formats used to represent audio and video. We'll also look at the time formats used for multimedia programming.

You can program your application to play audio content of different devices. Some devices use audio content that is already stored in files such as waveform files (with the .WAV extension). A device such as a CD-ROM player uses audio content stored on the CD. Video content is available in different formats such as AVI, MPEG, and so on. Still images and graphics are not covered here. Graphics using GDI programming are covered in Chapter 5, and sophisticated graphics using OpenGL are covered in Chapter 19. We will also not cover animation in this chapter. Animation using bitmaps is covered in Chapter 8, and animation using advanced controls is covered in Chapter 7.

Time Formats

Whenever we play audio or video, we need some method of specifying the play duration and to identify significant positions within the audio or video content (which tend to be large compared with other forms of computer content). Popular time formats used are *milliseconds*, *tracks* (commonly used with audio), and *frames* (commonly used with video). There are also other time formats such as SMPTE (Society of Motion Picture and Television Engineers) 24. Windows NT provides several macros to set and retrieve time formats. The macros are summarized in Table 17-1. Note that MCI stands for *Multimedia Control Interface*, which is an interface that Windows NT provides for audio-related programming. MCI is covered in detail later in this chapter in the section "Media Control Interface."

The macros and messages mentioned in Table 17-1 are specific to setting or changing time formats of MCI devices. You can also set the time format using the more general **MCI_SET** command, which sets device information, including time formats. You can set the **dwTimeFormat** member of the **MCI_SET_PARMS** structure to an appropriate constant. The valid values for the **dwTimeFormat** depend on the device type. Some common device types, the device constants defined for the device types in *Mmsystem.h*, and the time formats that can be used with them are shown in Table 17-2. Note that SMPTE has come up with a number of time formats based on number of frames, such as SMPTE 24 (which has 24 frames), SMPTE 25 (which has 25 frames), and so on.

Time Macro	Purpose
MCIWndSetTimeFormat	This sets the time format of an MCI device to a format supported by the device. Alternatively, you can explicitly send the MCIWNDM_SETTIMEFORMAT message or use one of the MCIWndUseTime/ MCIWndUseFrames macros if appropriate.
MCIWndUseTime	This sets the time format of an MCI device to milliseconds. Alternatively, you can explicitly send the MCIWNDM_SETTIMEFORMAT message or use the MCIWndSetTimeFormat macro.
MCIWndUseFrames	This sets the time format of an MCI device to frames. Alternatively, you can explicitly send the MCIWNDM_SETTIMEFORMAT message or use the MCIWndSetTimeFormat macro.
MCIWndGetTimeFormat	This retrieves the current time format for a file or an MCI device in string and numeric forms. Alternatively, you can explicitly send the MCIWNDM_GETTIMEFORMAT message.

Table 17-1. Time Macros and Their Purpose

Device Type	Device Constant	Applicable Time Formats
digitalvideo	MCI_DEVTYPE_DIGITAL_VIDEO	MCI_FORMAT_FRAMES (frames) MCI_FORMAT_MILLISECONDS (milliseconds)
vcr	MCI_DEVTYPE_VCR	MCI_FORMAT_FRAMES (frames) MCI_FORMAT_MILLISECONDS (milliseconds) MCI_FORMAT_HMS (hours/minutes/seconds) MCI_FORMAT_MSF (minutes/seconds/frames) MCI_FORMAT_SMPTE_24 (SMPTE 24 frame) MCI_FORMAT_SMPTE_25 (SMPTE 25 frame) MCI_FORMAT_SMPTE_30 (SMPTE 30 frame) MCI_FORMAT_SMPTE_30DROP (SMPTE 30 drop-frame) MCI_FORMAT_TMSF (tracks/minutes/seconds/frames)
videodisc	MCI_DEVTYPE_VIDEODISC	MCI_FORMAT_FRAMES (frames) MCI_FORMAT_MILLISECONDS (milliseconds) MCI_FORMAT_HMS (hours/minutes/seconds)
waveaudio	MCI_DEVTYPE_WAVEFORM_AUDIO	MCI_FORMAT_BYTES (bytes specific to a pulse code modulation data format) MCI_FORMAT_SAMPLES (samples) MCI_FORMAT_MILLISECONDS (milliseconds)
cdaudio	MCI_DEVTYPE_CD_AUDIO	MCI_FORMAT_MILLISECONDS (milliseconds) MCI_FORMAT_MSF (minutes/seconds/frames) MCI_FORMAT_TMSF (tracks/minutes/seconds/frames)

Table 17-2. Common Device Types, Associated Device Constants, and Applicable Time Formats

Device Type	Device Constant	Applicable Time Formats
sequencer (MIDI sequencer)	MCI_DEVTYPE_SEQUENCER	MCI_FORMAT_MILLISECONDS (milliseconds) MCI_FORMAT_SMPTE_24 (SMPTE 24 frame) MCI_FORMAT_SMPTE_25 (SMPTE 25 frame) MCI_FORMAT_SMPTE_30 (SMPTE 30 frame) MCI_FORMAT_SMPTE_30DROP (SMPTE 30 drop-frame)

Table 17-2.   Common Device Types, Associated Device Constants, and Applicable Time Formats (*continued*)

AUDIO PROGRAMMING

Windows NT provides different ways of audio-related programming in your applications. You can use some high-level functions, such as **MCIWnd**, **MessageBeep**, **PlaySound**, and **sndPlaySound**. The amount of code you need to add is reduced, but you also lose some control when you use the high-level functions. These functions are appropriate when you do not need the low-level control and the functions are adequate for your requirements.

Windows NT also provides the Multimedia Control Interface (MCI), an interface that includes a set of functions and commands that can be used to control audio (and other multimedia) devices. While using MCI may make your program code bigger than when you use high-level audio functions, the extra control you get can let you perform functions that may not be possible with high-level functions. For example, you cannot play large waveform files that do not fit completely in memory using the high-level functions, whereas you can use the media control interface to play such files.

Media Control Interface

While the capabilities of multimedia devices vary, MCI attempts to provide a standard generic interface to all multimedia devices. MCI provides two ways to communicate with a multimedia device (also called an *MCI device*). The two ways are command messages and command strings. The command message interface uses message-passing and is meant to be used by applications requiring a C-language interface. The command message interface uses the **mciSendCommand** function. Alternatively you can send string commands, parameters for the string commands, and a buffer for any returned information. The command string interface uses the **mciSendString** function. Use of the two functions is not mutually exclusive. You can use both in your application. The

MCI Function	Description
mciGetCreatorTask	Retrieves a handle to the creator task responsible for opening the specified device
mciGetDeviceID	Retrieves the device identifier assigned to a device when the device was opened
mciGetErrorString	Retrieves the string that contains descriptive text information about specific MCI error code
mciGetYieldProc	Retrieves the address of the current yield callback function associated with the MCI_WAIT flag
mciSendCommand	Sends a command message to an MCI device
mciSendString	Sends a command string to an MCI device
mciSetYieldProc	Sets the address of a callback function to be called periodically when an MCI device is waiting for a command to finish

Table 17-3. MCI Functions

command string format is easier to use, while the command message format generally offers better performance. The commands you can send to the multimedia device include *play* and *close*.

The MCI functions and their descriptions are summarized in Table 17-3.

Of these, **mciSendCommand** and **mciSendString** are by far the most commonly used. Let's take a closer look at these two functions. The prototype for the **mciSendCommand** function is shown here:

```
MCIERROR mciSendCommand( MCIDEVICEID DevID,
                         UINT uMsg,
                         DWORD fdwCmd,
                         DWORD dwParm

);
```

where

DevID is the device identifier to which the command message is sent *uMsg* is the specific command message

fdwCmd specifies the flags for the command message

dwParm points to the address of a structure that contains message command parameters

The **mciSendCommand** function returns zero if successful and an error otherwise. The low-order word of the returned doubleword value contains the error return value. You can use the **mciGetErrorString** function to retrieve the string that contains descriptive text from the error value returned. If the error is device specific, the high-order word of the return value is the driver identifier and is zero otherwise.

The prototype for the **mciSendString** function is shown here:

```
MCIERROR mciSendString( LPCTSTR lpszCmd,
                        LPTSTR lpszRtnString,
                        UINT cchRtn,
                        HANDLE hwndCallback
    );
```

where

lpszCmd is the MCI command string address.

lpszRtnString is the address of the buffer that will receive return information. You can set *lpszRtnString* to NULL, if you have no return information.

cchRtn is the return buffer size (in characters).

hwndCallback contains the handle of a callback window.

The **mciSendString** function returns zero if successful and an error otherwise. The low-order word of the returned doubleword value contains the error return value. You can use the **mciGetErrorString** function to retrieve the string that contains descriptive text from the error value returned. If the error is device specific, the high-order word of the return value is the driver identifier and is zero otherwise. The simple programming sequence for both the **mciSendString** and the **mciSendCommand** functions is to use the *open, play,* and *close* commands in that order. If at any point you get an error, then call **mciGetErrorString** to get descriptive text that can be displayed to the user by use of a function such as **MessageBox**.

The **mciSendString** function is easier to program than the **mciSendCommand** function, but is also somewhat less efficient (as the strings specified in **mciSendString** have to be parsed and interpreted, unlike the **mciSendCommand** function). The programming examples later in the chapter use both the **mciSendString** and the **mciSendCommand** functions.

Programming Using MCIWnd

You can use the functions, messages, and macros associated with the **MCIWnd** window class to perform audio and video playback and to record in your applications. The functions used with an **MCIWnd** class include the following:

MCIWnd-Related Function	Description
GetOpenFileNamePreview	This lets a user select files and preview some files, such as an AVI file.
GetSaveFileNamePreview	This is the same as GetOpenFileNamePreview, except that the dialog box displayed is the Save As dialog box, instead of the File Open dialog box.
MCIWndCreate	This registers the MCIWnd window class (you don't need a separate call to MCIWndRegisterClass) and creates an MCIWnd window. MCIWndCreate also opens an MCI device or file. This returns a window handle that you should use in MCIWnd macros.
MCIWndRegisterClass	This registers the MCI window class. If you use this function, use the CreateWindow or CreateWindowEx function to create an MCIWnd window (instead of using MCIWndCreate).

The most important of the **MCIWnd** functions is the **MCIWndCreate** function, whose prototype is shown here:

```
HWND MCIWndCreate( HWND hwndParnt,
                   HINSTANCE hInst,
                   DWORD dwStyle,
                   LPSTR szFl
);
```

where

hwndParnt is the parent window's handle (when this value is not NULL, **MCIWndCreate** automatically creates a child window).

hInst is the instance handle associated with the new MCIWnd window.

dwStyle specifies one or more flags that define the window style. You can use the window styles you specify for the window-create function commonly used, **CreateWindowEx**. **MCIWndCreate** also provides some additional flags that are unique to **MCIWndCreate**. **MCIWndCreate** is used in the programming example covered later in the chapter.

szFl is the name of the MCI device or data file to be opened.

MCIWndCreate returns the handle to the MCI window that is created if successful and zero otherwise.

Other Audio Programming Methods

You can also use the **MessageBeep** function for audio programming. You can specify the type of sound you want with **MessageBeep** (such as *SystemAsterisk*, *SystemExclamation*, and so on) by including the value in the *uType* parameter, as shown in the **MessageBeep** prototype here:

```
BOOL MessageBeep( UINT uType
);
```

Most of the choices in the Sounds icon in the control panel can be used with **MessageBeep**, including a simple beep. **MessageBeep** plays the waveform file identified in the registry for the type of sound selected asynchronously. If **MessageBeep** is unable to play the selected waveform file, it attempts to play the system default sound. **MessageBeep** is commonly used along with the **MessageBox** function to play a sound when a message box is displayed. **MessageBeep** returns a nonzero value when successful and zero otherwise.

While **MessageBeep** gives you the ability to play a set of predefined sounds, sometimes you may want to play the sound from other sources, such as a waveform file, that have not been predefined. You can use the **PlaySound** function to play sounds specified by a file, resource, or system event. The prototype for it is shown here:

```
BOOL PlaySound( LPCSTR pszSound,
                HMODULE hmod,
                DWORD fdwSound
);
```

where

pszSound specifies the name of the sound file or system event alias or resource identifier.

hmod contains the handle of the executable file that contains the resource to be loaded (used only if the sound source is a resource).

fdwSound specifies one or more flags. The flags are used to indicate whether the sound source is a waveform file (SND_FILENAME), a system event (SND_ALIAS), or resource (SND_RESOURCE), and whether any currently playing sound should be interrupted (SND_NOSTOP), and so on.

PlaySound returns TRUE, if successful, and FALSE otherwise. If you specify a filename for the sound, **PlaySound** searches for the file in a specific order (the current directory, the Windows directory, the Windows system directory, directories listed in the PATH environment variable, and so on), which is the same as that used by the **OpenFile** function. If **PlaySound** cannot find the sound you specified, it will attempt to play the default system event sound.

So far, we have been looking at representation of sound in the waveform format. Sound is also represented using the Musical Instrument Digital Interface (MIDI) protocol format. The primary difference between the two forms of representation is that waveforms record and reproduce sounds as is (without conversion to a notational format), which takes up a lot of space. MIDI, on the other hand, is actually a notational representation (much like a music sheet). A device capable of understanding the MIDI instructions (a MIDI synthesizer) can reproduce the sound from MIDI instructions. MCI includes a MIDI sequencer that can play (but not record) MIDI. Windows NT includes low-level functions such as **midiOutOpen** and **midiOutClose**, but these are not addressed in this book.

In addition to the methods mentioned earlier, Windows NT also provides some other low-level functions such as **waveOutOpen, waveOutWrite**, and **waveOutClose**. You normally should be able to address your audio programming needs using high-level functions and MCI. These low-level functions are not covered in this book.

Audio Programming Example

The *CDPlayer* sample application controls and plays a CD audio device. When the sample application is started, it opens the CD player, checks the CD, and displays the track and length information in a status window. It has buttons on the dialog box that can be used to control the CD player. Figures 17-1 through 17-3 show the dialog box when you run the *CDPlayer* sample. Figure 17-1 shows the dialog box when the *CDPlayer* program is started. The status window includes information obtained by querying the CD, such as the number of tracks present and the total time it would take to play the CD. Figure 17-2 shows the effect of clicking the Eject button. This ejects the CD and changes the button label to "Retract." Clicking the Retract button retracts the CD (if the CD-ROM drive supports it) and changes the button label to "Eject." Figure 17-3 shows the effect of pressing Pause. Pressing Pause changes the Pause label to "Resume" and pauses the playing of the CD.

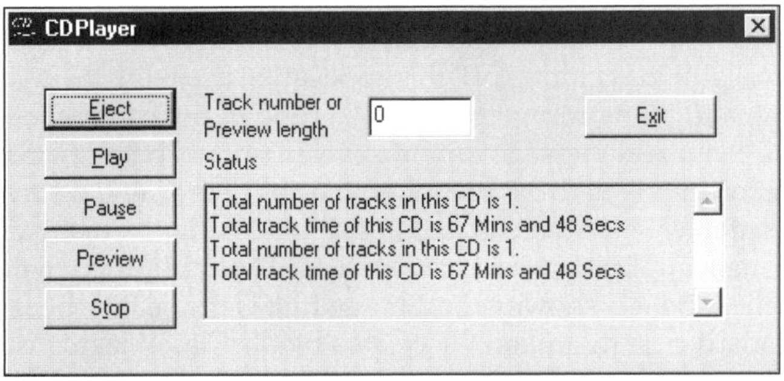

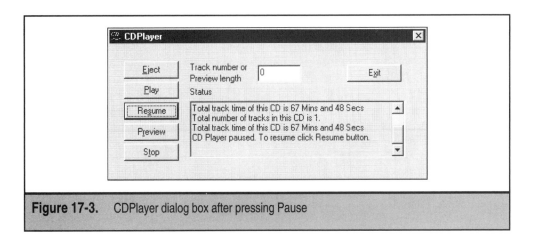

Figure 17-1. CDPlayer program dialog box

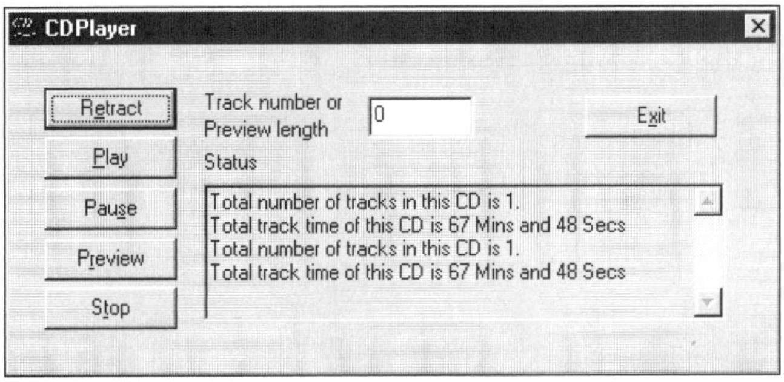

Figure 17-2. CDPlayer dialog box after pressing Eject

Figure 17-3. CDPlayer dialog box after pressing Pause

MCI supports command strings and command messages to control a media device. Both commands can be used in an application. To illustrate both sets of media control interface APIs available in Windows NT, this application uses both the command message format and command string format of the API. Though the command string format is easier to use, the command message format generally offers better performance.

The application is created by use of the AppWizard, and it is a dialog-based AppWizard executable. Since there is nothing significant in the main application class, the code for the main application is not shown here. The application dialog box class has all the functionality and it is shown here. Shown first is the header file.

This is a standard class definition file created by the ClassWizard. Member variables to retain the total tracks, device ID, whether the CD player door is open, whether the CD player is in a paused state, and a character buffer for holding the status information are declared here. Notice the member functions added by the ClassWizard that are invoked when the buttons are clicked on the dialog box. When the dialog box is initialized, the CD player device is opened, and the device ID is queried and stored in the member variable. This device ID is then used throughout the operation of the CD player. The number of tracks in the CD is also queried and initialized. A common character buffer to hold the status of the CD player is used.

```
// CDPlayerDlg.h : header file

#if !defined(AFX_CDPLAYERDLG_H)
#define AFX_CDPLAYERDLG_H

#if _MSC_VER >= 1000
#pragma once
#endif // _MSC_VER >= 1000

/////////////////////////////////////////////////////////////////////////////
// CCDPlayerDlg dialog

class CCDPlayerDlg : public CDialog
{
// Construction
public:
    CCDPlayerDlg(CWnd* pParent = NULL);     // standard constructor

// Dialog Data
    //{{AFX_DATA(CCDPlayerDlg)
    enum { IDD = IDD_CDPLAYER_DIALOG };
    CEdit    m_status;
    short    m_track;
    //}}AFX_DATA
```

```
        // ClassWizard generated virtual function overrides
        //{{AFX_VIRTUAL(CCDPlayerDlg)
        protected:
        virtual void DoDataExchange(CDataExchange* pDX);     // DDX/DDV support
        //}}AFX_VIRTUAL

// Implementation
protected:
    HICON m_hIcon;

    MCIDEVICEID    uDevID;
    short     sTotalTracks;
    BOOL      fDoorOpen;
    BOOL      fPaused;
    char      szStatus[256];
    // Generated message map functions
    //{{AFX_MSG(CCDPlayerDlg)
    virtual BOOL OnInitDialog();
    afx_msg void OnSysCommand(UINT nID, LPARAM lParam);
    afx_msg void OnPaint();
    afx_msg HCURSOR OnQueryDragIcon();
    afx_msg void OnPlay();
    afx_msg void OnPreview();
    afx_msg void OnDoor();
    afx_msg void OnPause();
    afx_msg void OnExit();
    afx_msg void OnStop();
    //}}AFX_MSG
    DECLARE_MESSAGE_MAP()
};
//{{AFX_INSERT_LOCATION}}
#endif //
```

The *CDPlayer* dialog box code is shown next. The framework code is generated by the ClassWizard. This generated code performs standard functions like handling the paint message, handling the About panel, and so on. First the code for the About dialog box is shown. This code is generated by ClassWizard, and no change has been made.

```
// CDPlayerDlg.cpp : implementation file
//

#include "stdafx.h"
#include "CDPlayer.h"
#include "CDPlayerDlg.h"
```

```cpp
#ifdef _DEBUG
#define new DEBUG_NEW
#undef THIS_FILE
static char THIS_FILE[] = __FILE__;
#endif

/////////////////////////////////////////////////////////////////////////////
// CAboutDlg dialog used for App About

class CAboutDlg : public CDialog
{
public:
    CAboutDlg();

// Dialog Data
    //{{AFX_DATA(CAboutDlg)
    enum { IDD = IDD_ABOUTBOX };
    //}}AFX_DATA

    // ClassWizard generated virtual function overrides
    //{{AFX_VIRTUAL(CAboutDlg)
    protected:
    virtual void DoDataExchange(CDataExchange* pDX);
    //}}AFX_VIRTUAL

// Implementation
protected:
    //{{AFX_MSG(CAboutDlg)
    //}}AFX_MSG
    DECLARE_MESSAGE_MAP()
};

CAboutDlg::CAboutDlg() : CDialog(CAboutDlg::IDD)
{
    //{{AFX_DATA_INIT(CAboutDlg)
    //}}AFX_DATA_INIT
}

void CAboutDlg::DoDataExchange(CDataExchange* pDX)
{
    CDialog::DoDataExchange(pDX);
    //{{AFX_DATA_MAP(CAboutDlg)
    //}}AFX_DATA_MAP
```

```
}

BEGIN_MESSAGE_MAP(CAboutDlg, CDialog)
    //{{AFX_MSG_MAP(CAboutDlg)
    // No message handlers
    //}}AFX_MSG_MAP
END_MESSAGE_MAP()
```

The *CDPlayer* dialog box code follows:

```
///////////////////////////////////////////////////////////////////////////
// CCDPlayerDlg dialog

CCDPlayerDlg::CCDPlayerDlg(CWnd* pParent /*=NULL*/)
    : CDialog(CCDPlayerDlg::IDD, pParent)
{
    //{{AFX_DATA_INIT(CCDPlayerDlg)
    m_track = 0;
    //}}AFX_DATA_INIT
    m_hIcon = AfxGetApp()->LoadIcon(IDR_MAINFRAME);
}

void CCDPlayerDlg::DoDataExchange(CDataExchange* pDX)
{
    CDialog::DoDataExchange(pDX);
    //{{AFX_DATA_MAP(CCDPlayerDlg)
    DDX_Control(pDX, IDC_STATUS, m_status);
    DDX_Text(pDX, IDC_TRACK, m_track);
    //}}AFX_DATA_MAP
}

BEGIN_MESSAGE_MAP(CCDPlayerDlg, CDialog)
    //{{AFX_MSG_MAP(CCDPlayerDlg)
    ON_WM_SYSCOMMAND()
    ON_WM_PAINT()
    ON_WM_QUERYDRAGICON()
    ON_BN_CLICKED(IDC_PLAY, OnPlay)
    ON_BN_CLICKED(IDC_PREVIEW, OnPreview)
    ON_BN_CLICKED(IDC_DOOR, OnDoor)
    ON_BN_CLICKED(IDC_PAUSE, OnPause)
    ON_BN_CLICKED(IDOK, OnExit)
    ON_BN_CLICKED(IDC_STOP, OnStop)
    //}}AFX_MSG_MAP
END_MESSAGE_MAP()
```

```
///////////////////////////////////////////////////////////////////////////
// CCDPlayerDlg message handlers

BOOL CCDPlayerDlg::OnInitDialog()
{
    CDialog::OnInitDialog();

    // Add "About..." menu item to system menu.
    // IDM_ABOUTBOX must be in the system command range.
    ASSERT((IDM_ABOUTBOX & 0xFFF0) == IDM_ABOUTBOX);
    ASSERT(IDM_ABOUTBOX < 0xF000);

    CMenu* pSysMenu = GetSystemMenu(FALSE);
    if (pSysMenu != NULL)
    {
        CString strAboutMenu;
        strAboutMenu.LoadString(IDS_ABOUTBOX);
        if (!strAboutMenu.IsEmpty())
        {
            pSysMenu->AppendMenu(MF_SEPARATOR);
            pSysMenu->AppendMenu(MF_STRING, IDM_ABOUTBOX, strAboutMenu);
        }
    }

    // Set the icon for this dialog.  The framework does this automatically
    //  when the application's main window is not a dialog
    SetIcon(m_hIcon, TRUE);         // Set big icon
    SetIcon(m_hIcon, FALSE);        // Set small icon
```

The following additional initialization is done during initialization. First the CD audio device is opened by sending the **MCI_OPEN** command message. The multimedia device *cdaudio*, which represents the CD player device, is passed in the **MCI_OPEN_PARMS** structure. The command message to open the multimedia device is **MCI_OPEN**. When this command message is sent, the device is opened and the device ID is returned in the *wDeviceID* field of the **MCI_OPEN_PARMS** structure. The device name can be specified in either case, but there cannot be any leading or trailing spaces. The MCI_OPEN_TYPE flag must be specified whenever a device is specified in the **mciSendCommand** function. The multimedia device can also be opened by specifying the device-type constants. For the CD player the device-type constant is MCI_DEVTYPE_CD_AUDIO.

Next the time format for the CD player is set to TMSF (track/minute/second/frame). For CD audio-type devices the preferred positioning is relative to tracks. That is, users want to play by tracks and not by minutes or frames. To specify a position relative to a track, the time format should be set to TMSF. As an exercise other time formats can be tried and results checked. The time format is set by sending the **MCI_SET** command message and MCI_SET_TIME_FORMAT flag.

This *CDPlayer* application enables the user to open the CD audio device by clicking on a button on the dialog box. For the application to open the CD audio device through software, the CD audio device should support this feature. To find out if the CD audio device supports this, the **MCI_GETDEVCAPS** command message is sent with the MCI_GETDEVCAPS_CAN_EJECT flag. Based on the result, the Eject button is grayed out on the dialog box if necessary. Though it serves no useful purpose here, the code also queries if the device can play. The **mciSendCommand** API returns zero if successful or a nonzero value if it failed. The error string can easily be obtained by calling the **mciGetErrorString** API and passing in the error code, the buffer for the error string, and the buffer size. This makes it convenient to handle errors and display them. Though it is wise to check for errors after each command, this application assumes successful completion at some places for simplicity.

One of the most useful command messages is the **MCI_STATUS**. This command message can be sent to find the status of the CD audio device—such as the track length, current mode (play, pause, open, and so on), readiness, whether there is a media present, and so forth. This application gets the total number of tracks in the CD and the total track length. This information is displayed in the dialog box. Notice that the limitation of this application is that it expects a CD to be present in the CD audio device when this application is started. However, this can be easily changed by checking whether the media is present and then proceeding based on the result.

```
// TODO: Add extra initialization here

    DWORD dwRC;
    MCI_OPEN_PARMS OpenParms;
    MCI_SET_PARMS SetParms;

    fDoorOpen = FALSE;
    fPaused = FALSE;

    OpenParms.lpstrDeviceType = "cdaudio";
    if (dwRC = mciSendCommand(NULL, MCI_OPEN | MCI_WAIT,
        MCI_OPEN_TYPE, (DWORD) &OpenParms))
    {
        return (FALSE);
    }
    uDevID = OpenParms.wDeviceID;
    SetParms.dwTimeFormat = MCI_FORMAT_TMSF;
    if (dwRC = mciSendCommand(uDevID, MCI_SET,
        MCI_SET_TIME_FORMAT, (DWORD) &SetParms))
    {
```

```
        mciSendCommand(uDevID, MCI_CLOSE, 0, NULL);
        return (FALSE);
}
MCI_GETDEVCAPS_PARMS CapsParms;
CapsParms.dwCallback = 0;
CapsParms.dwItem = MCI_GETDEVCAPS_CAN_PLAY;
if (dwRC = mciSendCommand(uDevID, MCI_GETDEVCAPS,
            MCI_GETDEVCAPS_CAN_PLAY | MCI_GETDEVCAPS_ITEM,
            (DWORD)&CapsParms))
{
    CHAR szError[128+1];
    mciGetErrorString(dwRC, szError, sizeof(szError));
    AfxMessageBox(szError);
}

CapsParms.dwItem = MCI_GETDEVCAPS_CAN_EJECT;
if (dwRC = mciSendCommand(uDevID, MCI_GETDEVCAPS,
            MCI_GETDEVCAPS_CAN_EJECT | MCI_GETDEVCAPS_ITEM,
            (DWORD)&CapsParms))
{
    CHAR szError[256];
    mciGetErrorString(dwRC, szError, sizeof(szError));
    AfxMessageBox(szError);
}

// If the drive cannot eject the CD, gray the Eject button.
if (!CapsParms.dwReturn)
{
    GetDlgItem(IDC_DOOR)->EnableWindow(FALSE);
}

MCI_STATUS_PARMS StatusParms;
StatusParms.dwItem = MCI_STATUS_NUMBER_OF_TRACKS;
if (dwRC = mciSendCommand(uDevID, MCI_STATUS,
            MCI_STATUS_ITEM, (DWORD)&StatusParms))
{// May be no disk in the CD drive.
    sTotalTracks = 0;
}
else
{
    sTotalTracks = (short)StatusParms.dwReturn;
}

StatusParms.dwItem = MCI_STATUS_LENGTH;
```

```
    if (dwRC = mciSendCommand(uDevID, MCI_STATUS,
              MCI_STATUS_ITEM, (DWORD)&StatusParms))
    {// May be no disk in the CD drive
        StatusParms.dwReturn = 0;
    }
    wsprintf (szStatus,
            "Total number of tracks in this CD is %d.\r\n\
             Total track time of this CD is %d Mins and %d Secs\r\n",
            sTotalTracks,
            MCI_MSF_MINUTE(StatusParms.dwReturn),
            MCI_MSF_SECOND(StatusParms.dwReturn));
    m_status.SetSel(-1,0);
    m_status.ReplaceSel(szStatus);

    return TRUE;  // return TRUE unless you set the focus to a control
}


void CCDPlayerDlg::OnSysCommand(UINT nID, LPARAM lParam)
{
    if ((nID & 0xFFF0) == IDM_ABOUTBOX)
    {
        CAboutDlg dlgAbout;
        dlgAbout.DoModal();
    }
    else
    {
        CDialog::OnSysCommand(nID, lParam);
    }
}


// If you add a minimize button to your dialog, you will need the code below
//  to draw the icon.  For MFC applications using the document/view model,
//  this is automatically done for you by the framework.

void CCDPlayerDlg::OnPaint()
{
    if (IsIconic())
    {
        CPaintDC dc(this); // device context for painting

        SendMessage(WM_ICONERASEBKGND, (WPARAM) dc.GetSafeHdc(), 0);

        // Center icon in client rectangle
        int cxIcon = GetSystemMetrics(SM_CXICON);
```

```
        int cyIcon = GetSystemMetrics(SM_CYICON);
        CRect rect;
        GetClientRect(&rect);
        int x = (rect.Width()-cxIcon + 1) / 2;
        int y = (rect.Height()-cyIcon + 1) / 2;

        // Draw the icon
        dc.DrawIcon(x, y, m_hIcon);
    }
    else
    {
        CDialog::OnPaint();
    }
}


// The system calls this to obtain the cursor to display while the user drags
//  the minimized window.
HCURSOR CCDPlayerDlg::OnQueryDragIcon()
{
    return (HCURSOR) m_hIcon;
}
```

When the user clicks on the Play button, the selected track's length is queried and the status message is displayed. If the user selects a track number greater than the total number of tracks, the entire CD is played. To play a track, the **MCI_PLAY** command message is sent. Depending on the track, additional flags, such as MCI_FROM and MCI_TO, are specified. If both these flags are specified, then the CD audio device will play starting from the From track specified in the **MCI_PLAY_PARMS** until the To track. If the To track is not specified, it will play until the end of the CD. If the MCI_FROM flag is not specified, it will start playing from the current track. After issuing the **MCI_PLAY** command message, the function returns immediately without waiting for the track to be completed. This should be the preferred way in order to yield to the Windows message loop.

If the track specified is less than or equal to zero, a waveform sound is played. The sound depends on the registry entry for the MB_ICONHAND sound type.

```
void CCDPlayerDlg::OnPlay()
{
    // TODO: Add your control notification handler code here
    DWORD dwRC;
    MCI_PLAY_PARMS PlayParms;
    MCI_STATUS_PARMS StatusParms;

    UpdateData(TRUE);
    if (m_track <= 0)
```

```
{
    MessageBeep(MB_ICONHAND);
    MessageBox("Track number should be greater than 0",
                "Error", MB_ICONHAND);
    return;
}
if (m_track <= sTotalTracks)
{
    StatusParms.dwItem = MCI_STATUS_LENGTH;
    StatusParms.dwTrack = m_track;
    if (dwRC = mciSendCommand(uDevID, MCI_STATUS,
                MCI_STATUS_ITEM | MCI_TRACK,
                (DWORD)&StatusParms))
    {
        CHAR szError[128+1];
        mciGetErrorString(dwRC, szError, sizeof(szError));
        AfxMessageBox(szError);
    }
    wsprintf (szStatus,
                "Length of track %d is %d Mins and %d Secs\r\n",
            m_track,
            MCI_MSF_MINUTE(StatusParms.dwReturn),
            MCI_MSF_SECOND(StatusParms.dwReturn));
}
else
{
    strcpy (szStatus, "Playing all tracks.\r\n");
}
m_status.SetSel(-1,0);
m_status.ReplaceSel(szStatus);

dwRC = 0;
PlayParms.dwFrom = 0L;
PlayParms.dwTo = 0L;
if (m_track < sTotalTracks)
{
    PlayParms.dwFrom = MCI_MAKE_TMSF(m_track, 0, 0, 0);
    PlayParms.dwTo = MCI_MAKE_TMSF(m_track + 1, 0, 0, 0);
    PlayParms.dwCallback = (DWORD) NULL;
    dwRC = mciSendCommand(uDevID, MCI_PLAY,
        MCI_FROM | MCI_TO , (DWORD)(LPVOID) &PlayParms);
}
else if (m_track == sTotalTracks)
{
```

```
            PlayParms.dwFrom = MCI_MAKE_TMSF(m_track, 0, 0, 0);
            PlayParms.dwCallback = (DWORD) NULL;
            dwRC = mciSendCommand(uDevID, MCI_PLAY,
                MCI_FROM, (DWORD)(LPVOID) &PlayParms);
    }
    else
    {   // Play all tracks
            PlayParms.dwFrom = MCI_MAKE_TMSF(1, 0, 0, 0);
            PlayParms.dwCallback = (DWORD) NULL;
            dwRC = mciSendCommand(uDevID, MCI_PLAY,
                MCI_FROM, (DWORD)(LPVOID) &PlayParms);
    }
    if (dwRC)
        {
            CHAR szError[128+1];
            mciGetErrorString(dwRC, szError, sizeof(szError));
            AfxMessageBox(szError);
            mciSendCommand(uDevID, MCI_CLOSE, 0, NULL);
        }
}
```

When the Preview button is selected, the CD audio device plays each track for a specified number of seconds. This is done by seeking each track, playing it for the specified amount of time, and then seeking the next track. The **MCI_SEEK** command message is used to jump to the track specified in the **MCI_SEEK_PARM** structures. This application takes a simple method of sleeping for a given number of milliseconds, thereby not yielding to the message loop. A better method would be to use the notification method by specifying the MCI_NOTIFY flag and giving a callback window handle in the **MCI_PLAY_PARMS** structure. MCI commands usually return immediately, even if the command could take several minutes to complete the action, as in the case of playing a track. If needed, the program can wait until the command is completed by specifying the MCI_WAIT flag. This will cause the device to wait until the command action is completed.

```
void CCDPlayerDlg::OnPreview()
{
    // TODO: Add your control notification handler code here
    DWORD dwRC;
    UpdateData(TRUE); // Get the preview time.
    for (int i = 1; i <= sTotalTracks; i++)
    {
        MCI_PLAY_PARMS PlayParms;
        MCI_SEEK_PARMS SeekParms;

        SeekParms.dwTo = i;
```

```
        dwRC = mciSendCommand(uDevID, MCI_SEEK,
            MCI_TO, (DWORD)(LPVOID) &SeekParms);

        if (i < sTotalTracks)
        {
            PlayParms.dwFrom = MCI_MAKE_TMSF(i, 0, 0, 0);
            PlayParms.dwTo = MCI_MAKE_TMSF(i + 1, 0, 0, 0);
            PlayParms.dwCallback = (DWORD) NULL;
            dwRC = mciSendCommand(uDevID, MCI_PLAY,
                MCI_FROM | MCI_TO , (DWORD)(LPVOID) &PlayParms);
        }
        else
        {
            PlayParms.dwFrom = MCI_MAKE_TMSF(i, 0, 0, 0);
            PlayParms.dwCallback = (DWORD) NULL;
            dwRC = mciSendCommand(uDevID, MCI_PLAY,
                    MCI_FROM, (DWORD)(LPVOID) &PlayParms);
        }

        Sleep(m_track*1000); // Data in track is the preview seconds.
    }
    dwRC = mciSendCommand(uDevID, MCI_STOP, 0, NULL);
    wsprintf (szStatus,
            "%d seconds preview of CD Player ended.\r\n",
            m_track);
    m_status.SetSel(-1,0);
    m_status.ReplaceSel(szStatus);

}
```

When the Eject button is pressed, the CD media is ejected from the CD audio device and the button is renamed "Retract." When the Retract button is pressed, it retracts the CD audio device door. Unlike earlier commands that were used, the application uses the command string format API, **mciSendString**. Using **mciSendString** is much easier, since the string form of the command is directly sent to the device. When the CD is ejected, the track information is reset; when the CD is loaded, information related to the track is reread and displayed on the status area.

```
void CCDPlayerDlg::OnDoor()
{
    // TODO: Add your control notification handler code here
    CButton *pDoorButton;
    MCI_STATUS_PARMS StatusParms;
    DWORD dwRC;
```

```
// Assume that the CD is in the drive and the door is closed
// to start with.

if (fDoorOpen)
{
    mciSendString( "set cdaudio door closed wait",
                    NULL, 0, NULL );
    pDoorButton = (CButton *)GetDlgItem(IDC_DOOR);
    pDoorButton->SetWindowText("&Eject");
    fDoorOpen = FALSE;

    while (1)
    {   // Loop till device is ready
        memset (&StatusParms, '\0', sizeof(StatusParms));
        StatusParms.dwItem = MCI_STATUS_MODE;
        if (dwRC = mciSendCommand(uDevID, MCI_STATUS,
                    MCI_STATUS_ITEM | MCI_WAIT,
                    (DWORD)&StatusParms))
        {
            break; // error assume no media!
        }
        else
        {
            if (StatusParms.dwReturn == MCI_MODE_NOT_READY ||
                StatusParms.dwReturn == MCI_MODE_OPEN)
            {
                continue; // Still not ready continue.
            }
            else
            {
                break;      // Ready to query.
            }
        }
    }
    memset (&StatusParms, '\0', sizeof(StatusParms));
    StatusParms.dwItem = MCI_STATUS_NUMBER_OF_TRACKS;
    if (mciSendCommand(uDevID, MCI_STATUS, MCI_STATUS_ITEM |
                    MCI_WAIT, (DWORD)&StatusParms))
    {// May be no disk in the CD drive.
        sTotalTracks = 0;
    }
    else
    {
```

```
                sTotalTracks = (short)StatusParms.dwReturn;
        }


        StatusParms.dwItem = MCI_STATUS_LENGTH;
        if (mciSendCommand(uDevID, MCI_STATUS, MCI_STATUS_ITEM,
                        (DWORD)&StatusParms))
        {// May be no disk in the CD drive
            StatusParms.dwReturn = 0;
        }
        wsprintf (szStatus,
                "Total number of tracks in this CD is %d.\r\n\
Total track time of this CD is %d Mins and %d Secs\r\n",
                sTotalTracks,
                MCI_MSF_MINUTE(StatusParms.dwReturn),
                MCI_MSF_SECOND(StatusParms.dwReturn));
        m_status.SetSel(-1,0);
        m_status.ReplaceSel(szStatus);

    }
    else
    {
        mciSendString( "set cdaudio door open", NULL, 0, NULL );
        pDoorButton = (CButton *)GetDlgItem(IDC_DOOR);
        pDoorButton->SetWindowText("R&etract");
        fDoorOpen = TRUE;
        sTotalTracks = 0;    // The CD is taken out. Reset total tracks.
    }
}
```

When the Pause button is pressed, it pauses the currently playing CD and changes the button text to "Resume." When the Resume button is pressed, the currently selected track continues to play. Here again the string format of the API is used.

```
void CCDPlayerDlg::OnPause()
{
    // TODO: Add your control notification handler code here
    CButton *pPauseButton;
    DWORD dwRC;
    char    szCmdBuffer[32];

    // Assume that the CD is in the drive and the door is closed
    // to start with.

    if (fPaused)
```

```
        {
            if (m_track < sTotalTracks)
            {
                wsprintf (szCmdBuffer,
                            "play cdaudio to %d",
                            m_track+1);
            }
            else
            {
                strcpy (szCmdBuffer, "play");
            }

            if (dwRC = mciSendString( szCmdBuffer, NULL, 0, NULL ))
            {
                CHAR szError[128+1];
                mciGetErrorString(dwRC, szError, sizeof(szError));
                AfxMessageBox(szError);
            }
            else
            {
                pPauseButton = (CButton *)GetDlgItem(IDC_PAUSE);
                pPauseButton->SetWindowText("Pau&se");
                fPaused = FALSE;
                strcpy (szStatus, "CD Player resumed.\r\n");
                m_status.SetSel(-1,0);
                m_status.ReplaceSel(szStatus);
            }
        }
        else
        {
            if(dwRC = mciSendString( "pause cdaudio", NULL, 0, NULL ))
            {
                CHAR szError[128+1];
                mciGetErrorString(dwRC, szError, sizeof(szError));
                AfxMessageBox(szError);
            }
            else
            {
                pPauseButton = (CButton *)GetDlgItem(IDC_PAUSE);
                pPauseButton->SetWindowText("Re&sume");
                fPaused = TRUE;
                strcpy (szStatus, "CD Player paused. To resume click Resume \
button.\r\n");
                m_status.SetSel(-1,0);
```

```
                m_status.ReplaceSel(szStatus);
        }
    }
}

void CCDPlayerDlg::OnStop()
{
    // TODO: Add your control notification handler code here
    mciSendCommand(uDevID, MCI_STOP, 0, NULL);

}
```

The **MCI_STOP** command message stops playing the CD. The difference between **MCI_PAUSE** and **MCI_STOP** is that **MCI_STOP** resets the current track position to zero, whereas **MCI_PAUSE** remembers the current track position and can resume at that point.

```
void CCDPlayerDlg::OnExit()
{
    // TODO: Add your control notification handler code here

    mciSendCommand(uDevID, MCI_CLOSE, 0, NULL);

    CDialog::OnOK();

}
```

When exiting the application, the CD audio device is closed by sending the **MCI_CLOSE** command message, which relinquishes the device. The device should be closed when exiting the application. Not doing so can leave the device inaccessible.

Though the sample application deals with the CD audio device, the MCI commands (both the message form and the string form) can be used to control any supported multimedia device including waveform audio devices, MIDI sequencers, digital video devices, and CD audio devices.

The libraries related to multimedia are *Vfw32.lib* and *Winmm.lib*, which are included as input to the project while building. Also not shown here is the inclusion of the *Vfw.h* header file, which is included in the *Stdafx.h* header file. This header file has all the definitions needed for multimedia.

VIDEO PROGRAMMING EXAMPLE

The next sample is an application that loads, plays, and controls an AVI file. When the application is started, a dialog box is displayed with buttons to open, play, pause, stop, step forward, step reverse, and change the speed of an AVI file. It also allows input of the

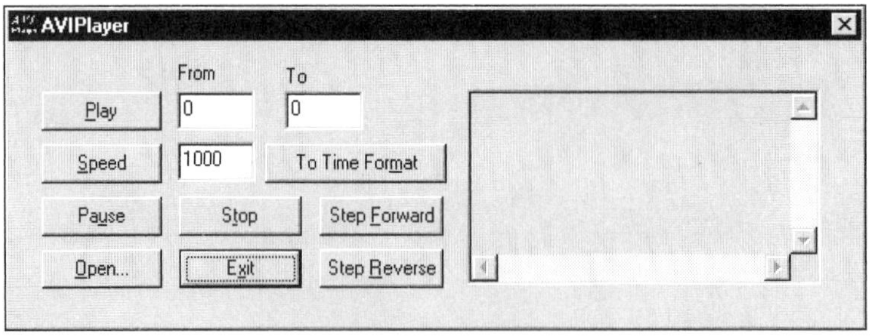

Figure 17-4. AVIPlayer dialog box

From and To location of the AVI segment to be played and provides a status area. Figure 17-4 shows the dialog box.

The application creates an *MCIWnd* window and uses it to play the AVI file. Like the CDPlayer sample application, this is also a dialog-based application whose framework is created by use of the AppWizard and ClassWizard. Since all the functionality that this application tries to show is in the *AVIPlayerDlg* dialog box, code related to this dialog box class is shown next. Shown is the class definition file for the **AVIPlayerDlg** class. The class maintains the information about the AVI window, its status, and the file information in member variables. Information conveyed by the user or to the user through the user interface, such as the frame numbers, speed, and status, is also maintained in member variables.

```
// AVIPlayerDlg.h : header file
#if !defined(AFX_AVIPLAYERDLG_H)
#define AFX_AVIPLAYERDLG_H
#if _MSC_VER >= 1000
#pragma once
#endif // _MSC_VER >= 1000


/////////////////////////////////////////////////////////////////////////////
// CAVIPlayerDlg dialog

class CAVIPlayerDlg : public CDialog
{
// Construction
public:
    CAVIPlayerDlg(CWnd* pParent = NULL);    // standard constructor

// Dialog Data
    //{{AFX_DATA(CAVIPlayerDlg)
```

```
    enum { IDD = IDD_AVIPLAYER_DIALOG };
    CEdit    m_status;
    long     m_from;
    short    m_speed;
    long     m_to;
    //}}AFX_DATA

    // ClassWizard generated virtual function overrides
    //{{AFX_VIRTUAL(CAVIPlayerDlg)
    protected:
    virtual void DoDataExchange(CDataExchange* pDX);
    //}}AFX_VIRTUAL

// Implementation
protected:
    HICON m_hIcon;
    BOOL     fPaused;
    BOOL     fTimeFormat;
    char     szStatus[256];
    char     szAVIFile[MAX_PATH];
    HWND     m_hwndAVIWindow;

    // Generated message map functions
    //{{AFX_MSG(CAVIPlayerDlg)
    virtual BOOL OnInitDialog();
    afx_msg void OnSysCommand(UINT nID, LPARAM lParam);
    afx_msg void OnPaint();
    afx_msg HCURSOR OnQueryDragIcon();
    afx_msg void OnOpen();
    afx_msg void OnPause();
    afx_msg void OnPlay();
    afx_msg void OnSpeed();
    afx_msg void OnStepf();
    afx_msg void OnStepr();
    afx_msg void OnStop();
    afx_msg void OnTimeformat();
    virtual void OnOK();
    //}}AFX_MSG
    DECLARE_MESSAGE_MAP()
};

//{{AFX_INSERT_LOCATION}}

#endif // !defined(AFX_AVIPLAYERDLG_H)
```

The implementation file for the **AVIPlayerDlg** class is shown next. Apart from the code for the application dialog box, it also has code to deal with the About panel. During **OnInitDialog** processing the member variables are initialized and displayed in the dialog box by calling **UpdateData**. **OnSystemCommand**, **OnPaint**, and **OnQueryDragIcon** are handled by the code generated by the ClassWizard and are unchanged, since no additional processing is required in this application.

```
// AVIPlayerDlg.cpp : implementation file
//

#include "stdafx.h"
#include "AVIPlayer.h"
#include "AVIPlayerDlg.h"

#ifdef _DEBUG
#define new DEBUG_NEW
#undef THIS_FILE
static char THIS_FILE[] = __FILE__;
#endif

/////////////////////////////////////////////////////////////////////////////
// CAboutDlg dialog used for App About

class CAboutDlg : public CDialog
{
public:
    CAboutDlg();

// Dialog Data
    //{{AFX_DATA(CAboutDlg)
    enum { IDD = IDD_ABOUTBOX };
    //}}AFX_DATA

    // ClassWizard generated virtual function overrides
    //{{AFX_VIRTUAL(CAboutDlg)
    protected:
    virtual void DoDataExchange(CDataExchange* pDX);
    //}}AFX_VIRTUAL

// Implementation
protected:
    //{{AFX_MSG(CAboutDlg)
    //}}AFX_MSG
    DECLARE_MESSAGE_MAP()
```

```
};

CAboutDlg::CAboutDlg() : CDialog(CAboutDlg::IDD)
{
    //{{AFX_DATA_INIT(CAboutDlg)
    //}}AFX_DATA_INIT
}

void CAboutDlg::DoDataExchange(CDataExchange* pDX)
{
    CDialog::DoDataExchange(pDX);
    //{{AFX_DATA_MAP(CAboutDlg)
    //}}AFX_DATA_MAP
}

BEGIN_MESSAGE_MAP(CAboutDlg, CDialog)
    //{{AFX_MSG_MAP(CAboutDlg)
        // No message handlers
    //}}AFX_MSG_MAP
END_MESSAGE_MAP()

/////////////////////////////////////////////////////////////////////////
// CAVIPlayerDlg dialog


CAVIPlayerDlg::CAVIPlayerDlg(CWnd* pParent /*=NULL*/)
    : CDialog(CAVIPlayerDlg::IDD, pParent)
{
    //{{AFX_DATA_INIT(CAVIPlayerDlg)
    m_from = 0;
    m_speed = 0;
    m_to = 0;
    //}}AFX_DATA_INIT
    // Note that LoadIcon does not require a subsequent DestroyIcon in Win32
    m_hIcon = AfxGetApp()->LoadIcon(IDR_MAINFRAME);
}

void CAVIPlayerDlg::DoDataExchange(CDataExchange* pDX)
{
    CDialog::DoDataExchange(pDX);
    //{{AFX_DATA_MAP(CAVIPlayerDlg)
    DDX_Control(pDX, IDC_MLE_STATUS, m_status);
    DDX_Text(pDX, IDC_EDIT_FROM, m_from);
    DDX_Text(pDX, IDC_EDIT_SPEED, m_speed);
```

```
    DDX_Text(pDX, IDC_EDIT_TO, m_to);
    //}}AFX_DATA_MAP
}


BEGIN_MESSAGE_MAP(CAVIPlayerDlg, CDialog)
    //{{AFX_MSG_MAP(CAVIPlayerDlg)
    ON_WM_SYSCOMMAND()
    ON_WM_PAINT()
    ON_WM_QUERYDRAGICON()
    ON_BN_CLICKED(IDC_OPEN, OnOpen)
    ON_BN_CLICKED(IDC_PAUSE, OnPause)
    ON_BN_CLICKED(IDC_PLAY, OnPlay)
    ON_BN_CLICKED(IDC_SPEED, OnSpeed)
    ON_BN_CLICKED(IDC_STEPF, OnStepf)
    ON_BN_CLICKED(IDC_STEPR, OnStepr)
    ON_BN_CLICKED(IDC_STOP, OnStop)
    ON_BN_CLICKED(IDC_TIMEFORMAT, OnTimeformat)
    //}}AFX_MSG_MAP
END_MESSAGE_MAP()


/////////////////////////////////////////////////////////////////////////////
// CAVIPlayerDlg message handlers

BOOL CAVIPlayerDlg::OnInitDialog()
{
    CDialog::OnInitDialog();

    // Add "About..." menu item to system menu.

    // IDM_ABOUTBOX must be in the system command range.
    ASSERT((IDM_ABOUTBOX & 0xFFF0) == IDM_ABOUTBOX);
    ASSERT(IDM_ABOUTBOX < 0xF000);

    CMenu* pSysMenu = GetSystemMenu(FALSE);
    if (pSysMenu != NULL)
    {
        CString strAboutMenu;
        strAboutMenu.LoadString(IDS_ABOUTBOX);
        if (!strAboutMenu.IsEmpty())
        {
            pSysMenu->AppendMenu(MF_SEPARATOR);
            pSysMenu->AppendMenu(MF_STRING, IDM_ABOUTBOX, strAboutMenu);
        }
    }
```

```
    // Set the icon for this dialog.  The framework does this automatically
    //  when the application's main window is not a dialog
    SetIcon(m_hIcon, TRUE);            // Set big icon
    SetIcon(m_hIcon, FALSE);          // Set small icon

    // TODO: Add extra initialization here

    fPaused = FALSE;
    fTimeFormat = FALSE;
    m_to = 0;
    m_from = 0;
    m_speed = 1000;

    UpdateData(FALSE);

    return TRUE;
}

void CAVIPlayerDlg::OnSysCommand(UINT nID, LPARAM lParam)
{
    if ((nID & 0xFFF0) == IDM_ABOUTBOX)
    {
        CAboutDlg dlgAbout;
        dlgAbout.DoModal();
    }
    else
    {
        CDialog::OnSysCommand(nID, lParam);
    }
}


void CAVIPlayerDlg::OnPaint()
{
    if (IsIconic())
    {
        CPaintDC dc(this); // device context for painting

        SendMessage(WM_ICONERASEBKGND, (WPARAM) dc.GetSafeHdc(), 0);

        // Center icon in client rectangle
        int cxIcon = GetSystemMetrics(SM_CXICON);
        int cyIcon = GetSystemMetrics(SM_CYICON);
```

```
            CRect rect;
            GetClientRect(&rect);
            int x = (rect.Width()—cxIcon + 1) / 2;
            int y = (rect.Height()—cyIcon + 1) / 2;

            // Draw the icon
            dc.DrawIcon(x, y, m_hIcon);
        }
        else
        {
            CDialog::OnPaint();
        }
    }


    // The system calls this to obtain the cursor to
    // display while the user drags
    // the minimized window.
    HCURSOR CAVIPlayerDlg::OnQueryDragIcon()
    {
        return (HCURSOR) m_hIcon;
    }
```

When the Open button is pressed, a file dialog box is displayed by calling the **DoModal** member function of the **CFileDialog** class. The class is initialized to display all the files with the .AVI extension and to pad .AVI as the extension if the user does not provide one. When the user selects an AVI file, an **MCIWnd** window is created and the selected file is passed to it by calling the **MCIWndCreate** function. This function registers the **MCIWnd** window class and creates an **MCIWnd** window to which various MCI command messages can be sent. The window is created without any menus (MCIWNDF_NOMENU), without the play bar that allows you to control the play (MCIWNDF_NOPLAYBAR), and is requested to show the mode on the title bar MCIWNDF_SHOWMODE). The menu and play bar are not shown since this application controls the entire functionality of the AVI file. As an exercise, the style can be modified and the effect can be observed. The AVI file is also passed to the function, and when the **MCIWnd** window is created, the AVI file is loaded.

```
void CAVIPlayerDlg::OnOpen()
{
    // TODO: Add your control notification handler code here
    CFileDialog   Filedlg (TRUE, "avi", "*.avi", OFN_HIDEREADONLY,
               "Video files (*.AVI)", this);
    if (IDOK == Filedlg.DoModal())
    {
        strcpy (szAVIFile, Filedlg.GetPathName());
```

```
        m_hwndAVIWindow = MCIWndCreate(NULL,
                        AfxGetInstanceHandle(),
                        MCIWNDF_NOMENU |
                        MCIWNDF_SHOWMODE |
                        MCIWNDF_NOPLAYBAR,
                        szAVIFile);
    long lAVILength = MCIWndGetLength(m_hwndAVIWindow);
    wsprintf (szStatus, "Window opened with %s.\r\n The file has
      %ld frames.\r\n", szAVIFile, lAVILength);
    m_status.SetSel(-1,0);
    m_status.ReplaceSel(szStatus);
    }
    else
    {
        return;
    }
}
```

When the Play button is pressed, the segment information (either frames or time) is retrieved and the segment is played by calling the **MCIWndPlay**, **MCIWndPlayTo**, **MCIWndPlayFrom**, or **MCIWndPlayFromTo** macro. Depending on the segment information, one of these macros is used. These macros in turn send a **MCI_PLAY**, **MCIWNDM_PLAYFROM**, or **MCIWNDM_PLAYTO** message to the **MCIWnd** window. In the case of **MCIWndPlayFromTo** the system first seeks to the starting segment by sending a **MCI_SEEK** message and then sending a **MCI_PLAYTO** message. The **MCI_PLAY** message plays from the current location till the end of the content, **MCIWNDM_PLAYTO** plays from the current location till the specified location, and **MCIWNDM_PLAYFROM** plays from the specified location till the end of the content. Note that if the From location is after the To location, the content is played in the reverse direction. After sending the message, the status edit control is updated with the status information.

```
void CAVIPlayerDlg::OnPlay()
{
    // TODO: Add your control notification handler code here
    UpdateData(TRUE);

    if (m_from == 0 && m_to == 0)
    {   // Play the entire segment
        MCIWndPlay(m_hwndAVIWindow);
        strcpy (szStatus, "Playing the AVI file\r\n");
    }
    else if (m_from == 0 && m_to != 0)
    {   // Play up to m_to segment
        MCIWndPlayTo(m_hwndAVIWindow, m_to);
```

```
        wsprintf (szStatus, "Playing up to %d\r\n", m_to);
    }
    else if (m_from !=0 && m_to == 0)
    {   // Play from m_from segment
        MCIWndPlayFrom(m_hwndAVIWindow, m_from);
        wsprintf (szStatus, "Playing from %d\r\n", m_from);
    }
    else
    {   // Play the selected segment
        MCIWndPlayFromTo(m_hwndAVIWindow, m_from, m_to);
        wsprintf (szStatus, "Playing from %d to %d\r\n",
                  m_from, m_to);
    }
    m_status.SetSel(-1,0);
    m_status.ReplaceSel(szStatus);
}
```

When the Pause button is pressed, the application sends an **MCI_PAUSE** or **MCI_RESUME** message to the **MCIWnd** window by calling the **MCIWndPause** or **MCIWndResume** macro. It also changes the button text from "Pause" to "Resume" or the other way around, depending on the current state. Information as to whether the player is paused is maintained in a member variable. To stop the player, the **MCI_STOP** message is sent to the **MCIWnd** window by use of the **MCIWndStop** macro.

```
void CAVIPlayerDlg::OnPause()
{
    // TODO: Add your control notification handler code here
    CButton *pPauseButton;

    if (fPaused)
    {
        MCIWndResume(m_hwndAVIWindow);
        pPauseButton = (CButton *)GetDlgItem(IDC_PAUSE);
        pPauseButton->SetWindowText("Pau&se");
        fPaused = FALSE;
        strcpy (szStatus, "Play resumed.\r\n");
    }
    else
    {
        MCIWndPause(m_hwndAVIWindow);
        pPauseButton = (CButton *)GetDlgItem(IDC_PAUSE);
        pPauseButton->SetWindowText("Re&sume");
        fPaused = TRUE;
        strcpy (szStatus,
```

```
                         "Play paused.\r\nTo resume click Resume button.\r\n");
    }

    m_status.SetSel(-1,0);
    m_status.ReplaceSel(szStatus);
}


void CAVIPlayerDlg::OnStop()
{
    // TODO: Add your control notification handler code here
    MCIWndStop(m_hwndAVIWindow);
    strcpy(szStatus, "Play stopped\r\n");
    m_status.SetSel(-1,0);
    m_status.ReplaceSel(szStatus);


}
```

The speed of the player can be controlled by sending the **MCIWNDM_SETSPEED** message. This *AVIPlayer* application provides a way to change the speed at which the player plays back the AVI file. The speed can be provided by the application through the Speed edit control in the dialog box and by setting the speed by clicking on the Speed button. A value of 1000 indicates a normal speed, any value above 1000 can be specified for more speed, and any value lower than 1000 but greater than 0 can be specified for less speed.

```
void CAVIPlayerDlg::OnSpeed()
{
    // TODO: Add your control notification handler code here
    UpdateData(TRUE);

    if( MCIWndSetSpeed (m_hwndAVIWindow, m_speed))
    {
        strcpy (szStatus, "Speed setting command failed\r\n");
    }
    else
    {
        wsprintf (szStatus, "Player speed set to %d\r\n", m_speed);
    }
    m_status.SetSel(-1,0);
    m_status.ReplaceSel(szStatus);


}


void CAVIPlayerDlg::OnStepf()
{
```

```
    // TODO: Add your control notification handler code here
    MCIWndStep(m_hwndAVIWindow, 1);
    strcpy(szStatus, "Step forward\r\n");
    m_status.SetSel(-1,0);
    m_status.ReplaceSel(szStatus);


}
```

Two buttons to step through the AVI player are provided. The Step Forward button steps one frame forward, and Step Reverse steps one frame backwards. The step can be modified to other values. For example, a step value of 5 will step forward 5 frames, and –5 will step 5 frames backwards.

```
void CAVIPlayerDlg::OnStepr()
{
    // TODO: Add your control notification handler code here
    MCIWndStep(m_hwndAVIWindow, -1);
    strcpy(szStatus, "Step backward\r\n");
    m_status.SetSel(-1,0);
    m_status.ReplaceSel(szStatus);


}

void CAVIPlayerDlg::OnTimeformat()
{
    // TODO: Add your control notification handler code here
    CButton *pTimeFormatButton;

    if (fTimeFormat)
    {   // Currently in Time Format
        MCIWndUseFrames(m_hwndAVIWindow);
        pTimeFormatButton = (CButton *)GetDlgItem(IDC_TIMEFORMAT);
        pTimeFormatButton->SetWindowText("To Ti&me Format");
        fTimeFormat = FALSE;
        strcpy (szStatus, "Changed to Frame Format\r\n");
    }
    else
    {   // Currently in Frame Format
        MCIWndUseTime(m_hwndAVIWindow);
        pTimeFormatButton = (CButton *)GetDlgItem(IDC_TIMEFORMAT);
```

```
        pTimeFormatButton->SetWindowText("To Fra&me Format");
        fTimeFormat = TRUE;
        strcpy (szStatus, "Changed to Time Format.\r\n");
    }

    m_status.SetSel(-1,0);
    m_status.ReplaceSel(szStatus);

}
```

This application allows the user to change the time format for the player. By default the time format is set to *frames*. But the time format can also be set to *ms* or milliseconds. Messages like **MCIWND_PLAYTO** and **MCIWND_PLAYFROM** are affected by the time format setting. Thus, if the time format is set to frames and "10" and "100," respectively, appear in the From and To entry fields, all frames from 10 until 100 are played. On the other hand, if the time format is set to *ms*, then the player will play 90ms of the segment beginning at 10ms from the start. Formats other than *frames* and *ms* can be set provided the MCI device supports them. To set the time format to *frames*, the **MCIWndUseFrames** macro is used; to set to *ms*, **MCIWndUseTime** is used.

Finally, when the user chooses the Exit button, the **MCIWnd** window is closed by sending an **MCI_CLOSE** message by use of the **MCIWndClose** macro. This closes the file associated with the **MCIWnd** window, but still keeps the window open and can be associated with a different file. Since this application processes the Exit button to exit, it also destroys the **MCIWnd** window by sending the **WM_CLOSE** message using the **MCIWndDestroy** macro. This macro destroys the **MCIWnd** window. (It also closes the MCI file associated with the window, and hence the **MCIWndClose** macro is irrelevant here.)

```
void CAVIPlayerDlg::OnOK()
{
    // TODO: Add extra validation here
    MCIWndClose(m_hwndAVIWindow);
    CDialog::OnOK();
}
```

If you do not have an AVI file to load, look at some of the television networks' web sites, like **www.abcnews.com**. They typically have AVI files for their news coverage.

The libraries related to multimedia are *Vfw32.lib* and *Winmm.lib*, which are included as input to the project while building. Also not shown here is the inclusion of the *Vfw.h* header file, which is included in the *Stdafx.h* header file. This header file has all the definitions needed for multimedia.

Conclusion

We started with a brief review of multimedia basics, including time formats. Then we looked at some audio programming methods such as using the media control interface and **MCIWnd**. We looked at a CD player programming example. Then we looked at video programming methods and looked at a video programming example that plays AVI video clips.

In the next chapter, we will look at the telephony interface TAPI.

CHAPTER 18

Telephony Programming Using TAPI

Computer Telephony Integration (CTI), also called "telephony" for short, is a fast developing field that attempts to integrate the functions of telephones, the telephone network, and computers. Traditionally, people in computers and communications have had different visions of the role of computers and communications. The computer-oriented people see, of course, the computer at the center and want transparent communications when one computer needs to communicate with another. The communications people, of course, see the communications network at the center and see computers and other devices at the endpoints. One consequence of this traditional difference in visions is that most of us still have a computer and a telephone on our desks with little, if any, interaction between the two. Yet the technology exists to let computers handle not only voice communications, but also video conferencing. Another consequence was that the first systems that came up to bridge the capabilities between computers and communications were proprietary systems that used their own user and programming interfaces.

Telephony Application Programming Interface (TAPI) and Telephony Service Provider Interface (TSPI) standardize the application programming and service programming interfaces so that applications written to these standard interfaces will work across different communications networks, and so the underlying communications networks and services are transparent to the telephony applications. For example, if you develop a TAPI application to communicate using a modem and subsequently the modem connection has an ISDN (Integrated Services Digital Network) connection, your TAPI application will not need to be changed. Of course, you will need an ISDN adapter, changes in drivers, and so on. Besides handling the simple dialing and receiving of voice calls, TAPI also supports the development of complex applications. Such applications handle data transmission; support different connections, such as connecting through a serial port, an add-in phone/fax card, and through LANs; and handle advanced features such as caller ID, call waiting, call conferencing, and voice mail. In short, TAPI gives your application access to the public switched telephone network (PSTN) and enables your application to handle functions that can be performed with phones and Private Branch Exchanges (PBXs). The phone service provided using PSTN is also called "plain old telephone service" (POTS).

As a business programmer, you are unlikely to develop full-scale telephony applications (unless you work for a company that builds telephony applications). When you use telephony functions, you are far more likely to use TAPI, unless you are providing a telephony service using TSPI. In this chapter, we will review telephony basics, look at the different functions and capabilities provided by TAPI for developing telephony applications, see the steps involved in developing a TAPI application, and discuss a simple TAPI programming example.

TELEPHONY BASICS

Let's consider POTS to your home. POTS provides you a *line* from your telephone to the telephone network. This part of the connection is also called a *local loop*. The local loop from your home to the telephone company's switching office is slowly being converted to digital, while other connections in the telephone network are mostly digital. Converting to digital provides some advantages, such as better quality connections and faster data transmission. More importantly, the telephone companies are now starting to offer ISDN service. Unlike regular phone service, which allows one *channel* on a line at a time (a channel is a communications conduit), ISDN enables you to have between three and 32 channels using the same line. This means that you can have a voice phone conversation using one channel while your computer is downloading a web page on another channel. You can use TAPI to develop telephony applications that can transparently use POTS, ISDN, or any telephone networking mechanism such as PBX, Centrex, cellular, and so on.

TAPI is a telephony facilitator, but not a processor of the data stream that is communicated. For example, you can develop a TAPI application that will place a call or receive a fax. But TAPI does not have any functions to process the WAV data type of the voice call or the G3 image of the fax. You can, of course, have a multimedia application process a WAV file received by TAPI, and this is one of the advantages of TAPI compared with proprietary communications-centric systems. You can have supporting Win32 API–based applications work with TAPI to provide enhanced telephony application functions.

TAPI SDK is integrated with the Win32 SDK, and TAPI is included as part of the Windows NT operating system (both Server and Workstation). Windows NT TAPI-related components include *Tapi32.dll* and *Tapisrv.exe*. The relationship between the components is shown in Figure 18-1.

Your TAPI application invokes the *Tapi32.dll*, which runs in your application's address space. *Tapi32.dll* communicates with the Windows NT service *Tapisrv.exe*, which in turn communicates with a service provider DLL. The service provider also provides a driver that is invoked by the service provider DLL. To develop TAPI applications, Micrsoft provides the TAPI header file *Tapi.h* and the library *Tapi32.lib*.

An *address* in TAPI is a telephone number, and a *call* is a connection between two or more addresses.

Device Classes and Media Modes

TAPI classifies telephony devices into two device classes. A *device class* is a group of related physical devices or device drivers through which applications send and receive information. There are primarily two classes of devices in TAPI—line devices and phone devices. *Line* devices are logical representations of physical devices, such as a modem, an ISDN adapter, a fax board, and so on. A *phone* device includes the traditional phone with a handset, hook switch, and so forth. A phone device could also be any device that is capable of performing the functions of the phone. For example, it could be an audio card installed in the PC with a microphone and headset connected to it.

The types of data carried by the telephone network are normally classified as the media stream or signals. The *media stream* is the actual data, such as a voice conversation or fax data. *Signals* are the associated data, such as the digits that are dialed to start a communication connection, caller ID, and so on. TAPI provides access to signal

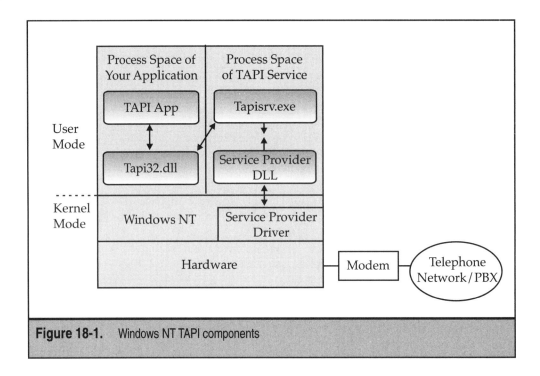

Figure 18-1.   Windows NT TAPI components

information. TAPI facilitates transmission of media streams, but does not provide any functions to process media streams.

Owner and Monitor Applications

In TAPIs each call typically has one owner application. In addition, each call may have one or more monitoring applications. If your application initiates a call, your application is automatically the call's owner. You can pass ownership to another application. For example, if your application initiates a voice call on a line and if you decide to send a fax on the same line, your application can pass ownership of the call to the fax application. Although it is possible for an application to retain ownership after passing (a call can thus have multiple owners), it is rarely required. When an incoming call is received, the highest priority application capable of handling the media type of the incoming call is selected as the owner, and the call is passed to the application. Priorities can be assigned by the user, and this information is typically stored in the Registry.

Monitoring applications commonly monitor the call status and produce logs.

Call States

A call goes through different states from the time it is originated to the time it is terminated. When a call is first initiated, it is in an *offering* state until the remote party responds and completes the connection, at which point the call is in the *connected* state. When your application disconnects a call, it goes to the *idle* state. If the remote party disconnects a call, the call goes to the *disconnected* state. It is important to understand the role of states, since the actions your application can perform on a call depend on its current state. Some other states a call can be in are *onholdpending* (the state of the calls waiting for a conference call to be initiated), *onhold* (when a call is placed on hold), and so on.

Address Translation

Often telephone numbers are stored in a database, and one or more numbers are selected from the database when dialing. The format of the stored numbers is normally not the same as the format of the number dialed. Typically the numbers are stored in a *canonical* address format and are translated into a *dialable* address format. This translation is handled by use of the TAPI **lineTranslateAddress** function. While the canonical format may contain the complete address, including country code and area code, the country code is not necessary when a call is made within the same country. **lineTranslateAddress** takes care of removing such unnecessary parts of the address and including other required data such as a prefix that may be needed to dial an outside call in an office, or the calling code of an alternate carrier if the call is to be placed using the alternate carrier. **lineTranslateAddress** retrieves information, such as the country and area code where the application is executing, from the Registry.

Although it is common for one line to have one channel and one address in POTS, this need not always be the case. For example, with *distinctive ringing,* the same channel supports multiple addresses, each with its own distinctive ring. Also, with an ISDN line, there are multiple channels, and each channel can have its own address.

Service Providers

Service providers use the TSPI interface to develop service provider applications that interface with your TAPI applications. For example, an incoming call is first detected by the service provider, which performs some initial functions, such as determining the media mode of the incoming call. Then the service provider passes it to *Tapi.dll* which selects an application and passes the call to the application. The media mode of an incoming call needs to be determined. For example, an incoming call may be a voice call or a fax. The process of determining the actual media mode of a call is called *probing* and is attempted first by the service provider. If the service provider is unable to determine the media mode, then an application has to do so.

TELEPHONY SERVICES

Windows NT provides four types of telephony services, as follows:

▼ Assisted

■ Basic

■ Supplemental

▲ Extended

Assisted telephony services are not considered part of TAPI, while the other three services are considered three levels of TAPI.

Assisted telephony services provide a simple way for any general application, such as a word processor or spreadsheet or any application you develop, to place a call. All your application has to do is to call **tapiRequestMakeCall** and provide an address to be dialed. The actual call is placed by a call-control application (Windows NT includes a default call-control application, which you can substitute with your own). Another assisted telephony function is the **tapiGetLocationInfo** function, which returns the country code and city (area) code that the user has set in the current location parameters (in the Telephony Control Panel).

TIP: It is not efficient to mix TAPI function calls and assisted telephony calls within the same application.

Basic telephony services are a set of functions that roughly corresponds to the capabilities of POTS. Every TAPI-capable line device and all TAPI service providers must support all the basic telephony functions. Thus, if you develop a TAPI application using only basic telephony services, your application will work in all TAPI environments regardless of the lines, service providers, and so on. However, the subset of telephony services available in basic telephony services is limited.

Supplemental telephony services provide support for advanced features such as call holding, conference calling, and so on. All supplemental telephony services are optional, and service providers can choose what they want to implement. Your TAPI application is portable across TAPI environments only if the service provider of the environment you are interested in supports the supplemental services you have used in your application. You can query a line or phone device to get the set of supplementary services it supports by using the **lineGetDevCaps** and **lineGetAddressCaps** functions.

Extended telephony functions enable a telephony service provider to provide additional services not available with TAPI in basic or supplemental telephony services. The functionality contained in the extended telephony functions is up to the service provider of such functions. Service providers offer additional special services by using new values for some enumeration types and bit flags, and by adding new members to many data structures.

TAPI provides a number of functions that let your applications perform a range of telephony functions from simply dialing and receiving voice calls to sophisticated call-center applications managing hundreds of lines and phone devices. Some common TAPI functions are summarized in Table 18-1.

TAPI provides many more functions in addition to the ones shown in Table 18-1. For more details, refer to the TAPI SDK.

Category	Sample TAPI Functions	Description
Call setup and termination	lineOpen	This opens a line and returns a handle. Your application can open as a monitor or an owner.
	lineClose	This closes a line.
	lineAnswer	This answers an incoming call.
	lineDial	This dials a number.
Conferencing functions	lineAddTo Conference	This adds a call to a conference call.
	lineRemoveFrom Conference	This removes a call from a conference call.
Line-related functions	lineSetMedia Control	This enables and disables control actions on the media stream associated with the specified line, address, or call.
	lineSetNumRings	This sets the number of times an incoming call will ring before it is answered. You can use this function in conjunction with the lineGetNumRings function to implement the popular toll-saver function.
	lineSetStatus Messages	This specifies the subset of notification messages to receive for events related to status changes for the specified line or any of its addresses.
	lineForward	This forwards calls for a given address to another address.
	lineHold	This holds a call.
	lineUnhold	This removes the hold and reactivates a call.

Table 18-1. TAPI Functions and Categories

Category	Sample TAPI Functions	Description
	lineSecureCall	This prevents interference from the network or switch while a call is in progress (for example, it disables call waiting).
Phone-related functions	phoneOpen	This opens a specified phone device.
	phoneClose	This closes a specified phone device.
	phoneGetDev Caps	This retrieves the capabilities of a phone device.
	phoneGetStatus Messages	This returns which phone-state changes generate a callback to the application.
	phoneSetStatus Messages	This enables an application to monitor a phone device for selected status events.

Table 18-1. TAPI Functions and Categories (*continued*)

Many TAPI functions are *asynchronous*. When your application calls an asynchronous function, the function returns a code to your application. The actual operation to be performed by calling the function is performed asynchronously while your application is doing something else. If the operation encounters problems, your application is notified by use of mechanisms such as event signaling. You specify the mechanism you want in the **lineInitializeEx** function (see step 1 in the "TAPI Application Execution Sequence" section later in this chapter).

TAPI MESSAGES

Besides the calls where TAPI responds to your application's function calls, TAPI also sends your application unsolicited messages. For example, when the remote party to the communication hangs up, this is communicated to your application by use of a message. Your application can respond to the message and take appropriate action. The most common use for messages is for TAPI to inform your application of changes in call states. Table 18-2 summarizes some of the common TAPI messages and their descriptions.

TAPI Message	Description
LINE_CALLSTATE	Indicates that the status of the specified call has changed
LINE_CLOSE	Indicates that the specified line device has been (forcibly) closed (to free up a line controlled exclusively by a misbehaving application)
LINE_LINEDEVSTATE	Indicates that the state of a line device has changed
LINE_CREATE	Indicates that a new line device has been created and provides the line device's new device identifier

Table 18-2. TAPI Messages

TELEPHONY CAPABILITIES PROVIDED BY TAPI

TAPI can be used to provide simple dialing and receiving capability to your application. It can also be used to develop sophisticated call-center applications that monitor and handle a lot of simultaneous calls. Some of the advanced capabilities of TAPI include

▼ Support for delayed dialing, where you dial part of a number and subsequently complete the remaining digits.

■ Support for long-distance calls to be routed by use of different carriers, and charging calls to credit cards.

■ Retrieving the caller ID in incoming calls, or blocking sending of caller ID on outgoing calls.

■ Building and using *toll lists* (a toll list is a list of prefixes within an area code whose addresses must be dialed as long-distance addresses).

■ *Securing* a call, which prevents interference from the network or switch while a call is in progress. For example, you can disable call waiting before sending or receiving faxes. You can secure a call using **lineMakeCall** or **lineSecureCall**.

■ TAPI can handle various computer and phone connection configurations. The configurations include the following:

■ The phone may be attached by use of a serial device to a computer's serial port.

■ The computer may be attached to the phone network directly by use of a modem.

■ The computer may be attached by use of a modem to a company's PBX, which in turn is connected to the telephone network.

■ The computer may not have a modem, but just have a LAN connection which can handle both voice and data traffic.

TAPI APPLICATION EXECUTION SEQUENCE

The following steps illustrate the sequence when an application uses TAPI:

1. The application initializes TAPI by calling the **lineInitializeEx** TAPI function. **lineInitializeEx** specifies the application's callback function, which is called by TAPI to notify the application of various events. **lineInitializeEx** returns a TAPI usage handle and the number of line devices available to the application. Unlike many TAPI functions, **lineInitializeEx** is a synchronous function. **lineInitializeEx** also specifies the communication mechanism that will be used by TAPI—posting to a window message, signaling an event, or posting to an I/O completion port to notify your application of events.

   In addition, the telephony environment is set up the first time an initialization call is made in a telephony session. Setting up the telephony environment includes loading *Tapi32.dll*, starting TAPI service *Tapisrv.exe* (if it is not already running), and loading the telephony-related device drivers specified in the Registry.

2. The application negotiates with TAPI the correct version to be used. The application uses the **lineNegotiateAPIVersion** function to inform TAPI of the least recent API version and the most recent version of the TAPI API that it can use. **lineNegotiateAPIVersion** returns the version that the application can use for all further communication with TAPI. It also retrieves any extension that the line device can support.

TIP: Don't be tempted to set the least supported version to 0x00000000 or the highest supported version to 0xFFFFFFFF as an alternative to specifying specific version numbers. If your application attempts to work with a new TAPI version released in the future, then TAPI may choose the new version during negotiation, and your application may not work properly.

3. After agreeing on a specific version, your application queries the capabilities of the line device by calling the **lineGetDevCaps** function, which returns a rich set of details about the line device in a structure of type **LINEDEVCAPS**. Line-device capabilities specified include information such as the TAPI service provider, switch information, string format used by the line, different bearer modes that the line can support, data rate for information exchange, and so on.

4. The application registers itself.

5. After user input, your application should call the **ResolveNumber** function. **ResolveNumber** modifies the user's input number, and the modified number is then used for dialing.

6. Your application should call the **lineOpen** function to open a line device. You can specify a particular line device using a line-device identifier, or get TAPI to allocate a line that matches the line properties you specify. **lineOpen** returns a handle to the line device. This handle is used in all subsequent operations on the line device. You can open more than one line in your application if you choose.

7. Your application should call the **lineTranslateAddress** function, which translates the number to be dialed into a format that is dialable. Options such as inserting the call-waiting cancellation string at the beginning of the number, forcing a number that could potentially be a long-distance number to a local number (for example, a local calling area might have two area codes), forcing a number that could potentially be a local to long-distance (for example, a long-distance calling area might have the same area code), and so on, can be specified in *dwTranslateOptions*. The translated number is returned in the **LINETRANSLATEOUTPUT** structure. After translation the call returns two numbers, one that can be used to place the call on the line device (which the line device can understand and interpret), and the other that can be displayed to the user.

8. Your application then makes the call using the **lineMakeCall** function. **lineMakeCall** gets a call appearance (connection to the switch), waits for the dial tone, and dials the specified address. **lineMakeCall** uses the line handle returned by **lineOpen**. The **lineMakeCall** function returns a handle with owner privileges to the current call, and the handle is used to identify the call in future telephony operations on the call. **lineMakeCall** returns immediately and the function completes asynchronously. If the call encounters any problem after **lineMakeCall** returns, a **LINE_REPLY** message provides the status of the call.

9. When the communication is complete, call the **lineDrop** function to terminate (hang up) the call. Optionally, you can specify some user-user information that is communicated to the remote party, if such communication is supported by the underlying network. **lineDrop** is an asynchronous function. Note that **lineDrop** does not release a call's handle. This is because you may still want to access the call's data structures for logging purposes. The call handle must, however, be released to free up resources. You can explicitly release the handle by calling **lineDeallocateCall** or by calling **lineClose**, which also releases the handle (see next step).

10. Your application then calls the **lineClose** function to close the line using the line handle, and the released line can then be used by other applications.

11. Finally, your application calls **lineShutdown** to indicate the termination of the use of TAPI. Although calling **lineShutdown** implicitly closes open lines, you should close the lines explicitly before calling **lineShutdown**

The preceding steps are illustrated with actual code in the following example.

TAPI PROGRAMMING EXAMPLE

The *PhDial* sample program is simple, and it illustrates the use of line-device functions. It just scratches the surface of TAPI and introduces you to TAPI programming. This sample enables the user to place a call through a line device. A modem is used to develop this program, and after placing the call, the user can use the handset of the phone connected to the line.

The *PhDial* application's dialog box when it starts executing is shown in Figure 18-2.

The sample is created by use of the AppWizard, and it is a dialog-based AppWizard executable. It has two entry fields—one for the name and the other for the number—and three buttons—one each for dialing the number, hanging up the call, and exiting the program. It also has a status area where the status of the call is shown.

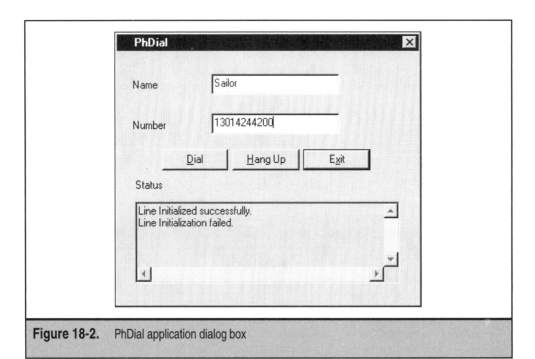

Figure 18-2. PhDial application dialog box

Shown next is the application dialog class header file. The sections of interest are highlighted. Member variables are used to save the handle to TAPI, the handle to the line, the negotiated version, the number of line devices, the handle to the currently placed call, a buffer for status, and so forth. Apart from the standard member functions to handle button actions, additional member functions to process the callback message and to display the status on the dialog box are also declared.

```
// PhDialDlg.h : header file

#if !defined(AFX_PHDIALDLG_H)
#define AFX_PHDIALDLG_H
#if _MSC_VER >= 1000
#pragma once
#endif // _MSC_VER >= 1000


/////////////////////////////////////////
// CPhDialDlg dialog

class CPhDialDlg : public CDialog
{
// Construction
public:
  CPhDialDlg(CWnd* pParent = NULL);// standard constructor

  afx_msg void DisplayCallBackInfo
        (DWORD   hDevice,
        DWORD   dwMsg,
        DWORD   dwCBInstance,
        DWORD   dwParam1,
        DWORD   dwParam2,
        DWORD   dwParam3
        );

// Dialog Data
  //{{AFX_DATA(CPhDialDlg)
  enum { IDD = IDD_PHDIAL_DIALOG };
  CEdit    m_status;
  CString  m_name;
  CString  m_number;
  //}}AFX_DATA

  // ClassWizard generated virtual function overrides
  //{{AFX_VIRTUAL(CPhDialDlg)
  protected:
```

```
  virtual void DoDataExchange(CDataExchange* pDX);
  //}}AFX_VIRTUAL

// Implementation
protected:
  HICON    m_hIcon;
  HLINEAPP  hLineApp;
  HLINE    hLine;
  DWORD    dwNumDevs;
  DWORD    dwNegVersion;
  HCALL    hCurrentCall;
  char    szStatus[256];

  afx_msg void WriteStatus();

  // Generated message map functions
  //{{AFX_MSG(CPhDialDlg)
  virtual BOOL OnInitDialog();
  afx_msg void OnSysCommand(UINT nID, LPARAM lParam);
  afx_msg void OnPaint();
  afx_msg HCURSOR OnQueryDragIcon();
  afx_msg void OnDial();
  virtual void OnOK();
  afx_msg void OnHang();
  //}}AFX_MSG
  DECLARE_MESSAGE_MAP()
};
#endif
```

Shown next is the implementation file for the application dialog class. The initial code handles the About dialog box, which is followed by the dialog initialization code.

```
// PhDialDlg.cpp : implementation file
//
#include "stdafx.h"
#include "PhDial.h"
#include "PhDialDlg.h"

#ifdef _DEBUG
#define new DEBUG_NEW
#undef THIS_FILE
```

```
static char THIS_FILE[] = __FILE__;
#endif


void CALLBACK PhDialCallback (
        DWORD   hDevice,
        DWORD   dwMsg,
        DWORD   dwCBInstance,
        DWORD   dwParam1,
        DWORD   dwParam2,
        DWORD   dwParam3);

void ResolveNumber(char *pszName, char *pszNumber);

/////////////////////////////////////
// CAboutDlg dialog used for App About

class CAboutDlg : public CDialog
{
public:
  CAboutDlg();

// Dialog Data
  //{{AFX_DATA(CAboutDlg)
  enum { IDD = IDD_ABOUTBOX };
  //}}AFX_DATA

  // ClassWizard generated virtual function overrides
  //{{AFX_VIRTUAL(CAboutDlg)
  protected:
  virtual void DoDataExchange(CDataExchange* pDX);
  //}}AFX_VIRTUAL

// Implementation
protected:
  //{{AFX_MSG(CAboutDlg)
  //}}AFX_MSG
  DECLARE_MESSAGE_MAP()
};

CAboutDlg::CAboutDlg() : CDialog(CAboutDlg::IDD)
{
```

```
  //{{AFX_DATA_INIT(CAboutDlg)
  //}}AFX_DATA_INIT
}

void CAboutDlg::DoDataExchange(CDataExchange* pDX)
{
  CDialog::DoDataExchange(pDX);
  //{{AFX_DATA_MAP(CAboutDlg)
  //}}AFX_DATA_MAP
}

BEGIN_MESSAGE_MAP(CAboutDlg, CDialog)
  //{{AFX_MSG_MAP(CAboutDlg)
    // No message handlers
  //}}AFX_MSG_MAP
END_MESSAGE_MAP()

/////////////////////////////////////
// CPhDialDlg dialog

CPhDialDlg::CPhDialDlg(CWnd* pParent /*=NULL*/)
  : CDialog(CPhDialDlg::IDD, pParent)
{
  //{{AFX_DATA_INIT(CPhDialDlg)
  m_name = _T("");
  m_number = _T("");
  //}}AFX_DATA_INIT
  m_hIcon = AfxGetApp()->LoadIcon(IDR_MAINFRAME);
}

void CPhDialDlg::DoDataExchange(CDataExchange* pDX)
{
  CDialog::DoDataExchange(pDX);
  //{{AFX_DATA_MAP(CPhDialDlg)
  DDX_Control(pDX, IDC_STATUS, m_status);
  DDX_Text(pDX, IDC_NAME, m_name);
  DDX_Text(pDX, IDC_NUMBER, m_number);
  //}}AFX_DATA_MAP
}

BEGIN_MESSAGE_MAP(CPhDialDlg, CDialog)
  //{{AFX_MSG_MAP(CPhDialDlg)
  ON_WM_SYSCOMMAND()
```

```
ON_WM_PAINT()
ON_WM_QUERYDRAGICON()
ON_BN_CLICKED(IDC_DIAL, OnDial)
ON_BN_CLICKED(IDC_HANG, OnHang)
//}}AFX_MSG_MAP
END_MESSAGE_MAP()
```

After the About menu item is added, the application-related initialization is done. First the application initializes the use of TAPI by calling the **lineInitialize** TAPI function. This function initializes the application's use of TAPI for future use of line abstraction. When TAPI is operational, it sends messages to the application to notify it of various events. These messages are sent to the application's callback function, which is provided to the TAPI through **lineInitialize**. When this function completes, it returns the application's TAPI usage handle and the number of line devices available to the application. For TAPI version 2.0 the **lineInitializeEx** function should be used. Before this application can communicate with TAPI, it should agree upon a version of TAPI that it can use to communicate. To do this, the application should tell TAPI the least recent API version and the most recent version of the TAPI API that it can use. This is done by calling **lineNegotiateAPIVersion**. When this function completes, it returns the version that the application can use for all further communication with TAPI. It also retrieves any extension that the line device can support. For this sample the line device extensions are ignored, since this application is a simple one. This sample uses the first line device, 0. **TAPI_CURRENT_VERSION** is defined by the TAPI toolkit to represent the most recent version of the toolkit. After a version number is established, the telephony capabilities of the line device are queried by calling the **lineGetDevCaps** function. This application does not depend on specific telephony capabilities, and this call serves no purpose other than showing the use of it. The **lineGetDevCaps** function returns a rich set of details about the line device. The line device capabilities are returned in a structure of type **LINEDEVCAPS**. Since the information is returned in the structure as the offset to the start of the structure, a big enough buffer should be passed to the call. Information such as the TAPI service provider, switch information, string format used by the line, different bearer modes that the line can support, data rate for information exchange, and much more is provided by this function. For a complete set of information returned by **lineGetDevCaps**, please refer to the TAPI SDK. Next the application registers itself as the recipient for the LINEREQUESTMODE_MAKECALL. With these initializations completed the application is ready to place calls.

```
/////////////////////////////////////
// CPhDialDlg message handlers

BOOL CPhDialDlg::OnInitDialog()
{
  CDialog::OnInitDialog();
```

```
// Add "About..." menu item to system menu.

// IDM_ABOUTBOX must be in the system command range.
ASSERT((IDM_ABOUTBOX & 0xFFF0) == IDM_ABOUTBOX);
ASSERT(IDM_ABOUTBOX < 0xF000);

CMenu* pSysMenu = GetSystemMenu(FALSE);
if (pSysMenu != NULL)
{
  CString strAboutMenu;
  strAboutMenu.LoadString(IDS_ABOUTBOX);
  if (!strAboutMenu.IsEmpty())
  {
    pSysMenu->AppendMenu(MF_SEPARATOR);
    pSysMenu->AppendMenu(MF_STRING, IDM_ABOUTBOX,
              strAboutMenu);
  }
}

// Set the icon for this dialog.
// The framework does this automatically
// when the application's main window is not a dialog
SetIcon(m_hIcon, TRUE);       // Set big icon
SetIcon(m_hIcon, FALSE);    // Set small icon

// TODO: Add extra initialization here

long  lRC;
LINEEXTENSIONID lineExtensionId;

lRC = lineInitialize (&hLineApp,
          AfxGetInstanceHandle(),
          (LINECALLBACK) PhDialCallback,
          "Phone Dialer Application",
           &dwNumDevs);
if (!lRC)
{
  strcpy(szStatus,"Line Initialized successfully.\r\n");
}
else
{
  strcpy (szStatus, "Line Initialization failed.\r\n");
}
```

```
WriteStatus();

lRC = lineNegotiateAPIVersion (
                hLineApp,
                0,
                0x00010003,
                TAPI_CURRENT_VERSION,
                &dwNegVersion,
                &lineExtensionId);
if (!lRC)

{
  wsprintf (szStatus, "Using Version %d.%d\r\n",
        HIWORD(dwNegVersion),
        LOWORD(dwNegVersion));
}
else
{
  strcpy (szStatus, "Line Initialization failed.\r\n");
}
WriteStatus();

LPLINEDEVCAPS lpDevCaps = NULL;

lpDevCaps = (LPLINEDEVCAPS)malloc(5*sizeof(LINEDEVCAPS));
lpDevCaps->dwTotalSize = 5*sizeof( LINEDEVCAPS );
lRC = lineGetDevCaps (
            hLineApp,
            0,
            dwNegVersion,
            0,
            lpDevCaps
            );

free (lpDevCaps);
lRC = lineRegisterRequestRecipient (
                hLineApp,
                0,
                LINEREQUESTMODE_MAKECALL,
                TRUE
                );

return TRUE;
```

```
}

void CPhDialDlg::OnSysCommand(UINT nID, LPARAM lParam)
{
  if ((nID & 0xFFF0) == IDM_ABOUTBOX)
  {
    CAboutDlg dlgAbout;
    dlgAbout.DoModal();
  }
  else
  {
    CDialog::OnSysCommand(nID, lParam);
  }
}


void CPhDialDlg::OnPaint()
{
  if (IsIconic())
  {
    CPaintDC dc(this); // device context for painting

    SendMessage(WM_ICONERASEBKGND,
          (WPARAM) dc.GetSafeHdc(), 0);

    // Center icon in client rectangle
    int cxIcon = GetSystemMetrics(SM_CXICON);
    int cyIcon = GetSystemMetrics(SM_CYICON);
    CRect rect;
    GetClientRect(&rect);
    int x = (rect.Width() - cxIcon + 1) / 2;
    int y = (rect.Height() - cyIcon + 1) / 2;

    // Draw the icon
    dc.DrawIcon(x, y, m_hIcon);
  }
  else
  {
    CDialog::OnPaint();
  }
}
```

```
HCURSOR CPhDialDlg::OnQueryDragIcon()
{
  return (HCURSOR) m_hIcon;
}
```

When the user clicks on the Dial button, the application picks up the user-entered data and calls the **ResolveNumber** function. This function, as you can see later, returns without modifying the data. For now assume that this function may modify the user's input for number, and the modified number is then used. The first step in placing a call is to open the line. This is done by calling the **lineOpen** function, which opens the specified line device and returns a handle to the line device. This line handle is used in subsequent operations on that line device. The first line device, 0, is used. Unique callback instance data can be passed to the function and will be passed back to the callback function. In a situation where there are multiple line devices and multiple threads opening the line devices, each can specify unique callback instance data, and the common callback function can then distinguish between various line devices based on the callback instance data. After completion of the function, a line handle is returned.

Before the call can be placed by use of the number, it should be translated to a format that TAPI can understand. This is done by calling the **lineTranslateAddress** API and passing in the user-entered number. **lineTranslateAddress** translates the given number to another format based on the options. Options such as inserting the call-waiting cancellation string at the beginning of the number, forcing a number that could potentially be a long-distance number to a local number (for example, a local calling area might have two area codes), forcing a number that could potentially be a local to long-distance (for example, a long-distance calling area might have the same area code), and so on, can be specified in *dwTranslateOptions*. The translated number is returned in the **LINETRANSLATEOUTPUT** structure. Note that since the translated number is appended to the end of the structure, enough memory should be allocated for the structure. The size of the structure is passed, and the call on its return fills in the size needed to translate and the size used in the structure. After translation the call returns two numbers, one that can be used to place the call on the line device (which the line device can understand and interpret), and the other that can be displayed to the user.

This translated number is used to place the call by use of the **lineMakeCall** function. This function places the call on the given line—in this sample, 0—to the given destination number. A **LINECALLPARAMS** structure with information on how the call is to be set up can optionally be passed to the **lineMakeCall** function. After completion of the call, a handle to the current call is given by the function that can be used to identify the call in future telephony operations on the call. The **lineMakeCall** function returns immediately and the function completes asynchronously. A **LINE_REPLY** message that has the status of the call is sent to the call.

```
void CPhDialDlg::OnDial()
{
  // TODO: Add your control notification handler code here
```

```
long  lRC;
LPLINETRANSLATEOUTPUT  lpTransOut;
char  szName[256];
char  szPhNumber[256];
UpdateData (TRUE);

strcpy (szPhNumber, m_number);
strcpy (szName, m_name);

ResolveNumber(szName, szPhNumber);

hCurrentCall = NULL;
lpTransOut = (LPLINETRANSLATEOUTPUT)
        malloc(5*sizeof(LINETRANSLATEOUTPUT));
lpTransOut->dwTotalSize = 5*sizeof(LINETRANSLATEOUTPUT);
lRC = lineOpen (
        hLineApp,
        0,
        &hLine,
        dwNegVersion,
        0,
        0,
        LINECALLPRIVILEGE_NONE,
        0,
         NULL
                    );
  lRC = lineTranslateAddress (
                              hLineApp,
                              0,
                              dwNegVersion,
                              szPhNumber,
                              0,
                              0,
                              lpTransOut
                              );
  char *lpNewNum;
  lpNewNum = (LPSTR)lpTransOut+lpTransOut
                    ->dwDialableStringOffset;
  wsprintf (szStatus, "Dialing %s\r\n", lpNewNum);
  WriteStatus();
  lRC = lineMakeCall (
                      hLine,
                      &hCurrentCall,
                      (LPSTR) lpTransOut +
```

```
                        lpTransOut-> dwDialableStringOffset,
                        0,
                        NULL
                        );

    free(lpTransOut);
}
```

When the user hangs up the call, the call is terminated by calling the **lineDrop** function followed by the **lineClose** function. The **lineDrop** function disconnects the given call. Optional user-user information can be specified, in which case it will be sent to the remote party as part of the call termination if the underlying network supports it. To make it generic, this sample does not send any user-user information. After terminating the call, the line is closed, so other applications can use it, by calling the **lineClose** function and specifying the line to be closed.

```
void CPhDialDlg::OnHang()
{
    // TODO: Add your control notification handler code here
    long lRC;

    if(hCurrentCall)
    {
        lRC = lineDrop (hCurrentCall, NULL, 0);
        hCurrentCall = NULL;
    }
    if (hLine)
    {
        lRC = lineClose(hLine);
        hLine = NULL;
    }
}
```

When the application terminates, the call is terminated if it is still connected and the line is closed. Before exiting, this application's use of TAPI is shut down by calling the **lineShutdown** function. If the line is still open, TAPI automatically closes all the open lines, and any pending request is canceled.

```
void CPhDialDlg::OnOK()
{
    // TODO: Add extra validation here
    long lRC;
    OnHang();
    lRC = lineShutdown(hLineApp);
```

```
        CDialog::OnOK();
}


void CPhDialDlg::WriteStatus()
{
    m_status.SetSel(-1,0);
    m_status.ReplaceSel(szStatus);
}
```

When TAPI needs to communicate to the application, it does so through the callback function. The function **PhDialCallback** is the callback function for this application. Since the information that is received in the callback is displayed in the dialog box, the callback function in turn passes the information that it receives to this member function. The processing by this member function when the callback function initiates is straightforward; it displays a message indicating what message was received. The only additional processing that it does is when it receives the **LINECALLSTATE_ DISCONNECT** message, which is triggered by hanging up the line through an external user interface, such as the call state dialog box displayed by TAPI. When it receives the disconnect message, it drops the call and closes the line.

```
void CPhDialDlg::DisplayCallBackInfo
                (DWORD   hDevice,
                 DWORD   dwMsg,
                 DWORD   dwCBInstance,
                 DWORD   dwParam1,
                 DWORD   dwParam2,
                 DWORD   dwParam3
                 )
{
    switch (dwMsg)
    {
        case LINE_ADDRESSSTATE:
            strcpy (szStatus,
                    "Line Address state received\r\n");
            WriteStatus();
            break;
        case LINE_CALLINFO:
            strcpy (szStatus,
                    "Line call info received\r\n");
            WriteStatus();
            break;

        case LINE_CALLSTATE:
            switch (dwParam1)
```

```
        {
            case LINECALLSTATE_DIALTONE:
                strcpy (szStatus,
                        "Dial tone received.\r\n");
                WriteStatus();
                break;

            case LINECALLSTATE_BUSY:
                strcpy (szStatus,
                        "Line is busy\r\n");
                WriteStatus();
                break;

            case LINECALLSTATE_DIALING:
                strcpy (szStatus,
                        "Dialing the number.\r\n");
                WriteStatus();
                break;

            case LINECALLSTATE_CONNECTED:
                strcpy (szStatus,
                        "Call has been established and\
connection made.\r\n");
                WriteStatus();
                break;

            case LINECALLSTATE_ACCEPTED:
                strcpy (szStatus,
                        "Call has been accepted.\r\n");
                WriteStatus();
                break;

            case LINECALLSTATE_DISCONNECTED:
                strcpy (szStatus,
                    "Call has been disconnected.\r\n");
                WriteStatus();
                OnHang();
                break;

            case LINECALLSTATE_PROCEEDING:
                strcpy (szStatus,
                        "Dialing has completed and the\
call is proceeding.\r\n");
```

```
                    WriteStatus();
                    break;

               case LINECALLSTATE_ONHOLD:
                    strcpy (szStatus,
                    "The call is on hold.\r\n");
                    WriteStatus();
                    break;
               default:
                    wsprintf(szStatus,
                              "Line call state received.\
dwParam1 = %1X, dwParam2 = %2X\r\n",
                    dwParam1, dwParam2);
                    WriteStatus();
          }

          break;

     case LINE_CLOSE:
          strcpy (szStatus,
                    "Line Close received\r\n");
          WriteStatus();
          break;

     case LINE_CREATE:
          strcpy (szStatus,
                    "Line create received\r\n");
          WriteStatus();
          break;

     case LINE_DEVSPECIFIC:
          strcpy (szStatus,
                    "Line dev specific received\r\n");
          WriteStatus();
          break;

     case LINE_DEVSPECIFICFEATURE:
          strcpy (szStatus,
                    "Line device spec feature received\r\n");
          WriteStatus();
          break;

     case LINE_GATHERDIGITS:
          strcpy (szStatus,
```

```
                              "Line gatherdigits received\r\n");
            WriteStatus();
            break;

        case LINE_GENERATE:
            strcpy (szStatus,
                    "Line generate received\r\n");
            WriteStatus();
            break;

        case LINE_LINEDEVSTATE:
            strcpy (szStatus,
                    "Line line dev state received\r\n");
            WriteStatus();
            break;

        case LINE_MONITORDIGITS:
            strcpy (szStatus,
                    "Line monitor digit received\r\n");
            WriteStatus();
            break;

        case LINE_MONITORMEDIA:
            strcpy (szStatus,
                    "Line monitor media received\r\n");
            WriteStatus();
            break;

        case LINE_MONITORTONE:
            strcpy (szStatus,
                    "Line monitor tone received\r\n");
            WriteStatus();
            break;

        case LINE_REPLY:
            if (!dwParam2)
            {
                strcpy (szStatus,
                        "Line Reply received. Function \
returned successfully\r\n");
            }
            else
            {
```

```
                    wsprintf(szStatus,
                        "Line Reply received. Error code\
%lX\r\n", dwParam2);
            }
            WriteStatus();
            break;

        case LINE_REQUEST:
            strcpy (szStatus,
                    "Line Request received\r\n");
            WriteStatus();
            break;
    }


}
```

Shown next is the callback function and the **ResolveNumber** function (which does not need to be in this module). The callback function basically turns around and passes the information to the application dialog box's member function, which takes care of sorting out the message and displaying it to the user. The pointer to the main application dialog class is externalized in the main application module.

```
// PhDialDlg.cpp : implementation file

#include "stdafx.h"
#include "PhDial.h"
#include "PhDialDlg.h"

#ifdef _DEBUG
#define new DEBUG_NEW
#undef THIS_FILE
static char THIS_FILE[] = __FILE__;
#endif

extern CPhDialDlg  *pdlg;

void CALLBACK PhDialCallback (
                DWORD   hDevice,
                DWORD   dwMsg,
                DWORD   dwCBInstance,
                DWORD   dwParam1,
```

```
                        DWORD     dwParam2,
                        DWORD     dwParam3);

void CALLBACK PhDialCallback (
                        DWORD     hDevice,
                        DWORD     dwMsg,
                        DWORD     dwCBInstance,
                        DWORD     dwParam1,
                        DWORD     dwParam2,
                        DWORD     dwParam3
                )
{
    pdlg->DisplayCallBackInfo(
                        hDevice,
                        dwMsg,
                        dwCBInstance,
                        dwParam1,
                        dwParam2,
                        dwParam3
                );


}
```

This module also has the **ResolveNumber** function, which takes the name and number as given by the user and can resolve it to an appropriate number. In this sample it basically assumes that the user typed in a correct number. But this sample can be extended by providing more functionality in this function. For example, when the application starts, it can load up the phone book (by means of a database or any other mechanism), and this function can use it. When the user provides the name, this function can do a lookup for the phone number or vice versa. It can also decide which long-distance carrier is most economical for dialing the given number, and prefix the number with that long-distance carrier's access code. Since the object of this sample is to show the functions of TAPI, this function does not do much and is provided as a hook for extending this sample.

```
void ResolveNumber(char *pszName, char *pszNumber)
{
    // Add your logic to translate the number
    // based on name and number.
    // Modify the same buffer.

    return; // Do nothing by default
}
```

TELEPHONY LOGGING

TAPI provides functions to log calls. Logging calls helps provide reports that show telephone incoming and outgoing usage by extension and call duration. Many firms use such reports to have employees pay for their personal calls. You can call the **lineGetCallInfo** function to get information about a call. **lineGetCallInfo** returns information about the call, such as the addresses of the originator and receiver of the call, whether the call was a direct call or a transferred call, and so on, in the **LINECALLINFO** structure. Each incoming and outgoing call has its own **LINECALLINFO** structure. However, data such as the start and stop times (and hence the duration of the call) must be maintained by applications. While it is possible for owners to do logging, it is more common for monitoring applications to do logging. Typically a logging application is the last application to deal with the data from a call, and as such, it should free the call's handle, using **lineDeallocateCall** to reclaim resources used by the call.

TIP: While freeing resources and avoiding memory leaks is important and a good programming practice, freeing memory is especially important in TAPI. With each incoming call, TAPI assigns system memory, and in TAPI applications that handle many calls it is very important that you free the memory as soon as possible.

Conclusion

We reviewed telephony basics, looked at the different functions and capabilities provided by TAPI for developing telephony applications, saw the steps involved in developing a TAPI application, and examined a simple TAPI programming example. As a business programmer, you are not likely to be developing telephony applications (unless you work for a company that develops telephony applications). But this chapter gave you an introduction to telephony and an insight into the capabilities of TAPI. As computer telephony integration improves, vendors are offering applications, that could, for example, read your e-mail over the phone. Or you may eventually be able to completely interact with your PC using only voice commands.

The next chapter looks at sophisticated two-dimensional and three-dimensional graphics programming using OpenGL.

WINDOWS
NT
Professional
Library

CHAPTER 19

OpenGL Programming

We looked at graphics programming using GDI in Chapter 5. While GDI can help you with some graphics, its capabilities are somewhat limited. If you want to program sophisticated three-dimensional graphics and want to include special effects such as shading, lighting, texture mapping, and so on, you need OpenGL.

OpenGL is an offshoot of IRIS GL graphics workstations developed by Silicon Graphics. It is now a standard supported across many computer systems, including many UNIX systems and Windows NT. The OpenGL language standard, including language features and conformance testing, is controlled by the OpenGL Architecture Review Board (OpenGL ARB), an industry consortium whose members include Silicon Graphics, Microsoft, IBM, Intel, and DEC. The OpenGL language itself is independent of hardware and underlying software, such as operating systems and windowing systems. You can port OpenGL applications written for one environment to another (see the section "Porting OpenGL Applications" later in this chapter). OpenGL is heavily used where three-dimensional object visualization and sophisticated graphics are required, such as in CAD/CAM applications.

We will start with a brief review of OpenGL basics, and then look at OpenGL data structures, OpenGL functions, and programming examples to draw and transform two-dimensional and three-dimensional objects. We will conclude the chapter with a look at porting OpenGL across environments.

OPENGL BASICS

OpenGL can handle geometric objects, images, and text. In OpenGL, the geometric objects are defined as sequences of vertices across different planes. The images are a collection of pixels. OpenGL support for text includes different fonts.

OpenGL handles geometric objects (which are made up of vertices) by rasterizing (the process of converting vector graphics to images consisting of pixels) and storing the pixels in a frame buffer. A *vertex* is a point, such as the endpoint of a line or a corner in a polygon. Besides the coordinates of the vertex, OpenGL also lets you associate other attributes, such as color, texture, and so on, with each vertex. OpenGL processes *primitives,* which are functions, to connect vertices and form geometric objects such as lines, polygons, and so on. Primitive processing includes evaluation, transforming vertices, lighting, and clipping to a viewport. Processed primitives are rasterized, which results in a series of frame buffer addresses and associated points. The rasterized output is stored as pixels in the frame buffer after some final processing, such as blending incoming pixel colors with existing colors. The OpenGL primitives execute in the order you specify them to complete the drawing of the geometric object. You can further control the final output using *modes* (see modes in the "OpenGL Programming Concepts" section).

OpenGL can handle image pixels directly (instead of using vertices). OpenGL provides pixel update functions to handle images. The pixels are either used in the rasterization stage or stored directly in frame buffers. You can use the standard GDI text functions to draw text if you are working with a single-buffered OpenGL window. If you are using a double-buffered window (see "Double Buffering" in the section "OpenGL

Programming Concepts"), you can draw text by creating display lists for characters in a font and executing the appropriate display list when the characters (of the text you want to display) are drawn.

These functions are just the beginning. OpenGL also provides transformation matrices, lighting equation coefficients, antialiasing methods, and so on, to significantly enhance the graphics effects in the final output.

OpenGL implementation, like other Windows NT functions, is implemented in a client/server fashion. Your application runs at the client and invokes the OpenGL APIs. The OpenGL client module communicates with an OpenGL server module and passes your application's OpenGL commands. The OpenGL server module invokes the Win32 Device Driver Interface (DDI) to drive the display driver. The OpenGL server may be on the same machine as the client, or it may be separated by a network. An OpenGL server typically maintains several OpenGL contexts. A *context* is an encapsulated OpenGL state that an OpenGL client connects to.

Graphics are typically resource intensive, and there are hardware accelerators available for improving specific graphics functions. Windows NT provides a mechanism for you to take advantage of such devices where available. However, Microsoft did not want its OpenGL implementation tied to specific hardware. So Windows NT OpenGL includes a *generic* implementation that is software based. You can take advantage of special hardware and device drivers by setting and using flags in appropriate data structures. The client module invokes hardware-specific device drivers at the client level. At the server level, hardware-specific device drivers are used by the server module to drive the display driver (instead of the Win32 DDI). Unlike in most other programming areas in Windows NT, you should check on the availability of add-ons before developing your OpenGL applications and take advantage of them where appropriate. While the add-ons may enhance your application's performance and other capabilities, keep in mind that the add-ons also make it more difficult to port your OpenGL application to another OpenGL environment where the add-on is not available or is not supported. Also note that resource-intensive OpenGL applications (including some OpenGL screen-savers) executed on a client machine only affect other applications at the client, whereas the same applications executed at the server may affect a number of users.

Windows NT implementation of OpenGL supports color processing in one of two ways—RGBA mode and color-index mode. Unlike GDI, where most applications use color indexing and logical palettes, OpenGL applications usually work better in the RGBA mode. RGBA tends to perform better than color indexing, particularly for shading, lighting, texture mapping, and so on. RGBA works better for OpenGL applications for both true-color devices and palette-based devices. Situations in which you may want to use color-index mode in your application include porting an existing application that uses color-index mode or if you want to use color-map animation (which is not possible on true-color devices).

OpenGL does not handle end-user input (which your application can do by use of the GUI mechanisms discussed in Part 2). In addition, OpenGL does not configure frame buffers (frame buffers are configured by the windowing subsystem) or initialize itself (initialization of OpenGL occurs when the windowing subsystem allocates a window for OpenGL).

Note for UNIX Programmers

As mentioned earlier OpenGL is standards based, and there are UNIX systems that support OpenGL. If you have used OpenGL in UNIX systems or developed IRIS GL applications, then the language part of your OpenGL application in Windows NT is pretty much the same. However, the windowing subsystems are different—X Window in UNIX and the Windows subsystem in Windows NT. The operating system calls in your OpenGL application will also be different.

OpenGL applications can print a rendered scene in one of two ways. The more difficult method (and the only method available prior to Windows NT 4.0) is to render the scene into a DIB section and then print the DIB section. Starting with Windows NT 4.0, OpenGL applications can print directly to a printer DC if a metafile spooler is used (by using a metafile DC when creating a rendering context). Keep in mind, though, that most OpenGL output requires more memory than is typically found in most printers. As such, OpenGL prints graphics in bands, which causes OpenGL printing to take more time than other output.

OPENGL PROGRAMMING CONCEPTS

There are many concepts that are almost unique to OpenGL that you should be familiar with to be able to write OpenGL programs. The concepts include rendering contexts, modes, double buffering, and OpenGL internal matrices such as projection, model view, and texture. These concepts are briefly addressed here.

Rendering Contexts

Rendering contexts are the link between OpenGL and the Windows NT windowing system. All your application's OpenGL calls pass through an OpenGL rendering context.

An application specifies a Windows NT device context when it creates a rendering context. You can create a rendering context after you set the pixel format (see **PIXELFORMATDESCRIPTOR** in the "OpenGL Data Structures" section) for the device context (and the rendering context has the same pixel format as the device context). This rendering context is now ready for drawing on the device referenced by the specified device context. Keep in mind, however, that this does not mean that the rendering context must use the device context created with it. It can use another device context as long as that device context references the same device and has the same pixel format.

Also, the preceding discussion does not mean that a rendering context is basically the same as a device context. A *device* context contains information related to GDI, while a *rendering* context contains information related to OpenGL. In addition, a device context is specified explicitly in a GDI call, while a rendering context is implicit in an OpenGL call.

A thread that makes OpenGL calls must have one (and only one) current rendering context. A rendering context can be current to only one thread. However, a window to which OpenGL outputs are being sent can have multiple rendering contexts drawing to it at one time. An application's OpenGL calls without a current rendering context have no effect. The typical sequence involving rendering contexts is as follows:

1. A rendering context is created.
2. The rendering context created is set as a thread's current rendering context.
3. The thread then performs initialization related to OpenGL.
4. The thread calls OpenGL rendering functions.
5. When OpenGL processing is complete, the rendering context is made not current (the rendering context is detached).
6. The rendering context is destroyed (when not needed).

Now let's look at the multithreading implications of OpenGL applications.

Multithreading OpenGL Applications

You can use multiple threads in your OpenGL application. If your application has multiple threads, then each thread that makes OpenGL calls must have its own (and only one) current rendering context. With multithreaded applications, you should take steps to ensure that one thread does not affect the output of another thread. For example, one thread may clear the window prior to displaying its OpenGL image, and this may inadvertently clear an image of another thread. Another example would be if you were to call **SwapBuffers** in one thread application, it could overwrite another thread's output. A common way to handle multithreaded OpenGL applications is to designate one thread for clearing and swapping the window, and to let other threads communicate with the designated thread. Multithreading and thread communication and synchronization are covered in detail in Chapter 10.

Now let's look at another OpenGL programming concept—modes.

Modes

Modes are OpenGL capabilities that can be used to enhance the final output. Modes are enabled by the **glEnable** function and disabled by the **glDisable** function. Modes are specified as parameters to these functions. There are a number of modes possible, and the following table lists only a small, selected subset of the modes.

Mode Parameter	Description
GL_BLEND	Bends the source RGBA color values with the RGBA values in the destination buffer using **glBlendFunc**
GL_TEXTURE_2D	Performs two-dimensional texturing using **glTexImage2D**

Mode Parameter	Description
GL_SCISSOR_TEST	Performs drawing functions only within the rectangle specified by the **glScissor** function
GL_POLYGON_ SMOOTH	Applies filtering specified by **glPolygonMode**

Double Buffering

Microsoft implementation of OpenGL supports double buffering. There are two buffers—an onscreen buffer and an offscreen buffer. By default, all your OpenGL drawing commands draw to the offscreen buffer. When the drawing is complete, the contents of the offscreen buffer are copied to the onscreen buffer (by use of the **SwapBuffers** function). Double buffering smoothes image transitions.

OPENGL DATA STRUCTURES

A pixel format specifies properties of an OpenGL drawing surface, such as whether the pixel buffer is single or double buffered, whether the pixel data is in RGBA or color-index form, and so on.

The **PIXELFORMATDESCRIPTOR** structure describes the pixel format of a drawing surface. It is probably the most important data structure related to OpenGL in Windows NT. The **PIXELFORMATDESCRIPTOR** structure is shown here:

```
typedef struct tagPIXELFORMATDESCRIPTOR { // pfd
    WORD   nSize;
    WORD   nVersion;
    DWORD  dwFlags;
    BYTE   iPixelType;
    BYTE   cColorBits;
    BYTE   cRedBits;
    BYTE   cRedShift;
    BYTE   cGreenBits;
    BYTE   cGreenShift;
    BYTE   cBlueBits;
    BYTE   cBlueShift;
    BYTE   cAlphaBits;
    BYTE   cAlphaShift;
    BYTE   cAccumBits;
    BYTE   cAccumRedBits;
    BYTE   cAccumGreenBits;
    BYTE   cAccumBlueBits;
    BYTE   cAccumAlphaBits;
```

```
    BYTE    cDepthBits;
    BYTE    cStencilBits;
    BYTE    cAuxBuffers;
    BYTE    iLayerType;
    BYTE    bReserved;
    DWORD   dwLayerMask;
    DWORD   dwVisibleMask;
    DWORD   dwDamageMask;
} PIXELFORMATDESCRIPTOR;
```

where

nSize is the size of the **PIXELFORMATDESCRIPTOR** structure and is set by use of **sizeof(PIXELFORMATDESCRIPTOR)**.

nVersion is the version of the **PIXELFORMATDESCRIPTOR** structure and is set to 1.

dwFlags is a set of bit flags that specify pixel buffer properties, such as whether the buffer supports GDI or OpenGL, whether the pixel format is supported by GDI or a device/driver or hardware, and so on. Most of the flags are not mutually exclusive (exceptions are noted in the description), and you can set a combination of bit flags to suit your application. The flag values and associated description are listed in Table 19-1.

Flag Value	Description
PFD_DRAW_TO_WINDOW	The buffer can draw to a window/device surface.
PFD_DRAW_TO_BITMAP	The buffer can draw to a memory bitmap.
PFD_SUPPORT_GDI	The buffer supports GDI. This flag is mutually exclusive with PFD_DOUBLEBUFFER in the current generic implementation.
PFD_SUPPORT_OPENGL	The buffer supports OpenGL.
PFD_GENERIC_ ACCELERATED	The pixel format is supported by a device driver that provides acceleration in the generic implementation.

Table 19-1.   Pixel Buffer Property Flags

Flag Value	Description
PFD_GENERIC_FORMAT	The pixel format is supported by the generic implementation (implementation by GDI without hardware acceleration).
PFD_NEED_PALETTE	The buffer uses RGBA pixels on a palette-managed device. You need a logical palette for this pixel type. Colors in the palette should be specified according to the values of cRedBits, cRedShift, and so on (see cRedBits, cRedShift, and so on, later in this section).
PFD_NEED_SYSTEM_PALETTE	This flag is used with hardware palettes. Some restrictions include support for one hardware palette in 256-color mode only, and the hardware palette must be in a fixed order (for example, 3-3-2) in RGBA mode or must match the logical palette in color-index mode.
	To use hardware palettes, call SetSystemPaletteUse in your program to force a one-to-one mapping of the logical palette and the system palette. You can clear this flag if your OpenGL hardware supports multiple hardware palettes and the device driver can assign spare hardware palettes for OpenGL.
PFD_DOUBLEBUFFER	The buffering uses double buffers (mutually exclusive with PFD_SUPPORT_GDI). See PFD_SUPPORT_GDI earlier in this table.
PFD_STEREO	The buffering is stereoscopic (there are separate left and right buffers). This flag is not supported in the current generic implementation.
PFD_SWAP_LAYER_BUFFERS	This specifies whether a device can swap individual layer planes with pixel formats. The layer planes could include double-buffered overlay or underlay planes. When this flag is not set, all layer planes are swapped together as a group. This flag must be set for the wglSwapLayerBuffers function to be supported.

Table 19-1. Pixel Buffer Property Flags (*continued*)

Flag Value	Description
PFD_DEPTH_DONTCARE	Selected pixel format can either have or not have a depth buffer
PFD_DOUBLEBUFFER_DONTCARE	Selected pixel format can be either single or double buffered
PFD_STEREO_DONTCARE	Selected pixel format can be either monoscopic or stereoscopic

Table 19-2. ChoosePixelFormat Function Flags

You can specify the bit flags listed in Table 19-2 when calling **ChoosePixelFormat** (which attempts to find the closest pixel format supported by a device context to that specified in your application).

With the **glAddSwapHintRectWIN** extension function, two new flags in Table 19-3 are included for the **PIXELFORMATDESCRIPTOR** pixel format structure.

Flag Value	Description
PFD_SWAP_COPY	This flag causes the content of the back buffer to be copied to the front buffer in the double-buffered main color plane without affecting the contents of the back buffer. PFD_SWAP_COPY is a hint to the device driver, which may opt not to support the function.
PFD_SWAP_EXCHANGE	This flag causes the exchange of the back buffer's content with the front buffer's content in the double-buffered main color plane. PFD_SWAP_COPY is a one-way copy from the back buffer to the front buffer, while PFD_SWAP_EXCHANGE is a two-way copy between the front and back buffers. PFD_SWAP_ EXCHANGE is a hint to the device driver, which may opt not to support the function.

Table 19-3. New Flags for the glAddSwapHintRectWIN Function

iPixelType specifies the type of pixel data. The types are defined in Table 19-4.

cColorBits is the number of color bitplanes in each color buffer. For RGBA pixel types, it is the size of the color buffer, excluding the alpha bitplanes. For color-index pixels, it is the size of the color-index buffer.

cRedBits is the number of red bitplanes in each RGBA color buffer.

cRedShift is the shift count for red bitplanes in each RGBA color buffer.

cGreenBits is the number of green bitplanes in each RGBA color buffer.

cGreenShift is the shift count for green bitplanes in each RGBA color buffer.

cBlueBits is the number of blue bitplanes in each RGBA color buffer.

cBlueShift is the shift count for blue bitplanes in each RGBA color buffer.

cAlphaBits is the number of alpha bitplanes in each RGBA color buffer (alpha bitplanes are not supported).

cAlphaShift is the shift count for alpha bitplanes in each RGBA color buffer (alpha bitplanes are not supported).

cAccumBits is the total number of bitplanes in the accumulation buffer.

cAccumRedBits is the number of red bitplanes in the accumulation buffer.

cAccumGreenBits is the number of green bitplanes in the accumulation buffer.

cAccumBlueBits is the number of blue bitplanes in the accumulation buffer.

cAccumAlphaBits is the number of alpha bitplanes in the accumulation buffer.

cDepthBits is the depth of the Z-axis (depth) buffer.

cStencilBits is the depth of the stencil buffer.

cAuxBuffers is the number of auxiliary buffers (auxiliary buffers are not supported in Release 1.0 of the generic implementation).

iLayerType is ignored. This parameter is included for compatibility.

bReserved is the number of overlay and underlay planes. Bits 0 through 3 specify up to 15 overlay planes, and bits 4 through 7 specify up to 15 underlay planes.

dwLayerMask is ignored. This parameter is included for compatibility.

dwVisibleMask is the transparent color value or the index of an underlay plane. When the pixel type is RGBA, *dwVisibleMask* is a transparent RGB color value. When the pixel type is a color index, it is a transparent index value.

dwDamageMask is ignored. This parameter is included for compatibility.

Flag Value	Description
PFD_TYPE_RGBA	These are RGBA pixels. Each pixel has four components (in red, green, blue, and alpha order).
PFD_TYPE_ COLORINDEX	These are color-index pixels. Each pixel uses a color-index value.

Table 19-4. Pixel Types

OPENGL FUNCTIONS

OpenGL implementation is in the form of a library of functions. Although there are a lot of OpenGL functions, many functions are variations of each other based on the data types of arguments. For example, there are two variations to the scaling function—**glScaled**, which uses double-precision arguments, and **glScalef**, which uses floating-point arguments. Keep in mind, however, that extensions supported in one rendering context are not necessarily supported in a different rendering context. The OpenGL functions can be classified as follows:

▼ *Core* OpenGL functions are for basic functions such as object shape description, matrix transformation, and so on. These core functions are prefixed by "gl" (such as **glDrawBuffer**).

■ *Utility* OpenGL functions provide functions such as texture support, rendering cylinders and other geometric objects, and so on. Utility functions are prefixed by "glu" (such as **gluPerspective**).

■ *Auxiliary* OpenGL functions are for simple window management and are prefixed by "aux" (such as **auxSphere**).

■ *WGL* functions connect OpenGL to a windowing subsystem and are prefixed by "wgl" (such as **wglGetCurrentDC**).

▲ *Win32* functions are related to OpenGL.

There are more than 300 core OpenGL functions (counting variations of functions) besides a lot of utility and auxiliary functions. Refer to MSDN and other OpenGL documentation such as the *OpenGL Reference Manual* and *OpenGL Programming Guide* (these are the official books on OpenGL published by the OpenGL ARB) for more details about these functions. Table 19-5 summarizes the Win32 functions related to OpenGL and their descriptions.

ENABLING MFC APPLICATIONS TO USE OPENGL

Before we look at programming examples, let's briefly review the steps involved for an MFC application to use OpenGL. These steps are a brief extract from the *MFCOGL.EXE* sample that is included on MSDN. This sample program is also available by anonymous FTP from **ftp.microsoft.com** in the SOFTLIB/MSLFILES directory.

1. Include required headers (such as *Gl.h*, *Glu.h*, and *Glaux.h*) and add required libraries (such as *Opengl32.lib*, *Glu32.lib*, and *Glaux.lib*) to the link project settings.

2. If your application uses palettes, add your implementations for the **OnPaletteChanged** and **OnQueryNewPalette** functions in the **CMainFrame** class.

3. Derive classes from **Cwnd**, including view classes.

4. Include implementations for initialization, window sizing (if necessary), and so on.

5. Include implementation for OpenGL rendering code.

6. Include implementation for cleanup.

Let's now take a look at some programming examples using OpenGL.

OPENGL PROGRAMMING EXAMPLES

There are three sample programs related to OpenGL that will be discussed here. The first sample program displays three 2-D objects—a triangle, a rectangle, and a pentagon—using OpenGL. In the second sample program a graphic object is transformed, and in the third sample, 3-D objects are drawn and transformed. The samples are AppWizard-generated SDI applications. The screen images generated by these samples

OpenGL Function	Description
ChoosePixel Format	This chooses a pixel format supported by a device context that is closest to a given pixel format specification. Although the closest format is chosen, the choice may not be acceptable, and you have to ensure that the selection is valid. For example, the closest format to a 24-bit RGB color format supported by the device context may be an 8-bit color format, but this may not be acceptable to your application.
DescribePixel Format	This loads the pixel format data of the specified pixel format and device in a PIXELFORMATDESCRIPTOR structure.
GetEnhMetaFile PixelFormat	This retrieves enhanced metafile pixel format data. You have to ensure that the buffer used to store the pixel format data is large enough.
GetPixelFormat	This obtains the index of the currently selected pixel format of the specified device context.
SetPixelFormat	This sets the pixel format of the specified device context to the specified format.
SwapBuffers	This exchanges contents of front (onscreen) and back (offscreen) buffers.

Table 19-5.   OpenGL Win32 Functions

are included in the CD that accompanies this book. There is no dependency of MFC when using OpenGL, and OpenGL can be used directly using the normal Windows SDK. However, for ease of programming the examples use MFC.

Programming Example to Display 2-D Objects

The code for the first sample program is shown next. It is basically an SDI application framework created by use of AppWizard. The only relevant changes that are made are in the view module that is shown.

There are a few standard steps that must be taken in an OpenGL application. They will be discussed as the sample application is discussed. The header file for the view class is shown next. A set of member variables, some relevant to OpenGL and others not, are added. Additional message handlers for **WM_CREATE**, **WM_DESTROY**, **WM_SIZE**, and **WM_MOUSEMOVE** are added, the use of which will become clear later.

```
// OglView.h : interface of the COglView class
//
#if !defined(AFX_OGLVIEW_H)
#define AFX_OGLVIEW_H

#if _MSC_VER >= 1000
#pragma once
#endif // _MSC_VER >= 1000

class COglView : public CView
{
protected: // create from serialization only
    COglView();
    DECLARE_DYNCREATE(COglView)

// Attributes
public:
    COglDoc* GetDocument();
// Operations
public:
// Overrides
    // ClassWizard generated virtual function overrides
    //{{AFX_VIRTUAL(COglView)
    public:
    virtual BOOL PreCreateWindow(CREATESTRUCT& cs);
    protected:
    virtual void OnDraw(CDC* pDC);
    //}}AFX_VIRTUAL
// Implementation
public:
```

```
        virtual ~COglView();
#ifdef _DEBUG
    virtual void AssertValid() const;
    virtual void Dump(CDumpContext& dc) const;
#endif
protected:
    int m_pixelformat;
    HGLRC m_hglRendContext;

    GLfloat vdColor1[3];
    GLfloat vdColor2[3];
    GLfloat vdColor3[3];
    GLfloat vdColor4[3];
    GLfloat vdColor5[3];
    GLfloat vdColor6[3];
    GLfloat vdColor7[3];
    GLfloat vdColor8[3];

    GLfloat *clrArray[8];

    BOOL InitPixelFormat(HDC hDC);
    void InitPFDStruc(PIXELFORMATDESCRIPTOR *ppfd);

// Generated message map functions
protected:
    //{{AFX_MSG(COglView)
    afx_msg int OnCreate(LPCREATESTRUCT lpCreateStruct);
    afx_msg void OnDestroy();
    afx_msg void OnPaint();
    afx_msg void OnSize(UINT nType, int cx, int cy);
    afx_msg void OnMouseMove(UINT nFlags, CPoint point);
    //}}AFX_MSG
    DECLARE_MESSAGE_MAP()
};

#ifndef _DEBUG  // debug version in OglView.cpp
inline COglDoc* COglView::GetDocument()
   { return (COglDoc*)m_pDocument; }
#endif

///////////////////////////////////////////////////////////////////////

//{{AFX_INSERT_LOCATION}}

#endif //
```

The implementation code for the view is shown next. When the view is created, the member variables are initialized. The member variable **m_pixelformat** maintains the chosen pixel format index. The member variable **m_hglRendContext** maintains the OpenGL rendering context. An array of colors is also maintained, which is used to add some interesting effects to the graphic objects that are drawn.

```cpp
// OglView.cpp : implementation of the COglView class
//
#include "stdafx.h"
#include "Ogl.h"

#include "OglDoc.h"
#include "OglView.h"

#ifdef _DEBUG
#define new DEBUG_NEW
#undef THIS_FILE
static char THIS_FILE[] = __FILE__;
#endif

/////////////////////////////////////////////////////////////////////////////
// COglView

IMPLEMENT_DYNCREATE(COglView, CView)

BEGIN_MESSAGE_MAP(COglView, CView)
    //{{AFX_MSG_MAP(COglView)
    ON_WM_CREATE()
    ON_WM_DESTROY()
    ON_WM_PAINT()
    ON_WM_SIZE()
    ON_WM_MOUSEMOVE()
    //}}AFX_MSG_MAP
END_MESSAGE_MAP()

/////////////////////////////////////////////////////////////////////////////
// COglView construction/destruction

COglView::COglView()
{
    // TODO: add construction code here
    m_pixelformat = 0;
    m_hglRendContext = NULL;
```

```
        vdColor1[0] = 1.0;
        vdColor1[1] = 0.0;
        vdColor1[2] = 0.0;
        vdColor2[0] = 0.0;
        vdColor2[1] = 1.0;
        vdColor2[2] = 0.0;
        vdColor3[0] = 1.0;
        vdColor3[1] = 1.0;
        vdColor3[2] = 0.0;
        vdColor4[0] = 0.0;
        vdColor4[1] = 1.0;
        vdColor4[2] = 1.0;
        vdColor5[0] = 1.0;
        vdColor5[1] = 0.0;
        vdColor5[2] = 1.0;
        vdColor6[0] = 0.0;
        vdColor6[1] = 1.0;
        vdColor6[2] = 1.0;
        vdColor7[0] = 1.0;
        vdColor7[1] = 1.0;
        vdColor7[2] = 1.0;
        vdColor8[0] = 0.0;
        vdColor8[1] = 0.0;
        vdColor8[2] = 0.0;

        clrArray[0] = vdColor1;
        clrArray[1] = vdColor2;
        clrArray[2] = vdColor3;
        clrArray[3] = vdColor4;
        clrArray[4] = vdColor5;
        clrArray[5] = vdColor6;
        clrArray[6] = vdColor7;
        clrArray[7] = vdColor8;
}


COglView::~COglView()
{
}
```

An OpenGL window has its own pixel format; thus, to draw into the window, the device contexts retrieved for the client area of an OpenGL window should be used. Therefore an OpenGL window should be created with the WS_CLIPCHILDREN and

WS_CLIPSIBLINGS style. Furthermore, the window class attribute should not include the CS_PARENTDC style. This is the first standard step and is performed by the **PreCreateWindow** member function.

```
        BOOL COglView::PreCreateWindow(CREATESTRUCT& cs)
{
    // TODO: Modify the Window class or styles here by modifying
    //  the CREATESTRUCT cs

    cs.style |= (WS_CLIPCHILDREN | WS_CLIPSIBLINGS);
    return CView::PreCreateWindow(cs);
}


////////////////////////////////////////////////////////////////////////////
// COglView drawing

void COglView::OnDraw(CDC* pDC)
{
    COglDoc* pDoc = GetDocument();
    ASSERT_VALID(pDoc);

    // TODO: add draw code for native data here
}


////////////////////////////////////////////////////////////////////////////
// COglView diagnostics

#ifdef _DEBUG
void COglView::AssertValid() const
{
    CView::AssertValid();
}

void COglView::Dump(CDumpContext& dc) const
{
    CView::Dump(dc);
}

COglDoc* COglView::GetDocument() // non-debug version is inline
{
    ASSERT(m_pDocument->IsKindOf(RUNTIME_CLASS(COglDoc)));
    return (COglDoc*)m_pDocument;
}
#endif //_DEBUG
```

The next step is to create a rendering context and make it current. But before a rendering context is created, the window's pixel format should be set. This is handled by the **OnCreate** member function. The actual setting of the pixel format is done in the **InitPixelFormat** member function. To set a pixel format, a **PIXELFORMATDESCRIPTOR** data structure is initialized with the requirements for this application, and a close match is requested from the system by calling the **ChoosePixelFormat** function. This function attempts to match an appropriate pixel format supported by a device context to the given pixel format and returns a pixel format index. The application may check to see if the returned pixel format matches the application's requirement. The **DescribePixelFormat** function can be used to get information about the pixel format given the pixel format index. This application overlooks this and assumes that it gets the correct or closest matching pixel format. **SetPixelFormat** is then used to set the pixel format for the device context. If the application does not get a pixel format, it tries to use the first pixel format, but checks that it is valid before using it by calling **DescribePixelFormat**.

After the pixel format is set, a rendering context is created by calling the **wglCreateContext** function. This creates a new rendering context that is made the current rendering context by calling the **wglMakeCurrent** function. Note that a rendering context is not the same as a device context. Typically a rendering context is created once and is used throughout the application. It is finally freed at the end. On the other hand, a device context is created when needed and freed immediately after that. This is to improve performance, since creation of a rendering context is quite expensive. When the application no longer needs the rendering context, it should be deleted by calling the **wglDeleteContext** function. This is done when the window is destroyed in the **OnDestroy** handler.

```
/////////////////////////////////////////////////////////////////////////
// COglView message handlers

int COglView::OnCreate(LPCREATESTRUCT lpCreateStruct)
{
    if (CView::OnCreate(lpCreateStruct) == -1)
        return -1;

    // TODO: Add your specialized creation code here
    HDC hDC = ::GetDC(GetSafeHwnd());
    if (InitPixelFormat(hDC) == FALSE)
        return 0;
    m_hglRendContext = wglCreateContext(hDC);
    wglMakeCurrent(hDC, m_hglRendContext);
    return 0;
}


BOOL COglView::InitPixelFormat(HDC hDC)
```

```
{
    PIXELFORMATDESCRIPTOR    PixForDesc;

    InitPFDStruc(&PixForDesc);
    m_pixelformat = ChoosePixelFormat( hDC, &PixForDesc);
    if (m_pixelformat == 0)
    {
        m_pixelformat = 1;
        if (DescribePixelFormat(hDC,  m_pixelformat,
            sizeof(PIXELFORMATDESCRIPTOR), &PixForDesc) == 0)
        {
            return FALSE;
        }
    }

    if (SetPixelFormat(hDC, m_pixelformat, &PixForDesc) == FALSE)
    {
        return FALSE;
    }

    return TRUE;

}
```

Only those fields that are supported are filled in the **PIXELFORMATDESCRIPTOR**
structure. The two variations of *dwFlags* that are seen in the code are discussed at the end.

```
void COglView::InitPFDStruc(PIXELFORMATDESCRIPTOR *ppfd)
{
    memset(ppfd, 0, sizeof(PIXELFORMATDESCRIPTOR));
    ppfd->nSize = sizeof(PIXELFORMATDESCRIPTOR);
    ppfd->nVersion = 1;
#if 1
    ppfd->dwFlags = PFD_DRAW_TO_WINDOW |
                    PFD_SUPPORT_OPENGL |
                    PFD_DOUBLEBUFFER;
#else
    ppfd->dwFlags = PFD_DRAW_TO_WINDOW |
                    PFD_SUPPORT_OPENGL |
                    PFD_DRAW_TO_BITMAP ;
#endif

    ppfd->iPixelType = PFD_TYPE_RGBA;
    ppfd->cColorBits = 24;
```

```
    ppfd->cDepthBits = 16;
    ppfd->iLayerType = PFD_MAIN_PLANE;
}
```

The objects are painted in the **OnPaint** handler member function shown next. First the buffers that are currently enabled for color are cleared by calling the **glClear** function. Then three polygons—a triangle, a rectangle, and a pentagon—are drawn by use of the **glVertex2f** function. For each vertex, the color is specified by calling the **glColor3fv** function. The **glBegin** and **glEnd** functions delimit the vertices of a primitive like point, line, and so on. The **glVertex** function commands should only be used within the **glBegin**/**glEnd** pair. Note that the application just sets the color of the vertex. OpenGL will automatically interpolate the color between the vertices. Finally the **glFlush** function is called to force execution of the previous graphic functions, which in this case are graphic primitives. Note that depending on the OpenGL implementation, the buffering of commands can be in a network buffer, graphic accelerator card, and so on. This application uses double buffering, and the call to **SwapBuffers** exchanges the front and the back buffers displaying the graphic objects.

```
void COglView::OnPaint()
{
    CPaintDC dc(this); // device context for painting
    // TODO: Add your message handler code here
    glClear(GL_COLOR_BUFFER_BIT);
    glBegin(GL_POLYGON);
        glColor3fv(clrArray[0]);
        glVertex2f(20.0f, 20.0f);
        glColor3fv(clrArray[1]);
        glVertex2f(175.0f, 20.0f);
        glColor3fv(clrArray[2]);
        glVertex2f(90.0f, 200.0f);
    glEnd();
    glBegin(GL_POLYGON);
        glColor3fv(clrArray[3]);
        glVertex2f(250.0f, 20.0f);
        glColor3fv(clrArray[4]);
        glVertex2f(400.0f, 20.0f);
        glColor3fv(clrArray[5]);
        glVertex2f(400.0f, 220.0f);
        glColor3fv(clrArray[6]);
        glVertex2f(250.0f, 220.0f);
    glEnd();
    glBegin(GL_POLYGON);
        glColor3fv(clrArray[7]);
        glVertex2f(150.0f, 250.0f);
```

```
            glColor3fv(clrArray[0]);
            glVertex2f(350.0f, 250.0f);
            glColor3fv(clrArray[1]);
            glVertex2f(400.0f, 375.0f);
            glColor3fv(clrArray[2]);
            glVertex2f(250.0f, 450.0f);
            glColor3fv(clrArray[3]);
            glVertex2f(100.0f, 375.0f);
        glEnd();
        glFlush();
#if 1
        SwapBuffers (wglGetCurrentDC());
#endif
        // Do not call CView::OnPaint() for painting messages
}
```

A *viewport* is the area in the window within which the OpenGL can draw. In this application whenever the window is resized, the entire client area of the window is set to be the viewport. The **gluOrtho2D** function defines the 2-D orthographic matrix. The aspect ratio passed to this function draws the graphic objects relative to the screen, so when the viewport becomes larger, the graphic objects appear larger, too.

```
void COglView::OnSize(UINT nType, int cx, int cy)
{
    CView::OnSize(nType, cx, cy);

    // TODO: Add your message handler code here
      glViewport(0, 0, cx, cy);
    if (cy == 0)
    {
        cy = 1;
    }
    glMatrixMode(GL_PROJECTION);
    glLoadIdentity();
    gluOrtho2D(0.0, (GLdouble)500.0*(cx/cy), 0.0, 500.0);
    glMatrixMode(GL_MODELVIEW);
    glLoadIdentity();
    glDrawBuffer(GL_BACK);
}
```

Just to add some dynamic features to the graphic objects that are drawn, the mouse movement is tracked and the events are handled by the next function. Earlier in the application, the code sets the color of the vertices, and OpenGL interpolates the color between the vertices. The vertex color is taken from a color array. This color array is manipulated in this function so that every time the mouse is moved, the color of the graphic objects drawn changes. This function can be commented out, and the difference can be seen.

```
void COglView::OnMouseMove(UINT nFlags, CPoint point)
{
    // TODO: Add your message handler code here and/or call default
    GLfloat *glfTemp;
    glfTemp = clrArray[0];
    for(int j=0; j<7; j++)
    {
        clrArray[j] = clrArray[j+1];
    }
    clrArray[7] = glfTemp;
    Invalidate(FALSE);
    CView::OnMouseMove(nFlags, point);
}


void COglView::OnDestroy()
{
    CView::OnDestroy();

    // TODO: Add your message handler code here
    HGLRC hRC;

    hRC = ::wglGetCurrentContext();
    ::wglMakeCurrent(NULL, NULL);
    if (hRC)
    {
        ::wglDeleteContext(hRC);
    }
}
```

This application used double buffering, which prevents the flicker every time the graphic objects are drawn. The difference between double buffering and drawing directly to the bitmap can be seen by changing the #if preprocessor directives and building the application not to use double buffering.

Programming Example to Transform 2-D Objects

The next sample extends the previous sample to illustrate pushing and popping the matrices, which are useful when you are transforming certain graphic objects while leaving the others in place. When the application is run and the mouse is moved over the application windows, the triangle object rotates about the lower-left corner of the screen, while the other two objects just change color. Part of the code that has changed is shown next.

To keep track of angle of rotation, a protected member variable **theta** is added in the view class. This is initialized to 0.0 degrees in the view constructor and is incremented by 5 degrees every time the application gets a mouse move message. The function that draws the graphic objects is shown next.

The idea of the application is to transform just the triangle. The transformation functions **glRotated** and **glTranslated** can be used to achieve these desired effects. The **glRotated** function computes a matrix that performs a counterclockwise rotation of the object by a given degree about the axis between the origin and the given vector. The **glTranslated** function moves the coordinate system origin to the point specified by the new coordinates. In both cases the current matrix is multiplied by the transformation matrix, and the resulting matrix replaces the current matrix. Thus, if the current matrix is not saved, then the result of one graphic object's translation will also be reflected in all other future graphic objects that are drawn. To overcome this situation, OpenGL maintains a stack of matrices. The stack depth is 32 for the GL_MODELVIEW mode and 2 for the GL_PROJECTION and GL_TEXTURE modes. It also provides two functions, **glPushMatrix** and **glPopMatrix**, that save and restore the current matrix. The **glPushMatrix** function pushes the current matrix in the stack, makes a copy of it, and leaves it at the top of the stack. The **glPopMatrix** function pops the top matrix from the stack, thereby making the next matrix current.

Before the triangle is transformed, the current matrix is saved by pushing it in the stack. The transformation is applied and the triangle is drawn. Before the next graphic object is drawn, the transformed matrix is replaced with the old matrix that was saved in the stack. Thus, the transformation only applies to the triangle graphic object and not the others. To gain more understanding, it would be worth trying out the application without the **glPushMatrix**/**glPopMatrix** functions. Then it would transform all three objects.

```
void COglView::OnPaint()
{
    CPaintDC dc(this); // device context for painting
    // TODO: Add your message handler code here

    glLoadIdentity();
    glClear(GL_COLOR_BUFFER_BIT);

    glPushMatrix();
        glRotated(theta, 0.0, 0.0, 1.0);
//      glTranslated(100.0, 100.0, 0);

        glBegin(GL_POLYGON);
            glColor3fv(clrArray[0]);
            glVertex2f(20.0f, 20.0f);
            glColor3fv(clrArray[1]);
            glVertex2f(175.0f, 20.0f);
            glColor3fv(clrArray[2]);
```

```
            glVertex2f(90.0f, 200.0f);
        glEnd();
    glPopMatrix();

    glBegin(GL_POLYGON);
        glColor3fv(clrArray[3]);
        glVertex2f(250.0f, 20.0f);
        glColor3fv(clrArray[4]);
        glVertex2f(400.0f, 20.0f);
        glColor3fv(clrArray[5]);
        glVertex2f(400.0f, 220.0f);
        glColor3fv(clrArray[6]);
        glVertex2f(250.0f, 220.0f);
    glEnd();

    glBegin(GL_POLYGON);
        glColor3fv(clrArray[7]);
        glVertex2f(150.0f, 250.0f);
        glColor3fv(clrArray[0]);
        glVertex2f(350.0f, 250.0f);
        glColor3fv(clrArray[1]);
        glVertex2f(400.0f, 375.0f);
        glColor3fv(clrArray[2]);
        glVertex2f(250.0f, 450.0f);
        glColor3fv(clrArray[3]);
        glVertex2f(100.0f, 375.0f);
    glEnd();
    glFlush();

    SwapBuffers (wglGetCurrentDC());

    // Do not call CView::OnPaint() for painting messages
}
```

When the mouse is moved, the angle of rotation is incremented by 5.0 degrees.

```
void COglView::OnMouseMove(UINT nFlags, CPoint point)
{
    // TODO: Add your message handler code here and/or call default

    GLfloat *glfTemp;
    glfTemp = clrArray[0];

    for(int j=0; j<7; j++)
```

```
        {
            clrArray[j] = clrArray[j+1];
        }
        clrArray[7] = glfTemp;
        theta += 5.0;
        Invalidate(FALSE);
        CView::OnMouseMove(nFlags, point);
}
```

Programming Example to Draw and Transform 3-D Objects

The next sample draws two 3-D graphic objects and transforms them. Most of the code
follows a pattern similar to that seen earlier. The changes related to the 3-D object are
highlighted here. Notice that in the **OnPaint** function the Z buffer is enabled by calling
the **glEnable** function. Since we are enabling the Z buffer, it is cleared before drawing by
calling **glClear** and adding GL_DEPTH_BUFFER_BIT to the parameter. The rest of the
logic of pushing and popping the matrix is similar to the earlier example. The coordinates
of the two boxes are calculated with respect to the origin being at the center of the 3-D
box. The sample can be modified and experimented with by changing the axis of rotation
of the 3-D boxes. Check the commented-out lines in the **OnPaint( )** function in the
following example.

```
// OglView.cpp : implementation of the COglView class
//

#include "stdafx.h"
#include "Ogl.h"

#include "OglDoc.h"
#include "OglView.h"

#ifdef _DEBUG
#define new DEBUG_NEW
#undef THIS_FILE
static char THIS_FILE[] = __FILE__;
#endif


/////////////////////////////////////////////////////////////////////////////
// COglView

IMPLEMENT_DYNCREATE(COglView, CView)

BEGIN_MESSAGE_MAP(COglView, CView)
        //{{AFX_MSG_MAP(COglView)
```

```
        ON_WM_CREATE()
        ON_WM_DESTROY()
        ON_WM_PAINT()
        ON_WM_SIZE()
        ON_WM_MOUSEMOVE()
        //}}AFX_MSG_MAP
END_MESSAGE_MAP()


//////////////////////////////////////////////////////////////////////////
// COglView construction/destruction

COglView::COglView()
{
        // TODO: add construction code here
    theta = 5.0;
    m_pixelformat = 0;
    m_hglRendContext = NULL;

    vdColor1[0] = 1.0;
    vdColor1[1] = 0.0;
    vdColor1[2] = 0.0;
    vdColor2[0] = 0.0;
    vdColor2[1] = 1.0;
    vdColor2[2] = 0.0;
    vdColor3[0] = 1.0;
    vdColor3[1] = 1.0;
    vdColor3[2] = 0.0;
    vdColor4[0] = 0.0;
    vdColor4[1] = 1.0;
    vdColor4[2] = 1.0;
    vdColor5[0] = 1.0;
    vdColor5[1] = 0.0;
    vdColor5[2] = 1.0;
    vdColor6[0] = 0.0;
    vdColor6[1] = 1.0;
    vdColor6[2] = 1.0;
    vdColor7[0] = 1.0;
    vdColor7[1] = 1.0;
    vdColor7[2] = 1.0;
    vdColor8[0] = 0.0;
    vdColor8[1] = 0.0;
    vdColor8[2] = 0.0;
```

```
        clrArray[0] = vdColor1;
        clrArray[1] = vdColor2;
        clrArray[2] = vdColor3;
        clrArray[3] = vdColor4;
        clrArray[4] = vdColor5;
        clrArray[5] = vdColor6;
        clrArray[6] = vdColor7;
        clrArray[7] = vdColor8;

}


COglView::~COglView()
{
}


BOOL COglView::PreCreateWindow(CREATESTRUCT& cs)
{
    // TODO: Modify the Window class or styles here by modifying
    //  the CREATESTRUCT cs

    cs.style |= (WS_CLIPCHILDREN | WS_CLIPSIBLINGS);
        return CView::PreCreateWindow(cs);
}


/////////////////////////////////////////////////////////////////////////
// COglView drawing

void COglView::OnDraw(CDC* pDC)
{
        COglDoc* pDoc = GetDocument();
        ASSERT_VALID(pDoc);

        // TODO: add draw code for native data here
}


/////////////////////////////////////////////////////////////////////////
// COglView diagnostics

#ifdef _DEBUG
void COglView::AssertValid() const
{
        CView::AssertValid();
}
```

```
void COglView::Dump(CDumpContext& dc) const
{
        CView::Dump(dc);
}


COglDoc* COglView::GetDocument() // non-debug version is inline
{
        ASSERT(m_pDocument->IsKindOf(RUNTIME_CLASS(COglDoc)));
        return (COglDoc*)m_pDocument;
}
#endif //_DEBUG


/////////////////////////////////////////////////////////////////////////////
// COglView message handlers

int COglView::OnCreate(LPCREATESTRUCT lpCreateStruct)
{
    if (CView::OnCreate(lpCreateStruct) == -1)
        return -1;
    // TODO: Add your specialized creation code here
    HDC hDC = ::GetDC(GetSafeHwnd());
    if (InitPixelFormat(hDC) == FALSE)
        return 0;
    m_hglRendContext = wglCreateContext(hDC);
    wglMakeCurrent(hDC, m_hglRendContext);
    return 0;
}


void COglView::OnDestroy()
{
        CView::OnDestroy();
        // TODO: Add your message handler code here
    HGLRC hRC;

    hRC = ::wglGetCurrentContext();
    ::wglMakeCurrent(NULL, NULL);
    if (hRC)
    {
        ::wglDeleteContext(hRC);
    }
}


BOOL COglView::InitPixelFormat(HDC hDC)
```

```
{
    PIXELFORMATDESCRIPTOR    PixForDesc;

    InitPFDStruc(&PixForDesc);
    m_pixelformat = ChoosePixelFormat( hDC, &PixForDesc);
    if (m_pixelformat == 0)
    {
        m_pixelformat = 1;
        if (DescribePixelFormat(hDC,  m_pixelformat,
            sizeof(PIXELFORMATDESCRIPTOR), &PixForDesc) == 0)
        {
            return FALSE;
        }
    }
    if (SetPixelFormat(hDC, m_pixelformat, &PixForDesc) == FALSE)
    {
        return FALSE;
    }
    return TRUE;
}


void COglView::InitPFDStruc(PIXELFORMATDESCRIPTOR *ppfd)
{
    memset(ppfd, 0, sizeof(PIXELFORMATDESCRIPTOR));

    ppfd->nSize = sizeof(PIXELFORMATDESCRIPTOR);
    ppfd->nVersion = 1;
    ppfd->dwFlags = PFD_DRAW_TO_WINDOW |
                    PFD_SUPPORT_OPENGL |
                    PFD_DOUBLEBUFFER;

    ppfd->iPixelType = PFD_TYPE_RGBA;
    ppfd->cColorBits = 24;
    ppfd->cDepthBits = 16;
    ppfd->iLayerType = PFD_MAIN_PLANE;

}


void COglView::OnPaint()
{
    CPaintDC dc(this); // device context for painting

    // TODO: Add your message handler code here
    glEnable( GL_DEPTH_TEST );
```

```
    glClear( GL_COLOR_BUFFER_BIT | GL_DEPTH_BUFFER_BIT);
    glMatrixMode( GL_MODELVIEW );
    glLoadIdentity();

    glTranslated( 0.0, 0.0, -9.0 );
    glRotated( theta, 1.0, 0.0, 0.0 ); // Sping along the X axis
// The next two lines can be uncommented to see rotation along Y and Z axis
//  glRotated( theta, 0.0, 1.0, 0.0 ); // Spin along the Y axis
//  glRotated( theta, 0.0, 0.0, 1.0 ); // Spin along the Z axis


    glPushMatrix();
// Commented-out lines can be uncommented to see rotation along X and Z axis
//     glRotated( theta, 1.0, 0.0, 0.0); // Spin along the X axis
       glRotated( theta, 0.0, 1.0, 0.0); // Spin along the Y axis
//     glRotated( theta, 0.0, 0.0, 1.0); // Spin along the Z axis

    glTranslated( 0.0, 0.05, 0.0 ); // Translate only along the Y axis
    DrawBox(0.5f, 0.5f, 0.5f);
    glPopMatrix();

    DrawBox(1.0f, 0.30f, 0.25f);
    glFlush();
    SwapBuffers( wglGetCurrentDC() );
        // Do not call CView::OnPaint() for painting messages
}

void COglView::OnSize(UINT nType, int cx, int cy)
{
    CView::OnSize(nType, cx, cy);

    // TODO: Add your message handler code here
    glViewport(0, 0, cx, cy);
    if (cy == 0)
    {
        cy = 1;
    }
    glMatrixMode(GL_PROJECTION);
    glLoadIdentity();
    gluPerspective(30.0f, cx/cy, 1.0, 20.0);
    glMatrixMode(GL_MODELVIEW);
    glLoadIdentity();
    glDrawBuffer(GL_BACK);
}
```

```
void COglView::OnMouseMove(UINT nFlags, CPoint point)
{
        // TODO: Add your message handler code here and/or call default

#if 0
    GLfloat *glfTemp;

    glfTemp = clrArray[0];
    for(int j=0; j<7; j++)
    {
        clrArray[j] = clrArray[j+1];
    }
    clrArray[7] = glfTemp;
#endif
    theta += 5.0;
    Invalidate(FALSE);
    CView::OnMouseMove(nFlags, point);
}


void COglView::DrawBox(GLfloat x, GLfloat y, GLfloat z)
{
    glBegin(GL_POLYGON);
        glColor3fv(clrArray[0]);
        glVertex3f(x,y,z);
        glColor3fv(clrArray[1]);
        glVertex3f(-x,y,z);
        glColor3fv(clrArray[2]);
        glVertex3f(-x,-y,z);
        glColor3fv(clrArray[3]);
        glVertex3f(x,-y,z);
    glEnd();
    glBegin(GL_POLYGON);
        glColor3fv(clrArray[4]);
        glVertex3f(x,y,-z);
        glColor3fv(clrArray[5]);
        glVertex3f(-x,y,-z);
        glColor3fv(clrArray[6]);
        glVertex3f(-x,-y,-z);
        glColor3fv(clrArray[7]);
        glVertex3f(x,-y,-z);
    glEnd();
    glBegin(GL_POLYGON);
```

```
        glColor3fv(clrArray[0]);
        glVertex3f(-x,y,z);
        glColor3fv(clrArray[1]);
        glVertex3f(-x,y,-z);
        glColor3fv(clrArray[2]);
        glVertex3f(-x,-y,-z);
        glColor3fv(clrArray[3]);
        glVertex3f(-x,-y,z);
    glEnd();
    glBegin(GL_POLYGON);
        glColor3fv(clrArray[4]);
        glVertex3f(x,y,z);
        glColor3fv(clrArray[5]);
        glVertex3f(x,y,-z);
        glColor3fv(clrArray[6]);
        glVertex3f(x,-y,-z);
        glColor3fv(clrArray[7]);
        glVertex3f(x,-y,z);
    glEnd();
    glBegin(GL_POLYGON);
        glColor3fv(clrArray[0]);
        glVertex3f(x,y,z);
        glColor3fv(clrArray[1]);
        glVertex3f(x,y,-z);
        glColor3fv(clrArray[2]);
        glVertex3f(-x,y,-z);
        glColor3fv(clrArray[3]);
        glVertex3f(-x,y,z);
    glEnd();
    glBegin(GL_POLYGON);
        glColor3fv(clrArray[4]);
        glVertex3f(x,-y,z);
        glColor3fv(clrArray[5]);
        glVertex3f(x,-y,-z);
        glColor3fv(clrArray[6]);
        glVertex3f(-x,-y,-z);
        glColor3fv(clrArray[7]);
        glVertex3f(-x,-y,z);
    glEnd();
}
```

Now that you have seen how to develop OpenGL applications, let's conclude this chapter with how to port an OpenGL application from one environment to another.

PORTING OPENGL APPLICATIONS

As mentioned earlier, the OpenGL standard helps in porting OpenGL applications from one environment to another. If you are porting OpenGL within Windows NT environments (such as Windows NT on Intel to Windows NT on Alpha), you should be able to make your application work by recompiling your OpenGL application source in the new environment (due to implementation differences, your application binaries are not normally portable).

If you are porting from a UNIX (or other) OpenGL environment to Windows NT or vice versa, then you have a lot more work to do. A typical OpenGL application will include OpenGL statements, calls to the operating system, calls to the windowing system, and potentially some calls for accessing databases. The OpenGL calls, for the most part, are standard. However, you may have to replace calls to the X Window subsystem in UNIX with equivalent calls to the Windows subsystem (for example, the **glXgetConfig** GLX X Window function may need to be replaced by the equivalent **DescribePixelFormat** function). While most GLX/Xlib functions have an equivalent Windows function, there are some GLX/Xlib functions that are not applicable in a Windows environment (such as **glXIsDirect**), or there is no equivalent Windows function (such as **glxWaitGl**). You may need to delete or rewrite functions that have no direct equivalence. You may need similar replacements for the operating system and database access calls.

Conclusion

We started with a brief review of OpenGL basics. We then looked at OpenGL data structures, OpenGL functions, and programming examples to draw and transform two-dimensional and three-dimensional objects. We concluded the chapter with a look at porting OpenGL across environments.

In the next chapter we will switch from multimedia to databases and take a look at database access by use of ODBC.

CHAPTER 20

Database Programming Using ODBC

L et's now look at another important programming aspect of Windows NT that you are likely to use a lot in business programming—accessing databases. Almost all business applications store and retrieve data from databases. Windows NT provides two primary ways to access databases—Data Access Objects (DAO) and Open Database Connectivity (ODBC). In this chapter, we will discuss ODBC. We will look at DAO in Chapter 21.

We will examine the need for ODBC, review ODBC basics, look at MFC library support for ODBC, review the steps involved in executing an ODBC API application, and see programming examples illustrating ODBC.

WHY ODBC?

Database applications belong to one of three categories: interactive, embedded, and module. *Interactive* database applications are typically ready-made database front-ends that include a GUI and that access a database in response to user queries. A module is a stand-alone usage. The most common form for database application development purposes is the *embedded* application, where an application program is developed with programming language statements interspersed with embedded database access statements. The most common language used for embedding is the structured query language (SQL). SQL is a widely accepted standard followed by almost all relational database product vendors. A recent enhancement to the standard addresses *call level interface (CLI)*. ODBC (also referred to as ODBC/SQL-3 CLI) provides database transparency to your application. As shown in Figure 20-1, your application interfaces with the ODBC driver manager using the same ODBC APIs or ODBC MFC library classes, regardless of which database it is accessing. This architecture permits easy access to heterogeneous databases as long as there is an ODBC driver for them. The databases need not be local to the machine your application is executing on, as indicated by the network connections between the drivers and the databases in Figure 20-1. When the database is on a network, a network library such as NetLib or SQLNet is also required to access the data, besides the ODBC drivers.

Note for UNIX Programmers

You can port Windows NT applications written to the Win32 API to run on UNIX using porting tools such as Wind/U from Bristol Technology and MainWin Studio from Mainsoft Corporation. If you are porting ODBC applications, you have to make sure that you are using the appropriate version of the ODBC driver for the UNIX system you are porting to.

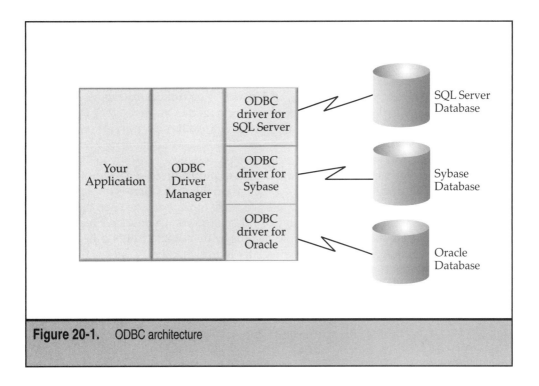

Figure 20-1. ODBC architecture

ODBC BASICS

An ODBC *data source* is a set of data together with the location of the data, information to access the data, and any intervening network connection. Your ODBC application can access multiple data sources at the same time. Examples of ODBC data sources could be an SQL server on the network or a local access database. Data sources must be registered and configured before they can be accessed by ODBC applications, and this function is typically performed by the ODBC administrator. See the programming example later in this chapter for more details about the ODBC administrator.

Your application must first establish a *connection* with the data source, and all communication with the data source is through that connection. You terminate the connection after you have finished accessing the data source. Besides being able to access multiple data sources at the same time, you can also have multiple connections at any given time to one data source.

Visual C++ includes ODBC drivers for a number of Microsoft databases, including SQL Server, Access, and FoxPro. Visual C++ also includes ODBC drivers for Microsoft's other products, such as Excel, and non-Microsoft databases, such as dBASE and Paradox. ODBC drivers are available from other vendors, too. When you connect to an ODBC data source using an ODBC driver, your application connects to the driver, which in turn connects to the ODBC data source. Typically the ODBC driver performs a translation from the format in which it receives the application's request to the format suitable for the target database. However, ODBC level 2 supports a *pass-through* function whereby the application request is sent to the target database without format translation.

ODBC data sources can be updated in *transaction* mode. In this mode, a series of updates to the ODBC data source can be bunched together so that either they are all performed (*commit transactions*), or none of the updates is performed (*rollback transactions*). This feature is useful to synchronize data across data sources. Many, but not all, ODBC data sources support transaction mode processing.

When you are updating data in a data source that could be accessed by multiple users, you may want to ensure that the integrity of the data in the data source is preserved using *locking* which prevents simultaneous update access by more than one user.

You can access records from a data source either a record at a time or access multiple records with one call. Accessing multiple records with a single call is called *bulk row fetching* (see the "Bulk Row Fetching" section later in this chapter).

Now that we have a basic understanding of what ODBC is, let's look at some advantages and disadvantages of using ODBC compared with direct SQL access, which are summarized in Table 20-1.

ODBC Advantages	ODBC Disadvantages
Transparent access to a variety of databases.	Small degradation in performance compared with invoking SQL directly, due to translation by the ODBC drivers.
No precompilation step required (unlike embedded SQL).	Vendor SQL extensions not supported at ODBC level 1. Some extensions may be accessed in ODBC level 2 using pass-through.
Besides SQL statements, your application can also initiate the execution of other database functions, such as stored procedures.	Absence of precompilation makes it difficult to detect or enforce coding standards.

Table 20-1.   Advantages and Disadvantages of ODBC

TIP: Both 16- and 32-bit ODBC drivers are available. Make sure that you use the 32-bit version when you are developing 32-bit applications for Windows NT.

MFC AND ODBC

MFC database classes let your application access data from any ODBC source database for which an ODBC driver is available. MFC provides the following classes for developing ODBC applications:

▼ CDatabase

■ CRecordset

■ CFieldExchange

■ CRecordView

■ CLongBinary

▲ CDBException

Let's look at these classes in detail.

CDatabase

A **CDatabase** class is derived from **CObject** and is used to construct a **CDatabase** object. The **CDatabase** object represents the connection between your application and the ODBC data source through which all interactions occur. The MFC library provides classes that are functionally similar for ODBC and DAO. The class names are different, and they are not interchangeable. For example, the DAO class similar to **CDatabase** is **CDAODatabase**. This class provides member functions to open and close the ODBC data source as well as to perform transactions. The important member functions of **CDatabase** are summarized in Table 20-2.

CRecordset

You typically derive an application-specific recordset class from **CRecordset** class to create a **CRecordset** object. A **CRecordset** object is a set of records selected from an ODBC data source. There are two types of recordsets: *dynasets* and *snapshots.* A dynaset is a recordset where the data reflects updates made to the record by your application or other applications. For example, when you scroll to a record in a dynaset, it reflects changes made to the record after the recordset was created. A snapshot is a static view of the data as of the time the recordset was created and is not updated. You can specify the type of recordset you want in the **Open** member function.

CDatabase Member Function	Description
Open	This opens a database connection after a database object is constructed and before recordsets are constructed.
OpenEx	This is a more general version of **Open** supporting more options.
Close	This closes a connection. **Close** does not destroy the CDatabase object, which can be reused for another connection to the same or even a different ODBC data source. You have to close associated recordsets before closing the connection.
BeginTrans	This starts a new transaction. The data source must support transaction processing. You can check if your driver supports transactions for a given database using the CanTransact member function. BeginTrans may lock data records in the data source. A transaction consists of one or more calls to the AddNew, Edit, Delete, and Update member functions of a CRecordset object (see the "CRecordset" section).
CommitTrans	This commits updates of the current transaction.
Rollback	This cancels updates of the current transaction.
ExecuteSQL	This executes an SQL statement. You normally would retrieve and update data in the data source using recordset objects. However, there may be a need to execute some SQL statements directly. You use ExecuteSQL for such purposes. ExecuteSQL does not return any data.

Table 20-2. CDatabase Member Functions

With either type of recordset, you can perform functions such as scrolling, filtering, sorting, and so on, of the records in the recordset. The important member functions of **CRecordset** are summarized in Table 20-3.

CRecordset Member Function	Description
AddNew	This prepares a new record using the recordset's field data members. The record's fields are initially set to NULL. After assigning values, call the Update member function (see Update member function in this table). You cannot use this member function in bulk row fetching.
Edit	This edits field data member values for existing records.
Update	This commits new records after AddNew or existing records after Edit.
Delete	This deletes a record.

Table 20-3.   CRecordset Member Functions

Recordset Locking

To ensure that updates to the ODBC data source are coordinated between multiple users of the data source, you can use locking. The typical update sequence is to use the **Edit** member function of **CRecordset** to get the data, update the desired fields, and use the **Update** member function to update the data. You can choose between two types of locking—*optimistic* and *pessimistic*. In optimistic locking mode, the lock is placed only for the **Update** call. In pessimistic locking mode, the lock is placed when the **Edit** member function is called, and the lock remains in place (affecting other potential users) until the **Update** member function is called. While the lock duration in optimistic mode is much shorter than in pessimistic mode, your application has to account for the possibility that some other application may apply a lock between the time your application called the **Edit** member function and called the **Update** member function. You can choose between the two locking modes using the **SetLockingMode** member function.

Consistent with the MFC design, the MFC library doesn't support all the functionality of the native APIs. You can call ODBC and DAO APIs directly from your MFC applications for functionality not supported by the MFC library (just as you can directly call any Win32 APIs). One such example would be the ODBC catalog functions, such as **::SQLTables**.

Bulk Row Fetching

Bulk row fetching lets multiple records be retrieved during a single fetch. You have to derive a class from the **CRecordset** class to implement bulk row fetching. The number of records you want to retrieve with a single fetch is specified as a parameter of the **SetRowsetSize** member function. You must also set the **CRecordset::useMultiRowFetch** option in the *dwOptions* parameter of the **Open** member function. Bulk row fetching uses *bulk record field exchange* to transfer data between the data source and the recordset. Bulk record field exchange uses arrays to store the multiple rows of data. You can assign the memory buffers to hold the multiple data rows, or the buffers can be allocated automatically. You assign the buffers by specifying the **CRecordset::user AllocMultiRowBuffers** option. **CRecordset** does not include a member function for bulk row data updates. If you want to update bulk row data, you have to use ODBC APIs directly. In addition, ClassWizard does not support bulk record field exchange. This implies that you must declare field data members and override **DoBulkFieldExchange**. Repositioning within records retrieved using bulk row fetching is by rowset.

CFieldExchange

The **CFieldExchange** class supports the record field exchange (RFX) and bulk record field exchange (Bulk RFX) routines. You will not normally use this class unless you are implementing bulk row fetching or writing custom RFX routines. The member functions provided by **CFieldExchange** are **IsFieldType**, which helps determine whether the current operation can be performed on a particular field or parameter, and **SetFieldType**, which specifies the type of access for a parameter or column as input, output, and so on.

CRecordView

A **CRecordView** object enables the records from an ODBC data source to be displayed in controls of a dialog box. **CRecordView** uses dialog data exchange (DDX) and record field exchange (RFX) to automate the movement of data between the controls and the fields of the recordset. The **CRecordView** class is commonly created with the AppWizard, which also creates an associated **CRecordset** class. You can also create the **CRecordView** class using ClassWizard.

CLongBinary

The **CLongBinary** class is used in constructing a **CLongBinary** object. A **CLongBinary** object can be used if you are working with *binary large objects* (*BLOBs*). A common example of a BLOB is a bitmap. If you want to store a BLOB as a field in a table row, declare a field data member of type **CLongBinary** in your recordset class. Once the **CLongBinary** object is constructed and ready to use, RFX queries the data source for the size of the binary large object, allocates storage, and stores an HGLOBAL handle to the data in the **m_hData**

data member of the **CLongBinary** object. RFX also stores the actual size of the data object in the **m_dwDataLength data** member of the **CLongBinary** object.

CDBException

The **CDBException** class includes the **m_nRetCode** data member that contains an ODBC return code in case of an exception. The data member **m_strError** contains an alphanumeric string that has the error description. You can also throw **CDBException** objects from your code with the **AfxThrowDBException** global function.

ODBC Application Using ODBC APIs

The sequence of steps followed by an ODBC application using ODBC APIs are summarized here:

1. Allocate the environment, connection, and statement handles using **SQLAllocHandle**. Allocating the environment handle initializes the ODBC call-level interface and must be called before any other ODBC call is made. Allocating the connection handle causes memory to be allocated for the connection. Allocating a statement handle provides access to statement information, such as the cursor name, error messages, and SQL status information and so on. The ODBC driver is then loaded and connected to the ODBC data source. You can access multiple ODBC data sources in your application, and you can create multiple connections to the same data source as long as the ODBC driver supports these functions. Also, if the driver is thread safe (that is, if the driver is capable of being invoked by multiple simultaneous threads), you can pass the environment, connection, and statement handles across different threads in your application.

2. Perform application processing such as requesting recordsets, managing transactions, or submitting SQL statements.

3. Receive results of requests from the ODBC data source such as recordsets, responses to SQL queries, and so on.

4. Process the received results. This may result in requesting additional recordsets or submitting additional SQL statements.

5. When you are done processing, free the environment, connection, and statement handles using **SQLFreeHandle**.

ODBC PROGRAMMING EXAMPLE

The *MyPhone* sample shown here provides a graphical interface for a Microsoft Access database that contains a list of names, phone numbers, and comments. This sample uses the document/view architecture and is created by use of the AppWizard. It also uses the MFC library database classes based on ODBC, which significantly reduces the complexity of the application. In later samples, this application will be extended to give the ability to add and delete the records in the database. The example shows the records from the database accessed and displayed on a dialog box. You can navigate through the records in the database using the Next, Previous, First, and Last Record menu selections or icons. Figure 20-2 shows the first record in the database when the example program starts execution.

Note that the First Record and Previous Record icons are grayed out, indicating that the record shown is the first record. You can also add and delete records to the database using the Add and Delete options in the Record pull-down menu. When you select Add, the example program clears all the entry fields in the dialog box, as shown in Figure 20-3.

The MFC library database classes are based on ODBC, and thus they provide access to any database so long as an ODBC driver is available for that database. The application based on ODBC can access data from many different data formats and different local and remote configurations, thereby elevating the application above the details of the database.

The database consists of four columns: first and last names, phone number, and a comment. The first step is to register the database that will be used, with an ODBC data source name. This data source name will be referred to by the sample application. This

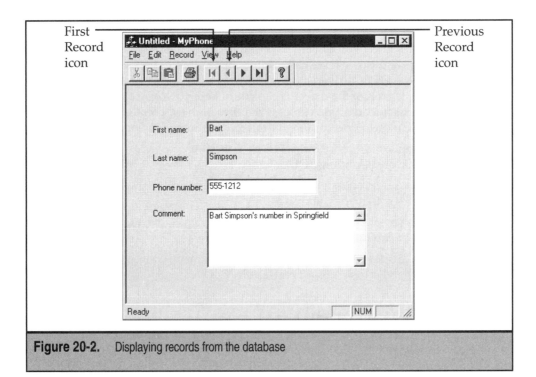

Figure 20-2. Displaying records from the database

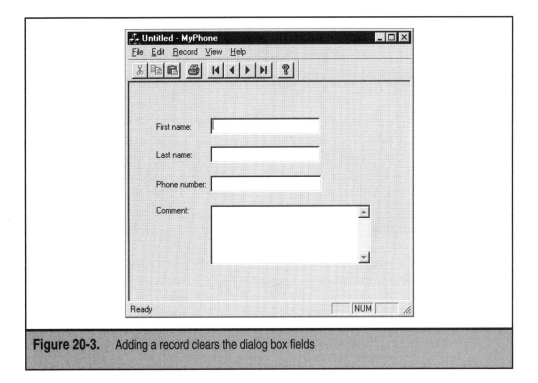

Figure 20-3.   Adding a record clears the dialog box fields

registration is done by use of the ODBC administrator from the Control Panel or by custom-written application. To register the data source using ODBC:

1. Open the Control Panel and double-click on the ODBC icon to bring up the ODBC Data Source Administrator.

2. Go to the User DSN page, and click on the Add button to add the new data source. The database that will be added is a Microsoft Access database.

3. Select Microsoft Access Driver and click on Finish in the Create New Data Source dialog box.

4. Type in **Phone Directory** as the data source name, and add description text for the data source name.

5. In the Database group box click on Select and provide the database name, which is **MyPhone.mdb**. (Make sure the fully qualified filename is provided. It may make it easier to navigate and locate the database file.)

6. Click on OK on all the dialog boxes to exit the ODBC Data Source Administrator.

Figure 20-4 shows the ODBC Data Source Administrator menu after registration is complete and the Phone Directory has been added.

The procedure to create this application through the AppWizard is as follows:

1. Start the Microsoft Visual C++ and select New from the File menu to create a new project.

2. Click on the Project tab, and select MFC AppWizard (exe) as the project type.

3. Type in the project name as **MyPhone** and select OK. The AppWizard creates the project directory, and the MFC AppWizard—Step 1 dialog box appears.

4. Make this application a single document application by clicking on the Single Document radio button, and then click on the Next button to go to the Step 2 Of 6 dialog box.

5. Click on Database View Without File Support, and then click on the Data Source button.

6. Click on the ODBC radio button and select the Phone Directory. Registering the database in the earlier step resulted in the availability of the data source. Clicking on OK will bring up the Select Database Tables dialog box.

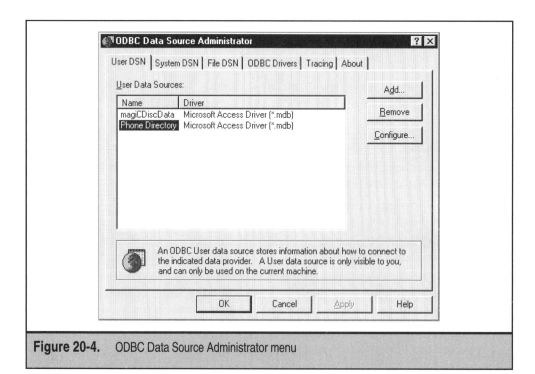

Figure 20-4.   ODBC Data Source Administrator menu

7. Select the *PhoneBook* table and click on OK. This will bring you back to the Step 2 Of 6 dialog box.

8. On the rest of the pages select Next to accept the default. (In the last page the filenames can be changed if needed. To illustrate this, the **CMyPhoneView** class file is renamed from the default *MyPhoneView* name to *MyPhoneForm* name. When the Finish button is clicked, the AppWizard will create the files related to the project.)

Shown next is the standard application class derived from **CWinApp** class. The only significant code to notice here is the registration of the application's document template with the framework. This document template serves as the connection between document, frame window, and view. This module also has the code to process the About dialog box.

```
// MyPhone.h : main header file for the MYPHONE application
//
#if !defined(AFX_MYPHONE_H)
#define AFX_MYPHONE_H

#if _MSC_VER >= 1000
#pragma once
#endif // _MSC_VER >= 1000

#ifndef __AFXWIN_H__
    #error include 'stdafx.h' before including this file for PCH
#endif

#include "resource.h"        // main symbols

/////////////////////////////////////////////////
// CMyPhoneApp:
// See MyPhone.cpp for the implementation of this class
//

class CMyPhoneApp : public CWinApp
{
public:
    CMyPhoneApp();

// Overrides
    // ClassWizard generated virtual function overrides
    //{{AFX_VIRTUAL(CMyPhoneApp)
    public:
    virtual BOOL InitInstance();
```

```
    //}}AFX_VIRTUAL

// Implementation

    //{{AFX_MSG(CMyPhoneApp)
    afx_msg void OnAppAbout();
        // NOTE - the ClassWizard will add and remove member functions here.
        //    DO NOT EDIT what you see in these blocks of generated code!
    //}}AFX_MSG
    DECLARE_MESSAGE_MAP()
};

//{{AFX_INSERT_LOCATION}}
#endif

// MyPhone.cpp : Defines the class behaviors for the application.
//

#include "stdafx.h"
#include "MyPhone.h"

#include "MainFrm.h"
#include "MyPhoneSet.h"
#include "MyPhoneDoc.h"
#include "MyPhoneForm.h"

#ifdef _DEBUG
#define new DEBUG_NEW
#undef THIS_FILE
static char THIS_FILE[] = __FILE__;

#endif
/////////////////////////////////////////////////
// CMyPhoneApp

BEGIN_MESSAGE_MAP(CMyPhoneApp, CWinApp)
    //{{AFX_MSG_MAP(CMyPhoneApp)
    ON_COMMAND(ID_APP_ABOUT, OnAppAbout)
        // NOTE - the ClassWizard will add and remove mapping macros here.
        //    DO NOT EDIT what you see in these blocks of generated code!
    //}}AFX_MSG_MAP
    // Standard print setup command
    ON_COMMAND(ID_FILE_PRINT_SETUP, CWinApp::OnFilePrintSetup)
END_MESSAGE_MAP()
```

```
/////////////////////////////////////////////////
// CMyPhoneApp construction

CMyPhoneApp::CMyPhoneApp()
{
    // TODO: add construction code here,
    // Place all significant initialization in InitInstance
}

/////////////////////////////////////////////////
// The one and only CMyPhoneApp object

CMyPhoneApp theApp;

/////////////////////////////////////////////////
// CMyPhoneApp initialization

BOOL CMyPhoneApp::InitInstance()
{
    AfxEnableControlContainer();

#ifdef _AFXDLL
    Enable3dControls();
#else
    Enable3dControlsStatic();
#endif

// Change the registry key under which our settings are stored.
// You should modify this string to be something appropriate
// such as the name of your company or organization.
    SetRegistryKey(_T("Local AppWizard-Generated Applications"));
    LoadStdProfileSettings();

    CSingleDocTemplate* pDocTemplate;
    pDocTemplate = new CSingleDocTemplate(
        IDR_MAINFRAME,
        RUNTIME_CLASS(CMyPhoneDoc),
        RUNTIME_CLASS(CMainFrame),        // main SDI frame window
        RUNTIME_CLASS(CMyPhoneForm));
    AddDocTemplate(pDocTemplate);

    CCommandLineInfo cmdInfo;
    ParseCommandLine(cmdInfo);
```

```
    // Dispatch commands specified on the command line
    if (!ProcessShellCommand(cmdInfo))
        return FALSE;

    // The one and only window has been initialized,
    // so show and update it.
    m_pMainWnd->ShowWindow(SW_SHOW);
    m_pMainWnd->UpdateWindow();

    return TRUE;
}

/////////////////////////////////////////////////////
// CAboutDlg dialog used for App About

class CAboutDlg : public CDialog
{
public:
    CAboutDlg();

// Dialog Data
    //{{AFX_DATA(CAboutDlg)
    enum { IDD = IDD_ABOUTBOX };
    //}}AFX_DATA

    // ClassWizard generated virtual function overrides
    //{{AFX_VIRTUAL(CAboutDlg)
    protected:
    virtual void DoDataExchange(CDataExchange* pDX);    // DDX/DDV support
    //}}AFX_VIRTUAL

// Implementation
protected:
    //{{AFX_MSG(CAboutDlg)
        // No message handlers
    //}}AFX_MSG
    DECLARE_MESSAGE_MAP()
};

CAboutDlg::CAboutDlg() : CDialog(CAboutDlg::IDD)
{
    //{{AFX_DATA_INIT(CAboutDlg)
    //}}AFX_DATA_INIT
```

```
}

void CAboutDlg::DoDataExchange(CDataExchange* pDX)
{
    CDialog::DoDataExchange(pDX);
    //{{AFX_DATA_MAP(CAboutDlg)
    //}}AFX_DATA_MAP
}

BEGIN_MESSAGE_MAP(CAboutDlg, CDialog)
    //{{AFX_MSG_MAP(CAboutDlg)
        // No message handlers
    //}}AFX_MSG_MAP
END_MESSAGE_MAP()

// App command to run the dialog
void CMyPhoneApp::OnAppAbout()
{
    CAboutDlg aboutDlg;
    aboutDlg.DoModal();
}
```

Shown next is the code for **CMyPhoneDoc** class, which is derived from the **CDocument** class of the framework. This is pretty much the boilerplate code. Just notice the member data **m_myPhoneSet**. In a typical application the document stores the data and serializes it to a file, reading all the data into the memory once and writing it back to disk. But in the database application the data is stored in the database and is commonly viewed one record at a time. So instead of serializing the data, the document encapsulates the recordset object. The recordset object **m_myPhoneSet** is encapsulated in the document and is automatically constructed when the document object is constructed, and deleted when the document object is deleted. This sample has only one recordset related to the phone list, so we have only one recordset object. The document can encapsulate more than one recordset object if the application has more than one recordset. Thus, the document acts as a proxy or front-end for the database.

```
// MyPhoneDoc.h : interface of the CMyPhoneDoc class
//
#if !defined(AFX_MYPHONEDOC_H)
#define AFX_MYPHONEDOC_H

#if _MSC_VER >= 1000
#pragma once
#endif // _MSC_VER >= 1000
```

```
class CMyPhoneDoc : public CDocument
{
protected: // create from serialization only
    CMyPhoneDoc();
    DECLARE_DYNCREATE(CMyPhoneDoc)

// Attributes
public:
    CMyPhoneSet m_myPhoneSet;

// Operations
public:

// Overrides
    // ClassWizard generated virtual function overrides
    //{{AFX_VIRTUAL(CMyPhoneDoc)
    public:
    virtual BOOL OnNewDocument();
    //}}AFX_VIRTUAL

// Implementation
public:
    virtual ~CMyPhoneDoc();
#ifdef _DEBUG
    virtual void AssertValid() const;
    virtual void Dump(CDumpContext& dc) const;
#endif

protected:

// Generated message map functions
protected:
    //{{AFX_MSG(CMyPhoneDoc)
        // NOTE - the ClassWizard will add and remove member functions here.
        //    DO NOT EDIT what you see in these blocks of generated code!
    //}}AFX_MSG
    DECLARE_MESSAGE_MAP()
};

//{{AFX_INSERT_LOCATION}}
// Microsoft Developer Studio will insert additional declarations
// immediately before the previous line.

#endif
```

```
// MyPhoneDoc.cpp : implementation of the CMyPhoneDoc class
//
#include "stdafx.h"
#include "MyPhone.h"
#include "MyPhoneSet.h"
#include "MyPhoneDoc.h"

#ifdef _DEBUG
#define new DEBUG_NEW
#undef THIS_FILE
static char THIS_FILE[] = __FILE__;
#endif

/////////////////////////////////////////////////
// CMyPhoneDoc

IMPLEMENT_DYNCREATE(CMyPhoneDoc, CDocument)

BEGIN_MESSAGE_MAP(CMyPhoneDoc, CDocument)
    //{{AFX_MSG_MAP(CMyPhoneDoc)
        // NOTE - the ClassWizard will add and remove mapping macros here.
        //    DO NOT EDIT what you see in these blocks of generated code!
    //}}AFX_MSG_MAP
END_MESSAGE_MAP()

/////////////////////////////////////////////////
// CMyPhoneDoc construction/destruction

CMyPhoneDoc::CMyPhoneDoc()
{
    // TODO: add one-time construction code here
}

CMyPhoneDoc::~CMyPhoneDoc()
{
}

BOOL CMyPhoneDoc::OnNewDocument()
{
    if (!CDocument::OnNewDocument())
        return FALSE;
    // TODO: add reinitialization code here
    // (SDI documents will reuse this document)
```

```
    return TRUE;
}
/////////////////////////////////////////////////
// CMyPhoneDoc diagnostics
#ifdef _DEBUG
void CMyPhoneDoc::AssertValid() const
{
    CDocument::AssertValid();
}

void CMyPhoneDoc::Dump(CDumpContext& dc) const
{
    CDocument::Dump(dc);
}
#endif //_DEBUG
```

Shown next are the **CMyPhoneSet** class-related modules. This class deals with the set of records selected from the database known as recordsets. Notice that the application-specific recordset, **CMyPhoneSet** class, is derived from **CRecordset**, which is typical. Recordsets select records from a data source, and these records can be scrolled through and updated if needed. A filter can also be specified to selectively retrieve the records from the data source. The records in the recordset can be sorted and the recordset can be parameterized to customize its selection with information not known until run time.

In the **CMyPhoneSet** class, notice that the columns of the phone book table appear as member variables. The AppWizard has bound all of the columns in the table to member variables in this class. These member variables are called *field data members*. The names for these member variables, as you can see, are automatically assigned by AppWizard. It also assigns the correct C++ or class library data type to them based on the column type. As expected, they are mapped to the **CString** type. Though AppWizard creates these automatically, not all columns need to be exposed to the user. Fields that need not be exposed can be removed from this list. This customization can be done through the ClassWizard.

To use a recordset, the ClassWizard constructs a recordset object and calls the **Open** member function to run the recordset's query and select the records. When this process is completed, the recordset is closed and the object is destroyed. In the following example these processes are triggered by the framework. The **GetDefaultConnect** member function, which is overridden here automatically by the ClassWizard, is called by the framework to get the default connect string for the data source on which the recordset is based. The ClassWizard implements this function by identifying the same data source that was identified to the ClassWizard to get information about tables and columns. The other member function that is overridden here is the **GetDefaultSQL**, which is also called by the framework to get the default SQL statement on which the recordset is based. The default SQL statement was indirectly defined by the ClassWizard when the recordset class was declared with it. The data exchange between the recordset and data source is achieved by the **DoFieldExchange** member function. The framework calls this member function to automatically exchange data between the field data members of the recordset object and the corresponding columns of the current record on the data source.

```
// MyPhoneSet.h : interface of the CMyPhoneSet class
//
#if !defined(AFX_MYPHONESET_H)
#define AFX_MYPHONESET_H

#if _MSC_VER >= 1000
#pragma once
#endif // _MSC_VER >= 1000

class CMyPhoneSet : public CRecordset
{
public:
    CMyPhoneSet(CDatabase* pDatabase = NULL);
    DECLARE_DYNAMIC(CMyPhoneSet)

// Field/Param Data
    //{{AFX_FIELD(CMyPhoneSet, CRecordset)
    CString     m_FirstName;
    CString     m_LastName;
    CString     m_Phone;
    CString     m_Notes;
    //}}AFX_FIELD

// Overrides
    // ClassWizard generated virtual function overrides
    //{{AFX_VIRTUAL(CMyPhoneSet)
    public:
    virtual CString GetDefaultConnect();    // Default connection string
    virtual CString GetDefaultSQL();     // default SQL for Recordset
    virtual void DoFieldExchange(CFieldExchange* pFX);    // RFX support
    //}}AFX_VIRTUAL

// Implementation
#ifdef _DEBUG
    virtual void AssertValid() const;
    virtual void Dump(CDumpContext& dc) const;
#endif
```

```cpp
};

//{{AFX_INSERT_LOCATION}}
// Microsoft Developer Studio will insert additional declarations
// immediately before the previous line.
#endif

// MyPhoneSet.cpp : implementation of the CMyPhoneSet class
//

#include "stdafx.h"
#include "MyPhone.h"
#include "MyPhoneSet.h"

#ifdef _DEBUG
#define new DEBUG_NEW
#undef THIS_FILE
static char THIS_FILE[] = __FILE__;
#endif

/////////////////////////////////////////////////////
// CMyPhoneSet implementation

IMPLEMENT_DYNAMIC(CMyPhoneSet, CRecordset)

CMyPhoneSet::CMyPhoneSet(CDatabase* pdb)
    : CRecordset(pdb)
{
    //{{AFX_FIELD_INIT(CMyPhoneSet)
    m_FirstName = _T("");
    m_LastName = _T("");
    m_Phone = _T("");
    m_Notes = _T("");
    m_nFields = 4;
    //}}AFX_FIELD_INIT
    m_nDefaultType = snapshot;
}

CString CMyPhoneSet::GetDefaultConnect()
{
    return _T("ODBC;DSN=Phone Directory");
}
```

```
CString CMyPhoneSet::GetDefaultSQL()
{
    return _T("[PhoneBook]");
}


void CMyPhoneSet::DoFieldExchange(CFieldExchange* pFX)
{
    //{{AFX_FIELD_MAP(CMyPhoneSet)
    pFX->SetFieldType(CFieldExchange::outputColumn);
    RFX_Text(pFX, _T("[FirstName]"), m_FirstName);
    RFX_Text(pFX, _T("[LastName]"), m_LastName);
    RFX_Text(pFX, _T("[Phone]"), m_Phone);
    RFX_Text(pFX, _T("[Notes]"), m_Notes);
    //}}AFX_FIELD_MAP
}


/////////////////////////////////////////////////////
// CMyPhoneSet diagnostics

#ifdef _DEBUG
void CMyPhoneSet::AssertValid() const
{
    CRecordset::AssertValid();
}


void CMyPhoneSet::Dump(CDumpContext& dc) const
{
    CRecordset::Dump(dc);
}
#endif //_DEBUG
```

Discussed next are the procedure to create the form that displays the phone numbers and how to bind the controls on the dialog box to the recordset fields. In ResourceView, the MyPhone folder is expanded and then the Dialog folder is expanded. IDD_MYPHONE_FORM is opened by double-clicking on it. The default static control that says "TODO: Place form controls on this dialog" is selected and deleted. Four pairs of static controls and edit controls are created, one each for First name, Last name, Phone number, and Comment. They are named IDC_FIRSTNAME, IDC_LASTNAME, IDC_PHONENUMBER, and IDC_NOTES. The style for the First name and Last name edit controls is set to read-only. The resource file is saved. The next step is to bind the controls to the recordset fields to indicate which control maps to which column in the table. This is done by use of the ClassWizard's "foreign object" mechanism. Typically ClassWizard binds controls in a dialog box or form to member variables of the class derived from **CDialog** or **CFormView**. In the case of **CRecordView** the controls are bound to data members of the recordset class associated with the record view. In this case the class derived from **CRecordView**, **CMyPhoneForm**, has a data member for **CMyPhoneSet**. The control bindings go through m_pSet to the corresponding field data members of **CMyPhoneSet**.

To bind a control in the dialog box to a recordset data member, the CTRL key is held down and the left mouse button (in right-handed button configuration) is double-clicked on the control in the dialog box. The ClassWizard's Add Member Variable dialog box appears with a proposed field name selected. This proposed name is accepted. All the controls in the dialog box are bound and the work is saved.

The **CMyPhoneForm** class-related code is shown next.

```cpp
// MyPhoneForm.h : interface of the CMyPhoneForm class
//

#if !defined(AFX_MYPHONEFORM_H)
#define AFX_MYPHONEFORM_H

#if _MSC_VER >= 1000
#pragma once
#endif // _MSC_VER >= 1000

class CMyPhoneSet;

class CMyPhoneForm : public CRecordView
{
protected: // create from serialization only
    CMyPhoneForm();
    DECLARE_DYNCREATE(CMyPhoneForm)

public:
    //{{AFX_DATA(CMyPhoneForm)
    enum { IDD = IDD_MYPHONE_FORM };
    CEdit       m_ctlLastName;
    CEdit       m_ctlFirstName;
    CMyPhoneSet* m_pSet;
    //}}AFX_DATA

// Attributes
public:
    CMyPhoneDoc* GetDocument();

// Operations
public:
```

```
// Overrides
    // ClassWizard generated virtual function overrides
    //{{AFX_VIRTUAL(CMyPhoneForm)
    public:
    virtual CRecordset* OnGetRecordset();
    virtual BOOL PreCreateWindow(CREATESTRUCT& cs);
    virtual BOOL OnMove(UINT nIDMoveCommand);
    protected:
    virtual void DoDataExchange(CDataExchange* pDX);    // DDX/DDV support
    virtual void OnInitialUpdate(); // called first time after construct
    virtual BOOL OnPreparePrinting(CPrintInfo* pInfo);
    virtual void OnBeginPrinting(CDC* pDC, CPrintInfo* pInfo);
    virtual void OnEndPrinting(CDC* pDC, CPrintInfo* pInfo);
    //}}AFX_VIRTUAL

// Implementation
public:
    virtual ~CMyPhoneForm();
#ifdef _DEBUG
    virtual void AssertValid() const;
    virtual void Dump(CDumpContext& dc) const;
#endif

protected:

// Generated message map functions
protected:

    //{{AFX_MSG(CMyPhoneForm)
    //}}AFX_MSG
    DECLARE_MESSAGE_MAP()
};

#ifndef _DEBUG  // debug version in MyPhoneForm.cpp
inline CMyPhoneDoc* CMyPhoneForm::GetDocument()
   { return (CMyPhoneDoc*)m_pDocument; }
#endif

/////////////////////////////////////////////////////

//{{AFX_INSERT_LOCATION}}
// Microsoft Developer Studio will insert additional declarations
// immediately before the previous line.
#endif //
```

```cpp
// MyPhoneForm.cpp : implementation of the CMyPhoneForm class
//

#include "stdafx.h"
#include "MyPhone.h"

#include "MyPhoneSet.h"
#include "MyPhoneDoc.h"
#include "MyPhoneForm.h"

#ifdef _DEBUG
#define new DEBUG_NEW
#undef THIS_FILE
static char THIS_FILE[] = __FILE__;
#endif

/////////////////////////////////////////////////////
// CMyPhoneForm

IMPLEMENT_DYNCREATE(CMyPhoneForm, CRecordView)

BEGIN_MESSAGE_MAP(CMyPhoneForm, CRecordView)
    //{{AFX_MSG_MAP(CMyPhoneForm)
    //}}AFX_MSG_MAP
    // Standard printing commands
    ON_COMMAND(ID_FILE_PRINT, CRecordView::OnFilePrint)
    ON_COMMAND(ID_FILE_PRINT_DIRECT, CRecordView::OnFilePrint)
    ON_COMMAND(ID_FILE_PRINT_PREVIEW, CRecordView::OnFilePrintPreview)
END_MESSAGE_MAP()

/////////////////////////////////////////////////////
// CMyPhoneForm construction/destruction

CMyPhoneForm::CMyPhoneForm()
    : CRecordView(CMyPhoneForm::IDD)
{
    //{{AFX_DATA_INIT(CMyPhoneForm)
    m_pSet = NULL;
    //}}AFX_DATA_INIT
    // TODO: add construction code here
}

CMyPhoneForm::~CMyPhoneForm()
```

```
{
}

void CMyPhoneForm::DoDataExchange(CDataExchange* pDX)
{
    CRecordView::DoDataExchange(pDX);
    //{{AFX_DATA_MAP(CMyPhoneForm)
    DDX_Control(pDX, IDC_LASTNAME, m_ctlLastName);
    DDX_Control(pDX, IDC_FIRSTNAME, m_ctlFirstName);
    DDX_FieldText(pDX, IDC_FIRSTNAME, m_pSet->m_FirstName, m_pSet);
    DDX_FieldText(pDX, IDC_LASTNAME, m_pSet->m_LastName, m_pSet);
    DDX_FieldText(pDX, IDC_PHONENUMBER, m_pSet->m_Phone, m_pSet);
    DDX_FieldText(pDX, IDC_NOTES, m_pSet->m_Notes, m_pSet);
    //}}AFX_DATA_MAP
}

BOOL CMyPhoneForm::PreCreateWindow(CREATESTRUCT& cs)
{
    // TODO: Modify the Window class or styles here by modifying
    //   the CREATESTRUCT cs
    return CRecordView::PreCreateWindow(cs);
}

void CMyPhoneForm::OnInitialUpdate()
{
    m_pSet = &GetDocument()->m_myPhoneSet;
    m_pSet->m_strSort="FirstName"; // sort by first name
    CRecordView::OnInitialUpdate();
}


/////////////////////////////////////////////////
// CMyPhoneForm printing

BOOL CMyPhoneForm::OnPreparePrinting(CPrintInfo* pInfo)
{
    // default preparation
    return DoPreparePrinting(pInfo);
}

void CMyPhoneForm::OnBeginPrinting(CDC* /*pDC*/, CPrintInfo* /*pInfo*/)
{
    // TODO: add extra initialization before printing
}
```

```
void CMyPhoneForm::OnEndPrinting(CDC* /*pDC*/, CPrintInfo* /*pInfo*/)
{
    // TODO: add cleanup after printing
}


//////////////////////////////////////////////////
// CMyPhoneForm diagnostics

#ifdef _DEBUG
void CMyPhoneForm::AssertValid() const
{
    CRecordView::AssertValid();
}

void CMyPhoneForm::Dump(CDumpContext& dc) const
{
    CRecordView::Dump(dc);
}

CMyPhoneDoc* CMyPhoneForm::GetDocument() // non-debug version is inline
{
    ASSERT(m_pDocument->IsKindOf(RUNTIME_CLASS(CMyPhoneDoc)));
    return (CMyPhoneDoc*)m_pDocument;
}
#endif //_DEBUG

//////////////////////////////////////////////////
// CMyPhoneForm database support
CRecordset* CMyPhoneForm::OnGetRecordset()
{
    return m_pSet;
}



//////////////////////////////////////////////////
// CMyPhoneForm message handlers

BOOL CMyPhoneForm::OnMove(UINT nIDMoveCommand)
{
    // TODO: Add your specialized code here and/or call the base class
    return CRecordView::OnMove(nIDMoveCommand);
}
```

The **OnInitialUpdate** member function that is overridden here is called by the framework after the view is attached to the document but before the view is initially displayed. When this is called, the sort order for the recordset is set by setting the **m_strSort** data member of the recordset. The string that appears in the SQL **ORDER BY** clause is set here. In this sample the records are sorted by the **FirstName** column. Later, when the **Open** member function of the recordset class is called, the records are retrieved and sorted by this column. Also notice that the **OnGetRecordset** member function is overridden here. This function should be overridden, and a recordset object or a pointer to a recordset object should be returned. Since this sample used the ClassWizard, **OnGetRecordSet** is automatically overridden and the pointer to the recordset is returned.

At this stage take a look at the **CRecordView** class implementation file, *Dbview.cpp*, that is shipped with Visual C++. When the user navigates through the records, the framework calls the **OnMove** member function, whose default implementation is shown in the *Dbview.cpp* file. If anything special needs to be done in response to scrolling of the record, it can be done here in the **OnMove** overridden function. This sample does not do any special processing and simply uses the default processing. The **OnMove** member function first gets the recordset from the application and checks if the record needs to be updated. If so, it collects the data from the dialog box and then updates the data to the database by calling the **Update** member function of the **CRecordset** class. Before a record is updated, the **Edit** member function of the **CRecordset** class should be called to allow changes to the current record. If a new record is added, then the **AddNew** member function of **CRecordset** should be called before calling the **Update** member function. The **Update** member function updates the record. Only those fields that are changed are updated. The record is then moved after proper boundary checking. The move can be done forward, backward, to the first record, to the last record, and to the *n*th record relative to the current by calling a variety of move-related member functions in the **CRecordset** class like **MoveNext**, **MovePrev**, **MoveFirst**, **MoveLast**, and **Move**. Helper functions like **IsEOF** and **IsBOF** help in determining the boundaries. Based on the original design, SQL provided only forward scrolling, but ODBC extends scrolling capabilities. However, the available level of scrolling support depends on the ODBC driver that is used by the application.

Earlier you saw how to implement sorting of the record by setting the **m_strSort** member data in the **CRecordset** class. A similar feature is also available to filter the records so that only a certain set of records is selected based on the filter. This is achieved by setting the **m_strFilter** member data in the **CRecordset** class. This is set to the contents of the SQL **WHERE** clause. For example, to locate the phone numbers of all the Johns, the filter can be set to

```
m_pSet->m_strFilter = "Firstname = 'John'";
```

This filter is also useful for joining tables, in which case the filter would be set as follows, where Table1 and Table2 are two tables and Column1 and Column2 are columns in Table1 and Table2 that are to be joined:

```
m_pSet->m_strFilter = "Table1.Column1=Table2.Column2";
```

Most of the functions that are needed for this simple sample program are done by default by the framework, and this sample does not need to bother about doing them. If an application is written not using AppWizard, then it should perform all these steps. By now you can see the advantages of using the AppWizard and ClassWizard for simple applications.

The preceding sample lets the user view the database and update an existing phone number or notes. The next example extends this sample to add a new record to the database. Since there is no change in the database schema, the changes to be made are very simple and are limited to the **CMyPhoneForm** class. The changes to the **CMyPhoneForm** class in *Myphoneform.h* and *MYphoneform.cpp* are highlighted in the following code:

```
// MyPhoneForm.h : interface of the CMyPhoneForm class
//

#if !defined(AFX_MYPHONEFORM_H)
#define AFX_MYPHONEFORM_H

#if _MSC_VER >= 1000
#pragma once
#endif // _MSC_VER >= 1000

class CMyPhoneSet;

class CMyPhoneForm : public CRecordView
{
protected: // create from serialization only
    CMyPhoneForm();
    DECLARE_DYNCREATE(CMyPhoneForm)

public:
    //{{AFX_DATA(CMyPhoneForm)
    enum { IDD = IDD_MYPHONE_FORM };
    CEdit    m_ctlLastName;
    CEdit    m_ctlFirstName;
    CMyPhoneSet* m_pSet;
    //}}AFX_DATA

// Attributes
public:
    CMyPhoneDoc* GetDocument();

// Operations
public:
```

```
// Overrides
    // ClassWizard generated virtual function overrides
    //{{AFX_VIRTUAL(CMyPhoneForm)
    public:
    virtual CRecordset* OnGetRecordset();
    virtual BOOL PreCreateWindow(CREATESTRUCT& cs);
    virtual BOOL OnMove(UINT nIDMoveCommand);
    protected:
    virtual void DoDataExchange(CDataExchange* pDX);     // DDX/DDV support
    virtual void OnInitialUpdate(); // called first time after construct
    virtual BOOL OnPreparePrinting(CPrintInfo* pInfo);
    virtual void OnBeginPrinting(CDC* pDC, CPrintInfo* pInfo);
    virtual void OnEndPrinting(CDC* pDC, CPrintInfo* pInfo);
    //}}AFX_VIRTUAL

// Implementation
public:
    virtual ~CMyPhoneForm();
#ifdef _DEBUG
    virtual void AssertValid() const;
    virtual void Dump(CDumpContext& dc) const;
#endif

protected:
    BOOL m_bAddMode;

// Generated message map functions
protected:
    //{{AFX_MSG(CMyPhoneForm)
    afx_msg void OnRecordAdd();
    //}}AFX_MSG
    DECLARE_MESSAGE_MAP()
};

#ifndef _DEBUG  // debug version in MyPhoneForm.cpp
inline CMyPhoneDoc* CMyPhoneForm::GetDocument()
    { return (CMyPhoneDoc*)m_pDocument; }
#endif
//{{AFX_INSERT_LOCATION}}
// Microsoft Developer Studio will insert additional declarations
// immediately before the previous line.

#endif
```

```cpp
// MyPhoneForm.cpp : implementation of the CMyPhoneForm class
//

#include "stdafx.h"
#include "MyPhone.h"

#include "MyPhoneSet.h"
#include "MyPhoneDoc.h"
#include "MyPhoneForm.h"

#ifdef _DEBUG
#define new DEBUG_NEW
#undef THIS_FILE
static char THIS_FILE[] = __FILE__;
#endif

/////////////////////////////////////////////////
// CMyPhoneForm

IMPLEMENT_DYNCREATE(CMyPhoneForm, CRecordView)

BEGIN_MESSAGE_MAP(CMyPhoneForm, CRecordView)
    //{{AFX_MSG_MAP(CMyPhoneForm)
    ON_COMMAND(ID_RECORD_ADD, OnRecordAdd)
    //}}AFX_MSG_MAP
    // Standard printing commands
    ON_COMMAND(ID_FILE_PRINT, CRecordView::OnFilePrint)
    ON_COMMAND(ID_FILE_PRINT_DIRECT, CRecordView::OnFilePrint)
    ON_COMMAND(ID_FILE_PRINT_PREVIEW, CRecordView::OnFilePrintPreview)
END_MESSAGE_MAP()

/////////////////////////////////////////////////
// CMyPhoneForm construction/destruction

CMyPhoneForm::CMyPhoneForm()
    : CRecordView(CMyPhoneForm::IDD)
{
    //{{AFX_DATA_INIT(CMyPhoneForm)
    m_pSet = NULL;
    //}}AFX_DATA_INIT
    // TODO: add construction code here
    m_bAddMode=FALSE;
}
```

```
CMyPhoneForm::~CMyPhoneForm()
{
}

void CMyPhoneForm::DoDataExchange(CDataExchange* pDX)
{
    CRecordView::DoDataExchange(pDX);
    //{{AFX_DATA_MAP(CMyPhoneForm)
    DDX_Control(pDX, IDC_LASTNAME, m_ctlLastName);
    DDX_Control(pDX, IDC_FIRSTNAME, m_ctlFirstName);
    DDX_FieldText(pDX, IDC_FIRSTNAME, m_pSet->m_FirstName, m_pSet);
    DDX_FieldText(pDX, IDC_LASTNAME, m_pSet->m_LastName, m_pSet);
    DDX_FieldText(pDX, IDC_PHONENUMBER, m_pSet->m_Phone, m_pSet);
    DDX_FieldText(pDX, IDC_NOTES, m_pSet->m_Notes, m_pSet);
    //}}AFX_DATA_MAP
}

BOOL CMyPhoneForm::PreCreateWindow(CREATESTRUCT& cs)
{
    // TODO: Modify the Window class or styles here by modifying
    //   the CREATESTRUCT cs

    return CRecordView::PreCreateWindow(cs);
}

void CMyPhoneForm::OnInitialUpdate()
{
    m_pSet = &GetDocument()->m_myPhoneSet;
    m_pSet->m_strSort="FirstName"; // sort by first name
    CRecordView::OnInitialUpdate();
}


/////////////////////////////////////////////////
// CMyPhoneForm printing

BOOL CMyPhoneForm::OnPreparePrinting(CPrintInfo* pInfo)
{
    // default preparation
    return DoPreparePrinting(pInfo);
}

void CMyPhoneForm::OnBeginPrinting(CDC* /*pDC*/, CPrintInfo* /*pInfo*/)
```

```
{
    // TODO: add extra initialization before printing
}

void CMyPhoneForm::OnEndPrinting(CDC* /*pDC*/, CPrintInfo* /*pInfo*/)
{
    // TODO: add cleanup after printing
}

/////////////////////////////////////////////////////
// CMyPhoneForm diagnostics

#ifdef _DEBUG
void CMyPhoneForm::AssertValid() const
{
    CRecordView::AssertValid();
}

void CMyPhoneForm::Dump(CDumpContext& dc) const
{
    CRecordView::Dump(dc);
}

CMyPhoneDoc* CMyPhoneForm::GetDocument() // non-debug version is inline
{
    ASSERT(m_pDocument->IsKindOf(RUNTIME_CLASS(CMyPhoneDoc)));
    return (CMyPhoneDoc*)m_pDocument;
}
#endif //_DEBUG

/////////////////////////////////////////////////////
// CMyPhoneForm database support
CRecordset* CMyPhoneForm::OnGetRecordset()
{
    return m_pSet;
}


/////////////////////////////////////////////////////
// CMyPhoneForm message handlers

void CMyPhoneForm::OnRecordAdd()
{
    // TODO: Add your command handler code here
```

```
        if (m_bAddMode) {
            OnMove(ID_RECORD_FIRST);
        }
        m_pSet->AddNew();
        m_pSet->SetFieldNull(NULL, FALSE);
        m_pSet->SetFieldNull(NULL, FALSE);
        m_bAddMode=TRUE;
        m_ctlFirstName.SetReadOnly(FALSE);
        m_ctlLastName.SetReadOnly(FALSE);
        UpdateData(FALSE);
    }


BOOL CMyPhoneForm::OnMove(UINT nIDMoveCommand)
{
    // TODO: Add your specialized code here and/or call the base class
    if (m_bAddMode) {
        if (!UpdateData()) {
            return FALSE;
        }
        try {
            m_pSet->Update();
        } catch (CDBException e) {
            AfxMessageBox(e.m_strError);
            return FALSE;
        }
        m_pSet->Requery();
        UpdateData(FALSE);
        m_ctlFirstName.SetReadOnly(TRUE);
        m_ctlLastName.SetReadOnly(TRUE);
        m_bAddMode=FALSE;
        return TRUE;
    } else {
        return CRecordView::OnMove(nIDMoveCommand);
    }
}
```

To add a new phone number, select Add from the Record pull-down menu. This transforms the application to add mode. In add mode all fields including the first name and last name can be entered, unlike the view mode, where only the phone number and the notes can be updated. A state flag, **m_bAddMode**, maintains the current mode of the application. The Add menu command is handled by the **OnRecordAdd** member function. To add a new record, the **AddNew** member function is first called. This does the preparation work for adding a new record to the table. The fields in the record are initially set to NULL fields. This should be followed by a call to the **Update** member function to save the record to the data source. This call is done in the **OnMove** member function, which is called when the user navigates to a different record. When **OnMove** is called, it calls **UpdateData( )** to set the values of the new record's field data members. The **Update** member function is later called to save the record. Note that only after calling the **Update** member function is the data stored. If **Update** is not called, the new record will be lost. The **Requery** member function is called to refresh the recordset. Optionally the **AddNew** call can be placed within a transaction if the database supports transactions.

The next example takes the preceding sample and extends the functionality to provide the Delete and Refresh capabilities. Here again the changes are made only to the **CMyPhoneForm** class. Shown next is the additional code to implement the **OnRecordDelete** and **OnRecordRefresh** member functions. Since the header file is very similar to the earlier header file except for the addition of two new member functions, it is not shown.

```
BEGIN_MESSAGE_MAP(CMyPhoneForm, CRecordView)
    //{{AFX_MSG_MAP(CMyPhoneForm)
    ON_COMMAND(ID_RECORD_ADD, OnRecordAdd)
    ON_COMMAND(ID_RECORD_DELETE, OnRecordDelete)
    ON_COMMAND(ID_RECORD_REFRESH, OnRecordRefresh)
    //}}AFX_MSG_MAP
    // Standard printing commands
    ON_COMMAND(ID_FILE_PRINT, CRecordView::OnFilePrint)
    ON_COMMAND(ID_FILE_PRINT_DIRECT, CRecordView::OnFilePrint)
    ON_COMMAND(ID_FILE_PRINT_PREVIEW, CRecordView::OnFilePrintPreview)
END_MESSAGE_MAP()


void CMyPhoneForm::OnRecordDelete()
{
    // TODO: Add your command handler code here
    try {
        m_pSet->Delete();
    } catch (CDBException e) {
        AfxMessageBox(e.m_strError);
        return;
    }

    m_pSet->MoveNext();

    if (m_pSet->IsEOF()) {
        m_pSet->MoveLast();
    }
    if (m_pSet->IsBOF()) {
```

```
            m_pSet->SetFieldNull(NULL);
    }
    UpdateData(FALSE);
}




void CMyPhoneForm::OnRecordRefresh()
{
    // TODO: Add your command handler code here

    m_pSet->Requery();
    m_ctlFirstName.SetReadOnly(TRUE);
    m_ctlLastName.SetReadOnly(TRUE);
    m_bAddMode=FALSE;
    UpdateData(FALSE);
}
```

The **OnRecordDelete** member function is called when the Delete menu item is selected. This function deletes the current record displayed on the screen by calling the **Delete** member function. The **Delete** member function deletes the current record from the open recordset object. After successful deletion, the field data members are set to a NULL value, and an explicit call to one of the recordset navigation member functions must be made. Here it calls the **MoveNext** member function and checks the boundary to adjust for the current record appropriately. Unlike **AddNew**, **Delete** had no corresponding **Update** call, since it immediately marks the record as deleted both in the recordset and on the data source. In the sample, notice that if the record that was deleted is scrolled back, the fields are shown as <Deleted>. Looking at the *Dbview.cpp* module, which is shipped with Visual C++, would make this immediately clear. If the record is deleted, it displays the string "<Deleted>". Another way to handle this is to check if the record is deleted by calling the **IsDeleted** member function while scrolling through the records and to jump over the deleted records. The recordset can also be refreshed by calling the **Requery** member function. To refresh the records, this sample provides another menu item called Refresh.

The **OnRecordRefresh** member function is called when the Refresh menu item is selected. This function refreshes the recordset, which moves the current record to the beginning of the recordset. The refresh is done by calling the **Requery** member function. **Requery** rebuilds the recordset and if records are returned, the first record is made the current record. If the data source can be accessed by multiple users, then the recordset should be refreshed by calling **Requery** to reflect the change to the data source.

This sample can easily be extended to search for a specific record. For example, if it needs to search for the phone number given the first name, then a filter can be added before getting the recordset. The filter can be set as discussed previously in the **m_strFilter** member data.

Conclusion

Quite often the ODBC application that you develop needs to be distributed and run in a number of environments. When you are distributing your ODBC applications, you have to ensure that the environment that will run your application uses the same ODBC driver, ODBC administrator functions, and so on, that you have used for your application to work successfully in the other environment.

We looked at the need for ODBC, reviewed ODBC basics, looked at MFC library support for ODBC, reviewed the steps involved in executing an ODBC API application, and looked at a programming example illustrating ODBC.

Chapter 21 looks at how you can use a similar mechanism—DAO—and compares ODBC and DAO.

CHAPTER 21

Database Programming
Using DAO

Continuing our database focus, let's take a look at another way that you can do database programming besides ODBC—using DAO. DAO stands for Data Access Objects.

We will look at what DAO is, compare and contrast DAO and ODBC, discuss the DAO software development kit (SDK), and learn about MFC support for DAO.

Let's start with a quick recap of DAO basics.

DAO BASICS

You can use DAO to access data from local as well as external data sources. Data sources can be local or networked versions of the following:

▼ Any Microsoft Jet (MDB) database

■ Any ODBC data source such as an ORACLE Server or a SYBASE SQL Server

▲ Any Indexed Sequential Access Method (ISAM) database such as a dBASE or Microsoft FoxPro database accessed through the Microsoft Jet database engine

Regardless of the data source, the common elements of any data source are tables, queries, fields, users, groups, and so on. In DAO, these elements are represented in a hierarchy as shown in Figure 21-1.

DAO Terminology

A *collection* is an object that is a group of (or contains) similar objects. In fact, the name of a collection is the plural of the object name contained in the collection. For example, a Databases collection contains database objects. The objects within a collection are numbered by use of a zero-based index. For example, DBEngine.Workspaces(0). Databases(1) refers to the second database in the Databases collection that is within the first Workspaces collection, which in turn is within DBEngine.

A *workspace* contains one or more open DAO database objects. A workspace manages sessions with the database engine. Multiple workspaces can be part of a DBEngine object. The default workspace is the first workspace in the Workspaces collection, and references to database objects and recordsets without an explicit workspace reference use the default workspace. Workspaces are not persistent across database engine sessions. You can use a workspace session to open multiple databases and perform transactions. You can create workspace objects using the **CreateWorkspace** method of a DBEngine object.

A DAO database contains elements such as tables, queries, and so on. Multiple DAO databases (a Databases collection) can be part of a workspace. You use the member functions to access underlying collections (except for the Recordsets collection, which you can directly access using **CDaoRecordset**). You can access a database object explicitly

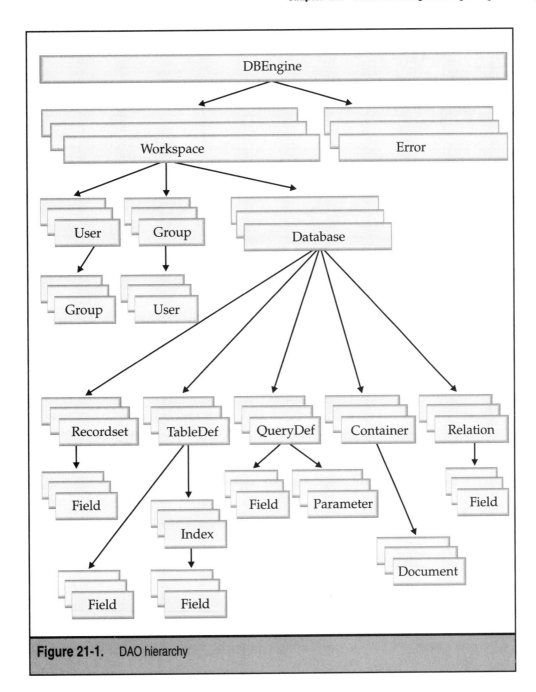

Figure 21-1. DAO hierarchy

or implicitly when you access a database element within the database. Databases are not persistent across database engine sessions.

MFC Support for DAO

Using the MFC DAO classes will substantially reduce the complexity of your application. MFC encapsulates DAO functionality, one for one, in a number of classes that correspond to DAO objects. Though it does this for many classes, not all DAO objects, including fields, indexes, parameters, and relations, are encapsulated. Interfaces for some of these DAO objects are provided via member functions of appropriate other MFC library classes. DAO objects that are not exposed in MFC can be accessed by non-MFC C++ classes provided with the DAO SDK or by calling DAO directly through a DAO interface pointer supplied by one of the MFC library classes.

MFC does not expose DAO's security features. You can, however, include DAO's security features by calling DAO directly in your program.

Let's look at some DAO classes in the MFC library.

▼ **CDaoDatabase**—This class constructs a **CDaoDatabase** object. To create a new database, use the **Create** member function. To access an existing database, use the **Open** member function. When you have finished using the database, use the **Close** member function.

■ **CDaoException**—This class constructs a **CDaoException** object. You normally would call the global function **AfxThrowDaoException** to throw an exception, but you would use the **CDaoException** class to explicitly create an exception object if you are making direct calls to DAO using the DAO interface pointers encapsulated by the MFC library classes.

■ **CDaoFieldExchange**—This class is used for record field exchange of custom data types between the field data members of your **CDaoRecordset** object and the corresponding fields in the current record on the data source. You would not normally use this class.

▲ **CDaoQueryDef**—This class is used to construct a **CDaoQueryDef** object that can be for an existing query, a new query which may or may not be saved as part of the QueryDefs collection. To create a new QueryDef that is to be saved, use the **Create** and **Append** member functions. To create a new QueryDef that is not to be saved, pass an empty string for the query name in **Create** and do not use the **Append** member function. To access an existing QueryDef, use the **Open** member function. When you have finished using the QueryDef, use the **Close** member function. You can use the member functions listed in Table 21-1 to set the QueryDef attributes.

CDaoRecordset—This class constructs a **CDaoRecordset** object that represents a set of records from a data source. The **CDaoRecordset** objects belong to one of three types, as shown in the following table:

CDaoRecordset Type	Description
Table	Data from a single database table
Dynaset	Updatable data from one or more tables
Snapshot	Nonupdatable data from one or more tables

Except for snapshot recordsets, you can perform operations such as add, change, and delete on the recordset data.

▼ **CDaoRecordView**—This class is used to create a **CDaoRecordView** object, which in conjunction with **CDaoRecordset** is used to display database records within controls. The **CDaoRecordView** object uses dialog data exchange (DDX) and DAO record field exchange (DFX) to automate the movement of data between the controls on the form and the recordset fields. While creating a **CDaoRecordView** object, the constructor is used to identify the form dialog resource that will be used in conjunction with the view object.

■ **CDaoTableDef**—This class is used to create a **CDaoTableDef** object. The **CDaoTableDef** object contains the stored definitions about the table contents, such as its fields and indexes. You use a **CDaoTableDef** object in conjunction

CDaoQueryDef Method	Description
SetName	Call before an **Append** to change the name of a nontemporary QueryDef.
SetSQL	Call to set the SQL statement that the QueryDef executes.
SetConnect	Call to set the QueryDef object's connect string, which passes additional information to ODBC (and some ISAM drivers).
SetODBC Timeout	Call to override the default timeout (60 seconds) for queries to an ODBC source.
SetReturns Records	Call to indicate if the external data source will return records. This member function is used in conjunction with **SetConnect** to set up an external pass-through query to an external database.

Table 21-1. CDaoQueryDef Member Functions

with a **CDaoRecordset** object. To create a new TableDef, use the **Create** member function and call the **Append** member function to store the TableDef in the TableDefs collection of the database. To access an existing TableDef, use the **Open** member function. When you have finished using the TableDef, use the **Close** member function.

▲ **CDaoWorkSpace**—This class is used to create a **CDaoWorkSpace** object. To create a new WorkSpace, use the **Create** member function and call the **Append** member function to store the WorkSpace in the WorkSpaces collection of the database. To access an existing WorkSpace, use the **Open** member function. When you have finished using the WorkSpace, use the **Close** member function. A **CDaoWorkspace** object handles a complete user database session. Typically, workspaces are opened implicitly when you open a database contained within a workspace.

When you use DAO to access databases, you will at a minimum use a **CDaoDatabase** object and a **CDaoRecordset** object.

DAO and External Databases

You can access tables in an external database in two ways using MFC DAO classes:

▼ Attach the tables (to an MDB database)

▲ Open the external database directly

Attaching tables is normally more efficient than opening the tables directly (particularly for ODBC sources). When an external table is attached, it can be accessed in the same way as a Microsoft Jet database table. The external table connection information is stored along with the table definition. While you can programmatically access the external table, the data still resides externally, and you cannot make structural changes, such as changing the table's schema. You can open a table directly by specifying the connection information each time you open the external database.

DAO and ODBC

Many databases, both local to a machine and external, can be accessed by use of either ODBC classes or DAO classes. You can decide between ODBC and DAO based on their features, which are summarized in Table 21-2.

DAO SDK

To facilitate DAO programming, Microsoft provides the DAO SDK. The SDK contains include files (such as *Dbdao.h* and *Dbdaoerr.h*), files for OLE support (such as *Dbdaoint.h* and *Daogetrw.h*), SRC files (such as *Dbdao.cpp* and *Dbdaouid.cpp*), LIB files (such as *Dbdao.rc* and *Dbdao3.lib*), program samples, and a setup program. Run the setup program to copy all

ODBC	DAO
Performs better with external client/server ODBC data sources	Performs better with databases using Microsoft Jet engine (MDB) and compatible databases that the Jet engine can access directly
Requires less disk space	Requires more disk space compared with ODBC
Does not work with database compaction	Works with database compaction
Vendor database engine (when using vendor database)	Microsoft's Jet database engine
MFC library classes have just the prefix "C"	MFC library classes have just the prefix "Cdao"
Field exchange with RFX routines	Field exchange with DFX routines

Table 21-2. Comparing DAO and ODBC

necessary DLLs, update the Registry, and to set up the directory structure for headers, libraries, and so on.

DAO Programming Examples

We will look at four samples that show how to create a database; create a table with fields; and view, add, update, and delete records from the database. The database creation sample uses the DAO SDK, and the rest of the samples use DAO through MFC.

Database Creation Example

The sample shown next creates a database called *PhoneDB* and adds a table called *PhoneBook* with four fields. The purpose of this sample and the samples that follow in this chapter is to create and maintain a telephone number database. To run this sample, type the program name followed by the database filename from the command prompt. Once the database is created, you can use the example in this chapter to add records to it. Alternatively, if you have Microsoft Access, you can use Microsoft Access and create a new database. The sample database, Phonelist, which is used by the examples in this chapter and included in the CD, was created using Microsoft Access. Let's look at the code in more detail.

To start with, the DAO-related header files are included. The code first checks to see if the database filename has been given. If not, it prompts the usage of the program and exits. A default instance of the **CdbDBEngine** is created. By use of the Workspaces collection, the reference to the first **CdbWorkspace** object is obtained. This workspace object defines a named session for a user and can be used to manage the current session or to start an additional session. The session creates a scope in which multiple databases can be opened. When the **CdbWorkspace** object is first referred to or used, a default workspace is automatically created. The Name property is set to *#Default Workspace* and the UserName property is set to *Admin*. The name of the user is used for UserName if security is enabled. Since multiple databases can be opened, note that when you're using transactions, all databases in the specified workspace are affected. This is not important in this sample since it only creates a database. But it is important when a program manages data by adding, updating, deleting, and using transactions across multiple databases, since a **Rollback** method will roll back the operation across all databases in the current workspace.

The **CreateDatabase** method is then used to create a new database on the disk. This database is saved on the disk, and a **CdbDatabase** object is returned. To create a database, the name of the database is specified along with connection information and other options. The name of the database can be up to 255 characters long with full path and filename, including a network path. If the filename extension is not specified, extension MDB is appended. As part of the connection information, the collating order and password can be specified. In this sample a general collating order is specified along with the *dbEncrypt* option, which creates an encrypted database.

Once the database is created, a table object is created by calling the **CreateTableDef** method. This creates a new **CdbTableDef** object to which fields can be added. A default table named *PhoneBook* is created. To this table object four fields—*FirstName*, *LastName*, *Phone*, and *Notes*—are added by first creating these **CdbField** objects and then adding them to the **CdbTableDef** object created earlier. When you're creating the **CdbField** objects, the name of the field, its type, and size can be specified. The types are set to *dbText* for *FirstName*, *LastName*, and *Phone*, which indicates regular text up to 255 characters, and to *dbMemo* for *Notes*, which is regular text up to 1.2Gb characters. The size is defaulted here. The size of fields can be limited by specifying the size parameter when you're creating the fields. The fields are added to the **CdbTableDef** object created earlier by calling the **Append** method, and the table is added to the **CdbDatabase** object by calling the **Append** method. If there are no fields in the **CdbTableDef** object, it cannot be appended to the **CdbDatabase** object.

Finally the **Close** method is used to close the **CdbDatabase** object, thereby creating the database. Any exception that may be thrown is handled, and the message is displayed on the console.

```
// CrtPhoneDB.cpp
#include    <afxole.h>
#include    <dbdao.h>
#include    <dbdaoerr.h>
```

```
#include    <stdio.h>
#include    <iostream.h>

void main(int argc, char **argv)
    {
    CdbDBEngine     dben;
    CdbWorkspace    wsDef;
    CdbDatabase     dbsPhone;
    CdbTableDef     tdfNew;
    CdbField        fld;
    CdbProperty     prp;
    COleVariant     vVal;

    // get new database name
    if (argc!=2)
    {
        cout << "Usage: CrtPhoneDB <database name>" << endl;
        exit(1);
    }
    try
    {
        //    Get default workspace.
        wsDef = dben.Workspaces[0L];

        //    Delete any old database with the given name
        cout << "removing previous database..." << endl;
        remove(_T(argv[1]));
        cout << "Creating new database: " << argv[1]
             << "..." << endl;
        //    Create a new database

dbsPhone = wsDef.CreateDatabase(_T(argv[1]),
                                   dbLangGeneral,
                                   dbEncrypt);

        //    Create a new TableDef object.
        cout << "Creating a new table: PhoneBook ..." << endl;
        tdfNew = dbsPhone.CreateTableDef(_T("PhoneBook"));
        fld = tdfNew.CreateField(_T("FirstName"), dbText);
        tdfNew.Fields.Append( fld );
        fld = tdfNew.CreateField(_T("LastName"), dbText);
        tdfNew.Fields.Append( fld );
        fld = tdfNew.CreateField(_T("Phone"), dbText);
        tdfNew.Fields.Append( fld );
```

```
        fld = tdfNew.CreateField(_T("Notes"), dbMemo);
        tdfNew.Fields.Append( fld );

        //Append the new TableDef object to the phone database
        cout << "Phonebook Table configured." << endl;
        dbsPhone.TableDefs.Append( tdfNew);

        // close the newly created and configured database
        dbsPhone.Close();

        cout << "Database created successfully." << endl;
    }
    catch (CdbException)
    {
        for (long ct = 0; ct < dben.Errors.GetCount(); ct++)
        {
            printf(_T("\t Error #%ld: #%ld -- %s\n"),
                ct,
                DBERR(dben.Errors[ct].GetNumber()),
                dben.Errors[ct].GetDescription()
                );
        }
    }
    catch (CException *e)
    {
        cout << "exception: MFC Exception" << endl;
        e->Delete();
    }
    catch (...)
    {
        cout << "exception: Win32 Exception" << endl;
    }
}
```

Database View, Add, Update, and Delete Example

The *PhoneBook* sample uses the phone database created earlier and implements the front-end to the database to view its contents. This sample uses the document/view architecture and is created by use of the AppWizard. It also uses the MFC DAO classes, which substantially reduces the complexity of the application. Figure 21-2 shows the Open dialog box to specify where the database resides.

Figure 21-3 shows the *PhoneBook* application dialog box. The dialog box is prefilled with data from the database.

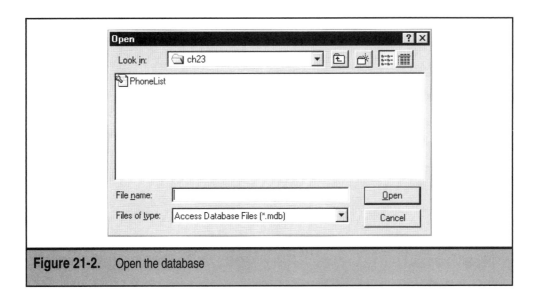

Figure 21-2. Open the database

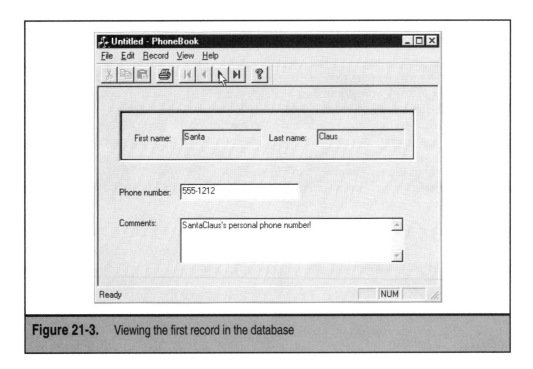

Figure 21-3. Viewing the first record in the database

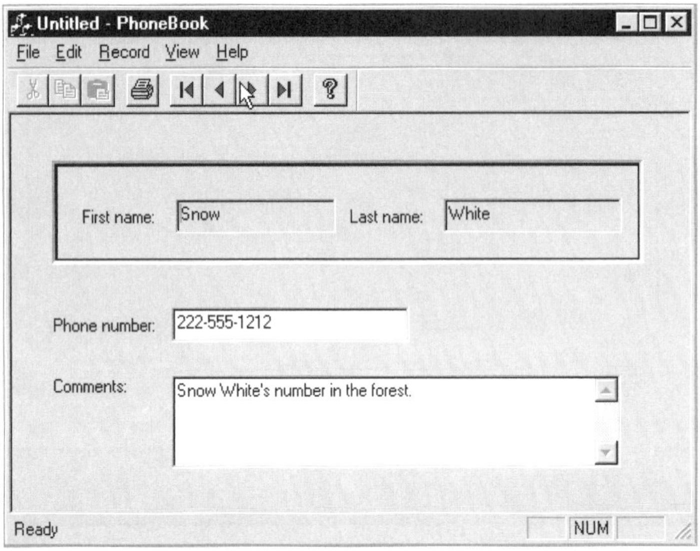

Figure 21-4. Viewing the next record in the database

You can see each record in the database in succession by clicking the Right Arrow icon or by clicking Record from the menu and selecting Next Record from the pull-down menu. Figure 21-4 shows the next record.

You can skip intermediate records and go to the last record using the appropriate icon or the pull-down menu. You can add records to the database by clicking Record on the menu bar and selecting Add Record from the pull-down menu. The dialog box is cleared, and you can input the data as shown in Figure 21-5.

You can delete records from the database by clicking Record from the menu bar and selecting Delete Record from the pull-down menu.

As mentioned earlier, the following examples use MFC. MFC encapsulates DAO functionality, one for one, in a number of classes that correspond to DAO objects.

Let's look at the program code in more detail. The procedure to create this application through the AppWizard is as follows:

1. Start the Microsoft Visual C++ and select New from the File menu to create a new project.

2. Click on the Projects tab, and select MFC AppWizard (EXE) as the project type.

3. Type in the project name as **PhoneBook** and select OK. The AppWizard creates the project directory and the MFC AppWizard—Step 1 dialog box appears.

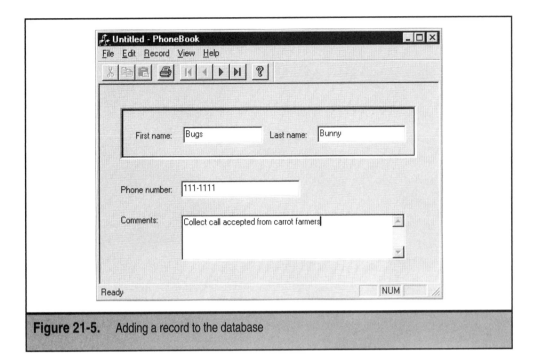

Figure 21-5.   Adding a record to the database

4. Make this application a single document application by selecting the Single Document radio button, and then click on the Next button to go to the Step 2 Of 6 dialog box.

5. Select Database View Without File Support, and then select the Data Source button to specify the database to be used with this application.

6. From the File Selection dialog box select the *Phonelist.mdb* database and click OK.

7. Accept the default for the rest of the steps, and click on the Finish button to create the project with the files. These files are shown shortly and discussed in detail.

Shown next is the standard application class derived from **CWinApp** class. What is significant to note here is the registration of the application's document template with the framework. This document template serves as the connection between document, frame window, and view. It also has the code to show the About dialog box.

```
// PhoneBook.h : main header file for the PHONEBOOK application

#if !defined(AFX_PHONEBOOK_H)
#define AFX_PHONEBOOK_H
```

```cpp
#if _MSC_VER >= 1000
#pragma once
#endif // _MSC_VER >= 1000

#ifndef __AFXWIN_H__
    #error include 'stdafx.h' before including this file for PCH
#endif

#include "resource.h"        // main symbols

/////////////////////////////////////////////////////
// CPhoneBookApp:
// See PhoneBook.cpp for the implementation of this class
//

class CPhoneBookApp : public CWinApp
{
public:
    CPhoneBookApp();

// Overrides
    // ClassWizard generated virtual function overrides
    //{{AFX_VIRTUAL(CPhoneBookApp)
    public:
    virtual BOOL InitInstance();
    //}}AFX_VIRTUAL

// Implementation

    //{{AFX_MSG(CPhoneBookApp)
    afx_msg void OnAppAbout();
    //}}AFX_MSG
    DECLARE_MESSAGE_MAP()
};


/////////////////////////////////////////////////////////////////////////////

//{{AFX_INSERT_LOCATION}}


#endif

// PhoneBook.cpp
```

```
//

#include "stdafx.h"
#include "PhoneBook.h"

#include "MainFrm.h"
#include "PhoneBookSet.h"
#include "PhoneBookDoc.h"
#include "PhoneBookView.h"

#ifdef _DEBUG
#define new DEBUG_NEW
#undef THIS_FILE
static char THIS_FILE[] = __FILE__;
#endif

/////////////////////////////////////////////////////////////////////////
// CPhoneBookApp

BEGIN_MESSAGE_MAP(CPhoneBookApp, CWinApp)
    //{{AFX_MSG_MAP(CPhoneBookApp)
    ON_COMMAND(ID_APP_ABOUT, OnAppAbout)
    //}}AFX_MSG_MAP
    // Standard print setup command
    ON_COMMAND(ID_FILE_PRINT_SETUP, CWinApp::OnFilePrintSetup)
END_MESSAGE_MAP()

/////////////////////////////////////////////////////////////////////////
// CPhoneBookApp construction

CPhoneBookApp::CPhoneBookApp()
{
    // TODO: add construction code here,
    // Place all significant initialization in InitInstance
}

/////////////////////////////////////////////////////////////////////////
// The one and only CPhoneBookApp object

CPhoneBookApp theApp;

/////////////////////////////////////////////////////////////////////////
// CPhoneBookApp initialization
```

```
BOOL CPhoneBookApp::InitInstance()
{
    AfxEnableControlContainer();

#ifdef _AFXDLL
    Enable3dControls();#else
    Enable3dControlsStatic();
#endif

    SetRegistryKey(_T("Local AppWizard-Generated Applications"));

    LoadStdProfileSettings();

    CSingleDocTemplate* pDocTemplate;
    pDocTemplate = new CSingleDocTemplate(
        IDR_MAINFRAME,
        RUNTIME_CLASS(CPhoneBookDoc),
        RUNTIME_CLASS(CMainFrame),          // main SDI frame window
        RUNTIME_CLASS(CPhoneBookView));
    AddDocTemplate(pDocTemplate);

    // Parse command line for standard
    // shell commands, DDE, file open
    CCommandLineInfo cmdInfo;
    ParseCommandLine(cmdInfo);

    // Dispatch commands specified on the command line
    if (!ProcessShellCommand(cmdInfo))
        return FALSE;

    m_pMainWnd->ShowWindow(SW_SHOW);
    m_pMainWnd->UpdateWindow();

    return TRUE;
}


/////////////////////////////////////////////////////////////////////////////
// CAboutDlg dialog used for App About

class CAboutDlg : public CDialog
{
public:
    CAboutDlg();
```

```
// Dialog Data
    //{{AFX_DATA(CAboutDlg)
    enum { IDD = IDD_ABOUTBOX };
    //}}AFX_DATA

    // ClassWizard generated virtual function overrides
    //{{AFX_VIRTUAL(CAboutDlg)
    protected:
    virtual void DoDataExchange(CDataExchange* pDX);
    //}}AFX_VIRTUAL

// Implementation
protected:
    //{{AFX_MSG(CAboutDlg)
        // No message handlers
    //}}AFX_MSG
    DECLARE_MESSAGE_MAP()
};

CAboutDlg::CAboutDlg() : CDialog(CAboutDlg::IDD)
{
    //{{AFX_DATA_INIT(CAboutDlg)
    //}}AFX_DATA_INIT
}

void CAboutDlg::DoDataExchange(CDataExchange* pDX)
{
    CDialog::DoDataExchange(pDX);
    //{{AFX_DATA_MAP(CAboutDlg)
    //}}AFX_DATA_MAP
}

BEGIN_MESSAGE_MAP(CAboutDlg, CDialog)
    //{{AFX_MSG_MAP(CAboutDlg)
        // No message handlers
    //}}AFX_MSG_MAP
END_MESSAGE_MAP()

// App command to run the dialog
void CPhoneBookApp::OnAppAbout()
{
    CAboutDlg aboutDlg;
    aboutDlg.DoModal();
}
```

Shown next is the **CphoneBookDoc** class, which is derived from the **CDocument** class of the framework. This is pretty much the boilerplate code for the member data **m_phoneBookSet**. In a typical application the document stores the data and serializes it to a file, reading the entire data into memory once and writing it back to disk. But in a database application the data is stored in the database and is typically viewed one record at a time. So instead of using the document to serialize the data, the document is used to encapsulate the recordset object. The recordset object **m_phoneBookSet** is encapsulated in the document object. It is automatically constructed when the document object is constructed, and automatically deleted when the document object is deleted. In this sample we have only one recordset related to the phone list. So we have only one recordset object. If the application has more than one recordset, then more recordset objects can be encapsulated in the document. Thus, the document acts as a proxy or front-end for the database.

```
// PhoneBookDoc.h : interface of the CPhoneBookDoc class
//

#if !defined(AFX_PHONEBOOKDOC_H)
#define AFX_PHONEBOOKDOC_H

#if _MSC_VER >= 1000
#pragma once
#endif // _MSC_VER >= 1000


class CPhoneBookDoc : public CDocument
{
protected: // create from serialization only
    CPhoneBookDoc();
    DECLARE_DYNCREATE(CPhoneBookDoc)

// Attributes
public:
    CPhoneBookSet m_phoneBookSet;

// Operations
public:

// Overrides
    // ClassWizard generated virtual function overrides
    //{{AFX_VIRTUAL(CPhoneBookDoc)
    public:
    virtual BOOL OnNewDocument();
    //}}AFX_VIRTUAL
```

```cpp
// Implementation
public:
    virtual ~CPhoneBookDoc();
#ifdef _DEBUG
    virtual void AssertValid() const;
    virtual void Dump(CDumpContext& dc) const;
#endif

protected:

// Generated message map functions
protected:
    //{{AFX_MSG(CPhoneBookDoc)
    //}}AFX_MSG
    DECLARE_MESSAGE_MAP()
};

/////////////////////////////////////////////////////////////////////////////

//{{AFX_INSERT_LOCATION}}


#endif

// PhoneBookDoc.cpp : implementation of the CPhoneBookDoc
//

#include "stdafx.h"
#include "PhoneBook.h"

#include "PhoneBookSet.h"
#include "PhoneBookDoc.h"

#ifdef _DEBUG
#define new DEBUG_NEW
#undef THIS_FILE
static char THIS_FILE[] = __FILE__;
#endif

/////////////////////////////////////////////////////////////////////////////
// CPhoneBookDoc

IMPLEMENT_DYNCREATE(CPhoneBookDoc, CDocument)
```

```
BEGIN_MESSAGE_MAP(CPhoneBookDoc,      CDocument)
    //{{AFX_MSG_MAP(CPhoneBookDoc)
    //}}AFX_MSG_MAP
END_MESSAGE_MAP()

/////////////////////////////////////////////////////////////////////////
// CPhoneBookDoc construction/destruction

CPhoneBookDoc::CPhoneBookDoc()
{
    // TODO: add one-time construction code here

}

CPhoneBookDoc::~CPhoneBookDoc()
{
}

BOOL CPhoneBookDoc::OnNewDocument()
{
    if (!CDocument::OnNewDocument())
        return FALSE;

    // TODO: add reinitialization code here
    // (SDI documents will reuse this document)

    return TRUE;
}



/////////////////////////////////////////////////////////////////////////
// CPhoneBookDoc diagnostics

#ifdef _DEBUG
void CPhoneBookDoc::AssertValid() const
{
    CDocument::AssertValid();
}

void CPhoneBookDoc::Dump(CDumpContext& dc) const
{
    CDocument::Dump(dc);
```

```
}
#endif //_DEBUG


//////////////////////////////////////////////////////////////////////////
// CPhoneBookDoc commands
```

Shown next are the *PhoneBookSet.h* and *PhoneBookSet.cpp* modules. These modules deal with the set of records selected from the database, known as recordsets. Note that the **CPhoneBookSet** class derives from the **CDaoRecordset** MFC DAO class. The **CDaoRecordset** class can be used directly, or another application-specific class can be derived from this and used. By using this object, you can scroll through the records in the database, quickly retrieve a record by setting up an index, update a record, specify a query and filter the recordset to constrain which record it selects from the set available in the database, and sort the recordset.

In the **CPhoneBookSet** class notice that the columns of the *PhoneBook* table appear as the member variables. These member variables are called *field data members*. AppWizard names these data members automatically, based on the column names from the data source. It also assigns the correct C++ or class library data type to the members based on the column type. Since in our case all the columns are text, they have been mapped to **CString** type. If some of the columns are not to be exposed to the user, then the field can be deleted from the recordset. This can be achieved by use of the ClassWizard. The **GetDefaultDBName** member function is overridden, and this member function provides the database name to the application. This function as seen in *PhoneBookSet.cpp* puts up the File dialog box and retrieves the database filename. The **DoFieldExchange** member function is called by the framework to automatically exchange data between the field data members of your recordset object and the corresponding columns of the current record on the data source.

```
// PhoneBookSet.h : interface of the CPhoneBookSet class
#if
!defined(AFX_PHONEBOOKSET_H)
#define AFX_PHONEBOOKSET_H

#if _MSC_VER >= 1000
#pragma once
#endif // _MSC_VER >= 1000


class CPhoneBookSet : public CDaoRecordset
{
public:
    CPhoneBookSet(CDaoDatabase* pDatabase = NULL);
    DECLARE_DYNAMIC(CPhoneBookSet)

// Field/Param Data
```

```
    //{{AFX_FIELD(CPhoneBookSet, CDaoRecordset)
    CString     m_FirstName;
    CString     m_LastName;
    CString     m_Phone;
    CString     m_Notes;
    //}}AFX_FIELD

// Overrides
    // ClassWizard generated virtual function overrides
    //{{AFX_VIRTUAL(CPhoneBookSet)
    public:
    virtual CString GetDefaultDBName();
    virtual CString GetDefaultSQL();
    virtual void DoFieldExchange(CDaoFieldExchange* pFX);
    //}}AFX_VIRTUAL

// Implementation
#ifdef _DEBUG
    virtual void AssertValid() const;
    virtual void Dump(CDumpContext& dc) const;
#endif

};

//{{AFX_INSERT_LOCATION}}
#endif

// PhoneBookSet.cpp : implementation of the CPhoneBookSet
//

#include "stdafx.h"
#include "PhoneBook.h"
#include "PhoneBookSet.h"

#ifdef _DEBUG
#define new DEBUG_NEW
#undef THIS_FILE
static char THIS_FILE[] = __FILE__;
#endif

/////////////////////////////////////////////////////////////////////////////
// CPhoneBookSet implementation

IMPLEMENT_DYNAMIC(CPhoneBookSet, CDaoRecordset)
```

```
CPhoneBookSet::CPhoneBookSet(CDaoDatabase* pdb)
    : CDaoRecordset(pdb)
{
    //{{AFX_FIELD_INIT(CPhoneBookSet)
    m_FirstName = _T("");
    m_LastName = _T("");
    m_Phone = _T("");
    m_Notes = _T("");
    m_nFields = 4;
    //}}AFX_FIELD_INIT
    m_nDefaultType = dbOpenDynaset;
}

CString CPhoneBookSet::GetDefaultDBName()
{
        while (true) {
        // allow user to select database to open
        CFileDialog    dlg (TRUE, _T("mdb"), NULL, OFN_HIDEREADONLY,
                    _T("Access Database Files (*.mdb)|*.mdb||"),
                    0);

        // if user selected a file then open it as a database
        if (IDOK == dlg.DoModal()) {
            // get full path to database file
            return dlg.GetPathName();
        } else {
            AfxMessageBox("Select a valid phone database");
        }
    }
}

CString CPhoneBookSet::GetDefaultSQL()
{
    return _T("[PhoneBook]");
}

void CPhoneBookSet::DoFieldExchange(CDaoFieldExchange* pFX)
{
    //{{AFX_FIELD_MAP(CPhoneBookSet)
    pFX->SetFieldType(CDaoFieldExchange::outputColumn);
    DFX_Text(pFX, _T("[FirstName]"), m_FirstName);
    DFX_Text(pFX, _T("[LastName]"), m_LastName);
    DFX_Text(pFX, _T("[Phone]"), m_Phone);
```

```
        DFX_Text(pFX, _T("[Notes]"), m_Notes);
        //}}AFX_FIELD_MAP
}


//////////////////////////////////////////////////////////////////////////
// CPhoneBookSet diagnostics

#ifdef _DEBUG
void CPhoneBookSet::AssertValid() const
{
        CDaoRecordset::AssertValid();
}

void CPhoneBookSet::Dump(CDumpContext& dc) const
{
        CDaoRecordset::Dump(dc);
}
#endif //_DEBUG
```

Discussed next are the procedure to create the form that displays the phone numbers and how to bind the controls to the recordset fields. In ResourceView the PhoneBook folder is expanded, and then the Dialog folder is expanded. IDD_PHONEBOOK_FORM is opened by double-clicking on it. The default static control that says "TODO: Place form controls on this dialog" is selected and deleted. Four edit controls—one each for First name, Last name, Phone number, and Comments—are created, and they are named IDC_FIRSTNAME, IDC_LASTNAME, IDC_PHONENUMBER, and IDC_NOTES, respectively. The names are given read-only style. The resource file is then saved. The next step is to bind the controls to the recordset fields to indicate which control maps to which column in the table. This is done by use of the ClassWizard's "foreign object" mechanism. Typically ClassWizard binds controls in a dialog box or form to member variables of the class derived from **CDialog** or **CFormView**. In the case of **CDaoRecordView** the controls are bound to data members of the recordset class associated with the record view. In this case the **CDaoRecordView** derived class is the **CPhoneBookView** class, and it has a data member for **CPhoneBookSet**. The control bindings go through **m_pSet** to the corresponding field data members of **CPhoneBookSet**. To bind a control to a recordset data member, hold down the CTRL key and double-click on the control in the dialog editor window. The ClassWizard's Add Member Variable dialog box appears with a proposed field name selected. All the controls in the dialog box are bound and the work is saved.

The **CPhoneBookView**-related code is shown next.

```
// PhoneBookView.h : interface of the CPhoneBookView class
//
```

```
#if
!defined(AFX_PHONEBOOKVIEW_H)
#define AFX_PHONEBOOKVIEW_H

#if _MSC_VER >= 1000
#pragma once
#endif // _MSC_VER >= 1000

class CPhoneBookSet;

class CPhoneBookView : public CDaoRecordView
{
protected: // create from serialization only
    CPhoneBookView();
    DECLARE_DYNCREATE(CPhoneBookView)

public:
    //{{AFX_DATA(CPhoneBookView)
    enum { IDD = IDD_PHONEBOOK_FORM };
    CPhoneBookSet* m_pSet;
    //}}AFX_DATA

// Attributes
public:
    CPhoneBookDoc* GetDocument();

// Operations
public:

// Overrides
    // ClassWizard generated virtual function overrides
    //{{AFX_VIRTUAL(CPhoneBookView)
    public:
    virtual CDaoRecordset* OnGetRecordset();
    virtual BOOL PreCreateWindow(CREATESTRUCT& cs);
    protected:
    virtual void DoDataExchange(CDataExchange* pDX);
    virtual void OnInitialUpdate();
    virtual BOOL OnPreparePrinting(CPrintInfo* pInfo);
    virtual void OnBeginPrinting(CDC* pDC, CPrintInfo* pInfo);
    virtual void OnEndPrinting(CDC* pDC, CPrintInfo* pInfo);
    //}}AFX_VIRTUAL

// Implementation
```

```
public:
    virtual ~CPhoneBookView();
#ifdef _DEBUG
    virtual void AssertValid() const;
    virtual void Dump(CDumpContext& dc) const;
#endif

protected:

// Generated message map functions
protected:
    //{{AFX_MSG(CPhoneBookView)
    //}}AFX_MSG
    DECLARE_MESSAGE_MAP()
};

#ifndef _DEBUG  // debug version in PhoneBookView.cpp
inline CPhoneBookDoc* CPhoneBookView::GetDocument()
    { return (CPhoneBookDoc*)m_pDocument; }
#endif

/////////////////////////////////////////////////////////////////////////////

//{{AFX_INSERT_LOCATION}}
#endif

// PhoneBookView.cpp : implementation of the CPhoneBookView
//

#include "stdafx.h"
#include "PhoneBook.h"

#include "PhoneBookSet.h"
#include "PhoneBookDoc.h"
#include "PhoneBookView.h"

#ifdef _DEBUG
#define new DEBUG_NEW
#undef THIS_FILE
static char THIS_FILE[] = __FILE__;
#endif

/////////////////////////////////////////////////////////////////////////////
// CPhoneBookView
```

```
IMPLEMENT_DYNCREATE(CPhoneBookView, CDaoRecordView)

BEGIN_MESSAGE_MAP(CPhoneBookView, CDaoRecordView)
    //{{AFX_MSG_MAP(CPhoneBookView)
    //}}AFX_MSG_MAP
    // Standard printing commands
    ON_COMMAND(ID_FILE_PRINT, CDaoRecordView::OnFilePrint)
    ON_COMMAND(ID_FILE_PRINT_DIRECT,
               CDaoRecordView::OnFilePrint)
ON_COMMAND(ID_FILE_PRINT_PREVIEW,
               CDaoRecordView::OnFilePrintPreview)
END_MESSAGE_MAP()

/////////////////////////////////////////////////////////////////////
// CPhoneBookView construction/destruction

CPhoneBookView::CPhoneBookView()
    : CDaoRecordView(CPhoneBookView::IDD)
{
    //{{AFX_DATA_INIT(CPhoneBookView)
    m_pSet = NULL;
    //}}AFX_DATA_INIT
    // TODO: add construction code here

}

CPhoneBookView::~CPhoneBookView()
{
}

void CPhoneBookView::DoDataExchange(CDataExchange* pDX)
{
    CDaoRecordView::DoDataExchange(pDX);
    //{{AFX_DATA_MAP(CPhoneBookView)
    DDX_FieldText(pDX, IDC_FIRSTNAME, m_pSet->m_FirstName,
                  m_pSet);
    DDX_FieldText(pDX, IDC_LASTNAME, m_pSet->m_LastName,
                  m_pSet);
    DDX_FieldText(pDX, IDC_PHONENUMBER, m_pSet->m_Phone,
                  m_pSet);
    DDX_FieldText(pDX, IDC_NOTES, m_pSet->m_Notes, m_pSet);
    //}}AFX_DATA_MAP
}
```

```
BOOL CPhoneBookView::PreCreateWindow(CREATESTRUCT& cs)
{
 // TODO: Modify the Window class or styles here by modifying
 //   the CREATESTRUCT cs

    return CDaoRecordView::PreCreateWindow(cs);
}

void CPhoneBookView::OnInitialUpdate()
{
    m_pSet = &GetDocument()->m_phoneBookSet;
    CDaoRecordView::OnInitialUpdate();
}

/////////////////////////////////////////////////////////////////////////////
// CPhoneBookView printing

BOOL CPhoneBookView::OnPreparePrinting(CPrintInfo* pInfo)
{
    // default preparation
    return DoPreparePrinting(pInfo);
}

void CPhoneBookView::OnBeginPrinting(CDC* /*pDC*/,
                                     CPrintInfo* /*pInfo*/)
{
    // TODO: add extra initialization before printing
}

void CPhoneBookView::OnEndPrinting(CDC* /*pDC*/,
                                   CPrintInfo* /*pInfo*/)
{
    // TODO: add cleanup after printing
}

/////////////////////////////////////////////////////////////////////////////
// CPhoneBookView diagnostics

#ifdef _DEBUG
void CPhoneBookView::AssertValid() const
```

```
{
    CDaoRecordView::AssertValid();
}


void CPhoneBookView::Dump(CDumpContext& dc) const
{
    CDaoRecordView::Dump(dc);
}


CPhoneBookDoc* CPhoneBookView::GetDocument()
{
    ASSERT(m_pDocument->IsKindOf(RUNTIME_CLASS(CPhoneBookDoc)));
    return (CPhoneBookDoc*)m_pDocument;
}
#endif //_DEBUG


/////////////////////////////////////////////////////////////////////////
// CPhoneBookView database support
CDaoRecordset* CPhoneBookView::OnGetRecordset()
{
    return m_pSet;
}



/////////////////////////////////////////////////////////////////////////
// CPhoneBookView message handlers
```

The **OnGetRecordSet** member function is overridden here. This function should be overridden, and a recordset object or a pointer to a recordset object should be returned. Since this sample used the ClassWizard, the function is automatically overridden and the data is returned. At this stage it is worth looking at the **CDaoRecordView** code that is shipped with Visual C++. The navigation through the records is handled by the **OnMove** member function.

The preceding sample lets the user view the database and update an existing record. The next sample extends this sample to add a new record to the database. Since there is no change in the database schema itself, the changes to be made are very simple and are limited to the **CPhoneBookView** class. The changes to *PhoneBookView.h* and *PhoneBookView.cpp* are highlighted in the following code.

To enter add mode, the user should select the Add menu item from the Record menu. This transforms the application to add mode. In add mode all fields, including the names, can be entered. In view mode the names fields are read-only fields. To change the style of the

First name and Last name controls to read-only and read/write, two **CEdit** classes are
defined in the **CPhoneBookView** class. A state flag to indicate whether the application is in
add mode is also added. The member function **OnRecordAdd** handles the selection Add
from the menu, and the member function **OnMove** overrides the **OnMove** function
provided by **CDaoRecordView** class to check if the data has to be added and if so, adds it.

```cpp
// PhoneBookView.h : interface of the CPhoneBookView class
//
#if
!defined(AFX_PHONEBOOKVIEW_H)
#define AFX_PHONEBOOKVIEW_H

#if _MSC_VER >= 1000
#pragma once
#endif // _MSC_VER >= 1000

class CPhoneBookSet;

class CPhoneBookView : public CDaoRecordView
{
protected: // create from serialization only
    CPhoneBookView();
    DECLARE_DYNCREATE(CPhoneBookView)

public:
    //{{AFX_DATA(CPhoneBookView)
    enum { IDD = IDD_PHONEBOOK_FORM };
    CEdit       m_ctlLastName;
    CEdit       m_ctlFirstName;
    CPhoneBookSet* m_pSet;
    //}}AFX_DATA

// Attributes
public:
    CPhoneBookDoc* GetDocument();

// Operations
public:

// Overrides
    // ClassWizard generated virtual function overrides
    //{{AFX_VIRTUAL(CPhoneBookView)
    public:
    virtual CDaoRecordset* OnGetRecordset();
```

```
    virtual BOOL PreCreateWindow(CREATESTRUCT& cs);
    virtual BOOL OnMove(UINT nIDMoveCommand);
    protected:
    virtual void DoDataExchange(CDataExchange* pDX);
    virtual void OnInitialUpdate();
    virtual BOOL OnPreparePrinting(CPrintInfo* pInfo);
    virtual void OnBeginPrinting(CDC* pDC, CPrintInfo* pInfo);
    virtual void OnEndPrinting(CDC* pDC, CPrintInfo* pInfo);
    //}}AFX_VIRTUAL

// Implementation
public:
    virtual ~CPhoneBookView();
#ifdef _DEBUG
    virtual void AssertValid() const;
    virtual void Dump(CDumpContext& dc) const;
#endif

protected:
    BOOL m_bAddMode;

// Generated message map functions
protected:
    //{{AFX_MSG(CPhoneBookView)
    afx_msg void OnRecordAdd();
    //}}AFX_MSG
    DECLARE_MESSAGE_MAP()
};

#ifndef _DEBUG  // debug version in PhoneBookView.cpp
inline CPhoneBookDoc* CPhoneBookView::GetDocument()
    { return (CPhoneBookDoc*)m_pDocument; }
#endif

/////////////////////////////////////////////////////////////////////////

//{{AFX_INSERT_LOCATION}}
#endif
!defined(AFX_PHONEBOOKVIEW_H)


// PhoneBookView.cpp : implementation of the CPhoneBookView class
//
#include "stdafx.h"
```

```
#include "PhoneBook.h"

#include "PhoneBookSet.h"
#include "PhoneBookDoc.h"
#include "PhoneBookView.h"

#ifdef _DEBUG
#define new DEBUG_NEW
#undef THIS_FILE
static char THIS_FILE[] = __FILE__;
#endif

/////////////////////////////////////////////////////////////////////////////
// CPhoneBookView

IMPLEMENT_DYNCREATE(CPhoneBookView, CDaoRecordView)

BEGIN_MESSAGE_MAP(CPhoneBookView, CDaoRecordView)
    //{{AFX_MSG_MAP(CPhoneBookView)
    ON_COMMAND(ID_RECORD_ADD, OnRecordAdd)
    //}}AFX_MSG_MAP
    // Standard printing commands
    ON_COMMAND(ID_FILE_PRINT, CDaoRecordView::OnFilePrint)
    ON_COMMAND(ID_FILE_PRINT_DIRECT,
                CDaoRecordView::OnFilePrint)
ON_COMMAND(ID_FILE_PRINT_PREVIEW,
                CDaoRecordView::OnFilePrintPreview)
END_MESSAGE_MAP()

/////////////////////////////////////////////////////////////////////////////
// CPhoneBookView construction/destruction

CPhoneBookView::CPhoneBookView()
    : CDaoRecordView(CPhoneBookView::IDD)
{
    //{{AFX_DATA_INIT(CPhoneBookView)
    m_pSet = NULL;
    //}}AFX_DATA_INIT
    // TODO: add construction code here
    m_bAddMode=FALSE;
}

CPhoneBookView::~CPhoneBookView()
{
```

```
}

void CPhoneBookView::DoDataExchange(CDataExchange* pDX)
{
    CDaoRecordView::DoDataExchange(pDX);
    //{{AFX_DATA_MAP(CPhoneBookView)
    DDX_Control(pDX, IDC_LASTNAME, m_ctlLastName);
    DDX_Control(pDX, IDC_FIRSTNAME, m_ctlFirstName);
    DDX_FieldText(pDX, IDC_FIRSTNAME, m_pSet->m_FirstName,
                m_pSet);
    DDX_FieldText(pDX, IDC_LASTNAME, m_pSet->m_LastName,
                m_pSet);
    DDX_FieldText(pDX, IDC_PHONENUMBER, m_pSet->m_Phone,
                m_pSet);
    DDX_FieldText(pDX, IDC_NOTES, m_pSet->m_Notes, m_pSet);
    //}}AFX_DATA_MAP
}

BOOL CPhoneBookView::PreCreateWindow(CREATESTRUCT& cs)
{
// TODO: Modify the Window class or styles here by modifying
//   the CREATESTRUCT cs

    return CDaoRecordView::PreCreateWindow(cs);
}
```

The sort order of the records is set by setting the string containing the **ORDER BY** clause of an SQL statement without the reserved words **ORDER BY** in the **m_strSort** member data of the **CDaoRecordset** class or its derived class, **CPhoneBookSet**. This sample requests the sort order to be *FirstName* and then *LastName*, which are the column names of the table.

```
void CPhoneBookView::OnInitialUpdate()
{
    m_pSet = &GetDocument()->m_phoneBookSet;
    m_pSet->m_strSort="FirstName, LastName";
    CDaoRecordView::OnInitialUpdate();
}

/////////////////////////////////////////////////////////////////////////
// CPhoneBookView printing

BOOL CPhoneBookView::OnPreparePrinting(CPrintInfo* pInfo)
{
```

```
    // default preparation
    return DoPreparePrinting(pInfo);
}

void CPhoneBookView::OnBeginPrinting(CDC* /*pDC*/,
                                     CPrintInfo* /*pInfo*/)
{
    // TODO: add extra initialization before printing
}

void CPhoneBookView::OnEndPrinting(CDC* /*pDC*/,
                                   CPrintInfo* /*pInfo*/)
{
    // TODO: add cleanup after printing
}

/////////////////////////////////////////////////////////////////////////////
// CPhoneBookView diagnostics

#ifdef _DEBUG
void CPhoneBookView::AssertValid() const
{
    CDaoRecordView::AssertValid();
}

void CPhoneBookView::Dump(CDumpContext& dc) const
{
    CDaoRecordView::Dump(dc);
}

CPhoneBookDoc* CPhoneBookView::GetDocument()
{
    ASSERT(m_pDocument->IsKindOf(RUNTIME_CLASS(CPhoneBookDoc)));
    return (CPhoneBookDoc*)m_pDocument;
}
#endif //_DEBUG

/////////////////////////////////////////////////////////////////////////////
// CPhoneBookView database support
CDaoRecordset* CPhoneBookView::OnGetRecordset()
{
    return m_pSet;
}
```

When the Add menu item is selected, the state flag is set to TRUE and the controls are enabled for data entry. A new record is added by calling the **AddNew** member function. The record fields are initially set to NULL. To complete the operation, the **Update** method should be called, which is done when the user moves to the next record with the **OnMove** member function. **Update** saves the changes to the database. The **AddNew** call can be placed within a transaction if the database supports transactions.

```
//////////////////////////////////////////////////////////////////////////
// CPhoneBookView message handlers

void CPhoneBookView::OnRecordAdd()
{
    // TODO: Add your command handler code here
    if (m_bAddMode) {
        OnMove(ID_RECORD_FIRST);
    }
    m_pSet->AddNew();
    m_pSet->SetFieldNull(&(m_pSet->m_FirstName),FALSE);
    m_pSet->SetFieldNull(&(m_pSet->m_LastName),FALSE);
    m_bAddMode=TRUE;
    m_ctlFirstName.SetReadOnly(FALSE);
    m_ctlLastName.SetReadOnly(FALSE);
    UpdateData(FALSE);
}
```

When the user moves to the next or previous record, the **OnMove** member function checks if the application is in add mode and if so, adds/updates the data to the database from the screen. After adding a record, the recordset maintained should be updated to reflect the new addition. The **Requery** member function rebuilds the recordset. Optionally a new filter or sort order can be set by setting **m_strFilter** and **m_strSort** before calling **Requery**.

```
BOOL CPhoneBookView::OnMove(UINT nIDMoveCommand)
{
    if (m_bAddMode) {
        if (!UpdateData()) {
            return FALSE;
        }
        try {
            m_pSet->Update();
        } catch (CDaoException* e) {
            AfxMessageBox(e->m_pErrorInfo->m_strDescription);
            e->Delete();
            return FALSE;
        }
```

```
        m_pSet->Requery();
        UpdateData(FALSE);
        m_ctlFirstName.SetReadOnly(TRUE);
        m_ctlLastName.SetReadOnly(TRUE);
        m_bAddMode=FALSE;
        return TRUE;
    } else {
        return CDaoRecordView::OnMove(nIDMoveCommand);
    }
}
```

The next sample takes the previous sample and extends it to provide the Delete functionality. It adds an additional menu item, Delete, to the Record menu, and the user can select it to delete the record shown currently. Here again, since there is no change in the database, the only changes are in the **CPhoneBookView** class. The code that has been added is highlighted next. The header file shows the addition of another member function that processes the Delete menu item.

```
// PhoneBookView.h : interface of the CPhoneBookView class
//
///////////////////////////////////////////////////////////////////

#if
!defined(AFX_PHONEBOOKVIEW_H)
#define AFX_PHONEBOOKVIEW_H

#if _MSC_VER >= 1000
#pragma once
#endif // _MSC_VER >= 1000

class CPhoneBookSet;

class CPhoneBookView : public CDaoRecordView
{
protected: // create from serialization only
    CPhoneBookView();
    DECLARE_DYNCREATE(CPhoneBookView)

public:
    //{{AFX_DATA(CPhoneBookView)
    enum { IDD = IDD_PHONEBOOK_FORM };
    CEdit   m_ctlLastName;
    CEdit   m_ctlFirstName;
    CPhoneBookSet* m_pSet;
    //}}AFX_DATA
```

```
// Attributes
public:
    CPhoneBookDoc* GetDocument();

// Operations
public:

// Overrides
    // ClassWizard generated virtual function overrides
    //{{AFX_VIRTUAL(CPhoneBookView)
    public:
    virtual CDaoRecordset* OnGetRecordset();
    virtual BOOL PreCreateWindow(CREATESTRUCT& cs);
    virtual BOOL OnMove(UINT nIDMoveCommand);
    protected:
    virtual void DoDataExchange(CDataExchange* pDX);
    virtual void OnInitialUpdate();
    virtual BOOL OnPreparePrinting(CPrintInfo* pInfo);
    virtual void OnBeginPrinting(CDC* pDC, CPrintInfo* pInfo);
    virtual void OnEndPrinting(CDC* pDC, CPrintInfo* pInfo);
    //}}AFX_VIRTUAL

// Implementation
public:
    virtual ~CPhoneBookView();
#ifdef _DEBUG
    virtual void AssertValid() const;
    virtual void Dump(CDumpContext& dc) const;
#endif

protected:
    BOOL m_bAddMode;

// Generated message map functions
protected:
    //{{AFX_MSG(CPhoneBookView)
    afx_msg void OnRecordAdd();
    afx_msg void OnRecordDelete();
    //}}AFX_MSG
    DECLARE_MESSAGE_MAP()
};

#ifndef _DEBUG  // debug version in PhoneBookView.cpp
```

```
inline CPhoneBookDoc* CPhoneBookView::GetDocument()
   { return (CPhoneBookDoc*)m_pDocument; }
#endif


/////////////////////////////////////////////////////////////////////////

//{{AFX_INSERT_LOCATION}}
#endif




// PhoneBookView.cpp : implementation of the CPhoneBookView
//

#include "stdafx.h"
#include "PhoneBook.h"

#include "PhoneBookSet.h"
#include "PhoneBookDoc.h"
#include "PhoneBookView.h"

#ifdef _DEBUG
#define new DEBUG_NEW
#undef THIS_FILE
static char THIS_FILE[] = __FILE__;
#endif

/////////////////////////////////////////////////////////////////////////
// CPhoneBookView

IMPLEMENT_DYNCREATE(CPhoneBookView, CDaoRecordView)

BEGIN_MESSAGE_MAP(CPhoneBookView, CDaoRecordView)
   //{{AFX_MSG_MAP(CPhoneBookView)
   ON_COMMAND(ID_RECORD_ADD, OnRecordAdd)
   ON_COMMAND(ID_RECORD_DELETE, OnRecordDelete)
   //}}AFX_MSG_MAP
   // Standard printing commands
   ON_COMMAND(ID_FILE_PRINT, CDaoRecordView::OnFilePrint)
   ON_COMMAND(ID_FILE_PRINT_DIRECT,
              CDaoRecordView::OnFilePrint)
ON_COMMAND(ID_FILE_PRINT_PREVIEW,
              CDaoRecordView::OnFilePrintPreview)
END_MESSAGE_MAP()
```

```
//////////////////////////////////////////////////////////////////////////
// CPhoneBookView construction/destruction

CPhoneBookView::CPhoneBookView()
    : CDaoRecordView(CPhoneBookView::IDD)
{
    //{{AFX_DATA_INIT(CPhoneBookView)
    m_pSet = NULL;
    //}}AFX_DATA_INIT
    // TODO: add construction code here
    m_bAddMode=FALSE;
}


CPhoneBookView::~CPhoneBookView()
{
}

void CPhoneBookView::DoDataExchange(CDataExchange* pDX)
{
    CDaoRecordView::DoDataExchange(pDX);
    //{{AFX_DATA_MAP(CPhoneBookView)
    DDX_Control(pDX, IDC_LASTNAME, m_ctlLastName);
    DDX_Control(pDX, IDC_FIRSTNAME, m_ctlFirstName);
    DDX_FieldText(pDX, IDC_FIRSTNAME, m_pSet->m_FirstName, m_pSet);
    DDX_FieldText(pDX, IDC_LASTNAME, m_pSet->m_LastName, m_pSet);
    DDX_FieldText(pDX, IDC_PHONENUMBER, m_pSet->m_Phone, m_pSet);
    DDX_FieldText(pDX, IDC_NOTES, m_pSet->m_Notes, m_pSet);
    //}}AFX_DATA_MAP
}


BOOL CPhoneBookView::PreCreateWindow(CREATESTRUCT& cs)
{
    // TODO: Modify the Window class or styles here by modifying
    //  the CREATESTRUCT cs

    return CDaoRecordView::PreCreateWindow(cs);
}

void CPhoneBookView::OnInitialUpdate()
{
    m_pSet = &GetDocument()->m_phoneBookSet;
    m_pSet->m_strSort="FirstName, LastName"; // sort by the first name
    CDaoRecordView::OnInitialUpdate();
}
```

```
//////////////////////////////////////////////////////////////////////
// CPhoneBookView printing

BOOL CPhoneBookView::OnPreparePrinting(CPrintInfo* pInfo)
{
    // default preparation
    return DoPreparePrinting(pInfo);
}

void CPhoneBookView::OnBeginPrinting(CDC* /*pDC*/,
                                     CPrintInfo* /*pInfo*/)
{
    // TODO: add extra initialization before printing
}

void CPhoneBookView::OnEndPrinting(CDC* /*pDC*/,
                                   CPrintInfo* /*pInfo*/)
{
    // TODO: add cleanup after printing
}

//////////////////////////////////////////////////////////////////////
// CPhoneBookView diagnostics

#ifdef _DEBUG
void CPhoneBookView::AssertValid() const
{
    CDaoRecordView::AssertValid();
}

void CPhoneBookView::Dump(CDumpContext& dc) const
{
    CDaoRecordView::Dump(dc);
}

CPhoneBookDoc* CPhoneBookView::GetDocument()
{
    ASSERT(m_pDocument->IsKindOf(RUNTIME_CLASS(CPhoneBookDoc)));
    return (CPhoneBookDoc*)m_pDocument;
}
#endif //_DEBUG

//////////////////////////////////////////////////////////////////////
```

```
// CPhoneBookView database support
CDaoRecordset* CPhoneBookView::OnGetRecordset()
{
    return m_pSet;
}



/////////////////////////////////////////////////////////////////////////
// CPhoneBookView message handlers

void CPhoneBookView::OnRecordAdd()
{
    // TODO: Add your command handler code here
    if (m_bAddMode) {
        OnMove(ID_RECORD_FIRST);
    }
    m_pSet->AddNew();
    m_pSet->SetFieldNull(&(m_pSet->m_FirstName),FALSE);
    m_pSet->SetFieldNull(&(m_pSet->m_LastName),FALSE);
    m_bAddMode=TRUE;
    m_ctlFirstName.SetReadOnly(FALSE);
    m_ctlLastName.SetReadOnly(FALSE);
    UpdateData(FALSE);
}

BOOL CPhoneBookView::OnMove(UINT nIDMoveCommand)
{
    // TODO: Add your specialized code here and/or call the base class
    if (m_bAddMode) {
        if (!UpdateData()) {
            return FALSE;
        }
        try {
            m_pSet->Update();
        } catch (CDaoException* e) {
            AfxMessageBox(e->m_pErrorInfo->m_strDescription);
            e->Delete();
            return FALSE;
        }
        m_pSet->Requery();
        UpdateData(FALSE);
        m_ctlFirstName.SetReadOnly(TRUE);
        m_ctlLastName.SetReadOnly(TRUE);
        m_bAddMode=FALSE;
```

```
            return TRUE;
        } else {
            return CDaoRecordView::OnMove(nIDMoveCommand);
        }
    }
```

The **OnRecordDelete** member function is called when the Delete menu item is selected. This function deletes the current record displayed on the screen by calling the **Delete** member function. The **Delete** member function deletes the current record from the open recordset object. After successful deletion, the field data members are set to a NULL value and an explicit call to one of the recordset navigation member functions must be made. Here it calls the **MoveNext** member function and checks the boundary to adjust the current record appropriately.

```
void CPhoneBookView::OnRecordDelete()
{
    // TODO: Add your command handler code here
    try {
        m_pSet->Delete();
    } catch (CDaoException* e) {
        AfxMessageBox(e->m_pErrorInfo->m_strDescription);
        e->Delete();
    }
    m_pSet->MoveNext();
    if (m_pSet->IsEOF()) {
        m_pSet->MoveLast();
    }
    if (m_pSet->IsBOF()) {
        m_pSet->SetFieldNull(NULL);
    }
    UpdateData(FALSE);
}
```

Conclusion

In this chapter, we looked at what DAO is, compared DAO with ODBC, discussed MFC support for DAO, and looked at some programming examples for DAO.

This concludes the book. As you are undoubtedly aware, there are many aspects of programming Windows NT, including communications, databases, graphics, multimedia, OLE, ActiveX, and so on. The text and the examples should have given you the ability not only to write a program related to these topics, but also the confidence to write programs involving all aspects of Windows NT programming.

WINDOWS
NT
Professional
Library

PART V

Appendixes

WINDOWS
NT
Professional
Library

APPENDIX A

Internationalization

One of the buzzwords of the '90s is "globalization." You undoubtedly have heard about a global economy, shrinking borders, the Internet bringing people together, and so on. All point to the fact that communication, distribution, and many other business functions now span the world. Consider two examples. Talking about shrinking borders, today you can buy a stock from the Tokyo stock exchange, turn around and sell it on the London stock exchange (and hopefully make a profit), and have the money taken from and deposited to your account in the United States—all through phone call(s) in a matter of minutes while you are vacationing on your boat in the Bahamas.

Let's take a simpler example. Books like this will be sold as-is in some countries and after translation in other countries. What does this globalization mean to you as a programmer? You may have faced this already. Even if you haven't, the chances are increasing that the program you write will execute in more than one country. If you are a product developer, then it would make good business sense to sell the product you have already developed (and spent development dollars on) in other markets. Even if you are not a product developer, if you work for a multinational organization, then the application you develop may need to run outside the United States. More and more international programmers routinely participate in programming newsgroups, and the road shows and conferences that software companies conduct to promote their products now include many international stops as well. I hope I have given you enough incentive to look at the topic of programming for the world in this chapter.

You may ask, "How come I have successfully developed programs all these years without worrying about all this international programming stuff?"

If you are like many programmers, you probably developed your application just fine without worrying about international programming, because Windows NT lets you develop applications at least three ways (using the default code page, multibyte characters, and Unicode), and you have been using one of the three.'

THE PROBLEM

Chances are, the programs you are developing every day will not work in Germany, Japan, or China. To understand why, let's start with the ANSI character set. In ANSI, each character is represented by 8 bits. With 8 bits, the maximum number of different characters you can represent is 2^8, which is 256 characters. Even if you count A through Z, a through z, the numbers 0–9, and special characters such as $, *, and so on, the total number is well within 256. Thus, the ANSI character set is large enough to handle the English language and other languages using the same character set. But what if the language needs more than 256 characters? There are a lot of languages based on other character sets such as Cyrillic and Kanji. You cannot represent ANSI and Cyrillic characters in the same set with just 8 bits. The problem gets worse when you consider some eastern languages whose alphabets are actually pictorial symbols—and there are thousands of these symbols.

Now that you know what the problem is, let's look at some solutions that will let you develop programs that will not only work in the United States, but also will require little or no effort to make them work elsewhere. We will look at four solutions and their programming aspects:

▼ Using code pages

■ Using Multi-Byte Character Sets (MBCS)

■ Using Unicode

▲ Of course, you can create a portable source and use a switch to generate applications for different environments

CODE PAGES

The first solution, which still permits use of only one byte per character, is the computer version of divide and conquer—using *code pages*. Each single-byte code page could still represent only 256 characters, but different code pages are used to support different character sets. Thus, there are a number of ANSI and OEM character sets, and corresponding code pages. Different versions of the same product are created, each one using a different code page. For example, the U.S. version of the Windows 95 operating system uses a code page that is different from the code page that can represent Cyrillic characters. Windows NT is available in several international versions including Chinese, French, German, Japanese, and so on. The most common code page used in the United States is OEM code page 437. The code page for Japanese is 932. As a programmer you do not have to do any special programming involving code pages, unlike MBCS and Unicode (discussed later in the chapter). You can tell the current code page by use of the C run-time function **_getmbcp**.

This solution works fine as long as you have applications that need to work with only one code page at a time. If within your application you wanted to support more than one code page at the same time, then you have problems. Consider, for example, a server in one of the European countries serving clients that run with different code pages within the same or different countries (a common situation). With the increased use of the Internet and intranets, more and more applications need to be able to handle this type of situation.

MULTI-BYTE CHARACTER SETS (MBCS)

By default you program using a character set where a single byte is a single character—a *Single Byte Character Set (SBCS)*. A logical solution is to have more than one byte represent the characters in the character set, if all the characters cannot be represented by one byte. Two bytes are used in *Double Byte Character Sets (DBCS)*—keep in mind that two bytes are only for *some* characters, not all. Of course, you are not restricted to two bytes. You can have multibyte character sets too, but DBCS is by far the most common. In fact, Visual C++ only supports up to two bytes per character (DBCS). If you want to develop a new application for the international market, you are better off using Unicode. But if you already have an application that you want to quickly enable for markets that will be satisfied with MBCS support, you may want to look at MBCS enabling your application.

Programming Aspects of DBCS

Visual C++ and MFC support DBCS. You have to watch out for data type differences (in particular, character strings) and run-time function differences. Character strings are a problem in DBCS. This is because each character in the string could either be a complete character or a partial character. How can you tell?—by looking at each byte. If the byte has a value in a reserved range and is the first of two bytes that make up the character (the first byte is also called the *lead byte*) then the character uses two bytes. The reserved range is dependent on the code page (for example, 0x81 through 0x9F for the code page 932). Although you can check for the lead byte yourself (find out the code page and use a table that specifies the appropriate range), it is a lot easier for you to use the function **IsDBCSLeadByteEx** to check if a byte is a lead byte. You can use the Input Method Editor to create double-byte characters (as well as single-byte characters). You use _MBCS in your build to specify that you are building an MBCS-enabled application. Some of the things you need to watch out for in DBCS programming are as follows:

▼ Operations such as inserting, deleting, and counting characters are normally synonymous with byte operations. In DBCS, you have to ensure that you deal with characters, not bytes.

■ In instances where you used str functions (such as **strlen** to get the number of characters in a string), you need to use **_mbs** functions (**strlen** will not return the right result on a string with both one-byte and two-byte characters).

■ Develop your application on an MBCS-enabled version of Windows NT to ensure that Visual C++ will accept DBCS characters.

■ Ensure that the application uses the right code page. You can change the default code page using the resource compiler's /c option.

▲ Ensure that you have the right target locale (country and language). You can use the pragma setlocale to change the default as required.

UNICODE

Developed by the Unicode Consortium, a nonprofit consortium sponsored by a number of computer companies, *Unicode* is a fixed-width encoding scheme where each character is represented by 16 bits. The number of characters that can be represented by Unicode is thus 2^{16} or 65,536.

Using Unicode, we can represent all the characters from character sets like ANSI, characters from the Cyrillic character set, special-purpose characters such as publishing characters, and mathematical symbols. In short, everything we want to represent (as of now). For a complete description of the Unicode standard, the characters represented, and so on, refer to *The Unicode Standard: Worldwide Character Encoding,* by Addison-Wesley Publishing Company, 1992.

The Win32 API and Windows NT support Unicode. Windows NT uses Unicode extensively in its internal operations. For example, all text strings in GDI are in Unicode, and NTFS uses Unicode for file, path and directory names, object names, and all system information files.

The subsystems take care of many of the conversions. For instance, the Win32 subsystem converts American Standard Code for Information Interchange (ASCII) characters it receives into Unicode strings and converts them back to ASCII, if necessary, for output.

Note for UNIX Programmers

Unicode is supported by many UNIX systems such as Digital UNIX. If you have done Unicode programming before in UNIX, then it is essentially the same in Windows NT.

The differences between SBCS, MBCS, and Unicode are summarized in Table A-1. Table A-1

Programming Using Unicode

Unicode programming is not a whole new way of programming. Using it is not as difficult as learning a new programming language. You just have to be aware of the differences in data types, function types, string handling, and so on, between using Unicode and not using Unicode.

SBCS	MBCS	Unicode
All characters use one byte.	Not all characters use two bytes.	All characters use two bytes.
Use str functions.	Use _mbs functions.	Use _wcs functions.
Don't include _MBCS or _UNICODE.	Include _MBCS for build.	Include _UNICODE for build.

Table A-1. SBCS, MBCS, and Unicode Programming Differences

To represent character constants, you normally would use char, which would take up one byte. In Unicode you use **wchar_t**, and the same character constant would take up two bytes (the Unicode character set is also called the *wide character set*, and the prefix "W" is used in functions and data types to indicate that the function or data type is Unicode related). A string such as "example string" becomes a Unicode string by prefixing it with "L," that is, the Unicode string is L"example string". You can include Unicode fonts in your program by using UNICODE_CHARSET for **lfCharSet** in your **LOGFONT** structure.

If you used the **CString** class to handle strings, you can continue to use **CString**, because **CString** is Unicode enabled.

To specify that your application uses Unicode, you use the #define _Unicode.

TIP: The libraries for the MFC library's Unicode support are copied only by selecting Custom Installation.

Win32 APIs and Unicode

Win32 APIs that use characters are actually implemented three ways:

▼ The most common, the ANSI version, is implemented with the suffix "A."

■ The Unicode version is implemented with the suffix "W."

▲ A portable version that can be compiled for either Unicode or ANSI is implemented without a suffix.

For example, if you specifically want the ANSI version of **SetWindowLong**, you call **SetWindowLongA**. When you specifically want the Unicode version, you call **SetWindowLongW**.

At times, you may need to translate strings from one form to another. Win32 includes functions that let you perform these translations as summarized in Table A-2.

WRITING PORTABLE APPLICATIONS

You don't have to choose between SBCS, MBCS, and Unicode. You can write portable applications and build your application in different ways—SBCS, MBCS, or Unicode—without changing your program source. The Microsoft run-time library provides mappings for many data types, routines that you can use to write generic code that can be compiled for single byte, multibyte, or Unicode. You make the selection between single byte, multibyte, or Unicode using a #define statement. You would also include the header file *Tchar.h*. As mentioned before, an ANSI character is char, while a

Function	Purpose
MultiByteToWideChar	Translates MBCS strings to Unicode strings
WideCharToMultiByte	Translates Unicode strings to MBCS strings
CharToOem or CharToOemBuff	Translates an ANSI or Unicode string to OEM characters
OemToChar or OemToCharBuff	Translates OEM characters to an ANSI or Unicode string

Table A-2.   Win32 String Translation Functions

Unicode character is wchar_t. You can use a generic character type TCHAR, and *Tchar.h* takes care of portability by switching the typedef as shown next:

```
#ifdef UNICODE
        typedef wchar_t TCHAR;
#else
        typedef unsigned char TCHAR;
#endif
```

Similar portability mappings occur for other data types besides the simple character type as shown in Table A-3.

Data Type	SBCS	MBCS	Unicode
_TINT	int	int	wint_t
_TSCHAR	Signed char	Signed char	wchar_t
_TUCHAR	Unsigned char	Unsigned char	wchar_t
_TXCHAR	Signed char	Unsigned char	wchar_t
_T or _TEXT	Not required	Not required	Prefixed by "L"

Table A-3.   Data Types Portability Mapping

Similarly, Tchar.h maps generic macros prefixed with _tcs to str (SBCS), _mbs (DBCS), or wcs (Unicode) functions as appropriate. Thus, what may appear in an SBCS program as

```
char * strcat(char *, const char *);
```

would appear in a Unicode program as

```
wchar_t * wcscat(wchar_t *, const wchar_t *);
```

For a complete list of the mappings, please refer to the *Microsoft Visual C++: Run-Time Library Reference*.

AN INTERNATIONALIZATION TECHNIQUE

When you program so that your program can be used internationally, you have to ensure that the end-user interface is usable in the countries you expect your program to run. A German user must see all end-user interface text, such as dialog titles, static controls, text in other controls, messages, and so on, in German. A French user would like to see all the user interface text in French.

One way of doing this would be to develop your program as you normally would, send all the relevant source to the countries you want your program to run in, and get some programmer there to change all the user interface text and rebuild the application. The advantage of this approach is that your program development is not slowed by the development and testing related to international requirements. But there are also problems with this approach. First, you may not be able to find the skills you need in all the countries—and even if you do, the countries may not have all the latest versions necessary to be able to develop the application. Second, you have multiple versions of your sources, and replicating future changes across different sources in different countries is a major problem.

The typical compromise is to ship the international versions a little bit after the U.S. version. Instead of shipping the complete source overseas, you just get the text of the various user interface elements translated here or abroad, and structure your application so that it can be quickly built by use of the translated user interface elements. The following program shows how to separate user interface text from your main executable so that changes to the user interface can be handled without changing or rebuilding your program. There are two ways you can get the program to pick up different user interface elements. You can swap text files and rebuild the *Intl* DLL, or you can copy the already generated DLLs to *Intl* DLL and rerun your application.

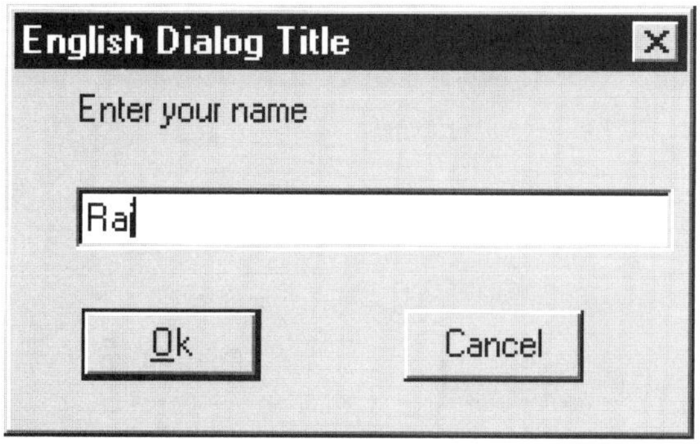

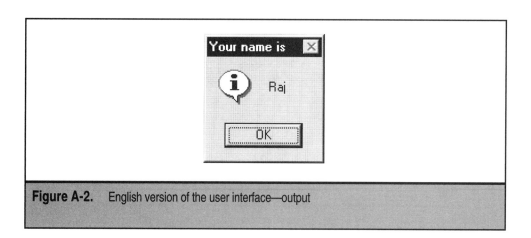

Figure A-1.   English version of the user interface—input

The Intl example is a simple example that displays an application window with a title. The menu has two choices: one brings up a dialog panel, and the other exits the program. The dialog panel gets an input from the user and displays that in a message box. The output of the program using the English version of the user interface elements is shown in Figures A-1 and A-2.

Figure A-2.   English version of the user interface—output

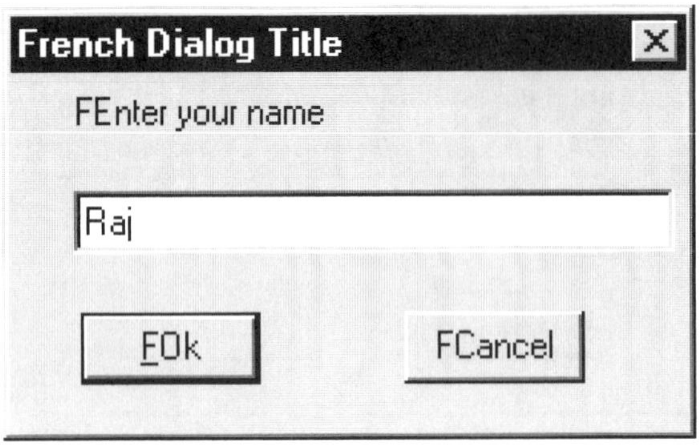

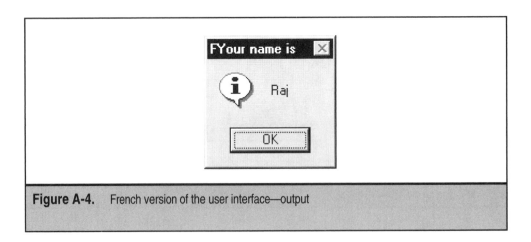

Figure A-3. French version of the user interface—input

The French version was then substituted by copying *French.dll* to *Intl.dll*. When the program is run, the French version of the user interface is shown. (For simplicity, the letter "F" prefixes all user interface elements, but in the real world you would insert the translated text into the *French.txt* file.) The output using the French version is shown in Figures A-3 and A-4.

Figure A-4. French version of the user interface—output

Finally, the German version is used, and that output is shown in Figures A-5 and A-6.

Now let's take a detailed look at the program to see how this is done.

The program's header files *Menus.h* and *Dialogs.h* are shown next:

```
// menus.h
// Constants for menu commands

#define IDM_NAME         1001
#define IDM_EXIT         1002

#define IDS_PROG_TITLE   2001
#define IDS_NAME_PROMPT  2002
#define IDS_MESSAGE_1    2003

// dialogs.h
#define IDC_NAME             101
#define IDC_LABEL            104
```

When developing software for international use, it is crucial to isolate all the language-dependent entities like prompt text, messages, icons, and so on, so that you do not end up creating one executable for each language. Obviously, having one executable for each language would be a maintenance nightmare, particularly when your program works in many other languages.

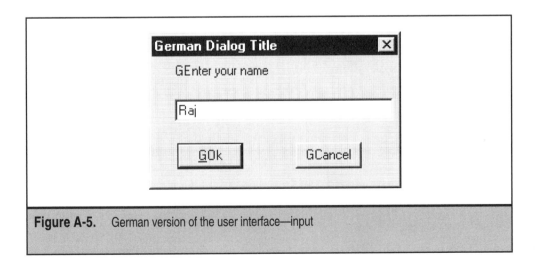

Figure A-5. German version of the user interface—input

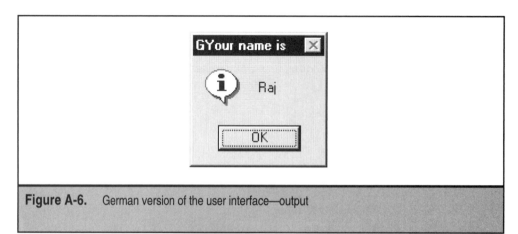

Figure A-6.   German version of the user interface—output

The Intl example shows one of the programming techniques that can be used to isolate all the strings and create a *resource DLL*. This resource DLL can then be loaded from the executable and used. When the time comes to translate the program to another language, the translators, who are typically translators and not programmers, can just translate the text files. These text files are included in the resource files, which can be compiled into a resource DLL. The program can then load the resource DLL and use it.

The idea behind the program is to show how the textual strings can be isolated to a resource file. The program is made up of one executable and one DLL. The executable is made of just the *Intl.cpp* module and the related header files *Dialog.h* and *Menus.h*. It does not include the resource file in the build process. That is part of the resource DLL, which will be discussed later.

The *Intl.cpp* module essentially has two classes. The **CWindow** class is the application's main class, and **CNameDialog** is the dialog panel class. The other class is the application class **CApp**.

```
// INTL.CPP

#include <afxwin.h>
#include <afxdlgs.h>
#include "dialogs.h"
#include "menus.h"


// Define the application object class
class CApp : public CWinApp
{
public:
    virtual BOOL InitInstance ();
```

```
};

// Define the window class
class CWindow : public CFrameWnd
{
public:
    CWindow();
    afx_msg void OnName();
    afx_msg void OnExit();
    DECLARE_MESSAGE_MAP()
};
```

What has been done here is the standard definition of our application class and the frame window class. The member function **OnName( )** will display a dialog panel, and **OnExit( )** will exit the application.

```
// Define the Name Dialog Class
class CNameDialog: public CDialog
{
private:
    CString m_nameString;
public:
    CNameDialog( CString defaultString = NULL,
        CWnd* pParentWnd = NULL )
        : CDialog( "NameDlg", pParentWnd )
        { m_nameString = defaultString; }

    virtual void OnOK();
    virtual BOOL OnInitDialog();
    CString& GetInputString()
        { return m_nameString; }
};

// OnInitDialog is called just before the dialog
// appears on the screen.

BOOL CNameDialog::OnInitDialog()
{
    SetDlgItemText( IDC_NAME, m_nameString );
    return TRUE;
}

void CNameDialog::OnOK()
{
```

```
    GetDlgItemText( IDC_NAME,
        m_nameString.GetBuffer(128), 128 );
    m_nameString.ReleaseBuffer();
    EndDialog( IDOK );
}
```

Next the dialog class **CNameDialog** is defined. Note that the string "NameDlg" is really immaterial for translation, and it could have been a dialog identification number instead. The **CNameDialog** constructor initializes the prompt string that would appear in the edit field of the dialog panel. The member function **GetInputString( )** returns the stored string inline. The **OnInitDialog( )** member function basically initializes the edit field in the dialog panel. The **OnOK( )** member function picks up the string and stores it in the member variable, m_nameString.

Next the **CWindow** constructor is defined:

```
// CWindow constructor
CWindow::CWindow()
{
        CString title;
        title.LoadString(IDS_PROG_TITLE);
        Create( NULL, "",
        WS_OVERLAPPEDWINDOW,
        rectDefault, NULL, "MainMenu" );
        SetWindowText(title);
}
```

The interesting piece of code starts here. Typically, when the frame window is created, the window title is explicitly given as a parameter to the **Create( )**. In the code here, a **CString** title is defined, and the title string is loaded from the resource file. This dynamically loaded string is used as the title. In the example here, the frame is created without any title text, and it is set later with **SetWindowText( )**. This is done assuming that some dynamic change to the loaded text will be made. If there is nothing to be made, the title can be directly passed in the **Create( )** member function.

```
void CWindow::OnName()
{
        CString namePrompt;
        CString messageText;
        namePrompt.LoadString(IDS_NAME_PROMPT);
        CNameDialog nameDialog( namePrompt, this );

        if( nameDialog.DoModal() == IDOK )
        {
```

```
                messageText.LoadString(IDS_MESSAGE_1);
                MessageBox( nameDialog.GetInputString(),messageText,
                    MB_ICONINFORMATION );
            }
}
```

The **OnName( )** member function processes the menu selection "Name Dialog." It loads the prompt text from the resource file and uses it to create the dialog panel. When the user is done with the dialog panel, the program retrieves the data entered in the edit field and displays the entered data in a message box. Note that the title for the message box is also loaded from the resource file.

The item to look at next is the **InitInstance** method of the main application class **CApp**:

```
// Initialize the CApp m_pMainWnd data member
BOOL CApp::InitInstance()
{
        HINSTANCE          ResourceHandle;

        ResourceHandle = AfxLoadLibrary ("Intl.DLL");
        AfxSetResourceHandle (ResourceHandle);

        m_pMainWnd = new CWindow();
        m_pMainWnd -> ShowWindow( m_nCmdShow );
        m_pMainWnd -> UpdateWindow();
        return( TRUE );
}
```

Here a resource instance handle, **ResourceHandle**, is defined, and the resource DLL *Intl.dll* is loaded using **AfxLoadLibrary**. **AfxSetResourceHandle** takes this handle and sets it as the application's resource handle. All resources that are needed by the application will use this resource handle. The rest of the code is the standard code.

As was seen earlier, the Intl.exe did not contain any resource files associated with the executable. The resources are separated and a resource DLL is created as discussed next. The files that create the resource DLL *Intl.dll* are *Resource.c, Intl.rc, Dialogs.dlg, Dialogs.h, Menus.h,* and *Intl.txt.*

```
// This is a dummy file used for creating the Resource DLL
void dialogs ()
{
}
```

The preceding is the *Resource.c* file. This is just a dummy file to create a DLL. It contains no code and the only reason for its existence is to create a DLL.

```
// Intl.rc
// The resource file for INTL.CPP sample

#include <windows.h>
#include <afxres.h>

#include "dialogs.h"
#include "dialogs.dlg"
#include "menus.h"
#include "intl.txt"

MainMenu MENU
BEGIN
    POPUP TXT_M_FILE
    BEGIN
      MENUITEM TXT_MI_NAME, IDM_NAME
      MENUITEM TXT_MI_EXIT, IDM_EXIT
    END
END
STRINGTABLE
BEGIN
    IDS_PROG_TITLE,        TXT_STR_PROG_TITLE
    IDS_NAME_PROMPT,       TXT_STR_NAME_PROMPT
    IDS_MESSAGE_1,         TXT_STR_MESSAGE_1
END
```

Just shown is the *Intl.rc* module. Apart from including the standard header files related to the resource ID, notice that it also includes a text file *Intl.txt*. At places where text is to appear in the resource, it is substituted with a macro. So instead of specifying the MainMenu as

```
MainMenu MENU
BEGIN
    POPUP "&File"
    BEGIN
      MENUITEM "&Name dialog", IDM_NAME
      MENUITEM "&Exit", IDM_EXIT
    END
END
```

it specifies it as

```
MainMenu MENU
BEGIN
    POPUP TXT_M_FILE
    BEGIN
      MENUITEM TXT_MI_NAME, IDM_NAME
      MENUITEM TXT_MI_EXIT, IDM_EXIT
    END
END
```

where TXT_M_FILE, TXT_MI_NAME, and TXT_MI_EXIT are defined in the *Intl.txt* file as shown next:

```
// This file contains the English text related to
// the International program.

// Main Window related text
#define TXT_M_FILE          "&File"
#define TXT_MI_NAME         "&Name dialog"
#define TXT_MI_EXIT         "&Exit"


// Name dialog related text
#define TXT_DIALOG_TITLE    "English Dialog Title"
#define TXT_OK              "&Ok"
#define TXT_CANCEL          "Cancel"
#define TXT_PROMPT1_STRING  "Enter your name"


// String Table text

#define TXT_STR_PROG_TITLE    "Sample for Internationalization"
#define TXT_STR_NAME_PROMPT   "Type your name here"
#define TXT_STR_MESSAGE_1     "Your name is"
```

With this structure, just the text file—*Intl.txt*—which contains minimal programming details, can be given to the translators for translation.

When this program is compiled and run, the characters appear in English text. Also found in the project are two more text files, *German.txt* and *French.txt*. These files are similar to *Intl.txt*, but the texts are German and French texts, respectively. The same English texts as found in *Intl.txt* are just prefixed with "G" in *German.txt* and "F" in *French.txt*. To create the German version of the resource file, just copy *German.txt* to *Intl.txt*, and rebuild the resource *DLL Intl.dll*. Now without making any change or rebuild of the executable, a German version of the program is created. While the size of the program and resource shown here are small and trivial, in a real project this would substantially increase the maintainability of the project.

There are some drawbacks in this approach to keep in mind. When translated, some strings, such as titles, may become too long and may not fit in the available space. You may also have a problem with the text direction (right to left versus left to right, as well as horizontal versus vertical). In such cases, you can create individual dialogs as needed.

GUIDELINES FOR INTERNATIONAL PROGRAMMING

If you use the technique illustrated by this program, here a few guidelines that you will find useful:

▼ The way numbers, dates, time, and currency are represented is different in different countries. You should account for this by using locale information and preferences. There are Win32 functions, such as **GetProfileInt**, **GetSystemDefaultSystemLCID**, and **GetLocaleInfoW**, to retrieve locale and preference information. There are also Win32 functions, such as **GetDateFormatW**, to convert dates to local formats.

■ Even though dialogs may have the same string repeated, use different string IDs for multiple occurrences of one string with the same name. This is because a given string may have a different meaning when translated, and the different instances where the string is used in dialogs may not always translate to the same target string.

■ To find out whether your application is running on an MBCS-enabled operating system, set a flag at program startup, and do not issue repeated API calls.

■ A translated string (particularly in German) may be longer than the source string. To ensure that the translated string will fit, allow approximately 30 percent extra space at the end of static text controls.

■ Keep the fonts available in your target systems in mind, as not all fonts will be available (by default). Try to use a least common subset.

■ Do not mix localized strings with those that are not localized. Assume that the string is localized if you are not sure.

■ Use *stringtable* resources to specify strings. Include strings in your application's RC file. This will avoid source code changes that will be required as a result of string changes due to translation.

▲ Keep in mind that even if you have taken care of all the programming issues, you may have difficulty testing. The real test is when a program meant for another market runs using the keyboard, the display, the code page, the international user, and so on. In many instances you will not be able to test your application without the right equipment. In such cases, make sure to allocate some extra time to get your software to the other market and tested under the right conditions.

CONCLUSION

As mentioned at the start of the chapter, advanced programmers are most likely to be required to write programs that will work internationally. There are some other cultural aspects that influence your application, but for which no general-purpose solution exists. The basic units of measurement for height, weight, distances, calendars, and so on, vary among countries. Some basic assumptions that are true in the United States may not be true elsewhere (for example, identifying a person by use of a social security number). The algorithms and keys you may have used in your application in the United States will not work properly elsewhere. You can try to modularize your code as was shown in the example to minimize country-specific changes.

There is more to Windows NT than meets the eye. As you get to use Windows NT more, you will soon appreciate all the functions and features it supports. As someone said, "Software, like wine, gets better with age." We have been through many operating systems, starting with IBM's MVS, VM, and so on, through the many UNIX variants, DOS, Windows, and Windows NT. Windows NT has picked up some of the best elements of operating systems. Programming using Windows NT is bound to be a rewarding experience from a programming-pleasure as well as a financial viewpoint.

1

APPENDIX B

About the CD

WHAT IS ON THE CD-ROM

The CD-ROM that accompanies this book contains all the source code and executable files from this book. These code samples and executables are in the *Book* subdirectory, with one directory for each applicable chapter. For your convenience, they are ready for use, rather than being compressed. They also come with complete project files.

You will also find shareware and demo/trial versions of many powerful software utilities used by advanced programmers every day. Take a look at each of them, and you may find one that will simplify some aspect of your program development. These utilities are available in the *Shareware* subdirectory. Some of them are listed below with their features.

▼ **WinZip** brings the convenience of Windows to the use of Zip files without requiring PKZIP and PKUNZIP. The new WinZip Wizard makes unzipping easier than ever. WinZip features built-in support for popular Internet file formats, including TAR, gzip, Unix compress, UUencode, BinHex, and MIME. ARJ, LZH, and ARC files are supported via external programs. WinZip interfaces to most virus scanners.

■ **Lemmy** is a vi editor for Windows NT. In addition to the usual things you've come to expect from a programmer's editor, Lemmy combines the familiar look and feel of the Unix VI editor with excellent Windows integration, including: Full Graphical Interface, File Type Contexts, Extensible Syntax Highlighting , Java and Visual Basic Scripting, OLE Automation, and Transparent Internet Access.

■ **Search and Replace** is an indispensable utility loved by programmers, webmasters, and novice computer users alike. If you need to find and replace text, or just find text, this utility is a must-have.

■ **Directory Toolkit** now has ZIP functions. It does what you simply can't do any other way. You can rename long filenames with wildcards, physically sort files in directories, compare directories, compare files, split and concatenate, encode and decode files, and much more.

■ **PR-Tracker** helps manage software development projects by tracking software bugs, action items, and change requests with problem reports. PR-Tracker runs on Windows, Windows 95 and Windows NT. Features include recording problem reports in a network database; supporting simultaneous access to the database by multiple users; supporting multiple projects; supporting configuration of data collection for each project; supporting configuration of workflow for each project; redundant data storage for speed and backup; classifying problems according to priority, type, and other properties; supporting sort and search operations on the database or problem reports; assigning personnel to perform the tasks required to correct bugs; tracking the tasks of problem investigation, resolution, and verification; determining which testing methods are most effective in detecting bugs; estimating the time required to complete projects; estimating personnel work load; and exporting reports in HTML format.

- **RSM,** or Resource Standard Metrics, is a tool that provides a standard method for analyzing C and C++ source code. RSM performs both quality analysis and metrics for C and C++ applicable to ISO9001, TickIt, and the SEI certification process. RSM is used world-wide by Fortune 500 companies to analyze software metrics, code quality and to enforce a coding standard. Resource Standard Metrics will notify you of the top 25 (or more) most common programming or quality problems not checked by a compiler. It will enforce standard programming practices and style. RSM greatly simplifies the analysis process for peer reviews, subcontract performance assessment, and quantifying the porting process. RSM provides the extensive metrics for measuring the actual work performed on a module, file, or project. A standard metrics measurement streamlines the project estimation process. RSM creates more accurate estimates with a standard basis of estimate.

- **SnagIt** captures anything on the Windows desktop quickly and easily. From one-step capture of scrolling web pages to video capture and text conversion, SnagIt does it all.

- **PMDiff** is an intuitive application that lets you visually compare different text files. It also lets you combine files using just a few mouse clicks.

- **WinImage** is a powerful disk utility that enables users to make a disk image from a floppy, extract files from image, make an empty image, put the image on blank disk, and more. WinImage also supports many different standard and non-standard formats, including Microsoft's new DMF format. WinImage has many great features like making a disk image from a floppy, extracting files from an image, creating empty disks, injecting files and directories into an image, changing an image format, defragmenting an image, supporting non-standard formats (such as DMF, 1.68MB), and has a powerful "Batch assistant" mode that lets you automate many operations.

- **FileAdmin** is a must-have tool to properly handle File System Permissions. Unlike the built-in NT security manager, FileAdmin allows a user to add, remove or modify account permission to a file, directory, or a group of files and propagate these changes without affecting other accounts' permissions. It provides advanced account-to-account replacement, comprehensive log information, and easy handling of deleted or unknown accounts.

- **RegAdmin**, unlike NT Registry Editor, allows an administrator to add, remove, or modify account permissions to a key value or a group of keys and propagate the changes without affecting other accounts' permissions. It provides advanced account-to-account replacement, comprehensive log of changes, easy handling of deleted or unknown accounts.

- **ScanNT Plus** is intended for use by system administrators in order to enhance the security of NT system. The program tests for sufficient complexity in the existing passwords. The program uses a plain text dictionary file as the file of assumed passwords to check whether a password is sufficiently complex or if it is easily breakable.

- **EasyHelp/Web** is designed for authors and programmers who want to make either Windows Help files or Internet web pages quickly and easily from Word for Windows documents. If you are familiar with Microsoft Word, you will be able to produce online hypertext versions of your paper-based documents in minutes.

- **BKReplace** is essentially a text search-and-replace program. However, unlike the search-replace functionality of a standard text editor, BK ReplaceEm is designed to operate on multiple text files at once. And you need not perform only one search-replace operation per file—you can set up a list of operations to perform. If different groups of files need to have different operations performed on them, that is no problem either. You can also specify a backup file for each file processed, just in case the replace operation didn't do exactly what you wanted.

- **SuperNoteTab** is not just another Windows Notepad replacement. It is a feature-rich and user-friendly editor with some very original productivity tools.

- **VMX32B** is a Shared Heap/Queue/Memory Manager for Windows NT.

- **Delete97** is an enhanced DEL command.

- ▲ **DBWin32** is a useful utility for debugging on Windows NT and 95.

These and more shareware tools and utilities are included in the CD-ROM.

NOTE:Italic page numbers refer to graphs, charts, or illustrations:

▼ NUMBERS

2-D display programming example, OpenGL, 719-728
2-D transform programming example, OpenGL, 728-731
3-D transform programming example, OpenGL, 731-738
32-bit data, Tree View control, 268

▼ A

About dialog box, ActiveX controls, 548-549
absolute paths, broken links and moniker, 474
Acceleration attribute, Spin control, *200*
accelerator keys, user interface programming, 45-47
accept, *Echocs* sockets programming example, 599
access control lists, Security Reference Monitor, 13
ACK message, DHCP (Dynamic Host Configuration Protocol), 65
activation, in-place (OLE), 467, *468*
Active Server Pages (ASP), defined, 611
ActiveX control security, 573-579
    certificates, 573

Internet Explorer and, *574*
IObjectSafety OLE interface, 573
    marking, 573, *574*, 575-579
    overview, 573
    programming example, 575-579
    signing, 573, *574*, 575-579
    viruses, 573
ActiveX controls, 479-482, 533-580
    About dialog box, 548-549
    Add, 539, 543, 549
    ClassWizard, 538, 539-540, 543, 545
    client programming, 481-482
    COleControl class, 534, 543
    COleControlModule class, 540
    COlePropertyPage class, 551
    connectable object interfaces, *480*
    connection point interface methods, *481*
    container communication, 534-537
    container programming example, 554-572
    containers, 553-572
    control IDs, 540
    ControlWizard, 538, 540
    creating, 537-553

CRecordsPropPage class, 539
CStringArray class, 549
custom events, 534, 544
DDP_Text macro, 552-553
DDX_Text macro, 552-553
DllRegisterServer, 540
DoPropExchange, 548
event maps, 544
events, 534, 539
ExitInstance, 540
FireAddressChanged, 549
FireNameChanged, 549
FireRemarksChanged, 549
GetClassID, 545
GetCount, 539, 543, 549
GetTypeLib, 545
IDispatch interface, 481-482
in-process and out-of-process servers, 479
InitInstance, 540
IUnknown interface, 479
location transparency, 479-480
marking, 573, *574*, 575-579
methods, 480-481, 535-537, 539
OnDraw, 547, 580
overview, 479, 534
programming example for creation of, 538-553
programming example for security, 575-579
programming tips, 579-580

N

▼ X

▼ Z